P9-DNR-508

Steps to Writing Well

with Additional Readings

Sixth Edition

Steps to Writing Well

with Additional Readings

Jean Wyrick   *Professor Emerita*
Colorado State University

THOMSON ™

WADSWORTH

Australia • Canada • Mexico • Spain • United Kingdom • United States

THOMSON
WADSWORTH

Steps to Writing Well with Additional Readings
Sixth Edition
Jean Wyrick

Publisher: *Michael Rosenberg*

Acquisitions Editor: *Dickson Musslewhite*

Development Editor: *Camille Adkins*

Production Project Manager: *Samantha Ross*

Executive Marketing Manager: *Carrie Brandon*

Manufacturing Manager: *Marcia Locke*

Compositor: *GEX Publishing Services*

Project Manager: *Matrix Productions*

Photography Manager: *Sheri Blaney*

Photo Researcher: *Cheri Throop*

Cover/Text Designer: *Brian Salisbury*

Cover Printer: *Coral Graphic Services*

Text Printer: *Quebecor World-Taunton*

Cover Images: Top Right: © Hemera Photo Objects; Middle Left: Keith Brofsky/Photodisc/Getty; Bottom Right: © Photodisc

Copyright © 2005, 2002, 1999, 1996, 1993, 1990 by Thomson Wadsworth. Thomson Wadsworth and the Thomson logo are trademarks used herein under license.

All rights reserved. No part of this work covered by the copyright hereon may be reproduced or used in any form or by any means—graphic, electronic, or mechanical, including photocopying, recording, taping, Web distribution or information storage and retrieval systems—without the written permission of the publisher.

Printed in the United States of America.

1 2 3 4 5 6 7 8 9 10 08 07 06 05 04

Credits appear on page 630, which constitutes an extension of this copyright page.

For permission to use material from this text or product, submit a request online at http://www.thomsonrights.com.

Any additional questions about permissions can be submitted by email to thomsonrights@thomson.com

For more information contact Thomson Wadsworth, 25 Thomson Place, Boston, Massachusetts 02210 USA, or you can visit our Internet site at http://www.thomson.com

ISBN: 1-4130-0109-2
(Student Edition)

ISBN: 1-4130-1043-1
(Instructor's Edition)

Library of Congress Control Number: 2004105796

Contents

List of Fine Art   xviii
To the Teacher   xix
To the Student   xxv

■ Part One The Basics of the Short Essay 1

1 Prewriting 3

Getting Started (or Soup-Can Labels Can Be Fascinating) 3
Selecting a Subject 4
Finding Your Essay's Purpose and Focus 6
Pump-Primer Techniques 7
After You've Found Your Focus 17
Practicing What You've Learned 18
Discovering Your Audience 19
How to Identify Your Readers 19
Practicing What You've Learned 22
Assignment 22
Keeping a Journal (Talking to Yourself *Does* Help) 25
Chapter 1 Summary 29

2 The Thesis Statement 31

What Is a Thesis? What Does a "Working Thesis" Do? 32
Can a "Working Thesis" Change? 32
Guidelines for Writing a Good Thesis 33
Avoiding Common Errors in Thesis Statements 37
Practicing What You've Learned 39
Assignment 40
Using the Essay Map 41
Practicing What You've Learned 42
Assignment 43
Chapter 2 Summary 45

3 The Body Paragraphs   47

Planning the Body of Your Essay   47

Composing the Body Paragraphs   50

The Topic Sentence   50

Focusing Your Topic Sentence   53

Placing Your Topic Sentence   53

Practicing What You've Learned   55

Assignment   58

Applying What You've Learned to Your Writing   58

Paragraph Development   59

Paragraph Length   62

Practicing What You've Learned   63

Assignment   63

Applying What You've Learned to Your Writing   64

Paragraph Unity   64

Practicing What You've Learned   66

Applying What You've Learned to Your Writing   67

Paragraph Coherence   68

Practicing What You've Learned   73

Paragraph Sequence   76

Transitions between Paragraphs   77

Applying What You've Learned to Your Writing   78

Chapter 3 Summary   78

4 Beginnings and Endings   79

How to Write a Good Lead-in   79

Avoiding Errors in Lead-ins   81

Practicing What You've Learned   82

How to Write a Good Concluding Paragraph   82

Avoiding Errors in Conclusions   84

Practicing What You've Learned   85

How to Write a Good Title   85

Assignment   86

Applying What You've Learned to Your Writing   86

Chapter 4 Summary   87

5 Drafting and Revising: Creative Thinking, Critical Thinking 89

What Is Revision? 89

When Does Revision Occur? 90

Myths about Revision 90

Can I Learn to Improve My Revision Skills? 91

Preparing to Draft: Some Time-Saving Hints 92
Additional Suggestions for Writers with Word Processors   93

Writing Centers, Computer Labs, and Computer Classrooms 95

A Revision Process for Your Drafts 96

What Is Critical Thinking? 98

Thinking Critically as a Writer 98

A Final Checklist for Your Essay 104
Practicing What You've Learned 104

Benefiting from Revision Workshops 106
Practicing What You've Learned 109
Assignment 110

Some Last Advice: How to Play with Your Mental Blocks 110

Chapter 5 Summary 113

6 Effective Sentences 115

Developing a Clear Style 116

Developing a Concise Style 122
Practicing What You've Learned 126
Assignment 128

Developing a Lively Style 128
Practicing What You've Learned 132
Assignment 132

Developing an Emphatic Style 133
Practicing What You've Learned 136
Assignment 138
Applying What You've Learned to Your Writing 139

Chapter 6 Summary 139

7 Word Logic 141

Selecting the Correct Words 141
Practicing What You've Learned 147

Selecting the Best Words 149
Practicing What You've Learned 159

Assignment 161
Applying What You've Learned to Your Writing 163
Chapter 7 Summary 164

8 The Reading-Writing Connection 165

How Can Reading Well Help Me Become a Better Writer? 165
How Can I Become an Analytical Reader? 166
Sample Annotated Essay: "Our Youth Should Serve" 168
Practicing What You've Learned 171
Assignment 171
Writing a Summary 171
Practicing What You've Learned 173
Benefiting from Class Discussions 173
Chapter 8 Summary 175

Part One Summary: The Basics of the Short Essay 176

■ Part Two   Purposes, Modes, and Strategies 177

9 Exposition 179

The Strategies of Exposition 179
Strategy One: Development by Example 180
Developing Your Essay 183
Problems to Avoid 184
Essay Topics 185
A Topic Proposal for Your Essay 186
Sample Student Essay 187

Professional Essay: "So What's So Bad about Being So-So?" 189
The drive for perfection is preventing too many people from enjoying sports and hobbies, says author Lisa Wilson Strick (who proudly plays the piano badly but with great pleasure).
A Revision Worksheet 192
Reviewing Your Progress 193
Strategy Two: Development by Process Analysis 193
Developing Your Essay 194
Problems to Avoid 196
Essay Topics 196
A Topic Proposal for Your Essay 198
Sample Student Essay 198

Professional Essay (Informative Process): "To Bid the World Farewell" 203
By describing the embalming process in vivid, step-by-step detail, social critic and author Jessica Mitford questions the value—and necessity—of the entire procedure.

Professional Essay (Directional Process): "Ditch Diving" 208
Humorist Tom Bodett offers precise instructions for achieving high scores in the winter sport of ditch diving, an unappreciated artistic activity that requires only a vehicle, a road, a ditch, and some snow.

A Revision Worksheet 210

Reviewing Your Progress 211

Strategy Three: Development by Comparison and Contrast 211

Developing Your Essay 211

Which Pattern Should You Use? 213

Problems to Avoid 214

Essay Topics 215

A Topic Proposal for Your Essay 217

Sample Student Essay (Point-by-Point Pattern) 217

Sample Student Essay (Block Pattern) 221

Professional Essay (Point-by-Point Pattern): "Grant and Lee: A Study in Contrasts" 223
Noted historian Bruce Catton compares and contrasts the two great generals of the Civil War, concluding that their roles at Appomattox made possible "a peace of reconciliation."

Professional Essay (Block Pattern): "Two Ways of Viewing the River" 227
One of the United States' most beloved writers, Samuel Clemens (Mark Twain), contrasts his earlier, romantic view of the Mississippi River to his later, more practical view as an experienced riverboat pilot.

A Revision Worksheet 229

A Special Kind of Comparison: The Analogy 229

Reviewing Your Progress 232

Strategy Four: Development by Definition 232

Why Do We Define? 233

Developing Your Essay 233

Problems to Avoid 235

Essay Topics 236

A Topic Proposal for Your Essay 237

Sample Student Essay 238

Professional Essay: "The Munchausen Mystery" 241
A Harvard professor of psychiatry explains a perplexing "medical madness" in which patients use extreme and sophisticated measures to fake illnesses—in some cases, all the way to the operating room.

A Revision Worksheet 244

Reviewing Your Progress 244

Strategy Five: Development by Division and Classification 245

Division 245

Classification 245

Developing Your Essay   246
Problems to Avoid   247

Essay Topics   247

A Topic Proposal for Your Essay   249

Sample Student Essay   249

Professional Essay (Classification): "The Plot against People"   252

According to well-known columnist Russell Baker, all inanimate objects may be classified into three categories: those that don't work, those that get lost, and those that break down.

Professional Essay (Division): "A Brush with Reality: Surprises in the Tube"   255

Do you really know what's in the toothpaste you use every day? In this unforgettable essay, science-writer David Bodanis analyzes the surprising (and sometimes shocking) ingredients.

A Revision Worksheet   258

Reviewing Your Progress   258

Strategy Six: Development by Causal Analysis   259

Developing Your Essay   259
Problems to Avoid   261

Essay Topics   262

A Topic Proposal for Your Essay   263

Sample Student Essay   264

Professional Essay: "How Mr. Dewey Decimal Saved My Life"   267

In this delightful essay recalling her teen years in rural Kentucky, award-winning novelist Barbara Kingsolver explains how books and a librarian with a hidden agenda rescued her from a dead-end life in a two-stop-light town.

A Revision Worksheet   270

Reviewing Your Progress   270

10 Argumentation   273

Developing Your Essay   273
Problems to Avoid   282

Common Logical Fallacies   282

Practicing What You've Learned   285

Assignment   287

Essay Topics   287

A Topic Proposal for Your Essay   288

Sample Student Essay   289

Professional Essays (Pro/Con): "Free Speech Zones"   292

Should demonstrators be restricted to "protest zones" far away from the speakers or sites they are protesting? No, says the editorial board of *USA Today*, an enforced confinement of citizens interferes with their basic right of free speech. Yes, says attorney Robert J. Scott, who argues that recent disruptive activity justifies such restrictions to maintain order.

Analyzing Advertisements 295
  Conflicting Positions: Gun Control 295
  Competing Products: Sources of Energy 299
  Popular Appeals: Spending Our Money 302
A Revision Worksheet 305
  Reviewing Your Progress 305

11 Description **307**

How to Write Effective Description 307
  Problems to Avoid 311
Practicing What You've Learned: "Aboard the Sleeper" by Verlyn Klinkenborg 312
Assignment: "Nighthawks" by Edward Hopper 313
Essay Topics 313
  A Topic Proposal for Your Essay 315

Sample Student Essay 315

Professional Essay: "Still Learning from My Mother" 319
  Not only did Mom throw a mean fast ball in her younger days, at almost 80 she
    continues to achieve new goals with determination and spirit, as described by son
    Cliff Schneider in this charming tribute.
A Revision Worksheet 322
  Reviewing Your Progress 323

12 Narration **325**

Writing the Effective Narrative Essay 326
  Problems to Avoid 327
Practicing What You've Learned: "Tornado Over Kansas" by John Steuart Curry 328
Essay Topics 329
  A Topic Proposal for Your Essay 330

Sample Student Essay 331

Professional Essay: "Sister Flowers" 333
  Multi-talented writer and performer Maya Angelou remembers a special time in her life
    and shows how one person's kindness and respect can dramatically change a child's
    life for the better.
A Revision Worksheet 338
  Reviewing Your Progress 339

13 Writing Essays Using Multiple Strategies **341**

  Choosing the Best Strategies 342
  Problems to Avoid 343

Sample Student Essay 343

Professional Essay: "Don't Let Stereotypes Warp Your Judgments" 347
  Are Gloria and Richard better looking than Bertha or Cuthbert? Do you vote for the
    candidate who looks like a winner? In this essay, Professor Robert L. Heilbroner

addresses the complex issue of stereotyping, first by citing some fascinating experiments that illustrate the problem. He then analyzes the causes of type-casting, explains the harmful effects, and offers some steps for changing this negative behavior.

A Revision Worksheet 351
   Reviewing Your Progress 352

■ Part Three   Special Assignments 353

14 Writing a Paper Using Research 355

Focusing Your Topic 355

Beginning Your Library Research 356
   General Reference Works 357
   Online Catalogs 357
   Indexes 358
   Databases 358
   The Internet 361
   Special Collections 363

Conducting the Personal Interview 363

Preparing a Working Bibliography 365

Choosing and Evaluating Your Sources 368

Preparing an Annotated Bibliography 370

Taking Notes 371
   Distinguishing Paraphrase from Summary 373

Incorporating Your Source Material 374

Avoiding Plagiarism 376
Practicing What You've Learned 378
Assignment 379

Choosing the Documentation Style for Your Essay 380
   MLA Style 380
   APA Style 391
   Footnote and Bibliography Form 395

Using Supplementary Notes 396

Sample Student Paper Using MLA Style 397

15 Writing in Class: Exams and "Response" Essays 407

Steps to Writing Well under Pressure 407
   Problems to Avoid 413
Practicing What You've Learned 413
Assignment 414

Writing the Summary-and-Response Essay 414

Sample Student Essay 417
Practicing What You've Learned 419
Assignment 419

16 Writing about Literature **421**

Using Literature in the Composition Classroom 421
Suggestions for Close Reading of Literature 422
Steps to Reading a Story 423
Annotated Story: "The Story of an Hour" 424
In this ironic story by Kate Chopin, a woman receives some bad news about her husband—not once, but twice.
Sample Student Essay 428
Steps to Reading a Poem 430
Annotated Poem: "When I Heard the Learn'd Astronomer" 433
Poet Walt Whitman contrasts two ways of knowing and responding to the marvels of the night sky.
Sample Student Essay 434
Guidelines for Writing about Literature 437
Problems to Avoid 438
Practicing What You've Learned:"Snow" by Julia Alverez and "Those Winter Sundays" by Robert Hayden 439
Suggestions for Writing 441

17 Writing about Film **443**

Using Film in the Composition Classroom 443
Guidelines for Writing about Film 445
Problems to Avoid 448
Sample Student Essay 448
Practicing What You've Learned: "Cat in the Hat Coughs Up Mayhem" by David Germain 452
Suggestions for Writing 453
Glossary of Film Terms 454

18 Writing in the World of Work **457**

Composing Business Letters 458
Business Letter Format 459
Practicing What You've Learned 462
Assignment 462
Sample Business Letter 463
Creating Memos 464

Sending Professional E-Mail 465

Designing Résumés 467
Critique Your Page Appeal 470
Problems to Avoid 470
Assignment 471

Sample Résumés 471

Writing Post-Interview Letters 474

■ **Part Four** A Concise Handbook **475**

19 Major Errors in Grammar 477

Errors with Verbs 477
Practicing What You've Learned 481

Errors with Nouns 482

Errors with Pronouns 482
Practicing What You've Learned 485

Errors with Adverbs and Adjectives 486
Practicing What You've Learned 488

Errors in Modifying Phrases 488
Practicing What You've Learned 489

Errors in Sentences 490
Practicing What You've Learned 490
Practicing What You've Learned 492
Practicing What You've Learned 494
Practicing What You've Learned 496

20 A Concise Guide to Punctuation 499

The Period 500

The Question Mark 500

The Exclamation Point 500
Practicing What You've Learned 500

The Comma 501
Practicing What You've Learned 504

The Semicolon 505
Practicing What You've Learned 506

The Colon 507
Practicing What You've Learned 508

The Apostrophe 509
Practicing What You've Learned 510

Quotation Marks 510
Practicing What You've Learned 512
Parentheses 512
Brackets 513
The Dash 514
Practicing What You've Learned 515
The Hyphen 515
Practicing What You've Learned 516
Underlining 517
Ellipsis Points 517
Practicing What You've Learned 518

21 A Concise Guide to Mechanics 521

Capitalization 521
Practicing What You've Learned 522
Abbreviations 523
Numbers 524
Practicing What You've Learned 524
Spelling 525

■ Part Five Additional Readings 529

22 Exposition: Development By Example 531

"Darkness at Noon" by Harold Krents 531
"Black Men and Public Space" by Brent Staples 533
"Relying on the Kindness of Strangers" by Deborah Mathis 535

23 Exposition: Process Analysis 537

"The Jeaning of America" by Carin C. Quinn 537
"Skiing Lessons: The Cold, Hard Facts" by Dave Barry 539
"Autumn Leaves" by Diane Ackerman 540

24 Exposition: Comparison/Contrast 543

"My Real Car" by Bailey White 543
"Dearly Disconnected" by Ian Frazier 545
"Once More to the Lake" by E. B. White 548

25 Exposition: Definition 553

"The Heroes Among Us" by Stephen M. Wolf 553

"Celebrating Nerdiness" by Tom Rogers 554

"What Is Poverty?" by Jo Goodwin Parker 556

26 Exposition: Division/Classification 561

"Hoppers" by Garrison Keillor 561

"Party Manners" by Richard Grossman 562

"College Pressures" by William Zinsser 565

27 Exposition: Causal Analysis 571

"The Teacher Who Changed My Life" by Nicholas Gage 571

"They Have to Keep It: People Who Save Everything" by Lynda W. Warren and Jonnae C. Ostrom 575

"You Call This Progress?" by Seth Shostak 577

28 Argumentation 581

"A Scientist: 'I Am the Enemy'" by Ron Kline 581

"Sack Athletic Scholarships" by Allen Barra 583

"Judging by the Cover" by Bonny Gainley 584

29 Description 587

"A Day at the Theme Park" by W. Bruce Cameron 587

"Hush, Timmy—This Is Like a Church" by Kurt Anderson 588

"In the Land of 'Coke-Cola'" by William Least Heat-Moon 590

30 Narration 593

"38 Who Saw Murder Didn't Call the Police" by Martin Gansberg 593

"When Father Doesn't Know Best" by Andrew Merton 596

"The Talkies" by James Lileks 598

31 Essays for Further Analysis: Multiple Strategies and Styles 601

"I Have a Dream" by Martin Luther King, Jr. 601

"Crossing the Great Divide" by Peter Fish 604

"Beauty: When the Other Dancer Is the Self" by Alice Walker 606

32 Literature 613

"Child of the Americas" by Aurora Levins Morales 613
"Ozymandias" by Percy Bysshe Shelley 614
"A Mystery of Heroism" by Stephen Crane 615

33 Writing and Language 621

"Life at Close Range" by Gretel Ehrlich 621
"Notes on Punctuation" by Lewis Thomas 624
"Mother Tongue" by Amy Tan 626

Credits   630
Index   635

List of Fine Art

The Letter, by Johannes Vermeer 25

Sliding in Yankee Stadium, by Lance Richbourg 74

The Scream, by Edvard Munch 111

Breadline during the Louisville Flood, Kentucky 1937, by Margaret Bourke-White 216

The Subway, by George Tooker 237

Nighthawks, by Edward Hopper 313

The Water-Lily Pond, by Claude Monet 314

Migrant Mother, by Dorothea Lange 322

Tornado Over Kansas, by John Steuart Curry 328

Repose [Nonchaloir], by John Singer Sargent 427

Starry Night, by Vincent Van Gogh 433

To the Teacher

The sixth edition of *Steps to Writing Well with Additional Readings* has been written for teachers of composition who have had trouble finding a textbook that students can easily understand. Too many books on today's market, these teachers rightfully complain, are still unnecessarily complex, dry, or massive for the majority of students. Written simply, in an informal style and addressed to the student, this textbook offers a step-by-step guide to writing a variety of 500-to-800-word essays. The combination of concise, practical advice, a number of student and professional samples, and a brief handbook should provide more than enough helpful information for students enrolled in a one-semester course, without intimidating them. Teachers of this new edition may appreciate the book's four-color design and the addition of artwork, including thirty-six paintings and photographs, many used as writing prompts for today's visually oriented students.

Although many parts of the book have been revised or expanded for this edition, its organization remains essentially the same. Part One offers advice on "The Basics of the Short Essay"; Part Two discusses "Purposes, Modes, and Strategies"; Part Three focuses on "Special Assignments"; and Part Four presents "A Concise Handbook." Part Five contains thirty-six additional readings. This textbook still begins with the essay "To the Student," which not only argues that students can learn to write better with practice and dedication but also gives them a number of practical reasons why they *should* learn to write better.

Part One, containing eight chapters, moves students through the process of writing the short essay. Chapter 1, on prewriting, stresses finding the proper attitude ("the desire to communicate") and presents helpful suggestions for selecting a subject. This chapter then offers students ten methods for finding a significant purpose and focus for their essays. In addition, a section on using the journal explains more than a dozen ways that students may improve their skills by writing a variety of nonthreatening—and even playful—assignments. The section on audience should also help student writers identify their particular readers and communicate more effectively with them. After finding a topic and identifying their audience, students are ready for Chapter 2, devoted almost entirely to a discussion of the thesis statement. This chapter first explains the role of the "working thesis" in early drafts and then clearly outlines what a good thesis is and isn't by presenting a host of examples to illustrate the advice. Also included in this chapter is an explanation of the "essay map," an organizational tool that can help students structure their essays and plan their body paragraphs.

Chapter 3 discusses in detail the requirements of good body paragraphs: topic sentences, unity, order and coherence, adequate development, use of specific detail, and logical sequence. Over forty paragraphs illustrate both strengths and weaknesses of student writing. These paragraphs are not complex literary or professional excerpts but rather well-designed, precise examples of the principles under examination, written on subjects students can understand and appreciate. This chapter twice provides the opportunity for students to see how a topic may progress from a working thesis statement to an informal essay outline, which in turn helps produce well-developed paragraphs in the body of an essay. To complete the overview of the short essay, Chapter 4 explains, through a number of samples, how to write good introductions, conclusions, and titles.

Chapter 5, "Drafting and Revising: Creative Thinking, Critical Thinking," focuses on the revision process. Because too many students still think of revision as merely proofreading their essays rather than as an essential, recursive activity, this chapter emphasizes the importance of revision in all good writing. These pages offer a system for revising drafts in stages, including a discussion of drafting and revising on a word processor. A section on critical thinking shows students how to analyze and evaluate their ideas and those of others and stresses the role of critical thinking skills in the selection of evidence for all writing assignments. Chapter 5 also offers advice for participants in "peer workshops" (instructors may also find useful advice on organizing effective peer workshops in the Instructor's Manual for this edition). Also included in this chapter is a student essay, annotated to show how a writer (or a workshop partner) might use the questions suggested in the discussion of the revision process. This chapter ends with a list of suggestions for beating Writer's Block.

Chapter 6, on effective sentences, emphasizes the importance of clarity, conciseness, and vividness, with nearly one hundred and fifty sample sentences illustrating the chapter's advice. Chapter 7, on word choice, presents practical suggestions for selecting accurate, appropriate words that are specific, memorable, and persuasive. This chapter also contains sections on avoiding sexist language and "bureaucratese." Chapter 8, "The Reading-Writing Connection," maintains that by learning to read analytically, students can improve their own writing skills. The chapter contains step-by-step directions for reading and annotating essays and suggests many ways students may profit from studying the rhetorical choices of other writers. A professional essay, annotated according to these steps, is included, as well as guid-ance for writing summaries of reading selections. A new section offers students suggestions for effective participation in class discussions, with advice for improving comprehension and note-taking skills. Teachers may wish to assign this chapter before asking students to read the professional essays that appear throughout this textbook.

Each chapter in Part One contains samples and exercises. As in the previous editions, the "Practicing What You've Learned" exercises follow each major section in each chapter so that both teacher and students may quickly discover if particular material needs additional attention. Moreover, by conquering small steps in the writing process, one at a time, students should feel more confident and should learn more rapidly. Assignments, which also follow each major section in these chapters, suggest class activities and frequently emphasize "peer teaching," a useful method that asks students to prepare appropriate exercises for classmates and then to evaluate the results. Such assignments, operating under the premise that "you don't truly learn a subject until you teach it," provide engaging classroom activity for all the students and also remove from the teacher some of the burden of creating exercises.

Throughout the chapters in Part One, activities called "Applying What You've Learned to *Your* Writing" follow the exercises and assignments. Each of these activities encourages students to "follow through" by incorporating into a current draft the skill they have just read about and practiced. By following a three-step procedure—reading the advice in the text, practicing the advice through the exercises, and then applying the advice directly to their own prose—students should improve their writing processes. In addition, each of the chapters in Part One concludes with a summary, designed to help students review the important points in the material under study.

 Part Two presents discussion of the kinds of essays students are most often asked to write. Chapter 9, on exposition, is divided into separate discussions of the expository strategies: example, process, comparison/contrast, definition, division and classification, and causal analysis. A new section explaining analogy expands the discussion of comparison/contrast. Discussions in Chapter 9 and the chapters on argument, description, and narration follow a similar format by offering the students (a) a clear definition of the mode (or strategy), explained with familiar examples; (b) practical advice on developing each essay; (c) warnings about common problems; (d) suggested essay topics; (e) a topic proposal sheet; (f) sample student essay(s) with marginal notes; (g) professional essay(s) followed by questions on content, structure, and style, writing suggestions, and a vocabulary list; (h) a revision worksheet to guide student writers through their rough drafts; and (i) a progress report. In this edition, a new feature has been added to Part Two: in the lists of suggested essay topics, each #20 uses one or more of the artworks in this book as a writing prompt. Teachers now have the option of using paintings and photographs such as *Nighthawks* and *Migrant Mother* to encourage thoughtful essays organized in a variety of ways.

The sixteen student essays in this text should encourage student writers by showing them that others in their situation can indeed compose organized, well-developed essays. The student essays that appear here are not perfect; consequently, teachers may use them in class to generate suggestions for still more revision. The twenty-one professional readings in Parts Two and Three were also selected to spur class discussion and to illustrate the rhetorical principles presented throughout the text. (The process analysis and comparison/contrast sections of Chapter 9 contain two professional essays so that students may see examples of two commonly used methods of organization; both division and classification are now illustrated by professional writing.) Those professional reading in Parts Two and Three most popular with the users of the fifth edition have been retained; six selections are new to this edition.

 Chapter 10 discusses the argumentative essay, presenting a new pair of professional essays with opposing views and new advertisements, selected to help students analyze rhetorical appeals and supporting evidence. Chapters 11 and 12, on writing description and narration, may be assigned prior to the expository strategies or may be used as supplementary material for any kind of writing incorporating descriptive language or extended example. Chapter 11 now includes two professional essays, illustrating both description of a person and of a place. Both chapters contain art work designed to help students understand the importance of vivid details in support of a dominant effect.

Although this text shows students how to master individual rhetorical strategies, one essay at a time, experienced writers often choose a combination, or blending, of strategies to best accomplish their purpose. "Writing Essays Using Multiple Strategies," Chapter 13, concludes Part Two by offering advice to writers who are ready to address more complex topics and essay organization. This chapter also contains both student and professional essays to illustrate clear use of multiple strategies to accomplish the writer's purpose.

Part Three, called "Special Assignments," allows instructors to design their composition courses in a variety of ways, perhaps by adding a research paper, a literary analysis, an in-class essay, a movie review, or a business writing assignment. Chapter 14, "Writing a Paper Using Research," shows students how to focus a topic, search for information in a variety of ways, choose and evaluate evidence, avoid plagiarism, and effectively incorporate and cite source material in their essays. This edition contains updated discussions of electronic sources and offers students a free, four-month subscription to *InfoTrac College* *Edition*, an easy-to-use online database of full-text articles from nearly 5,000 magazines, journals, newspapers, and other sources. To provide students with another avenue for collecting information, a new section on the art of interviewing has been added. This chapter also presents updated MLA and APA documentation styles and includes a student essay illustrating MLA citations.

Chapter 15, "Writing in Class: Exams and 'Response' Essays," is designed to help students respond quickly and accurately to a variety of in-class assignments by understanding their task's purpose and by recognizing key directional words. Advice for successfully organizing and completing timed writing should also help decrease students' anxiety. Because so many composition courses today include some variation of the "summary-and-response" assignment (used not only as an in- or out-of-class essay but also as a placement or exit test), this chapter also addresses this kind of writing and offers a sample student essay.

"Writing about Literature," Chapter 16, discusses multiple ways literary selections may be used in the composition class, either as prompts for personal essays or for papers of literary analysis. Students are offered a series of suggestions for close reading of both poetry and short fiction. The chapter contains an annotated poem, an annotated short story, and two student essays analyzing those works. Another poem and story, without marginal notes, are included for classroom discussion or assignment.

An entirely new Chapter 17, "Writing about Film," offers an opportunity for students to practice good writing skills in essays using movies as subject matter in a variety of ways. Suggestions for critical thinking and writing about films and a glossary of cinematic terms are included, as well as a student essay and a brief movie review that may be critiqued in class.

Chapter 18, "Writing in the World of Work," allows students to practice composing business letters, office memos, electronic mail, and résumés. With the increasing use of technology in the workplace, students may also profit from a section discussing "netiquette" that encourages writers to cultivate a sense of civility and professionalism, as well as clarity, in their electronic communications. A second sample résumé and a brief section on writing the post-interview letter have been added to this chapter.

Part Four presents a concise handbook with accessible explanations and examples showing how to correct the most common errors in grammar, punctuation, and mechanics. To satisfy requests from teachers, the number of grammar and punctuation exercises has been greatly expanded.

Part Five gives instructors the opportunity to choose among thirty-six additional professional readings. These selections—some serious, some humorous, some familiar, fifteen new to this edition—offer a variety of ideas, structures, and styles to consider. A new section, "Writing and Language," presents essays by three well-known authors thinking about their craft. Studying the professional selections presented in Part Five should help novice writers as they make their own rhetorical choices.

Once again, readers of this edition may note an occasional attempt at humor. The lighthearted tone of some samples and exercises is the result of the author's firm belief that while learning to write is serious business, solemn composition classrooms are not always the most beneficial environments for anxious beginning writers. The author takes full responsibility (and all of the blame) for the bad jokes and even worse puns.

UPDATED

Finally, a complimentary Instructor's Manual, updated for this edition by Colleen Schaeffer, is available, containing suggestions for teaching and answers to exercises and essay questions. Teachers interested in additional information regarding the *InfoTrac College Edition* subscription offer should contact their Thomson sales representative or visit www.thomsonlearning.com.

Although a new edition of this textbook has allowed its author to make a number of changes and additions, the book's purpose remains as stated in the original preface: "While there are many methods of teaching composition, *Steps to Writing Well* tries to help inexperienced writers by offering a clearly defined sequential approach to writing the short essay. By presenting simple, practical advice directly to the students, this text is intended to make the demanding jobs of teaching and learning the basic principles of composition easier and more enjoyable for everyone."

Acknowledgments

Once again I'd like to express my deep appreciation to all the good people at Thomson Wadsworth who helped with this new edition. I'm grateful to Acquisitions Editor Dickson Musslewhite for his kind and generous support, especially for the artwork, which adds a new dimension to this text. The loudest and longest applause goes, as always, to Camille Adkins, the best development editor a textbook author could imagine. Without Camille's advice, creative suggestions, tireless efforts, and incredible patience, there would be no new edition of *Steps*. Thank you, Camille, for your expertise, your hard work, and your good humor throughout this revision.

Special thanks to Samantha Ross, Production Project Manager, who helped guide this edition to print in so many ways; to Karyn Morrison, who once again did such a conscientious job of obtaining permissions for the professional writing in this edition; and to Cheri Throop for her valuable assistance securing the new art and photography.

Merrill Peterson of Matrix Productions must also be highly praised for his excellent work on this book. Merrill's dedication to the production of a quality product was so admirable—and so very appreciated. Another big thank you goes to Holly Aldis and Lauren Root for their professional proofreading and editing skills and to Carrie Brandon, Marlene Veach, and many others in marketing who spread the word of this new edition.

Colleen Schaeffer at California State University, Northridge, has once again created a useful Instructor's Manual, with many good suggestions for discussion and writing.

On-going gratitude is due the students at Colorado State University who allowed me to reprint their writing and also to Sharon Straus, whose essay "Treeclimbing" was a prize winner at the College of Charleston.

In addition, I would like to acknowledge a number of colleagues across the country who offered many helpful suggestions for this edition:

Edith Burford, *Pan American University*
Emily Golson, *University of Northern Colorado*

Sara McKinnon, *Pueblo Community College*
Taylor Emery, *Austin Peay State University*
Keri Bjorklund, *Laramie County Community College*

Many thanks to Professors Joan Beam at Colorado State University's Morgan Library and Scott Douglass at Chattanooga State College for their careful review and contributions to Chapter 14.

Finally, thanks to my husband, David Hall, and to our children, Sarah, Kate, and Austin, for their patience and flexibility during the many phases of this revision process.

To the Student

Finding the Right Attitude

If you agree with one or more of the following statements, we have some serious myth-killing to do before you begin this book:

1. I'm no good in English—never have been, never will be.

2. Only people with natural talent for writing can succeed in composition class.

3. My composition teacher is a picky, comma-hunting old fogey/radical, who will insist I write just like him or her.

4. I write for myself, not for anyone else, so I don't need this class or this book.

5. Composition classes are designed to put my creativity in a straitjacket.

The notion that good writers are born, not made, is a widespread myth that may make you feel defeated before you start. But the simple truth is that good writers *are* made—simply because *effective writing is a skill that can be learned*. Despite any feelings of insecurity you may have about composition, you should realize that you already know many of the basic rules of good writing; after all, you've been writing since you were six years old. What you need now is some practical advice on composition, some coaching to sharpen your skills, and a strong dose of determination to practice those skills until you can consistently produce the results you want. Talent, as the French writer Flaubert once said, is nothing more than long patience.

Think about learning to write well as you might consider your tennis game. No one is born a tennis star. You first learn the basic rules and movements and then go out on the court to practice. And practice. No one's tennis will improve if he or she stays off the court; similarly, you must write regularly and receive feedback to improve your composition skills. Try to see your teacher not as Dr. Frankenstein determined to reproduce his or her style of writing in you, but rather as your coach, your loyal trainer who wants you to do the very best you can. Like any good coach, your teacher will point out your strengths and weaknesses; she or he will often send you to this text for practical suggestions for improvement. And while there are no quick, magic solutions for learning to write well, the most important point to remember is this: with this text, your own common sense, and determination, *you can improve your writing*.

Why Write?

"OK," you say, "so I can improve if I try—but why should I bother? Why should I write well? I'm not going to be a professional writer."

In the first place, writing helps us explore our own thoughts and feelings. Writing forces us to articulate our ideas, to discover what we really think about an issue. For example, let's suppose you're faced with a difficult decision and that the arguments pro and con are jumbled in your head. You begin to write down all the pertinent facts and feelings, and suddenly, you begin to see that you do, indeed, have stronger arguments for one side of the question than the other. Once you "see" what you are thinking, you may then scrutinize your opinions for any logical flaws or weaknesses and revise your argument accordingly. In other words, writing lays out our ideas for examination, analysis, and thoughtful reaction. Thus when we write, we (and the world at large) see who we are, and what we stand for, much more clearly. Moreover, writing can provide a record of our thoughts that we may study and evaluate in a way that conversation cannot. In short, writing well enables us to see and know ourselves—our feelings, ideas, and opinions—better.

On a more practical level, we need to write effectively to communicate with others. While some of our writing may be done solely for ourselves, the majority of it is created for others to share. In this world, it is almost impossible to claim that we write only for ourselves. We are constantly asked to put our feelings, ideas, and knowledge in writing for others to read. During your college years, no matter what your major, you will be repeatedly required to write essays, tests, reports, and exercises (and possibly e-mail or letters home). Later, you may need to write formal letters of application for jobs or graduate training. And on a job you may have to write numerous kinds of reports, proposals, analyses, and requisitions. To be successful in any field, you must make your correspondence with business associates and co-workers clearly understood; remember that enormous amounts of time, energy, and profit have been lost because of a single unclear office memo.

There's still a third—more cynical—reason for studying writing techniques. Once you begin to improve your ability to use language, you will become more aware of the ways others write and speak. Through today's mass media and electronic highways, we are continually bombarded with words from politicians, advertisers, scientists, preachers, teachers, and self-appointed "authorities." We need to understand and evaluate what we are hearing, not only for our benefit but also for self-protection. Language is frequently manipulated to manipulate us. For example, the CIA has long referred to the "neutralization" of enemies, and on occasion, Pentagon officials have carefully avoided discussion of times when misdirected "physics packages" (bombs) fell on "soft targets" (civilians). (One year not so long ago, the National Council of Teachers of English gave their Doublespeak Award to the U.S. officers who, after accidentally shooting down a plane of civilians, reported that the plane didn't crash—rather, it had "uncontrolled contact with the ground.") Some members of Congress have seen no recessions, just "meaningful downturns in aggregate output," so they have treated themselves to a "pay equalization concept," rather than a raise. Advertisers frequently try to disguise their pitches through "infomercials" and "advertorials;" the television networks treat us to "encore presentations" that are the same old summer reruns. And "fenestration engineers" are still window cleaners; "environmental superintendents" are still janitors; "drain surgeons" are still plumbers.

By becoming better writers ourselves, we can learn to recognize and reject the irresponsible, cloudy, or dishonest language of others before we become victims of their exploitation.

A Good Place to Start

If improving writing skills is not only possible but important, it is also something else: hard work. H. L. Mencken, American critic and writer, once remarked that "for every difficult and complex problem, there is an obvious solution that is simple, easy and wrong." No composition textbook can promise easy formulas guaranteed to improve your writing overnight. Nor is writing always fun for everyone. But this text can make the learning process easier, less painful, and more enjoyable than you might anticipate. Written in plain, straightforward language addressed to you, the student, this book will suggest a variety of practical ways for you to organize and write clear, concise prose. Because each of your writing tasks will be different, this textbook cannot provide a single, simple blueprint that will apply in all instances. Later chapters, however, will discuss some of the most common methods of organizing essays, such as development by example, definition, classification, causal analysis, comparison/contrast, and argument. As you become more familiar with, and begin to master, these patterns of writing, you will find yourself increasingly able to assess, organize, and explain the thoughts you have about the people, events, and situations in your own life. And while it may be true that in learning to write well there is no free ride, this book, along with your own willingness to work and improve, can start you down the road with a good sense of direction.

J.W.

Part 1

The Basics
of the Short Essay

The first section of this text is designed to move you through the writing process as you compose a short essay, the kind you are most likely to encounter in composition class and in other college courses. Chapters 1 and 2, on prewriting and the thesis statement, will help you find a topic, purpose, and focus for your essay. Chapter 3, on paragraphs, will show you how to plan, organize, and develop your ideas; Chapter 4 will help you complete your essay. Chapter 5 offers suggestions for revising your writing, and Chapters 6 and 7 present additional advice on selecting your words and composing your sentences. Chapter 8 explains the important reading-writing connection and shows how learning to read analytically can sharpen your writing skills. ■

Chapter 1

Prewriting

■ Getting Started (or Soup-Can Labels Can Be Fascinating)

For many writers, getting started is the hardest part. You may have noticed that when it is time to begin a writing assignment, you suddenly develop an enormous desire to straighten your books, water your plants, or sharpen your pencils for the fifth time. If this situation sounds familiar, you may find it reassuring to know that many professionals undergo these same strange compulsions before they begin writing. Jean Kerr, author of *Please Don't Eat the Daisies*, admitted that she often found herself in the kitchen reading soup-can labels—or anything—in order to prolong the moments before taking pen in hand. John C. Calhoun, vice president under Andrew Jackson, insisted he had to plow his fields before he could write, and Joseph Conrad, author of *Lord Jim* and other novels, is said to have cried on occasion from the sheer dread of sitting down to compose his stories.

To spare you as much hand-wringing as possible, this chapter presents some practical suggestions on how to begin writing your short essay. Although all writers must find the methods that work best for them, you may find some of the following ideas helpful.

But no matter how you actually begin putting words on paper, it is absolutely essential to maintain two basic ideas concerning your writing task. Before you write a single sentence, you should always remind yourself that

1. You have some valuable ideas to tell your reader, and
2. More than anything, you want to communicate those ideas to your reader.

These reminders may seem obvious to you, but without a solid commitment to your own opinions as well as to your reader, your prose will be lifeless and boring. If *you* don't care about your subject, you can't very well expect anyone else to. Have confidence that your ideas are worthwhile and that your reader genuinely wants, or needs, to know what you think.

Equally important, you must also have a strong desire to tell others what you are thinking. One of the most common mistakes inexperienced writers make is failing to move past early stages in the writing process in which they are writing for—or writing to—themselves only. In the first stages of composing an essay, writers frequently "talk" on paper to themselves, exploring thoughts, discovering new insights, making connections, selecting examples, and so on. The ultimate goal of a finished essay, however, is to communicate your opinions to *others* clearly and persuasively. Whether you wish to inform your readers, change their minds, or stir them to action, you cannot accomplish your purpose by writing so that only you understand what you mean. The burden of communicating your thoughts falls on *you*, not the reader, who is under no obligation to struggle through confused, unclear prose, paragraphs that begin and end for no apparent reason, or sentences that come one after another with no more logic than lemmings following one another to the sea.

Therefore, as you move through the drafting and revising stages of your writing process, commit yourself to becoming increasingly aware of your reader's reactions to your prose. Ask yourself as you revise your drafts, "Am I moving beyond writing just to myself? Am I making myself clear to others who may not know what I mean?" Much of your success as a writer depends on an unflagging determination to communicate clearly with your readers.

■ Selecting a Subject

Once you have decided that communicating clearly with others is your ultimate goal, you are ready to select the subject of your essay. Here are some suggestions on how to begin:

Start early. Writing teachers since the earth's crust cooled have been pushing this advice, and for good reason. It's not because teachers are egoists competing for the dubious honor of having the most time-consuming course; it is because few writers, even experienced ones, can do a good job when rushed. You need time to mull over ideas, organize your thoughts, revise and polish your prose. Rule of thumb: always give yourself twice as much time as you think you'll need to avoid the 2:00-A.M.-why-did-I-come-to-college panic.

Find your best space. Develop some successful writing habits by thinking about your very own writing process. When and where do you usually do your best composing? Some people write best early in the morning; others think better later in the day. What time of day seems to produce your best efforts? Where are you working? At a desk? In your room or in a library? Do you start drafting ideas on a computer or do you begin with paper or a yellow pad? With a certain pen or sharpened pencil? Most writers avoid noise and interruptions (TV, telephone, friends, etc.), although some swear by music in the background. If you can identify a previously successful writing experience, try duplicating its location, time, and tools to help you calmly address your new writing task. Or consider trying new combinations of time and place if your previous choices weren't as productive as you would have liked. Recognition and repeated use of your most comfortable writing "spot" may shorten your hesitation to begin composing; your subconscious may recognize the pattern ("Hey, it's time to write!") and help you start in a positive frame of mind. (Remember that it's not just writers who repeat such rituals—think of the athletes you've heard about who won't begin a game without wearing their lucky socks. If it works for them, it can work for you!)

Select something in which you currently have a strong interest. If the essay subject is left to you, think of something fun, fascinating, or frightening you've done or seen lately, perhaps something you've already told a friend about. The subject might be the pleasure of a new hobby, the challenge of a recent book or movie, or even the harassment of registration—anything in which you are personally involved. If you aren't enthusiastic enough about your subject to want to spread the word, pick something else. Bored writers write boring essays.

Don't feel you have nothing from which to choose your subject. Your days are full of activities, people, joys, and irritations. Essays do not have to be written on lofty intellectual or poetic subjects—in fact, some of the world's best essays have been written on such subjects as china teacups, roast pig, and chimney sweeps. Think: what have you been talking or thinking about lately? What have you been doing that you're excited about? Or what about your past? Reflect a few moments on some of your most vivid memories—special people, vacations, holidays, childhood hideaways, your first job or first date—all are possibilities.

Still searching? Make a list of all the subjects on which you are an expert. None, you say? Think again. Most of us have an array of talents we hardly acknowledge. Perhaps you play the guitar or make a mean pot of chili or know how to repair a sports car. You've trained a dog or become a first-class house-sitter or gardener. You know more about computers or old baseball cards than any of your friends. You play soccer or volleyball or Ping-Pong. In other words, take a fresh, close look at your life. You know things that others don't . . . now is your chance to enlighten them!

If a search of your immediate or past personal experience doesn't turn up anything inspiring, you might try looking in the campus newspaper for stories that arouse your strong feelings; don't skip the "Letters to the Editor" column. What are the current topics of controversy on your campus? How do you feel about open admissions? A particular graduation requirement? Speakers or special-interest groups on campus? Financial aid applications? Registration procedures? Parking restrictions? Consider the material you are studying in your other classes: reading *The Jungle* in a literature class may spark an investigative essay on the hot dog industry today, or studying previous immigration laws in your history class may lead you to an argument for or against current immigration practices. Similarly, your local newspaper or national magazines might suggest essay topics to you on local, national, or international affairs that affect your life. Browsing the Internet can provide you with literally thousands of diverse opinions and controversies that invite your response.

In other words, when you're stuck for an essay topic, take a closer look at your environment: your own life—past, present, and future; your hometown; your college town; your state; your country; and your world. You'll probably discover more than enough subjects to satisfy the assignments in your writing class.

Narrow a large subject. Once you've selected a general subject to write on, you may find that it is too broad for effective treatment in a short essay; therefore, you may need to narrow it somewhat. Suppose, for instance, you like to work with plants and have decided to make them the subject of your essay. The subject of "plants," however, is far too large and unwieldy for a short essay, perhaps even for a short book. Consequently, you must make your subject less general. "Houseplants" is more specific, but, again, there's too much to say. "Minimum-care houseplants" is better, but you still need to pare this large, complex subject further so that you may treat it in depth in your short essay. After all, there are many houseplants that require little attention. After several more tries, you might arrive at more specific, manageable topics, such as "houseplants that thrive in dark areas" or "the easy-care Devil's Ivy."

Then again, let's assume you are interested in sports. A 500-to-800-word essay on "sports" would obviously be superficial because the subject covers so much ground. Instead, you might divide the subject into categories such as "sports heroes," "my years on the high school tennis team," "women in gymnastics," "my love of running," and so forth. Perhaps several of your categories would make good short essays, but after looking at your list, you might decide that your real interest at this time is running and that it will be the topic of your essay.

■ Finding Your Essay's Purpose and Focus

Even after you've narrowed your large subject to a more manageable topic, you still must find a specific *purpose* for your essay. Why are you writing about this topic? Do your readers need to be informed, persuaded, entertained? What do you want your writing to accomplish?

In addition to knowing your purpose, you must also find a clear *focus* or direction for your essay. You cannot, for example, inform your readers about every aspect of running. Instead, you must decide on a particular part of the sport and then determine the main point you want to make. If it helps, think of a camera: you see a sweeping landscape you'd like to photograph but you know you can't get it all into one picture, so you pick out a particularly interesting part of the scene. Focus in an essay works in the same way; you zoom in, so to speak, on a particular part of your topic and make that the focus of your paper.

Sometimes part of your problem may be solved by your assignment; your teacher may choose the focus of your essay for you by asking for certain specific information or by prescribing the method of development you should use (compare running to aerobics, explain the process of running properly, analyze the effects of daily running, and so forth). But if the purpose and focus of your essay are decisions you must make, you should always allow your interest and knowledge to guide you. Often a direction or focus for your essay will surface as you narrow your subject, but don't become frustrated if you have to discard several ideas before you hit the one that's right. For instance, you might first consider writing on how to select running shoes and then realize that you know too little about the shoe market, or you might find that there's just too little of importance to say about running paths to make an interesting 500-word essay.

Let's suppose for a moment that you have thought of a subject that interests you—but now you're stuck. Deciding on something to write about this subject suddenly looks as easy as nailing Jell-O to your kitchen wall. What should you say? What would be the purpose of your essay? What would be interesting for you to write about and for readers to hear about?

At this point, you may profit from trying more than one prewriting exercise, designed to help you generate some ideas about your topic. The exercises described next are, in a sense, "pump primers" that will get your creative juices flowing again. Because all writers compose differently, not all of these exercises will work for you—in fact, some of them may lead you nowhere. Nevertheless, try all of them at least once or twice; you may be surprised to discover that some pump-primer techniques work better with some subjects than with others.

■ Pump-Primer Techniques

1. Listing

Try jotting down all the ideas that pop into your head about your topic. Free-associate; don't hold back anything. Try to brainstorm for at least ten minutes.

A quick list on running might look like this:

fun	training for races
healthy	both sexes
relieves tension	any age group
no expensive equipment	running with friend or spouse
shoes	too much competition
poor shoes won't last	great expectations
shin splints	good for lungs
fresh air	improves circulation
good for heart	firming
jogging paths vs. streets	no weight loss
hard surfaces	warm-ups before run
muscle cramps	cool-downs after
going too far	getting discouraged
going too fast	hitting the wall
sense of accomplishment	marathons

As you read over the list, look for connections between ideas or one large idea that encompasses several small ones. In this list, you might first notice that many of the ideas focus on improving health (heart, lungs, circulation), but you discard that subject because a "running improves health" essay is too obvious; it's a topic that's been done too many times to say anything new. A closer look at your list, however, turns up a number of ideas that concern how *not* to jog or reasons why someone might become discouraged and quit a running program. You begin to think of friends who might have stuck with running as you have if only they'd warmed up properly beforehand, chosen the right places to run, paced themselves more realistically, and so on. You decide, therefore, to write an essay telling first-time runners how to start a successful program, how to avoid a number of problems, from shoes to track surfaces, that might otherwise defeat their efforts before they've given the sport a chance.

2. Freewriting

Some people simply need to start writing to find a focus. Take out several sheets of blank paper, give yourself at least ten to fifteen minutes, and begin writing whatever comes to mind on your subject. Don't worry about spelling, punctuation, or even complete sentences. Don't change, correct, or delete anything. If you run out of things to say, write "I can't think of anything to say" until you can find a new thought. At the end of the time period you may discover that by continuously writing you will have written yourself into an interesting topic.

Here are examples of freewriting from students who were given ten minutes to write on the general topic of "nature."

STUDENT 1:

I'm really not the outdoorsy type. I'd rather be inside somewhere than out in Nature tromping through the bushes. I don't like bugs and snakes and stuff like that. Lots of my friends like to go hiking around or camping but I don't. Secretly, I think maybe one of the big reasons I really don't like being out in Nature is because I'm deathly afraid of bees. When I was a kid I was out in the woods and ran into a swarm of bees and got stung about a million times, well, it felt like a million times. I had to go to the hospital for a few days. Now every time I'm outside somewhere and something, anything, flies by me I'm terrified. Totally paranoid. Everyone kids me because I immediately cover my head. I keep hearing about killer bees heading this way, my worst nightmare come true. . . .

STUDENT 2:

We're not going to have any Nature left if people don't do something about the environment. Despite all the media attention to recycling, we're still trashing the planet left and right. People talk big about "saving the environment" but then do such stupid things all the time. Like smokers who flip their cigarette butts out their car windows. Do they think those filters are just going to disappear overnight? The parking lot by this building is full of butts this morning where someone dumped their car ashtray. This campus is full of pop cans, I can see at least three empties under desks in this classroom right now. . . .

These two students reacted quite differently to the same general subject. The first student responded personally, thinking about her own relationship to "nature" (defined as being out in the woods), whereas the second student obviously associated nature with environmental concerns. More freewriting might lead student 1 to a humorous essay on her bee phobia or even to an inquiry about those dreaded killer bees; student 2 might write an interesting paper suggesting ways college students could clean up their campus or easily recycle their aluminum cans.

Often freewriting will not be as coherent as these two samples; sometimes freewriting goes nowhere or in circles. But it's a technique worth trying. By allowing our minds to roam freely over a subject, without worrying about "correctness" or organization, we may remember or discover topics we want to write about or investigate, topics we feel strongly about and wish to introduce to others.

3. Looping*

Looping is a variation on freewriting that works amazingly well for many people, including those who are frustrated rather than helped by freewriting.

Let's assume you've been assigned that old standby "My Summer Vacation." Obviously you must find a focus, something specific and important to say. Again, take out several sheets of blank paper and begin to freewrite, as described previously. Write for at least ten minutes. At the end of this period read over what you've written and try to identify a central idea that has emerged. This idea may be an important thought that occurred to you in the middle or at the end of your writing, or perhaps it was the idea you liked best for whatever reason. It may be the idea that was pulling you onward when time ran out. In other words, look for the thought that stands out, that seems to indicate the direction of your thinking. Put this thought or idea into one sentence called the "center-of-gravity sentence." You have now completed loop 1.

To begin loop 2, use your center-of-gravity sentence as a jumping-off point for another ten minutes of freewriting. Stop, read what you've written, and complete loop 2 by composing another center-of-gravity sentence. Use this second sentence to start loop 3. You should write at least three loops and three center-of-gravity sentences. At the end of three loops, you may find that you have focused on a specific topic that might lead to a good essay. If you're not satisfied with your topic at this point, by all means try two or three more loops until your subject is sufficiently narrowed and focused.

Here's an example of one student's looping exercise:

SUMMER VACATION

Loop 1

    I think summer vacations are very important aspects of living. They symbolize getting away from daily routines, discovering places and people that are different. When I think of vacations I think mostly of traveling somewhere too far to go, say, for a weekend. It is a chance to get away and relax and not think about most responsibilities. Just have a good time and enjoy yourself. Vacations can also be a time of gathering with family and friends.

Center-of-gravity sentence

    Vacations are meant to be used for traveling.

Loop 2

    Vacations are meant for traveling. Last summer my family and I drove to Yellowstone National Park. I didn't want to go at first. I thought looking at geysers would be dumb and boring. I was really

---

* This technique is suggested by Peter Elbow in *Writing Without Teachers* (New York: Oxford University Press, 1975).

obnoxious all the way up there and made lots of smart remarks about getting eaten by bears. Luckily, my parents ignored me and I'm glad they did, because Yellowstone turned out to be wonderful. It's not just Old Faithful—there's lots more to see and learn about, like these colorful boiling pools and boiling patches of mud. I got interested in the thermodynamics of the pools and how new ones are surfacing all the time, and how algae make the pools different colors.

Center-of-gravity sentence

Once I got interested in Yellowstone's amazing pools, my vacation turned out great.

Loop 3

Once I got interested in the pools, I had a good time, mainly because I felt I was seeing something really unusual. I knew I'd never see anything like this again unless I went to Iceland or New Zealand (highly unlikely!). I felt like I was learning a lot, too. I liked the idea of learning a lot about the inside of the earth without having to go to class and study books. I really hated to leave—Mom and Dad kidded me on the way back about how much I'd griped about going on the trip in the first place. I felt pretty dumb. But I was really glad I'd given the Park a closer look instead of holding on to my view of it as a boring bunch of water fountains. I would have had a terrible time, but now I hope to go back someday. I think the experience made me more open-minded about trying new places.

Center-of-gravity sentence

My vacation this summer was special because I was willing to put aside my expectations of boredom and learn some new ideas about the strange environment at Yellowstone.

At the end of three loops, this student has moved from the general subject of "summer vacation" to the more focused idea that her willingness to learn about a new place played an important part in the enjoyment of her vacation. Although her last center-of-gravity sentence still contains some vague words ("special," "new ideas," "strange environment"), the thought stated here may eventually lead to an essay that will not only say something about this student's vacation but may also persuade the readers to reconsider their attitude toward taking trips to new places.

4. The Boomerang

Still another variation on freewriting is the technique called the boomerang, named appropriately because, like the Australian stick, it invites your mind to travel over a subject from opposite directions to produce new ideas.

Suppose, for example, members of your class have been asked to write about their major field of study, which in your case is Liberal Arts. Begin by writing a statement that comes into your mind about majoring in the Liberal Arts and then freewrite on that statement for five minutes. Then write a second statement that approaches the subject from an opposing point of view, and freewrite again for five minutes. Continue this pattern several times. Boomeranging, like looping, can help writers see their subject in a new way and consequently help them find an idea to write about.

Here's an abbreviated sample of boomeranging:

1. Majoring in the Liberal Arts is impractical in today's world.

   [Freewrite for five minutes.]

2. Majoring in the Liberal Arts is practical in today's world.

   [Freewrite for five minutes.]

3. Liberal Arts is a particularly enjoyable major for me.

   [Freewrite for five minutes.]

4. Liberal Arts is not always an enjoyable major for me.

   [Freewrite for five minutes.]

And so on.

By continuing to "throw the boomerang" across your subject, you may not only find your focus but also gain insight into other people's views of your topic, which can be especially valuable if your paper will address a controversial issue or one that you feel is often misunderstood.

5. Clustering

Another excellent technique is clustering (sometimes called "mapping"). Place your general subject in a circle in the middle of a blank sheet of paper and begin to draw other lines and circles that radiate from the original subject. Cluster those ideas that seem to fall together. At the end of ten minutes see if a topic emerges from any of your groups of ideas.

Ten minutes of clustering on the subject of "A Memorable Holiday" might look like the drawing on page 12.

This student may wish to brainstorm further on the Christmas he spent in the hospital with a case of appendicitis or perhaps on the Halloween he first experienced a house of horrors. By using clustering, he has recollected some important details about a number of holidays that may help him focus on an occasion he wants to describe in his paper.

6. Cubing

Still another way to generate ideas is cubing. Imagine a six-sided cube that looks something like the figure on page 13.

Mentally, roll your subject around the cube and freewrite the answers to the questions that follow. Write whatever comes to mind for ten or fifteen minutes; don't concern yourself with the "correctness" of what you write.

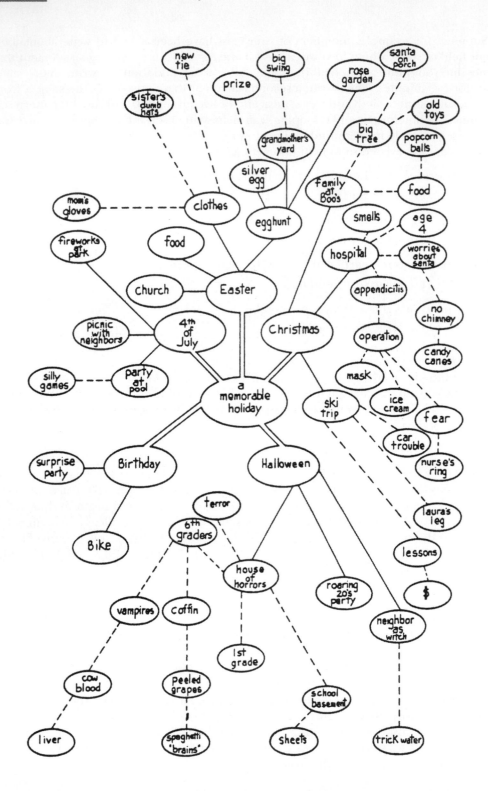

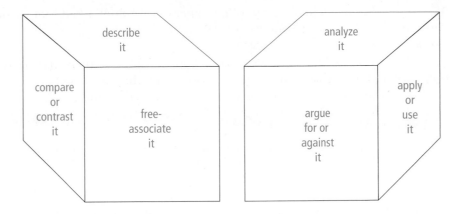

a. *Describe it:* What does your subject look like? What size, colors, textures does it have? Any special features worth noting?

b. *Compare or contrast it:* What is your subject similar to? What is your subject different from? In what ways?

c. *Free-associate it:* What does this subject remind you of? What does it call to mind? What memories does it conjure up?

d. *Analyze it:* How does it work? How are the parts connected? What is its significance?

e. *Argue for or against it:* What arguments can you make for or against your subject? What advantages or disadvantages does it have? What changes or improvements should be made?

f. *Apply it:* What are the uses of your subject? What can you do with it?

A student who had recently volunteered at a homeless shelter wrote the following responses about her experience:

a. *Describe it:* I and five other members of my campus organization volunteered three Saturdays to work at the shelter here in town. We mainly helped in the kitchen, preparing, serving, and cleaning up after meals. At the dinners we served about 70 homeless people, mostly men but also some families with small children and babies.

b. *Compare or contrast it:* I had never done anything like this before so it's hard to compare or contrast it to anything. It was different though from what I expected. I hadn't really thought much about the people who would be there— or to be honest I think I thought they would be pretty weird or sad and I was kind of dreading going there after I volunteered. But the people were just regular normal people. And they were very, very polite to us.

c. *Free-associate it:* Some of the people there reminded me of some of my relatives! John, the kitchen manager, said most of the people were just temporarily "down on their luck" and that reminded me of my aunt and uncle who came to stay with us for a while when I was in high school after my uncle lost his job.

d. *Analyze it:* I feel like I got a lot out of my experience. I think I had some wrong ideas about "the homeless" and working there made me think more about them as real people, not just a faceless group.

e. *Argue for or against it:* I would encourage others to volunteer there. The work isn't hard and it isn't scary. It makes you appreciate what you've got and also makes you think about what you or your family might do if things went wrong for a while. It also makes you feel good to do something for people you don't even know.

f. *Apply it:* I feel like I am more knowledgeable when I hear people talk about the poor or the homeless in this town, especially those people who criticize those who use the shelter.

After you've written your responses, see if any one or more of them give you an idea for a paper. The student who wrote the preceding responses decided she wanted to write an article for her campus newspaper encouraging people to volunteer at the shelter not only to provide much-needed help but also to challenge their own preconceived notions about the homeless in her college town. Cubing helped her realize she had something valuable to say about her experience and gave her a purpose for writing.

7. Interviewing

Another way to find a direction for your paper is through interviewing. Ask a classmate or friend to discuss your subject with you. Let your thoughts range over your subject as your friend asks you questions that arise naturally in the conversation. Or your friend might try asking what are called "reporter's questions" as she or he "interviews" you on your subject:

Who?   When?
What?   Why?
Where?   How?

Listen to what you have to say about your subject. What were you most interested in talking about? What did your friend want to know? Why? By talking about your subject, you may find that you have talked your way into an interesting focus for your paper. If, after the interview, you are still stumped, question your friend: if he or she had to publish an essay based on the information from your interview, what would that essay focus on? Why?

8. The Cross-Examination

If a classmate isn't available for an interview, try interviewing, or cross-examining, yourself. Ask yourself questions about your general subject, just as a lawyer might if you were on the witness stand. Consider using the five categories described on the next page, which are adapted from those suggested by Aristotle, centuries ago, to the orators of his day. Ask yourself as many questions in each category as you can think of, and then go on to the next category. Jot down brief notes to yourself as you answer.

Here are the five categories, plus six sample questions for each to illustrate the possibilities:

1. Definition
   a. How does the dictionary or encyclopedia define or explain this subject?
   b. How do most people define or explain it?
   c. How do I define or explain it?
   d. What do its parts look like?
   e. What is its history or origin?
   f. What are some examples of it?

2. Comparison and Contrast
   a. What is it similar to?
   b. What does it differ from?
   c. What does it parallel?
   d. What is it opposite to?
   e. What is it better than?
   f. What is it worse than?

3. Relationship
   a. What causes it?
   b. What are the effects of it?
   c. What larger group or category is it a part of?
   d. What larger group or category is it in opposition to?
   e. What are its values or goals?
   f. What contradictions does it contain?

4. Circumstance
   a. Is it possible?
   b. Is it impossible?
   c. When has it happened before?
   d. What might prevent it from happening?
   e. Why might it happen again?
   f. Who has been or might be associated with it?

5. Testimony
   a. What do people say about it?
   b. What has been written about it?
   c. What authorities exist on the subject?
   d. Are there any relevant statistics?
   e. What research has been done?
   f. Have I had any direct experience with it?

Some of the questions suggested here, or ones you think of, may not be relevant to or useful for your subject. But some may lead you to ideas you wish to explore in more depth, either in a discovery draft or by using another prewriting technique described in this chapter, such as looping or mapping.

9. Sketching

Sometimes when you have found or been assigned a general subject, the words to explain or describe it just won't come. Although listing or freewriting or one of the other methods suggested here work well for some people, other writers find these techniques intimidating or unproductive. Some of these writers are visual learners—that is, they respond better to pictorial representations of material than they do to written descriptions or explanations. If, on occasion, you are stuck for words, try drawing or sketching or even cartooning the pictures in your mind.

You may be surprised at the details that you remember once you start sketching. For example, you might have been asked to write about a favorite place or a special person in your life or to compare or contrast two places you have lived in or visited. See how many details you can conjure up by drawing the scenes or the people; then look at your details to see if some dominant impression or common theme has emerged. Your Aunt Sophie's insistence on wearing two pounds of costume jewelry might become the focus of a paragraph on her sparkling personality, or the many details you recalled about your grandfather's barn might lead you to a paper on the hardships of farm life. For some writers, a picture can be worth a thousand words—especially if that picture helps them begin putting those words on paper.

10. Dramatizing the Subject

Some writers find it helpful to visualize their subject as if it were a drama or play unfolding in their minds. Kenneth Burke, a thoughtful writer himself, suggests that writers might think about human action in dramatists' terms and then see what sorts of new insights arise as the "drama" unfolds. Burke's dramatists' terms might be adapted for our use and pictured this way:

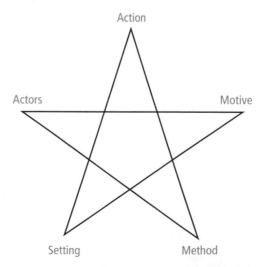

Action

Actors   Motive

Setting   Method

Just as you did in the cubing exercise, try mentally rolling your subject around the star and explore the possibilities that emerge. For example, suppose you want to write about your recent decision to return to college after a long period of working, but you don't know what you want to say about your decision. Start thinking about this decision as a drama and jot down brief answers to such questions as these:

Action:	What happened?
	What were the results?
	What is going to happen?
Actors:	Who was involved in the action?
	Who was affected by the action?
	Who caused the action?
	Who was for it and who was opposed?
Motive:	What were the reasons behind the action?
	What forces motivated the actors to perform as they did?
Method:	How did the action occur?
	By what means did the actors accomplish the action?
Setting:	What was the time and place of the action?
	What did the place look like?
	What positive or negative feelings are associated with this time or place?

These are only a few of the dozens of questions you might ask yourself about your "drama." (If it helps, think of your "drama" as a murder mystery and answer the questions the police detective might ask: what happened here? to whom? who did it? why? with what? when? where? and so on.)

You may find that you have a great deal to write about the combination of actor and motive but very little to say in response to the questions on setting or method. That's fine—simply use the "dramatists' approach" to help you find a specific topic or idea you want to write about.

> ☑ If at any point in this stage of the writing process you are experiencing *Writer's Block*, you might turn to the suggestions for overcoming this common affliction that appear on pages 110–112 in Chapter 5. You might also find it helpful to read the section on *Keeping a Journal*, pages 25–28, because writing in a relaxed mood on a regular basis may be the best long-term cure for your writing anxiety.

■ After You've Found Your Focus

Once you think you've found the focus of your essay, you may be ready to compose a *working thesis statement*, an important part of your essay discussed in great detail in the next chapter. If you've used one of the prewriting exercises outlined in this chapter, by all means hang onto it. The details and observations you generated as you focused your topic may be useful to you as you begin to organize and develop your body paragraphs.

■ PRACTICING WHAT YOU'VE LEARNED

A. Some of the subjects listed below are too broad for a 500-to-800-word essay. Identify those topics that might be treated in short papers and those that still need to be narrowed.

1. The role of the modern university

2. My first (and last) experience with roller blading

3. The characters of William Shakespeare

4. Solar energy

5. Collecting baseball cards

6. Gun-control laws

7. Down with throwaway bottles

8. Computers

9. The best teacher I've ever had

10. Selecting the right bicycle

B. Select two of the large subjects that follow and, through looping or listing details or another prewriting technique, find focused topics that would be appropriate for essays of three to five pages.

1. music

2. cars

3. education

4. jobs

5. television commercials

6. politics

7. animals

8. childhood

9. pollution

10. athletics

■ Discovering Your Audience

Once you have a focused topic and perhaps some ideas about developing your essay, you need to stop a moment to consider your *audience*. Before you can decide what information needs to go into your essay and what should be omitted, you must know who will be reading your paper and why. Knowing your audience will also help you determine what *voice* you should use to achieve the proper tone in your essay.

Suppose, for example, you are attending a college organized on the quarter system, and you decide to write an essay arguing for a switch to the semester system. If your audience is composed of classmates, your essay will probably focus on the advantages to the student body, such as better opportunities for in-depth study in one's major, the ease of making better grades, and the benefits of longer midwinter and summer vacations. However, if you are addressing the Board of Regents, you might emphasize the power of the semester system to attract more students, cut registration costs, and use professors more efficiently. If your audience is composed of towns-people who know little about either system, you will have to devote more time to explaining the logistics of each one and then discuss the semester plan's advantages to the local merchants, realtors, restauranteurs, and so on. *In other words, such factors as the age, education, profession, and interests of your audience can make a difference in determining which points of your argument to stress or omit, which ideas need additional explanation, and what kind of language to adopt.*

■ How to Identify Your Readers

To help you analyze your audience before you begin writing your working thesis statement and rough drafts, here are some steps you may wish to follow:

1. First, see if your writing assignment specifies a particular audience (editors of a journal in your field or the Better Business Bureau of your town, for example) or a general audience of your peers (your classmates or readers of the local newspaper, for instance). Even if your assignment does not mention an intended audience, try to imagine one anyway. Imagining specific readers will help you stick to your goal of communicating clearly, in engaging detail.

2. If a specific audience is designated, ask yourself some questions about their motivation or *reasons for reading* your essay.

- What do these readers want to learn?
- What do they hope to gain?
- Do they need your information to make a decision? Formulate a new plan? Design a new project?
- What action do you want them to take?

The answers to such questions will help you find both your essay's purpose and its content. If, for example, you're trying to persuade an employer to hire you for a particular job, you certainly would write your application in a way that stresses the skills and training the company is searching for. You may have a fine hobby or wonderful family, but if your prospective employer-reader doesn't need to hear about that particular part of your life, toss it out of this piece of writing.

3. Next, try to discover what *knowledge* your audience has of your subject.

- What, if anything, can you assume that your readers already know about your topic?
- What background information might they need to know to understand a current situation clearly?
- What facts, explanations, or examples will best present your ideas? How detailed should you be?
- What terms need to be defined? Equipment explained?

Questions like these should guide you as you collect and discard information for your paper. An essay written to your colleagues in electrical engineering, for instance, need not explain commonly used technical instruments; to do so might even insult your readers. But the same report read by your composition classmates would probably need more detailed explanation in order for you to make yourself understood. Always put yourself in your readers' place and then ask: what else do they need to know to understand this point completely?

4. Once you have decided what information is necessary for your audience, dig a little deeper into your readers' identities. Pose some questions about their *attitudes* and emotional states.

- Are your readers already biased for or against your ideas in some way?
- Do they have positive or negative associations with your subject?
- Are they fearful or anxious, reluctant or bored?
- Do they have radically different expectations or interests?

It helps enormously to know the emotional attitudes of your readers toward your subject. Let's suppose you were arguing for the admission of a young child with AIDS into a local school system, and your audience was the parent-teacher organization. Some of your readers might be frightened or even hostile; knowing this, you would wisely begin your argument with a disarming array of information showing that no cases of AIDS have developed from the casual contact of schoolchildren. In other words, the more you know about your audience's attitudes before you begin writing, the more convincing your prose, because you will make the best choices about both content and organization.

5. Last, think of any *special qualities* that might set your audience apart from any other.

- Are they older or younger than your peers?
- Do they share similar educational experiences or training?
- Are they from a particular part of the world or country that might affect their perspective? Urban or rural?
- Are they in positions of authority?

Knowing special facts about your audience makes a difference, often in your choice of words and tone. You wouldn't, after all, use the same level of vocabulary addressing a group of fifth-graders as you would writing to the children's teacher or principal. Similarly, your tone and word choice probably wouldn't be as formal in a letter to a friend as in a letter to the telephone company protesting your most recent bill.

Without question, analyzing your specific audience is an important step to take before you begin to shape your rough drafts. And before you move on to writing a working thesis, here are a few tips to keep in mind about *all* audiences, no matter who your readers are or what their reasons for reading your writing.

1. **Readers don't like to be bored.** Grab your readers' attention and fight to keep it. Remember the last dull movie you squirmed—or slept—through? How much you resented wasting not only your money but your valuable time as well? How you turned it off mentally and drifted away to someplace more exciting? As you write and revise your drafts, keep imagining readers who are as intelligent—and busy—as you are. Put yourself in their place: would you find this piece of writing stimulating enough to keep reading?

2. **Readers hate confusion and disorder.** Can you recall a time when you tried to find your way to a party, only to discover that a friend's directions were so muddled you wound up hours later, out of gas, cursing in a cornfield? Or the afternoon you spent trying to follow a friend's notes for setting up a chemistry experiment, with explanations that twisted and turned as often as a wandering stray cat? Try to relive such moments of intense frustration as you struggle to make *your* writing clear and direct.

3. **Readers want to think and learn (whether they realize it or not).** Every time you write, you strike a bargain of sorts with your readers: in return for their time and attention, you promise to inform and interest them, to tell them something new or show them something familiar in a different light. You may enlighten them or amuse them or even try to frighten them—but they must feel, in the end, that they've gotten a fair trade. As you plan, write, and revise, ask yourself, "What are my readers learning?" If the honest answer is "nothing important," you may be writing only for yourself. (If you yourself are bored rereading your drafts, you're probably not writing for anybody at all.)

4. **Readers want to see what you see, feel what you feel.** Writing that is vague keeps your readers from fully sharing the information or experience you are trying to communicate. Clear, precise language—full of concrete details and specific examples—lets your readers know that you understand your subject and that you want them to understand it, too. Even a potentially dull topic such as tuning a car can become engaging to a reader if the right details are provided in the right places: your terror as blue sparks leap under your nose when the wrong wire is touched, the depressing sight of the screwdriver squirming from your greasy fingers and disappearing into the oil pan, the sudden shooting pain when the wrench slips and turns your knuckles to raw hamburger. Get your readers involved and interested—and they'll listen to what you have to say. (Details also persuade your reader that you're an authority on your subject; after all, no reader likes to waste time listening to someone whose tentative, vague prose style announces "I only sort-of know what I'm talking about here.")

5. Readers are turned off by writers with pretentious, phony voices. Too often inexperienced writers feel they must sound especially scholarly, scientific, or sophisticated for their essays to be convincing. In fact, the contrary is true. When you assume a voice that is not yours, when you pretend to be someone you're not, you don't sound believable at all—you sound phony. Your readers want to hear what *you* have to say, and the best way to communicate with them is in a natural voice. You may also believe that to write a good essay it is necessary to use a host of unfamiliar, unpronounceable, polysyllabic words gleaned from the pages of your thesaurus. Again, the opposite is true. Our best writers agree with Mark Twain, who once said, "Never use a twenty-five-cent word when a ten-cent word will do." In other words, avoid pretension in your writing just as you do in everyday conversation. Select simple, direct words you know and use frequently; keep your voice natural, sincere, and reasonable. (For additional help choosing the appropriate words and the level of your diction, see Chapter 7.)

> ☑ **Don't Ever Forget Your Readers!**
> Thinking about them as you write will help you choose your ideas, organize your information effectively, and select the best words.

■ PRACTICING WHAT YOU'VE LEARNED

Find a piece of writing in a magazine or newspaper. Identify as specifically as you can the intended audience and main purpose of the selection. How did you arrive at your conclusion?

■ ASSIGNMENT

The article that follows appeared in newspapers across the country some time ago. Read about the diet called "Breatharianism" and then write one or more of the assignments that follow the article.

The Ultimate in Diet Cults: Don't Eat Anything at All

1   CORTE MADERA, CALIF.—Among those seeking enlightenment through diet cults, Wiley Brooks seemed to have the ultimate answer—not eating at all. He called himself a "Breatharian" and claimed to live on air, supplemented only by occasional fluids taken to counteract the toxins of urban environments.

2   "Food is more addictive than heroin," the tall, gaunt man told hundreds of people who paid $500 each to attend five-day "intensives," at which he would stand before them in a camel velour sweatsuit and talk for hours without moving, his fingers meditatively touching at their tips.

3   Brooks, 46, became a celebrity on the New Age touring circuit. ABC-TV featured him in October, 1980, as a weight lifter; he allegedly hoisted 1,100 pounds, about 10 times his own weight. He has also been interviewed on radio and in newspapers.

4   Those who went to his sessions during the past six months on the West Coast and in Hawaii were not just food faddists, but also physicians and other professionals who—though not necessarily ready to believe—thought this man could be onto something important. Some were convinced enough by what they saw to begin limiting their own diets, taking the first steps toward Breatharianism.

5   In his intensives, Brooks did not recommend that people stop eating altogether. Rather, he suggested they "clean their blood" by starting with the "yellow diet"—24 food items including grapefruit, papaya, corn products, eggs, chicken, fish, goat's milk, millet, salsa piquante (Mexican hot sauce) and certain flavors of the Häagen Dazs brand ice cream, including "rum raisin." These foods, he said, have a less toxic effect because, among other things, "their vibrational quality is yellow."

6   Last week, however, aspirants toward Breatharianism were shocked by reports that Brooks had been eating—and what's more, eating things that to health food purists are the worst kind of junk.

7   Word spread that during an intensive in Vancouver, Brooks was seen emerging from a 7-Eleven store with a bag of groceries. The next morning there were allegedly room service trays outside his hotel room, while inside, the trash basket held empty containers of chicken pot pie, chili and biscuits.

8   Kendra Wagner, regional Breatharian coordinator, said she herself had seen Brooks drinking a Coke. "When I asked him about it he said, 'That's how dirty the air is here,'" she explained. "We (the coordinators) sat down with Wiley after the training and said, 'We want you to tell us the truth.' He denied everything. We felt tricked and deceived."

9   As the rumors grew, some Breatharians confronted their leader at a lecture in San Francisco. Brooks denied the story and said that the true message of Breatharianism did not depend on whether he ate or not, anyway.

10   The message in his promotional material reads that "modern man is the degenerate descendant of the Breatharian," and that "living on air alone leads to perfect health and perfect happiness." Though followers had the impression Brooks has not eaten for 18 years, his leaflets merely declare that "he does not eat, and seldom drinks any fluid. He sleeps less than seven hours a week and is healthier, more energetic and happier than he ever dreamed possible."

11   In a telephone interview, Brooks acknowledged that this assertion is not quite correct. "I'm sure I've taken some fruit, like an apple or an orange, but it's better in public to keep it simple." He again staunchly denied the 7-Eleven story.

12   Among those who have been on the yellow diet for months is Jime Collison, 24, who earlier tried "fruitarianism," fasting and other special regimens, and moved from Texas to the San Francisco Bay area just to be around the Breatharian movement. "Now I'm a basket case," he said. "My world revolved around Wiley's philosophy." He had thought Wiley "made the jump to where all of us health food fanatics were going," Collison said.

13   Other Brooks disciples, though disappointed, feel they nevertheless benefited from their experience. Said a physician who has been on the yellow diet for four months: "I feel very good. I still don't know what the truth is, but I do know that Wiley is a good salesman. So I'll be patient, keep an open mind and continue to observe."

14   "Breatharianism is the understanding of what the body really needs, not whether Wiley eats or doesn't," said James Wahler, 35, who teaches a self-development technique called "rebirthing," in Marin County. "I'm realizing that the less I eat the better I feel." He also suggested that Brooks may have lied for people's own good, to get them to listen.

15   "Everyone has benefited from what I'm saying," Brooks said. "There will be a food shortage and a lot of unhappy people when they realize that I was trying to save their lives."

Each of the assignments that follow is directed to a different audience, none of whom know much about Breatharianism. What information does each audience need to know? What kinds of details will be the most persuasive? What sort of organization will work best for each purpose and audience?

1. Write a brief radio advertisement for the five-day intensives. What appeals might persuade people to pay $500 each to attend a seminar to learn to eat air?

2. Assume you are a regional Breatharian coordinator. Write a letter to your city council petitioning for a parade permit that will allow members of your organization to parade down your main street in support of this diet and its lifestyle. What do council members need to know before they vote on such a permit?

3. You are a former Breatharian who is now unhappy with the diet and its unfulfilled promises. Write a report for the vice squad calling for an investigation into the organization. Convince the investigators that the organization is defrauding local citizens and should be stopped.

After writing these assignments, you might exchange them with those written by some of your classmates. Which ads, petitions, and reports are the most persuasive and why?

The Letter, 1670, by Johannes Vermeer

■ Keeping a Journal (Talking to Yourself Does Help)

Many professional writers carry small notebooks with them so they can jot down ideas and impressions for future use. Other people have kept daily logs or diaries for years to record their thoughts for their own enjoyment. In your composition class, you may find it useful to keep a journal that will help you with your writing process, especially in the early stages of prewriting. Journals can also help you to prepare for class discussions and to remember important course material.

You may have kept a journal in another class. There, it may have been called a day-book or learning log or some other name. Although the journal has a variety of uses, it frequently is assigned to encourage you to record your responses to the material read or discussed in class as well as your own thoughts and questions. Most often the journal is kept in a notebook you can carry with you (spiral is fine, although a prong or ring notebook allows you to add or remove pages when you wish); some writers with word processors may prefer to collect their thoughts in designated computer files. Even if a journal is not assigned in your composition class, it is still a useful tool.

Writers who have found journal writing effective advise trying to write a minimum of three entries a week, with each entry at least a half page. To keep your notebook organized, you might start each entry on a new page and date each entry you write. You might also leave the backs of your pages blank so that you can return and respond to an entry at a later date if you wish.

Uses of the Journal

Here are some suggested uses for your journal as you move through the writing process. You may want to experiment with a number of these suggestions to see which are the most productive for you.

1. Use the journal, especially in the first weeks of class, to confront your fears of writing, to conquer the blank page. Write anything you want to—thoughts, observations, notes to yourself, letters home, anything at all. Best your enemy by writing down that witty retort you thought of later and wished you had said. Write about your ideal job, vacation, car, or home. Write a self-portrait or make a list of all the subjects on which you are (or would like to become) an "authority." The more you write, the easier writing becomes—or at least, the easier it is to begin writing because, like a sword swallower, you know you have accomplished the act before and lived to tell about it.

2. Improve your powers of observation. Record interesting snippets of conversations you overhear or catalog noises you hear in a ten-minute period in a crowded place, such as your student center, a bookstore, or a mall. Eat something with multiple layers (a piece of fruit such as an orange) and list all the tastes, textures, and smells you discover. Look around your room and write down a list of everything that is yellow. By becoming sensitive to the sights, sounds, smells, and textures around you, you may find that your powers of description and explanation will expand, enabling you to help your reader "see" what you're talking about in your next essay.

3. Save your own brilliant ideas. Jot down those bright ideas that might turn into great essays. Or save those thoughts you have now for the essay you know is coming later in the semester so you won't forget them. Expand or elaborate on any ideas you have; you might be able to convert your early thoughts into a paragraph when it's time to start drafting.

4. Save other people's brilliant ideas. Record interesting quotations, facts, and figures from other writers and thinkers. You may find some of this information useful in one of your later essays. It's also helpful to look at the ways other writers make their words emphatic, moving, and arresting so you can try some of their techniques in your own prose. (Important: Don't forget to note the source of any material you record, so if you do quote any of it in a paper later, you will be able to document it properly.)

5. Be creative. Write a poem or song or story or joke. Parody the style of someone you've heard or read. Become an inanimate object and complain to the humans around you (for example, what would a soft-drink machine like to say to those folks constantly beating on its stomach?). Become a little green creature from Mars and convince a human to accompany you back to your planet as a specimen of Earthlings (or be the invited guest and explain to the creature why you are definitely not the person to go). The possibilities are endless, so go wild.

6. Prepare for class. If you've been given a reading assignment (an essay or article or pages from a text, for instance), try a split-page entry. Draw a line down the middle of a page in your journal and on the left side of the page write a summary of what you've read or perhaps list the main points. Then on the right side of the same page, write your responses to the material. Your responses might be your personal reaction to the content (what struck you hardest? why?), or it might be your agreement or disagreement with a particular point or two. Or the material might call up some long-forgotten idea or memory. By thinking about your class material both analytically and personally, you almost certainly will remember it for class discussion. You might also find that a good idea for an essay will arise as you think about the reading assignments in different ways.

7. Record responses to class discussions. A journal is a good place to jot down your reactions to what your teacher and your peers are saying in class. You can ask yourself questions ("What did Megan mean when she said . . .") or note any confusion ("I got mixed up when . . .") or record your own reactions ("I disagreed with Jamal when he argued that . . ."). Again, some of your reactions might become the basis of a good essay.

8. Focus on a problem. You can restate the problem or explore the problem or solve the problem. Writing about a problem often encourages the mind to flow over the information in ways that allow discoveries to happen. Sometimes, too, we don't know exactly what the problem is or how we feel about it until we write about it. (You can see the truth of this statement almost every week if you're a reader of advice columns such as "Dear Abby"—invariably someone will write a letter asking for help and end by saying, "Thanks for letting me write; I know now what I should do.")

9. Practice audience awareness. Write letters to different companies, praising or panning their product; then write advertising copy for each product. Become the third critic on a popular movie-review program and show the other two commentators why your review of your favorite movie is superior to theirs. Thinking about a specific audience when you write will help you plan the content, organization, and tone of each writing assignment.

10. Describe your own writing process. It's helpful sometimes to record how you go about writing your essays. How do you get started? How much time do you spend getting started? Do you write an "idea" draft or work from an outline? How do you revise? Do you write multiple drafts? These and many other questions may give you a clue to any problems you may have as you write your next essay. If, for example, you see that you're having trouble again and again with conclusions, you can turn to Chapter 4 for some extra help. Sometimes it's hard to see that there's a pattern in our writing process until we've described it several times.

11. Write a progress report. List all the skills you've mastered as the course progresses. You'll be surprised at how much you have learned. Read the list over if you're ever feeling frustrated or discouraged, and take pride in your growth.

12. Become sensitive to language. Keep a record of jokes and puns that play on words. Record people's weird-but-funny uses of language (overheard at the dorm cafeteria: "She was so skinny she was emancipated" and "I'm tired of being the escape goat"). Rewrite some of today's bureaucratic jargon or retread a cliché. Come up with new images of your own. Playing with language in fun or even silly ways may make writing tasks seem less threatening. (A newspaper recently came up with this language game: change, add, or subtract one letter in a word and provide a new definition. Example: intoxication/intaxication—the giddy feeling of getting a tax refund; graffiti/giraffiti—spray paint that appears on tall buildings; sarcasm/sarchasm—the gulf between the witty speaker and the listener who doesn't get it.)

13. Write your own textbook. Make notes on material that is important for you to remember. For instance, make your own grammar or punctuation handbook with only those rules you find yourself referring to often. Or keep a list of spelling rules that govern the words you misspell frequently. Writing out the rules in your own words and having a convenient place to refer to them may help you teach yourself quicker than studying any textbook (including this one).

These suggestions are some of the many uses you may find for your journal once you start writing in one on a regular basis. Obviously, not all the suggestions here will be appropriate for you, but some might be, so you might consider using a set of divider tabs to separate the different functions of your journal (one section for class responses, one section for your own thoughts, one for your own handbook, and so on).

You may find, as some students have, that the journal is especially useful during the first weeks of your writing course when putting pen to paper is often hardest. Many students, however, continue to use the journal throughout the entire course, and others adapt their journals to record their thoughts and responses to their other college courses and experiences. Whether you continue using a journal beyond this course is up to you, but consider trying the journal for at least six weeks. You may find that it will improve your writing skills more than anything else you have tried before.

★ CHAPTER 1 SUMMARY

Here is a brief summary of what you should know about the prewriting stage of your writing process:

1. Before you begin writing anything, remember that you have valuable ideas to tell your readers.

2. It's not enough that these valuable ideas are clear to you, the writer. Your single most important goal is to communicate those ideas clearly to your readers, who cannot know what's in your mind until you tell them.

3. Whenever possible, select a subject to write on that is of great interest to you, and always give yourself more time than you think you'll need to work on your essay.

4. Try a variety of prewriting techniques to help you find your essay's purpose and a narrowed, specific focus.

5. Review your audience's knowledge of and attitudes toward your topic before you begin your first draft; ask yourself questions such as "Who needs to know about this topic, and why?"

6. Consider keeping a journal to help you explore good ideas and possible topics for writing assignments in your composition class.

Chapter 2

The Thesis Statement

The famous American author Thomas Wolfe had a simple formula for beginning his writing: "Just put a sheet of paper in the typewriter and start bleeding." For some writers, the "bleeding" method works well. You may find that, indeed, you are one of those writers who must begin by freewriting or by writing an entire "discovery draft"* to find your purpose and focus—you must write yourself into your topic, so to speak. Other writers are more structured; they may prefer prewriting in lists, outlines, or cubes. Sometimes writers begin certain projects by composing one way, whereas other kinds of writing tasks profit from another method. There is no right or wrong way to find a topic or to begin writing; simply try to find the methods that work best for you.

Let's assume at this point that you have identified a topic you wish to write about—perhaps you found it by working through one of the prewriting activities mentioned in Chapter 1 or by writing in your journal. Perhaps you had an important idea you have been wanting to write about for some time, or perhaps the assignment in your class suggested the topic to you. Suppose that through one of these avenues you have focused on a topic and you have given some thought to a possible audience for your paper. You may now find it helpful to formulate a *working thesis*.

---

* If you do begin with a discovery draft, you may wish to turn at this point to the manuscript suggestions on pages 92–95 in Chapter 5.

■ What Is a Thesis? What Does a "Working Thesis" Do?

The thesis statement declares the main point or controlling idea of your entire essay. Frequently located near the beginning of a short essay, the thesis answers these questions: "What is the subject of this essay?" "What is the writer's opinion on this subject?" "What is the writer's purpose in this essay?" (to explain something? to argue a position? to move people to action? to entertain?).

Consider a "working thesis" a statement of your main point in its trial or rough-draft form. Allow it to "work" for you as you move from prewriting through drafts and revision. Your working thesis may begin as a very simple sentence. For example, one of the freewriting exercises on nature in Chapter 1 (page 8) might lead to a working thesis such as "Our college needs an on-campus recycling center." Such a working thesis states an opinion about the subject (the need for a center) and suggests what the essay will do (give arguments for building such a center). Similarly, the prewriting list on running (page 7) might lead to a working thesis such as "Before beginning a successful program, novice runners must learn a series of warm-up and cool-down exercises." This statement not only tells the writer's opinion and purpose (the value of the exercises) but also indicates an audience (novice runners).

A working thesis statement can be your most valuable organizational tool. Once you have thought about your essay's main point and purpose, you can begin to draft your paper to accomplish your goals. *Everything in your essay should support your thesis.* Consequently, if you write your working thesis statement at the top of your first draft and refer to it often, your chances of drifting away from your purpose should be reduced.

■ Can a "Working Thesis" Change?

It's important for you to know at this point that there may be a difference between the working thesis that appears in your rough drafts and your final thesis. As you begin drafting, you may have one main idea in mind that surfaced from your prewriting activities. But as you write, you may discover that what you really want to write about is different. Perhaps you discover that one particular part of your essay is really what you want to concentrate on (instead of covering three or four problems you have with your current job, for instance, you decide you want to explore in depth only the difficulties with your boss), or perhaps in the course of writing you find another approach to your subject more satisfying or persuasive (explaining how employees may avoid problems with a particular kind of difficult boss as opposed to describing various kinds of difficult bosses in your field).

Changing directions is not uncommon: *writing is an act of discovery.* Frequently we don't know exactly what we think or what we want to say until we write it. A working thesis appears in your early drafts to help you focus and organize your essay; don't feel it's carved in stone.

A warning comes with this advice, however. If you do write yourself into another essay—that is, if you discover as you write that you are finding a better topic or main point to make, consider this piece of writing a "discovery draft," extended prewriting that has helped you find your real focus. Occasionally, your direction changes so slightly that you can rework or expand your thesis to accommodate your new ideas. But more frequently you may find that it's necessary to begin another draft with your newly discovered working thesis as the controlling idea. When this is the case, don't be discouraged—this kind of "reseeing" or revision of your topic is a common practice among experienced writers (for more advice on revising as rethinking, see Chapter 5). Don't be tempted at this point to leave your original thesis in an essay that has clearly changed its point, purpose, or approach—in other words, don't try to pass off an old head on the body of a new statue! Remember that ultimately you want your thesis to guide your readers rather than confuse them by promising an essay they can't find as they read on.

■ Guidelines for Writing a Good Thesis

To help you draft your thesis statement, here is some advice:

A good thesis states the writer's clearly defined opinion on some subject. You must tell your reader what you think. Don't dodge the issue; present your opinion specifically and precisely. For example, if you were asked to write a thesis statement expressing your position on the national law that designates twenty-one as the legal minimum age to purchase or consume alcohol, the first three theses listed below would be confusing:

Poor	Many people have different opinions on whether people under twenty-one should be permitted to drink alcohol, and I agree with some of them. [The writer's opinion on the issue is not clear to the reader.]
Poor	The question of whether we need a national law governing the minimum age to drink alcohol is a controversial issue in many states. [This statement might introduce the thesis, but the writer has still avoided stating a clear opinion on the issue.]
Poor	I want to give my opinion on the national law that sets twenty-one as the legal age to drink alcohol and the reasons I feel this way. [What is the writer's opinion? The reader still doesn't know.]
Better	To reduce the number of highway fatalities, our country needs to enforce the national law that designates twenty-one as the legal minimum age to purchase and consume alcohol. [The writer clearly states an opinion that will be supported in the essay.]
Better	The legal minimum age for purchasing alcohol should be eighteen rather than twenty-one. [Again, the writer has asserted a clear position on the issue that will be argued in the essay.]

If you want to write about a personal experience but are finding it difficult to find your clearly defined thesis idea, try asking yourself questions about the topic's significance or value. (Examples: Why is this topic important to me? What was so valuable about my year on newspaper staff? What was the most significant lesson I learned? What was an unexpected result of this experience?). Often the answer to one of your questions will show you the way to a working thesis. (Example: Writing for the school newspaper teaches time-management skills that are valuable both in and out of class).

A good thesis asserts one main idea. Many essays drift into confusion because the writer is trying to explain or argue two different, large issues in one essay. You can't effectively ride two horses at once; pick one main idea and explain or argue it in convincing detail.

Poor	The proposed no-smoking ordinance in our town will violate a number of our citizens' civil rights, and no one has proved secondary smoke is dangerous anyway. [This thesis contains two main assertions—the ordinance's violation of rights and secondary smoke's lack of danger—that require two different kinds of supporting evidence.]
Better	The proposed no-smoking ordinance in our town will violate our civil rights. [This essay will show the various ways the ordinance will infringe on personal liberties.]
Better	The most recent U.S. Health Department studies claiming that secondary smoke is dangerous to nonsmokers are based on faulty research. [This essay will also focus on one issue: the validity of the studies on secondary smoke danger.]
Poor	High school athletes shouldn't have to maintain a certain grade-point average to participate in school sports, and the value of sports is often worth the lower academic average. [Again, this thesis moves in two different directions.]
Better	High school athletes shouldn't have to maintain a certain grade-point average to participate in school sports. [This essay will focus on one issue: reasons why a particular average shouldn't be required.]
Better	For some students, participation in sports may be more valuable than achieving a high grade-point average. [This essay will focus on why the benefits of sports may sometimes outweigh those of academics.]

Incidentally, at this point you may recall from your high school days a rule about always expressing your thesis in one sentence. Writing teachers often insist on this rule to help you avoid the double-assertion problem just illustrated. Although not all essays have one-sentence theses, many do, and it's a good habit to strive for in this early stage of your writing.

A good thesis has something worthwhile to say. Although it's true that almost any subject can be made interesting with the right treatment, some subjects are more predictable and therefore more boring than others. Before you write your thesis, think hard about your subject: does your position lend itself to stale or overly obvious ideas? For example, most readers would find the following theses tiresome unless the writers had some original method of developing their essays:

Poor	Dogs have always been man's best friends. [This essay might be full of ho-hum clichés about dogs' faithfulness to their owners.]
Poor	Friendship is a wonderful thing. [Again, watch out for tired truisms that restate the obvious.]
Poor	Food in my dorm is horrible. [Although this essay might be enlivened by some vividly repulsive imagery, the subject itself is ancient.]

Frequently in composition classes you will be asked to write about yourself; after all, you are the world's authority on that subject, and you have many significant interests to talk about whose subject matter will naturally intrigue your readers. However, some topics you may consider writing about may not necessarily appeal to other readers because the material is simply too personal or restricted to be of general interest. In these cases, it often helps to *universalize* the essay's thesis so your readers can also identify with or learn something about the general subject, while learning something about you at the same time:

Poor	The four children in my family have completely different personalities. [This statement may be true, but would anyone other than the children's parents really be fascinated with this topic?]
Better	Birth order can influence children's personalities in startling ways. [The writer is wiser to offer this controversial statement, which is of more interest to readers than the preceding one because many readers have brothers and sisters of their own. The writer can then illustrate her claims with examples from her own family, and from other families, if she wishes.]
Poor	I don't like to take courses that are held in big lecture classes at this school. [Why should your reader care one way or another about your class preference?]
Better	Large lecture classes provide a poor environment for the student who learns best through interaction with both teachers and peers. [This thesis will allow the writer to present personal examples that the reader may identify with or challenge, without writing an essay that is exclusively personal.]

In other words, try to select a subject that will interest, amuse, challenge, persuade, or enlighten your readers. If your subject itself is commonplace, find a unique approach or an unusual, perhaps even controversial, point of view. If your subject is personal, ask yourself if the topic alone will be sufficiently interesting to readers; if not, think about universalizing the thesis to include your audience. Remember that a good thesis should encourage readers to read on with enthusiasm rather than invite groans of "not this again" or shrugs of "so what."

A good thesis is limited to fit the assignment. Your thesis should show that you've narrowed your subject matter to an appropriate size for your essay. Don't allow your thesis to promise more of a discussion than you can adequately deliver in a short essay. You want an in-depth treatment of your subject, not a superficial one. Certainly you may take on important issues in your essays; don't feel you must limit your topics to local or personal subjects. But one simply cannot refight the Vietnam War or effectively defend U.S. foreign policy in Central America in five to eight paragraphs. Focus your essay on an important part of a broader subject that interests you. (For a review of ways to narrow and focus your subject, see pages 6–17.)

Poor	Nuclear power should be banned as an energy source in this country. [Can the writer give the broad subject of nuclear power a fair treatment in three to five pages?]

Better	Because of its poor safety record during the past two years, the Collin County nuclear power plant should be closed. [This writer could probably argue this focused thesis in a short essay.]
Poor	The parking permit system at this college should be completely revised. [An essay calling for the revision of the parking permit system would involve discussion of permits for various kinds of students, faculty, administrators, staff, visitors, delivery personnel, disabled persons, and so forth. Therefore, the thesis is probably too broad for a short essay.]
Better	Because of the complicated application process, the parking permit system at this college penalizes disabled students. [This thesis is focused on a particular problem and could be argued in a short paper.]
Poor	African-American artists have always contributed a lot to many kinds of American culture. ["African-American artists," "many kinds," "a lot," and "culture" cover more ground than can be dealt with in one short essay.]
Better	Scott Joplin was a major influence in the development of the uniquely American music called ragtime. [This thesis is more specifically defined.]

A good thesis is clearly stated in specific terms. More than anything, a vague thesis reflects lack of clarity in the writer's mind and almost inevitably leads to an essay that talks around the subject but never makes a coherent point. Try to avoid words whose meanings are imprecise or those that depend largely on personal interpretation, such as "interesting," "good," and "bad."

Poor	The women's movement is good for our country. [What group does the writer refer to? How is it good? For whom?]
Better	The Colorado Women's Party is working to ensure the benefits of equal pay for equal work for both males and females in our state. [This tells who will benefit and how—clearly defining the thesis.]
Poor	Registration is a big hassle. [No clear idea is communicated here. How much trouble is a "hassle"?]
Better	Registration's alphabetical fee-paying system is inefficient. [The issue is specified.]
Poor	Living in an apartment for the first time can teach you many things about taking care of yourself. ["Things" and "taking care of yourself" are both too vague—what specific ideas does the writer want to discuss? And who is the "you" the writer has in mind?]
Better	By living in an apartment, first-year students can learn valuable lessons in financial planning and time management. [The thesis is now clearly defined and directed.]

A good thesis is easily recognized as the main idea and is often located in the first or second paragraph. Many students are hesitant to spell out a thesis at the beginning of an essay. To quote one student, "I feel as if I'm giving everything away." Although you may feel uncomfortable "giving away" the main point so soon, the alternative of waiting until the last page to present your thesis can seriously weaken your essay.

Without an assertion of what you are trying to prove, your reader does not know how to assess the supporting details your essay presents. For example, if your roommate comes home one afternoon and points out that the roof on your apartment leaks, the rent is too high, and the closet space is too small, you may agree but you may also be confused. Does your roommate want you to call the owner or is this merely a gripe session? How should you respond? On the other hand, if your roommate first announces that he wants the two of you to look for a new place, you can put the discussion of the roof, rent, and closets into its proper context and react accordingly. Similarly, you write an essay to have a specific effect on your readers. You will have a better chance of producing this effect if readers easily and quickly understand what you are trying to do.

Granted, some essays whose position is unmistakably obvious from the outset can get by with a strongly *implied thesis*, and it's true that some essays, often those written by professional writers, are organized to build dramatically to a climax. But if you are an inexperienced writer, the best choice at this point still may be a direct statement of your main idea. It is, after all, your responsibility to make your purpose clear, with as little expense of time and energy on the readers' part as possible. Readers should not be forced to puzzle out your essay's main point—it's your job to tell them.

Remember: an essay is not a detective story, so don't keep your readers in suspense until the last minute. Until you feel comfortable with more sophisticated patterns of organization, plan to put your clearly worded thesis statement near the beginning of your essay.

■ Avoiding Common Errors in Thesis Statements

Here are five mistakes to avoid when forming your thesis statements:

1. Don't make your thesis merely an announcement of your subject matter or a description of your intentions. State an attitude toward the subject.

Poor	The subject of this essay is my experience with a pet boa constrictor. [This is an announcement of the subject, not a thesis.]
Poor	I'm going to discuss boa constrictors as pets. [This represents a statement of intention but not a thesis.]
Better	Boa constrictors do not make healthy indoor pets. [The writer states an opinion that will be explained and defended in the essay.]
Better	My pet boa constrictor, Sir Pent, was a much better bodyguard than my dog, Fang. [The writer states an opinion that will be explained and illustrated in the essay.]

2. Don't clutter your thesis with such expressions as "in my opinion," "I believe," and "in this essay I'll argue that. . . ." These unnecessary phrases weaken your thesis statement because they often make you sound timid or uncertain. This is your essay; therefore, the opinions expressed are obviously yours. Be forceful: speak directly, with conviction.

Poor	My opinion is that the federal government should devote more money to solar energy research.

Poor	My thesis states that the federal government should devote more money to solar energy research.
Better	The federal government should devote more money to solar energy research.
Poor	In this essay I will present lots of reasons why horse racing should not be legalized in Texas.
Better	Horse racing should not be legalized in Texas.

3. Don't be unreasonable. Making irrational or oversimplified claims will not persuade your reader that you have a thorough understanding of the issue. Don't insult any reader; avoid irresponsible charges, name-calling, and profanity.

Poor	Radical religious fanatics across the nation are trying to impose their right-wing views by censoring high school library books. [Words such as "radical," "fanatics," "right-wing," and "censoring" will antagonize many readers immediately.]
Better	Only local school board members—not religious leaders or parents—should decide which books high school libraries should order.
Poor	Too many corrupt books in our high school libraries selected by liberal, atheistic educators are undermining the morals of our youth. [Again, some readers will be offended.]
Better	To ensure that high school libraries contain books that reflect community standards, parents should have a voice in selecting new titles.

4. Don't merely state a fact. A thesis is an assertion of opinion that leads to discussion. Don't select an idea that is self-evident or dead-ended.

Poor	Child abuse is a terrible problem. [Yes, of course, who wouldn't agree that child abuse is terrible?]
Better	Child-abuse laws in this state are too lenient for repeat offenders. [This thesis will lead to a discussion in which supporting arguments and evidence will be presented.]
Poor	Advertisers often use attractive models in their ads to sell products. [True, but rather obvious. How could this essay be turned into something more than a list describing one ad after another?]
Better	A number of liquor advertisers, well known for using pictures of attractive models to sell their products, are now using special graphics to send subliminal messages to their readers. [This claim is controversial and will require persuasive supporting evidence.]
Better	Although long criticized for their negative portrayal of women in television commercials, the auto industry is just as often guilty of stereotyping men as brainless idiots unable to make a decision. [This thesis makes a point that may lead to an interesting discussion.]

5. Don't express your thesis in the form of a question unless the answer is already obvious to the reader.

Poor	Why should every college student be required to take two years of foreign language?

Better   Chemistry majors should be exempt from the foreign-language requirement.

✓ **REMEMBER:** Many times writers "discover" a better thesis near the end of their first draft. That's fine—consider that draft a prewriting or focusing exercise and begin another draft, using the newly discovered thesis as a starting point.

■ PRACTICING WHAT YOU'VE LEARNED

A. Identify each of the following thesis statements as adequate or inadequate. If the thesis is weak or insufficient in some way, explain the problem.

  1. I think *Schindler's List* is a really interesting movie that everyone should see.

  2. Which cars are designed better, Japanese imports or those made in America?

  3. Some people think that the state lottery is a bad way to raise money for parks.

  4. My essay will tell you how to apply for a college loan with the least amount of trouble.

  5. During the fall term, final examinations should be given before the Winter Break, not after the holidays as they are now.

  6. Raising the cost of tuition will be a terrible burden on the students and won't do anything to help the quality of education at this school.

  7. I can't stand to even look at people who are into body piercing, especially in their face.

  8. The passage of the newly proposed health-care bill for the elderly will lead to socialized medicine in this country.

  9. Persons over seventy-five should be required to renew their driver's licenses every year.

  10. Having a close friend you can talk to is very important.

B. Rewrite the following sentences so that each one is a clear thesis statement. Be prepared to explain why you changed the sentences as you did.

  1. Applying for a job can be a negative experience.

  2. Skiing is a lot of fun, but it can be expensive and too dangerous.

3. There are many advantages and disadvantages to the county's new voting machines.

4. The deregulation of the telephone system has been one big headache.

5. In this paper I will debate the pros and cons of the controversial motorcycle helmet law.

6. We need to do something about the billboard clutter on the main highway into town.

7. The insurance laws in this country need to be rewritten.

8. Bicycle riding is my favorite exercise because it's so good for me.

9. In my opinion, Santa Barbara is a fantastic place.

10. The Civil Rights Movement of the 1960s had a tremendous effect on this country.

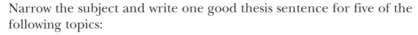 

■ ASSIGNMENT

Narrow the subject and write one good thesis sentence for five of the following topics:

1. A political or social issue
2. College or high school
3. Family
4. A hobby or pastime
5. A recent book or movie
6. Vacations
7. An environmental issue
8. A current fad or fashion
9. A job or profession
10. A rule, law, or regulation

■ Using the Essay Map*

Many thesis sentences will benefit from the addition of an *essay map*, a brief statement in the introductory paragraph introducing the major points to be discussed in the essay. Consider the analogy of beginning a trip by checking your map to see where you are headed. Similarly, an essay map allows the readers to know in advance where you, the writer, will be taking them in the essay.

Let's suppose you have been assigned the task of praising or criticizing some aspect of your campus. You decide that your thesis will be "The Study Skills Center is an excellent place for first-year students to receive help with basic courses." Although your thesis does take a stand ("excellent place"), your reader will not know why the Center is helpful or what points you will cover in your argument. With an essay map added, the reader will have a brief but specific idea where the essay is going and how it will be developed:

Thesis	The Study Skills Center is an excellent place for first-year students to receive help with basic courses. <u>The Center's numerous free services,</u>
Essay map (underlined)	<u>well-trained tutors, and variety of supplementary learning materials can often mean the difference between academic success and failure for many students.</u>

Thanks to the essay map, the reader knows that the essay will discuss the Center's free services, tutors, and learning materials.

Here's another example—this time let's assume you have been frustrated trying to read articles that have been placed "on reserve" in your campus library, so you have decided to criticize your library's reserve facility:

Thesis	The library's reserve facility is badly managed. <u>Its unpredictable</u>
Essay map (underlined)	<u>hours, poor staffing, and inadequate space discourage even the most dedicated students.</u>

After reading the introductory paragraph, the reader knows the essay will discuss the reserve facility's problematic hours, staff, and space. In other words, the thesis statement defines the main purpose of your essay, and the essay map indicates the route you will take to accomplish that purpose.

The essay map often follows the thesis, but it can also appear before it. It is, in fact, frequently part of the thesis statement itself, as illustrated in the following examples:

Thesis with underlined essay map	<u>Because of its free services, well-trained tutors, and useful learning aids,</u> the Study Skills Center is an excellent place for students seeking academic help.
Thesis with underlined essay map	For those students who need extra help with their basic courses, the Study Skills Center is one of the best resources <u>because of its numerous free services, well-trained tutors, and variety of useful learning aids.</u>
Thesis with underlined essay map	<u>Unreasonable hours, poor staffing, and inadequate space</u> make the library reserve facility difficult to use.

---

* I am indebted to Susan Wittig for this useful concept, introduced in *Steps to Structure: An Introduction to Composition and Rhetoric* (Cambridge, MA: Winthrop Publishers, 1975), pages 125–126.

In addition to suggesting the main points of the essay, the map provides two other benefits. It will provide a set of guidelines for organizing your essay, and it will help keep you from wandering off into areas only vaguely related to your thesis. A clearly written thesis statement and essay map provide a skeletal outline for the sequence of paragraphs in your essay, frequently with one body paragraph devoted to each main point mentioned in your map. (Chapter 3, on paragraphs, will explain in more detail the relationships among the thesis, the map, and the body of your essay.) Note that the number of points in the essay map may vary, although three or four may be the number found most often in 500-to-800-word essays. (More than four main points in a short essay may result in underdeveloped paragraphs; see pages 59–62 for additional information.)

Some important advice: although essay maps can be helpful to both writers and readers, they can also sound too mechanical, repetitive, or obvious. If you choose to use a map, always strive to blend it with your thesis as smoothly as possible.

Poor   The Study Skills Center is a helpful place for three reasons. The reasons are its free services, good tutors, and lots of learning materials.

Better   Numerous free services, well-trained tutors, and a variety of useful learning aids make the Study Skills Center a valuable campus resource.

If you feel your essay map is too obvious or mechanical, try using it only in your rough drafts to help you organize your essay. Once you're sure it isn't necessary to clarify your thesis or to guide your reader, consider dropping it from your final draft.

■ PRACTICING WHAT YOU'VE LEARNED

A. Identify the thesis and the essay map in the following sentences by underlining the map.

1. *Citizen Kane* deserves to appear on a list of "Top Movies of All Times" because of its excellent ensemble acting, its fast-paced script, and its innovative editing.

2. Our state should double the existing fines for first-offense drunk drivers. Such a move would lower the number of accidents, cut the costs of insurance, and increase the state revenues for highway maintenance.

3. To guarantee sound construction, lower costs, and personalized design, more people should consider building their own log cabin home.

4. Apartment living is preferable to dorm living because it's cheaper, quieter, and more luxurious.

5. Not everyone can become an astronaut. To qualify, a person must have intelligence, determination, and training.

6. Through unscrupulous uses of propaganda and secret assassination squads, Hitler was able to take control of an economically depressed Germany.

7. Because it builds muscles, increases circulation, and burns harmful fatty tissue, weightlifting is a sport that benefits the entire body.

8. The new tax bill will not radically reform the loophole-riddled revenue system: deductions on secondary residences will remain, real estate tax shelters will be untouched, and nonprofit health organizations will be taxed.

9. Avocados make excellent plants for children. They're inexpensive to buy, easy to root, quick to sprout, and fun to grow.

10. His spirit of protest and clever phrasing blended into unusual musical arrangements have made Bob Dylan a recording giant for over thirty-five years.

B. Review the thesis statements you wrote for the Assignment on page 40. Write an essay map for each thesis statement. You may place the map before or after the thesis, or you may make it part of the thesis itself. Identify which part is the thesis and which is the essay map by underlining the map.

■ ASSIGNMENT

Use one of the following quotations to help you think of a subject for an essay of your own. Don't merely repeat the quotation itself as your thesis statement but, rather, allow the quotation to lead you to your subject and a main point of your own creation that is appropriately narrowed and focused. Don't forget to designate an audience for your essay, a group of readers who need or want to hear what you have to say.

1. "It is never too late to be what one might have been"—George Eliot (Mary Ann Evans), writer

2. "It is amazing how complete is the delusion that beauty is goodness"—Leo Tolstoy, writer

3. "The world is a book and those who don't travel read only a page" —St. Augustine, cleric

4. "Sports do not build character. They reveal it"—Heywood Hale Broun, sportscaster

5. "It is never too late to give up your prejudices"—Henry Thoreau, writer and naturalist

6. "When a thing is funny, search it carefully for a hidden truth"—George Bernard Shaw, writer

7. "I am a great believer in luck, and I find the harder I work the more I have of it"—Stephen Leacock, economist and humorist

8. "Noncooperation with evil is as much a moral obligation as is cooperation with good"—Martin Luther King, Jr., statesman and civil-rights activist

9. "When an old person dies, a library burns to the ground"—African proverb

10. "In this world there are only two tragedies. One is not getting what one wants, and the other is getting it"—Oscar Wilde, writer

11. "Few things are harder to put up with than the annoyance of a good example"—Mark Twain, writer and humorist

12. "The journey is the reward"—Taoist proverb

13. "You can discover more about a person in an hour of play than in a year of conversation"—Plato, philosopher

14. "Nobody can make you feel inferior without your consent"—Eleanor Roosevelt, stateswoman

15. "When a person declares that he's going to college, he's announcing that he needs four more years of coddling before he can face the real world"—Al Capp, creator of the *Li'l Abner* cartoon

16. "If you are patient in one moment of anger, you will escape a hundred days of sorrow"—Chinese proverb

17. "Nobody ever went broke underestimating the intelligence of the American public"—H. L. Mencken, writer and critic

18. "Even if you are on the right track, you will get run over if you just sit there"—Will Rogers, humorist and writer

Eleanor Roosevelt (1884–1962)

© Life Time Pictures/Getty Images

19. "No matter what accomplishments you make, somebody helps you"—Althea Gibson, tennis champion

20. "Human beings are like tea bags. You don't know your own strength until you get into hot water"—Bruce Laingen, U.S. diplomat

21. "Los secretos ni oirlos ni decirlos" (Don't listen to secrets, and don't tell them)—Spanish proverb

★ CHAPTER 2 SUMMARY

Here's a brief review of what you need to know about the thesis statement:

1. A thesis statement declares the main point of your essay; it tells the reader what clearly defined opinion you hold.

2. Everything in your essay should support your thesis statement.

3. A good thesis statement asserts one main idea, narrowed to fit the assignment, and is stated in clear, specific terms.

4. A good thesis statement makes a reasonable claim about a topic that is of interest to its readers as well as to its writer.

5. The thesis statement is often presented near the beginning of the essay, frequently in the first or second paragraph, or is so strongly implied that readers cannot miss the writer's main point.

6. A "working" or trial thesis is an excellent organizing tool to use as you begin drafting because it can help you decide which ideas to include.

7. Because writing is an act of discovery, you may write yourself into a better thesis statement by the end of your first draft. Don't hesitate to begin a new draft with the new thesis statement.

8. Some writers may profit from using an essay map, a brief statement accompanying the thesis that introduces the supporting points discussed in the body of the essay.

C h a p t e r   3

The Body Paragraphs

The middle—or *body*—of your essay is composed of paragraphs that support the thesis statement. By citing examples, explaining causes, offering reasons, or using other strategies in these paragraphs, you supply enough specific evidence to persuade your reader that the opinion expressed in your thesis is a sensible one. Each paragraph in the body usually presents and develops one main point in the discussion of your thesis. Generally, but not always, a new body paragraph signals another major point in the discussion.

■ Planning the Body of Your Essay

Many writers like to have a plan before they begin drafting the body of their essay. To help you create a plan, first look at your thesis. If you used an essay map, as suggested in Chapter 2, you may find that the points mentioned there will provide the basis for the body paragraphs of your essay. For example, recall from Chapter 2 a thesis and essay map praising the Study Skills Center: "Because of its free services, well-trained tutors, and useful learning aids, the Study Skills Center is an excellent place for students seeking academic help." Your plan for developing the body of your essay might look like this:

Body paragraph one: discussion of free services

Body paragraph two: discussion of tutors

Body paragraph three: discussion of learning aids

At this point in your writing process you may wish to sketch in some of the supporting evidence you will include in each paragraph. You might find it helpful to go back to your prewriting activities (listing, looping, freewriting, mapping, cubing, and so on) to see what ideas surfaced then. Adding some examples and supporting details might make an informal outline of the Study Skills paper appear like this:

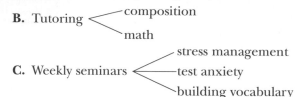

I. Free services
   A. Minicourse on improving study skills
   B. Tutoring ⟨ composition
                 math
   C. Weekly seminars ⟨ stress management
                        test anxiety
                        building vocabulary
   D. Testing for learning disabilities

II. Tutors
   A. Top graduate students in their fields
   B. Experienced teachers
   C. Some bilingual
   D. Have taken training course at Center

III. Learning aids
   A. Supplementary texts
   B. Workbooks
   C. Audiovisual aids

Notice that this plan is an *informal* or *working outline* rather than a *formal outline*—that is, it doesn't have strictly parallel parts nor is it expressed in complete sentences. Unless your teacher requests a formal sentence or topic outline, don't feel you must make one at this early stage. Just consider using the informal outline to plot out a tentative plan that will help you start your first draft.

Here's an example of an informal outline at work: let's suppose you have been asked to write about your most prized possession—and you've chosen your 1966 Mustang, a car you have restored. You already have some ideas but as yet they're scattered and too few to make an interesting, well-developed essay. You try an informal outline, jotting down your ideas thus far:

©Bettmann/CORBIS

I. Car is special because it was a gift from Dad
II. Fun to drive
III. Looks great—new paint job
IV. Engine in top condition

   V. Custom features
  VI. Car shows—fun to be part of

After looking at your outline, you see that some of your categories overlap and could be part of the same discussion. For example, your thoughts about the engine are actually part of the discussion of "fun to drive," and "custom features" are what make the car look great. Moreover, the outline may help you discover new ideas—custom features could be divided into those on the interior as well as those on the exterior of the car. The revised outline might look like this:

   I. Gift from Dad
  II. Fun to drive
     A. Engine
     B. Steering
 III. Looks great
     A. New paint job
     B. Custom features
       1. exterior
       2. interior
  IV. Car shows

You could continue playing with this outline, even moving big chunks of it around; for example, you might decide that what really makes the car so special is that it was a graduation gift from your dad and that is the note you want to end on. So you move "I. Gift from Dad" down to the last position in your outline.

The important point to remember about an informal or working outline is that it is there to help you—not control you. The value of an outline is its ability to help you plan, to help you see logical connections between your ideas, and to help you see obvious places to add new ideas and details. (The informal outline is also handy to keep around in case you're interrupted for a long period while you're drafting; you can always check the outline to see where you were and where you were going when you stopped.) In other words, *don't be intimidated by the outline!*

Here's one more example of an informal outline, this time for the thesis and essay map on the library reserve facility, from Chapter 2:

Thesis-Map: Unpredictable hours, poor staffing, and inadequate space make the library's reserve facility difficult for students to use.

   I. Unpredictable hours
     A. Hours of operation vary from week to week
     B. Unannounced closures
     C. Closed on some holidays, open on others

  II. Poor staffing
     A. Uninformed personnel at reserve desk
     B. Too few on duty at peak times

 III. Inadequate space
     A. Room too small for number of users
     B. Too few chairs, tables
     C. Weak lighting

You may have more than three points to make in your essay. And, on occasion, you may need more than one paragraph to discuss a single point. For instance, you might discover that you need two paragraphs to explain fully the many services at the Study Skills Center (for advice on splitting the discussion of a single point into two or more paragraphs, see page 62). At this stage, you needn't bother trying to guess whether you'll need more than one paragraph per point; just use the outline to get going. Most writers don't know how much they have to say before they begin writing—and that's fine because *writing itself is an act of discovery and learning.*

When you are ready to begin drafting, read Chapter 5 for advice on composing and revising. Remember, too, that Chapter 5 contains suggestions for beating Writer's Block, should this condition arise while you are working on any part of your essay, as well as some specific hints on formatting your draft that may make revision easier (pages 92–95).

■ Composing the Body Paragraphs

There are many ways to organize and develop body paragraphs. Paragraphs developed by common patterns, such as example, comparison, and definition, will be discussed in specific chapters in Part Two; at this point, however, here are some comments about the general nature of all good body paragraphs that should help as you draft your essay.

 REMEMBER: Most of the body paragraphs in your essay will profit from a focused *topic sentence*. In addition, body paragraphs should have adequate *development*, *unity*, and *coherence*.

■ The Topic Sentence

Most body paragraphs present one main point in your discussion, expressed in a *topic sentence*. The topic sentence of a body paragraph has three important functions:

1. It supports the thesis by clearly stating a main point in the discussion.
2. It announces what the paragraph will be about.
3. It controls the subject matter of the paragraph. The entire discussion—the examples, details, and explanations—in a particular paragraph must directly relate to and support the topic sentence.

Think of a body paragraph (or a single paragraph) as a kind of mini-essay in itself. The topic sentence is, in a sense, a smaller thesis. It too asserts one main idea on a limited subject that the writer can explain or argue in the rest of the paragraph. Like the thesis, the topic sentence should be stated in as specific language as possible.

To see how a topic sentence works in a body paragraph, study this sample:

Essay Thesis: The Study Skills Center is an excellent place for students who need academic help.

Topic Sentence
1. The topic sentence supports the thesis by stating a main point (one reason why the Center provides excellent academic help).
2. The topic sentence announces the subject matter of the paragraph (a variety of free services that improve basic skills).
3. The topic sentence controls the subject matter (all the examples—the mini course, the tutoring, the seminars, and the testing—support the claim of the topic sentence).

The Center offers students a variety of free services designed to improve basic skills. Those who discover their study habits are poor, for instance, may enroll in a six-week minicourse in study skills that offers advice on such topics as how to read a text, take notes, and organize material for review. Students whose math or writing skills are below par can sign up for free tutoring sessions held five days a week throughout each semester. In addition, the Center presents weekly seminars on special topics such as stress management and overcoming test anxiety for those students who are finding college more of a nerve-wracking experience than they expected; other students can attend evening seminars in such worthwhile endeavors as vocabulary building or spelling tips. Finally, the Center offers a series of tests to identify the presence of any learning disabilities, such as dyslexia, that might prevent a student from succeeding academically. With such a variety of free services, the Center can help almost any student.

Here's another example from the essay on the library reserve:

Essay Thesis: The library's reserve facility is difficult for students to use.

Topic Sentence
1. The topic sentence supports the thesis by stating a main point (one reason why the facility is difficult to use).
2. The topic sentence announces the subject matter of the paragraph (the unpredictable hours).
3. The topic sentence controls the subject matter (all the examples—the changing hours, the sudden closures, the erratic holiday schedule—support the claim of the topic sentence).

The library reserve facility's unpredictable hours frustrate even the most dedicated students. Instructors who place articles on reserve usually ask students to read them by a certain date. Too often, however, students arrive at the reserve desk only to find it closed. The facility's open hours change from week to week: students who used the room last week on Tuesday morning may discover that this week on Tuesday the desk is closed, which means another trip. Perhaps even more frustrating are the facility's sudden, unannounced closures. Some of these closures allow staff members to have lunch or go on breaks, but, again, they occur without notice on no regular schedule. A student arrives, as I did two weeks ago, at the desk to find a "Be Back Soon" sign. In my case, I waited for nearly an hour. Another headache is the holiday schedule, which is difficult to figure out. For example, this year the reserve room was closed without advance notice on Presidents' Day but open on Easter; open during Winter Break but closed some days during Spring Break, a time many students use to catch up on their reserve assignments. Overall, the reserve facility would be much easier for students to use if it adopted a set schedule of operating hours, announced these times each semester, and maintained them.

Always be sure your topic sentences actually support the particular thesis of your essay. For example, the second topic sentence presented here doesn't belong in the essay promised by the thesis:

Thesis: Elk hunting should be permitted because it financially aids people in our state.

Topic Sentences

1. Fees for hunting licenses help pay for certain free, state-supported social services.
2. Hunting helps keep the elk population under control.
3. Elk hunting offers a means of obtaining free food for those people with low incomes.

Although topic sentence 2 is about elk and may be true, it doesn't support the thesis's emphasis on financial aid and therefore should be tossed out of this essay.

Here's another example:

Thesis: During the past fifty years, movie stars have often tried to change the direction of America's politics.

Topic Sentences

1. During World War II, stars sold liberty bonds to support the country's war effort.
2. Many stars refused to cooperate with the blacklisting of their colleagues during the McCarthy Era in the 1950s.
3. Some stars were actively involved in protests against the Vietnam War.
4. More recently, stars have appeared in Congress criticizing the lack of legislative help for struggling farmers.

Topic sentences 2, 3, and 4 all show how stars have tried to effect a change. But topic sentence 1 says only that stars sold bonds to support, not *change*, the political direction of the nation. Although it does show stars involved in politics, it doesn't illustrate the claim of this particular thesis.

Sometimes a topic sentence needs only to be rewritten or slightly recast to fit:

Thesis: The recent tuition hike may discourage students from attending our college.

Topic Sentences

1. Students already pay more here than at other in-state schools.
2. Out-of-state students will have to pay an additional "penalty" to attend.
3. Tuition funds should be used for scholarships.

As written, topic sentence 3 doesn't show why students won't want to attend the school. However, a rewritten topic sentence does support the thesis:

3. Because the tuition money will not be used for scholarships, some students may not be able to afford this higher-priced school.

In other words, always check carefully to make sure that *all* your topic sentences clearly support your thesis's assertion.

Focusing Your Topic Sentence

A vague, fuzzy, or unfocused topic sentence most often leads to a paragraph that touches only on the surface of its subject or that wanders away from the writer's main idea. On the other hand, a topic sentence that is tightly focused and stated precisely will not only help the reader to understand the point of the paragraph but will also help you select, organize, and develop your supporting details.

Look, for example, at these unfocused topic sentences and their revisions:

Unfocused	Too many people treat animals badly in experiments. [What people? Badly how? What kinds of experiments?]
Focused	The cosmetic industry often harms animals in unnecessary experiments designed to test their products.
Unfocused	Grades are an unfair pain in the neck. [Again, the focus is too broad. All grades? Unfair how?]
Focused	A course grade based on one multiple-choice exam doesn't accurately measure a student's knowledge of the subject.
Unfocused	Getting the right job is important and can lead to rewarding experiences. [Note both vague language and a double focus— "important" and "can lead to rewarding experiences."]
Focused	Getting the right job can lead to an improved sense of self-esteem.

Before you practice writing focused topic sentences, you may wish to review pages 33–37, the advice on composing good thesis statements, as the same rules generally apply.

Placing Your Topic Sentence

Although the topic sentence most frequently occurs as the first sentence in the body paragraph, it also often appears as the second or last sentence. A topic sentence that directly follows the first sentence of a paragraph usually does so because the first sentence provides an introductory statement or some kind of "hook" to the preceding paragraph. A topic sentence frequently appears at the end of a paragraph that first presents particular details and then concludes with its central point. Here are two paragraphs in which the topic sentences do not appear first:

Introductory sentence   Millions of Americans have watched the elaborate Rose Bowl Parade televised nationally each January from Pasadena, California. *Less well known, but growing in popularity, is*

Topic sentence   *Pasadena's Doo Dah Parade, an annual parody of the Rose Bowl spectacle, that specializes in wild-and-crazy participants.* Take this year's Doo Dah Precision Drill Team, for instance. Instead of marching in unison, the members cavorted down the avenue displaying—what else—a variety of precision electric drills. In heated competition with this group was the Synchronized Briefcase Drill Team, whose male and female members wore gray pinstripe suits and performed a series of tunes by tapping on their briefcases. Another crowd-pleasing entry was the Citizens for the Right to Bare Arms, whose members sang while carrying aloft unclothed mannequin arms. The zany procession, led this year as always by the All-Time Doo Dah Parade Band, attracted more than 150,000 fans and is already preparing for its next celebration.

In the preceding paragraph, the first sentence serves as an introduction leading directly to the topic sentence. In the following example, the writer places the topic sentence last to sum up the information in the paragraph:

Rumors certainly fly around Washington's Capitol Building—but ghosts too? According to legend, the building was cursed in 1808 by construction superintendent John Lenthall, crushed by a falling ceiling following a feud with his architect over the wisdom of ceiling braces. Some workers in the building swear they have heard both the ghostly footsteps of James Garfield, who was assassinated after only four months as president, and the spooky last murmurings of John Quincy Adams, who died mid-speech on the House floor. Others claim to have seen a demon cat, so large and terrifying that it caused a guard to suffer a fatal heart attack. Perhaps the most cheerful ghosts appear on the night of a new president's swearing-in ceremony when the statues in Statuary Hall are said to leave their pedestals and dance at their own Inaugural Ball. *Whether these stories are true or merely the products of rich imaginations, the U.S. Capitol Building boasts the reputation as one of the most haunted buildings in America.*

Topic sentence

As you can see, the position of topic sentences largely depends on what you are trying to do in your paragraph. And it's true that the purposes of some paragraphs are so obvious that no topic sentences are needed. However, if you are a beginning writer, you may want to practice putting your topic sentences first for a while to help you organize and unify your paragraphs.

Some paragraphs with a topic sentence near the beginning also contain a concluding sentence that makes a final general comment based on the supporting details. The last sentence below, for example, reemphasizes the main point of the paragraph.

Topic sentence

Of all nature's catastrophes, tornadoes may cause the most bizarre destruction. Whirling out of the sky at speeds up to 300 miles per hour, tornadoes have been known to drive broom handles through brick walls and straws into tree trunks. In one extreme case, a Kansas farmer reported that his prize rooster had been sucked into a two-gallon distilled-water bottle. More commonly, tornadoes lift autos and deposit them in fields miles away or uproot trees and drop them on lawns in neighboring towns. One tornado knocked down every wall in a house but one—luckily, the very wall shielding the terrified family. *Whenever a tornado touches the earth, spectacular headlines are sure to follow.*

Concluding sentence

Warning: Although topic sentences may appear in different places in a paragraph, there is one common error you should be careful to avoid. Do *not* put a topic sentence at the end of one body paragraph that belongs to the paragraph that follows it. For example, let's suppose you were writing an essay discussing a job you had held recently, one that you enjoyed because of the responsibilities you were given, the training program you participated in, and the interaction you experienced with your coworkers. The body paragraph describing your responsibilities may end with its own topic sentence or with a concluding sentence about those responsibilities. However, that paragraph should not end with a sentence such as "Another excellent feature of this job was the training program for the next level of management." This "training program" sentence belongs in the *following* body paragraph as its topic sentence. Similarly, you would not end the paragraph on the training program with a topic sentence praising your experience with your coworkers.

If you feel your paragraphs are ending too abruptly, consider using a concluding sentence, as described previously. Later in this chapter you will also learn some ways to smooth the way from one paragraph to the next by using transitional devices and "idea hooks" (page 77). For now, remember: do *not* place a topic sentence that introduces and controls paragraph "B" at the end of paragraph "A." In other words, always place your topic sentence in the paragraph to which it belongs, to which it is topic-related, not at the end of the preceding paragraph.

▪ PRACTICING WHAT YOU'VE LEARNED

A. Point out the topic sentences in the following paragraphs; identify those paragraphs that also contain concluding sentences. Cross out any stray topic sentences that belong elsewhere.

Denim is one of America's most widely used fabrics. It was first introduced during Columbus's voyage, when the sails of the Santa Maria were made of the strong cloth. During our pioneer days, denim was used for tents, covered wagons, and the now-famous blue jeans. Cowboys found denim an ideal fabric for protection against sagebrush, cactus, and saddle sores. World War II also gave denim a boost in popularity when sailors were issued jeans as part of their dress code. Today, denim continues to be in demand as more and more casual clothes are cut from the economical fabric. Because of its low cost and durability, manufacturers feel that denim will continue as one of America's most useful fabrics.

Adlai Stevenson, American statesman and twice an unsuccessful presidential candidate against Eisenhower, was well known for his intelligence and wit. Once on the campaign trail, after he had spoken eloquently and at length about several complex ideas, a woman in the audience was moved to stand and cheer, "That's great! Every thinking person in America will vote for you!" Stevenson immediately retorted, "That's not enough. I need a majority!" Frequently a reluctant candidate but never at a loss for words, Stevenson once defined a politician as a person who "approaches every question with an open mouth." Stevenson was also admired for his work as the Governor of Illinois and, later, as Ambassador to the United Nations.

Almost every wedding tradition has a symbolic meaning that originated centuries ago. For example, couples have been exchanging rings to symbolize unending love for over a thousand years. Most often, the rings are worn on the third finger of the left hand, which was thought to contain a vein that ran directly to the heart. The rings in ancient times were sometimes made of braided grass, rope, or leather, giving rise to the expression "tying the knot." Another tradition, the bridal veil, began when marriages were arranged by the families and the groom was not allowed to see his choice until the wedding. The tossing of rice at newlyweds has long signified fertility blessings, and the sweet smell of the bride's bouquet was present to drive away evil spirits, who were also diverted by the surrounding bridal attendants. Weddings may vary enormously today, but many couples still include ancient traditions to signify their new life together.

You always think of the right answer five minutes after you hand in the test. You always hit the red light when you're already late for class. The one time you skip class is the day of the pop quiz. Back-to-back classes are always held in buildings at opposite ends of campus. The one course you need to graduate will not be offered your last semester. If any of these sound familiar, you've obviously been a victim of the "Murphy's Laws" that govern student life.

Want to win a sure bet? Then wager that your friends can't guess the most widely sold musical instrument in America today. Chances are they won't get the answer right—not even on the third try. In actuality, the most popular instrument in the country is neither the guitar nor the trumpet but the lowly kazoo. Last year alone, some three and one-half million kazoos were sold to music lovers of all ages. Part of the instrument's popularity arises from its availability, since kazoos are sold in variety stores and music centers nearly everywhere; another reason is its inexpensiveness—it ranges from the standard thirty-nine-cent model to the five-dollar gold-plated special. But perhaps the main reason for the kazoo's popularity is the ease with which it can be played by almost anyone—as can testify the members of the entire Swarthmore College marching band, who have now added a marching kazoo number to their repertoire. Louis Armstrong, move over!

It's a familiar scenario: Dad won't stop the car to ask directions, despite the fact that he's been hopelessly lost for over forty-five minutes. Mom keeps nagging Dad to slow down and finally blows up because your little sister suddenly remembers she's left her favorite doll, the one she can't sleep without, at the rest stop you left over an hour ago. Your legs are sweat-glued to the vinyl seats, you need desperately to go to the bathroom, and your big brother has just kindly acknowledged that he will relieve you of your front teeth if you allow any part of your body to extend over the imaginary line he has drawn down the back seat. The wonderful tradition known as the "family vacation" has begun.

B. Rewrite these topic sentences so that they are clear and focused rather than fuzzy or too broad.

1. My personality has changed a lot in the last year.
2. His date turned out to be really great.
3. The movie's special effects were incredible.
4. The Memorial Day celebration was more fun than ever before.
5. The evening with her parents was an unforgettable experience.

C. Add topic sentences to the following paragraphs:

Famous inventor Thomas Edison, for instance, did so poorly in his first years of school that his teachers warned his parents that he'd never be a success at anything. Henry Ford, the father of the auto industry, also had trouble in school with both reading and writing. But perhaps the best example is Albert Einstein, whose parents and teachers suspected that he was mentally disabled because he responded to questions so slowly and in a stuttering voice. Einstein's high school record was poor in everything but math, and he failed his college entrance exams the first time. Even out of school the man had trouble holding a job—until he announced the theory of relativity.

A 1950s felt skirt with Elvis's picture on it, for example, now sells for $150, and Elvis scarves go for as much as $200. Elvis handkerchiefs, originally 50 cents or less, fetch $150 in today's market as do wallets imprinted with the singer's face. Original posters from the Rock King's movies can sell for $500, and cards from the chewing gum series can run $30 apiece. Perhaps one of the most expensive collectors' items is the Emene Elvis guitar that can cost a fan at least $1000, regardless of musical condition.

When successful playwright Jean Kerr once checked into a hospital, the receptionist asked her occupation and was told, "Writer." The receptionist said, "I'll just put down 'housewife.'" Similarly, when a British official asked W. H. Auden, the award-winning poet and essayist, what he did for a living, Auden replied, "I'm a writer." The official jotted down "no occupation."

Cumberland College, for example, set the record back in 1916 for the biggest loss in college ball, having allowed Georgia Tech to run up 63 points in the first quarter and ultimately succumbing to them with a final score of 222 to nothing. In pro ball, the Washington Redskins are the biggest losers, going down in defeat 73 to 0 to the Chicago Bears in 1940. The award for the longest losing streak, however, goes to Northwestern University's team, who by 1981 had managed to lose 29 consecutive games. During that year, morale was so low that one disgruntled fan passing a local highway sign that read "Interstate 94" couldn't resist adding "Northwestern 0."

D. Write a focused topic sentence for five of the following subjects:

1. Job interviews
2. Friends
3. Food
4. Money
5. Selecting a major or occupation
6. Clothes
7. Music
8. Dreams
9. Housing
10. Childhood

■ ASSIGNMENT

Review the thesis statements with essay maps you wrote for the practice exercise on page 43. Choose two, and from each thesis create at least three topic sentences for possible body paragraphs.

■ APPLYING WHAT YOU'VE LEARNED TO *YOUR* WRITING

If you currently have a working thesis statement you have written in response to an assignment in your composition class, try sketching out an outline or a plan for the major ideas you wish to include. After you write a draft, underline the topic sentences in your body paragraphs. Do your topic sentences directly support your thesis? If you find that they do not clearly support your thesis, you must decide if you need to revise your draft's organization or whether you have, in fact, discovered a new, and possibly better, subject to write about. If the latter is true, you'll need to redraft your essay so that your readers will not be confused by a paper that announces one subject but discusses another. (See Chapter 5 for more information on revising your drafts.)

■ Paragraph Development

Possibly the most serious—and most common—weakness of all essays by novice writers is *the lack of effectively developed body paragraphs.* The information in each paragraph must adequately explain, exemplify, define, or in some other way support your topic sentence. Therefore, you must include *enough supporting information* or *evidence* in each paragraph to make your readers understand your topic sentence. Moreover, you must make the information in the paragraph clear and specific enough for the readers to accept your ideas.

The next paragraph is *underdeveloped.* Although the topic sentence promises a discussion of Jesse James as a Robin Hood figure, the paragraph does not provide enough specific supporting evidence (in this case, examples) to explain this unusual view of the gunfighter.

> Although he was an outlaw, Jesse James was considered a Robin Hood figure in my hometown in Missouri. He used to be generous to the poor, and he did many good deeds, not just robberies. In my hometown people still talk about how lots of the things James did weren't all bad.

Rewritten, the paragraph might read as follows:

> Although he was an outlaw, Jesse James was considered a Robin Hood figure in my hometown in Missouri. Jesse and his gang chose my hometown as a hiding place, and they set out immediately to make friends with the local people. Every Christmas for four years, the legend goes, he dumped bags of toys on the doorsteps of poor children. The parents knew the toys had been bought with money stolen from richer people, but they were grateful anyway. On three occasions, Jesse gave groceries to the dozen neediest families—he seemed to know when times were toughest—and once he supposedly held up a stage to pay for an old man's operation. In my hometown, some people still sing the praises of Jesse James, the outlaw who wasn't all bad.

The topic sentence promises a discussion of James's generosity and delivers just that by citing specific examples of his gifts to children, the poor, and the sick. The paragraph is, therefore, better developed.

The following paragraph offers reasons but no specific examples or details to support those claims:

> Living with my ex-roommate was unbearable. First, she thought everything she owned was the best. Second, she possessed numerous filthy habits. Finally, she constantly exhibited immature behavior.

The writer might provide more evidence this way:

> Living with my ex-roommate was unbearable. First, she thought everything she owned, from clothes to cosmetics, was the best. If someone complimented my pants, she'd point out that her designer jeans looked better and would last longer because they were made of better material. If she borrowed my shampoo, she'd let me know that it didn't get her hair as clean and shiny as hers did. My hand cream wasn't as smooth; my suntan lotion wasn't as protective; not even my wire clothes hangers were as good as her padded ones! But despite her pickiness about products, she had numerous filthy habits. Her dirty dishes remained in the sink for days before she felt the need to wash them. Piles of the "best" brand

of tissues were regularly discarded from her upper bunk and strewn about the floor. Her desk and closets overflowed with heaps of dirty clothes, books, cosmetics, and whatever else she owned, and she rarely brushed her teeth (when she did brush, she left oozes of toothpaste in the sink). Finally, she constantly acted immaturely by throwing tantrums when things didn't go her way. A poor grade on an exam or paper, for example, meant books, shoes, or any other small object within her reach would hit the wall flying. Living with such a person taught me some valuable lessons about how not to win friends or keep roommates.

By adding more supporting evidence—specific examples and details—to this paragraph, the writer has a better chance of convincing the reader of the roommate's real character.

Where does evidence come from? Where do writers find their supporting information? Evidence comes from many sources. Personal experiences, memories, observations, hypothetical examples, reasoned arguments, facts, statistics, testimony from authorities, many kinds of studies and research—all these and more can help you make your points clear and persuasive. In the paragraph on Jesse James, for example, the writer relied on stories and memories from his hometown. The paragraph on the obnoxious roommate was supported by examples gained through the writer's personal observation. The kind of supporting evidence you choose for your paragraphs depends on your purpose and your audience; as the writer, you must decide what will work best to make your readers understand and accept each important point in your discussion. (For advice on ways to think critically about evidence, see Chapter 5; for more information on incorporating research material into your essays, see Chapter 14.)

Having a well-developed paragraph is more than a matter of adding material or expanding length, however. The information in each paragraph must effectively explain or support your topic sentence. *Vague generalities or repetitious ideas are not convincing.* Look, for example, at the following paragraph, in which the writer offers only generalities:

> We ought to ban the use of cell phones in moving vehicles. Some people who have them think they're a really good idea but a lot of us don't agree. Using a phone while driving causes too many dangerous accidents to happen, and even if there's no terrible accident, people using them have been known to do some really stupid things in traffic. Drivers using phones are constantly causing problems for other drivers; pedestrians are in big trouble from these people too. I think car phone use is getting to be a really dangerous nuisance and we ought to do something about it soon.

This paragraph is weak because it is composed of repetitious general statements using vague, unclear language. None of its general statements is supported with specific evidence. Why is car phone use not a "good" idea? How does it cause accidents? What are the "problems" and "trouble" the writer refers to? What exactly does "do something about it" mean? The writer obviously had some ideas in mind, but these ideas are not clear to the reader because they are not adequately developed with specific evidence and language.

By adding supporting examples and details, the writer might revise the paragraph this way:

> Although cell phones may be a time-saving convenience for busy people, they are too distracting for use by drivers of moving vehicles, whose lack of full attention poses a serious threat to other drivers and to pedestrians. The simple act

of dialing or answering a phone, for example, may take a driver's eyes away from traffic signals or other cars. Moreover, involvement in a complex or emotional conversation could slow down a driver's response time just when fast action is needed to avoid an accident. Last week I drove behind a man using his cell phone. As he drove and talked, I could see him gesturing wildly, obviously agitated with the other caller. His speed repeatedly slowed and then picked up, slowed and increased, and his car drifted more than once, on a street frequently crossed by schoolchildren. Because the man was clearly not in full, conscious control of his driving, he was dangerous. My experience is not isolated; a recent study by the Foundation for Traffic Safety has discovered that using a cell phone is far more distracting to drivers than listening to the radio or talking to a rider. With additional studies in progress, voters should soon be able to demand legislation to restrict phone use to passengers or to drivers when the vehicles are not in motion.

The reader now has a better idea why the writer feels such cell phone use is distracting and, consequently, dangerous. By using two hypothetical examples (looking away, slowed response time), one personal experience (observing the agitated man), and one reference to research (the safety study), the writer offers the reader three kinds of supporting evidence for the paragraph's claim.

After examining the following two paragraphs, decide which explains its point more effectively.

1	Competing in an Ironman triathlon is one of the most demanding feats known to amateur athletes. First, they have to swim many miles and that takes a lot of endurance. Then they ride a bicycle a long way, which is also hard on their bodies. Last, they run a marathon, which can be difficult in itself but is especially hard after the first two events. Competing in the triathlon is really tough on the participants.

2	Competing in an Ironman triathlon is one of the most demanding feats known to amateur athletes. During the first stage of the triathlon, the competitors must swim 2.4 miles in the open ocean. They have to battle the constantly choppy ocean, the strong currents, and the frequent swells. The wind is often an adversary, and stinging jellyfish are a constant threat. Once they have completed the ocean swim, the triathletes must ride 112 miles on a bicycle. In addition to the strength needed to pedal that far, the bicyclists must use a variety of hand grips to assure the continued circulation in their fingers and hands as well as to ease the strain on the neck and shoulder muscles. Moreover, the concentration necessary to steady the bicycle as well as the attention to the inclines on the course and the consequent shifting of gears causes mental fatigue for the athletes. After completing these two grueling segments, the triathletes must then run 26.2 miles, the length of a regular marathon. Dehydration is a constant concern as is the prospect of cramping. Even the pain and swelling of a friction blister can be enough to eliminate a contestant at this late stage of the event. Finally, disorientation and fatigue can set in and distort the athlete's judgment. Competing in an Ironman triathlon takes incredible physical and mental endurance.

The first paragraph contains, for the most part, repetitious generalities; it repeats the same idea (the triathlon is hard work) and gives few specific details to illustrate the point presented in the topic sentence. The second paragraph, however, does offer many specific examples and details—the exact mileage figures, the currents, jellyfish, inclines, grips, blisters, and so forth—that help the reader understand why the event is so demanding.

Joseph Conrad, the famous novelist, once remarked that a writer's purpose was to use "the power of the written word to make you hear, to make you feel . . . before all, to make you *see*. That—and no more, and it is everything." By using specific details instead of vague, general statements, you can write an interesting, convincing essay. Ask yourself as you revise your paragraphs, "Have I provided enough information, presented enough clear, precise details to make my readers see what I want them to?" In other words, a well-developed paragraph effectively makes its point with *an appropriate amount of specific supporting evidence*. (Remember that a handwritten paragraph in a rough draft will look much shorter when it is typed. Therefore, if you can't think of much to say about a particular idea, you should gather more information or consider dropping it as a major point in your essay.)

■ Paragraph Length

"How long is a good paragraph?" is a question novice writers often ask. Like a teacher's lecture or a preacher's sermon, paragraphs should be long enough to accomplish their purpose and short enough to be interesting. In truth, there is no set length, no prescribed number of lines or sentences, for any of your paragraphs. In a body paragraph, your topic sentence presents the main point, and the rest of the paragraph must give enough supporting evidence to convince the reader. Although too much unnecessary or repetitious detail is boring, too little discussion will leave the reader uninformed, unconvinced, or confused.

Although paragraph length varies, beginning writers should avoid the one- or two-sentence paragraphs frequently seen in newspapers or magazine articles. (Journalists have their own rules to follow; paragraphs are shorter in newspapers for one reason, because large masses of print in narrow columns are difficult to read quickly.) Essay writers do occasionally use the one-sentence paragraph, most often to produce some special effect, when the statement is especially dramatic or significant and needs to call attention to itself or when an emphatic transition is needed. For now, however, you should concentrate on writing well-developed body paragraphs.

One more note on paragraph length: sometimes you may discover that a particular point in your essay is so complex that your paragraph is growing far too long—well over a typed page, for instance. If this problem occurs, look for a logical place to divide your information and start a new paragraph. For example, you might see a convenient dividing point between a series of actions you're describing or a break in the chronology of a narrative or between explanations of arguments or examples. Just make sure you begin your next paragraph with some sort of transitional phrase or key words to let the reader know you are still discussing the same point as before ("Still another problem caused by the computer's faulty memory circuit is. . .").

■ PRACTICING WHAT YOU'VE LEARNED

Analyze the following paragraphs. Explain how you might improve the development of each one.

1. Professor Wilson is the best teacher I've ever had. His lectures are interesting, and he's very concerned about his students. He makes the class challenging but not too hard. On tests he doesn't expect more than one can give. I think he's a great teacher.

2. Newspaper advice columns are pretty silly. The problems are generally stupid or unrealistic, and the advice is out of touch with today's world. Too often the columnist just uses the letter to make a smart remark about some pet peeve. The columns could be put to some good uses, but no one tries very hard.

3. Driving tests do not adequately examine a person's driving ability. Usually the person being tested does not have to drive very far. The test does not require the skills that are used in everyday driving situations. Supervisors of driving tests tend to be very lenient.

4. Nursing homes are often sad places. They are frequently located in ugly old buildings unfit for anyone. The people there are lonely and bored. What's more, they're sometimes treated badly by the people who run the homes. It's a shame something better can't be done for the elderly.

5. There is a big difference between acquaintances and friends. Acquaintances are just people you know slightly, but friends give you some important qualities. For example, they can help you gain self-esteem and confidence just by being close to you. By sharing their friendship, they also help you feel happy about being alive.

■ ASSIGNMENT

A. Select two of the paragraphs from above and rewrite them, adding enough specific details to make well-developed paragraphs.

B. Write a paragraph composed of generalities and vague statements. Exchange this paragraph with a classmate's, and turn each other's faulty paragraph into a clearly developed one.

C. Find at least two well-developed paragraphs in an essay or book; explain why you think the two paragraphs are successfully developed.

■ APPLYING WHAT YOU'VE LEARNED TO *YOUR* WRITING

If you are currently drafting an essay, look closely at your body paragraphs. Find the topic sentence in each paragraph and circle the key words that most clearly communicate the main idea of the paragraph. Then ask yourself if the information in each paragraph effectively supports, explains, or illustrates the main idea of the paragraph's topic sentence. Is there enough information? If you're not sure, try numbering your supporting details. Are there too few to be persuasive? Does the paragraph present clear, specific supporting material or does it contain too many vague generalities to be convincing? Where could you add more details to help the reader understand your ideas better and to make each paragraph more interesting? (For more help revising your paragraphs, see Chapter 5.)

■ Paragraph Unity

Every sentence in a body paragraph should relate directly to the main idea presented by the topic sentence. A paragraph must stick to its announced subject; it must not drift away into another discussion. In other words, a good paragraph has *unity*.

Examine the unified paragraph below; note that the topic sentence clearly states the paragraph's main point and that each sentence thereafter supports the topic sentence.

> (1) Frank Lloyd Wright, America's leading architect of the first half of the twentieth century, believed that his houses should blend naturally with their building sites. (2) Consequently, he designed several "prairie houses," whose long, low lines echoed the flat earth plane. (3) Built of brick, stone, and natural wood, the houses shared a similar texture with their backgrounds. (4) Large windows were often used to blend the interior and exterior of the houses. (5) Wright also punctuated the lines and spaces of the houses with greenery in planters to further make the buildings look like part of nature.

The first sentence states the main idea, that Wright thought houses should blend with their location, and the other sentences support this assertion:

Topic Sentence: Wright's houses blend with their natural locations

(2) long, low lines echo flat prairie

(3) brick, stone, wood provide same texture as location

(4) windows blend inside with outside

(5) greenery in planters imitates the natural surroundings

Now look at the next paragraph, in which the writer strays from his original purpose:

> (1) Cigarette smoke is unhealthy even for people who don't have the nicotine habit themselves. (2) Secondhand smoke can cause asthmatics and sufferers of sinusitis serious problems. (3) Doctors regularly advise heart

patients to avoid confined smoky areas because coronary attacks might be triggered by the lack of clean air. [4] Moreover, having the smell of smoke in one's hair and clothes is a real nuisance. [5] Even if a person is without any health problems, exhaled smoke doubles the amount of carbon monoxide in the air, a condition that may cause lung problems in the future.

Sentence 4 refers to smoke as a nuisance and therefore does not belong in a paragraph that discusses smoking as a health hazard to nonsmokers.

Sometimes a large portion of a paragraph will drift into another topic. In the paragraph below, did the writer wish to focus on her messiness or on the beneficial effects of her engagement?

> I have always been a very messy person. As a child, I was a pack rat, saving every little piece of insignificant paper that I thought might be important when I grew up. As a teenager, my pockets bulged with remnants of basketball tickets, hall passes, gum wrappers, and other important articles from my high school education. As a college student, I became a boxer—not a fighter, but someone who cannot throw anything away and therefore it winds up in a box in my closet. But my engagement has changed everything. I'm really pleased with the new stage of my life, and I owe it all to my fiancé. My overall outlook on life has changed because of his influence on me. I'm neater, much more cheerful, and I'm even getting places on time like I never did before. It's truly amazing what love can do.

Note shift from the topic of messiness

This writer may wish to discuss the changes her fiancé has inspired and then use her former messiness, tardiness, and other bad habits as examples illustrating those changes; however, as presented here, the paragraph is not unified around a central idea. On the contrary, it first seems to promise a discussion of her messiness but then wanders into comments on "what love can do."

Also beware a tendency to end your paragraph with a new idea. A new point calls for an entirely new paragraph. For example, the following paragraph focuses on the *origins* of Muzak; the last sentence, on Muzak's *effects* on workers, should be omitted or moved to a paragraph on Muzak's uses in the workplace.

> Muzak, the ever-present sound of music that pervades elevators, office buildings, and reception rooms, was created over fifty years ago by George Owen Squier, an army general. A graduate of West Point, Squier was also an inventor and scientist. During World War I he headed the Signal Corps where he began experimenting with the notion of transmitting simultaneous messages over power lines. When he retired from the army in 1922, he founded Wired Radio, Inc., and later, in 1934, the first Muzak medley was heard in Cleveland, Ohio, for homeowners willing to pay the great sum of $1.50 a month. That year he struck upon the now-famous name, which combined the idea of music with the brand name of the country's most popular camera, Kodak. *Today, experiments show that workers get more done when they listen to Muzak.*

Breaks unity

In general, think of paragraph unity in terms of the diagram below:

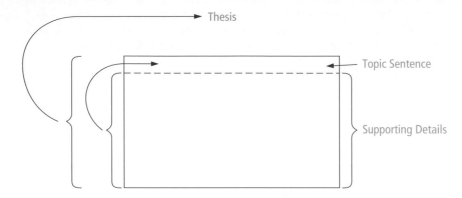

Thesis

Topic Sentence

Supporting Details

The sentences in the paragraph support the paragraph's topic sentence; the paragraph, in turn, supports the thesis statement.

■ PRACTICING WHAT YOU'VE LEARNED

In each of the following examples, delete or rewrite any information that interferes with the unity of the paragraph:

In the Great Depression of the 1930s, American painters suffered severely because few people had the money to spend on the luxury of owning art. To keep our artists from starving, the government ultimately set up the Federal Art Project, which paid then little-known painters such as Jackson Pollock, Arshile Gorky, and Willem de Kooning to paint murals in post offices, train stations, schools, housing projects, and other public places. During this period, songwriters were also affected by the Depression, and they produced such memorable songs as "Buddy, Can You Spare a Dime?" The government-sponsored murals, usually depicting familiar American scenes and historical events, gave our young artists an opportunity to develop their skills and new techniques; in return, our country obtained thousands of elaborate works of art in over one thousand American cities. Sadly, many of these artworks were destroyed in later years, as public buildings were torn down or remodeled.

After complaining in vain about the quality of food in the campus restaurant, University of Colorado students are having their revenge after all. The student body recently voted to rename the grill after Alferd Packer, the only American ever convicted of cannibalism. Packer was a Utah prospector trapped with an expedition of explorers in the southwest Colorado mountains during the winter of 1874; the sole survivor of the trip, he was later tried by a jury and sentenced to hang for dining on at least five of his companions. Colorado students are now holding an annual "Alferd Packer Day" and have installed a mural relating the prospector's story on the main wall of the restaurant. Some local wits have also suggested a new motto for the bar and grill: "Serving our fellow man since 1874." Another well-known incident of cannibalism in the West occurred in the winter of 1846, when the Donner party, a wagon train of eighty-seven California-bound immigrants, became trapped by ice and snow in the Sierra Nevada mountain range.

Inventors of food products often name their new creations after real people. In 1896 Leo Hirschfield hand-rolled a chewy candy and named it after his daughter Tootsie. In 1920 Otto Schnering gave the world the Baby Ruth candy bar, named after the daughter of former President Grover Cleveland. To publicize his new product, Schnering once dropped the candy tied to tiny parachutes from an airplane flying over Pittsburgh. And one of our most popular soft drinks was named by a young suitor who sought to please his sweetheart's physician father, none other than old Dr. Pepper. Despite the honor, the girl's father never approved of the match and the young man, Wade Morrison, married someone else.

States out West have often led the way in recognizing women's roles in politics. Wyoming, for example, was the first state to give women the right to vote and hold office, back in 1869 while the state was still a territory. Colorado was the second state to grant women's suffrage; Idaho, the third. Wyoming was also the first state to elect a woman as governor, Nellie Tayloe Ross, in 1924. Montana elected Jeanette Rankin as the nation's first congresswoman in 1916. Former U.S. Representative from Colorado, Patricia Schroeder, claims to be the first person to take the congressional oath of office while clutching a handbag full of diapers. Ms. Schroeder later received the National Motherhood Award.

Living in a college dorm is a good way to meet people. There are activities every weekend such as dances and parties where one can get acquainted with all kinds of students. Even just sitting by someone in the cafeteria during a meal can start a friendship. Making new friends from foreign countries can teach students more about international relations. A girl on my dorm floor, for example, is from Peru, and I've learned a lot about the customs and culture in her country. She's also helping me with my study of Spanish. I hope to visit her in Peru some day.

■ APPLYING WHAT YOU'VE LEARNED TO *YOUR* WRITING

If you have written a draft of an essay, underline the topic sentence in each body paragraph and circle the key words. For example, if in an essay on America's growing health consciousness, one of your topic sentences reads "In an effort to improve their health, Americans have increased the number of vitamins they consume," you might circle "Americans," "increased," and "vitamins." Then look closely at your paragraph. All the information in that paragraph should support the idea expressed in your topic sentence; nothing should detract from the idea of showing that Americans have increased their vitamin consumption. Now study the paragraphs in your draft, one by one. Cross out any sentence or material that interferes with the ideas in your topic sentences. If one of your paragraphs begins to drift away from its topic-sentence idea, you will need to rethink the purpose of that paragraph and rewrite so that the reader will understand what the paragraph is about. (For additional help revising your drafts, turn to Chapter 5.)

■ Paragraph Coherence

In addition to unity, *coherence* is essential to a good paragraph. Coherence means that all the sentences and ideas in your paragraph flow together to make a clear, logical point about your topic. Your paragraph should not be a confusing collection of ideas set down in random order. The readers should be able to follow what you have written and see easily and quickly how each sentence grows out of, or is related to, the preceding sentence. To achieve coherence, you should have a smooth connection or transition between the sentences in your paragraphs.

There are five important means of achieving coherence in your paragraphs:

1. A natural or easily recognized order
2. Transitional words and phrases
3. Repetition of key words
4. Substitution of pronouns for key nouns
5. Parallelism

These transitional devices are similar to the couplings between railroad cars; they enable the controlling engine to pull the train of thought along as a unit.

A Recognizable Ordering of Information

Without consciously thinking about the process, you may often organize paragraphs in easily recognized patterns that give the reader a sense of logical movement and order. Four common patterns of ordering sentences in a paragraph are discussed next:

The Order of Time

Some paragraphs are composed of details arranged in chronological order. You might, for example, explain the process of changing an oil filter on your car by beginning with the first step, draining the old oil, and concluding with the last step, installing the new filter. Here is a paragraph on black holes in which the writer chronologically orders her details:

> A black hole in space, from all indications, is the result of the death of a
> star. Scientists speculate that stars were first formed from the gases floating in

the universe at the beginning of time. In the first stage in the life of a star, the hot gas is drawn by the force of gravity into a burning sphere. In the middle stage—our own sun being a middle-aged star—the burning continues at a regular rate, giving off enormous amounts of heat and light. As it grows old, however, the star eventually explodes to become what is called a nova, a superstar. But gravity soon takes over again, and the exploded star falls back in on itself with such force that all the matter in the star is compacted into a mass no larger than a few miles in diameter. At this point, no heavenly body can be seen in that area of the sky, as the tremendous pull of gravity lets nothing escape, not even light. A black hole has thus been formed.

The Order of Space

When your subject is a physical object, you should select some orderly means of describing it: from left to right, top to bottom, inside to outside, and so forth. For example, you might describe a sculpture as you walk around it from front to back. Below is a paragraph describing a cowboy in which the writer has ordered the details of his description in a head-to-feet pattern.

Big Dave was pure cowboy. He wore a black felt hat so big that it kept his face in perpetual shade. Around his neck was knotted a red bandana stained with sweat from long hot days in the saddle. An oversized blue denim shirt hung from his shoulders to give him plenty of arm freedom, and his faded jeans were held up by a broad leather belt with a huge silver buckle featuring a snorting bronc in full buck. His boots, old and dirt-colored, kicked up little dust storms as he sauntered across the corral.

Deductive Order

A paragraph ordered deductively moves from a generalization to particular details that explain or support the general statement. Perhaps the most common pattern of all paragraphs, the deductive paragraph begins with its topic sentence and proceeds to its supporting details, as illustrated in the following example:

If a group of 111 ninth-graders is typical of today's teenagers, spelling and social science teachers may be in for trouble. In a recent experiment, not one of the students tested could write the Pledge of Allegiance correctly. In addition, the results showed that the students apparently had little understanding of the pledge's meaning. For example, several students described the United States as a "nation under guard" instead of "under God," and the phrase "to the Republic for which it stands" appeared in several responses as "of the richest stand" or "for Richard stand." Many students changed the word "indivisible" to the phrase "in the visible," and over 9 percent of the students, all of whom are Americans from varying racial and ethnic backgrounds, misspelled the word "America."

Inductive Order

An inductive paragraph begins with an examination of particular details and then concludes with a larger point or generalization about those details. Such a paragraph often ends with its topic sentence, as does the following paragraph on Little League baseball:

> At too many Little League baseball games, one or another adult creates a minor scene by yelling rudely at an umpire or a coach. Similarly, it is not uncommon to hear adults whispering loudly with one another in the stands over which child should have caught a missed ball. Perhaps the most astounding spectacle of all, however, is an irate parent or coach yanking a child off the field after a bad play for a humiliating lecture in front of the whole team. Sadly, Little League baseball today often seems intended more for childish adults than for the children who actually play it.

Transitional Words and Phrases

Some paragraphs may need internal transitional words to help the reader move smoothly from one thought to the next so that the ideas do not appear disconnected or choppy.

Here is a list of common transitional words and phrases and their uses:

giving examples	for example, for instance, specifically, in particular, namely, another, other
comparison	similarly, not only . . . but also, in comparison
contrast	although, but, while, in contrast, however, though, on the other hand
sequence	first . . . second . . . third, finally, moreover, also, in addition, next, then, after, furthermore, and
results	therefore, thus, consequently, as a result

Notice the difference the use of transitional words makes in the paragraphs below:

> Working in the neighborhood grocery store as a checker was one of the worst jobs I've ever had. In the first place, I had to wear an ugly, scratchy uniform cut at least three inches too short. My schedule of working hours was another inconvenience; because my hours were changed each week, it was impossible to make plans in advance, and getting a day off was out of the question. In addition, the lack of working space bothered me. Except for a half-hour lunch break, I was restricted to three square feet of room behind the counter and consequently felt as if I were no more than a cog in the cash register.

The same paragraph rewritten without transitional words sounds choppy and childish:

> Working in the neighborhood grocery store as a checker was one of the worst jobs I've ever had. I had to wear an ugly, scratchy uniform. It was cut at least three inches too short. My schedule of working hours was inconvenient. My hours changed each week. It was impossible to make plans in advance. Getting a day off was out of the question. The lack of working space bothered me. Except for a half-hour break, I was restricted to three square feet of room behind the counter. I felt like a cog in the cash register.

Although transitional words and phrases are useful in bridging the gaps between your ideas, don't overuse them. Not every sentence needs a transitional phrase, so use one only when the relationship between your thoughts needs clarification. It's also a mistake to place the transitional word in the same position in your sentence each time. Look at the paragraph that follows:

> It's a shame that every high school student isn't required to take a course in first aid. *For example*, you might need to treat a friend or relative for drowning during a family picnic. Or, *for instance*, someone might break a bone or receive a snakebite on a camping trip. *Also*, you should always know what to do for a common cut or burn. *Moreover*, it's important to realize when someone is in shock. *However*, very few people take the time to learn the simple rules of first aid. *Thus*, many injured or sick people suffer more than they should. *Therefore*, everyone should take a first aid course in school or at the Red Cross center.

As you can see, a series of sentences each beginning with a transitional word quickly becomes repetitious and boring. To hold your reader's attention, use transitional words only when necessary to avoid choppiness, and vary their placement in your sentences.

Repetition of Key Words

Important words or phrases (and their synonyms) may be repeated throughout a paragraph to connect the thoughts into a coherent statement:

> One of the most common, and yet most puzzling, phobias is the *fear* of *snakes*. It's only natural, of course, to be afraid of a poisonous *snake*, but many people are just as frightened of the harmless varieties. For such people, a tiny green grass *snake* is as terrifying as a cobra. Some researchers say this unreasonable *fear* of any and all *snakes* is a legacy left to us by our cave-dwelling ancestors, for whom these *reptiles* were a real and constant danger. Others maintain that the *fear* is a result of our associating the *snake* with the notion of evil, as in the Garden of Eden. Whatever the reason, the fact remains that for many otherwise normal people, the mere sight of a *snake* slithering through the countryside is enough to keep them city dwellers forever.

The repeated words "fear" and "snake" and the synonym "reptile" help tie one sentence to another so that the reader may follow the ideas easily.

Pronouns Substituted for Key Nouns

A pronoun is a word that stands for a noun. In your paragraph you may use a key noun in one sentence and then use a pronoun in its place in the following sentences. The pronoun "it" often replaces "shark" in the description that follows:

> (1) The great white shark is perhaps the best equipped of all the ocean's predators. (2) *It* can grow up to twenty-one feet and weigh three tons, with

two-inch teeth that can replace themselves within twenty-four hours when damaged. (3) The shark's sense of smell is so acute *it* can detect one ounce of fish blood in a million ounces of water. (4) In addition, *it* can sense vibrations from six hundred feet away.

Sentences 2, 3, and 4 are tied to the topic sentence by the use of the pronoun "it."

Parallelism

Parallelism in a paragraph means using the same grammatical structure in several sentences to establish coherence. The repeated use of similar phrasing helps tie the ideas and sentences together. Next, for example, is a paragraph predominantly unified by its use of grammatically parallel sentences:

(1) The weather of Texas offers something for everyone. (2) If you are the kind who likes to see snow drifting onto mountain peaks, a visit to the Big Bend area will satisfy your eye. (3) If, on the other hand, you demand a bright sun to bake your skin a golden brown, stop in the southern part of the state. (4) And for hardier souls, who ask from nature a show of force, the skies of the Panhandle regularly release ferocious springtime tornadoes. (5) Finally, if you are the fickle type, by all means come to central Texas, where the sun at any time may shine unashamed throughout the most torrential rainstorm.

The parallel structures of sentences 2, 3, and 5 ("if you" + verb) keep the paragraph flowing smoothly from one idea to the next.

Using a Variety of Transitional Devices

Most writers use a combination of transitional devices in their paragraphs. In the following example, three kinds of transitional devices are circled. See if you can identify each one.

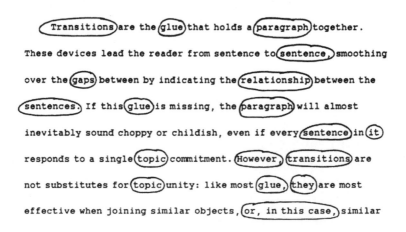

Transitions are the glue that holds a paragraph together. These devices lead the reader from sentence to sentence, smoothing over the gaps between by indicating the relationship between the sentences. If this glue is missing, the paragraph will almost inevitably sound choppy or childish, even if every sentence in it responds to a single topic commitment. However, transitions are not substitutes for topic unity: like most glue, they are most effective when joining similar objects, or, in this case, similar

ideas. (For example,) in a (paragraph) describing a chicken egg, no
(transition) could bridge the (gap) created by the inclusion of a
(sentence) concerned with naval losses in the Civil War. (In other)
(words,) (transitions) can call attention to the (topic) (relationships)
between (sentences,) but (they) cannot create those (relationships.)

transitional	repetition	repetition
words	of pronouns	of key words

■ PRACTICING WHAT YOU'VE LEARNED

A. Identify each of the following paragraphs as ordered by time, space, or parallelism:

My apartment is so small that it will no longer hold all my possessions. Every day when I come in the door, I am shocked by the clutter. The wall to my immediate left is completely obscured by art and movie posters that have become so numerous they often overlap, hiding even each other. Along the adjoining wall is my sound system: CDs and tapes are stacked several feet high on two long, low tables. The big couch that runs across the back of the room is always piled so high with schoolbooks and magazines that a guest usually ends up sitting on the floor. To my right is a large sliding glass door that opens onto a balcony—or at least it used to, before it was permanently blocked by my tennis gear, golf clubs, and ten-speed bike. Even the tiny closet next to the front door is bursting with clothes, both clean and dirty. I think the time has come for me to move.

Once-common acts of greeting may be finding renewed popularity after three centuries. According to one historian, kissing was at the height of its popularity as a greeting in seventeenth-century England, when ladies and gentlemen of the court often saluted each other in this affectionate manner. Then the country was visited by a strange plague, whose cause was unknown. Because no one knew how the plague was spread, people tried to avoid physical contact with others as much as possible. Both kissing and the handshake went out of fashion and were replaced by the bow and curtsy, so people could greet others without having to touch them. The bow and curtsy remained in vogue for over a hundred years, until the handshake—for men only—returned to popularity in the nineteenth century. Today, both men and women may shake hands upon meeting others, and kissing as a greeting is making a comeback—especially among the jet-setters and Hollywood stars.

Students have diverse ways of preparing for final exams. Some stay up the night before, trying to cram into their brains what they avoided all term. Others pace themselves, spending a little time each night going over the notes they took in class that day. Still others just cross their fingers, assuming they absorbed enough along the way from lectures and readings. In the end, though, everyone hopes the tests are easy.

B. Circle and identify the transitional devices in the following paragraphs:

Each year I follow a system when preparing firewood to use in my stove. First, I hike about a mile from my house with my bow saw in hand. I then select three good-size oak trees and mark them with orange ties. Next, I saw through the base of each tree about two feet from the ground. After I fell the trees, not only do I trim away the branches, but I also sort the scrap from the usable limbs. I find cutting the trees into manageable-length logs is too much for one day; however, I roll them off the ground so they will not begin to rot. The next day I cut the trees into eight-foot lengths, which allows me to handle them more easily. Once they are cut, I roll them along the fire lane to the edge of the road, where I stack them neatly but not too high. The next day I borrow my uncle's van, drive to the pile of logs, and load as many logs as I can, thus reducing the number of trips. When I finally have all the logs in my backyard, I begin sawing them into eighteen-inch lengths. I create large piles that consequently have to be split and finally stacked. The logs will age and dry until winter when I will make daily trips to the woodpile.

Fans of professional baseball and football argue continually over which is America's favorite spectator sport. Though the figures on attendance for each vary with every new season, certain arguments remain the same, spelling out both the enduring appeals of each game and something about the people who love to watch. Football, for instance, is a quicker, more physical sport, and football fans enjoy the

Sliding in Yankee Stadium, by Lance Richbourg

© Lance Richbourg/SuperStock

emotional involvement they feel while watching. Baseball, on the other hand, seems more mental, like chess, and attracts those fans who prefer a quieter, more complicated game. In addition, professional football teams usually play no more than fourteen games a year, providing fans with a whole week between games to work themselves up to a pitch of excitement and expectation. Baseball teams, however, play almost every day for six months, so that the typical baseball fan is not so crushed by missing a game, knowing there will be many other chances to attend. Finally, football fans seem to love the half-time pageantry, the marching bands, the cheers, and the mascots, whereas baseball fans are often more content to concentrate on the game's finer details and spend the breaks between innings filling out their own private scorecards.

C. The following paragraph lacks common transitional devices. Fill in each blank with the appropriate transitional word or key word.

Scientists continue to debate the cause of the dinosaurs' disappearance. One group claims the _____ vanished after a comet smashed into the Earth; dust and smoke _____ blocked the sun for a long time. _____ of no direct sunlight, the Earth underwent a lengthy "winter," far too cold for the huge _____ to survive. A University of California paleontologist, _____, disputes this claim. He argues that _____ we generally think of _____ living in swampy land, fossils found in Alaska show that _____ could live in cold climates _____ warm ones. _____ group claims that the _____ became extinct following an intense period of global volcanic activity. _____ to killing the _____ themselves, these scientists _____ believe the volcanic activity killed much of the plant life that the _____ ate and, _____, many of the great _____ who survived the volcanic eruptions starved to death. Still _____ groups of _____ claim the _____ were destroyed by acid rain, by a passing "death star," _____ even by visitors from outer space.

D. The sentences in each of the following exercises are out of order. By noting the various transitional devices, you should be able to arrange each group of sentences into a coherent paragraph.

Paragraph 1: How to Purchase a New Car

- If you're happy with the car's performance, find out about available financing arrangements.
- Later, at home, study your notes carefully to help you decide which car fits your needs.
- After you have discussed various loans and interest rates, you can negotiate the final price with the salesperson.
- A visit to the showroom also allows you to test-drive the car.

- Once you have agreed on the car's price, feel confident you have made a well-chosen purchase.
- Next, a visit to a nearby showroom should help you select the color, options, and style of the car of your choice.
- First, take a trip to the library to read the current auto magazines.
- As you read, take notes on models and prices.

Paragraph 2: Henry VIII and the Problems of Succession

- After Jane, Henry took three more wives, but all these marriages were childless.
- Jane did produce a son, Edward VI, but he died at age fifteen.
- The problem of succession was therefore an important issue during the reign of Henry VIII.
- Still hoping for a son, Henry beheaded Anne and married Jane Seymour.
- Thus, despite his six marriages, Henry failed in his attempts to produce a male heir for the British throne.
- In sixteenth-century England it was considered essential for a son to assume the throne.
- Henry's first wife, Catherine of Aragon, had only one child, the Princess Mary.
- Anne and Henry also produced a daughter, the future Queen Elizabeth I.
- Consequently, he divorced Catherine and married Anne Boleyn.

■ Paragraph Sequence

The order in which you present your paragraphs is another decision you must make. In some essays, the subject matter itself will suggest its own order.* For instance, in an essay designed to instruct a beginning runner, you might want to discuss the necessary equipment—good running shoes, loose-fitting clothing, and a sweatband—before moving to a discussion of where to run and how to run. Other essays, however, may not suggest a natural order, in which case you must decide which order will most effectively reach and hold the attention of your audience. Frequently, writers withhold their strongest point until last. (Lawyers often use this technique; they first present the jury with the weakest arguments, then pull out the most incriminating evidence—the "smoking pistol." Thus the jury members retire with the strongest argument freshest in their minds.) Sometimes, however, you'll find it necessary to present one particular point first so that the other points

---

* For more information on easily recognized patterns of order, see pages 68–70.

make good sense. Study your own major points and decide which order will be the most logical, successful way of persuading your reader to accept your thesis.

■ Transitions between Paragraphs

As you already know, each paragraph usually signals a new major point in your discussion. These paragraphs should not appear as isolated blocks of thought but rather as parts of a unified, step-by-step progression. To avoid a choppy essay, link each paragraph to the one before it with *transitional devices.* Just as the sentences in your paragraphs are connected, so are the paragraphs themselves; therefore, you can use the same transitional devices suggested on pages 70–73.

The first sentence of most body paragraphs frequently contains the transitional device. To illustrate this point, here are some topic sentences lifted from the body paragraphs of a student essay criticizing a popular sports car, renamed the 'Gator to protect the guilty and to prevent lawsuits. The transitional devices are italicized.

Thesis: The *'Gator* is one of the worst cars on the market.

- When you buy a *'Gator,* you buy physical inconvenience. [repetition of key word from thesis]

- *Another* reason the *'Gator* is a bad buy is the cost of insurance. [transitional word, key word]

- You might overlook the *inconvenient* size and exorbitant *insurance* rates if the *'Gator* were a strong, reliable car, *but* this automobile constantly needs repair. [key words from preceding paragraphs, transitional word]

- When you decide to sell this *car,* you face *still another* unpleasant surprise: the extremely low resale value. [key word, transitional phrase]

- The most serious drawback, *however,* is the *'Gator'*s safety record. [transitional word, key word]

Sometimes, instead of using transitional words or repetition of key words or their synonyms, you can use an *idea hook.* The last idea of one paragraph may lead you smoothly into your next paragraph. Instead of repeating a key word from the previous discussion, find a phrase that refers to the entire idea just expressed. If, for example, the previous paragraph discussed the highly complimentary advertising campaign for the 'Gator, the next paragraph might begin, "This view of the 'Gator as an economy car is ridiculous to anyone who's pumped a week's salary into this gas guzzler." The phrase "this view" connects the idea of the first paragraph with the one that follows. Idea hooks also work well with transitional words: "This view, however, is ridiculous. . . ."

If you do use transitional words, don't allow them to make your essay sound mechanical. For example, a long series of paragraphs beginning "first . . . second . . . third . . ." quickly becomes boring. Vary the type and position of your transitional devices so that your essay has a subtle but logical movement from point to point.

■ APPLYING WHAT YOU'VE LEARNED TO *YOUR* WRITING

If you are currently working on a draft of an essay, check each body paragraph for coherence, the smooth connection of ideas and sentences in a logical, easy-to-follow order. You might try placing brackets around key words, pronouns, and transitional words that carry the reader's attention from thought to thought and from sentence to sentence. Decide whether you have enough ordering devices, placed in appropriate places, or whether you need to add (or delete) others. (For additional help revising your drafts, turn to Chapter 5.)

★ CHAPTER 3 SUMMARY

Here is a brief restatement of what you should know about the paragraphs in the body of your essay:

1. Each body paragraph usually contains one major point in the discussion promised by the thesis statement.

2. Each major point is presented in the topic sentence of a paragraph.

3. Each paragraph should be adequately developed with clear supporting detail.

4. Every sentence in the paragraph should support the topic sentence.

5. There should be an orderly, logical flow from sentence to sentence and from thought to thought.

6. The sequence of your essay's paragraphs should be logical and effective.

7. There should be a smooth flow from paragraph to paragraph.

8. The body paragraphs should successfully persuade your reader that the opinion expressed in your thesis is valid.

Chapter 4

Beginnings and Endings

As you work on your rough drafts, you might think of your essay as a coherent, unified whole composed of three main parts: the introduction (lead-in, thesis, and essay map), the body (paragraphs with supporting evidence), and the conclusion (final address to the reader). These three parts should flow smoothly into one another, presenting the reader with an organized, logical discussion. The following pages will suggest ways to begin, end, and also name your essay effectively.

■ How to Write a Good Lead-in

The first few sentences of your essay are particularly important; first impressions, as you know, are often lasting ones. The beginning of your essay, then, must catch the readers' attention and make them want to keep reading. Recall the way you read a magazine: if you are like most people, you probably skim the magazine, reading a paragraph or two of each article that looks promising. If the first few paragraphs hold your interest, you read on. When you write your own introductory paragraph, assume that you have only a few sentences to attract your reader. Consequently, you must pay particular attention to making those first lines especially interesting and well written.

In some essays, your thesis statement alone may be controversial or striking enough to capture the readers. At other times, however, you will want to use the introductory device called a *lead-in*.* The lead-in (1) catches the readers' attention; (2) announces the subject

_____

* Do note that for some writing assignments, such as certain kinds of technical reports, attention-grabbing lead-ins are not appropriate. Frequently, these reports are directed toward particular professional audiences and have their own designated format; they often begin, for example, with a statement of the problem under study or with a review of pertinent information or research.

matter and tone of your essay (humorous, satiric, serious, etc.); and (3) sets up, or leads into, the presentation of your thesis and essay map.

Here are some suggestions for and examples of lead-ins:

1. A paradoxical or intriguing statement

> "Eat two chocolate bars and call me in the morning," says the psychiatrist to his patient. Such advice sounds like a sugar fanatic's dream, but recent studies have indeed confirmed that chocolate positively affects depression and anxiety.

2. An arresting statistic or shocking statement

> One of every nine women will develop breast cancer this year, according to a recent report prepared by the Health Information Service.

3. A question

> It is three times the number of people who belong to the Southern Baptist Convention, nine times the number who serve in the U.S. armed forces, and more than twice the number who voted for Barry Goldwater for president in 1964. What is it? It's the number of people in the United States who admit to having smoked marijuana: a massive 70 million.

4. A quotation or literary allusion

> "I think onstage nudity is disgusting, shameful, and damaging to all things American," says actress Shelley Winters. "But if I were twenty-two with a great body, it would be artistic, tasteful, patriotic, and a progressive religious experience."

5. A relevant story, joke, or anecdote

> Writer and witty critic Dorothy Parker was once assigned a remote, out-of-the-way office. According to the story, she became so lonely, so desperate for company, that she ultimately painted "Gentlemen" on the door. Although this university is large, no one on this campus needs to feel as isolated as Parker obviously did: our excellent Student Activity Office offers numerous clubs, programs, and volunteer groups to involve students of all interests.

6. A description, often used for emotional appeal

> With one eye blackened, one arm in a cast, and third-degree burns on both her legs, the pretty, blond two-year-old seeks corners of rooms, refuses to speak, and shakes violently at the sound of loud noises. Tammy is not the victim of a war or a natural disaster; rather, she is the helpless victim of her parents, one of the thousands of children who suffer daily from America's hidden crime, child abuse.

7. A factual statement or a summary who-what-where-when-why lead-in

> Texas's first execution of a woman in twenty-two years occurred September 17 at the Huntsville Unit of the state's Department of Corrections, despite the protests of various human rights groups around the country.

8. An analogy or comparison

> The Romans kept geese on their Capitol Hill to cackle alarm in the event of attack by night. Modern Americans, despite their technology, have hardly improved on that old system of protection. According to the latest Safety Council report, almost any door with a standard lock can be opened easily with a common plastic credit card.

9. A contrast

> I used to search for toast in the supermarket. I used to think "blackened"—as in blackened Cajun shrimp—referred to the way I cooked anything in a skillet. "Poached" could only have legal ramifications. But all that has changed! Attending a class in basic cooking this summer has transformed the way I purchase, prepare, and even talk about food.

10. A personal experience

> I realized times were changing for women when I overheard my six-year-old nephew speaking to my sister, a prominent New York lawyer. As we left her elaborate, luxurious office one evening, Tommy looked up at his mother and queried, "Mommy, can little boys grow up to be lawyers, too?"

11. A catalog of relevant examples

> A two-hundred-pound teenager quit school because no desk would hold her. A three-hundred-pound chef who could no longer stand on his feet was fired. A three-hundred-fifty-pound truck driver broke furniture in his friends' houses. All these people are now living healthier, happier, and thinner lives, thanks to the remarkable intestinal bypass surgery first developed in 1967.

12. Statement of a problem or a popular misconception

> Some people believe that poetry is written only by aging beatniks or solemn, mournful men and women with suicidal tendencies. The Poetry in the Schools Program is working hard to correct that erroneous point of view.

Thinking of a good lead-in is often difficult when you sit down to begin your essay. Many writers, in fact, skip the lead-in until the first draft is written. They compose their working thesis first and then write the body of the essay, saving the lead-in and conclusion for last. As you write the middle of your essay, you may discover an especially interesting piece of information you might want to save to use as your lead-in.

■ Avoiding Errors in Lead-ins

In addition to the previous suggestions, here is some advice to help you avoid common lead-in errors:

Make sure your lead-in introduces your thesis. A frequent weakness in introductory paragraphs is an interesting lead-in but no smooth or clear transition to the thesis statement. To avoid a gap or awkward jump in thought in your introductory paragraph, you may need to add a connecting sentence or phrase between your lead-in and thesis. Study the paragraph below, which uses a comparison as its lead-in. The italicized transitional sentence takes the reader from a general comment about Americans who use wheelchairs to information about those in Smallville, smoothly preparing the reader for the thesis that follows.

Lead-in

Transitional sentence

Thesis

> In the 1950s African Americans demanded the right to sit anywhere they pleased on public buses. Today, Americans who use wheelchairs are fighting for the right to board those same buses. *Here in Smallville, the lack of proper boarding facilities often denies disabled citizens basic transportation to jobs, grocery stores, and medical centers.* To give persons in wheelchairs the same opportunities as other residents, the City Council should vote the funds necessary to convert the public transportation system.

Keep your lead-in brief. Long lead-ins in short essays often give the appearance of a tail wagging the dog. Use a brief, attention-catching hook to set up your thesis; don't make your introduction the biggest part of your essay.

Don't begin with an apology or complaint. Such statements as "It's difficult to find much information on this topic . . ." and "This controversy is hard to understand, but . . ." do nothing to entice your reader.

Don't assume your audience already knows your subject matter. Identify the pertinent facts even though you know your teacher knows the assignment. ("The biggest problem with the new requirement. . . ." What requirement?) If you are writing about a particular piece of literature, identify the title of the work and its author, using the writer's full name in the first reference.

Stay clear of overused lead-ins. If composition teachers had a nickel for every essay that began with a dry dictionary definition, they could all retire to Bermuda. Leave *Webster's* alone and find a livelier way to begin. Asking a question as your lead-in is becoming overworked, too, so use it only when it is obviously the best choice for your opener.

■ PRACTICING WHAT YOU'VE LEARNED

Find three good lead-ins from essays, magazine articles, or newspaper feature stories. Identify the kinds of lead-ins you found, and tell why you think each effectively catches the reader's attention and sets up the thesis.

■ How to Write a Good Concluding Paragraph

Like a good story, a good essay should not stop in the middle. It should have a satisfying conclusion, one that gives the reader a sense of completion on the subject. Don't allow your essay to drop off or fade out at the end—instead, use the concluding paragraph to emphasize the validity and importance of your thinking. Remember that the concluding paragraph is your last chance to convince the reader. (As one cynical but realistic student pointed out, the conclusion may be the last part of your essay the teacher reads before putting a grade on your paper.) Therefore, make your conclusion count.

Some people feel that writing an essay shares a characteristic with a romantic fling—both activities are frequently easier to begin than they are to end. If you find, as many writers do, that you often struggle while searching for an exit with the proper emphasis and grace, here are some suggestions, by no means exhaustive, that might spark some good ideas for your conclusions:

1. A restatement of the thesis and the essay's major points (most useful in long essays)

> The destruction of the rainforests must be stopped. Although developers protest that they are bringing much-needed financial aid into these traditionally poverty-stricken areas, no amount of money can compensate for what is being lost. Without the rainforests, we not only are contributing to the global warming of the entire planet, we are losing indigenous trees and plants that might someday provide new medicines or vaccines for diseases. Moreover, the replacement of indigenous peoples with corporation-run ranches robs the world of cultural diversity. For the sake of the planet's well-being, Project Rainforest should be implemented.

2. An evaluation of the importance of the essay's subject

> These amazing, controversial photographs of the comet will continue to be the subject of debate because, according to some scientists, they yield the most important clues yet revealed about the origins of our universe.

3. A statement of the essay's broader implications

> Because these studies of feline leukemia may someday play a crucial role in the discovery of a cure for AIDS in human beings, the experiments, as expensive as they are, must continue.

4. A call to action

> The specific details surrounding the death of World War II hero Raoul Wallenberg are still unknown. Although Russia has recently admitted—after 50 years of denial—that Wallenberg was murdered by the KGB in 1947, such a confession is not enough. We must write our congressional representatives today urging their support for the new Swedish commission investigating the circumstances of his death. No hero deserves less.

5. A warning based on the essay's thesis

> Understanding the politics that led to Hiroshima is essential for all Americans—indeed, for all the world's peoples. Without such knowledge, the frightful possibility exists that somewhere, sometime, someone may drop the bomb again.

6. A quotation from an authority or someone whose insight emphasizes the main point

> Even though I didn't win the fiction contest, I learned so much about my own powers of creativity. I'm proud that I pushed myself in new directions. I know now I will always agree with Herman Melville, whose writing was unappreciated in his own times, that "it is better to struggle with originality than to succeed in imitation."

7. An anecdote or witticism that emphasizes or sums up the point of the essay

> Bette Davis's role on and off the screen as the catty, wisecracking woman of steel helped make her an enduring star. After all, no audience, past or present, could ever resist a dame who drags on a cigarette and then mutters about a passing starlet, "There goes a good time that was had by all."

Bette Davis (1908–1989)

8. An image or description that lends finality to the essay

> As the last of the Big Screen's giant ants are incinerated by the army scientist, one can almost hear the movie audiences of the 1950s breathing a collective sigh of relief, secure in the knowledge that once again the threat of nuclear radiation had been vanquished by the efforts of the U.S. military.

(For another brief image that captures the essence of an essay, see also the "open house" scene that concludes "To Bid the World Farewell," page 206.)

9. A rhetorical question that makes the readers think about the essay's main point

> No one wants to see hostages put in danger. But what nation can afford to let terrorists know they can get away with murder?

10. A forecast based on the essay's thesis

> Soap operas will continue to be popular not only because they distract us from our daily chores but also because they present life as we want it to be: fast-paced, glamorous, and full of exciting characters.

■ Avoiding Errors in Conclusions

Try to omit the following common errors in your concluding paragraphs:

Avoid a mechanical ending. One of the most frequent weaknesses in student essays is the conclusion that merely restates the thesis, word for word. A brief essay of five hundred to seven hundred and fifty words rarely requires a flat, point-by-point conclusion—in fact, such an ending often insults the readers' intelligence by implying that their attention spans are extremely short. Only after reading long essays do most readers need a precise recap of all the writer's main ideas. Instead of recopying your thesis and essay map, try finding an original, emphatic way to conclude your essay—or as a well-known newspaper columnist described it, a good ending should snap with grace and authority, like the close of an expensive sports car door.

Don't introduce new points. Treat the major points of your essay in separate body paragraphs rather than in your exit.

Don't tack on a conclusion. There should be a smooth, logical flow of thought from your last body paragraph into your concluding statements.

Don't change your stance. Sometimes writers who have been critical of something throughout their essays will soften their stance or offer apologies in their last paragraph. For instance, someone complaining about the poor quality of a particular college course might abruptly conclude with statements that declare the class wasn't so bad after all, maybe she should have worked harder, or maybe she really did learn something after all. Such reneging may seem polite, but in actuality it undercuts the thesis and confuses the reader who has taken the writer's criticisms seriously. Instead of contradicting themselves, writers should stand their ground, forget about puffy clichés or "niceties," and find an emphatic way to conclude that is consistent with their thesis.

Avoid trite expressions. Don't begin your conclusions by declaring, "in conclusion," "in summary," or "as you can see, this essay proves my thesis that. . . ." End your essay so that the reader clearly senses completion; don't merely announce that you're finished.

■ PRACTICING WHAT YOU'VE LEARNED

Find three good concluding paragraphs. Identify each kind of conclusion and tell why you think it is an effective ending for the essay or article.

■ How to Write a Good Title

As in the case of lead-ins, your title may be written at any time, but many writers prefer to finish their essays before naming them. A good title is similar to a good newspaper headline in that it attracts the readers' interest and makes them want to investigate the essay. Like the lead-in, the title also helps announce the tone of the essay. An informal or humorous essay, for instance, might have a catchy, funny title. Some titles show the writer's wit and love of wordplay; a survey of recent magazines revealed these titles: "Bittersweet News about Saccharin," "Coffee: New Grounds for Concern," and "The Scoop on the Best Ice Cream."

On the other hand, a serious, informative essay should have a more formal title that suggests its content as clearly and specifically as possible. Let's suppose, for example, that you are researching the meaning of color in dreams, and you see an article in a database list titled merely "Dreams." You don't know whether you should bother to read it. To avoid such confusion in your own essay and to encourage readers' interest, always use a specific title: "Interpreting Animal Imagery in Dreams," "Dream Research: An Aid to Diagnosing Depression," and so forth. Moreover, if your subject matter is controversial, let the reader know which side you're on (e.g., "The Advantages of Solar Power"). Never substitute a mere label, such as "Football Games" or "Euthanasia," for a meaningful title. And never, never label your essays "Theme One" or "Comparison and Contrast Essay." In all your writing, including the title, use your creativity to attract the readers' attention and to invite their interest in your ideas.

If you're unsure about how to present your title, here are two basic rules:

1. Your own title should *not* be underlined or put in quotation marks. It should be written at the top of page one of your essay or on an appropriate cover sheet with no special marks of punctuation.

2. Only the first word and the important words of your title should be capitalized. Generally, do not capitalize such words as "an," "and," "a," or "the," or prepositions, unless they appear as the first word of the title.

■ Assignment

Select any three of the student or professional essays in this text; give the first one a new title; the second, an interesting lead-in; the third, a different conclusion. Why are your choices as effective as (or even better than) those of the original writers?

■ Applying What You've Learned to *Your* Writing

Look at the draft of the essay you are currently working on and ask yourself these questions:

- Does the opening of my essay make my reader want to continue reading? Does the lead-in smoothly set up my thesis or do I need to add some sort of transition to help move the reader to my main idea? Is the lead-in appropriate in terms of the tone and length of my essay?

- Does the conclusion of my essay offer an emphatic ending, one that is consistent with my essay's purpose? Have I avoided a mechanical, trite, or tacked-on closing paragraph? Have I refrained from adding a new point in my conclusion that belongs in the body of my essay or in another essay?

- Does my title interest my reader? Is its content and tone appropriate for this particular essay?

If you have answered "no" to any of the above questions, you should continue revising your essay. (For more help revising your prose, turn to Chapter 5.)

★ CHAPTER 4 SUMMARY

Here is a brief restatement of what you should remember about writing introductions, conclusions, and titles:

1. Many essays will profit from a lead-in, the first sentences of the introductory paragraph that attract the reader's attention and smoothly set up the thesis statement.

2. Essays should end convincingly, without being repetitious or trite, with thoughts that emphasize the writer's main purpose.

3. Titles should invite the reader's interest by indicating the general nature of the essay's content and its tone.

Chapter 5

Drafting and Revising: Creative Thinking, Critical Thinking

There is no good writing, only rewriting.
—JAMES THURBER

When I say writing, O, believe me, it is rewriting that I have chiefly in mind.
—ROBERT LOUIS STEVENSON

The absolute necessity of revision cannot be overemphasized. All good writers rethink, rearrange, and rewrite large portions of their prose. The French novelist Colette, for instance, wrote everything over and over. In fact, she often spent an entire morning working on a single page. Hemingway, to cite another example, rewrote the ending to *A Farewell to Arms* thirty-nine times "to get the words right." Although no one expects you to make thirty-nine drafts of each essay, the point is clear: writing well means revising. **All good writers revise their prose.**

■ What Is Revision?

Revision is a *thinking process* that occurs any time you are working on a writing project. It means looking at your writing with a "fresh eye"—that is, reseeing your writing in ways that will enable you to make more effective choices throughout your essay. Revision often entails rethinking what you have written and asking yourself questions about its effectiveness; it involves discovery as well as change. As you write, new ideas surface, prompting you to revise what you have planned or have just written. Or perhaps these new ideas will cause changes in earlier parts of your essay. In some cases, your new ideas will encourage you to begin an entirely new draft with a different focus or approach. Revision means making important decisions about the best ways to focus, organize, develop, clarify, and emphasize your ideas.

■ When Does Revision Occur?

Revision, as previously noted, occurs throughout your writing process. Early on, you are revising as you sort through ideas to write about, and you almost certainly revise as you define your purpose and audience and sharpen your thesis. Some revising may be done in your head, and some may be on paper or computer screen as you plan, sketch, or "discovery-write" your ideas. Later, during drafting, revision becomes more individualized and complex. Many writers find themselves sweeping back and forth over their papers, writing for a bit and then rereading what they wrote, making changes, and then moving ahead. Some writers like to revise "lumps," or pieces of writing, perhaps reviewing one major idea or paragraph at a time. Frequently, writers discover that a better idea is occurring almost at the very moment they are putting another thought on paper. And virtually all writers revise after "reseeing" a draft in its entirety.

Revision, then, occurs before drafting, during drafting, between parts of drafts, and at the ends of drafts. You can revise a word, a sentence, a paragraph, or an entire essay. If you are like most writers, you sometimes revise almost automatically as you write (deleting one word or line and quickly replacing it with another as you move on, for example), and at other times you revise very deliberately (concentrating on a conclusion you know is weak, for example). Revision is "rethinking," and that activity can happen any time, in many ways, in any part of your writing.

■ Myths about Revision

If revision is rethinking, what is it not? Three misconceptions about revision are addressed here.

1. Revision Is Not Autopsy

Revision is not an isolated stage of writing that occurs *only* after your last draft is written or right before your paper is due. Revising is not merely a postmortem procedure, to be performed only after your creative juices have ceased to flow. Good writing, as Thurber noted, *is* revision, and revision occurs throughout the writing process.

2. Revision Is Not Limited to Editing or Proofreading

Too many writers mistakenly equate revision with editing and proofreading. *Editing* means revising for "surface errors"—mistakes in spelling, grammar, punctuation, sentence sense, and word choice. Certainly, good writers comb their papers for such errors, and they edit their prose extensively for clarity, conciseness, and emphasis, too. *Proofreading* to search out and destroy errors and typos that distort meaning or distract the reader is also important. Without question, both editing and proofreading are essential to a polished paper. But revision is not *limited* to such activities. It includes them but also encompasses those larger, global changes writers may make in purpose, focus, organization, and development. Writers who revise effectively not only change words and catch mechanical errors but also typically add, delete, rearrange, and rewrite large chunks of prose. In other words, revision is not cosmetic surgery on a body that may need major resuscitation.

3. Revision Is Not Punishment or Busywork

At one time or another, most of us have found ourselves guilty of racing too quickly through a particular job and then moving on. And perhaps just as often we have found ourselves redoing such jobs because the results were so disappointing. Some people may regard revising in a similar light—as the repeat performance of a job done poorly the first time. But that attitude isn't productive. Revising isn't punishment for failing to produce a perfect first draft. Rarely, if ever, does anyone—even our most admired professional writers—produce the results he or she wants without revising.* Remember that revising is not a tacked-on stage nor is it merely a quick touch-up; it's an integral part of the entire writing process itself. It's an ongoing opportunity to discover, remember, reshape, and refine your ideas.

If you've ever created something you now treasure—a piece of jewelry, furniture, painting, or music—recall the time you put into it. You probably thought about it from several angles, experimented with it, crafted it, worked it through expected and unexpected problems, and smoothed out its minor glitches, all to achieve the results you wanted. Similarly, with each revision you make, your paper becomes clearer, truer, more satisfying to you and to your readers. With practice, you will produce writing you are proud of—and you will discover that revising has become not only an essential but also a natural part of your writing process.

■ Can I Learn to Improve My Revision Skills?

Because revision is such a multifaceted and individual activity, no textbook can guide you through all the rethinking you may do as you move through each sentence of every writing project. But certainly you can learn to improve your ability to think creatively and critically about your prose. To sharpen your thinking and revision skills, this chapter will suggest a step-by-step method of self-questioning designed to help you achieve your writing goals.

---

* All of us have heard stories about famous essays or poems composed at one quick sitting. Bursts of creativity do happen. But it's also highly likely that authors of such pieces revise extensively in their heads before they write. They rattle ideas around in their brains for such a prolonged period that the actual writing does in fact flow easily or may even seem "dictated" by an inner voice. This sort of lengthy internal "cooking" may work well at various times for you, too.

■ Preparing to Draft: Some Time-Saving Hints

Before you begin drafting (either a "discovery" draft or a draft from your working thesis), remember this important piece of advice: no part of your draft is sacred or permanent. No matter what you write at this point, you can always change it. Drafting is discovering and recollecting as well as developing ideas from your earlier plans. Take the pressure off yourself: no one expects blue-ribbon prose in early drafts. (If you can't seem to get going or if you do become stuck along the way, try turning to pages 110–112 of this chapter for suggestions to help you confront your case of Writer's Block.)

At this point, too, you might consider the actual format of your drafts. Because you will be making many changes in your writing, you may find revising less cumbersome and time-consuming if you prepare your manuscripts as described below and in the following section on word processors.

1. If you are handwriting your first drafts, always write on one side of your paper only, in case you want to cut and tape together portions of drafts or you want to experiment with interchanging parts of a particular draft. (If you have written on both sides, you may have to recopy the parts of your essay you want to save; your time is better spent creating and revising.)

2. Leave big margins on *both* sides of any handwritten pages so you can add information later or jot down new ideas as they occur. (Some writers also skip lines for this reason. If you choose to write on every other line, however, do remember that you may not be getting a true picture of your paragraph development or essay length. A handwritten double-spaced body paragraph, for example, may appear skimpy in your typed final copy.)

3. Devise a system of symbols (circles, stars, checks, asterisks, etc.) that will remind you of changes you want to make later. For example, if you're in hot pursuit of a great idea but can't think of the exact word you want, put down a word that's close, circle it (or type three XXXs by it), and go on so that your thinking is not derailed. Similarly, a check in the margin might mean "return to this tangled sentence." A question mark might mean a fuzzy idea, and a star, a great idea that needs expanding. A system of symbols can save you from agonizing over every inch of your essay while you are still trying to discover and clarify your ideas.

4. If your ideas are flowing well but you realize you need more supporting evidence for some of your points, consider leaving some blank spots to fill in later. For example, let's say you are writing about the role of television in our presidential elections; your ideas are good but in a particular body paragraph you decide some statistics on commercial frequency would be most convincing. Or perhaps you need to cite an example of a particular kind of advertisement but you just can't think of a good one at that moment. Leave a spot for the piece of evidence with a key word or two to remind you of what's needed, and keep writing. Later, when you come back to that spot, you can add the appropriate support; if you can't find or think of the right supporting evidence to insert, you may decide to omit that point.

5. If you do decide to rewrite or omit something—a sentence or an entire passage—in a handwritten draft, mark a single "X" or line through it lightly.

Don't scratch it out or destroy it completely; you may realize later that you want to reinsert the material there or move it to another, better place. If you are composing on a computer, highlight or put brackets around material you may want to use elsewhere. Or consider moving a larger chunk of prose to a "holding page" or to the end of the current draft so you can take another look at it later.

6. If you begin with a handwritten draft, do eventually work on a typed copy. Frankly, the more compact spacing of typed prose allows you to see more clearly the relationship of the parts in your essay, making it easier for you to organize and develop your ideas. It is also far more likely that you will catch spelling and other mechanical errors in a printed draft.

7. Always keep your notes, outlines, drafts, and an extra copy of your final paper. Never burn your bridges—or your manuscripts! Sometimes essays change directions, and writers find they can return to prewriting or earlier drafts to recover ideas, once rejected, that now work well. Drafts also may contain ideas that didn't work in one paper but that look like great starts for another assignment. Tracking revisions from draft to draft can give writers a sense of accomplishment and insight into their composing processes. And drafts can be good insurance in case final copies of papers are lost or accidentally destroyed.

Additional Suggestions for Writers with Word Processors

If you have access to a computer and any of the many word-processing programs available today, you probably have already discovered how helpful this technology can be to writers in all stages of the writing process. You can, for example, compose and store your prewriting activities, journal entries, notes, or good ideas in various files until you need to recall certain information, and you can easily produce extra copies of your drafts or finished essays without having to search out a copy machine and correct change. Spell-checkers and dictionaries may help you correct many of your errors and typos.

But the most important use of the computer to a writer may be what it can do as you draft and revise your prose. At your command, a word-processing program enables you to add, delete, or change words easily; it allows you to move words, sentences, and even paragraphs or larger pieces of your essay. On a computer, for example, you can play "what if" by dropping the cursor below what you have written and phrasing your idea in another way. With some programs, you can even compare drafts side by side or with special "windows" that help you see your choices more clearly. In other words, computers can help us as writers do the kind of deep-structure revision necessary to produce our best, most effective prose—the kind of major changes

© Royalty Free/CORBIS

that, in the past, we may have been hesitant to make because of the time involved in recopying or retyping major portions of our drafts.

Although computers have made composing and revising easier and more effective for many writers, such technology provides its own special temptations and potential problems. Here, in addition to the hints in the previous section, are a few more suggestions for drafting and revising your essay on a computer:

1. To avoid the "agony of delete," always "save" what you have composed every ten minutes or so, and do print out a copy after each drafting session in case your system crashes or gobbles your work. Remember that all sorts of events, from electrical storms to carpet cleaning, have caused the tiny leprechauns in computers to behave badly; having "hard" (printed) copies of your notes and latest revisions will help you reconstruct your work should disaster strike. (Also, if you are working on multiple writing tasks, as most students are, or if you are just the forgetful type, develop the habit of noting on each print copy the name you have given the file. Doing so may save you from a frustrating search through your list of existing documents, especially if several days have elapsed between drafts.)

2. Do learn to use the editing tools that your word-processing program offers. In addition to making changes and moving text, most programs offer a dictionary to help you check the proper spelling, meaning, and use of your words; a thesaurus may help you expand your vocabulary, avoid repetition of words, or find just the right word to express the shade of meaning you want. Even the "word count" command can help writers who want to trim the fat from their essays.

One of the most prized tools the computer offers writers is the spell-checker. For poor spellers and bad typists, the invention of the spell-checker ranks right up there with penicillin as a boon to humankind. The spell-checker performs minor miracles as it asks writers to reconsider certain words as typed on the page. If you have one available, by all means run it! But be aware of its limitations: spell-checkers only highlight words whose order of assembled letters they do not recognize or whose capitalization they question. They do not recognize confused words (its/it's; you're/your; their/there; to/too), incorrect usage of words, or typos that are correctly spelled words. To underscore this point, here's a sample of writing that any spell-checker would happily pass over:

> Eye have a knew spell checker
> That tells me wrong from write;
> It marks four me miss steaks
> My ayes kin knot high lite.
>
> I no its let her perfect,
> Sew why due I all ways get
> Re quests to proof reed bet her
> Win my checker says I'm set?

The message of this brilliantly crafted poem? Don't rely on your spell-checker to catch all the errors in your final draft! Learn to edit, question your word choice, and proofread carefully with your own eyes and brain. (The same advice holds true for grammar-check and "style" programs, too. Although such programs have improved over the past several years, they are still limited in their ability to catch errors and see distinctions among usage and punctuation choices. Such programs may help you take a second look at your grammatical decisions, but do not rely on *any* computer program to do your editing and proofreading work for you!)

3. Use the computer to help you double-check for your own common errors. By using the "search," "find," or similar command, many writers can highlight words they know they frequently misuse. For example, on a final sweep of editing, you might take one last look at each highlighted "its" you wrote to determine whether the usage truly calls for the possessive pronoun "its" or rather should be the contraction for "it is" (it's). Or perhaps you have an ongoing struggle with the uses of "affect" and "effect" and know that you have used these words often in your essay of causal analysis. Reviewing your word-choice decisions in the proofreading stage could make an important difference to your readers, who wish to travel smoothly through the ideas in your essay without annoying errors flagging down their attention. Also consider searching for and replacing words that you know you overuse or those that are lazy or vague. For example, until you break yourself of the habit, highlight any use of the word "thing." In each case, are you really discussing an unknown quantity—or do you need to press yourself to find a more specific or vivid word to communicate what you mean?

4. Even if you are comfortable drafting on your computer, resist doing all your work there. It's a good idea from time to time to read your screen version in its printed form—the format your readers will most likely see. Many—if not most—writers move back and forth multiple times between the computer screen and printed copies of their drafts. Experiment to discover the best ways for you to revise. Remember that a neatly typed draft can look professional but still need much rethinking, restructuring, and polishing!

■ Writing Centers, Computer Labs, and Computer Classrooms

Today many schools have professionally staffed writing centers and computer labs open to composition students. The writing center or laboratory computers may have a variety of software designed to help you brainstorm, focus your ideas, organize a working structure, compose your drafts, revise your essay, and proofread. These computers may also help you research a topic by allowing you to check information available in your campus library as well as providing access to other libraries and sources on the Internet. Many writing centers have special tutors on hand to answer your questions about your drafts as well as explain effective uses of the available computer programs. In addition, some schools now have labs and special classrooms in which the computers are part of a network, linked together so that a specific group of writers may communicate with each other and/or with their instructor. In such a lab or classroom, for example, students might read each other's drafts and make suggestions or post comments about a current reading assignment on an electronic bulletin board for their classmates to consider.

Whether the program you are using at home or at school is a series of simple commands or an elaborate instructional system, make a point of getting to know how to use the computer in the most effective ways. Study the advice that accompanies your word-processing program (or one of the many self-help manuals now on the market), and don't be afraid to ask your instructor or computer-lab tutor for assistance. The more you practice using your program to help you organize, develop, and revise your prose, the better your writing will be.

■ A Revision Process for Your Drafts

Let's assume at this point that you have completed a draft, using the first four chapters of this book as a guide. You feel you've chosen an interesting topic and collected some good ideas. Perhaps the ideas came quickly or perhaps you had to coax them. However your thoughts came, they're now in print—you have a draft with meaning and general order, although it's probably much rougher in some spots than in others. Now it's time to "resee" this draft in a comprehensive way.

But wait. If possible, put a night's sleep or at least a few hours between this draft and the advice that appears on the next few pages. All writers become tired when they work on any project for too long at one sitting, and then they lose a sense of perspective. When you've looked at a piece of prose again and again, you may begin to read what's written in your head instead of what's on the page—that is, you may begin to "fill in" for yourself, reading into your prose what you meant to say rather than what your reader will actually see. Always try to start your writing process early enough to give yourself a few breaks from the action. You'll find that you will be better able to evaluate the strengths and weaknesses of your prose when you are fresh.

When you do return to your draft, *don't try to look at all the parts of your paper, from ideas to organization to mechanics, at the same time.* Trying to resee everything at once is rarely possible and will only overload and frustrate you. It may cause you to overlook some important part of your paper that needs your full attention. Overload can also block your creative ideas. Therefore, instead of trying to revise an entire draft in one swoop, break your revising process into a series of smaller, more manageable steps. Here is a suggested process:

I.	rethink	purpose, thesis, and audience
II.	rethink	ideas and evidence
III.	rethink	organization
IV.	rethink	clarity and style
V.	edit	grammar, punctuation, and spelling
VI.	proofread	entire essay

IMPORTANT: Please note that these steps are not necessarily distinct, nor must you always follow this suggested order. You certainly might, for instance, add details to a paragraph when you decide to move or reorder it. Or you might replace a vague word with a specific one after thinking about your audience and their needs. After strengthening a particular point, you might decide to offer it last, and therefore you rearrange the order of your paragraphs. In other words, the steps offered above are not part of a forced march—they are here simply to remind you to rethink and improve any part of your essay that needs work.

Now let's look at each of the steps in the revision process suggested above in more detail.

I. Revising for Purpose, Thesis, and Audience

To be effective, writers need a clear sense of purpose and audience. Their essays must present (or clearly imply) a main idea or thesis designed to fulfill that purpose and to inform their audience. As you reread your draft, ask yourself the following questions:

- Have I fulfilled the objectives of my assignment? (For example, if you were asked to analyze the causes of a problem, did you merely describe or summarize it instead?)

- Did I follow directions carefully? (If you were given a three-part assignment, did you treat all parts as requested?)

- Do I understand the purpose of my essay? Am I trying to inform, persuade, or amuse my readers? Spur them to action? Convince them to change their minds? Give them a new idea? Am I myself clear about my exact intent—what I want to do or say—in this essay?

- Does my essay reflect my clearly understood purpose by offering an appropriately narrowed and focused thesis? (After reading through your essay once, could a reader easily state its purpose and main point?)

- Do I have a clear picture of my audience—their character, knowledge, and expectations?

- Have I addressed both my purpose and my readers' needs by selecting appropriate strategies of development for my essay? (For example, would it be better to write an essay primarily developed with examples illustrating the community's need for a new hospital or should you present a more formal argument that also rebuffs objections to the project? Should you narrate the story of your accident or analyze its effects on your family?)

If you feel that your draft needs work in any of these areas, make changes. You might find it helpful to review Chapters 1 and 2 of this text to guide you as you revise.

II. Revising for Ideas and Evidence

If you're satisfied that your purpose and thesis are clear to your readers, begin to look closely at the development of your essay's ideas.

You want your readers to accept your thesis. To achieve this goal, you must offer body paragraphs whose major points clearly support that main idea. As you examine the body of your essay, you might ask yourself questions such as these:

- Is there a clear relationship between my thesis and each of the major points presented in the body of my essay? That is, does each major point in my essay further my readers' understanding, and thus their acceptance, of my thesis's general claim?

- Did I write myself into a new or slightly different position as I drafted my essay? If so, do I need to begin another draft with a new working thesis?

- Have I included all the major points necessary to the readers' understanding of my subject or have I omitted pertinent ones? (On the other hand, have I included major ideas that aren't relevant or that actually belong in a different essay?)

- Are my major points located and stated clearly in specific language so readers can easily see what position I am taking in each part of my discussion?

If you are happy with your choice and presentation of the major ideas in the body of your essay, it's time to look closely at the evidence you are offering to support those ideas (which, in turn, support the claim of your thesis). To choose the best supporting evidence for their major points, effective writers use *critical thinking skills.*

■ What Is Critical Thinking?

Critical thinking means the ability to analyze and evaluate our own ideas and those of others. Because we are constantly bombarded today with all kinds of information and differing points of view, we need skills to examine ideas carefully before we accept or reject them.

Here's a common situation in which critical thinking comes into play: two of your friends are arguing over the use of fetal tissue in medical research. Each friend has many points to offer; each is presenting statistics, examples of actual case studies, the words of experts, and hypothetical situations that might arise. Many of the statistics and experts on one side of the argument seem to contradict directly the figures and authorities on the other side. Which side do you take? Why? Are there other points of view to consider? How can you know what to think?

Every day we are faced with just such decisions. We must be able to judge intelligently the merits of what we hear and read before we can feel confident about what we think of a particular issue. We must practice analyzing our beliefs and those held by others to evaluate the reasons for maintaining those views. To think critically about ideas doesn't mean being constantly hostile or negative; it simply means that we need to examine opinions closely and carefully before we accept them.

■ Thinking Critically as a Writer

As a writer, you will be thinking critically in two important ways. First, you will need to think critically about any information you may be collecting to use as evidence in your essay. You will, for example, need to be a critical reader as you consider information from books, journals, or electronic sources. You almost certainly will need to be a critical listener as you hear other people talk about their experiences and beliefs.

As you draft and revise your essay, you must become a critical thinker in a second way: you must become your own toughest reader-critic. To convince your readers that your essay has merit, you must stand back and assess objectively what you have written. Are your ideas clear not only to you but to your readers as well? Will readers find your opinions well developed, logical, and supported? In other words, to revise more effectively, try role-playing one of your own most thoughtful critical readers, someone who will be closely examining the ideas and evidence in your essay before agreeing with its position.

Here are six suggestions to help you think critically as you draft and revise:

1. Learn to distinguish fact from opinion. A *fact* is an accepted truth whose verification is not affected by its source. No matter who presents it, a fact remains true. We accept some statements as facts because we can test them personally (fire is hot) or because they have been verified frequently by others (penguins live in Antarctica). We accept as fact, for example, that President John F. Kennedy was killed on November 22, 1963, in Dallas, Texas, while riding in a motorcade. However, even though much investigation and debate have focused on the assassination, the question of who was responsible for the murder is for many people still a matter of *opinion.* Some people believe that Lee Harvey Oswald was the lone gunman; others insist that there were two shooters; still others claim involvement by a foreign government, the Mafia, or even the CIA. Opinions, then, are often based on personal feelings or beliefs or on one's interpretation of information. As you think about your evidence, be careful that you don't present your opinions as facts accepted by everyone. Opinions are debatable, and therefore you must always support them before your readers will be convinced.

2. Support your opinions with evidence. To support your opinions, you must offer evidence of one or more kinds. You have a variety of options to choose from. You might support one idea by using personal experiences. Or you might describe the experiences of friends or family. In another place you might decide to offer detailed examples or to cite statistics or to quote an expert on your subject. You can also use hypothetical examples, researched material, vivid descriptions, reasoned arguments, revealing comparisons, case studies, or testimony of relevant participants, just to name a few other strategies. Consider your purpose and your audience, review the possibilities, and choose the most effective kind of support. The more convincing the support, the more likely your readers are to accept your opinions as true. (If you need to review some sample paragraphs developed by various types of evidence, turn to pages 59–62 of Chapter 3.)

3. Evaluate the strength of your evidence. As you choose your evidence, you should consider its value for the particular point it will support. Scrutinize the nature and source of your evidence carefully. If you are using examples, do they clearly illustrate your claim? Does this example or a different one (or both?) provide the best illustration of your particular point? Is description alone enough support here? Are your statistics or researched material from a reliable, current source? Was information from your research collected in a careful, professional way? Are your experts unbiased authorities from the field under discussion? Where did your experts obtain their information? (For example, are you claiming that crystals possess healing powers because a woman on a talk show said so and she sounded reasonable to you? Just how much do you know about the source of a particular Web site?) Asking yourself the kinds of questions posed here (and others suggested throughout Part Two of this textbook) will help you develop a critical eye for choosing the best evidence to support your opinions.

4. Use enough specific supporting evidence. Readers need to see strong, relevant supporting evidence throughout your essay. You must be sure, therefore, that you have enough clearly stated evidence for each of your major points. If you present, for instance, too few examples or only a vague reference to an event that supports one of your ideas, a reader may remain unconvinced or may even be confused. As you revise, ask yourself questions such as these: "Do I need to provide additional information here?" "Do I need more details to develop the supporting evidence already present?" "Is any of my evidence clouded by vague or fuzzy language?" If you feel additional supporting evidence or details are needed, take another look at any prewriting you did—or use one of the "pump-primer" techniques described in Chapter 1 now to discover some new creative thoughts. For some topics, you may need to do more research or interviewing to find the information you need. (Writers occasionally need to prune ideas too, especially if they're repetitious or off the topic. But, in general, most early drafts are thin or overly general and will profit from more, rather than less, specific supporting evidence.)

5. Watch for biases and strong emotions that may undermine evidence. As you think critically about evidence you are using, monitor any biases and emotional attitudes that may distort information you wish to incorporate into your essay. If you are using personal experiences, for example, have you calmed down enough from your anger over your landlord's actions to write about the clash in a rational, persuasive way? In an essay criticizing a particular product, are you so familiar with the frustrating item that you are making ambiguous claims? (If you write, "The new instructions for use are more confusing than ever," have you shown that they were confusing in the first place? Or why they are more so now?) Be sensitive to any racial, ethnic, cultural, religious, or gender-based assumptions you or your sources may have. Opinions based on generalizations and stereotypes ("Japanese cars are good buys because Asians are more efficient workers than Americans"; "Women should stay home because they are better with children than men") are not convincing to thinking readers.

6. Check your evidence for logical fallacies. Thinking critically about your drafts should help you support your ideas with reasonable, logical explanations and arguments. Logical fallacies are common errors in reasoning that good writers try to avoid. Those fallacies found most often today are explained on pages 282–285 of this text; reviewing them will enable you to identify problems in logic that might appear in the writing of others or in your own drafts.

Critical thinking is not, of course, limited to the six suggestions offered here. But by practicing this advice, you will begin to develop and sharpen analytical skills that should improve any writing project.

III. Revising for Organization

In reality, you have probably already made several changes in the order and organization of ideas in your draft. As noted before, it's likely that when you thought about your essay's meaning—its major points and their supporting evidence—you also thought about the arrangement of those ideas. As you take another look at your draft's organization, use these questions as a guide:

- Am I satisfied with the organizational strategy I selected for my purpose? (For example, would an essay primarily developed by comparison and contrast achieve your purpose better than a narrative approach?)
- Are my major points ordered in a logical, easy-to-follow pattern? Would readers understand my thinking better if certain paragraphs or major ideas were rearranged? Added? Divided? Omitted? Expanded?

- Are my major points presented in topic sentences that state each important idea clearly and specifically? (If any of your topic sentences are implied rather than stated, are you absolutely, 100 percent sure that your ideas cannot be overlooked or even slightly misunderstood by your readers?)

- Is there a smooth flow between my major ideas? Between paragraphs? Within paragraphs? Have I used enough transitional devices to guide the reader along?

- Are any parts of my essay out of proportion? Too long or too brief to do their job effectively?

- Do my title and lead-in draw readers into the essay and toward my thesis?

- Does my conclusion end my discussion thoughtfully? Emphatically or memorably?

Don't be afraid to restructure your drafts. Most good writers rearrange and recast large portions of their prose. Reviewing Chapters 3 and 4 may help you address questions on organization, beginnings, or endings.

IV. Revising for Clarity and Style

As you've revised for purpose, ideas, and organization, you have also taken steps to clarify your prose. Making a special point now of focusing on sentences and word choice will ensure your readers' complete understanding of your thinking. Read through your draft, asking these kinds of questions:

- Is each of my sentences as clear and precise as it could be for readers who do not know what I know? Are there sentences that contain misplaced words or convoluted phrases that might cause confusion?

- Are there any sentences that are unnecessarily wordy? Is there deadwood that could be eliminated? (Remember that concise prose is more effective than wordy, "fat" prose because readers can more easily find and follow key ideas and terms. Nearly every writer has a wordiness problem that chokes communication, so now is the season to prune.)

- Do any sentences run on for too long to be fully understood? Can any repetitive or choppy sentences be combined to achieve clarity and a pleasing variation of sentence style? (To help you decide if you need to combine sentences, you might try this experiment. Select a body paragraph and count the number of words it contains. Then count the number of sentences; divide the number of words by the number of sentences to discover the average number of words per sentence. If your score is less than 15–18, you may need to combine *some* sentences. Good prose offers a variety of sentence lengths and patterns.)

- Are all my words and their connotations accurate and appropriate?

- Can I clarify and energize my prose by adding "showing" details and by replacing bland, vague words with vivid, specific ones? By using active verbs rather than passive ones?

- Can I eliminate any pretentious or unnecessary jargon or language that's inappropriate for my audience? Replace clichés and trite expressions with fresh, original phrases?

■ Is my voice authentic, or am I trying to sound like someone else? Is my tone reasonable, honest, and consistent?

The issues raised by these questions—and many others—are discussed in detail in Chapters 6 and 7, on effective sentences and words, which offer more advice on clarifying language and improving style.

V. Editing for Errors

Writers who are proud of the choices they've made in content, organization, and style are, to use a baseball metaphor, rounding third base and heading for home. But there's more to be done. Shift from a baseball metaphor to car maintenance for a moment. All good essays are not only fine-tuned but also waxed and polished—they are edited and proofread repeatedly for errors until they shine. To help you polish your prose by correcting errors in punctuation, grammar, spelling, and diction, here are some hints for effective editing:

Read aloud. In addition to repeatedly reading your draft silently, reading your draft aloud is a good technique because it allows your ears to hear ungrammatical "clunks" or unintended gaps in sense or sound you may otherwise miss. (Reading aloud may also flag omitted words. If, for example, the mother had reread this note to her child's teacher, she might have noticed a missing word: "Please excuse Ian for being. It was his father's fault.")

Know your enemies. Learn to identify your particularly troublesome areas in punctuation and grammar and then read through your draft for one of these problems at a time: once for fragments, once for comma splices, once for run-ons, and so on. (If you try to look for too many errors at each reading, you'll probably miss quite a few.)

Read backwards. Try reading your draft one sentence at a time starting at the *end* of your essay and working toward the beginning. Don't read each sentence word-for-word backwards—just read the essay one sentence at a time from back to front. When writers try to edit (or proofread) starting at the beginning of their essays, they tend to begin thinking about the ideas they're reading rather than concentrating on the task of editing for errors. By reading one sentence at a time from the back, you will find that the sentences will still make sense but that you are less likely to wander away from the job at hand.

Learn some tricks. There are special techniques for treating some punctuation and grammar problems. If you have trouble, for example, with comma splices, turn to the FANBOYS hint on page 133. If fragments plague your writing, try the "it is true that" test explained on page 490. Consider designating a special part of your journal or class notebook to record in your own words these tricks and other useful pieces of advice so that you can refer to them easily and often.

Eliminate common irritants. Review your draft for those diction and mechanical errors many readers find especially annoying because they often reflect sheer carelessness. For example, look at these frequently confused words: *it's/its, your/you're, there/their/they're, who's/whose* (other often-confused words are listed on pages 141–142). Some readers are ready for a national march to protest the public's abandonment of the apostrophe, the Amelia Earhart of punctuation. (Apostrophes *can* change the meaning of sentences: "The teacher called the students names." Was the instructor being rude or just taking roll?) It's a grammatical jungle out there, so be sensitive to your weary readers.

Use your tools. Keep your dictionary handy to check the spelling, usage, and meanings of words in doubt. A thesaurus can also be useful if you can restrain any tendencies you might have for growing overly exotic prose. If you are using a word processor with a spell-checker, by all means run it after your last revisions are completed. Do remember, as noted earlier in this chapter, that such programs only flag words whose spelling they don't recognize; they will not alert you to omitted or confused words (*affect/effect*), nor will they signal when you've typed in a wrong, but correctly spelled, word (*form* for *from*).

Use Part Four of this text to help resolve any questions you may have about grammar, mechanics, and spelling. Advice on untangling sentences and clarifying word choice in Chapters 6 and 7 may be useful, too.

VI. Proofreading

Proofread your final draft several times, putting as much time between the last two readings as possible. Fresh eyes catch more typographical or careless errors. Remember that typing errors—even the simple transposing of letters—can change the meaning of an entire thought and occasionally bring unintended humor to your prose. (Imagine, for example, the surprise of restaurant owners whose new lease instructed them to "Please sing the terms of the agreement." Or consider the ramifications of the newspaper ad offering "Great dames for sale" or the 1716 Bible whose advice "sin no more" was misprinted as "sin on more.")

Make sure, too, that your paper looks professional before you turn it in. You wouldn't, after all, expect to be taken seriously if you went to an executive job interview dressed in cutoffs. Turning in a paper with a coffee stain or ink smear on it has about the same effect as a blob of spinach in your teeth—it distracts folks from hearing what you have to say. If your final draft has typos or small blemishes, you may use correction fluid to conceal them; if you've patched so frequently that your paper resembles the medicine-dotted face of a kindergartner with chicken pox, reprint or photocopy your pages for a fresh look.

Check to be sure you've formatted your paper exactly as your assignment requested. Some instructors ask for a title page; others want folders containing all your drafts and prewriting. Most teachers appreciate typed papers with pages that are numbered, ordered correctly, paper clipped or stapled, with clean edges (no sheets violently ripped from a spiral notebook still dribbling angry confetti down one side; no pages mutilated at the corners by the useless "tear-and-fold-tab" technique). Putting your name on each page will identify your work if papers from a particular class are accidentally mixed up.

As it's often been said, essays are never really done—only due. Take a last reading using the checklist that follows, make some notes on your progress as a writer and thinker, and congratulate yourself on your fine efforts and accomplishment.

■ A Final Checklist for Your Essay

If you have written an effective essay, you should be able to answer "yes" to the following questions:

1. Do I feel I have something important to say to my reader?

2. Am I sincerely committed to communicating with my reader and not just with myself?

3. Have I considered my audience's needs? (See Chapter 1.)

4. Do my title and lead-in attract the reader's attention and help set up my thesis? (See Chapter 4.)

5. Does my thesis statement assert one main, clearly focused idea? (See Chapter 2.)

6. Does my thesis and/or essay map give the reader an indication of what points the essay will cover? (See Chapter 2.)

7. Do my body paragraphs contain the essential points in the essay's discussion, and are those points expressed in clearly stated or implied topic sentences? (See Chapter 3.)

8. Is each major point in my essay well developed with enough detailed supporting evidence? (See Chapter 3.)

9. Does each body paragraph have unity and coherence? (See Chapter 3.)

10. Are all the paragraphs in my essay smoothly linked in a logical order? (See Chapter 3.)

11. Does my concluding paragraph provide a suitable ending for the essay? (See Chapter 4.)

12. Are all my sentences clear, concise, and coherent? (See Chapter 6.)

13. Are my words accurate, necessary, and meaningful? (See Chapter 7.)

14. Have I edited and proofread for errors in grammar, punctuation, spelling, or typing? (See Part Four.)

And most important:

15. Has my essay been effectively revised so that I am proud of this piece of writing?

■ PRACTICING WHAT YOU'VE LEARNED

The draft of the student essay below has been annotated by its own writer according to some—*but not all*—of the questions presented in this chapter's discussion of revision. As you read the draft and the writer's marginal

---

(Writing)

comments, think of specific suggestions you might offer to help this writer improve her essay. What other changes, in addition to the ones mentioned here, would you encourage this writer to make? What strengths do you see in this draft?

DORM LIFE

My title and lead-in are too bland to attract reader's attention.

Would my thesis be clearer if I said what I did find?

My supporting examples could use more "showing" details so the readers can really see the unfriendliness.

Contradicts my point

This paragraph has some specific details but it rambles and repeats ideas. Needs tighter organization.

Contradicts my ¶'s point

Dorm life is not at all what I had expected it to be. I had anticipated meeting friendly people, quiet hours for studying, eating decent food, and having wild parties on weekends. My dreams, I soon found out, were simply illusions, erroneous perceptions of reality.

My roommate, Kathy, and I live in Holland Hall on the third floor. The people on our dorm floor are about as unfriendly as they can possibly be. I wonder whether or not they're just shy and afraid or if they are simply snobs. Some girls, for example, ignore my roommate and me when we say "hello." Occasionally, they stare straight ahead and act like we aren't even there. Other girls respond, but it's as if they do it out of a sense of duty rather than being just friendly. The guys seem nice, but some are just as afraid or snobby as the girls.

I remember signing up for "quiet hours" when I put in my application for a dorm room last December. Unfortunately, I was assigned to a floor that doesn't have any quiet hours at all. I am a person who requires peace and quiet when studying or reading. The girls in all the rooms around us love to stay up until early in the morning and yell and turn up their music full blast. They turn music on at about eight o'clock at night and turn it off early in the morning. There is always at least one girl who has music playing at maximum volume. Now, I am very appreciative of music, but listening to "heavy metal" until three in the morning isn't really my idea of what music is. The girls right across from us usually play Bonnie Raitt or the Dixie Chicks and I enjoy them. On the other hand, though, the girls on either side of our room love to listen to Metallica or Linkin Park into the wee hours of the morning. It is these girls who run up and down the hall, yell at each other, laugh obnoxiously, and try to attract attention. All this continuous racket makes it nearly impossible to study, read, or get any sleep. Kathy and I usually end up going to the library or student cafeteria to study. As far as sleep goes, it doesn't matter what time we go to bed, but rather it depends on how noisy it is, and how late the music is on. Sometimes the noise gets so loud and goes on for so long that even when it stops, my ears are ringing and my stomach keeps churning. It is on nights like this that I never go to sleep. I wish the people here were a little more considerate of the people around them.

This paragraph doesn't support my thesis claim—do I mean the dorm has no good parties or not enough parties? Rethink so my point is clear.

As stated, this topic sentence contradicts my thesis.

Some good examples— could I use even more descriptive language?

Unity?

Parties, on weekends, are supposedly the most important part of dorm life. Parties provide the opportunity to meet others and have a good time. Holland Hall has had two parties that are even worth mentioning. One of them was a Fifties dance held in the courtyard approximately three weeks ago. Unfortunately, all the other dormitories, the fraternities, and the sororities heard about it, and by eight o'clock at night there were masses of people. It was so packed that it was hard to move around. The other party, much to my dismay, turned out to be a luau party. I do not really care for roast pig, and my stomach turned from the scent of it when I entered the room. Our floor never has parties. Everyone leaves their doors open, turns up the music, and yells back and forth. I suppose that there will be more floor parties once everyone becomes adjusted to this life and begins to socialize.

Dorm food is what I anticipated it would be, terrible, and I was right, it is awful. Breakfast is probably the hardest meal to digest. The bacon and sausage are cold, slightly uncooked, and very greasy. Sometimes, it's as though I am eating pure grease. The eggs look and taste like nothing I ever had before. They look like plastic and they are never hot. I had eggs once and I vowed I would never have another one as long as I lived in Holland Hall. The most enjoyable part of breakfast is the orange juice. It's always cold and it seems to be fresh. No one can say dorm food is totally boring because the cooks break up the monotony of the same food by serving "mystery meat" at least once every two weeks. This puts a little excitement in the student's day because everyone cracks jokes and wonders just what's in this "mystery meat." I think a lot of students are afraid to ask, fearful of the answer, and simply make snide remarks and shovel it in.

Can I conclude emphatically without switching positions?

All in all, I believe dorm life isn't too great, even though there are some good times. Even though I complain about dorm food, the people, the parties, and everything else, I am glad I am here. I am happy because I have learned a lot about other people, responsibilities, consideration, and I've even learned a lot about myself.

■ Benefiting from Revision Workshops

Many writing courses today include revision workshops in which students comment help-fully on one another's drafts. This sort of revision activity may also be called peer editing, classroom critique, or reader review. Peer workshops may be arranged in a variety of ways, though frequently students will work in pairs or in small groups of three to five. Sometimes writers will simply talk about their papers or read them aloud; at other times students will be asked to write suggestions on one another's drafts. Sometimes instructors will give stu-dent-reviewers a list of questions to answer; at other times, the writers themselves will voice their concerns directly to their reviewers. Structured in many effective ways, peer workshops can be extremely valuable to writers, who will invariably profit from seeing their drafts from a reader's point of view.

Students taking part in revision workshops for the first time often have questions about the reviewing process. Some student-reviewers may feel uneasy about their role, wondering, "What if I can't think of any suggestions for the writer? How can I tell someone that the essay is really terrible? What if I sense something's wrong but I'm not sure what it is—or how to fix it?" Writers, too, may feel apprehensive or even occasionally defensive about receiving criticism of their papers. Because these concerns are genuine and widespread, here is some advice to help you get the most out of your participation in revision workshops, in the role of writer or reviewer.

When you are the writer:

1. Develop a constructive attitude. Admittedly, receiving criticism—especially on a creation that has required hard work—can sometimes be difficult, particularly if your self-image has become mixed up with your drafts. Try to realize that your reviewer is not criticizing *you* personally but rather is trying to help you by offering fresh insights. All drafts can be improved, and no writer need feel embarrassed about seeking or receiving advice. (Take comfort in the words of writer Somerset Maugham: "Only the mediocre person is always at his best.") See the workshop as a nonthreatening opportunity to reconsider your prose and improve your audience awareness.

2. Come prepared. If your workshop structure permits, tell your reviewer what sort of help you need at this point in your drafting or revising process. Ask for suggestions to fix a particularly troublesome area or ask for feedback on a choice you've made but are feeling unsure of. Don't hesitate to ask your reviewer for assistance with any part of your essay.

3. Evaluate suggestions carefully. Writing isn't math: most of the time there are no absolutely right or wrong answers—just better or worse rhetorical choices. That is, there are many ways to communicate an idea to a set of readers. You, as the writer, must decide on an effective way, the way that best serves your purpose and your readers' needs. Sometimes your reviewer will suggest a change that is brilliant or one so obviously right you will wonder why in the world you didn't think of it yourself. At other times you may weigh your reviewer's suggestion and decide that your original choice is just as good or perhaps even better. Be open to suggestions, but learn to trust thyself as well.

4. Find the good in bad advice. Occasionally you may have a reviewer who seems to miss a crucial point or misunderstands your purpose entirely, whose suggestions for revising your paper seem uniformly unproductive for one reason or another. You certainly shouldn't take bad advice—but do think about the issues it raises. Although it's helpful to receive a dynamite suggestion you can incorporate immediately, the real value of a revision workshop is its ability to encourage you to rethink your prose. Readers' responses (yes, even the bizarre ones) challenge writers to take still another look at their rhetorical choices and ask themselves, "Is this clear after all? Does this example really work here? Did something in my essay throw this reader off the track?" Revision workshops offer you benefits, even if you ultimately decide to reject many of your reviewer's suggestions.

When you are the reviewer:

1. Develop a constructive attitude. Sometimes it's hard to give honest criticism—most of us are uncomfortable when we think we might hurt someone's feelings—but remember that the writer has resolved to develop a professional attitude, too. The writer expects (and is sometimes desperately begging for) sincere feedback, so be honest as you offer your best advice.

2. Be clear and specific. Vague or flippant responses ("This is confusing"; "Huh?") don't help writers know what or how to revise. Try putting some of your comments into this format: your response to X, the reason for your response, a request for change, and, if possible, a specific suggestion for the change. ("I'm confused when you say you enjoy some parts of breakfast because this seems to contradict your thesis claim of 'wretched dorm food.' Would it be clearer to modify your thesis to exclude breakfast or to revise this paragraph to include only discussion of the rubbery eggs?")

3. Address important issues. Unless you have workshop directions that request certain tasks, read through the draft entirely at least once and then comment on the larger issues first. Writers want to know if they are achieving their overall purpose, if their thesis is clear and convincing, if their major points and evidence make sense, and if their paper seems logical and ordered. Editing tips are fine, too, but because workshops encourage authors to rewrite large portions of their prose, attention to minor details may be less valuable early on than feedback on ideas, organization, and development. (Of course, an editing workshop later in the revision process may be exclusively focused on sentence and word problems. Workshops may be designed to address specific problems that writers face.)

4. Encourage the writer. Writers with confidence write and revise better than insecure or angry writers. Praise honestly wherever you can, as specifically as you can. When weaknesses do appear, show the writer that you know she or he is capable of doing better work by linking the weakness to a strength elsewhere in the draft. ("Could you add more 'showing' details here so that your picture of the dentist is as vivid as your description of the nurse?") Substitute specific responses and suggestions for one-word labels such as "awk" (awkward) or "unclear." Even positive labels don't always help writers repeat effective techniques. ("Good!" enthusiastically inscribed in the margin by a well-developed paragraph feels nice but might cause the writer to wonder, "'Good' what? Good point? Good supporting evidence? Good detail? How can I do 'good' again if I don't know exactly what it is?")

5. Understand your role as critical reader. Sometimes it's easy for a reviewer to take ownership of someone else's paper. Keep the writer's purpose in mind as you respond; don't insist on revisions that produce the essay that's in *your* head. Be sensitive to your own voice and language as a reviewer. Instead of making authoritative pronouncements that might offend, ask reader-based questions ("Will all your readers know the meaning of this technical term?" "Would some readers profit from a brief history of this controversy?"). If you're unsure about a possible error, request verification ("Could you recheck this quotation? Its wording here is confusing me because. . . ."). Practice offering criticism in language that acknowledges the writer's hard work and accentuates the positive nature of revision ("Would citing last year's budget figures make your good argument against the fish market even stronger?").

Last, always look over your own draft in light of the insightful suggestions you are offering your classmates. You may feel at first that it is far simpler to analyze someone else's writing than your own. As you participate in revision workshops, however, you will find it increasingly easy to transfer those same critical reading skills to your own work. Becoming a good reader-reviewer for your composition colleagues can be an important part of your training as a first-rate writer.

■ PRACTICING WHAT YOU'VE LEARNED

A. Assume that the essay below is a draft written by one of your classmates who has asked you for help during a class workshop. Using your best critical thinking skills, offer some marginal comments and questions that will guide this writer through an effective revision process.

MAYBE YOU SHOULDN'T GO AWAY TO COLLEGE

Going away to college is not for everyone. There are good reasons why a student might choose to live at home and attend a local school. Money, finding stability while changes are occurring, and accepting responsibility are three to consider.

Money is likely to be most important. Not only is tuition more expensive, but extra money is needed for room and board. Whether room and board is a dorm or an apartment, the expense is great.

Most students never stop to consider that the money that could be saved from room and board may be better spent in future years on graduate school, which is likely to be more important in their careers.

Going to school is a time of many changes anyway, without adding the pressure of a new city or even a new state. Finding stability will be hard enough, without going from home to a dorm. Starting college could be an emotional time for some, and the security of their home and family might make everything easier.

When students decide to go away to school, sometimes because their friends are going away, or maybe because the school is their parents' alma mater, something that all need to decide is whether or not they can accept the responsibility of a completely new way of life.

Everyone feels as if they are ready for total independence when they decide to go away to college, but is breaking away when they are just beginning to set their futures a good idea?

Going away to school may be the right road for some, but those who feel that they are not ready might start looking to a future that is just around the corner.

B. Continue to practice your revision skills by writing a one-to-two-page evaluation of the letter that follows. Help out poor Bubba by telling him what he might do in another draft to accomplish his purpose more effectively and better address his audience. Has he, for example, made the best choices in organization, selection and development of ideas, paragraph structure, and diction? Discuss why and how his letter needs revision.

Dear Mom and Dad,

This week at college has been very interesting.

My roommate is gone and so is my wallet and computer. I tried to tell the police that the stacks of phony $3 bills by his copier weren't mine but I don't know if they believed me.

And, hey, the car thing isn't my fault either. Despite the testimony of all those witnesses. Who knew the entire back end would crumple like that? The other guy's lawyer will be in touch.

Without any transportation, I don't know when I can come home. Maybe at Thanksgiving. The doctor says the rash shouldn't be contagious by then. The arm, after the fight at the party, is another matter altogether.

I have a new girlfriend! Bambi's real nice and the age difference between us is no big deal. I hope you like her, despite how you feel about tattoos. I have a funny story to tell you about how the stuff in her face set off the airport metal detector last weekend. I just wish her sick grandmother didn't need me to help out so much with her expensive operation. Bambi and her brother are pressuring me a lot.

As you can plainly see, I need more financial help! Please send money right away!

Your devoted son,
Bubba

■ ASSIGNMENT

Select a body paragraph from "Dorm Life" (pages 105–106) or "Maybe You Shouldn't Go Away to College" (page 109) and revise it, making any changes in focus, organization, development, sentence construction, or word choice you think necessary. (Feel free to elaborate on, eliminate, or change the content to improve the paragraph's effectiveness.)

■ Some Last Advice: How to Play with Your Mental Blocks

Every writer, sooner or later, suffers from some form of Writer's Block, the inability to think of or organize ideas. Symptoms may include sweaty palms, pencil chewing, and a pronounced tendency to sit in corners and weep. Although not every "cure" works for everyone, here are a few suggestions to help minimize your misery:

Try to give yourself as much time as possible to write your essay. Don't try to write the entire paper in one sitting. By doing so, you place yourself under too much pressure. Writer's Block often accompanies the "up against the wall" feeling that strikes at 2:00 a.m. the morning your essay is due at 9:00. Rome wasn't constructed in a day, and neither are most good essays.

Because most of us have had more experience talking than writing, try verbalizing your ideas. Sometimes it's helpful to discuss your ideas with friends or classmates. Their questions and comments (not to mention their sympathy for your temporary block) will often trigger the thoughts you need to begin writing again. Or you might try talking into a recorder so you can hear what you want to say.

When an irresistible force meets an immovable object, something's going to give. Conquer the task: break the paper into manageable bits. Instead of drooping with despair over the thought of a ten-page research paper, think of it as a series of small parts (explanation of the problem, review of current research, possible solutions, etc.). Then tackle one part at a time and reward yourself when that section's done.

Get the juices flowing and the pen moving. Try writing the easiest or shortest part of your essay

Sometimes writer's block makes you want to . . .

The Scream, 1893, by Edvard Munch

Copyright © 1992 Munch Museum, Oslo/Eric Lessing/Art Resource, NY

first. A feeling of accomplishment may give you the boost of confidence you need to undertake the other, more difficult sections. If no part looks easy or inviting, try more prewriting exercises, as described in Chapter 1, until you feel prepared to begin the essay itself.

Play "Let's Make a Deal" with yourself. Sometimes we just can't face the failure that we are predicting for ourselves. Strike a bargain with yourself: promise yourself that you are only going to work on your paper for twenty minutes—absolutely, positively only twenty minutes, not a second more, no sir, no way. If in twenty minutes, you're on to something good, ignore your promise to yourself and keep going. If you're not, then leave and come back for another twenty-minute session later (if you started early enough, you can do this without increasing your anxiety).

Give yourself permission to write garbage. Take the pressure off yourself by agreeing in advance to tear up the first page or two of whatever you write. You can always change your mind if the trash turns out to be treasure; if it isn't, so what? You said you were going to tear it up anyway.

Imagine that your brain is a water faucet. If you're like most people, you've probably lived in a house or apartment containing a faucet that needed to run a few minutes before the hot water came out. Think of your brain in the same way, and do some other, easier writing task to warm up. Write a letter, send an e-mail, make a grocery list, copy notes, whatever, to get your brain running. When you turn to your essay, your ideas may be hotter than you thought.

Remove the threat by addressing a friendly face. Sometimes we can't write because we are too worried about what someone else will think about us or maybe we can't write because we can't figure out who would want to read this stuff anyway. Instead of writing into a void or to an audience that seems threatening, try writing to a friend. Imagine what that friend's responses might be and try to elaborate or clarify wherever necessary. If it helps, write the first draft as a letter ("Dear Clyde, I want to tell you what happened to me last week. . ."), and then redraft your ideas as an essay when you've found your purpose and focus, making whatever changes in tone or development are necessary to fit your real audience.

If Writer's Block does hit, remember that it is a temporary bogdown, not a permanent one. Other writers have had it—and survived to write again. Try leaving your draft and taking a walk outdoors or at least into another room. Think about your readers—what should they know or feel at this point in your essay? As you walk, try to complete this sentence: "What I am trying to say is. . . ." Keep repeating this phrase and your responses aloud until you find the answer you want.

Sometimes while you're blocked at one point, a bright idea for another part of your essay will pop into your head. If possible, skip the section that's got you stuck and start working on the new part. (At least jot down the new idea somewhere so it won't be lost when you need it later.)

Change partners and dance. If you're thoroughly overcome by the vast white wasteland on the desk (or screen) before you, get up and do something else for a while. Exercise, balance your checkbook, or put on music and dance. (Mystery writer Agatha Christie claimed she did her best planning while washing the dishes.) Give your mind a break and refresh your spirit. When you come back to the paper or computer, you may be surprised to discover that your subconscious writer has been working while the rest of you played.

Here's the single most important piece of advice to remember: relax. No one—not even the very best professional writer—produces perfect prose every time pen hits paper. If you're blocked, you may be trying too hard; if your expectations of your first draft are too high, you may not be able to write at all for fear of failure. You just might be holding yourself back by being a perfectionist at this point. You can always revise and polish your prose in another draft—the first important step is jotting down your ideas. Remember that once the first word or phrase appears on your blank page or screen, a major battle has been won.

★ CHAPTER 5 SUMMARY

Here is a brief summary of what you should remember about revising your writing:

1. Revision is an activity that occurs in all stages of the writing process.

2. All good writers revise their prose extensively.

3. Revision is not merely editing or last-minute proofreading; it involves important decisions about the essay's ideas, organization, and development.

4. To revise effectively, novice writers might review their drafts in steps, to avoid the frustration that comes with trying to fix everything at once.

5. Critical thinking skills are vitally important today to all good readers and writers.

6. Most writers experience Writer's Block at some time but live through it to write again.

Chapter 6

Effective Sentences

An insurance agent was shocked to open his mail one morning and read the following note from one of his clients: "In accordance with your instructions, I have given birth to twins in the enclosed envelope." However, he may not have been more surprised than the congregation who read this announcement in their church bulletin: "There will be a discussion tomorrow on the problem of adultery in the minister's office." Or the patrons of a health club who learned that "guest passes will not be given to members until the manager has punched each of them first."

Certainly, there were no babies born in an envelope, nor was there adultery in the minister's office, and one doubts that the club manager was planning to assault the membership. But the implications (and the unintended humor) are nevertheless present—solely because of the faulty ways in which the sentences were constructed.

To improve your own writing, you must express your thoughts in clear, coherent sentences that produce precisely the reader response you want. Effective sentences are similar to the threads in a piece of knitting or weaving: each thread helps form the larger design; if any one thread becomes tangled or lost, the pattern becomes muddled. In an essay, the same is true: if any sentence is fuzzy or obscure, the reader may lose the point of your discussion and in some cases never bother to regain it. Therefore, to retain your reader, you must concentrate on writing informative, effective sentences that continuously clarify the purpose of your essay.

Many problems in sentence clarity involve errors in grammar, punctuation, word choice, and usage; the most common of these errors are discussed in Chapter 7, "Word Logic," and throughout Part Four, the handbook section of this text. In this chapter you'll find some general suggestions for writing clear, concise, engaging sentences. However, *don't try to apply all the rules to the first draft of your essay*. Revising sentences before your ideas are firmly in place may be a waste of effort if your essay's stance or structure changes. Concentrate your efforts in early drafts on your thesis, the development of your important supporting points, and the essay's general organization; then, in a later draft, rework your sentences so that each one is informative and clear. Your reader reads only the words on the page, not those in your mind—so it's up to you to make sure the sentences in your essay express the thoughts in your head as closely and vividly as possible.

 REMEMBER: All good writers revise and polish their sentences.

■ Developing a Clear Style

When you are ready to revise the sentences in your rough draft for clarity, try to follow the following five rules.

Give Your Sentences Content

Fuzzy sentences are often the result of fuzzy thinking. When you examine your sentences, ask yourself, "Do I know what I'm talking about here? Or are my sentences vague or confusing because I'm really not sure what my point is or where it's going?" Look at this list of content-poor sentences taken from student essays; how could you put more information into each one?

If you were to observe a karate class, you would become familiar with all the aspects that make it up.

The meaning of the poem isn't very clear the first time you read it, but after several readings, the poet's meaning comes through.

One important factor that is the basis for determining a true friend is the ability that person has for being a real human being.

Listening is important because we all need to be able to sit and hear all that is said to us.

Don't pad your paragraphs with sentences that run in circles, leading nowhere; rethink your ideas and revise your writing so that every sentence—like each brick in a wall—contributes to the construction of a solid discussion. In other words, commit yourself to a position and make each sentence contain information pertinent to your point; leave the job of padding to mattress manufacturers.

Sometimes, however, you may have a definite idea in mind but still continue to write "empty sentences"—statements that alone do not contain enough information to make a specific point in your discussion. Frequently, an empty sentence may be revised by combining it with the sentence that follows, as shown in the examples here. The empty, or overly general, sentences are underlined.

Poor	<u>There are many kinds of beautiful tropical fish.</u> The kind most popular with aquarium owners is the angelfish.
Better	Of the many kinds of beautiful tropical fish, the angelfish is the most popular with aquarium owners.
Poor	<u>D. W. Griffith introduced many new cinematic techniques.</u> Some of these techniques were contrast editing, close-ups, fade-outs, and freeze-frame shots.
Better	D. W. Griffith made movie history by introducing such new cinematic techniques as contrast editing, close-ups, fade-outs, and the freeze-frame shot.
Poor	<u>There is a national organization called The Couch Potatoes.</u> The group's 8,000 members are devoted television watchers.
Better	The Couch Potatoes is a national organization whose 8,000 members are devoted television watchers.

For more help on combining sentences, see pages 133–136.

Make Your Sentences Specific

In addition to containing an informative, complete thought, each of your sentences should give readers enough clear details for them to "see" the picture you are creating. Sentences full of vague words produce blurry, boring prose and drowsy readers. Remember your reaction the last time you asked a friend about a recent vacation? If the only response you received was something like, "Oh, it was great—a lot of fun," you probably yawned and proceeded quickly to a new topic. But if your friend had begun an exciting account of a wilderness rafting trip, with detailed stories about narrow escapes from freezing white water, treacherous rocks, and uncharted whirlpools, you'd probably have stopped and listened. The same principle works in your writing—clear, specific details are the only sure way to attract and hold the reader's interest. Therefore, make each sentence contribute something new and interesting to the overall discussion.

The following examples first show sentences far too vague to sustain anyone's attention. Rewritten, these sentences contain specific details that add clarity and interest:

Vague	She went home in a bad mood. [What kind of a bad mood? How did she act or look?]
Specific	She stomped home, hands jammed in her pockets, angrily kicking rocks, dogs, small children, and anything else that crossed her path.
Vague	His neighbor bought a really nice old desk. [Why nice? How old? What kind of desk?]
Specific	His neighbor bought a solid-oak rolltop desk made in 1885 that contains a secret drawer triggered by a hidden spring.

Vague	My roommate is truly horrible. ["Horrible" in what ways? To what extent? Do you "see" this person?]
Specific	My thoughtless roommate leaves dirty dishes under the bed, sweaty clothes in the closet, and toenail clippings in the sink.

For more help selecting specific "showing" words, see pages 149–152 in Chapter 7.

Avoid Overpacking Your Sentences

Because our society is becoming increasingly specialized and highly technical, we tend to equate complexity with excellence and simplicity with simplemindedness. This assumption is unfortunate because it often leads to a preference for unnecessarily complicated and even contorted writing. In a recent survey, for example, a student chose a sample of bureaucratic hogwash over several well-written paragraphs, explaining his choice by saying that it must have been better because he didn't understand it.

Our best writers have always worked hard to present their ideas simply and specifically so that their readers could easily understand them. Mark Twain, for instance, once praised a young author this way: "I notice that you use plain simple language, short words, and brief sentences. This is the way to write English. It is the modern way and the best way. Stick to it." And when a critic asked Hemingway to define his theory of writing, he replied, "[I] put down what I see and what I feel in the best and simplest way I can tell it."

In your own writing, therefore, work for a simple, direct style. Avoid sentences that are overpacked (too many ideas or too much information at once) as in the following example on racquetball:

> John told Phil that to achieve more control over the ball, he should practice flicking or snapping his wrist, because this action is faster in the close shots and placing a shot requires only a slight change of the wrist's angle instead of an acute movement of the whole arm, which gives a player less reaction time.

To make the overpacked sentence easier to understand, try dividing the ideas into two or more sentences:

> John told Phil that to achieve more control over the ball, he should practice flicking or snapping his wrist, because this action is faster in the close shots. Placing a shot requires only a slight change of the wrist's angle instead of an acute movement of the whole arm, which gives a player less reaction time.

Don't ever run the risk of losing your reader in a sentence that says too much to comprehend in one bite. This confusing notice, for example, came from a well-known credit card company:

> The Minimum Payment Due each month shall be reduced by the amounts paid in excess of the Minimum Payment Due during the previous three months which have not already been so applied in determining the Minimum Payment Due in such earlier months, unless you have exceeded your line of credit or have paid the entire New Balance shown on your billing statement.

Or consider the confusion of soccer players whose coach warned them in this manner:

> It is also a dangerous feeling to consider that where we are in the league is of acceptable standard because standard is relevant to the standards we have set, which thereby may well indicate that we have not aspired to the standard which we set ourselves.

Try too for a straightforward construction; this sentence by former president Ronald Reagan early in his campaign for office, for example, takes far too many twists and turns for anyone to follow it easily on the first reading:

> My goal is an America where something or anything that is done to or for anyone is done neither because of nor in spite of any difference between them, racially, religiously or ethnic-origin-wise.

If any sentences in your rough draft are overpacked or contorted, try rephrasing your meaning in shorter sentences and then combining thoughts where most appropriate. (Help with sentence variety may be found on pages 133–136 of this chapter.)

Pay Attention to Word Order

The correct word order is crucial for clarity. Always place a modifier (a word or group of words that affects the meaning of another word) near the word it modifies. The position of a modifier can completely change the meaning of your sentence; for example, each sentence presented here offers a different idea because of the placement of the modifier "only."

1. Eliza said she loves only me.
   [Eliza loves me and no one else.]
2. Only Eliza said she loves me.
   [No other person said she loves me.]
3. Eliza only said she loves me.
   [Eliza said she loves me, but said nothing other than that.]
4. Eliza said only she loves me.
   [Eliza says no one else loves me.]

To avoid confusion, therefore, place your modifiers close to the words or phrases they describe.

A modifier that seems to modify the wrong part of a sentence is called "misplaced." Not only can misplaced modifiers change or distort the meaning of your sentence, they can also provide unintentional humor, as illustrated by the following excerpt from the 1929 Marx Brothers' movie *Coconuts:*

Woman: There's a man waiting outside to see you with a black mustache.
Groucho: Tell him I've already got one.

Of course, the woman didn't mean to imply that the man outside was waiting with (that is, accompanied by) a mustache; she meant to say, "There's a man with a black mustache who is waiting outside."

A poster advertising a lecture on campus provided this opportunity for humor: "Professor Elizabeth Sewell will discuss the latest appearance of Halley's Comet in room 104." Under the announcement a local wit had scribbled, "Shall we reserve room 105 for the tail?" Or take the case of this startling headline: "Calf Born to Rancher with Two Heads."

Here are some other examples of misplaced modifiers:

Misplaced	Dilapidated and almost an eyesore, Shirley bought the old house to restore it to its original beauty. [Did the writer mean that Shirley needed a beauty treatment?]
Revised	Shirley bought the old house, which was dilapidated and almost an eyesore, to restore it to its original beauty.
Misplaced	Because she is now thoroughly housebroken, Sarah can take her dog almost anywhere she goes. [Did the writer mean that Sarah once had an embarrassing problem?]
Revised	Because she is now thoroughly housebroken, Sarah's dog can accompany her almost anywhere she goes.
Misplaced	Three family members were found bound and gagged by the grandmother. [Did the writer mean that the grandmother had taken up a life of crime?]
Revised	The grandmother found the three family members who had been bound and gagged.
Misplaced	The lost child was finally found wandering in a frozen farmer's field. [Did the writer mean to say that the farmer was that cold?]
Revised	The lost child was finally found wandering in a farmer's frozen field.

In each of the preceding examples the writer forgot to place the modifying phrase so that it modifies the correct word. In most cases, a sentence with a misplaced modifier can be corrected easily by moving the word or phrase closer to the word that should be modified.

In some sentences, however, the word being modified is missing entirely. Such a phrase is called a "dangling modifier." Think of these phrases as poor orphans, waiting out in the cold, without a parent to accompany them. Most of these errors may be corrected by adding the missing "parent"—the word(s) described by the phrase. Here are some examples followed by their revisions:

Dangling	Waving farewell, the plane began to roll down the runway. [Did the writer mean the plane was waving farewell?]
Revised	Waving farewell, <u>we</u> watched as the plane began to roll down the runway.
Dangling	After spending hours planting dozens of strawberry plants, the gophers came back to the garden and ate every one of them. [Did the writer mean that the gophers had a good meal after putting in such hard work?]
Revised	After spending hours planting dozens of strawberry plants, <u>Ralph</u> realized that the gophers had come back to the garden and eaten every one of them.

Dangling	While telling a joke to my roommate, a cockroach walked across my soufflé. [Did the writer mean that the cockroach was a comedian?]
Revised	While telling a joke to my roommate, <u>I</u> noticed a cockroach walking across my soufflé.
Dangling	Having tucked the children into bed, the cat was put out for the night. [Did the writer mean that the family pet had taken up nanny duties?]
Revised	Having tucked the children into bed, <u>Mother and Father</u> put the cat out for the night.

Misplaced and dangling modifiers (and many other kinds of sentence errors) often occur as you write your first "idea" drafts. Later, when you are satisfied with your content and organization, you can smooth out these confusing or unintentionally humorous constructions. At first you may agree with well-known essayist Annie Dillard, who notes that writing sometimes feels like alligator wrestling: "With your two bare hands, you hold and fight a sentence's head while its tail tries to knock you over." By practicing good revision skills, however, you soon should be able to wrestle your sentence problems to the ground. (For additional examples of misplaced and dangling modifiers, see pages 488–489 in Part Four.)

Avoid Mixed Constructions and Faulty Predication

Sometimes you may begin with a sentence pattern in mind and then shift, midsentence, to another pattern—a change that often results in a generally confusing sentence. In many of these cases, you will find that the subject of your sentence simply doesn't fit with the rest of the sentence (the predicate). Look at the following examples and note their corrections:

Faulty	Financial aid is a growing problem for many college students. [Financial aid itself isn't a problem; rather, it's the lack of aid.]
Revised	College students are finding it harder to obtain financial aid.
Faulty	Pregnant cows are required to teach a portion of two courses in Animal Science, AS100 (Breeding of Livestock) and AS200 (Problems in Reproduction of Cattle). [Obviously, the cows will not be the instructors for the classes.]
Revised	The Animal Science Department needs to purchase pregnant cows for use in two courses, AS100 (Breeding of Livestock) and AS200 (Problems in Reproduction of Cattle).
Faulty	Love is when you start rehearsing dinner-date conversation before breakfast. [A thing is never a "when" or a "where"; rewrite all "is when" or "is where" constructions.]
Revised	You're in love if you start rehearsing dinner-date conversation before breakfast.
Faulty	My math grade is why I'm so depressed.
Revised	I'm so depressed because of my math grade. [A grade is not a "why"; rewrite "is why" constructions.]
Faulty	"Fans, don't fail to miss tomorrow's game." [A contorted line from Dizzy Dean, baseball star and sportscaster]
Revised	"Fans, don't miss tomorrow's game."

Many mixed constructions occur when a writer is in a hurry; read your rough drafts carefully to see if you have sentences in which you started one pattern but switched to another. (For more help on faulty predications and mixed constructions, see pages 495–496 in Part Four.)

■ Developing a Concise Style

Almost all writing suffers from wordiness—the tendency to use more words than necessary. When useless words weigh down your prose, the meaning is often lost, confused, or hidden. Flabby prose calls for a reducing plan: put those obese sentences on a diet by cutting out unnecessary words, just as you avoid too many fatty foods to keep yourself at a healthy weight. Mushy prose is ponderous and boring; crisp, to-the-point writing, on the other hand, is both accessible and pleasing. Beware, however, a temptation to overdiet—you don't want your prose to become so thin or brief that your meaning disappears completely. Therefore, cut out only the *unessential* words and phrases.

Wordy prose is frequently the result of using one or more of the following: (1) deadwood constructions, (2) redundancies, (3) pretentious diction.

Avoid Deadwood Constructions

Always try to cut empty "deadwood" from your sentences. Having a clear, concise style does not mean limiting your writing to choppy, childish Dick-and-Jane sentences; it only means that all unnecessary words, phrases, and clauses should be deleted. Here are some sentences containing common deadwood constructions and ways they may be pruned:

Poor	The *reason* the starving novelist drove 50 miles to a new restaurant was *because* it was serving his favorite chicken dish, Pullet Surprise. ["The reason . . . was because" is both wordy and ungrammatical. If you have a reason, you don't need a "reason because."]
Revised	The starving novelist drove 50 miles to a new restaurant because it was serving his favorite chicken dish, Pullet Surprise.
Poor	The land settlement *was an example where* my client, Ms. Patti O. Furniture, did not receive fair treatment.
Revised	The land settlement was unfair to my client, Ms. Patti O. Furniture.
Poor	Because *of the fact that* his surfboard business failed after only a month, my brother decided to leave Minnesota.
Revised	Because his surfboard business failed after only a month, my brother decided to leave Minnesota.

Other notorious deadwood constructions include the following:

regardless of the fact that	(use "although")
due to the fact that	(use "because")
the reason is that	(omit)
as to whether or not to	(omit "as to" and "or not")
at this point in time	(use "now" or "today")

it is believed that	(use a specific subject and "believes")
concerning the matter of	(use "about")
by means of	(use "by")
these are the kinds of . . . that	(use "these" plus a specific noun)
on account of	(use "because")

Watch a tendency to tack on empty "fillers" that stretch one word into a phrase:

Wordy	Each candidate will be evaluated *on an individual basis.*
Concise	Each candidate will be evaluated *individually.*
Wordy	Television does not portray violence in a *realistic fashion.*
Concise	Television does not portray violence *realistically.*
Wordy	The New York blackout produced a *crisis-type situation.*
Concise	The New York blackout produced a *crisis.*

To retain your reader's interest and improve the flow of your prose, trim all the fat from your sentences.

"There are," "It is."   These introductory phrases are often space wasters. When possible, omit them or replace them with specific subjects, as shown in the following:

Wordy	*There are* ten dental students on Full-Bite Scholarships attending this university.
Revised	Ten dental students on Full-Bite Scholarships attend this university.
Wordy	*It is* true that the County Fair still offers many fun contests, including the ever-popular map fold-off.
Revised	The County Fair still offers many fun contests, including the ever-popular map fold-off.

"Who" and "which" clauses.   Some "who" and "which" clauses are unnecessary and may be turned into modifiers placed before the noun:

Wordy	The getaway car, *which* was stolen, turned the corner.
Revised	The stolen getaway car turned the corner.
Wordy	The chef, *who was* depressed, ordered his noisy lobsters to simmer down.
Revised	The depressed chef ordered his noisy lobsters to simmer down.

When adjective clauses are necessary, the words "who" and "which" may sometimes be omitted:

Wordy	Sarah Bellam, *who* is a local English teacher, was delighted to hear that she had won the annual lottery, *which is* sponsored by the Shirley Jackson Foundation.
Revised	Sarah Bellam, a local English teacher, was delighted to hear that she had won the annual lottery, sponsored by the Shirley Jackson Foundation.

"To be." Most "to be" phrases are unnecessary and ought not to be. Delete them every time you can.

Wordy	She seems *to be* angry.
Revised	She seems angry.
Wordy	Herb's charisma-bypass operation proved *to be* successful.
Revised	Herb's charisma-bypass operation proved successful.
Wordy	The new governor wanted his archenemy, the local movie critic, *to be* arrested.
Revised	The new governor wanted his archenemy, the local movie critic, arrested.

"Of" and infinitive phrases. Many "of" and infinitive ("to" plus verb) phrases may be omitted or revised by using possessives, adjectives, and verbs, as shown below:

Wordy	At the *time of registration*, students are required *to make* payment *of their library fees.*
Revised	At registration students must pay their library fees.
Wordy	The producer fired the mother *of the director of the movie.*
Revised	The producer fired the movie director's mother.

Including deadwood phrases makes your prose puffy; streamline your sentences to present a simple, direct style.

Avoid Redundancy

Many flabby sentences contain *redundancies* (words that repeat the same idea or whose meanings overlap). Consider the following examples, currently popular in the Department of Redundancy Department:

In this *day and age*, people expect to live at least seventy years. ["Day" and "age" present a similar idea. "Today" is less wordy.]

He repeated the winning bingo number *over again*. ["Repeated" means "to say again," so there is no need for "over again."]

The *group* consensus *of opinion* was that the pizza crust tasted like cardboard. ["Consensus" means "collective opinion," so it's unnecessary to add "group" or repeat "opinion."]

She thought his hot-lava necklaces were *really very* unique. [Because "unique" means "being the only one of its kind," the quality described by "unique" cannot vary in degree. Avoid adding modifiers such as "very," "most," or "somewhat" to the word "unique."]

Some other common redundancies include:

reverted ~~back~~	~~new~~ innovation
reflected ~~back~~	red ~~in color~~

retreated ~~back~~	burned ~~down~~ up
fell ~~down~~	~~pair of~~ twins/~~two~~ twins
climb ~~up~~	~~resulting~~ effect (or "result")
a ~~true~~ fact	~~final~~ outcome
large ~~in size~~	at this point ~~in time~~ (or "now")
joined ~~up~~	8 P.M. ~~at night~~

Carefully Consider Your Passive Verbs

When the subject of the sentence performs the action, the verb is *active;* when the subject of the sentence is acted on, the verb is *passive.* You can recognize some sentences with passive verbs because they often contain the word "by," telling who performed the action.

Passive	The wedding date *was announced* by the young couple.
Active	The young couple *announced* their wedding date.
Passive	His letter of resignation *was accepted* by the Board of Trustees.
Active	The Board of Trustees *accepted* his letter of resignation.
Passive	The trivia contest *was won* by the popular Boulder team, The Godzillas Must Be Crazy.
Active	The popular Boulder team, The Godzillas Must Be Crazy, *won* the trivia contest.

In addition to being wordy and weak, passive sentences often disguise the performer of the action in question. You might have heard a politician, for example, say something similar to this: "It was decided this year to give all the senators an increase in salary." The question of *who* decided to raise salaries remains foggy—perhaps purposefully so. In your own prose, however, you should strive for clarity and directness; therefore, use active verbs as often as you can except when you wish to stress the person or thing that receives the action, as shown in the following samples:

Their first baby was delivered September 30, 1980, by a local midwife.

The elderly man was struck by a drunk driver.

Special note: Authorities in some professional and technical fields still prefer the passive construction because they wish to put emphasis on the experiment or process rather than on the people performing the action. If the passive voice is preferred in your field, you should abide by that convention when you are writing reports or papers for your professional colleagues.

Avoid Pretentiousness

Another enemy of clear, concise prose is *pretentiousness.* Pompous, inflated language surrounds us, and because too many people think it sounds learned or official, we may be tempted to use it when we want to impress others with our writing. But as George Orwell, author of *1984,* noted, an inflated style is like "a cuttlefish squirting out ink." If you want your prose easily understood, write as clearly and plainly as possible.

To illustrate how confusing pretentious writing can be, here is a copy of a government memo announcing a blackout order, issued in 1942 during World War II:

> Such preparations shall be made as will completely obscure all Federal buildings and non-Federal buildings occupied by the Federal government during an air raid for any period of time from visibility by reason of internal or external illumination.

President Franklin Roosevelt intervened and rewrote the order in plain English, clarifying its message and reducing the number of words by half:

> Tell them that in buildings where they have to keep the work going to put something across the windows.

By translating the obscure original memo into easily understandable language, Roosevelt demonstrated that a natural prose style can communicate necessary information to readers more quickly and efficiently than bureaucratic jargon. (For more advice on ridding your prose of jargon, see pages 152–154.)

> ✓ **REMEMBER:** In other—shorter—words, to attract and hold your readers' attention, to communicate clearly and quickly, make your sentences as informative, straightforward, specific, and concise as possible.

■ PRACTICING WHAT YOU'VE LEARNED

A. The following sentences are vague, "empty," overpacked, or confused. Rewrite each one so that it is clear and specific, combining or dividing sentences and adding content as necessary.

1. Roger was an awesome guy who was really a big part of his company.

2. There's a new detective show on television. It stars Phil Noir and is set in the 1940s.

3. Sarah's room is always a huge disaster.

4. The book *Biofeedback: How to Stop It* is a good one because of all the ideas the writer put into it.

5. I can't help but wonder whether or not he isn't unwelcome.

6. Afraid poor repair service will ruin your next road trip? Come to the Fix-It Shop and be sure. If your car has a worn-out part, we'll replace it with one just like it.

7. I've signed up for a course at my local college. It is "Cultivating the Mold in Your Refrigerator for Fun and Profit."

8. For some people, reading your horoscope is a fun way to learn stuff about your life, but some people think it's too weird, even though the others don't.

9. I'm not sure but I think that Lois is the author of *The Underachiever's Guide to Very Small Business Opportunities* or is she the writer of *Whine Your Way to Success* because I know she's written several books since she's having an autograph party at the campus bookstore either this afternoon or tomorrow.

10. Upon being asked if she would like to live forever, one contestant in the 1994 Miss USA contest replied: "I would not live forever, because we should not live forever, because if we were supposed to live forever, then we would live forever, but we cannot live forever, which is why I would not live forever."

B. The following sentences contain misplaced words and phrases as well as other faulty constructions. Revise them so that each sentence is clear.

1. If you are accosted in the subway at night, you should learn to escape harm from the police.

2. The bride was escorted down the aisle by her stepfather wearing an antique family wedding gown.

3. Almost dead for five years now, I miss my dog so much.

4. For sale: unique gifts for that special, hard-to-find person in your life.

5. The reason why I finally got my leg operated on over Thanksgiving break is because it had been hanging over my head for years.

6. We need to hire two three-year-old teachers for preschool kids who don't smoke.

7. The story of Rip Van Winkle is one of the dangers endured by those who oversleep.

8. We gave our waterbed to friends we didn't want anymore.

9. People who are allergic to chocolate and children under 6 should not be given the new vaccine.

10. At 7:00 A.M., Kate starts preparing for another busy day as an executive in her luxurious bathroom.

C. The following sentences are filled with deadwood, redundancies, awkward phrases, and passive constructions. Rewrite each one so that it is concise and direct.

1. In point of fact, the main reason he lost the editing job was primarily because of his being too careless and sloppy in his proofreading work.

2. It was revealed to us by staff members today that there were many adults at the company picnic throwing their trash on the ground as well as their children.

3. My brother Austin, who happens to be older than me, can't drive to work this week due to the fact that he was in a wreck in his car at 2:00 A.M. early Saturday morning.

4. In this modern world of today, we often criticize or disapprove of advertising that is thought to be damaging to women by representing them in an unfair way.

5. When the prosecution tried to introduce the old antique gun, this was objected to by the attorney defending the two twin brothers.

6. It seems to me in my opinion that what the poet is trying to get across to the reader in the poem "Now Is the Winter of Our Discount Tent" is her feeling of disgust with camping.

7. We very often felt that although we expressed our deepest concerns and feelings to our boss, she often just sat there and gave us the real impression that she was taking what we said in a very serious manner although, in our opinion, she did not really and truly care about our concerns.

8. It is a true fact that certainly bears repeating over and over again that learning computer skills and word processing can help you perform in a more efficient way at work and school and also can save you lots of time in daily life too.

9. Personally, I believe that there are too many people who go to eat out in restaurants who always feel they must continually assert their superior natures by acting in a rude, nasty fashion to the people who are employed to wait on their tables.

10. In order to enhance my opportunities for advancement in the workplace at this point in time, I arrived at the decision to seek the hand of my employer's daughter in the state of matrimony.

■ ASSIGNMENT

Write a paragraph of at least five sentences as clearly and concisely as you can. Then rewrite this paragraph, filling it with as many vague words, redundancies, and deadwood constructions as possible. Exchange this rewritten paragraph for a similarly faulty one written by a classmate; give yourselves fifteen minutes to "translate" each other's sentences into effective prose. Compare the translations to the original paragraphs. Which version is clearer? Why?

■ Developing a Lively Style

Good writing demands clarity and conciseness—but that's not all. Good prose must also be lively, engaging, and interesting. It should excite, intrigue, and charm; each line should seduce the reader into the next. Consider, for example, a dull article you've read lately. It may have been written clearly, but perhaps it failed to interest or inform because of its insufferably bland tone; by the time you finished a few pages, you had discovered a new cure for insomnia.

You can prevent your readers from succumbing to a similar case of the blahs by developing a vigorous prose style that continually surprises and pleases them. As one writer has pointed out, all subjects—with the possible exceptions of sex and money—are dull until somebody makes them interesting. As you revise your rough drafts, remember: bored readers are not born but made. Therefore, here are some practical suggestions to help you transform ho-hum prose into lively sentences and paragraphs:

Use specific, descriptive verbs. Avoid bland verbs that must be supplemented by modifiers.

Bland	His fist *broke* the window *into many little pieces.*
Better	His fist *shattered* the window.
Bland	Dr. Love *asked* his congregation about donating money to his "love mission" *over and over again.*
Better	Dr. Love *hounded* his congregation into donating money to his "love mission."
Bland	The exhausted runner *went* up the last hill *in an unsteady way.*
Better	The exhausted runner *staggered* up the last hill.

To cut wordiness that weighs down your prose, try to use an active verb instead of a noun plus a colorless verb such as "to be," "to have," "to get," "to do," and "to make." Avoid unnecessary uses of "got."

Wordy	At first the players and managers *had an argument* over the money, but finally they *came to an agreement that got* the contract dispute settled.
Better	At first the players and managers *argued* over the money, but finally they *settled* the contract dispute.
Wordy	The executives *made the decision* to *have another meeting* on Tuesday.
Better	The executives *decided* to *meet again* on Tuesday.
Wordy	The family *made many enjoyable trips* to Hawaii before their daughter *got married* there in 2002.
Better	The family *enjoyed* many trips to Hawaii before their daughter *married* there in 2002.

Use specific, precise modifiers that help the reader see, hear, or feel what you are describing. Adjectives such as "good," "bad," "many," "more," "great," "a lot," "important," and "interesting" are too vague to paint the reader a clear picture. Similarly, the adverbs "very," "really," "too," and "quite" are overused and add little to sentence clarity. The following are examples of weak sentences and their revisions:

Imprecise	The potion changed the scientist into a *really old* man.
Better	The potion changed the scientist into a *one-hundred-year-old* man.
Imprecise	Marcia is a very *interesting* person.
Better	Marcia is *witty, intelligent,* and *talented.*
Imprecise	The vegetables tasted *funny.*
Better	The vegetables tasted *like moss mixed with Krazy Glue.*

(For more advice on using specific, colorful words, see pages 149–152 in Chapter 7.)

Emphasize people when possible. Try to focus on human beings rather than abstractions whenever you can. Next to our fascinating selves, we most enjoy hearing about other people. Although all the sentences in the first paragraph below are correct, the second one, revised by a class of composition students at Brown University, is clearer and more useful because the jargon has been eliminated and the focus changed from the tuition rules to the students.

Original	Tuition regulations currently in effect provide that payment of the annual tuition entitles an undergraduate-degree candidate to full-time enrollment, which is defined as registration for three, four, or five courses per semester. This means that at no time may an undergraduate student's official registration for courses drop below three without a dean's permission for part-time status and that at no time may the official course registration exceed five. (Brown University Course Announcement)
Revised	If students pay their tuition, they may enroll in three, four, or five courses per semester. Fewer than three or more than five can be taken only with a dean's permission.

Here's a similar example with a bureaucratic focus rather than a personal one:

Original	The salary deflations will most seriously impact the secondary educational profession.
Revised	High school teachers will suffer the biggest salary reductions.

Obviously, the revised sentence is the more easily understood of the two because the reader knows exactly who will be affected by the pay cuts. In your own prose, wherever appropriate, try to replace vague abstractions, such as "society," "culture," "administrative concerns," "programmatic expectations," and so forth, with the human beings you're thinking about. In other words, remember to talk *to* people *about* people.

Vary your sentence style. The only torture worse than listening to someone's nails scraping across a blackboard is being forced to read a paragraph full of identically constructed sentences. To illustrate this point, the following are a few sentences composed in the all-too-common "subject + predicate" pattern:

Soccer is the most popular sport in the world. Soccer exists in almost every country. Soccer players are sometimes more famous than movie stars. Soccer teams compete every few years for the World Soccer Cup. Soccer fans often riot if their team loses. Soccer fans even commit suicide. Soccer is the only game in the world that makes people so crazy.

Excruciatingly painful, yes? Each of us has a tendency to repeat a particular sentence pattern (though the choppy "subject + predicate" is by far the most popular); you can often detect your own by reading your prose aloud. To avoid overdosing your readers with the same pattern, vary the length, arrangement, and complexity of your sentences. Of course, this doesn't mean that you should contort your sentences merely for the sake of illustrating variety; just read your rough draft aloud, listening carefully to the rhythm of your prose so you can revise any monotonous passages or disharmonious sounds. (Try also to avoid the hiccup syndrome, in which you begin a sentence with the same word that ends the preceding sentence: "The first president to install a telephone on his desk was Herbert *Hoover. Hoover* refused to use the telephone booth outside his office.")

Avoid overuse of any one kind of construction in the same sentence. Don't, for example, pile up too many negatives, "who" or "which" clauses, and prepositional or infinitive phrases in one sentence.

> He *couldn't* tell whether she *didn't* want him to go or *not.*

> I gave the money to my brother, *who* returned it to the bank president, *who* said the decision to prosecute was up to the sheriff, *who* was out of town.

> I went to the florist *for* my roommate *for* a dozen roses *for* his date.

Try also to avoid stockpiling nouns, one on top of another, so that your sentences are difficult to read. Although some nouns may be used as adjectives to modify other nouns ("book mark," "gasoline pump," "food processor"), too many nouns grouped together sound awkward and confuse readers. If you have run too many nouns together, try using prepositional phrases ("an income tax bill discussion" becomes "discussion of an income tax bill") or changing the order or vocabulary of the sentence:

Confusing	The legislators are currently considering the *liability insurance multiple-choice premium proposal.*
Clearer	The legislators are currently considering the proposal that suggests *multiple-choice premiums* for *liability insurance.*
Confusing	We're concerned about the low *female labor force participation figures* in our department.
Clearer	We're concerned about the low *number of women working* in our department.

Don't change your point of view between or within sentences. If, for example, you begin your essay discussing students as "they," don't switch midway—or midsentence—to "we" or "you."

Inconsistent	Students pay tuition, which should entitle *them* to some voice in the university's administration. Therefore, *we* deserve one student on the Board of Regents.
Consistent	Students pay tuition, which should entitle *them* to some voice in the university's administration. Therefore, *they* deserve one student on the Board of Regents.
Inconsistent	*I* like my photography class because *we* learn how to restore *our* old photos and how to take better color portraits of *your* family.
Consistent	*I* like my photography class because *I'm* learning how to restore *my* old photos and how to take better color portraits of *my* family.

Perhaps this is a good place to dispel the myth that the pronoun "I" should never be used in an essay; on the contrary, many of our best essays have been written in the first person. Some of your former teachers may have discouraged the use of "I" for these two reasons: (1) personal opinion does not belong in the essay (2) writing in the first person often produces too many empty phrases, such as "I think that" and "I believe that." Nevertheless, if the personal point of view is appropriate in a particular assignment, you may use the first person in moderation, making sure that every other sentence doesn't begin with "I" plus a verb.

▪ PRACTICING WHAT YOU'VE LEARNED

Replace the following underlined words so that the sentences are clear and vivid. In addition, rephrase any awkward constructions or unnecessarily abstract words you find.

1. Judging from the <u>crazy</u> sound of the reactor, it isn't obvious to me that nuclear power as we know it today isn't a technology with a less than wonderful future.
2. The City Council felt <u>bad</u> because the revised tourist development activities grant fund application form letters were mailed without stamps.
3. To watch Jim Bob eat pork chops was <u>most interesting</u>.
4. For sale: <u>very nice</u> antique bureau suitable for ladies or gentlemen with thick legs and extra-large side handles.
5. There are many <u>things</u> people shouldn't eat, especially the elderly.
6. My roommate is <u>sort of different</u>, but he's a <u>good</u> guy at heart.
7. After reading the <u>great</u> new book, "The Looter's Guide to Riot-Prone Cities," Eddie <u>asked to have</u> a transfer <u>really soon</u>.
8. The wild oats soup was <u>fantastic</u>, so we drank <u>a lot of it very fast</u>.
9. When his new cat Chairman Meow won the pet show, owner Warren Peace got <u>pretty excited</u>.
10. The new diet <u>made me feel awful</u>, and it <u>did many horrible things</u> to my body.

▪ ASSIGNMENT

Find a short piece of writing you think is too bland, boring, vague, or confusing. (Possible sources: your college catalog, a business contract, a form letter, or your student health insurance policy.) In a well-written paragraph of your own, identify the sample's major problems and offer some specific suggestions for improving the writing. (If time permits, read aloud several of the samples and vote one the winner of the Most Lifeless Prose Award.)

■ Developing an Emphatic Style

Some words and phrases in your sentences are more important than others and, therefore, need more emphasis. Three ways to vary emphasis are by (1) word order, (2) coordination, and (3) subordination.

Word Order

The arrangement of words in a sentence can determine which ideas receive the most emphasis. To stress a word or phrase, place it at the end of the sentence or at the beginning of the sentence. Accordingly, a word or phrase receives least emphasis when buried in the middle of the sentence. Compare the following examples, in which the word "murder" receives varying degrees of emphasis:

Least emphatic	For Colonel Mustard *murder* was the only solution.
Emphatic	*Murder* was Colonel Mustard's only solution.
Most Emphatic	Colonel Mustard knew only one solution: *murder.*

Another use of word order to vary emphasis is *inversion,* taking a word out of its natural or usual position in a sentence and relocating it in an unexpected place.

Usual order	Parents who give their children both roots and wings are *wise.*
Inverted order	*Wise* are the parents who give their children both roots and wings.

Not all your sentences will contain words that need special emphasis; good writing generally contains a mix of some sentences in natural order and others rearranged for special effects.

Coordination

When you want to stress two closely related ideas equally, coordinate them.* In coordination, you join two sentences with a coordinating conjunction. To remember the coordinating conjunctions ("for," "and," "nor," "but," "or," "yet," "so"), think of the acronym FANBOYS; then always join two sentences with a comma and one of the FANBOYS. Here are two samples:

Choppy	The most popular girl's name today is Emily. The most popular boy's name today is Jacob.
Coordinated	The most popular girl's name today is Emily, *and* the most popular boy's name is Jacob.
Choppy	Imelda brought home a pair of ruby slippers. Ferdinand made her return them.
Coordinated	Imelda brought home a pair of ruby slippers, *but* Ferdinand made her return them.

---

* To remember that the term "coordination" refers to equally weighted ideas, think of other words with the prefix "co" such as "copilots," "co-authors," or "cooperation."

You can use coordination to show a relationship between ideas and to add variety to your sentence structures. Be careful, however, to select the right words while linking ideas, unlike the sentence that appeared in a church newsletter: "The ladies of the church have discarded clothing of all kinds, and they have been inspected by the minister." In other words, writers often need to slow down and make sure their thoughts are not joined in unclear or even unintentionally humorous ways: "For those of you who have children and don't know it, we have a nursery downstairs."

Sometimes when writers are in a hurry, they join ideas that are clearly related in their own minds, but whose relationship is confusing to the reader:

Confusing	My laboratory report isn't finished, and today my sister is leaving for a visit home.
Clear	I'm still working on my laboratory report, so I won't be able to catch a ride home with my sister who's leaving today.

You should also avoid using coordinating conjunctions to string too many ideas together like linked sausages:

Poor	We went inside the famous cave and the guide turned off the lights and we saw the rocks that glowed.
Revised	After we went inside the famous cave, the guide turned off the lights so we could see the rocks that glowed.

Subordination

Some sentences contain one main statement and one or more less emphasized elements; the less important ideas are subordinate to, or are dependent on, the sentence's main idea.* Subordinating conjunctions introducing dependent clauses show a variety of relationships between the clauses and the main part of the sentence. Here are four examples of subordinating conjunctions and their uses:

1. To show time without subordination	Superman stopped changing his clothes. He realized the phone booth was made of glass.
with subordination	Superman stopped changing his clothes *when* he realized the phone booth was made of glass.
2. To show cause without subordination	The country-western singer failed to gain success in Nashville. She sadly returned to Snooker Hollow to work in the sequin mines.
with subordination	*Because* the country-western singer failed to gain success in Nashville, she sadly returned to Snooker Hollow to work in the sequin mines.

---

* To remember that the term "subordination" refers to sentences containing dependent elements, think of such words as "a subordinate" (someone who works for someone else) or a post office "substation" (a branch of the post office less important than the main branch).

3. To show condition without subordination	Susan ought to study the art of tattooing. She will work with colorful people.
with subordination	*If* Susan studies the art of tattooing, she will work with colorful people.
4. To show place without subordination	Bulldozers are smashing the old movie theater. That's the place I first saw Roy Rogers and Dale Evans ride into the sunset.
with subordination	Bulldozers are smashing the old movie theater *where* I first saw Roy Rogers and Dale Evans ride into the sunset.

Subordination is especially useful in ridding your prose of choppy Dick-and-Jane sentences and those "empty sentences" discussed on pages 116–117. Here are some examples of choppy, weak sentences and their revisions, which contain subordinate clauses:

Choppy	Lew makes bagels on Tuesday. Lines in front of his store are a block long.
Revised	When Lew makes bagels on Tuesday, lines in front of his store are a block long.
Choppy	I have fond memories of Zilker Park. My husband and I met there.
Revised	I have fond memories of Zilker Park because my husband and I met there.

Effective use of subordination is one of the marks of a sophisticated writer because it presents adequate information in one smooth flow instead of in monotonous drips. Subordination, like coordination, also adds variety to your sentence construction.

Generally, when you subordinate one idea, you emphasize another, so to avoid the tail-wagging-the-dog problem, put your important idea in the main clause. Also, don't let your most important idea become buried under an avalanche of subordinate clauses, as in the sentence that follows:

When he was told by his boss, *who* had always treated him fairly, *that* he was being fired from a job *that* he had held for twenty years at a factory *where* he enjoyed working *because* the pay was good, Henry felt angry and frustrated.

Practice blending choppy sentences by studying the following sentence-combining exercise. In this exercise, a description of a popular movie or book has been chopped into simple sentences and then combined into one complex sentence.

1. *Psycho* (1960)
   Norman Bates manages a motel.
   It is remote.
   It is dangerous.
   Norman has a mother.
   She seems overly fond of knives.
   He tries to protect his mom.

   In a remote—and dangerous—motel, manager Norman Bates tries to protect his mother, who seems overly fond of knives.

2. *King Kong* (1933)

A showman goes to the jungle.
He captures an ape.
The ape is a giant.
The ape is taken to New York City.
He escapes.
He dies fighting for a young woman.
He loves her.
She is beautiful.

A giant ape, captured in the jungle by a showman, is taken to New York City, where he escapes and dies fighting for the beautiful young woman he loves.

3. *Casablanca* (1942)

Rick is an American.
He is cynical.
He owns a café.
He lives in Casablanca.
He meets his former love.
She is married.
Her husband is a French resistance fighter.
Rick helps the couple.
He regains self-respect.

When Rick, a cynical American café-owner in Casablanca, helps his former love and her husband, a French resistance fighter, he regains his self-respect.

Please note that the sentences in these exercises may be combined effectively in a number of ways. For instance, the description of *King Kong* might be rewritten this way: "After a showman captures him in the jungle, a giant ape escapes in New York City but dies fighting for the love of a beautiful young woman." How might you rewrite the other two sample sentences?

■ PRACTICING WHAT YOU'VE LEARNED

A. Revise the following sentences so that the underlined words receive more emphasis.

1. A remark attributed to the one-time heavyweight boxing champion <u>Joe Louis</u> is "I don't really like money, but it quiets my nerves."

2. According to recent polls, <u>television</u> is where most Americans get their news.

3. Of all the world's problems, it is <u>hunger</u> that is most urgent.

4. I enjoyed visiting many foreign countries last year, with <u>Greece</u> being my favorite of all of them.

5. The annoying habit of <u>knuckle-cracking</u> is something I can't stand.

B. Combine the following sentences using coordination or subordination.

1. The guru rejected his dentist's offer of novocaine. He could transcend dental medication.

2. John failed his literature test. John incorrectly identified Harper Lee as the author of the south-of-the-border classic *Tequila Mockingbird.*

3. Peggy Sue's house burned. She dialed a "9." She couldn't find "11" on the dial.

4. The police had only a few clues. They suspected Jean and David had strangled each other in a desperate struggle over control of the thermostat.

5. Bubba's favorite movie is *Sorority Babes in the Slimeball Bowl-O-Rama* (1988). A film critic called it "a pinhead chiller."

6. We're going to the new Psychoanalysis Restaurant. Their menu includes banana split personality, repressed duck, shrimp basket case, and self-expresso.

7. Kato lost the junior high spelling bee. He could not spell *DNA.*

8. Colorado hosts an annual BobFest to honor all persons named Bob. Events include playing softbob, bobbing for apples, listening to bob-pipes, and eating bob-e-que.

9. The earthquake shook the city. Louise was practicing primal-scream therapy at the time.

10. In 1789 many Parisians bought a new perfume called "Guillotine." They wanted to be on the cutting edge of fashion.

C. Combine the following simple sentences into one complex sentence. See if you can guess the name of the books or movies described in the sentences. (Answers appear on page 139.)

1. A boy runs away from home.
   His companion is a runaway slave.
   He lives on a raft.
   The raft is on the Mississippi River.
   He has many adventures.
   The boy learns many lessons.
   Some lessons are about human kindness.
   Some lessons are about friendship.

2. A young man returns from prison.
   He returns to his family.
   His family lives in the Dust Bowl.
   The family decides to move.
   The family expects to find jobs in California.
   The family finds intolerance.
   They also find dishonest employers.

3. A scientist is obsessed.
He wants to re-create life.
He creates a monster.
The monster rebels against the scientist.
The monster kills his creator.
The villagers revolt.
The villagers storm the castle.

■ ASSIGNMENT

A. Make up your own sentence-combining exercise by finding or writing one-sentence descriptions of popular or recent movies, books, or television shows. Divide the complex sentences into simple sentences and exchange papers with a classmate. Give yourselves ten minutes to combine sentences and guess the titles.

B. The following two paragraphs are poorly written because of their choppy, wordy, and monotonous sentences. Rewrite each passage so that it is clear, lively, and emphatic.

1. There is a new invention on the market. It is called a "dieter's conscience." It is a small box to be installed in one's refrigerator. When the door of the refrigerator is opened by you, a tape recorder begins to start. A really loud voice yells, "You eating again? No wonder you're getting fat." Then the very loud voice says, "Close the door; it's getting warm." Then the voice laughs a lot in an insane and crazy fashion. The idea is one that is designed to mock people into a habit of stopping eating.

2. In this modern world of today, man has come up with another new invention. This invention is called the "Talking Tombstone." It is made by the Gone-But-Not-Forgotten Company, which is located in Burbank, California. This company makes a tombstone that has a device in it that makes the tombstone appear to be talking aloud in a realistic fashion when people go close by it. The reason is that the device is really a recording machine that is turned on due to the simple fact of the heat of the bodies of the people who go by. The closer the people get, the louder the sound the tombstone makes. It is this device that individual persons who want to leave messages after death may utilize. A hypochondriac, to cite one example, might leave a recording of a message that says over and over again in a really loud voice, "See, I told you I was sick!" It may be assumed by one and all that this new invention will be a serious aspect of the whole death situation in the foreseeable future.

■ APPLYING WHAT YOU'VE LEARNED TO *YOUR* WRITING

If you have drafted a piece of writing and are satisfied with your essay's ideas and organization, begin revising your sentences for clarity, conciseness, and emphasis. As you move through your draft, think about your readers. Ask yourself, "Are any of my sentences too vague, overpacked, or contorted for my readers to understand? Can I clarify any of my ideas by using more precise language or by revising confusing sentence constructions?

If you can't easily untangle a jumbled sentence, try following the sentence-combining exercise described on pages 137–138 of this chapter—but in reverse. Instead of combining ideas, break your thought into a series of simpler sentences. Think about what you want to say and put the person or thing of importance in the *subject* position at the beginning of the sentences. Then select a verb and a brief phrase to complete each of the sentences. You will most likely need several of these simpler constructions to communicate the complexity of your original thought. Once you have your thought broken into smaller, simpler units, carefully begin to combine some of them as you strive for clarity and sentence variety.

Remember that it's not enough for you, the writer, to understand what your sentences mean—your readers must be able to follow your ideas, too. When in doubt, always revise your writing so that it is clear, concise, and inviting. (For more help, turn to Chapter 5, on revision.)

CHAPTER 6 SUMMARY

Here is a brief summary of what you should remember about writing effective sentences:

1. All good writers revise and polish their sentences.

2. You can help clarify your ideas for your readers by writing sentences that are informative, straightforward, and precise.

3. You can communicate your ideas more easily to your readers if you cut out deadwood, redundancies, confusing passives, and pretentious language.

4. You can maintain your readers' interest in your ideas if you cultivate an engaging style offering a variety of pleasing sentence constructions.

---

* Answers to sentence-combining exercise (pp. 137–138):

1. *Huckleberry Finn*
2. *The Grapes of Wrath*
3. *Frankenstein*

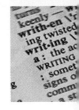

Chapter 7

Word Logic

The English language contains over a half million words—quite a selection for you as a writer to choose from. But such a wide choice may make you feel like a starving person confronting a six-page, fancy French menu. Which choice is best? How do I choose? Is the choice so important?

Word choice can make an enormous difference in the quality of your writing for at least one obvious reason: if you substitute an incorrect or vague word for the right one, you risk being misunderstood. Ages ago Confucius noted the same point: "If language is incorrect, then what is said is not meant. If what is said is not meant, then what ought to be done remains undone." It isn't enough that you know what you mean; you must transfer your thoughts onto paper in the proper words so that others clearly understand your ideas.

To help you avoid possible paralysis from indecision over word choice, this chapter offers some practical suggestions for selecting words that are not only accurate and appropriate but also memorable and persuasive.

■ Selecting the Correct Words

Accuracy: Confused Words

Unless I get a bank loan soon, I will be forced to lead an *immortal* life.

Dobermans make good pets if you train them with enough *patients*.

He dreamed of eating *desert* after *desert*.

She had dieted for so long that she had become *emancipated*.

The young man was completely in *ah* of the actress's beauty.

Socrates died from an overdose of *wedlock*.

© Richard Orton/Index

The preceding sentences share a common problem: each one contains an error in word choice. In each sentence, the italicized word is incorrect, causing the sentence to be nonsensical or silly. (Consider a sign recently posted in a local night spot: "No miners allowed." Did the owner think the lights on their hats would bother the other customers? Did the student with "duel majors" imagine that his two areas of study were squaring off with pistols at twenty paces?) To avoid such confusion in word choice, check your words for *accuracy*. Select words whose precise meaning, usage, and spelling you know; consult your dictionary for any words whose definitions (or spellings) are fuzzy to you. As Mark Twain noted, the difference between the right word and the wrong one is the difference between lightning and the lightning bug.

Here is a list of words that are often confused in writing. Use your dictionary to determine the meanings or usage of any word unfamiliar to you.

its/it's	lead/led	choose/chose
to/too/two	cite/sight/site	accept/except
there/their/they're	affect/effect	council/counsel
your/you're	good/well	reign/rein
complement/compliment	who's/whose	lose/loose
stationary/stationery	lay/lie	precede/proceed
capitol/capital	than/then	illusion/allusion
principal/principle	insure/ensure	farther/further

Special note: Some "confused" words don't even exist! Here are four commonly used nonexistent words and their correct counterparts:

No Such Word or Spelling	Use Instead
irregardless	regardless
allready	already *or* all ready
alot	a lot
its'	its or it's

Accuracy: Idiomatic Phrases

Occasionally you may have an essay returned to you with words marked "awkward diction" or "idiom." In English, as in all languages, we have word groupings that seem governed by no particular logic except the ever-popular "that's-the-way-we-say-it" rule. Many of these idiomatic expressions involve prepositions that novice writers sometimes confuse or misuse. Some common idiomatic errors and their corrected forms are listed here.

regardless ~~to~~ of   different ~~than to~~ from   relate ~~with~~ to
insight ~~of~~ into   must ~~of~~ have known   capable ~~to~~ of
similar ~~with~~ to   superior ~~than~~ to   aptitude ~~toward~~ for
comply ~~to~~ with   ~~to~~ in my opinion   prior ~~than~~ to
off ~~of~~   meet ~~to~~ her standards   should ~~of~~ have

To avoid idiomatic errors, consult your dictionary and read your essay aloud; often your ears will catch mistakes in usage that your eyes have overlooked.*

Levels of Language

In addition to choosing the correct word, you should also select words whose status is suited to your purpose. For convenience here, language has been classified into three categories, or levels, of usage: (1) colloquial, (2) informal, and (3) formal.

Colloquial language is the kind of speech you use most often in conversation with your friends, classmates, and family. It may not always be grammatically correct ("it's me"); it may include fragments, contractions, some slang, words identified as nonstandard by the dictionary (such as "yuck" or "lousy"), and shortened or abbreviated words ("grad school," "photos," "TV"). Colloquial speech is everyday language, and although you may use it in some writing (personal letters, journals, memos, and so forth), you should think carefully about using colloquial language in most college essays or in professional letters, reports, or papers because such a choice implies a casual relationship between writer and reader.

Informal language is called for in most college and professional assignments. The tone is more formal than in colloquial writing or speech; no slang or nonstandard words are permissible. Informal writing consistently uses correct grammar; fragments are used for special effect or not at all. Authorities disagree on the use of contractions in informal writing: some say avoid them entirely; others say they're permissible; still others advocate using them only to avoid stilted phrases ("let's go," for example, is preferable to "let us go"). Most, if not all, of your essays in English classes will be written in informal language.

Formal language is found in important documents and in serious, often ceremonial, speeches. Characteristics include an elevated—but not pretentious—tone, no contractions, and correct grammar. Formal writing often uses inverted word order and balanced sentence

---

* You may not immediately recognize what's wrong with words your teacher has labeled "diction" or "idiom." If you're uncertain about an error, ask your teacher for clarification; after all, if you don't know what's wrong with your prose, you can't avoid the mistake again. To illustrate this point, here's a true story: A bright young woman was having trouble with prepositional phrases in her essays, and although her professor repeatedly marked her incorrect expressions with the marginal note "idiom," she never improved. Finally, one day near the end of the term, she approached her teacher in tears and wailed, "Professor Jones, I know I'm not a very good writer, but must you write 'idiot,' 'idiot,' 'idiot' all over my papers?" The moral of this story is simple: it's easy to misunderstand a correction or misread your teacher's writing. Because you can't improve until you know what's wrong, always ask when you're in doubt.

structure. John F. Kennedy's 1960 Inaugural Address, for example, was written in a formal style ("Ask not what your country can do for you; ask what you can do for your country"). Most people rarely, if ever, need to write formally; if you are called on to do so, however, be careful to avoid diction that sounds pretentious, pompous, or phony.

Tone

Tone is a general word that describes writers' attitudes toward their subject matter and audience. There are as many different kinds of tones as there are emotions. Depending on how the writer feels, an essay's "voice" may sound light-hearted, indignant, sarcastic, or solemn, to name but a few of the possible choices. In addition to presenting a specific attitude, a good writer gains credibility by maintaining a tone that is generally reasonable, sincere, and authentic.

Although it is impossible to analyze all the various kinds of tones one finds in essays, it is nevertheless beneficial to discuss some of those that repeatedly give writers trouble. Here are some tones that should be used carefully or avoided altogether:

Invective

Invective is unrestrained anger, usually expressed in the form of violent accusation or denunciation. Let's suppose, for example, you hear a friend argue, "Anyone who votes for Joe Smith is a Fascist pig." If you are considering Smith, you are probably offended by your friend's abusive tone. Raging emotion, after all, does not sway the opinions of intelligent people; they need to hear the facts presented in a calm, clear discussion. Therefore, in your own writing, aim for a reasonable tone. You want your readers to think, "Now here is someone with a good understanding of the situation, who has evaluated it with an unbiased, analytical mind." Keeping a controlled tone doesn't mean you shouldn't feel strongly about your subject—on the contrary, you certainly should—but you should realize that a hysterical or outraged tone defeats your purpose by causing you to sound irrational and therefore untrustworthy. For this reason, you should probably avoid using profanity in your essays; the shock value of an obscenity may not be worth what you might lose in credibility. (Besides, is anyone other than your Great-Aunt Fanny really amazed by profanity these days?) The most effective way to make your point is by persuading, not offending, your reader.

Sarcasm

In most of your writing you'll discover that a little sarcasm—bitter, derisive remarks—goes a long way. Like invective, too much sarcasm can damage the reasonable tone your essay should present. Instead of saying, "You can recognize the supporters of the new tax law by the points on the tops of their heads," give your readers some reasons why you believe the tax bill is flawed. Sarcasm can be effective, but realize that it often backfires by causing the writer to sound like a childish name-caller rather than a judicious commentator.

Irony

Irony is a figure of speech whereby the writer or speaker says the opposite of what is meant; for the irony to be successful, however, the audience must understand the writer's true intent. For example, if you have slopped to school in a rainstorm and your drenched teacher enters the classroom saying, "Ah, nothing like this beautiful, sunny weather," you know that your teacher is being ironic. Perhaps one of the most famous cases of irony occurred in 1938, when Sigmund Freud, the famous Viennese psychiatrist, was arrested by the Nazis. After being harassed by the Gestapo, he was released on the condition that he sign a statement swearing he had been treated well by the secret police. Freud signed it, but he added a few words after his signature: "I can heartily recommend the Gestapo to anyone." Looking back, we easily recognize Freud's jab at his captors; the Gestapo, however, apparently overlooked the irony and let him go.

Although irony is often an effective device, it can also cause great confusion, especially when it is written rather than spoken. Unless your readers thoroughly understand your position in the first place, they may become confused by what appears to be a sudden contradiction. Irony that is too subtle, too private, or simply out of context merely complicates the issue. Therefore, you must make certain that your reader has no trouble realizing when your tongue is firmly embedded in your cheek. And unless you are assigned to write an ironic essay (in the same vein, for instance, as Swift's "A Modest Proposal"), don't overuse irony. Like any rhetorical device, its effectiveness is reduced with overkill.

Flippancy or Cuteness

If you sound too flip, hip, or bored in your essay ("People with IQs lower than their sunscreen number will object. . ."), your readers will not take you seriously and, consequently, will disregard whatever you have to say. Writers suffering from cuteness will also antagonize their readers. For example, let's assume you're assigned the topic "Which Person Did the Most to Arouse the Laboring Class in Twentieth-Century England?" and you begin your essay with a discussion of the man who invented the alarm clock. Although that joke might be funny in an appropriate situation, it's not likely to impress your reader, who's looking for serious commentary. How much cuteness is too much is often a matter of taste, but if you have any doubts about the quality of your humor, leave it out. Also, omit personal messages or comic asides to your reader (such as "Ha, ha, just kidding!" or "I knew you'd love this part"). Humor is often effective, but remember that the purpose of any essay is to persuade an audience to accept your thesis, not merely to entertain with freestanding jokes. In other words, if you use humor, make sure it is appropriate for your subject matter and that it works to help you make your point.

Sentimentality

Sentimentality is the excessive show of cheap emotions—"cheap" because they are not deeply felt but evoked by clichés and stock, tear-jerking situations. In the nineteenth century, for example, a typical melodrama played on the sentimentality of the audience by presenting a black-hatted, cold-hearted, mustache-twirling villain tying a golden-haired, pure-hearted "Little Nell" to the railroad tracks after driving her ancient, sickly mother out into a snowdrift. Today, politicians (among others) often appeal to our sentimentality by conjuring up vague images they feel will move us emotionally rather than rationally to take their side: "My friends," says Senator Stereotype, "this fine nation of ours was founded by men like myself, dedicated to the principles of family, flag, and freedom. Vote for me, and let's get back to those precious basics that make life in America so grand." Such gush is hardly convincing; good writers and speakers use evidence and logical reason to persuade their audience. In personal essays, guard against becoming too carried away with emotion, as did this student: "My dog, Cuddles, is the sweetest, cutest, most precious little puppy dog in the whole wide world, and she will always be my best friend." In addition to sending the reader into sugar shock, this description fails to present any specific reasons why anyone should appreciate Cuddles. In other words, be sincere in your writing, but don't lose so much control of your emotions that you become mushy or maudlin.

Preachiness

Even if you are so convinced of the rightness of your position that a burning bush couldn't change your mind, try not to sound smug about it. No one likes to be lectured by someone perched atop the mountain of morality. Instead of preaching, adopt a tone that says, "I believe my position is correct, and I am glad to have this opportunity to explain why." Then give your reasons and meet objections in a positive but not holier-than-thou manner.

Pomposity

The "voice" of your essay should sound as natural as possible; don't strain to sound scholarly, scientific, or sophisticated. If you write "My summer sojourn through the Western states of this grand country was immensely pleasurable" instead of "My vacation last summer in the Rockies was fun," you sound merely phony, not dignified and learned. Select only words you know and can use easily. Never write anything you wouldn't say in an intelligent classroom conversation. (For more information on correcting pretentious writing, see pages 125–126 and pages 152–155.)

 To achieve the appropriate tone, be as sincere, forthright, and reasonable as you can. Let the tone of your essay establish a basis of mutual respect between you and your reader.

Connotation and Denotation

A word's *denotation* refers to its literal meaning, the meaning defined by the dictionary; a word's *connotation* refers to the emotional associations surrounding its meaning. For example, "home" and "residence" both may be defined as the place where one lives, but "home" carries connotations of warmth, security, and family that "residence" lacks. Similarly, "old" and "antique" have similar denotative meanings, but "antique" has the more positive connotation because it suggests something that also has value. Reporters and journalists do the same job, but the latter name somehow seems to indicate someone more sophisticated and professional. Because many words with similar denotative meanings do carry different connotations, good writers must be careful with their word choice. *Select only words whose connotations fit your purpose.* If, for example, you want to describe your grandmother in a positive way as someone who stands up for herself, you might refer to her as "assertive" or "feisty"; if you want to present her negatively, you might call her "aggressive" or "pushy."

In addition to selecting words with the appropriate connotations for your purpose, be careful to avoid offending your audience with particular connotations. For instance, if you were trying to persuade a group of politically conservative doctors to accept your stand on a national health-care program, you would not want to refer to your opposition as "right-wingers" or "reactionaries," extremist terms that have negative connotations. Remember, you want to inform and persuade your audience, not antagonize them.

You should also be alert to the use of words with emotionally charged connotations, especially in advertising and propaganda of various kinds. Car manufacturers, for example, have often used names of swift, bold, or graceful animals (Jaguar, Cougar, Impala) to sway prospective buyers; cosmetic manufacturers in recent years have taken advantage of the trend toward lighter makeup by associating such words as "nature," "natural," and "healthy glow" with their products. Diet-conscious Americans are now deluged with "light" and "organic" food products. Politicians, too, are heavy users of connotation; they often drop in emotionally positive, but virtually meaningless, words and phrases such as "defender of the American Way," "friend of the common man," and "visionary" to describe themselves, while tagging their opponents with such negative, emotionally charged labels as "radical," "elitist," and "anti-family." Intelligent readers, like intelligent voters and consumers, want more than emotion-laden words; they want facts and logical argument. Therefore, as a good writer, you should use connotation as only one of many persuasive devices to enhance your presentation of evidence; never depend solely on an emotional appeal to convince your audience that your position—or thesis—is correct.

■ PRACTICING WHAT YOU'VE LEARNED

A. Some of the following underlined words are used incorrectly; some are correct. Substitute the accurate word wherever necessary.

1. Vacations of <u>to</u> weeks with <u>to</u> friends are always <u>to</u> short, and although <u>you're</u> <u>to</u> tired <u>to</u> return to work, <u>your</u> <u>to</u> broke not <u>to</u>.

2. The professor, <u>whose</u> famous for his <u>photogenic</u> memory, graciously <u>excepted</u> a large <u>amount</u> of <u>complements</u>.

3. <u>Its</u> <u>to</u> bad you don't like <u>they're</u> new Popsicle stick sculpture since <u>their</u> giving it <u>to</u> you for <u>you're</u> birthday.

4. The finances of the chicken ranch are in <u>fowl</u> shape because the hens are <u>lying</u> down on the job.

5. Sara June said she deserved an "A" in math, <u>irregardless</u> of her 59 average in the <u>coarse</u>, but her arguments were in <u>vein</u>.

6. Does the pamphlet "Ridding Your Home of Pesky <u>Aunts</u>" belong in the domestic-relations area of the public library?

7. Did the high school <u>principal</u> <u>loose</u> <u>you're</u> heavy <u>medal</u> CD and <u>it's</u> case <u>too</u>?

8. The new city <u>counsel</u> parade ordinance will <u>effect</u> everyone in the <u>capitol</u> city <u>except</u> members of the Lawn Chair Marching Band.

B. The following sentences contain words and phrases that interfere with the sincere, reasonable tone good writers try to create. Rewrite each sentence, replacing sentimentality, cuteness, and pretentiousness with more appropriate language.

1. The last dying rays of day were quickly ebbing in the West as if to signal the feline to begin its lonely vigil.

2. Because of seasonal unproductivity, it has been deemed an unfortunate fiscal necessity to terminate your valuable association with our store in order to meet our projected growth estimates.

3. I was desirous of acquiring knowledge about members of our lower income brackets.

4. If the bill to legalize marijuana is passed, we can safely assume that the whole country will soon be going to pot (heh, heh!).

5. I just love to look at those little critters with their itty-bitty mousey eyes.

C. In each of the following groups of words, identify the words with the most pleasing and least positive (or even negative) connotations.

1. dull/drab/quiet/boring/colorless/serene

2. slender/slim/skinny/thin/slight/anorexic

3. famous/notorious/well known/infamous

4. wealthy/opulent/rich/affluent/privileged

5. teacher/instructor/educator/professor/lecturer

D. Replace the underlined words in the following sentences with words arousing more positive feelings:

1. The <u>stench</u> from Jean's kitchen meant dinner was ready and was about to be served.

2. My neighbor was a <u>fat spinster lady</u> known for finding <u>cheap deals</u> on the Internet.

3. The coach had <u>rigid</u> rules for all her players.

4. His <u>obsession</u> with his yard pleased the city's beautification committee.

5. The <u>slick</u> car salesman made a <u>pitch</u> to the <u>old geezer</u> who walked in the door.

6. Textbook writers admit to having a few <u>bizarre</u> habits.

7. Carol was a <u>mediocre</u> student.

8. His <u>odd</u> clothes made Mary think he was a <u>bum</u>.

9. The High Priest explained his tribe's <u>superstitions</u>.

10. Many of the board members were amazed to see how Algernon <u>dominated</u> the meeting.

■ Selecting the Best Words

In addition to selecting the correct word and appropriate tone, good writers also choose words that firmly implant their ideas in the minds of their readers. The best prose not only makes cogent points but also states these points memorably. To help you select the best words to express your ideas, the following is a list of do's and don't's covering the most common diction (word choice) problems in students' writing today.

Do make your words as precise as possible. Always choose vigorous, active verbs and colorful, specific nouns and modifiers. "The big tree was hit by lightning," for example, is not as informative or interesting as "Lightning splintered the neighbors' thirty-foot oak." *Don't* use words whose meanings are unclear:

Vague Verbs

Unclear	She *got involved* in a lawsuit. [How?]
Clear	She is suing her dentist for filling the wrong tooth.
Unclear	Tom can *relate* to Jennifer. [What's the relationship?]
Clear	Tom understands Jennifer's financial problem.
Unclear	He won't *deal* with his ex-wife. [In what way?]
Clear	He refuses to speak to his ex-wife.
Unclear	Clyde *participated* in an off-Broadway play. [How?]
Clear	Clyde held the cue cards for the actors in an off-Broadway play.

Vague Nouns

Unclear	The burglar took several valuable *things* from our house.* [What items?]
Clear	The burglar took a *color television*, a *DVD player*, and a *microwave oven* from our house.
Unclear	When I have my car serviced, there is always *trouble*. [What kind?]
Clear	When I have my car serviced, *the mechanics always find additional repairs and never have the car ready when it is promised.*
Unclear	When I have *problems*, I always call my friends for advice. [What problems?]
Clear	*If my girlfriend breaks up with me, my roof needs repairing, or my dog needs surgery,* I always call my friends for advice.
Unclear	I like to have *fun* while I'm on vacation. [What sort of activities?]
Clear	I like to *eat in fancy restaurants, fly stunt kites,* and *walk along the beach* when I'm on vacation.

---

* Advice that bears repeating: banish the word "thing" from your writing. In nine out of ten cases, it is a lazy substitute for some other word. Unless you mean a nameless inanimate object, replace "thing" with the specific word it represents.

Vague Modifiers

Unclear	His *terrible* explanation left me *very* confused. [Why "terrible"? How confused?]
Clear	His *disorganized* explanation left me *too confused to begin the project.*
Unclear	The boxer hit the punching bag *really* hard. [How hard?]
Clear	The boxer hit the punching bag *so hard it split open.*
Unclear	*Casablanca* is a *good* movie *with something for everyone.* [Why "good" and for everyone?]
Clear	*Casablanca* is a *witty, sentimental* movie that *successfully combines an adventure story and a romance.*

To help you recognize the difference between general and specific language, consider the following series of words:

General→ →**Specific**

food→snack food→chips→potato chips→Red Hot Jalapeño Potato Chips

car→red car→red sports car→classic red Corvette→1966 red Corvette convertible

building→house→old house→big old fancy house→19th-century Victorian mansion

The preceding examples illustrate varying degrees of generality, with the words becoming more specific as they move to the right. Sometimes in your writing you will, of course, need to use general words to communicate your thought. However, most writers need practice finding specific language to substitute for bland, vague, or overly general diction that doesn't clearly present the precise picture the writer has in mind. For instance, look at the difference between these two sentences:

- My date arrived at the restaurant in an older car and then surprised us by ordering snack food.

- My date arrived at the restaurant in a rusted-out, bumperless '52 Cadillac DeVille and then surprised us by ordering only a small bowl of organic cheesy puffs.

Which description better conveys the start of an unusual evening? Which sentence would make you want to hear more?

Not all occasions call for specific details, to be sure. Don't add details that merely clutter if they aren't important to the idea or mood you are creating. If all your readers need to know is "I ate dinner alone and went to bed early," you don't need to write "Alone, I ate a dinner of lasagna, green salad, and ice cream before putting on my Gap cowgirl pajamas and going to sleep under my yellow comforter at 9 o'clock."

Most of the time, however, writers can improve their drafts by giving their language a close look, considering places where a vigorous verb or a "showing" adjective or a specific noun might make an enormous difference to the reader. As you revise and polish your own essays, ask yourself if you can clarify and enliven your writing by replacing dull, lifeless words with engaging, vivid, specific ones. Challenge yourself to find the best words possible—it's a writing habit that produces effective, reader-pleasing results. (For more help converting vague sentences to clear, inviting prose, see pages 117–118 in Chapter 6.)

Do make your word choices as fresh and original as possible. Instead of saying, "My hometown is very quiet," you might say, "My hometown's definition of an orgy is a light burning after midnight." In other words, if you can make your readers admire and remember your prose, you have a better chance of persuading them to accept your ideas.

Conversely, to avoid ho-hum prose, *don't* fill your sentences with clichés and platitudes—overworked phrases that cause your writing to sound lifeless and trite. Although we use clichés in everyday conversation, good writers avoid them in writing because (1) they are often vague or imprecise (just how pretty is "pretty as a picture?") and (2) they are used so frequently that they rob your prose style of personality and uniqueness ("It was raining cats and dogs"—does that phrase help your reader "see" the particular rainstorm you're trying to describe?).

Novice writers often include trite expressions because they do not recognize them as clichés; therefore, here is a partial list (there are literally thousands more) of phrases to avoid. Instead of using a cliché, try substituting an original phrase to describe what you see or feel. Never try to disguise a cliché by putting it in quotation marks—a baboon in dark glasses and a wig is still a baboon.

crack of dawn	needle in a haystack	gentle as a lamb
a crying shame	bed of roses	blind as a bat
white as a sheet	cold as ice	strong as an ox
depths of despair	hard as nails	sober as a judge
dead of night	white as snow	didn't sleep a wink
shadow of a doubt	almighty dollar	face the music
hear a pin drop	busy as a bee	out like a light
blessed event	to make a long story short	the last straw
first and foremost	pale as a ghost	solid as a rock

It would be impossible, of course, to memorize all the clichés and trite expressions in our language, but do check your prose for recognizable, overworked phrases so that your words will not be predictable and, consequently, dull. If you aren't sure if a phrase is a cliché—but you've heard it used frequently—your prose will probably be stronger if you substitute an original phrase for the suspected one.

Some overused words and phrases might better be called "Insta-Prose" rather than clichés. Similar to those instant "just add water and stir" food mixes on grocery shelves, Insta-Prose occurs when writers grab for the closest words within thought-reach rather than taking time to create an original phrase or image. It's easy, for example, to recognize such overused phrases as "last but not least," "easier said than done," and "when all was said and done." But Insta-Prose may pop up in essays almost without a writer's awareness. For instance, using your very first thoughts, fill in the blanks in the following sentence:

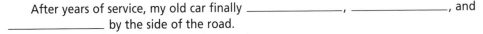

    After years of service, my old car finally _____, _____, and _____ by the side of the road.

If your immediate responses were the three words printed at the bottom of page 163, don't be surprised! Most people who have taken this simple test responded that way too, either entirely or in part. So what's the problem, you might ask. The writer describing the car wanted her readers to see *her* particular old car, not some bland image identically reproduced in her readers' minds. To show readers her car—as opposed to thousands of

other old cars—she needs to substitute specific, "showing" language for the Insta-Prose.*
(Retest yourself: what might she have said about this car that would allow you, the reader,
to see what happened that day?)

As a writer, you also want your readers to "see" your specific idea and be engaged by
your prose, rather than skipping over canned-bland images. When you are drafting for
ideas early in the writing process, Insta-Prose pours out—and that's as expected because
you are still discovering your thoughts. But, later, when you revise your drafts, be sensitive to predictable language in all its forms. Stamp out Insta-Prose! Cook up some fresh
language to delight your reader!

Don't use trendy expressions or slang in your essays. Slang generally consists of commonly used words made up by special groups to communicate among themselves. Slang
has many origins, from sports to space travel; for example, surfers gave us the expression
"to wipe out" (to fail), soldiers lent "snafu" (from the first letters of "situation normal—
all fouled up"), and astronauts provided "A-OK" (all systems working).

Although slang often gives our speech color and vigor, it is unacceptable in most writing
assignments for several reasons. First, slang is often part of a private language understood
only by members of a particular professional, social, or age group. Second, slang often
presents a vague picture or one that changes meanings from person to person or from context to context. More than likely, each person has a unique definition for a particular slang
expression, and, although these definitions may overlap, they are not precisely the same.
Consequently, your reader could interpret your words in one way whereas you mean them
in another, a dilemma that might result in total miscommunication.

Too often, beginning writers rely on vague, popular phrases ("The party was way awesome") instead of thinking of specific words to explain specific ideas. Slang expressions
frequently contain nontraditional grammar and diction that is inappropriate for college
work. Moreover, slang becomes dated quickly, and almost nothing sounds worse than
yesterday's "in" expressions. (Can you seriously imagine calling a friend "Daddy-O" or
telling someone you're "feelin' groovy"?)

Try to write so that your prose will be as fresh and pleasing ten years from now as today.
Don't allow slang to give your writing a tone that detracts from a serious discussion. Putting
slang in quotation marks isn't the solution—omit the slang and use precise words instead.

Do select simple, direct words your readers can easily understand. Don't use pompous or
pseudo-sophisticated language in place of plain speech. Wherever possible, avoid *jargon*—
that is, words and phrases that are unnecessarily technical, pretentious, or abstract.

Technical jargon—terms specific to one area of study or specialization—should be
omitted or clearly defined in essays directed to a general audience because such language is often inaccessible to anyone outside the writer's particular field. By now most of
us are familiar with bureaucratese, journalese, and psychobabble, in addition to gobbledygook from business, politics, advertising, and education. If, for example, you worry

---

* Some prose is so familiar that it is now a joke. The phrase "It was a dark and stormy night," the beginning of an 1830 Edward George Bulwer-Lytton novel, has been parodied in the Peanuts comic strip (plagiarized without shame by Snoopy). It also prompted a bad-writing contest sponsored since 1982 by the
English Department at San José State University, in which entrants are challenged to "compose the opening sentence to the worst of all possible novels."

that "a self-actualized person such as yourself cannot transcend either your hostile environment or your passive-aggressive behavior to make a commitment to a viable lifestyle and meaningful interpersonal relationships," you are indulging in psychological or sociological jargon; if you "review existing mechanisms of consumer input, thruput, and output via the consumer communications channel module," you are speaking business jargon. Although most professions do have their own terms, you should limit your use of specialized language to writing aimed solely at your professional colleagues; always try to avoid technical jargon in prose directed at a general audience.

Today the term "jargon" also refers to prose containing an abundance of abstract, pretentious, multisyllabic words. The use of this kind of jargon often betrays a writer's attempt to sound sophisticated and intellectual; actually, it only confuses meaning and delays communication. Here, for instance, is a sample of incomprehensible jargon from a college president who obviously prefers twenty-five-cent words to simple, straightforward, nickel ones: "We will divert the force of this fiscal stress into leverage energy and pry important budgetary considerations and control out of our fiscal and administrative procedures." Or look at the thirty-eight-word definition of "exit" written by an Occupational Safety and Health Administration bureaucrat: "That portion of a means of egress which is separated from all spaces of the building or structure by construction or equipment as required in this subpart to provide a protected way of travel to the exit discharge." Such language is not only pretentious and confusing but almost comic in its wordiness.

Legal jargon, complicating even the smallest transaction, has become so incomprehensible that some lawmakers and consumers have begun to fight back. Today in Texas, for example, any firm lending $500 or less must use a model plain-English contract or submit its contract for approval to the Office of Consumer Credit. The new, user-friendly contract replaces "Upon any such default, and at any time thereafter, Secured party may declare the entire balance of the indebtedness secured hereby, plus any other sums owed hereunder, immediately due and payable without demand or notice, less any refund due, and Secured Party shall have all the remedies of the Uniform Commercial Code" with a clear, easy-to-understand statement: "If I break any of my promises in this document, you can demand that I immediately pay all that I owe." Hooray for the gobbledygook squashers in the Lone Star State!

To avoid such verbal litter in your own writing, follow these rules:

1. Always select the plainest, most direct words you know.

Jargon	The editor wanted to halt the proliferation of the product because she discovered an error on the page that terminates the volume.
Revised	The editor wanted to stop publishing the book because she found an error on the last page.

2. Replace nominalizations (nouns that are made from verbs and adjectives, usually by adding endings such as *-tion*, *-ism*, *-ness*, or *-al*) with simpler verbs and nouns.

Jargon	The departmental head has come to the recognition that the utilization of verbose verbalization renders informational content inaccessible.

Revised   The head of the department recognizes that wordiness confuses
                     meaning.

3. Avoid adding *-ize* or *-wise* to verbs and adverbs.

   Jargon   *Weatherwise*, it looked like a good day to *finalize* her report on
                     wind tunnels.
   Revised   The day's clear weather would help her finish her report on
                     wind tunnels.

4. Drop out meaningless tack-on words such as "factor," "aspect," and "situation."

   Jargon   The convenience *factor* of the neighborhood grocery store is
                     one *aspect* of its success.
   Revised   The convenience of the neighborhood grocery store contributes
                     to its success.

Remember that good writing is clear and direct, never wordy, cloudy, or ostentatious.
(For more hints on developing a clear style, see pages 116–122.)

Do call things by their proper names. Don't sugarcoat your terms by substituting
euphemisms—words that sound nice or pretty applied to subjects some people find distasteful. For example, you've probably heard someone say, "she passed away" instead of
"she died," or "he was under the influence of alcohol" instead of "he was drunk." Flight
attendants refer to a "water landing" rather than an ocean crash. "Senior Citizens" (or
worse, the "chronologically advantaged") may receive special discounts. Often,
euphemisms are used to soften names of jobs: "sanitary engineer" for garbage collector,
"field representative" for salesperson, "information processor" for typist, "vehicle
appearance specialist" for car washer, and so forth.

Some euphemisms are dated and now seem plain silly: in Victorian times, for example, the word "leg" was considered unmentionable in polite company, so people spoke of
"piano limbs" and asked for the "first joint" of a chicken. The phrases "white meat" and
"dark meat" were euphemisms some people used to avoid asking for a piece of chicken
breast or thigh.

Today, euphemisms still abound. Though our generation is perhaps more direct about
sex and death, many current euphemisms gloss over unpleasant or unpopular business, military, and political practices. Some stockbrokers, for example, once referred to an October
market crash as "a fourth-quarter equity retreat," and General Motors didn't really shut
down one of its plants—the closing was merely a "volume-related production schedule
adjustment." Similarly, Chrysler didn't lay off workers; it simply "initiated a career alternative enhancement program." Nuclear power plants no longer have dumps; they have "con-
tainment facilities" with radiation "migration" rather than leaks and "inventory
discrepancies" rather than thefts of plutonium. Simple products are now complex technology: clocks are "analog temporal displacement monitors," toothbrushes are "home plaque
removal instruments," sinks are part of the "hygienic hand-washing media," and pencils are
"portable hand-held communications inscribers." Vinyl is now "vegetarian leather."

Euphemisms abound in governments and official agencies when those in charge try
to hide or disguise the truth from the public. On the national level, a former budget
director gave us "revenue enhancements" instead of new taxes, and a former Secretary

of Health, Education, and Welfare once tried to camouflage cuts in social services by calling them "advance downward adjustments." Wiretaps once became "technical collection sources" used by "special investigators units" instead of burglars, and plain lying became on one important occasion merely "plausible deniability." Other lies or exaggerations have been "strategic misrepresentations" and convenient "reality augmentations." Interestingly enough, even Washington staff members in charge of prettying up the truth for the public have earned their own euphemistic title: "spin doctors."

In a large Southwestern city, people may have been surprised to learn that there were no potholes in the streets—only "pavement deficiencies." Garbage no longer stinks; instead, it "exceeds the odor threshold." In some jails, a difficult prisoner who once might have been sent to solitary confinement is now placed in the "meditation room" or the "adjustment center." In some hospitals, sick people do not die—they experience "negative patient care outcome"; if they died because of a doctor's mistake, they underwent a "diagnostic misadventure of a high magnitude." Incidentally, those patients who survive no longer receive greeting cards; instead, they open "social expression products." During their recovery, patients might watch the "choreographed reality" of TV wrestling, while their dogs enjoy "play activities" at a local "pet lodge."

Perhaps the military, however, is the all-time winner of the "substitute-a-euphemism" contest. Over the years, the military has used a variety of words, such as "neutralization," "pacification," and "liberation," to mean the invasion and destruction of other countries and governments. During the first Gulf War with Iraq, for example, bombs that fell on civilians were referred to as "incontinent ordnance," with the dead becoming "collateral damage." Earlier, to avoid publicizing a retreat, the military simply called for "backloading our augmentation personnel." On the less serious side, the Navy changes ocean waves into "climatic disturbances at the air-sea interface," and the Army, not to be outdone, transforms the lowly shovel into a "combat emplacement evacuator."

Although many euphemisms seem funny and harmless, too many of them are not because people—often those with power to shape public opinion—have intentionally designed them to obscure the reality of a particular situation or choice of action. Because euphemisms can be used unscrupulously to manipulate people, you should always avoid them in your own prose and be suspicious of them in the writing of others. As Aldous Huxley, author of *Brave New World*, noted, "An education for freedom is, among other things, an education in the proper uses of language."

In addition to weakening the credibility of one's ideas, euphemisms can make prose unnecessarily abstract, wordy, pretentious, or even silly. For a clear and natural prose style, use terms that are straightforward and simple. In other words, call a spade a spade, not "an implement for use in horticultural environments."

Avoid sexist language. Most people will agree that language helps shape thought. Consequently, writers should avoid using any language that promotes demeaning stereotypes. Sexist language, in particular, often subtly suggests that women are less rational, intelligent, or capable of handling certain tasks or jobs. To make your writing as accurate and unbiased as possible, here are some simple suggestions for writing nonsexist prose:

1. Try using plural nouns to eliminate the need for the singular pronouns "he" and "she":

   Original   Today's *doctor* knows *he* must carry extra malpractice insurance.
   Revision   Today's *doctors* know *they* must carry extra malpractice insurance.

2. Try substituting gender-neutral occupational titles for those ending in "man" or "woman":

   Original   The *fireman* and the *saleslady* watched the *policeman* arrest the former *chairman* of the Physics Department.
   Revision   The *firefighter* and the *sales clerk* watched the *police officer* arrest the former *chair* of the Physics Department.

3. Don't contribute to stereotyping by assigning particular roles solely to men or women:

   Original   *Mothers* concerned about the possibility of Reyes syndrome should avoid giving aspirin to their sick children.
   Revision   *Parents* concerned about the possibility of Reyes syndrome should avoid giving aspirin to their sick children.

4. Try substituting such words as "people," "persons," "one," "voters," "workers," "students," and so on, for "man" or "woman":

   Original   Any *man* who wants to become a corporation executive before thirty should buy this book.
   Revision   *Anyone* who wants to become a corporation executive before thirty should buy this book.

5. Don't use inappropriate diminutives:

   Original   In the annual office picture, the photographer asked the men to stand behind the *girls.*
   Revision   In the annual office picture, the photographer asked the men to stand behind the *women.*

6. Consider avoiding words that use "man" to describe the actions or characteristics of a group ("man the barricades") or that refer to people in general.

   Original   Rebuilding the space shuttle will call for extra money and *manpower,* but such an endeavor will benefit *mankind* in the generations to come.
   Revision   Rebuilding the space shuttle will call for extra money and *employees,* but such an endeavor will benefit future *generations.*

7. Be consistent in your treatment of men's and women's names, marital status, professional titles, and physical appearances:

   Original   Neither Herman Melville, the inspired novelist, nor *Miss* Emily Dickinson, the *spinster poetess* of Amherst, gained fame or fortune in their lifetimes.
   Revision   Neither Herman Melville, the novelist, nor Emily Dickinson, the *poet,* gained fame or fortune in their lifetimes.

8. If a situation demands multiple hypothetical examples, consider including references to both genders, when appropriate.

> **Original**   In a revision workshop, one writer may request help with *his* concluding paragraph. Another writer may want reaction to *his* essay's introduction.
>
> **Revision**   In a revision workshop, one writer may request help with *his* concluding paragraph. Another writer may want reaction to *her* essay's introduction.

Revising your writing to eliminate certain kinds of gender-specific references does not mean turning clear phrases into awkward or confusing jumbles of "he/she told him/her that the car was his/hers." By following the previous suggestions, you should be able to make your prose both clear and inoffensive to all members of your audience.*

Do enliven your writing with figurative language, when appropriate. Figurative language produces pictures or images in a reader's mind, often by comparing something unfamiliar to something familiar. The two most common figurative devices are the simile and the metaphor. A *simile* is a comparison between two people, places, feelings, or things, using the word "like" or "as"; a more forceful comparison, omitting the word "like" or "as," is a *metaphor*. Here are two examples:

> **Simile**   George eats his meals like a hog.
>
> **Metaphor**   George is a hog at mealtime.

In both sentences, George, whose eating habits are unfamiliar to the reader, is likened to a hog, whose sloppy manners are generally well known. By comparing George to a hog, the writer gives the reader a clear picture of George at the table. Figurative language not only can help you present your ideas in clear, concrete, economical ways but also can make your prose more memorable—especially if the image or picture you present is a fresh, arresting one. Here are some examples of striking images designed to catch the reader's attention and to clarify the writer's point:

- An hour away from him felt like a month in the country.
- The atmosphere of the meeting room was as tense as a World Series game tied in the ninth inning.
- The woman's earrings were as big as butter plates.
- The angry accusation flew like a spear: once thrown, it could not be retrieved and it cut deeply.
- Out of the night came the convoy of brown trucks, modern-day buffalo thundering single-file across the prairie, eyes on fire.
- Behind her broad polished desk, Matilda was a queen bee with a swarm of office drones buzzing at her door.

---

* Some writers now use "s/he" to promote gender inclusivity in their informal prose. Be aware, however, that this usage is nontraditional and not accepted universally. Always check with your instructors, or the publication for which you are writing, for the appropriate and preferred style.

■ The factory squatted on the bank of the river like a huge black toad.

Sometimes, in appropriate writing situations, exaggerated similes and metaphors may be used humorously to underscore a particular point: "I felt so stupid that day. I'm sure my colleagues thought my brain was so small that if they placed it on the head of a pin, it would roll around like a marble on a six-lane highway."

Figurative language can spice up your prose, but like any spice, it can be misused, thus spoiling your soup. Therefore, don't overuse figurative language; not every point needs a metaphor or simile for clarity or emphasis. Too many images are confusing. Moreover, don't use stale images. (Clichés—discussed on pages 151–152—are often tired metaphors or similes: snake in the grass, hot as fire, quiet as a mouse, etc.) If you can't catch your readers' attention with a fresh picture, don't bore them with a stale one.

Finally, don't mix images—this too often results in a confusing or unintentionally comic scene. For example, a former mayor of Denver once responded to a question about city fiscal requirements this way: "I think the proper approach is to go through this Garden of Gethsemane that we're in now, give birth to a budget that will come out of it, and then start putting our ducks in order with an appeal and the backup we would need to get something done at the state level." Or consider the defense attorney who didn't particularly like his client's plea-bargaining deal but nevertheless announced, "Given the attitude of the normal jury on this type of crime, I feel we would be paddling up a stream behind the eight ball." Perhaps a newspaper columnist wins the prize for confusion with this triple-decker: "The Assemblymen also were miffed at their Senate counterparts because they have refused to bite the bullet that now seems to have grown to the size of a millstone to the Assemblymen whose necks are on the line."

Think of figurative language as you might regard a fine cologne on the person sitting next to you in a crowded theater: just enough is engaging; too much is overpowering.

(For more discussion of similes, metaphors, and other figurative language, see pages 310–311 in Chapter 11.)

Do vary your word choice so that your prose does not sound wordy, repetitious, or monotonous. Consider the following sentence:

> According to child psychologists, depriving a child of artistic stimulation in the earliest stages of childhood can cause the child brain damage.

Reworded, the following sentence eliminates the tiresome, unnecessary repetition of the word "child":

> According to child psychologists, depriving infants of artistic stimulation can cause brain damage.

By omitting or changing repeated words, you can add variety and crispness to your prose. Of course, don't ever change your words or sentence structure to achieve variety at the expense of clarity or precision; at all times, your goal is to make your prose clear to your readers.

Do remember that wordiness is a major problem for all writers, even the professionals. State your thoughts directly and specifically in as few words as necessary to communicate your meaning clearly. In addition to the advice given here on avoiding wordy or vague jargon, euphemisms, and clichés, you might also review the sections on simplicity and conciseness in Chapter 6.

> **THE MOST IMPORTANT KEY TO EFFECTIVE WORD CHOICE IS REVISION.**
> As you write your first draft, don't fret about selecting the best words to communicate your ideas; in later drafts, one of your main tasks will be replacing the inaccurate or imprecise words with better ones. (Dorothy Parker, famous for her witty essays, once lamented, "I can't write five words but that I change seven.") All good writers rewrite, so revise your prose to make each word count.

■ PRACTICING WHAT YOU'VE LEARNED

A. Underline the vague nouns, verbs, and modifiers in the sentences that follow. Then rewrite each sentence so that it says something clear and specific.

1. The experiment had very bad results.

2. The speaker came up with some odd items.

3. The house was big, old, and ugly.

4. The man was a nice guy with a good personality.

5. I felt that the whole ordeal was quite an experience.

6. The machine we got was missing a few things.

7. The woman was really something special.

8. The classroom material wasn't interesting.

9. The child made a lot of very loud noises.

10. The cost of the unusual meal was amazing.

B. Rewrite the following sentences, eliminating all clichés, slang, mixed metaphors, euphemisms, and sexist language you find.

1. When our mother didn't return from the little girl's room, we agreed she was slow as molasses.

2. Anyone who wants to be elected the next congressman from our state must clearly recognize that our tourist industry is sitting on a launching pad, ready to flex its muscles, and become a dynamo.

3. It goes without saying that all of us silver foxes over the ripe old age of 65 should exercise our most sacred democratic privilege every November.

4. I thought the whole deal was sweet but then my sister goes "whatever"; I think she got a special delivery from the duh truck.

5. After all is said and done, agricultural producers may be forced to relocate to urban environments settling in substandard housing with other members of the disadvantaged class until the day they expire.

6. Both Ron Howard and Shirley Temple were popular child actors; as adults, Howard moved on to directing movies but Shirley left show business to serve Old Glory by becoming ambassadoress to Ghana and Czechoslovakia, believe it or not.

7. Each commander realizes that he may one day be called upon to use the peacekeepers to depopulate an emerging nation in a lethal intervention.

8. Although Jack once regarded her as sweet and innocent, he knew then and there that Jill was really a wolf in sheep's clothing with a heart of stone.

9. The city councilman was stewing in his juices when he learned that his goals-impaired son had been arrested for fooling around with the funds for the fiscal underachievers' home.

10. The automobile company sent a complimentary letter warning that driving their preowned 2002 cars with the factory-installed set of bearings could adversely affect vehicle control.

C. Rewrite the following sentences, replacing the jargon and cloudy language with clear, precise words and phrases.

1. To maintain a state of high-level wellness, one should use a wooden interdental stimulator at least once a day and avoid spending time at fake-bake salons.

2. According to the military, one should not attempt a predawn vertical insertion without an aerodynamic personnel decelerator because it could lead to sudden deceleration trauma upon landing.

3. American Airlines' passengers can now arrive and depart planes on customer conveyance mobile lounges.

4. If you are in the armed services, you should avoid receiving a ballistically induced aperture in the subcutaneous environment that might lead to your being terminated with extreme prejudice.

5. The U.S. Embassy in Budapest once warned its employees: "It must be assumed that available casual indigenous female companions work for or cooperate with the Hungarian government security establishment."

6. At a 2003 press conference on the war in Iraq, Defense Secretary Donald Rumsfeld announced the following: "Reports that say something hasn't happened are always interesting to me, because as we know, there are known knowns, there are things we know we know. We also know there are known unknowns; that is to say we know there are some things we do not know. But there are also unknown unknowns— the ones we don't know we don't know."*

7. The employee was outplaced for a lack of interpersonal skills and for failing to optimize productivity.

8. My institute of higher learning announced today that its academic evaluation program had been delayed and in all probability indefinitely postponed due to circumstances relating to financial insolvency.

9. All of us could relate to Mabel's essay on the significant educational factors involved in the revenue enhancement tax-base erosion control program.

10. "We were not micromanaging Grenada intelligencewise until about that time frame," said Admiral Wesley L. McDonald, when asked what was happening on the island just prior to the United States' 1983 rescue mission.

■ ASSIGNMENT

A. The following recipe, which first appeared in *The Washington Post*, pokes fun at bureaucratic jargon. See if you can translate the bureaucratese into clear, simple instructions. Then look at your writing to make certain that you are not guilty of using similar gobbledygook in your own prose.

Input to Output, 35 Minutes

For government employees and bureaucrats who have problems with standard recipes, here's one that should make the grade—a classic version of the chocolate-chip cookie translated for easy reading.

Total Lead Time: 35 minutes.

---

*Incidentally, this comment won Rumsfeld the "Foot in Mouth" prize for the most confusing public statement of the year, awarded by Britain's Plain English Campaign, a group dedicated to ridding the language of jargon and legalese.

Inputs:
1 cup packed brown sugar
½ cup granulated sugar
½ cup softened butter
½ cup shortening
2 eggs
1½ teaspoons vanilla
2½ cups all-purpose flour
1 teaspoon baking soda
½ teaspoon salt
12-ounce package semi-sweet chocolate pieces
1 cup chopped walnuts or pecans

Guidance:

After procurement actions, decontainerize inputs. Perform measurement tasks on a case-by-case basis. In a mixing type bowl, impact heavily on brown sugar, granulated sugar, softened butter and shortening. Coordinate the interface of eggs and vanilla, avoiding an overrun scenario to the best of your skills and abilities.

At this point in time, leverage flour, baking soda and salt into a bowl and aggregate. Equalize with prior mixture and develop intense and continuous liaison among inputs until well-coordinated. Associate key chocolate and nut subsystems and execute stirring operations.

Within this time frame, take action to prepare the heating environment for throughput by manually setting the oven baking unit by hand to a temperature of 375 degrees Fahrenheit (190 Celsius). Drop mixture in an ongoing fashion from a teaspoon implement onto an ungreased cookie sheet at intervals sufficient enough apart to permit total and permanent separation of throughputs to the maximum extent practicable under operating conditions.

Position cookie sheet in a bake situation and survey for 8 to 10 minutes or until cooking action terminates. Initiate coordination of outputs within the cooling rack function. Containerize, wrap in red tape and disseminate to authorized staff personnel on a timely and expeditious basis.

Output:

Six dozen official government chocolate-chip cookie units.

B. Fill in the blanks with colorful words. Make the paragraph as interesting, exciting, or humorous as you can. Avoid clichés and Insta-Prose (those predictable phrases that first come to mind). Make your responses original and creative.

As midnight approached, Janet and Brad _____ toward the

_____ mansion to escape the _____ storm. Their

_____ car had _____ on the road nearby. The night was

_____, and Brad _____ at the shadows with

_____ and _____ . As they _____ up the

_____ steps to the _____ door, the _____

wind was filled with _____ and _____ sounds. Janet

_____ on the door, and moments later, it opened to reveal the

_____ scientist, with a face like a _____ . Brad and Janet

_____ at each other and then _____ (complete this sen-

tence and then end the paragraph and the story).

▪ APPLYING WHAT YOU'VE LEARNED TO *YOUR* WRITING

If you have drafted a piece of writing and you are satisfied with the
development and organization of your ideas, you may want to begin
revising your word choice. First, read your draft for accuracy, looking up in your dictionary any words you suspect may have been used incorrectly. Then, focus your
attention on your draft's tone, on the "voice" your words are creating. Have you
selected the right words for your purpose, subject, and audience?

If you need a word with a slightly different connotation, use your thesaurus to suggest choices (for example, is the person you're discussing best described as smart,
intellectual, studious, or wise?). Next, go on a Bland Verb Hunt. Try to replace at
least five colorless verbs (such as "are," "get," or "make") with active, vivid ones.
Revise vague nouns ("thing") and dull adjectives ("very," "really"); if you're stuck,
think of words with strong sensory appeal (sight, smell, taste, sound, touch) to
enliven your prose. Last, mine-sweep for any clichés, slang, or jargon. Make each
word count: each choice should clarify, not muddy, your meaning.

_____

Answer for page 151:

Most people respond with "coughed, sputtered, and died."

CHAPTER 7 SUMMARY

Here is a brief restatement of what you should remember about word choice:

1. Consult a dictionary if you are in doubt about the meaning or usage of a particular word.

2. Choose words that are appropriate for your purpose and audience.

3. Choose words that are clear, specific, and fresh rather than vague, bland, or clichéd.

4. Avoid language that is sexist, trendy, or that tries to disguise meaning with jargon or euphemisms.

5. Work for prose that is concise rather than wordy, precise rather than foggy.

Chapter 8

The Reading-Writing Connection

It's hardly surprising that good readers often become good writers themselves. Good readers note effectiveness in the writing of others and use these observations to help clarify their own ideas and rhetorical choices about organization, development, and style. Analogies abound in every skill: singers listen to vocalists they admire, tennis players watch championship matches, actors evaluate their colleagues' award-winning performances, medical students observe famous surgeons, all with an eye to improving their own craft. Therefore, to help you become a better writer, your instructor may ask you to study some of the professional essays included in other sections of this text. Learning to read these essays analytically will help when you face your own writing decisions. To sharpen your reading skills, follow the steps suggested in this chapter. After practicing these steps several times, you should discover that the process is becoming a natural part of your reading experience.

■ How Can Reading Well Help Me Become a Better Writer?

Close reading of the professional essays in this text should help you become a better writer in several ways. First, understanding the opinions expressed in these essays may spark interesting ideas for your own essays; second, discovering the various ways other writers have organized and explained their material should give you some new ideas about selecting your own strategies and supporting evidence. Familiarizing yourself with

© Michael Newman/PhotoEdit

the effective stylistic devices and diction of other writers may also encourage you to use language in ways you've never tried before.

Perhaps most important, analyzing the prose of others should make you more aware of the writing process itself. Each writer represented in this text faced a series of decisions regarding organization, development, and style, just as you do when you write. By asking questions (Why did the writer begin the essay this way? Why compare this event to that one? Why use a personal example in that paragraph?), you will begin to see how the writer put the essay together—and that knowledge will help you plan and shape your own essay. Questioning the rhetorical choices of other writers should also help you revise your prose because it promotes the habit of asking yourself questions that consider the reader's point of view (Does the point in paragraph three need more evidence to convince my reader? Will the reader be confused if I don't add a smoother transition from paragraph four to five? Does the conclusion fall flat?).

In other words, the skills you practice as an analytical reader are those you'll use as a good writer.

■ How Can I Become an Analytical Reader?

Becoming an analytical reader may, at first, demand more time—and involvement—than you have previously devoted to a reading assignment. Analytical reading requires more than allowing your eyes to pass over the words on the page; it's not like channel-surfing through late-night TV shows, stopping here or there as interest strikes. Analytical reading asks you not only to understand the writer's ideas, but also to consider *how* those ideas were presented, *why* the writer presented them that way, and whether that presentation was *effective*. Consequently, to improve your understanding of the reading-writing connection, you should plan on two readings of the assigned essay, some note-taking, and some marking of the text (called *annotating*). This procedure may seem challenging at first, but the benefits to you as both reader and writer will be well worth the extra minutes.

Steps to Reading Well

1. Before you begin the essay itself, note the *publication information* and *biographical data* on the author in the paragraph that precedes each selection in this text. Where and when was the essay originally published? Was it directed toward a particular or a general audience? Was it written in response to some event or controversy? Is the essay still timely or is it dated? Does the author seem qualified to write about this subject? Does the introduction offer any other information that might help you assess the essay's effectiveness?

2. Next, note the *title* of the essay. Does it draw you into the essay? Does it suggest a particular tone or image?

3. You're now ready to begin your first reading of the essay. Some readers like to read through the essay without stopping; others feel comfortable at this point underlining a few main ideas or making checks in the margins. You may also have to make a dictionary stop if words you don't know appear in key places in the essay. Many times you can figure out definitions from context—that is, from the words and ideas surrounding the unknown word—but don't miss the point of a major part of an essay because of failure to recognize an important word, especially if that word is repeated or emphasized in some way.

When you finish this reading, write a sentence or two summarizing your general impression of the essay's content or ideas. Consider the author's *purpose:* what do you think the writer was trying to do? Overall, how well did he or she succeed? (A typical response might be "argued for tuition hike—unconvincing, boring—too many confusing statistics.")

Now prepare to take another, closer look at the essay. Make some notes in the margins or in another convenient place as you respond to the following questions. Remember that analytical reading is not a horse race: there are no trophies for finishing quickly! Fight the bad habit of galloping at breakneck speed through an essay; slow down to admire the verbal roses the writer has tried to place in your path.

4. Look at the *title* (again) and at the essay's *introductory paragraph(s)*. Did they effectively set up your expectations? Introduce the essay's topic, main idea, tone? (Would some other title or introductory "hook" have worked better?)

5. Locate the writer's main point or *thesis*; this idea may be stated plainly or it may be clearly implied. If you didn't mark this idea on your first reading, do so now by placing a "T" in the margin so you can refer to the thesis easily. (If the thesis is implied, you may wish to mark places that you think most clearly indicate the writer's stance.)

6. As you reread the essay, look for important statements that support or illustrate the thesis. (As you know, these are often found as *topic sentences* occurring near the beginning or end of the body paragraphs.) Try numbering these supporting points or ideas and jotting a key word by each one in the margin.

7. As you identify each important supporting point, ask yourself how the writer develops, explains, or argues that idea. For example, does the writer clarify or support the point by providing examples, testimony, or statistics? By comparing or contrasting one idea to another? By showing a cause-effect relationship? Some other method? A combination of methods? A writer may use one or many methods of development, but each major point in an essay should be explained clearly and logically. Make brief marginal notes to indicate how well you think the writer has succeeded ("convincing example," "generalization without support," "questionable authority cited," "good comparison," etc.). Practice using marginal symbols, such as stars (for especially effective statements, descriptions, arguments) or question marks (for passages you think are confusing, untrue, or exaggerated).

Make up your own set of symbols to help yourself remember your evaluations of the writer's ideas and techniques.

8. Look back over the essay's general *organization*. Did the writer use one of the expository, descriptive, narrative, or argumentative strategies to structure the essay? Some combination of strategies? Was this choice effective? (Always consider alternate ways: Would another choice have allowed the writer to make his or her main point more emphatically? Why or why not?)

9. Does the essay flow logically and coherently? If you are having trouble with *unity* or *coherence* in your own essays, look closely at the transitional devices used in a few paragraphs; bracketing transitional words or phrases you see might show you how the writer achieved a sense of unity and flow.

10. Consider the writer's *style* and the essay's *tone*. Does the writer use figurative language in an arresting way? Specialized diction for a particular purpose? Repetition of words or phrases? Any especially effective sentence patterns? Does the writer's tone of voice come through clearly? Is the essay serious, humorous, angry, consoling, happy, sad, sarcastic, or something else? Is the tone appropriate for the purpose and audience of this essay? Writers use a variety of stylistic devices to create prose that is vivid and memorable; you might mark new uses of language you would like to try in essays of your own.

Now is also the time to look up meanings of any words you felt you could skip during your first time through the essay, especially if you sense that these words are important to the writer's tone or use of imagery.

Once you have completed these steps and added any other comments that seem important to the analysis of the essay, review your notes. Is this an effective essay? Is the essay's thesis explained or supported adequately with enough logically developed points and evidence? Is the essay organized as effectively as it could have been? What strengths and weaknesses did you find after this analytical reading? Has your original evaluation of this essay changed in any way? If so, write a new assessment, adding any other notes you want to help you remember your evaluation of this essay.

Finally, after this close reading of the essay, did you discover any new ideas, strategies, or techniques you might incorporate into *your* current piece of writing?

■ Sample Annotated Essay

Here is a professional essay annotated according to the steps listed on the previous pages.

By closely reading and annotating the professional essays in this text, you can improve your own writing in numerous ways. Once you have practiced analyzing essays by other writers, you may discover that you can assess your own drafts' strengths and weaknesses more easily and with more confidence.

■ Our Youth Should Serve

Steven Muller

title forecasts thesis

Steven Muller is President Emeritus of The Johns Hopkins University, founded in 1876 in Baltimore, Maryland. This essay first appeared in *Newsweek* in 1978 and has been reprinted often.

educator

general audience

1   Too many young men and women now leave school without a well-developed sense of purpose. If they go right to work after high school, many are not properly prepared for careers. But if they enter college instead, many do not really know what to study or what to do afterward. Our society does not seem to be doing much to encourage and use the best instincts and talents of our young.

Introduction presents subject: how to use talents of young people

2   On the other hand, I see the growing problems of each year's new generation of high-school graduates. After twelve years of schooling— and television—many of them want to participate actively in society; but they face either a job with a limited future or more years in educational institutions. Many are wonderfully idealistic: they have talent and energy to offer, and they seek the meaning in their lives that comes from giving of oneself to the common good. But they feel almost rejected by a society that has too few jobs to offer them and that asks nothing of them except to avoid trouble. They want to be part of a new solution; instead society perceives them as a problem. They seek a cause; but their elders preach only self-advancement. They need experience on which to base choice; yet society seems to put a premium on the earliest possible choice, based inescapably on the least experience.

Problem for youth: idealism, talent, and energy but too few jobs and little experience

3   On the other hand, I see an American society sadly in need of social services that we can afford less and less at prevailing costs of labor. Some tasks are necessary but constitute no career; they should be carried out, but not as anyone's lifetime occupation. Our democracy profoundly needs public spirit, but the economy of our labor system primarily encourages self-interest. The Federal government spends billions on opportunity grants for post-secondary education, but some of us wonder about money given on the basis only of need. We ask the young to volunteer for national defense, but not for the improvement of our society. As public spirit and public services decline, so does the quality of life. So I ask myself why cannot we put it all together and ask our young people to volunteer in peacetime to serve America.

Problem for society: social services are needed but labor costs are high

✱ *Thesis: youth should volunteer to serve America's public service needs*

4   I recognize that at first mention, universal national youth service may sound too much like compulsory military service or the Hitler Youth or the Komsomol. I do not believe it has to be like that at all. It need not require uniforms or camps, nor a vast new Federal bureaucracy, nor vast new public expenditures. And it should certainly not be compulsory.

¶ clarifies proposal by contrast : not like military, not political, not required (Komsomol: youth section of the Soviet Communist Party)

5 A voluntary program of universal national youth service does of course require compelling incentives. Two could be provided. Guaranteed job training would be one. Substantial Federal assistance toward post-secondary education would be the other. This would mean that today's complex measures of Federal aid to students would be ended, and that there would also be no need for tuition tax credits for post-secondary education. Instead, prospective students would *earn* their assistance for post-secondary education by volunteering for national service, and only those who earned assistance would receive it. Present Federal expenditures for the assistance of students in post-secondary education would be converted into a simple grant program, modeled on the post-World War II GI Bill of Rights.

1. Incentives
—job training
— Federal money
for college

Comparison:
education grants like
those given to returning WWII soldiers

6 But what, you say, would huge numbers of high-school graduates do as volunteers in national service? They could be interns in public agencies, local, state, and national. They could staff day-care programs, neighborhood health centers, centers to counsel and work with children; help to maintain public facilities, including highways, railbeds, waterways and airports; engage in neighborhood-renewal projects, both physical and social. Some would elect military service, others the Peace Corps. Except for the latter two alternatives and others like them, they could live anywhere they pleased. They would not wear uniforms. They would be employed and supervised by people already employed locally in public-agency careers.

2. Kinds of jobs

examples

7 Volunteers would be paid only a subsistence wage, because they would receive the benefits of job training (not necessarily confined to one task) as well as assistance toward post-secondary education if they were so motivated and qualified. If cheap mass housing for some groups of volunteers were needed, supervised participants in the program could rebuild decayed dwellings in metropolitan areas. . . .

3. support costs
—wages
—housing

problem?

8 The direct benefits of such a universal national-youth-service program would be significant. Every young man and woman would face a meaningful role in society after high school. Everyone would receive job training, and the right to earn assistance toward post-secondary education. Those going on to post-secondary education would have their education interrupted by a constructive work experience. There is evidence that they would thereby become more highly motivated and successful students, particularly if their work experience related closely to subsequent vocational interests. Many participants might locate careers by means of their national-service assignments.

* 4. Direct benefits for youth:
—meaningful role in society
—job training
—money for education
—work experience
—success in school
—career direction

such as?

9 No union jobs need be lost, because skilled workers would be needed to give job training. Many public services would be performed by cheap labor, but there would be no youth army. And the intangible indirect benefits would be the greatest of all. Young people could regard themselves as more useful and needed. They could serve this country for a two-year period as volunteers, and earn job

addresses possible
criticism

training and/or assistance toward post-secondary education. There is more self-esteem and motivation in earned than in unearned benefits. Universal national youth service may be no panacea. But in my opinion the idea merits serious and imaginative consideration.

First impression: Muller proposes a volunteer youth corps to provide some public services. Many benefits for both country and young people.

Notes: Muller uses comparisons, contrasts, and examples to explain the proposed youth corps, and he clearly shows the benefits (training, grants, self-esteem). His arguments might be even more effective if he had added some specific examples and testimony from students and people in social services. Or maybe from participants in similar kinds of programs, such as VISTA?

Personal response: Although the low wages might be a problem for many people, I like this program. It might have helped me decide on a career path sooner and definitely would help with tuition now.

Conclusion summarizes advantages, emphasizes the benefit of earning self-esteem, and calls for consideration of this proposal

■ PRACTICING WHAT YOU'VE LEARNED

Select one of the professional essays reprinted in this text and annotate it according to the steps described in this chapter. Note at least one strength in the essay that you would like to incorporate into your own writing.

■ ASSIGNMENT

Select one of the professional essays in this text to read analytically and annotate. Then write a one-page explanation of the essay's major strengths (or weaknesses), showing how the writer's rhetorical choices affected you, the reader.

■ Writing a Summary

Frequently, writing teachers will ask students to read an essay and briefly summarize it. A *summary* is an objective, condensed version of a reading selection, containing the author's main ideas. Although summaries are always more concise than the original texts, the length of a particular summary often depends on the length and complexity of the original reading and the purpose of the summary.

Learning to summarize reading material is a valuable skill, useful in many classes and in professional work. In one of your college classes, for example, your instructor might ask you to summarize an article pertinent to an upcoming lecture or class discussion, thus ensuring that you have thoroughly understood the information; at other times, you may need to summarize material for your own research. On a job, you might want to share a summary of an important report with colleagues, or you might be asked to present a summary of project results to your boss.

Because summarizing is such a useful skill, here are a few guidelines:

1. Read the selection carefully, as many times as it takes for you to understand and identify the author's thesis and main ideas. You might underline or take notes on the key ideas as you read, using the suggestions in the previous pages of this chapter to help you.

2. When you begin to draft your summary, always include the author's name and the title of the original text in your first sentence. Many times it's important to include the source of the work and its publication date, too.

3. Using your own words, present the author's thesis and other main ideas in a few concise sentences. Do not merely copy sentences directly from the original text. Use your own words to convey the main ideas as clearly and concisely as possible.

4. Omit all references to the supporting examples and details in the selection, unless you have been instructed to include these.

5. If, for clarity or emphasis, you do need to include an exact word or phrase from the original text, be certain to enclose the words in quotation marks.

6. Do not give your own opinion or interpretation of the material you are summarizing. Your goal is an objective, accurate, condensed overview of the selection that does not reveal your attitude toward the ideas presented.

To illustrate the preceding guidelines, here is a brief summary of the essay that appears on pages 169–171 of this chapter.

> In the *Newsweek* essay "Our Youth Should Serve," Steven Muller proposes a voluntary youth corps that would address America's need for social services and benefit our nation's youth. Muller, a former university president, believes the talents of too many bright, idealistic, but inexperienced high school graduates are wasted because the students must choose too soon between a low-paying job or more education with an undefined goal. Muller argues that a voluntary, non-partisan civilian youth corps would provide cheap labor for short-term public service projects while offering young people job training, work experience, assistance toward post-secondary education, and a sense of self-esteem.

Note that the writer of the summary did not offer her opinion of Muller's proposal, but, instead, objectively presented the essay's main ideas.

For additional discussion clarifying the difference between *summary* and *paraphrase*, see pages 372–373 in Chapter 14. For suggestions on writing the assignment known as the "summary-and-response essay," see pages 414–416 in Chapter 15; this section also contains a sample student paper written in response to Steven Muller's essay "Our Youth Should Serve."

■ **PRACTICING WHAT YOU'VE LEARNED**

Read one of the professional essays in this textbook and annotate it according to the steps outlined earlier in this chapter. After you are sure you clearly understand the author's thesis and main ideas, write a one-paragraph summary of the essay. Use your own words to convey the essay's main ideas, but remember to remain objective in your summary.

■ Benefiting from Class Discussions

If you have been practicing the steps for close reading of essays, you are on your way to becoming a better writer. By analyzing the rhetorical choices of other writers, you are gathering new ideas and techniques as well as improving your ability to look thoughtfully at your own drafts. To continue this progress, your composition instructor may devote class time to discussing sample professional or student essays that appear in this text.

Active participation in these discussions will contribute to your growth as a writer as you share ideas about effective prose with your classmates. To benefit from such discussions, consider these suggestions for improving your classroom skills:

Try to arrive a few minutes before class begins so that you can look over the reading and your marginal notes (and any other homework assigned to accompany the essay, such as questions or a summary). Remind yourself that it is time to become an "active listener," so if sitting by friends or near a window is a distraction, move to another seat. Sitting up front is encouraged not only because you can hear your instructor better, but also because he or she can see and hear you more clearly if you have questions. (Be sure you have turned off your cell phone, pager, or any other electronic device, and remember that gum-popping, pencil tapping, and knuckle-cracking may lead to bad-karma thoughts from nearby students who are also trying to listen without distraction.)

During the class period, your teacher may ask for responses to questions that follow selected essays in this text or he or she may pose new questions. If you've prepared by closely reading and annotating the assigned essay as outlined on pages 166–168, you should be able to join these discussions. Listen carefully to your classmates' opinions; offer your own insights and be willing to voice agreement or polite disagreement. If participating in class makes you so nervous you fear you will break out in spots, prepare one or two comments out of class in such clear detail that speaking about them will be easier for you, and then volunteer when those topics arise in the discussion. Don't hesitate to ask questions or request additional explanations; remember that if you don't understand something, it's a good bet others in the class are puzzled too.

As discussion of a sample essay unfolds, practice thinking critically on two levels. First, think of the essay as a draft in which the writer made certain choices to communicate meaning, just as you do in your essays. Trading ideas with your classmates may help you see why the writer chose as he or she did—and whether those decisions work effectively. As you gain a clear understanding of the strengths and weaknesses in the sample essay, move to the second level by considering the choices you are making in your own writing.

For example, if you struggle with conclusions to your essays, listen attentively to the discussion of the writer's choice and then consider whether this kind of ending might work in your essay. If a writer has failed to provide enough examples or details to illustrate a particular point, think about a paragraph in your current rough draft. Do you now see a similar problem in need of revision? In other words, as you and your classmates analyze essays in class, *actively make the essential connection between the samples and your own work.*

To remember important points in any class discussion, sharpen your note-taking skills. If you use a notebook for this course, you may find it helpful to leave a wide margin on the left side of your paper, giving yourself space to write key words, questions, or ideas for your own writing. Start each day's notes on a new page with the day's date to help you locate material later. Acquire the habit of stapling or taping handouts to blank pages that immediately follow notes from a particular class period (handouts stuck in your textbook or in your backpack are easily lost). As you take notes, pay special attention to any words your teacher considers significant enough to write on the board and to those concepts that merit treatment in handouts or other visual aids (transparencies, slides, PowerPoint, etc.). Be sensitive to the verbal cues your instructor uses to emphasize essential material (words such as "key terms," "main reasons," and "central idea," as well as repetition and even a louder tone of voice).

Because class discussion often moves quickly, you'll need to develop a shorthand method of note-taking. Some students write out an important term the first time (development) and then abbreviate it thereafter (dev). You can devise your own system of symbols but included here are some abbreviations common to note-taking you may find handy. Most of these abbreviations are for notes only, although some (such as e.g., i.e., cf., and ca.) may be used in college and professional writing; consult your instructor or the appropriate style manual if you are in doubt.

b/c = because	→ = causes, leads to, produces
b/4 = before	cf. = compare
w/ = with	↑ = increases, higher than
w/o = without	↓ = decreases, lower than
w/i = within	esp. = especially
e.g. = for example	re = regarding
i.e. = that is	ca. = approximately (use with dates or figures)
& = and	∴ = therefore
@ = at	≠ = not equal to, not the same, differs from
# = number	N.B. = "nota bene," Latin for "note well"

Later, after class, you may want to underline, star, or highlight important material. Fill in any gaps and rewrite any illegible words now before you forget what you meant. Use the wide left-hand margin to make some notes about applying the ideas and techniques discussed in class to your own writing. Reread these notes before you begin drafting or revising your essay.

Here's the last, and possibly most important, piece of advice for every student of writing: *attend every class session!* There is a logical progression in all composition courses; each day's lesson emphasizes and builds on the previous one. By conscientiously attending every class discussion and actively participating in your own learning process, you *will* improve your writing skills.

CHAPTER 8 SUMMARY

1. Reading and analyzing essays can improve your writing skills.

2. Learning to recognize and evaluate the strategies and stylistic techniques of other writers will help you plan and shape your own essays.

3. Reading analytically takes time and practice but is well worth the extra effort.

4. Learning to summarize reading material accurately and objectively is an important skill, useful in school and at work.

5. Active participation in class discussions of sample essays can help you strengthen your own writing.

★ PART ONE SUMMARY: THE BASICS OF THE SHORT ESSAY

Here are ten suggestions to keep in mind while you are working on the rough drafts of your essay:

1. Be confident that you have something important and interesting to say.

2. Identify your particular audience and become determined to communicate effectively with them.

3. Use prewriting techniques to help you focus on one main idea that will become the thesis of your essay.

4. Organize your essay's points logically, in a persuasive and coherent order.

5. Develop each of your ideas with enough evidence and specific details.

6. Delete any irrelevant material that disrupts the smooth flow from idea to idea.

7. Compose sentences that are clear, concise, and informative; choose accurate, vivid words.

8. Improve your writing by learning to read analytically.

9. Revise your prose.

10. Revise your prose!

Part 2

Purposes, Modes, and Strategies

Communication may be divided into four types (or "modes" as they are often called): exposition, argumentation, description, and narration. Although each one will be explained in greater detail in this section of the text, the four modes may be defined briefly as follows:

Exposition
The writer intends to explain or inform.

Argumentation
The writer intends to convince or persuade.

Description
The writer intends to create in words a picture of a person, place, object, or feeling.

Narration
The writer intends to tell a story or recount an event.

Although we commonly refer to exposition, argumentation, description, and narration as the basic types of prose, in reality it is difficult to find any one mode in a pure form. In fact, almost all essays are combinations of two or more modes; it would be virtually impossible, for instance, to write a story—narration—without including description or to argue without also giving some information. Nevertheless, by determining a writer's main purpose, we can usually identify an essay or prose piece as primarily exposition, argumentation, description, or narration. In other words, an article may include a brief description of a new mousetrap, but if the writer's main intention is to explain how the trap works, then we may designate the essay as exposition. In most cases, the primary mode of any essay will be readily apparent to the reader.

In Part Two of this text, you will study each of the four modes in detail and learn some of the patterns of development, called *strategies*, that will enable you to write the kind of prose most frequently demanded in college and professional work. Mastering the most common prose patterns in their simplest forms now will help you successfully assess and organize any kind of complex writing assignment you may face in the future. Chapter 13 concludes this section by discussing the more complex essay, developed through use of multiple strategies. ■

Chapter 9

Exposition

Exposition refers to prose whose primary purpose is giving information. Some familiar examples of expository writing include encyclopedias, dictionaries, news magazines, and textbooks. In addition, much of your own college work may be classified as exposition: book reports, political analyses, laboratory and business reports, and most essay exams, to cite only a few of the possibilities.

Although expository writing does present information, a good expository essay is more than a collection of facts, figures, and details. First, each essay should contain a thesis statement clarifying the writer's purpose and position. Then the essay should be organized so that the body paragraphs explain and support that thesis. In an expository essay the writer says, in effect, here are the facts *as I see them;* therefore, the writer's main purpose is not only to inform the readers but also to convince them that this essay explains the subject matter in the clearest, most truthful way.

■ The Strategies of Exposition

There are a variety of ways to organize an expository essay, depending on your purpose. The most common strategies, or patterns, of organization include development by *example, process analysis, comparison and contrast, definition, classification*, and *causal analysis*. However, an essay is rarely developed completely by a single strategy (an essay developed by comparison and contrast, for instance, may also contain examples; a classification essay may contain definitions, and so forth); therefore, as in the case of the four modes, we identify the kind of expository essay by its *primary* strategy of development. To help you understand every expository strategy thoroughly before going on to the next, each is presented here separately. Each discussion section follows a similar pattern, which includes explanation of the strategy, advice on developing your essay, a list of essay topics, a topic proposal sheet, a revision checklist, sample essays (by students and by professional writers), and a progress report.

■ Strategy One: Development by Example

Perhaps you've heard a friend complain lately about a roommate. "Tina is an inconsiderate boor, impossible to live with," she cries. Your natural response might be to question your friend's rather broad accusation: "What makes her so terrible? What does she do that's so bad?" Your friend might then respond with specific examples of Tina's insensitivity: she never washes her dishes, she ties up the telephone for hours, and she plays her radio until three every morning. By citing several examples, your friend clarifies and supports her general criticism of Tina, thus enabling you to understand her point of view.

Examples in an essay work precisely the same way as in the hypothetical story above: they *support, clarify, interest,* and *persuade.*

In your writing assignments, you might want to assert that dorm food is cruel and inhuman punishment, that recycling is a profitable hobby, or that the cost of housing is rising dramatically. But without some carefully chosen examples to show the truth of your statements, these remain unsupported generalities or mere opinions. Your task, then, is to provide enough specific examples to support your general statements, to make them both clear and convincing. Here is a statement offering the reader only hazy generalities:

> Our locally supported TV channel presents a variety of excellent educational shows. The shows are informative on lots of different subjects for both children and adults. The information they offer makes channel 19 well worth the public funds that support it.

Rewritten, the same paragraph explains its point clearly through the use of specific examples:

> Our locally supported TV channel presents a variety of excellent educational shows. For example, young children can learn their alphabet and numbers from *Sesame Street;* imaginative older children can be encouraged to create by watching *Kids' Writes*, a show on which four hosts read and act out stories written and sent in by youngsters from eight to fourteen. Adults may enjoy learning about antiques and collectibles from a program called *The Collector;* each week the show features an in-depth look at buying, selling, trading, and displaying collectible items, from Depression glass to teddy bears to Shaker furniture. Those folks wishing to become handy around the home can use information on repairs from plumbing to wiring on *This Old House*, while the nonmusical can learn the difference between scat singing and arias on such programs as *Jazz!* and *Opera Today*. And the money-minded can profit from the tips dropped by stockbrokers who appear on *Wall Street Week*. The information

offered makes these and other educational shows on channel 19 well worth the public funds that support the station.

Although the preceding example is based on real shows, you may also use personal experiences, hypothetical situations, anecdotes, research material, facts, testimony, or any combination thereof, to explain, illustrate, or support the points in your essays.

In some cases you may find that a series of short examples fits your purpose, illustrating clearly the idea you are presenting to your reader:

> In the earlier years of Hollywood, actors aspiring to become movie stars often adopted new names that they believed sounded more attractive to the public. Frances Ethel Gumm, for instance, decided to change her name to Judy Garland long before she flew over any rainbows, and Alexander Archibald Leach became Cary Grant on his way from England to America. Alexandra Cymboliak and Merle Johnson, Jr., might not have set teenage hearts throbbing in the early 1960s, but Sandra Dee and Troy Donahue certainly did. And while some names were changed to achieve a smoother flow (Frederic Austerlitz to Fred Astaire, for example), some may have also been changed to ensure a good fit on movie theater marquees as well as a place in their audience's memory: the little Turner girl, Julia Jean Mildred Frances, for instance, became just Lana.

Or you may decide that two or three examples, explained in some detail, provide the best support for your topic rather than a series of short examples. In the paragraph that follows, the writer chose to develop two examples to illustrate her point about the unusual dog her family owned when she was a young girl in the late 1970s:

> Our family dog Sparky always let us know when he wasn't getting enough attention. For instance, if he thought we were away from home too much, he'd perform his record trick. While we were out, Sparky would push an album out of the record rack and then tap the album cover in just such a way that the record would roll out. Then he would chomp the record! We'd return to find our favorite LP (somehow, always our current favorite) chewed into tiny bits of black vinyl scattered about the room. Another popular Sparky trick was the cat-sit. If the family was peacefully settled on the porch, not playing with him, Sparky would grab the family cat by the ear and drag her over to the steps, whereupon he would sit on top of her until someone paid attention to him. He never hurt the cat; he simply sat on her as one would sit on a fine cushion, with her head poking out under his tail, and a silly grin on his face that said, "See, if you'd play with me, I wouldn't get into such mischief."

You may also find that in some cases, one long, detailed example (called an *extended example*) is more useful than several shorter ones. If you were writing a paragraph urging the traffic department to install a stop sign at a particularly dangerous corner, you probably should cite numerous examples of accidents there. On the other hand, if you were praising a certain kind of local architecture, you might select one representative house and discuss it in detail. In the following paragraph, for instance, the writer might have supported his main point by citing a number of cases in which lives had been saved by seat belts; he chose instead to offer one detailed example, in the form of a personal experience:

> Wearing seat belts can protect people from injury, even in serious accidents. I know because seat belts saved me and my Dad two years ago when we were driving to see my grandparents who live in California. Because of the distance, we had to travel late on a rainy, foggy Saturday night. My Dad was driving, but what he didn't know was that there was a car a short way behind us driven by a drunk who was following our car's tail lights in order to keep himself on the road. About midnight, my Dad decided to check the map to make sure we were headed in the right direction, so he signaled, pulled over to the shoulder, and began to come to a stop. Unfortunately for us, the drunk didn't see the signal and moved his car over to the shoulder thinking that the main road must have curved slightly since our car had gone that way. As Dad slowed our car, the other car plowed into us at a speed estimated later by the police as over eighty miles an hour. The car hit us like Babe Ruth's bat hitting a slow pitch; the force of the speeding car slammed us hard into the dashboard, but not through the windshield and out onto the rocky shoulder, because, lucky for us, we were wearing our seat belts. The highway patrol, who arrived quickly on the scene, testified later at the other driver's trial that without question my Dad and I would have been seriously injured, if not killed, had it not been for our seat belts restraining us in the front seat.

The story of the accident illustrates the writer's claim that seat belts can save lives; without such an example, the writer's statement would be only an unsupported generalization.

In addition to making general statements specific and thus more convincing, good examples can explain and clarify unfamiliar, abstract, or difficult concepts for the reader. For instance, Newton's law of gravity might be more easily understood once it is explained through the simple, familiar example of an apple falling from a tree.

Moreover, clear examples can add to your prose vivid details that hold the reader's attention while you explain your points. A general statement decrying animal abuse, for instance, may be more effective accompanied by several examples detailing the brutal treatment of one particular laboratory's research animals.

The use of good examples is not, however, limited only to essays primarily developed by example. In reality, you will probably use examples in every essay you write. You couldn't, for instance, write an essay classifying kinds of popular movies without including examples to help identify your categories. Similarly, you couldn't write an essay defining the characteristics of a good teacher or comparing two kinds of cars without ample use of specific examples. To illustrate the importance of examples in all patterns of essay development, here are two excerpts from student essays reprinted in other parts of this textbook. The first excerpt comes from an essay classifying the Native American eras at Mesa Verde National Park (pages 249–252). In his discussion of a particular time period, the writer uses Balcony House pueblo as an example to illustrate the Native Americans' skills in building construction.

> The third period lasted until A.D. 1300 and saw the innovation of pueblos, or groups of dwellings, instead of single-family units. Nearly eight hundred dwellings

show the large number of people who inhabited the complex, tunneled houses, shops, storage rooms, courtyards, and community centers whose masonry walls, often elaborately decorated, were three and four stories high. At the spacious Balcony House pueblo, for example, an adobe court lies beneath another vaulted roof; on three sides stand two-story houses with balconies that lead from one room to the next. In back of the court is a spring, and along the front side is a low wall that kept the children from falling down the seven-hundred-foot cliff to the canyon floor below. Balcony House pueblo also contains two kivas, circular subterranean ceremonial chambers that show the importance of fellowship and religion to the people of this era.

Another student uses a personal example to help her support a point in her essay that contrasts a local food co-op to a big chain grocery store (pages 217–220). By using her friend's experience as an example, the writer shows the reader how a co-op may assist local producers in the community:

> Direct selling offers two advantages for producers: they get a better price for their wares than by selling them through a middleman, and at the same time they establish an independent reputation for their business, which can be immensely valuable to their success later on. In Fort Collins, for example, Luna tofu (bean curd) stands out as an excellent illustration of this kind of mutual support. Several years ago my friend Carol Jones began making tofu in small batches to sell to the co-op as a way to earn a part-time income as well as to contribute to the co-op. Her enterprise has now grown so well that last year her husband quit his job to go into business with her full time. She currently sells to distributors and independent stores from here to Denver; even Lane Grocer, who earlier would not consider selling her tofu even on a trial basis, is now thinking about changing its policy.

Learning to support, explain, or clarify your assertions by clear, thoughtful examples will help you develop virtually every piece of writing you are assigned, both in school and on the job. Development by example is the most widely used of all the expository strategies and by far the most important.

Developing Your Essay

An essay developed by example is one of the easiest to organize. In most cases, your first paragraph will present your thesis; each body paragraph will contain a topic sentence and as many effectively arranged examples as necessary to explain or support each major point; your last paragraph will conclude your essay in some appropriate way. Although the general organization is fairly simple, you should revise the examples in your rough draft by asking these questions:

Are all my examples relevant? Each specific example should support, clarify, or explain the general statement it illustrates; each example should provide readers with additional insight into the subject under discussion. Keep the purpose of your paragraphs in mind: don't wander off into an analysis of the causes of theft if you are only supposed to show examples of it on your campus. Keep your audience in mind, too: Which examples will provide the kinds of information that your particular readers need to understand your point?

Are my examples well chosen? To persuade your readers to accept your opinion, you should select those examples that are the strongest and most convincing. Let's say you were writing a research paper exposing a government agency's wastefulness. To illustrate your claim, you would select those cases that most obviously show gross or ridiculous expenditures rather than asking your readers to consider some unnecessary but minor expenses. And you would try to select cases that represent recent or current examples of wastefulness rather than discussing expenditures too dated to be persuasive. In other words, when you have a number of examples to choose from, evaluate them and then select the best ones to support your point.

Are there enough examples to make each point clear and persuasive? Put yourself in your reader's place: would you be convinced with three brief examples? Five? One extended example? Two? Use your own judgment, but be careful to support or explain your major points adequately. It's better to risk overexplaining than to leave your reader confused or unconvinced.

Problems to Avoid

By far, the most common weakness in essays developed by example is a lack of specific detail. Too often novice writers present a sufficient number of relevant, well-chosen examples, but the illustrations themselves are too general, vague, or brief to be helpful. Examples should be clear, specific, and adequately detailed so that the reader receives the full persuasive impact of each one. For instance, in an essay claiming that college football has become too violent, don't merely say, "Too many players were hurt last year." Such a statement only hints; it lacks enough development to be fully effective. Go into more detail by giving actual examples of jammed fingers, wrenched backs, fractured legs, crushed kneecaps, and broken dreams. Present these examples in specific, vivid language; once your readers begin to "see" that field covered with blood and bruised bodies, you'll have less trouble convincing them that your point of view is accurate. (For more help incorporating specific details into your paragraph development, review pages 59–64 in Chapter 3.)

The second biggest problem in example essays is the lack of coherence. The reader should never sense an interruption in the flow of thought from one example to the next in paragraphs containing more than one example. Each body paragraph of this kind should be more than a topic sentence and a choppy list of examples. You should first arrange the examples in an order that best explains the major point presented by your topic sentence; then carefully check to make sure each example is smoothly connected in thought to the statements preceding and following it. You can avoid a listing effect by using transitional devices where necessary to ensure easy movement from example to example and from point to point. A few common transitional words often found in essays of example include "for instance," "for example," "to illustrate," "another," and "in addition." (For a list of other transitional words and additional help on writing coherent paragraphs, review pages 68–73 and pages 76–77.)

■ ESSAY TOPICS

Use the following statements to help you discover and focus an essay topic of your own design. For additional ideas, turn to the "Suggestions for Writing" section following the professional essay (page 192).

1. Heroes today are merely media creations rather than truly admirable people.
2. First impressions are often the best/worst means of judging people.
3. Failure is a better teacher than success.
4. My fear of flying (or some other fear) prevents me from living a normal life.
5. The willingness to undertake adventure is a necessary part of a happy existence.
6. Everyone should see/flee this movie. (See Chapter 17 for help with this topic.)
7. Complaining can produce unforeseen results.
8. Travel can be the best medicine.
9. Consumers are often at the mercy of unscrupulous companies.
10. Visits to the doctor/dentist/veterinarian can prove more traumatic than the illness.
11. Failure to keep my mouth shut (or some other bad habit) leads me into trouble.
12. Participation in (a particular sport, club, hobby, event) teaches valuable lessons.
13. Modern technology can produce more inconvenience than convenience.
14. Job hunting today is a difficult process.
15. Moving frequently has its advantages (or disadvantages).
16. Good deeds can backfire (or make a wonderful difference).
17. Many required courses are/are not relevant to a student's education.
18. High schools do/do not adequately prepare students for college.
19. One important event can change the course of a life.

20. To persuade people to buy their products, advertisements often try to present well-selected examples of satisfied customers. (Consider, for instance, the "Got Milk?" ad that follows. What stated—and implied—claims are the white-mustached women intended to illustrate? Who are these women and for what reasons were they chosen for this particular ad? Is this a successful choice? To what audience is this ad most likely addressed? Would other examples of milk drinkers be more or less persuasive to that audience?)

A Topic Proposal for Your Essay

Selecting the right subject matter is important to every writer. To help you clarify your ideas and strengthen your commitment to your topic, here is a proposal sheet that asks you to describe some of your preliminary ideas about your subject before you begin drafting.

Although your ideas may change as you draft (they will almost certainly become more refined), thinking through your choice of topic now may help you avoid several false starts.

1. In a few words, identify the subject of your essay as you have narrowed and focused it for this assignment. Write a rough statement of your opinion or attitude toward this topic.

2. Why are you interested in this topic? Do you have a personal or professional connection to the subject? State at least one reason for your choice of topic.

3. Is this a significant topic of interest to others? Why? Who specifically might find it interesting, informative, or entertaining?

4. Describe in one or two sentences the primary effect you would like to have on your audience. After they read your essay, what do you want your audience to think, feel, or do? (In other words, what is your *purpose* in writing this essay?)

5. Writers use examples to explain and clarify their ideas. Briefly list two or three examples you might develop in your essay to support discussion of your chosen topic.

6. What difficulties, if any, might this topic present during your drafting? For example, do you know enough about this topic to illustrate it with specific rather than vague examples? Might the topic still be too broad or unfocused for this assignment? Revise your topic now or make notes for an appropriate plan of action to resolve any difficulties you foresee.

■ Sample Student Essay

Study the use of specific examples in the brief student essay that follows. If the writer were to revise this essay, where might he add more examples or details?

RIVER RAFTING TEACHES WORTHWHILE LESSONS

1   Sun-warmed water slaps you in the face, the blazing sun beats down on your shoulders, and canyon walls speed by as you race down rolling waves of water. No experience can equal that of river rafting. In addition to being fun and exciting, rafting has many educational advantages as well, especially for those involved in school-sponsored rafting trips. River trips teach students how to prevent some of the environmental destruction that concerns the park officials, and, in addition, river trips teach students to work together in a way few other experiences can.

Introduction: A description

Thesis

Essay map

Paragraphs in the Sample Student Essays are numbered for ease of discussion; do not number your own paragraphs.

2   The most important lesson a rafting trip teaches students is respect for the environment. When students are exposed to the outdoors, they can better learn to appreciate its beauty and feel the need to preserve it. For example, I went on a rafting trip three summers ago with the biology department at my high school. Our trip lasted seven days down the Green River through the isolated Desolation Canyon in Utah. After the first day of rafting, I found myself surrounded by steep canyon walls and saw virtually no evidence of human life. The starkly beautiful, unspoiled atmosphere soon became a major influence on us during the trip. By the second day I saw classmates, whom I had previously seen fill an entire room with candy wrappers and empty soda cans, voluntarily inspecting our campsite for trash. And when twenty-four high school students sacrifice washing their hair for the sake of a suds-less and thus healthier river, some new, better attitudes about the environment have definitely been established.

Topic sentence one: Trip teaches respect for environment

Two brief examples illustrating respect:
1. Cleaning up trash
2. Foregoing suds in river

3   In addition to the respect for nature a rafting trip encourages, it also teaches the importance of group cooperation. Since school-associated trips put students in command of the raft, the students find that in order to stay in control, each member must be reliable, be able to do his or her own part, and be alert to the actions of others. These skills are quickly learned when students see the consequences of noncooperation. Usually this occurs the first day, when the left side of the raft paddles in one direction, and the right the other way, and half the crew ends up seasick from going in circles. An even better illustration is another experience I had on my river trip. Because an upcoming rapid was usually not too rough, our instructor said a few of us could jump out and swim in it. Instead of deciding as a group who should go, though, five eager swimmers bailed out. This left me, our

Topic sentence two: Trip teaches cooperation

Two examples of the need for cooperation:

1. Difficulties in paddling raft

2. A near accident

angry instructor, and another student to steer the raft. As it turned out, the rapid was fairly rough, and we soon found ourselves heading straight for a huge hole (a hole is formed from swirling funnel-like currents and can pull a raft under). The combined effort of the three of us was not enough to get the raft completely clear of the hole, and the raft tipped up vertically on its side, spilling us into the river. Luckily, no one was hurt, and the raft did not topple over, but the near loss of our food rations for the next five days, not to mention the raft itself, was enough to make us all more willing to work as a group in the future.

4   Despite the obvious benefits rafting offers, the number of river permits issued to school groups continues to decline because of financial cutbacks. It is a shame that those in charge of these cutbacks do not realize that in addition to having fun and making discoveries about themselves, students are learning valuable lessons through rafting trips—lessons that may help preserve the rivers for future rafters.

Conclusion:
Importance
of lessons

Professional Essay*

■ So What's So Bad about Being So-So?

Lisa Wilson Strick

Lisa Wilson Strick is a freelance writer who publishes in a variety of magazines, frequently on the subjects of family and education. She is co-author of *Learning Disabilities, A to Z: A Parent's Complete Guide to Learning Disabilities from Preschool to Adulthood* (1997). This essay first appeared in *Woman's Day* in 1984.

1   The other afternoon I was playing the piano when my seven-year-old walked in. He stopped and listened awhile, then said: "Gee, Mom, you don't play that thing very well, do you?"

---

* To help you read this essay analytically, review pages 166–168.

2   No, I don't. I am a piano lesson dropout. The fine points of fingering totally escape me. I play everything at half-speed, with many errant notes. My performance would make any serious music student wince, but I don't care. I've enjoyed playing the piano badly for years.

3   I also enjoy singing badly and drawing badly. (I used to enjoy sewing badly, but I've been doing that so long that I finally got pretty good at it.) I'm not ashamed of my incompetence in these areas. I do one or two other things well and that should be enough for anybody. But it gets boring doing the same things over and over. Every now and then it's fun to try something new.

4   Unfortunately, doing things badly has gone out of style. It used to be a mark of class if a lady or a gentleman sang a little, painted a little, played the violin a little. You didn't have to be *good* at it; the point was to be fortunate enough to have the leisure time for such pursuits. But in today's competitive world we have to be "experts"—even in our hobbies. You can't tone up your body by pulling on your sneakers and slogging around the block a couple of times anymore. Why? Because you'll be laughed off the street by the "serious" runners—the ones who log twenty-plus miles a week in their headbands, sixty-dollar running suits and fancy shoes. The shoes are really a big deal. If you say you're thinking about taking up almost any sport, the first thing the aficionados will ask is what you plan to do about shoes. Leather or canvas? What type of soles? Which brand? This is not the time to mention that the gym shoes you wore in high school are still in pretty good shape. As far as sports enthusiasts are concerned, if you don't have the latest shoes you are hopelessly committed to mediocrity.

5   The runners aren't nearly so snobbish as the dance freaks, however. In case you didn't know, "going dancing" no longer means putting on a pretty dress and doing a few turns around the ballroom with your favorite man on Saturday night. "Dancing" means squeezing into tights and a leotard and leg warmers, then sweating through six hours of warm-ups and five hours of ballet and four hours of jazz classes. Every week. Never tell anyone that you "like to dance" unless this is the sort of activity you enjoy. (At least the costume isn't so costly, as dancers seem to be cultivating a riches-to-rags look lately.)

6   We used to do these things for fun or simply to relax. Now the competition you face in your hobbies is likely to be worse than anything you run into on the job. "Oh, you've taken up knitting," a friend recently said to me. "Let me show you the adorable cable-knit, popcorn-stitched cardigan with twelve tiny reindeer prancing across the yoke that I made for my daughter. I dyed the yarn myself." Now why did she have to go and do that? I was getting a kick out of watching my yellow stockinette muffler grow a couple of inches a week up till then. And all I wanted was something to keep my hands busy while I watched television anyway.

7   Have you noticed what this is doing to our children? "We don't want that dodo on our soccer team," I overheard a ten-year-old sneer the other day. "He doesn't know a goal kick from a head shot." As it happens, the boy was talking about my son, who did not—like some of his friends—start soccer instruction at age three (along with preschool diving, creative writing and Suzuki clarinet). I'm sorry, Son, I guess I blew it. In *my* day when we played softball on the corner lot, we expected to give a little instruction to the younger kids who didn't know how. It didn't matter if they were terrible; we weren't out to slaughter the other team. Sometimes we didn't even keep score. To

us, sports were just a way of having a *good time*. Of course we didn't have some of the nifty things kids have today—such as matching uniforms and professional coaches. All we had was a bunch of kids of various ages who enjoyed each other's company.

8   I don't think kids have as much fun as they used to. Competition keeps getting in the way. The daughter of a neighbor is a nervous wreck worrying about getting into the *best* gymnastics school. "I was a late starter," she told me, "and I only get to practice five or six hours a week, so my technique may not be up to their standards." The child is nine. She doesn't want to *be* a gymnast when she grows up; she wants to be a nurse. I asked what she likes to do for fun in her free time. She seemed to think it was an odd question. "Well, I don't actually *have* a lot of free time," she said. "I mean homework and gymnastics and flute lessons kind of eat it all up. I have flute lessons three times a week now, so I have a good shot at getting into the all-state orchestra."

9   Ambition, drive and the desire to excel are all admirable within limits, but I don't know where the limits are anymore. I know a woman who has always wanted to learn a foreign language. For years she has complained that she hasn't the time to study one. I've pointed out that an evening course in French or Italian would take only a couple of hours a week, but she keeps putting it off. I suspect that what she hasn't got the time for is to become completely fluent within the year—and that any lesser level of accomplishment would embarrass her. Instead she spends her evenings watching reruns on television and tidying up her closets—occupations at which no particular expertise is expected.

10   I know others who are avoiding activities they might enjoy because they lack the time or the energy to tackle them "seriously." It strikes me as so silly. We are talking about *recreation*. I have nothing against self-improvement. But when I hear a teenager muttering "practice makes perfect" as he grimly makes his four-hundred-and-twenty-seventh try at hooking the basketball into the net left-handed, I wonder if some of us aren't improving ourselves right into the loony bin.

11   I think it's time we put a stop to all this. For sanity's sake, each of us should vow to take up something new this week—and to make sure we never master it completely. Sing along with grand opera. Make peculiar-looking objects out of clay. I can tell you from experience that fallen soufflés still taste pretty good. The point is to enjoy being a beginner again; to rediscover the joy of creative fooling around. If you find it difficult, ask any two-year-old to teach you. Two-year-olds have a gift for tackling the impossible with zest; repeated failure hardly discourages them at all.

12   As for me, I'm getting a little out of shape so I'm looking into tennis. A lot of people I know enjoy it, and it doesn't look too hard. Given a couple of lessons I should be stumbling gracelessly around the court and playing badly in no time at all.

Questions on Content, Structure, and Style

1. Why does Strick begin her essay with the comment from her son and the list of activities she does badly?

2. What is Strick's thesis? Is it specifically stated or clearly implied?

3. What examples does Strick offer to illustrate her belief that we no longer take up hobbies for fun? Are there enough well-chosen examples to make her position clear?

4. What is the effect, according to Strick, of too much competition on kids? In what ways does she show this effect?

5. Does Strick use enough details in her examples to make them clear, vivid, and persuasive? Point out some of her details to support your answer.

6. What does Strick gain by using dialogue in some of her examples?

7. What solution to the problem does Strick offer? How does she clarify her suggestion?

8. Characterize the tone of Strick's essay. Is it appropriate for her purpose and for her intended audience? Why or why not?

9. Evaluate Strick's conclusion. Does it effectively wrap up the essay?

10. Do you agree or disagree with Strick? What examples could you offer to support your position?

Suggestions for Writing

Try using Lisa Strick's essay "So What's So Bad about Being So-So?" as a stepping-stone, moving from one or more of her ideas to a subject for your own essay. For instance, you might write an essay based on your personal experience that illustrates or challenges Strick's view that competition is taking all the fun out of recreation. Or perhaps Strick's advice urging her readers to undertake new activities might lead you to an essay about your best or worst "beginner" experience. Look through Strick's essay once more to find other springboard ideas for *your* writing.

Vocabulary*

errant (2)   mediocrity (4)   fluent (9)
incompetence (3)   excel (9)   zest (11)
aficionados (4)

■ A REVISION WORKSHEET

As you write your rough drafts, consult Chapter 5 for guidance through the revision process. In addition, here are a few questions to ask yourself as you revise your example essay:

1. Is the essay's thesis clear to the reader?

2. Do the topic sentences support the thesis?

3. Does each body paragraph contain examples that effectively illustrate the claim of the topic sentence rather than offering mere generalities?

4. Are there enough well-chosen examples to make each point clear and convincing?

---

* Numbers in parentheses following vocabulary words refer to paragraphs in the essay.

5. Is each example developed in enough specific detail? Where could more details be added? More precise language?

6. If a paragraph contains multiple examples, are they arranged in the most effective order, with a smooth transition from one to another?

7. If a paragraph contains an extended example, does the discussion flow logically and with coherence?

After you've revised your essay extensively, you might exchange rough drafts with a classmate and answer these questions for each other, making specific suggestions for improvement wherever appropriate. (For advice on productive participation in classroom workshops, see pages 106–109.)

Reviewing Your Progress

After you have completed your essay developed by examples, take a moment to measure your progress as a writer by responding to the following questions. Such analysis will help you recognize growth in your writing skills and may enable you to identify areas that are still problematic.

1. What is the best feature of your essay? Why?

2. After considering your essay's supporting examples, which one do you think most effectively explains or illustrates your ideas? Why?

3. What part of your essay gave you the most trouble? How did you overcome the problem?

4. If you had more time to work on this essay, what would receive additional attention? Why?

5. What did you learn about your topic from writing this essay? About yourself as a writer?

■ Strategy Two: Development by Process Analysis

Process analysis identifies and explains what steps must be taken to complete an operation or procedure. There are two kinds of process analysis essays: directional and informative.

A *directional process* tells the reader how to do or make something. In simple words, it gives directions. You are more familiar with directional process than you might think; when you open a telephone book, for example, you see the pages in the front explaining how to make a three-way long-distance call. When you tell friends how to find your house, you're asking them to follow a directional process. If you use a computer, you can learn how to transfer files or download attachments or any one of hundreds of other options by following step-by-step directions often found on a "Help" menu. The most widely read books in American libraries fall into the how-to-do-it (or how-to-fix-it) category: how to wire a house, how to repair a car, how to play winning poker, how to become a millionaire overnight, and so forth. And almost every home contains at least one cookbook full of recipes providing directions for preparing various dishes. (Even Part One of this text is, in detailed fashion, a directional process telling how to write a short essay, beginning with the selection of a topic and concluding with advice on revision.)

An *informative process* tells the reader how something is or was made or done or how something works. Informative process differs from directional process in that it is not designed primarily to tell people how to do it; instead, it describes the steps by which someone other than the reader does or makes something (or how something was made or done in the past). For example, an informative process essay might describe how scientists discovered polio vaccine, how a bill passes through Congress, how chewing gum is made, how roller blades were invented, or how an engine propels a jet. In other words, this type of essay gives information on processes that are not intended to be—or cannot be—duplicated by the individual reader.

Developing Your Essay

Of all the expository essays, students usually agree that the process paper is the easiest to organize, mainly because it is presented in simple, chronological steps. To prepare a well-written process essay, however, you should remember the following advice:

Select an appropriate subject. First, make sure you know your subject thoroughly; one fuzzy step could wreck your entire process. Second, choose a process that is simple and short enough to describe in detail. In a 500-to-800-word essay, for instance, it's better to describe how to build a ship in a bottle than how to construct a life-size replica of Noah's Ark. On the other hand, don't choose a process so simpleminded, mundane, or mechanical that it insults your readers' intelligence or bores them silly. (Some years ago at a large state university, students were asked to write a process essay on "How to Sharpen a Pencil"; with the assignment of such stirring, creative topics, it's a wonder that particular English department produced any majors at all that year.)

Describe any necessary equipment and define special terms. In some process essays, you will need to indicate what equipment, ingredients, or tools are required. Such information is often provided in a paragraph following the thesis, before the process itself is described; in other cases, the explanation of proper equipment is presented as the need arises in each step of the process. As the writer, you must decide which method is best for your subject. The same is true for any terms that need defining. Don't lose your reader by using terms only you, the specialist, can comprehend. Always remember that you're trying to tell people about a process they don't understand.

State your steps in a logical, chronological order. Obviously, if someone wanted to know how to bake bread, you wouldn't begin with "Put the prepared dough in the oven." Start at the beginning and carefully follow through, step by step, until the process is completed. Don't omit any steps or directions, no matter how seemingly insignificant. Without complete instructions, for example, the would-be baker might end up with a gob of dough rather than a loaf of bread—simply because the directions didn't say to heat the oven to a certain temperature.

Explain each step clearly, sufficiently, and accurately. If you've ever tried to assemble a child's toy or a piece of furniture, you probably already know how frustrating—and infuriating—it is to work from vague, inadequate directions. Save your readers from tears and tantrums by describing each step in your process as clearly as possible. Use enough specific details to distinguish one step from another. As the readers finish each step, they should know how the subject matter is supposed to look, feel, smell, taste, or sound at that stage of the process. You might also explain why each step is necessary ("Cutting back the young avocado stem is necessary to prevent a spindly plant"; "Senator Snort then had to win over the chair of the Arms Committee to be sure his bill would go to the Senate floor for a vote"). In some cases, especially in directional processes, it's helpful to give warnings ("When you begin tightrope walking, the condition of your shoes is critical; be careful the soles are not slick") or descriptions of errors and how to rectify them ("If you pass a white church, you've gone a block too far, so turn right at the church and circle back on Candle Lane"; "If the sauce appears gray and thin, add one teaspoon more of cornstarch until the gravy is white and bubbly").

Organize your steps effectively. If you have a few big steps in your process, you probably will devote a paragraph to each one. On the other hand, if you have several small steps, you should organize them into a few manageable units. For example, in the essay "How to Prepare Fresh Fish," the list of small steps on the left has been grouped into three larger units, each of which becomes a body paragraph:

1. scaling	I. Cleaning
2. beheading	A. scaling
3. gutting	B. beheading
4. washing	C. gutting
5. seasoning	II. Cooking
6. breading	A. washing
7. frying	B. seasoning
8. draining	C. breading
9. portioning	D. frying
10. garnishing	III. Serving
	A. draining
	B. portioning
	C. garnishing

In addition, don't forget to use enough transitional devices between steps to avoid the effect of a mechanical list. Some frequently used linking words in process essays include the following:

next	first, second, third, etc.
then	at this point
now	following
to begin	when
finally	at last
before	afterward

Vary your transitional words sufficiently so that your steps are not linked by a monotonous repetition of "and then" or "next."

Problems to Avoid

Don't forget to include a thesis. You already know, of course, that every essay needs a thesis, but the advice bears repeating here because for some reason some writers often omit the statement in their process essays. Your thesis might be (1) your reason for presenting this process—why you feel it's important or necessary for the readers to know it ("Because rescue squads often arrive too late, every adult should know how to administer CPR to accident victims") or (2) an assertion about the nature of the process itself ("Needlepoint is a simple, restful, fun hobby for both men and women"). Here are some other subjects and sample theses:

- Donating blood is not the painful process one might suspect.
- The raid on Pearl Harbor wasn't altogether unexpected.
- Returning to school as an older-than-average student isn't as difficult as it may look.
- Sponsoring a five-mile run can be a fun way for your club or student organization to raise money for local charities.
- Challenging a speeding ticket is a time-consuming, energy-draining, but financially rewarding endeavor.
- The series of public protests that led to the return of the traditional Coca-Cola was an unparalleled success in the history of American consumerism.

Presenting a thesis and referring to it appropriately gives your essay unity and coherence, as well as ensuring against a monotonous list of steps.

Pay special attention to your conclusion. Don't allow your essay to grind to an abrupt halt after the final step. You might conclude the essay by telling the significance of the completed process or by explaining other uses it may have. Or, if it is appropriate, finish your essay with an amusing story or emphatic comment. However you conclude, leave the reader with a feeling of satisfaction, with a sense of having completed an interesting procedure. (For more information on writing good conclusions, see pages 82–85.)

■ ESSAY TOPICS

Here are suggested topics for both directional and informative process essays. Some of the topics may be used in humorous essays, such as "How to Flunk a Test," "How to Remain a Bench Warmer," or "How to Say Nothing in Eight Hundred Words." For additional ideas, turn to the "Suggestions for Writing" sections following the professional essays (page 207 and page 210).

1. How you arrived at a major decision or solved an important problem
2. How to survive some aspect of a first year at college
3. How to begin a collection or hobby or acquire a skill
4. How to buy a computer, CD player, camera, or other recreational product
5. How a popular product or fad originated or grew

6. How to manage stress, stagefright, homesickness, or an irrational fear

7. How something in nature works or was formed

8. How a company makes or sells a product

9. How a piece of equipment or a machine works

10. How to cure a cold, the hiccups, insomnia, or some other common ailment

11. How to get in shape/develop physical fitness

12. How to stop smoking (or break some other bad habit)

13. How to select a car (new or used), house, apartment, roommate

14. How to earn money quickly or easily (and legally)

15. How a famous invention or discovery occurred

16. How to lodge a complaint and win

17. How to succeed or fail in a job interview (or in some other important endeavor)

18. How to build or repair some small item

19. How to plan the perfect party, wedding, holiday, birthday, or some other celebration

20. How a historical event occurred or an important law was passed (e.g., Rosa Parks's arrest, Civil Rights Act of 1964, Title IX)

Rosa Parks, whose refusal to give up her bus seat in Montgomery, Alabama, helped ignite the Civil Rights Movement

A Topic Proposal for Your Essay

Selecting the right subject matter is important to every writer. To help you clarify your ideas and strengthen your commitment to your topic, here is a proposal sheet that asks you to describe some of your preliminary ideas about your subject before you begin drafting. Although your ideas may change as you write (they will almost certainly become more refined), thinking through your choice of topic now may help you avoid several false starts.

1. What process will you explain in your essay? Is it a directional or an informative process? Can you address the complexity of this process in a short essay?

2. Why did you select this topic? Are you personally or professionally interested in this process? Cite at least one reason for your choice.

3. Why do you think this topic would be of interest to others? Who might find it especially informative or enjoyable?

4. Describe in one or two sentences the ideal response from your readers. What would you like them to do or know after reading about your topic?

5. List at least three of the larger steps or stages in the process.

6. What difficulties might this topic present during your drafting? Will this topic require any additional research on your part?

■ Sample Student Essay

The following essay is a directional process telling readers how to run a successful garage sale. To make the instructions clear and enjoyable, the writer described seven steps and offered many specific examples, details, and warnings.

CATCHING GARAGE SALE FEVER

Introduction: A series of questions to hook the reader

1   Ever need some easy money fast? To repay those incredible overdue library fines you ran up writing your last research paper? Or to raise money for that much-needed vacation to Mexico you put on credit cards last Spring Break? Or maybe you feel you simply have to clear out some junk before the piles block the remaining sunlight from your windows? Whether the problem is cash flow or trash flow, you can solve it easily by holding what is fast becoming an all-American sport: the weekend garage sale. As a veteran of some half-dozen

successful ventures, I can testify that garage sales are the easiest way to make quick money, with a minimum of physical labor and the maximum of fun.

Thesis

2   Most garage sale "experts" start getting ready at least two weeks before the sale by taking inventory. Look through your closets and junk drawers to see if you actually have enough items to make a sale worthwhile. If all you have is a mass of miscellaneous small items, think about waiting or joining a friend's sale, because you do need at least a couple of larger items (furniture is always a big seller) to draw customers initially. Also, consider whether the season is appropriate for your items: sun dresses and shorts, for example, sell better in the spring and summer; coats and boots in the fall. As you collect your items, don't underestimate the "saleability" of some of your junk—the hideous purple china bulldog Aunt Clara gave you for Christmas five years ago may be perfect for someone's Ugly Mutt Collection.

Step one: Taking inventory

3   As you sort through your closets, begin thinking about the time and place of your sale. First, decide if you want a one- or two-day sale. If you opt for only one day, Saturdays are generally best because most people are free that day. Plan to start early—by 8 A.M. if possible— because the experienced buyers get up and get going so they can hit more sales that way. Unless you have nothing else to do that day, plan to end your sale by mid-afternoon; most people have run out of buying energy (or money) by 3 P.M. Deciding on the location of your sale depends, of course, on your housing situation, but you still might need to make some choices. For instance, do you want to put your items out in a driveway, a front yard, or actually in the garage (weather might affect this decision)? Or perhaps a side yard gets more passers-by? Wherever you decide, be sure that there are plenty

Step two: Deciding when and where

of places for customers to park close by without blocking your neighbors' driveways.

Step three: 4 Unless you live in a very small town or on a very busy street,
Advertising you'll probably want to place an inexpensive ad in the "garage sale"
the sale column of your local newspaper, scheduled to run a day or two before, and the day of, your sale. Your ad should tell the times and place of the sale (give brief directions or mention landmarks if the location is hard to find) as well as a short list of some of your items. Few people will turn out for "household goods" alone; some popular items include bookcases, antiques, books, fans, jewelry, toys, baby equipment, and name-brand clothes. One other piece of advice
A warning about the ad copy: it should include the phrase "no early sales" unless you want to be awakened at 6:30 A.M., as I was one Saturday, by a bunch of semi-pro garage sale buyers milling restlessly around in your yard, looking like zombies out of a George Romero horror movie. In addition to your newspaper ad, you may also wish to put up posters in places frequented by lots of people; laundromats and grocery stores often have bulletin boards for such announcements.
Another warning You can also put up signs on nearby well-traveled streets, but one warning: in some towns it's illegal to post anything on utility poles or traffic signs, so be sure to check your local ordinances first.

Step four: 5 Tagging your items with their prices is the least fun, and it can
Pricing the take a day or a week depending on how many items you have and
merchandise how much time each day you can devote to the project. You can buy sheets of little white stickers or use pieces of masking tape to stick on the prices, but if you want to save time, consider grouping some items and selling them all for the same price—all shirts, for example, are 50¢. Be realistic about your prices; the handcrafted rug from Greece may have been expensive and important to you, but to

others, it's a worn doormat. Some experts suggest pricing your articles at about one-fourth their original value, unless you have special reasons not to (an antique or a popular collectors' item, for instance, may be more valuable now than when you bought it). Remember that you can always come down on your prices if someone is interested in a particular item.

6   By the day before your sale you should have all your items clean and tagged. One of the beauties of a garage sale is that there's very little equipment to collect. You'll need tables, benches, or boards supported by bricks to display your goods; a rope tied from side to side of your garage can double as a clothes rack. Try to spread out your merchandise rather than dumping articles in deep boxes; customers don't want to feel like they're rummaging through a trash barrel. Most important, you'll need a chair and a table to hold some sort of money box, preferably one with a lock. The afternoon before the sale, take a trip to the bank if you need to, to make sure you have enough one-dollar bills and coins to make plenty of change. The evening before the sale, set up your items on your display benches in the garage or indoors near the site of your sale so that you can quickly set things out in the morning. Get a good night's sleep so you can get up to open on time: the early bird does get the sales in this business.

Step five: Setting up your sale

A note on equipment

7   The sale itself is, of course, the real fun. Half the enjoyment is haggling with the customers, so be prepared to joke and visit with the shoppers. Watching the different kinds of people who show up is also a kick—you can get a cross section from college students on a tight budget to harried mothers toting four kids to real eccentrics in fancy cars who will argue about the price of a 75¢ item (if you're a creative writer, don't forget to take notes for your next novel). If the

Step six: Running the sale

action slows in the afternoon, you can resort to a half-price or two-for-one sale by posting a large sign to that effect; many shoppers can't resist a sale at a sale!

Step seven: 8 Closing up

8   By late afternoon you should be richer and junk-free, at least to some extent. If you do have items left after the half-price sale, decide whether you want to box them up for the next sale or drop them by a charitable organization such as Goodwill (some organizations will even pick up your donations; others have convenient drop boxes). After you've taken your articles inside, don't forget to take down any signs you've posted in the neighborhood; old, withered garage sale signs fluttering in the breeze are an eyesore. Last, sit down and count your profits, so you can go out in the evening to celebrate a successful business venture.

Conclusion: A summary of the benefits and a humorous warning

9   The money you make is, of course, the biggest incentive for having one or two sales a year. But the combination of money, clean closets, and memories of the characters you met can be irresistible. Garage sales can rapidly get in your blood; once you hold a successful one, you're tempted to have another as soon as the junk starts to mount up. And having sales somehow leads to attending them too, as it becomes fun to see what other folks are selling at bargain prices. So be forewarned: you too can be transformed into a garage sale junkie, traveling with a now-popular car bumper sticker that proudly proclaims to the world: "Caution! I brake for garage sales"!

■ Professional Essays*

Because there are two kinds of process essays, informative and directional, this section presents two professional essays to illustrate each type.

---

* To help you read these essays analytically, review pages 166–168.

I. The Informative Process Essay

■ To Bid the World Farewell

Jessica Mitford

As an investigative reporter, Jessica Mitford wrote many articles and books, including *Kind and Unusual Punishment: The Prison Business* (1973), *A Fine Old Conflict* (1977), *Poison Penmanship* (1979), and *The American Way of Birth* (1979). This essay is from her best-selling book *The American Way of Death* (1963), which scrutinizes the funeral industry.

1   Embalming is indeed a most extraordinary procedure, and one must wonder at the docility of Americans who each year pay hundreds of millions of dollars for its perpetuation, blissfully ignorant of what it is all about, what is done, how it is done. Not one in ten thousand has any idea of what actually takes place. Books on the subject are extremely hard to come by. They are not to be found in most libraries or bookshops.

2   In an era when huge television audiences watch surgical operations in the comfort of their living rooms, when, thanks to the animated cartoon, the geography of the digestive system has become familiar territory even to the nursery school set, and in a land where the satisfaction of curiosity about almost all matters is a national pastime, the secrecy surrounding embalming can, surely, hardly be attributed to the inherent gruesomeness of the subject. Custom in this regard has within this century suffered a complete reversal. In the early days of American embalming, when it was performed in the home of the deceased, it was almost mandatory for some relative to stay by the embalmer's side and witness the procedure. Today, family members who might wish to be in attendance would certainly be dissuaded by the funeral director. All others, except apprentices, are excluded by law from the preparation room.

3   A close look at what does actually take place may explain in large measure the undertaker's intractable reticence concerning a procedure that has become his major *raison d'être*. Is it possible he fears that public information about embalming might lead patrons to wonder if they really want this service? If the funeral men are loath to discuss the subject outside the trade, the reader may, understandably, be equally loath to go on reading at this point. For those who have the stomach for it, let us part the formaldehyde curtain. . . .

4   The body is first laid out in the undertaker's morgue—or rather, Mr. Jones is reposing in the preparation room—to be readied to bid the world farewell.

5   The preparation room in any of the better funeral establishments has the tiled and sterile look of a surgery, and indeed the embalmer-restorative artist who does his chores there is beginning to adopt the term "dermasurgeon" (appropriately corrupted by some mortician-writers as "demisurgeon") to describe his calling. His equipment, consisting of scalpels, scissors, augers, forceps, clamps, needles, pumps, tubes, bowls and basins, is crudely imitative of the surgeon's as is his technique, acquired in a nine- or twelve-month post-high-school course in an embalming school. He is supplied by an advanced chemical industry with a bewildering array of fluids, sprays, pastes, oils, powders, creams, to fix or soften tissue, shrink or distend it as needed, dry it here, restore the moisture there. There are cosmetics, waxes and

paints to fill and cover features, even plaster of Paris to replace entire limbs. There are ingenious aids to prop and stabilize the cadaver: a Vari-Pose Head Rest, the Edwards Arm and Hand Positioner, the Repose Block (to support the shoulders during the embalming), and the Throop Foot Positioner, which resembles an old-fashioned stocks.

6   Mr. John H. Eckels, president of the Eckels College of Mortuary Science, thus describes the first part of the embalming procedure: "In the hands of a skilled practitioner, this work may be done in a comparatively short time and without mutilating the body other than by slight incision—so slight that it scarcely would cause serious inconvenience if made upon a living person. It is necessary to remove the blood, and doing this not only helps in the disinfecting, but removes the principal cause of disfigurement due to discoloration."

7   Another textbook discusses the all-important time element: "The earlier this is done, the better, for every hour that elapses between death and embalming will add to the problems and complications encountered. . . ." Just how soon should one get going on the embalming? The author tells us, "On the basis of such scanty information made available to this profession through its rudimentary and haphazard system of technical research, we must conclude that the best results are to be obtained if the subject is embalmed before life is completely extinct—that is, before cellular death has occurred. In the average case, this would mean within an hour after somatic death." For those who feel that there is something a little rudimentary, not to say haphazard, about this advice, a comforting thought is offered by another writer. Speaking of fears entertained in early days of premature burial, he points out, "One of the effects of embalming by chemical injection, however, has been to dispel fears of live burial." How true; once the blood is removed, chances of live burial are indeed remote.

8   To return to Mr. Jones, the blood is drained out through the veins and replaced by embalming fluid pumped in through the arteries. As noted in *The Principles and Practices of Embalming*, "every operator has a favorite injection and drainage point—a fact which becomes a handicap only if he fails or refuses to forsake his favorites when conditions demand it." Typical favorites are the carotid artery, femoral artery, jugular vein, subclavian vein. There are various choices of embalming fluid. If Flextone is used, it will produce a "mild flexible rigidity. The skin retains a velvety softness, the tissues are rubbery and pliable. Ideal for women and children." It may be blended with B. and G. Products Company's Lyf-Lyk tint, which is guaranteed to reproduce "nature's own skin texture . . . the velvety appearance of living tissue." Suntone comes in three separate tints: Suntan; Special Cosmetic Tint, a pink shade "especially indicated for young female subjects"; and Regular Cosmetic Tint, moderately pink.

9   About three to six gallons of a dyed and perfumed solution of formaldehyde, glycerin, borax, phenol, alcohol and water is soon circulating through Mr. Jones, whose mouth has been sewn together with a "needle directed upward between the upper lip and gum and brought out through the left nostril," with the corners raised slightly "for a more pleasant expression." If he should be bucktoothed, his teeth are cleaned with Bon Ami and coated with colorless nail polish. His eyes, meanwhile, are closed with flesh-tinted eye caps and eye cement.

10   The next step is to have at Mr. Jones with a thing called a trocar. This is a long, hollow needle attached to a tube. It is jabbed into the abdomen, poked around the entrails and chest cavity, the contents of which are pumped out and replaced with

"cavity fluid." This done, and the hole in the abdomen sewn up, Mr. Jones' face is heavily creamed (to protect the skin from burns which may be caused by leakage of the chemicals), and he is covered with a sheet and left unmolested for a while. But not for long—there is more, much more, in store for him. He has been embalmed, but not yet restored, and the best time to start the restorative work is eight to ten hours after embalming, when the tissues have become firm and dry.

11   The object of all this attention to the corpse, it must be remembered, is to make it presentable for viewing in an attitude of healthy repose. "Our customs require the presentation of our dead in the semblance of normality . . . unmarred by the ravages of illness, disease or mutilation," says Mr. J. Sheridan Mayer in his *Restorative Art.* This is rather a large order since few people die in the full bloom of health, unravaged by illness and unmarked by some disfigurement. The funeral industry is equal to the challenge: "In some cases the gruesome appearance of a mutilated or disease-ridden subject may be quite discouraging. The task of restoration may seem impossible and shake the confidence of the embalmer. This is the time for intestinal fortitude and determination. Once the formative work is begun and affected tissues are cleaned or removed, all doubts of success vanish. It is surprising and gratifying to discover the results which may be obtained."

12   The embalmer, having allowed an appropriate interval to elapse, returns to the attack, but now he brings into play the skill and equipment of sculptor and cosmetician. Is a hand missing? Casting one in plaster of Paris is a simple matter. "For replacement purposes, only a cast of the back of the hand is necessary; this is within the ability of the average operator and is quite adequate." If a lip or two, a nose or an ear should be missing, the embalmer has at hand a variety of restorative waxes with which to model replacements. Pores and skin texture are simulated by stippling with a little brush, and over this cosmetics are laid on. Head off? Decapitation cases are rather routinely handled. Ragged edges are trimmed, and head joined to torso with a series of splints, wires and sutures. It is a good idea to have a little something at the neck— a scarf or high collar—when time for viewing comes. Swollen mouth? Cut out tissue as needed from inside the lips. If too much is removed, the surface contour can easily be restored by padding with cotton. Swollen necks and cheeks are reduced by removing tissue through vertical incisions made down each side of the neck. "When the deceased is casketed, the pillow will hide the suture incisions . . . as an extra precaution against leakage, the suture may be painted with liquid sealer."

13   The opposite condition is more likely to present itself—that of emaciation. His hypodermic syringe now loaded with massage cream, the embalmer seeks out and fills the hollowed and sunken areas by injection. In this procedure the backs of the hands and fingers and the under-chin area should not be neglected.

14   Positioning the lips is a problem that recurrently challenges the ingenuity of the embalmer. Closed too tightly, they tend to give a stern, even disapproving expression. Ideally, embalmers feel, the lips should give the impression of being ever so slightly parted, the upper lip protruding slightly for a more youthful appearance. This takes some engineering, however, as the lips tend to drift apart. Lip drift can sometimes be remedied by pushing one or two straight pins through the inner margin of the lower lip and then inserting them between the two front teeth. If Mr. Jones happens to have no teeth, the pins can just as easily be anchored in his Armstrong Face Former and

Denture Replacer. Another method to maintain lip closure is to dislocate the lower jaw, which is then held in its new position by a wire run through holes which have been drilled through the upper and lower jaws at the midline. As the French are fond of saying, *il faut souffrir pour être belle.**

15   If Mr. Jones has died of jaundice, the embalming fluid will very likely turn him green. Does this deter the embalmer? Not if he has intestinal fortitude. Masking pastes and cosmetics are heavily laid on, burial garments and casket interiors are color-correlated with particular care, and Jones is displayed beneath rose-colored lights. Friends will say, "How *well* he looks." Death by carbon monoxide, on the other hand, can be rather a good thing from the embalmer's viewpoint: "One advantage is the fact that this type of discoloration is an exaggerated form of a natural pink coloration." This is nice because the healthy glow is already present and needs but little attention.

16   The patching and filling completed, Mr. Jones is now shaved, washed and dressed. Cream-based cosmetic, available in pink, flesh, suntan, brunette and blond, is applied to his hands and face, his hair is shampooed and combed (and, in the case of Mrs. Jones, set), his hands manicured. For the horny-handed son of toil special care must be taken; cream should be applied to remove ingrained grime, and the nails cleaned. "If he were not in the habit of having them manicured in life, trimming and shaping is advised for better appearance—never questioned by kin."

17   Jones is now ready for casketing (this is the present participle of the verb "to casket"). In this operation his right shoulder should be depressed slightly "to turn the body a bit to the right and soften the appearance of lying flat on the back." Positioning the hands is a matter of importance, and special rubber positioning blocks may be used. The hands should be cupped slightly for a more lifelike, relaxed appearance. Proper placement of the body requires a delicate sense of balance. It should lie as high as possible in the casket, yet not so high that the lid, when lowered, will hit the nose. On the other hand, we are cautioned, placing the body too low "creates the impression that the body is in a box."

18   Jones is next wheeled into the appointed slumber room where a few last touches may be added—his favorite pipe placed in his hand or, if he was a great reader, a book propped into position. (In the case of little Master Jones a Teddy bear may be clutched.) Here he will hold open house for a few days, visiting hours 10 A.M. to 9 P.M.

Questions on Content, Structure, and Style

1. By studying the first three paragraphs, summarize both Mitford's reason for explaining the embalming process and her attitude toward undertakers who wish to keep their patrons uninformed about this procedure.

2. Does Mitford use enough specific details to help you visualize each step as it occurs? Point out examples of details that create vivid descriptions by appealing to your sense of sight, smell, or touch.

3. How does the technique of using the hypothetical "Mr. Jones" make the explanation of the process more effective? Why didn't Mitford simply refer to "the corpse" or "a body" throughout her essay?

---

* "One must suffer to be beautiful."

4. What is Mitford's general attitude toward this procedure? The overall tone of the essay? Study Mitford's choice of words and then identify the tone in each of the following passages:

> "The next step is to have at Mr. Jones with a thing called a trocar." (10)*

> "The embalmer, having allowed an appropriate interval to elapse, returns to the attack. . . ." (12)

> "Friends will say, 'How *well* he looks.'" (15)

> "On the other hand, we are cautioned, placing the body too low 'creates the impression that the body is in a box.'" (17)

> "Here he will hold open house for a few days, visiting hours 10 A.M. to 9 P.M." (18)

What other words and passages reveal Mitford's attitude and tone?

5. Why does Mitford repeatedly quote various undertakers and textbooks on the embalming and restorative process ("'needle directed upward between the upper lip and gum and brought out through the left nostril'")? Why is the quotation in paragraph 7 that begins "'On the basis of such scanty information made available to this profession through its rudimentary and haphazard system of technical research'" particularly effective in emphasizing Mitford's attitude toward the funeral industry?

6. What does Mitford gain by quoting euphemisms used by the funeral business, such as "dermasurgeon," "Repose Block," and "slumber room"?

7. What are the connotations of the words "poked," "jabbed," and "left unmolested" in paragraph 10? What effect is Mitford trying to produce with the series of questions (such as "Head off?") in paragraph 12?

8. Does this process flow smoothly from step to step? Identify several transitional devices connecting the paragraphs.

9. Evaluate Mitford's last sentence. Does it successfully sum up the author's attitude and conclude the essay?

10. By supplying information about the embalming process, did Mitford change your attitude toward this procedure or toward the funeral industry? Are there advantages Mitford fails to mention?

Suggestions for Writing

Try using Jessica Mitford's "To Bid the World Farewell" as a stepping-stone to your own writing. Mitford's graphic details and disparaging tone upset some readers who feel funerals are important for the living. If you agree, consider writing an essay that challenges Mitford's position. Or adopt Mitford's role as an investigative reporter exposing a controversial process. For example, how is toxic waste disposed of at the student health center? What happens to unclaimed animals at your local shelter? Or try a more lighthearted investigation: just how do they obtain that mystery meat served in the dorm cafeteria? Use Mitford's vivid essay as a guide as you present your discoveries.

---

* Numbers in parentheses following quoted material and vocabulary words refer to paragraphs in the essay.

Vocabulary

docility (1)	*raison d'être* (3)	pliable (8)
perpetuation (1)	ingenious (5)	semblance (11)
inherent (2)	cadaver (5)	ravages (11)
mandatory (2)	somatic (7)	stippling (12)
intractable (3)	rudimentary (7)	emaciation (13)
reticence (3)	dispel (7)	

II. The Directional Process Essay

■ Ditch Diving

Tom Bodett

Tom Bodett has been a logger, sailor, builder, radio show host, and the voice of popular commercials. Known for his humorous appearances on National Public Radio, Bodett has also published several collections of essays, including *As Far As You Can Go Without a Passport* (1985), *The End of the Road* (1989), *The Big Garage on Clear Shot* (1990), and *Small Comforts* (1987), from which this essay was taken. He hosted the PBS series *America's Historic Trails, with Tom Bodett*, and his latest books are *Williwaw!* (1999) and *Norman Tuttle on the Last Frontier* (2004), novels for young readers.

1   The graceful winter sports of skiing, skating, and dog-sledding get a lot of attention around Alaska,* but there's another winter activity that nobody seems to appreciate for the art that it actually is—ditch diving. We all become practitioners of this art at one time or another, but none of us seem to hold proper appreciation of what we're doing, perhaps because its aesthetics have never been fully defined for us. Allow me.

2   To dive you need a road, a ditch, some snow on the ground, and any licensed highway vehicle or its equivalent. Nothing else is required, but a good freezing rain will speed up the process.

3   The art of the dive is in the elegance with which you perform three distinct actions. The first one, of course, is that you and your car *leave the roadway*. Not so fast there, hotshot—remember, this is an art. The manner and theme of your dive are weighed heavily in this maneuver.

4   For instance, the "I wasn't looking and drove into the ditch" dive will gain you nothing with the critics. The "He wasn't looking and drove me into the ditch" dive is slightly better, but lacks character. The "It sucked me into the ditch" dive shows real imagination, and the "We spun around three times, hit the ditch going backwards, and thought we were all going to die" dive will earn you credits for sheer drama. The "I drove in the ditch rather than slide past the school bus" dive might win the humanitarian award, but only if you can explain to the police why you were going that fast in the first place.

5   Okay, so now you've left the road. Your second challenge is to *place the vehicle*. Any dumbbell can put a car in a ditch, but it takes an artist to put one there with panache. The overall appeal of you installation is gauged by how much the traffic slows down to gawk at it.

---

* Bodett has lived in Alaska and the Pacific Northwest for over twenty years.

6   Nosed-in within ten degrees of level won't even turn a head. Burrowed into a snowbank with one door buried shut is better, and if you're actually caught in the act of climbing out a window, you're really getting somewhere. Letting your car sit overnight so the snowplows can bury it is a good way of gaining points with the morning commuter traffic. Any wheel left visibly off the ground is good for fifty points each, with a hundred-point bonus for all four. Caution: Only master-class ditch divers should endeavor to achieve this bonus positioning.

7   All right, there you are, nicely featured alongside your favorite roadway. The third part of your mission is to *ask for assistance*. Simply walking to a phone and calling a tow truck will prove you a piker and not an artist at all. Hit the showers, friend. The grace and creativity you display getting back on the road must at least equal those you employed while leaving it.

8   Let's say you were forced into the ditch and are neatly enshrined with one rear wheel off the ground and the hood buried in the berm. Wait until any truck bigger than your bathroom happens along and start walking in that direction with a pronounced limp. Look angry but not defeated, as if you'd walk all night to find the guy who ran you off the road. Look the driver in the eye like it would have been him if he'd been there sooner. This is a risky move, but it's been proven effective. If the truck has personalized license plates and lights mounted all over it, you're in good shape. Those guys love to show how hard their trucks can pull on things.

9   I prefer, however, to rely on the softer side of human nature. Addle-brained people hold a special place in our hearts, and I like to play on these protective instincts. If my car is buried beyond hope, I'll display my tongue in the corner of my mouth and begin frantically digging at the snow drift with my hands until someone stops to talk me out of it. If my hands get cold and still nobody's stopped, I'll crawl head-first into the hole I've dug and flail my legs around like I was thrown clear of the wreck. This works every time and has won me many a ditch-diving exhibition over the years.

10   I certainly hope I've enlarged your appreciation of this undervalued creative medium. I warn against exercising this art to excess, but when the opportunity arises, remember: Hit 'er hard, sink 'er deep, get 'er out, and please, dive carefully.

Questions on Content, Structure, and Style

1. What, according to Bodett, is his reason for writing this essay? What unappreciated activity is explained here?
2. Overall, what is the tone of the essay? At what point was this tone clear to you?
3. Bodett explains his process in language associated with what sport? Cite some examples of this language as he instructs his readers in ditch diving.
4. What are the three steps in this process? By what criteria are these steps judged?
5. What "equipment" is necessary for this activity?
6. Point out some of the most effective examples and details Bodett uses to illustrate and clarify the steps in his process.
7. Effective process analysis sometimes offers readers warnings and advice on what not to do. How does Bodett make use of this technique?
8. How does Bodett make clear the transition from one step in the process to the next?

9. Identify some of Bodett's uses of colloquial language and exaggeration. What do these uses of language add to the tone and real purpose of this essay?

10. Evaluate Bodett's summary conclusion with its pun in the last line. Do you find the conclusion effective for this process essay? Why/why not?

Suggestions for Writing

Try using Tom Bodett's "Ditch Diving" as a stepping-stone to your own writing. Select an activity that you think is not appreciated for the fine "art" it truly is, and defend your position by explaining its intricate steps in a humorous or "mock heroic" process essay. The art of last-minute studying? The art of non-housekeeping? Consider using language lifted from a sport or another art form to add to the comic effect. (For example, might the steps you must take to arrive at your 8 A.M. class with mere seconds to spare parallel the labors of a triathlon athlete?)

Vocabulary

aesthetics (1)   berm (8)
panache (5)   addle-brained (9)
piker (7)

■ A REVISION WORKSHEET

As you write your rough drafts, consult Chapter 5 for guidance through the revision process. In addition, here are a few questions to ask yourself as you revise your process essay:

1. Is the essay's purpose clear to the reader?

2. Has the need for any special equipment been noted and explained adequately? Are all terms unfamiliar to the reader defined clearly?

3. Does the essay include all the steps (and warnings, if appropriate) necessary to understanding the process?

4. Is each step described in enough detail to make it understandable to all readers? Where could more detail be effectively added?

5. Are all the steps in the process presented in an easy-to-follow chronological order, with smooth transitions between steps or stages?

6. Are there any steps that should be combined in a paragraph describing a logical stage in the process?

7. Does the essay have a pleasing conclusion?

After you've revised your essay extensively, you might exchange rough drafts with a classmate and answer these questions for each other, making specific suggestions for improvement wherever appropriate. (For advice on productive participation in classroom workshops, see pages 106–109.)

Reviewing Your Progress

After you have completed your process essay, take a moment to measure your progress as a writer by responding to the following questions. Such analysis will help you recognize growth in your writing skills and may enable you to identify areas that are still problematic.

1. Which part of your essay is most successful? Why?

2. Select two details that contribute significantly to the clarity of your explanation. Why are these details effective?

3. What part of your essay gave you the most trouble? How did you overcome the problem?

4. If you had more time to work on this essay, what would receive additional attention? Why?

5. What did you learn about your topic from writing this essay? About yourself as a writer?

■ Strategy Three: Development by Comparison and Contrast

Every day you exercise the mental process of comparison and contrast. When you get up in the morning, for instance, you may contrast two choices of clothing—a short-sleeved shirt versus a long-sleeved one—and then make your decision after hearing the weather forecast. Or you may contrast and choose between Sugar-Coated Plastic Pops and Organic Mullet Kernels for breakfast, between the health advantages of walking to campus and the speed afforded by your car or bicycle. Once on campus, preparing to register, you may first compare both professors and courses; similarly, you probably compared the school you attend now to others before you made your choice. In short, you frequently use the process of comparison and contrast to come to a decision or make a judgment about two or more objects, persons, ideas, or feelings.

When you write a comparison or contrast essay, your opinion about the two elements* in question becomes your thesis statement; the body of the paper then shows why you arrived at that opinion. For example, if your thesis states that Mom's Kum-On-Back Hamburger Haven is preferable to McPhony's Mystery Burger Stand, your body paragraphs might contrast the two restaurants in terms of food, service, and atmosphere, revealing the superiority of Mom's on all three counts.

Developing Your Essay

There are two principal patterns of organization for comparison or contrast essays. For most short papers you should choose one of the patterns and stick with it throughout the essay. Later, if you are assigned a longer essay, you may want to mix the patterns for variety as some professional writers do, but do so only if you can maintain clarity and logical organization.

---

* It is possible to compare or contrast more than two elements. But until you feel confident about the organizational patterns for this kind of essay, you should probably stay with the simpler format.

Pattern One: Point by Point

This method of organization calls for body paragraphs that compare or contrast the two subjects first on point one, then on point two, then point three, and so on. Study the following example:

Thesis: Mom's Hamburger Haven is a better family restaurant than McPhony's because of its superior food, service, and atmosphere.

Point 1:   Food
    A. Mom's
    B. McPhony's

Point 2:   Service
    A. Mom's
    B. McPhony's

Point 3:   Atmosphere
    A. Mom's
    B. McPhony's

Conclusion

If you select this pattern of organization, you must make a smooth transition from subject "A" to subject "B" in each discussion to avoid a choppy seesaw effect. Be consistent: present the same subject first in each discussion of a major point. In the essay outlined above, for instance, Mom's is always introduced before McPhony's.

Pattern Two: The Block

This method of organization presents body paragraphs in which the writer first discusses subject "A" on points one, two, three, and so on, and then discusses subject "B" on the same points. The following model illustrates this Block Pattern:

Thesis: Mom's Hamburger Haven is a better family restaurant than McPhony's because of its superior food, service, and atmosphere.

    A. Mom's
       1. Food
       2. Service
       3. Atmosphere
    B. McPhony's
       1. Food
       2. Service
       3. Atmosphere

Conclusion

If you use the Block Pattern, you should discuss the three points—food, service, atmosphere—in the same order for each subject. In addition, you must include in your discussion of subject "B" specific references to the points you made earlier about subject "A" (see outline). In other words, because your statements about Mom's superior food may be several pages away by the time your comments on McPhony's food appear, the readers may not remember precisely what you said. Gently, unobtrusively, remind them with a specific reference to the earlier discussion. For instance, you might begin your paragraph on McPhony's service like this: "Unlike the friendly, attentive help at Mom's, service at McPhony's features grouchy persons who wait on you as if they consider your presence an intrusion on their privacy." The discussion of atmosphere might begin, "McPhony's atmosphere is as cold, sterile, and plastic as its decor, in contrast to the warm, homey feeling that pervades Mom's." Without such connecting phrases, what should be one unified essay will look more like two distinct mini-essays, forcing readers to do the job of comparing or contrasting for you.

Which Pattern Should You Use?

As you prepare to compose your first draft, you might ask yourself, "Which pattern of organization should I choose—Point by Point or Block?" Indeed, this is not your simple "paper or plastic" supermarket choice. It's an important question—to which there is no single, easy answer.

For most writers, choosing the appropriate pattern of organization involves thinking time in the prewriting stage, before beginning a draft. Many times, your essay's subject matter itself will suggest the most effective method of development. The Block Method might be the better choice when a complete, overall picture of each subject is desirable. For example, you might decide that your "then-and-now" essay (your disastrous first day at a new job contrasted with your success at that job today) would be easier for your readers to understand if your description of "then" (your first day) was presented in its entirety, followed by the contrasting discussion of "now" (current success). Later in this section, you will see that Mark Twain chose this method in his essay "Two Ways of Viewing the River" to contrast his early and later impressions of the Mississippi.

On the other hand, your essay topic might best be discussed by presenting a number of distinct points for the reader to consider one by one. Essays that evaluate, that argue the superiority or advantage of one thing over another ("A cat is a better pet for students than a dog because of X, Y, and Z"), often lend themselves to Point-by-Point Method because each of the writer's claims may be clearly supported by the side-by-side details. "Bringing Back the Joy of Market Day," a student essay in this section, employs this method to emphasize three ways in which a small food cooperative is preferable to a chain grocery store.

However, none of the above advice always holds true. There are no hard-and-fast rules governing this rhetorical choice. Each writer must decide which method of organization works best in any particular comparison/contrast essay. Before drafting begins, therefore, writers are wise to sketch out an informal outline or rough plan using one method and then the other to see which is more effective for their topic, their purpose, and their audience. By spending time in the prewriting stage "auditioning" each method of development, you may spare yourself the frustration of writing an entire draft whose organization doesn't work well for your topic.

Problems to Avoid

The single most serious error is the "so-what" thesis. Writers of comparison and contrast essays often wish to convince their readers that something—a restaurant, a movie, a product—is better (or worse) than something else: "Mom's Haven is a better place to eat than McPhony's." But not all comparison or contrast essays assert the absolute superiority or inferiority of their subjects. Sometimes writers simply want to point out the similarities or differences in two or more people, places, or objects, and that's fine, too—*as long as the writer avoids the "so-what" thesis problem.*

Too often novice writers will present thesis statements such as "My sister and I are very different" or "Having a blended family with two stepbrothers and stepsisters has advantages and disadvantages for me." To such theses, readers can only respond, "So what? Who cares?" There are many similarities and differences (or advantages and disadvantages) between countless numbers of things—but why should your readers care about those described in your essay? Comparing or contrasting for no apparent reason is a waste of the readers' valuable time; instead, find a purpose that will draw in your audience. You may indeed wish to write an essay contrasting the pros and cons of your blended family, but do it in a way that has a universal appeal or application. For instance, you might revise your thesis to say something like "Although a blended family often does experience petty jealousies and juvenile bickering, the benefits of having stepsiblings as live-in friends far outweigh the problems," and then use your family to show the advantages and disadvantages. In this way, your readers realize they will learn something about the blended family, a common phenomenon today, as well as learning some information about you and your particular family.

Another way to avoid the "so-what" problem is to direct your thesis to a particular audience. For instance, you might say that "Although Stella's Sweatateria and the Fitness Fanatics Gym are similar in their low student-membership prices and excellent instructors, Stella's is the place to go for those seeking a variety of exercise classes rather than hard-core bodybuilding machines." Or your thesis may wish to show a particular relationship between two subjects. Instead of writing "There are many similarities between the movie *Riot of the Killer Snails* and Mary Sheeley's novel *Salt on the Sidewalk*," write "The many similarities in character and plot (the monster, the scientist, and vegetable garden scene) clearly suggest that the movie director was greatly influenced by—if not actually guilty of stealing—parts of Mary Sheeley's novel."

In other words, tell your readers your point and then use comparison or contrast to support that idea; don't just compare or contrast items in a vacuum. Ask yourself, "What is the significant point I want my readers to learn or understand from reading this comparison/contrast essay? Why do they need to know this?"

Describe your subjects clearly and distinctly. To comprehend a difference or a similarity between two things, the reader must first be able to "see" them as you do. Consequently, you should use as many vivid examples and details as possible to describe both your subjects. Beware a tendency to overelaborate on one subject and then grossly skimp on the other, an especially easy trap to fall into in an essay that asserts "X" is preferable to "Y." By giving each side a reasonable treatment, you will do a better job of convincing your reader that you know both sides and have made a valid judgment.

Avoid a choppy essay. Whether you organize your essay by the point-by-point pattern or the block pattern, you need to use enough transitional devices to ensure a smooth flow from one subject to another and from one point to the next. Without transitions, your essay may assume the distracting movement of a Ping-Pong game, as you switch back and forth between discussions of your two subjects. Listed below are some appropriate words to link your points:

Comparison	Contrast
also	however
similarly	on the contrary
too	on the other hand
both	in contrast
like	although
not only . . . but also	unlike
have in common	though
share the same	instead of
in the same manner	but

(For a review of other transitional devices, see pages 70–73.)

■ ESSAY TOPICS

Here are some topics that may be compared or contrasted. Remember to narrow your subject, formulate a thesis that presents a clear point, and follow one of the two organizational patterns discussed on pages 212–213. For additional ideas, turn to the "Suggestions for Writing" sections following the professional essays (page 226 and page 228).

1. An expectation and its reality
2. A first impression and a later point of view
3. Two views on a current controversial issue (campus, local, national)
4. Two conflicting theories you are studying in another college course
5. A memory of a person or place and a more recent encounter
6. Coverage of the same story by two newspapers or magazines (the *National Enquirer* and the *Dallas Morning News,* for example, or *Time* and *Newsweek*)
7. A hero today and yesterday
8. Two essays or pieces of literature with similar themes but different styles
9. Two pieces of technology or two pieces of sports equipment
10. Two paintings/photographs/posters/advertisements (You might select any two of the many images in this text. For example, consider the depiction of urban life in *Nighthawks* [page 313] and *The Subway* [page 237]; the representation of women in *Repose* [page 425] and *Rosie the Riveter* [page 263]; the Depression era in *Breadline during the Louisville Flood, Kentucky 1937* [page 216] and *Migrant Mother* [page 322]; the appeals of various ads [page 186 and pages 296–304 to sway readers.)

11. Two solutions to a problem in your professional field

12. One of today's popular entertainments and one from an earlier era

13. Two places you've lived or visited or two schools you've attended

14. Two instructors or coaches whose teaching styles are effective but different

15. Two movies; a book and its movie; a movie and its sequel (For help writing about film, see Chapter 17.)

16. Two jobs, bosses, or employers (or your current job and your dream job)

17. Two places that are special for you in different ways

18. An opinion you held before coming to college that has changed

19. Your attitude toward a social custom or political belief and your parents' (or grandparents') attitude toward that belief or custom

20. Artwork or advertising developed by comparison/contrast (Consider, for example, *Breadline during the Louisville Flood, Kentucky 1937*, shown below. During the Great Depression, when floods were ravaging parts of the South previously gutted by drought, Margaret Bourke-White photographed people patiently standing in a breadline that stretched in front of a billboard advertising a new car. What comments on American society was Bourke-White's photo, with its powerful use of contrasts, making in 1937?)

Breadline during the Louisville Flood, Kentucky 1937, by Margaret Bourke-White

A Topic Proposal for Your Essay

Selecting the right subject matter is important to every writer. To help you clarify your ideas and strengthen your commitment to your topic, here is a proposal sheet that asks you to describe some of your preliminary ideas about your subject before you begin drafting. Although your ideas may change as you write (they will almost certainly become more refined), thinking through your choice of topic now may help you avoid several false starts.

1. What two subjects will your essay discuss? In what ways are these subjects similar? Different?

2. Do you plan to compare or contrast your two subjects?

3. Write one or two sentences describing your attitude toward these two subjects. Are you stating a preference for one or are you making some other significant point? In other words, what is the purpose of this essay?

4. Why would other people find this topic interesting and important? Would a particular group of people be more affected by your topic than others? Are you avoiding the "so-what" thesis problem?

5. List three or four points of comparison or contrast that you might include in this essay.

6. What difficulties might this topic present during your drafting? For example, would your topic be best explained using the Block or Point-by-Point pattern?

■ Sample Student Essays

Because there are two popular ways to develop comparison/contrast essays, this section offers two student essays so that each pattern is illustrated.

I. The Point-by-Point Pattern

Note that this writer takes a definite stand—that local food co-ops are superior to chain grocery stores—and then contrasts two local stores, Lane Grocer and the Fort Collins, Colorado, Co-op, to prove her thesis. She selected the Point-by-Point Pattern to organize her essay, contrasting prices, atmosphere, and benefits to local producers. See if you can identify her transitional devices as well as some of her uses of detail that make the essay more interesting and convincing.

BRINGING BACK THE JOY OF MARKET DAY

1   Now that the old family-run corner grocery is almost extinct, many people are banding together to form their own neighborhood stores as food cooperatives. Locally owned by their members, food

---

Thesis

Essay map

Point one:
Prices

Examples of
Lane Grocer's
prices
contrasted to
examples of
co-op prices

co-ops such as the one here in Fort Collins are welcome alternatives to the impersonal chain-store markets such as Lane Grocer. In exchange for volunteering a few hours each month, co-op members share savings and a friendly experience while they shop; local producers gain loyal, local support from the members as well as better prices for their goods in return for providing the freshest, purest food possible.

2   Perhaps the most crucial distinction between the two kinds of stores is that while supermarkets are set up to generate profit for their corporations, co-ops are nonprofit groups whose main purpose is to provide their members and the community with good, inexpensive food and basic household needs. At first glance, supermarkets such as Lane Grocer may appear to be cheaper because they offer so many specials, which they emphasize heavily through ads and in-store promotions. These special deals, known as "loss-leaders" in the retail industry, are more than compensated by the extremely high markups on other products. For example, around Thanksgiving Lane Grocer might have a sale on flour and shortening and then set up the displays with utmost care so that as customers reach for the flour they will be drawn to colorful bottles of pie spices, fancy jars of mincemeat, or maybe an inviting bin of fresh-roasted holiday nuts, all of which may be marked up 100% or more—way above what is being lost on the flour and shortening.

3   The Fort Collins Co-op rarely bothers with such pricing gimmicks; instead, it tries to have a consistent markup—just enough to meet overhead expenses. The flour at the co-op may cost an extra few cents, but that same fancy spice bottle that costs over $1.00 from the supermarket display can be refilled at the co-op for less than 25¢. The nuts, considered by regular groceries as a seasonal "gourmet" item,

are sold at the co-op for about two-thirds the price. Great savings like these are achieved by buying in bulk and having customers bag their own groceries. Recycled containers are used as much as possible, cutting down substantially on overhead. Buying in bulk may seem awkward at first, but the extra time spent bagging and weighing their own food results in welcome savings for co-op members.

4   Once people have become accustomed to bringing their own containers and taking part in the work at the co-ops, they often find that it's actually more fun to shop in the friendly, relaxed atmosphere of the co-ops. At Lane Grocer, for example, I often find shopping a battle of tangled metal carts wielded by bored customers who are frequently trying to manage one or more cranky children. The long aisles harshly lit by rows of cold fluorescent lights and the bland commercial music don't make the chore of shopping any easier either. On the other hand, the Fort Collins Co-op may not be as expertly planned, but at least the chaos is carried on in a friendly way. Parents especially appreciate that they can safely let their children loose while they shop because in the small, open-spaced co-op even toddlers don't become lost as they do in the aisles of towering supermarket shelves. Moreover, most members are willing to look after the children of other members if necessary. And while they shop, members can choose to listen to the FM radio or simply to enjoy each other's company in relative quiet.

Point two: Atmosphere

Description of Lane Grocer's atmosphere contrasted to description of the co-op's atmosphere

5   As well as benefiting member consumers, co-ops also help small local producers by providing a direct market for their goods. Large chain stores may require minimum wholesale quantities far beyond the capacity of an individual producer, and mass markets like Lane Grocer often feel they are "too big" to negotiate with small local producers. But because of their small, independent nature, co-ops

Point three: Benefits to local producers

No benefits at Lane Grocer contrasted to two benefits at the co-op

welcome the chance to buy direct from the grower or producer. Direct selling offers two advantages for producers: they get a better price for their wares than by selling them through a middleman, and at the same time they establish an independent reputation for their business, which can be immensely valuable to their success later on. In Fort Collins, for example, Luna tofu (bean curd) stands out as an excellent illustration of this kind of mutual support. Several years ago my friend Carol Jones began making tofu in small batches to sell to the co-op as a way to earn a part-time income as well as to contribute to the co-op. Her enterprise has now grown so well that last year her husband quit his job to go into business with her full time. She currently sells to distributors and independent stores from here to Denver; even Lane Grocer, who earlier would not consider selling her tofu even on a trial basis, is now thinking about changing its policy.

Conclusion: Summarizing the advantages of co-ops over chain stores

6   Of course, not all co-ops are like the one here in Fort Collins, but that is one of their best features. Each one reflects the personalities of its members, unlike the supermarket chain stores that vary only slightly. Most important, though, while each has a distinctive character, co-ops share common goals of providing members with high-quality, low-cost food in a friendly, cooperative spirit.

II. The Block Pattern

After thinking through both methods of development, a second student writer chose the Block Pattern to contrast two kinds of backyards. He felt it was more effective to give his readers a complete sense of his first backyard, with its spirit of wildness, instead of addressing each point of the contrast separately, as did the first student writer in this section. Do you agree with his choice? Why or why not? Note, too, the ways in which this writer tries to avoid the "split essay" problem by making clear connections between the new yard and the older one.

BACKYARDS: OLD AND NEW

1   Most of the time I like getting something new—new clothes, new CDs, new video games. I look forward to making new friends and visiting new places. But sometimes new isn't better than old. Five years ago, when my family moved to a house in a new area, I learned that a new, neat backyard can never be as wonderful as a rambling, untamed yard of an older house.

2   My first yard, behind our older house, was huge, the size of three normal backyards, but completely irregular in shape. Our property line zagged in and out around old, tall trees in a lot shaped like a large pie piece from which some giant had taken random bites. The left side was taken up by a lopsided garden that sometimes grew tomatoes but mainly wild raspberries, an odd assortment of overgrown bushes, and wildflowers of mismatched shapes and sizes. The middle part had grass and scattered shade trees, some that were good for climbing. The grassy part drifted off into an area with large old evergreen trees surrounded by a tall tangle of vines and bushes that my parents called "the Wild Spot," which they had carefully ignored for years. The whole yard sloped downhill, which with the irregular shape and the trees, made my job of mowing the grass a creative challenge.

3   Despite the mowing problem, there was something magical about that untamed yard. We kids made a path through the Wild Spot and had a secret hideout in the brush. Hidden from adult eyes, my friends and I sat around a pretend fire ring, made up adventures (lost in the jungle!), asked each other Important Questions (better to be a rock star or a baseball player?), and shared our secret fears (being asked to dance). The yard's grassy section was big enough for

Thesis

Block A: The older, "untamed" backyard

(Landscape variety: Irregular lot size and shape; trees, rambling mix of bushes, flowers, berries, and vines)

(Family activities)

throwing a football with my brother (the here-and-there trees made catching long passes even more spectacular), and my twin sisters invented gymnastic routines that rolled them downhill. Mom picked vegetables and flowers when she felt like it. It seemed like someone, family or friend, was always in our yard doing something fun.

Transition to Block B: The new backyard (contrasting bland landscape)

4   When all the kids were teenagers, my parents finally decided we needed more space, so we moved into a house in a new development. Although the house itself was better (more bathrooms), the new backyard, in comparison to our older one, was a total disappointment. New Backyard was neat, tidy, tiny, flat, square, and completely fenced. There were not only no big old trees for shade or for climbing—there were no trees at all. My parents had to plant a few, which looked like big twigs stuck in the ground. No untamed tangles of bushes and flowers there—only identical fire hydrant-sized shrubs planted evenly every few feet in narrow, even beds along the fence. The rest of this totally flat yard was grass, easy to mow in mere minutes, but no challenge either. No wild berry bushes or rambling vegetable gardens were allowed in the new development. No wild anything at all, to be exact.

5   Nothing wild and no variety: that was the problem. To put it bluntly, the yard was neat but boring. Every inch of it was open to inspection; it held no secret spaces for the imagination to fill. There was no privacy either as our yard looked directly into the almost duplicate bland yards of the neighbors on all sides. The yard was too small to do any real physical activity in it; going out for a long pass would mean automatic collision with the chain fence in any direction.

(Few activities)

My sisters' dance routines soon dissolved under our neighbor's eyes, and our tomatoes came from the grocery store. With no hidden nooks, no interesting landscape, and no tumbling space, our family just didn't go into the backyard very often. Unlike the older, overgrown backyard that was always inviting someone to play, the new backyard wasn't fun for anyone.

6   Over the last five years, the trees have grown and the yard looks better, not so sterile and empty. I guess all new yards are on their way to becoming old yards eventually. But it takes decades and that is too slow for me. New houses have lots of modern conveniences, but I hope if I am lucky enough to own my own place someday, I will remember that when it comes to backyards, old is always better than new.

Conclusion: A future preference based on essay's thesis

Professional Essays*

Because there are two common ways to develop comparison/contrast essays, this section offers two professional essays to illustrate each pattern.

I. The Point-by-Point Pattern

■ Grant and Lee: A Study in Contrasts

Bruce Catton

Bruce Catton, an authority on the Civil War, won both the Pulitzer Prize for historical work and the National Book Award in 1955. He wrote numerous books, including *Mr. Lincoln's Army* (1951), *A Stillness at Appomattox* (1953), *Never Call Retreat* (1966), and *Gettysburg: The Final Fury* (1974). This essay is a chapter of *The American Story* (1956), a collection of essays by noted historians.

1   When Ulysses S. Grant and Robert E. Lee met in the parlor of a modest house at Appomattox Court House, Virginia, on April 9, 1865, to work out the terms for the surrender of Lee's Army of Northern Virginia, a great chapter in American life came to a close, and a great new chapter began.

2   These men were bringing the Civil War to its virtual finish. To be sure, other armies had yet to surrender, and for a few days the fugitive Confederate government would struggle desperately and vainly, trying to find some way to go on living now

* To help you read these essays analytically, review pages 166–168.

that its chief support was gone. But in effect it was all over when Grant and Lee signed the papers. And the little room where they wrote out the terms was the scene of one of the poignant, dramatic contrasts in American history.

3   They were two strong men, these oddly different generals, and they represented the strengths of two conflicting currents that, through them, had come into final collision.

4   Back of Robert E. Lee was the notion that the old aristocratic concept might somehow survive and be dominant in American life.

5   Lee was tidewater Virginia, and in his background were family, culture, and tradition . . . the age of chivalry transplanted to a New World which was making its own legends and its own myths. He embodied a way of life that had come down through the age of knighthood and the English country squire. America was a land that was beginning all over again, dedicated to nothing much more complicated than the rather hazy belief that all men had equal rights, and should have an equal chance in the world. In such a land Lee stood for the feeling that it was somehow of advantage to human society to have a pronounced inequality in the social structure. There should be a leisure class, backed by ownership of land; in turn, society itself should be keyed to the land as the chief source of wealth and influence. It would bring forth (according to this ideal) a class of men with a strong sense of obligation to the community; men who lived not to gain advantage for themselves, but to meet the solemn obligations which had been laid on them by the very fact that they were privileged. From them the country would get its leadership; to them it could look for the higher values—of thought, of conduct, of personal deportment—to give it strength and virtue.

6   Lee embodied the noblest elements of this aristocratic ideal. Through him, the landed nobility justified itself. For four years, the Southern states had fought a desperate war to uphold the ideals for which Lee stood. In the end, it almost seemed as if the Confederacy fought for Lee; as if he himself was the Confederacy . . . the best thing that the way of life for which the Confederacy stood could ever have to offer. He had passed into legend before Appomattox. Thousands of tired, underfed, poorly clothed Confederate soldiers, long-since past the simple enthusiasm of the early days of the struggle, somehow considered Lee the symbol of everything for which they had been willing to die. But they could not quite put this feeling into words. If the Lost Cause, sanctified by so much heroism and so many deaths, had a living justification, its justification was General Lee.

7   Grant, the son of a tanner on the Western frontier, was everything Lee was not. He had come up the hard way, and embodied nothing in particular except the eternal toughness and sinewy fiber of the men who grew up beyond the mountains. He was one of a body of men who owed reverence and obeisance to no one, who were self-reliant to a fault, who cared hardly anything for the past but who had a sharp eye for the future.

8   These frontier men were the precise opposites of the tidewater aristocrats. Back of them, in the great surge that had taken people over the Alleghenies and into the opening Western country, there was a deep, implicit dissatisfaction with a past that had settled into grooves. They stood for democracy, not from any reasoned conclusion about the proper ordering of human society, but simply because they had grown up in the middle of democracy and knew how it worked. Their society might have privileges, but they would be privileges each man had won for himself. Forms and patterns meant nothing. No man was born to anything, except perhaps to a chance to show how far he could rise. Life was competition.

9   Yet along with this feeling had come a deep sense of belonging to a national community. The Westerner who developed a farm, opened a shop, or set up in business as a trader could hope to prosper only as his own community prospered—and his community ran from the Atlantic to the Pacific and from Canada down to Mexico. If the land was settled, with towns and highways and accessible markets, he could better himself. He saw his fate in terms of the nation's own destiny. As its horizons expanded, so did his. He had, in other words, an acute dollars-and-cents stake in the continued growth and development of his country.

10   And that, perhaps, is where the contrast between Grant and Lee becomes most striking. The Virginia aristocrat, inevitably, saw himself in relation to his own region. He lived in a static society which could endure almost anything except change. Instinctively, his first loyalty would go to the locality in which that society existed. He would fight to the limit of endurance to defend it, because in defending it he was defending everything that gave his own life its deepest meaning.

11   The Westerner, on the other hand, would fight with an equal tenacity for the broader concept of society. He fought so because everything he lived by was tied to growth, expansion, and a constantly widening horizon. What he lived by would survive or fall with the nation itself. He could not possibly stand by unmoved in the face of an attempt to destroy the Union. He would combat it with everything he had, because he could only see it as an effort to cut the ground out from under his feet.

12   So Grant and Lee were in complete contrast, representing two diametrically opposed elements in American life. Grant was the modern man emerging; beyond him, ready to come on the stage, was the great age of steel and machinery, of crowded cities and a restless, burgeoning vitality. Lee might have ridden down from the old age of chivalry, lance in hand, silken banner fluttering over his head. Each man was the perfect champion of his cause, drawing both his strengths and his weaknesses from the people he led.

13   Yet it was not all contrast, after all. Different as they were—in background, in personality, in underlying aspiration—these two great soldiers had much in common. Under everything else, they were marvelous fighters. Furthermore, their fighting qualities were really very much alike.

14   Each man had, to begin with, the great virtue of utter tenacity and fidelity. Grant fought his way down the Mississippi Valley in spite of acute personal discouragement and profound military handicaps. Lee hung on in the trenches at Petersburg after hope itself had died. In each man there was an indomitable quality . . . the born fighter's refusal to give up as long as he can still remain on his feet and lift his two fists.

15   Daring and resourcefulness they had, too; the ability to think faster and move faster than the enemy. These were the qualities which gave Lee the dazzling campaigns of Second Manassas and Chancellorsville and won Vicksburg for Grant.

16   Lastly, and perhaps greatest of all, there was the ability, at the end, to turn quickly from war to peace once the fighting was over. Out of the way these two men behaved at Appomattox came the possibility of a peace of reconciliation. It was a possibility not wholly realized, in the years to come, but which did, in the end, help the two sections to become one nation again . . . after a war whose bitterness might have seemed to make such a reunion wholly impossible. No part of either man's life became him more than the part he played in their brief meeting in the McLean house at Appomattox. Their behavior there put all succeeding generations of Americans in their debt. Two

great Americans, Grant and Lee—very different, yet under everything very much alike. Their encounter at Appomattox was one of the great moments of American history.

Questions on Content, Style, and Structure

1. What is Catton's thesis?

2. According to Catton, how did Lee view society? Summarize the aristocratic ideal that Lee symbolized.

3. Who did Grant represent? How did they view the country's social structure?

4. After carefully studying paragraphs 4 through 16, describe the pattern of organization Catton uses to present his discussion.

5. What new means of development begins in paragraph 13?

6. How does Catton avoid the choppy seesaw effect as he compares and contrasts his subjects? Point out ways in which Catton makes a smooth transition from point to point.

7. Evaluate Catton's ability to write unified, coherent paragraphs with clearly stated topic sentences. Are his paragraphs adequately developed with enough specific detail? Cite evidence to support your answer.

8. What is the advantage or disadvantage of having only one sentence in paragraph 3? In paragraph 4?

9. What is Catton's opinion of these men? Select words and passages to support your answer. How does Catton's attitude affect the tone of this essay? Is his tone appropriate? Why or why not?

10. Instead of including a separate paragraph, Catton presents his concluding remarks in paragraph 16, in which he discusses his last major point about Grant and Lee. Many essays lacking concluding paragraphs end too abruptly or merely trail off; how does Catton avoid these weaknesses?

Suggestions for Writing

Try using Bruce Catton's "Grant and Lee: A Study in Contrasts" as a stepping-stone to your writing. Comparing public figures is a familiar activity. People often discuss the styles and merits of various politicians, writers, business leaders, humanitarians, sports celebrities, and media stars. Write your own essay about two public figures who interest you. Similar or different, these people may have lived in the same times (Winston Churchill and Franklin D. Roosevelt, Ernest Hemingway and F. Scott Fitzgerald, Babe Didrikson Zaharias and Babe Ruth), or you might choose two people from different eras (Clara Barton and Mother Teresa, Mozart and Madonna, Susan B. Anthony and Cesar Chavez, Harriet Tubman and Martin Luther King, Jr.). The possibilities are endless and thought-provoking; use your essay to make an interesting specific point about the fascinating (and perhaps heretofore unrecognized) differences/similarities between the people you choose.

Vocabulary

chivalry (5)	tenacity (11)	indomitable (14)
deportment (5)	diametrically (12)	reconciliation (16)
embodied (6)	burgeoning (12)	

II. The Block Pattern

■ Two Ways of Viewing the River

Samuel Clemens

Samuel Clemens, whose pen name was Mark Twain, is regarded as one of America's most outstanding writers. Well known for his humorous stories and books, Twain was also a pioneer of fictional realism and local color. His most famous novel, *The Adventures of Huckleberry Finn* (1884), is often hailed as a masterpiece. This selection is from the autobiographical book *Life on the Mississippi* (1883), which recounts Clemens's job as a riverboat pilot.

1   Now when I had mastered the language of this water and had come to know every trifling feature that bordered the great river as familiarly as I knew the letters of the alphabet, I had made a valuable acquisition. But I had lost something, too. I had lost something which could never be restored to me while I lived. All the grace, the beauty, the poetry, had gone out of the majestic river! I still kept in mind a certain wonderful sunset which I witnessed when steamboating was new to me. A broad expanse of the river was turned to blood; in the middle distance the red hue brightened into gold, through which a solitary log came floating, black and conspicuous; in one place a long, slanting mark lay sparkling upon the water; in another the surface was broken by boiling, tumbling rings, that were as many-tinted as an opal; where the ruddy flush was faintest, was a smooth spot that was covered with graceful circles and radiating lines, ever so delicately traced; the shore on our left was densely wooded and the somber shadow that fell from this forest was broken in one place by a long, ruffled trail that shone like silver; and high above the forest wall a clean-stemmed dead tree waved a single leafy bough that glowed like a flame in the unobstructed splendor that was flowing from the sun. There were graceful curves, reflected images, woody heights, soft distances, and over the whole scene, far and near, the dissolving lights drifted steadily, enriching it every passing moment with new marvels of coloring.

2   I stood like one bewitched. I drank it in, in a speechless rapture. The world was new to me and I had never seen anything like this at home. But as I have said, a day came when I began to cease from noting the glories and the charms which the moon and the sun and the twilight wrought upon the river's face; another day came when I ceased altogether to note them. Then, if that sunset scene had been repeated, I should have looked upon it without rapture, and should have commented upon it inwardly after this fashion: "This sun means that we are going to have wind tomorrow; that floating log means that the river is rising, small thanks to it; that slanting mark on the water refers to a bluff reef which is going to kill somebody's steamboat one of these nights, if it keeps on stretching out like that; those tumbling 'boils' show

a dissolving bar and a changing channel there; the lines and circles in the slick water over yonder are a warning that that troublesome place is shoaling up dangerously; that silver streak in the shadow of the forest is the 'break' from a new snag and he has located himself in the very best place he could have found to fish for steamboats; that tall dead tree, with a single living branch, is not going to last long, and then how is a body ever going to get through this blind place at night without the friendly old landmark?"

3   No, the romance and beauty were all gone from the river. All the value any feature of it had for me now was the amount of usefulness it could furnish toward compassing the safe piloting of a steamboat. Since those days, I have pitied doctors from my heart. What does the lovely flush in a beauty's cheek mean to a doctor but a "break" that ripples above some deadly disease? Are not all her visible charms sown thick with what are to him the signs and symbols of hidden decay? Does he ever see her beauty at all, or doesn't he simply view her professionally and comment upon her unwholesome condition all to himself? And doesn't he sometimes wonder whether he has gained most or lost most by learning his trade?

Questions on Content, Structure, and Style

1. What is Clemens contrasting in this essay? Identify his thesis.
2. What organizational pattern does he choose? Why is this an appropriate choice for his purpose?
3. How does Clemens make a smooth transition to his later view of the river?
4. Why does Clemens refer to doctors in paragraph 3?
5. What is the purpose of the questions in paragraph 3? Why is the last question especially important?
6. Characterize the language Clemens uses in his description in paragraph 1. Is his diction appropriate?
7. Point out several examples of similes in paragraph 1. What do they add to the description of the sunset?
8. How does the language in the description in paragraph 2 differ from the diction in paragraph 1? What view of the river is emphasized there?
9. Identify an example of personification in paragraph 2. Why did Clemens add it to his description?
10. Describe the tone of this essay. Does it ever shift?

Suggestions for Writing

Try using Samuel Clemens' "Two Ways of Viewing the River" as a stepping-stone to your own writing. Consider, as Clemens did, writing about a subject before and after you experienced it from a more technically informed point of view. Did your appreciation of your grandmother's quilt increase after you realized how much skill went into making it? Did a starry night have a different appeal after your astronomy course? Did your admiration of a story or poem diminish or increase after you studied its craft? Clemens felt a certain loss came with his expertise, but was this the case in your experience?

Vocabulary

trifling (1)	ruddy (1)
acquisition (1)	wrought (2)
conspicuous (1)	compassing (3)

■ A REVISION WORKSHEET

As you write your rough drafts, consult Chapter 5 for guidance through the revision process. In addition, here are a few questions to ask yourself as you revise your comparison/contrast essay:

1. Does the essay contain a thesis that makes a significant point instead of a "so-what" thesis?

2. Is the material organized into the best pattern for the subject matter?

3. If the essay is developed by the Point-by-Point Pattern, are there enough transitional words used to avoid the see-saw effect?

4. If the essay is developed by the Block Pattern, are there enough transitional devices and references connecting the two subjects to avoid the split-essay problem?

5. Are the points of comparison/contrast presented in a logical, consistent order that the reader can follow easily?

6. Are both subjects given a reasonably balanced treatment?

7. Are both subjects developed in enough specific detail so that the reader clearly understands the comparison or contrast? Where might more detail be added?

After you've revised your essay extensively, you might exchange rough drafts with a classmate and answer these questions for each other, making specific suggestions for improvement wherever appropriate. (For advice on productive participation in classroom workshops, see pages 106–109.)

A Special Kind of Comparison: The Analogy

In the last few pages of this text, you've learned about essays developed by comparison/contrast, which generally point out similarities and differences between two things with enough common ground to merit meaningful discussion (two apartments, two computers, a book and its movie, etc.). In comparison/contrast essays, two subjects ("X" and "Y") are explained to make a point. An *analogy* is slightly different: it is a comparison that uses one thing ("X") only to clarify or argue a second thing ("Y"). In an analogy, one element is the main focus of attention.

You've probably heard several colorful analogies this week. Perhaps a friend who holds a hectic, dead-end job has tried to explain life at that moment by comparing herself to a crazed gerbil on a cage treadmill—always running, getting nowhere, feeling trapped in a never-changing environment. Or perhaps your science teacher explained the behavior of cancer cells by comparing them in several ways to an invading army on a destructive mission. If you read the Preface to this text, you were asked to see your writing instructor as a coach who helps you practice your skills, gives constructive criticism, and encourages your successes. Analogies are plentiful in our conversations and in both our reading and writing.

Writers often find analogies useful in three ways:

1. *To clarify and explain:* Most often writers use analogies to clarify an abstract, unfamiliar, or complex element by comparing it to something that is familiar to the reader, often something that is more concrete or easier to understand. For example, raising children has often been compared to nourishing baby birds, with parents feeding and nurturing but ultimately nudging offspring out of the nest. A relationship might be explained as having grown from a seed that eventually blossomed into a flower (or a weed!). Popular novelist Stephen King has used a roller coaster analogy to explain some people's enjoyment of horror movies.

Frequently, scientific and medical topics profit from analogies that a general audience of readers can more readily understand. A technical discussion of the human eye, for instance, might be explained using the analogy of a camera lens; photosynthesis might compared to the process of baking bread. One biology teacher explains the semipermeability of a cell membrane with a football analogy: the offensive line wants to let out the running back with the ball but keep the defensive line in. In short, analogies can make new or difficult material easier to grasp.

2. *To argue and persuade:* Writers often use analogies to try to convince their audience that what is true about "X" would also be true about "Y" because the two elements have so many important similarities. For example, someone against new anti-drug laws might argue that they are similar to those passed under Prohibition, the banning of alcohol in the 1930s, and thus the drug laws are doomed to failure. Or perhaps a NASA official might argue for more money for space exploration by comparing trips into outer space with those expeditions to the New World by explorers such as Columbus. How convincing an analogy is depends to a large extent on how similar the two elements appear to be. Remember, however, that analogies by themselves cannot *prove* anything; they can merely suggest similarities between two cases or things.

3. *To dramatize or capture an image:* Writers (and speakers) often use analogies because they wish their audience to remember a particular point or to see something in a new way. Using a vivid analogy—sometimes referred to as an extended metaphor or simile—can effectively impress an image upon the reader or listener's mind ("Using crack is like burning down your own house. And the insurance policy ran out a long time ago . . ."). Analogies can be enjoyable too for their sheer inventiveness and their colorful language. Perhaps one of the most well-known analogies in American literature is Thoreau's description, in *Walden*, of a battle between two ant colonies, with the tiny creatures drawn as rival warriors fighting to the death in classical epic style. Analogies may even be used for comic effect in appropriate situations (moving into your third-floor apartment in sweltering August heat as analogous to a trip to the Underworld, for instance). Fresh, creative analogies can delight your readers and hold their attention.

Although analogies can be helpful and memorable, they can also present problems if they are trite, unclear, or illogical. Analogies can be especially harmful to a writer's credibility in an argument if readers don't see enough logical similarities to make the comparison convincing. Some faulty analogies may seem acceptable on first glance but fall apart when the details of the comparison are considered closely. For example, perhaps you have seen a recent bumper sticker that reads "Giving money and power to the government is like giving whisky and car keys to teenage boys." Are the two situations really alike? Do government agencies/officials and adolescents share many similarities in maturity, experience, and goals? Does financial support have the same effect as alcohol? If too many points of comparison are weak, readers will not find the analogy persuasive. Or perhaps you have read that "America is like a lifeboat already full of people; letting in more immigrants will cause the boat to sink." If readers do not accept the major premise—that America, a country with many renewable resources, closely resembles a lifeboat, a confined space with unchanging dimensions—they are likely to reject the argument.

Also beware those writers who try to substitute an analogy in place of any other kind of evidence to support their points in an argument, and be especially suspicious of those using analogies as "scare tactics" ("This proposed legislation is just like laws passed in Nazi Germany"). As a writer, use only those analogies that will help your reader understand, remember, or accept your ideas; as a reader, always protect yourself by questioning the validity of the analogy offered to you. (For more on *faulty analogy* as a logical fallacy, see page 285.)

To illustrate use of analogy, here are three examples from professional writers. In each case, what was the writer's purpose? How is "X" used to clarify or argue for "Y"? Which of these analogies do you find the most effective, and why?

A good lab course is an exercise in *doing* science. As such it differs totally in mission from a good lecture course where the object is learning *about* science. In the same way that one can gain vastly greater insight into music by learning to play an instrument, one can experience the doing of science only by going into the lab and trying one's hand at measurement.

—Miles Pickering, "Are Lab Courses a Waste of Time?"

For a long time now, since the beginning, in fact, men and women have been sparring and dancing around with each other, each pair trying to get it together and boogie to the tune called Life. For some people, it was always a glide, filled with grace and ease. For most of us, it is a stumble and a struggle, always trying to figure out the next step, until we find a partner whose inconsistencies seem to fit with ours, and the two of us fit into some kind of rhythm. Some couples wind up struggling and pulling at cross purposes; and of course, some people never get out on the floor, just stand alone in the corners, looking hard at the dancers.

— Jay Molishever, "Changing Expectations of Marriage"

One afternoon while we were there at that lake a thunderstorm came up. It was like the revival of an old melodrama that I had seen long ago with childish awe. The second-act climax of the drama of the electrical disturbance over a lake in America had not changed in any important respect. This was the big scene, still the big scene. The whole thing was so familiar, the first feeling of oppression and heat and a general air around camp of not wanting to go very far away. In midafternoon (it was all the same) a curious darkening of the sky, and a lull in everything that had made life tick; and then the way the boats suddenly swung the other

way at their moorings with the coming of a breeze out of the new quarter, and the premonitory rumble. Then the kettle drum, then the snare, then the bass drum and cymbals, then
crackling light against the dark. . . . Afterward the calm, the rain steadily rustling in the calm
lake, the return of light and hope and spirits, and the campers running out in joy.

—E. B. White, "Once More to the Lake"

Analogies come in a variety of lengths, from several sentences to an entire essay,
depending upon the writer's purpose. As you practice your writing in this composition
class, you may find that incorporating an analogy into one of your essays is an effective
way to explain, emphasize, or help support an idea.

Reviewing Your Progress

After you have completed your essay developed by comparison/contrast, take a moment
to measure your progress as a writer by responding to the following questions. Such
analysis will help you to recognize growth in your writing skills and may enable you to
identify areas that are still problematic.

1. Which part of your essay do you like the best? Why?

2. Which point of comparison or contrast do you think is the most successful? Why
   is it effective?

3. What part of your essay gave you the most trouble? How did you overcome the
   problem?

4. If you had more time to work on this essay, what would receive additional attention? Why?

5. What did you learn about your topic from writing this essay? About yourself as
   a writer?

■ Strategy Four: Development by Definition

Frequently in conversation we must stop to ask, "What do you mean by that?" because in
some cases our failure to comprehend just one particular term may lead to total misunderstanding. Suppose, for example, in a discussion with a friend, you refer to a new law as
a piece of "liberal legislation"; if you and your friend do not share the same definition of
"liberal," your remark may be completely misinterpreted. Here's another example: if you
ask your grandparents for some dead presidents because you're in desperate need of bling
bling, will they know to open their wallets for your shopping trip? In other words, a clear
understanding of terms or ideas is often essential to meaningful communication.

Sometimes a dictionary definition or a one- or two-sentence explanation is all a term
needs (Hemingway, for example, once defined courage as "grace under pressure"). And
sometimes a brief, humorous definition can cut right to the heart of the matter (comedian Robin Williams, for instance, once defined "cocaine" as "God's way of saying you're
making too much money").*

---

* Even graffiti employ definition. One bathroom wall favorite: "Death is Nature's way of telling you to
slow down." Another, obviously written by an English major: "A double negative is a no-no."

Frequently, however, you will find it necessary to provide an *extended definition*—that is, a longer, more detailed explanation that thoroughly defines the subject. Essays of extended definitions are quite common; think, for instance, of the articles you've seen on "mercy killing," "assisted suicide," or abortion that define "life" in a variety of ways. Other recent essays have grappled with defining such complex concepts as free speech, animal rights, pornography, affirmative action, and gun control.

Many national discussions center on controversial definitions. Following the events of September 11, 2001, the "War on Terrorism" has produced a host of terms whose meanings are frequently debated. For example, does legislation such as the USA Patriot Act ensure "homeland security" or legitimize unlawful invasions of privacy? Is "racial profiling" acceptable in the search for terrorists? Is it "patriotic" to oppose military actions of one's country? What is the difference between a "political prisoner," a "detainee," and a "prisoner of war"? What roles do official "spin doctors" play in distribution of public information? Today, perhaps more than ever, we need to clearly understand specific meanings of language before we can make intelligent choices or take appropriate actions.

Why Do We Define?

Essays of extended definition are usually written for one or more of the following reasons:

1. To clarify an abstract term or concept ("hero," "success," "friendship," "loyalty")

2. To provide a personal interpretation of a term that the writer feels is vague, controversial, misused, or misunderstood ("feminist," "eco-terrorist," "senior citizen," "multiculturalism")

3. To explain a new or unusual term or phrase found in popular culture, slang, dialect, or within a particular geographic area or cultural group ("hip hop," "flash mob," "McJobs," "metrosexual," "lagniappe")

4. To make understandable the jargon or technical terms of a particular field of study, a profession, or an industry ("deconstruction," "blogs," "retinitis pigmentosa," "accelerated amortization")

5. To offer information about a term or an idea to a particular interested audience (antique collectors learning about "Depression glass," movie buffs understanding "film noir")

6. To inform and entertain by presenting the colorful history, uses, effects, or examples of a word, expression, or concept ("soul food," "Zydeco music," "urban legends," "Kwanzaa")

Developing Your Essay

Here are four suggestions to help you prepare your essay of extended definition:

Know your purpose. Sometimes we need to define a term as clearly and objectively as possible. As a laboratory assistant, for instance, you might need to explain a technical measuring instrument to a group of new students. At other times, however, we may wish to persuade as well as inform our readers. People's interpretations of words, especially abstract or controversial terms, can, and often do, differ greatly depending on their point of view. After all, one person's protest march can be another person's street riot. Consequently, before you begin writing, decide on your purpose. If your readers need objective information only, make your definition as unbiased as you can; if your goal is to convince them that your point of view is the right or best one, you may adopt a variety of persuasive techniques as well as subjective language. For example, readers of a paper entitled "Doc in the Box" should quickly realize that they are not getting an objective treatment of the twenty-four-hour emergency-care offices springing up around the country.

Give your readers a reason to read.   One way to introduce your subject is to explain the previous use, misuse, or misunderstanding of the term; then present your new or better interpretation of the term or concept. An introduction and thesis defining a new word in popular usage might state, "Although people who suffer from weak immune systems might suddenly fear breathing the same air as someone suffering from affluenza, they needn't worry. 'Affluenza' isn't germ-laden; it's simply a colorful term describing the out-of-control consumerism spreading like an epidemic through America today." Or consider this introduction and thesis aimed at a word the writer feels is unclear to many readers: "When the credits roll at the end of a movie, much of the audience may be perplexed to see the job of 'best boy' listed. No, the 'best boy' isn't the nicest kid on the set—he (or she) is, in fact, the key electrician's first assistant, who helps arrange the lights for the movie's director of photography."

Keep your audience in mind to anticipate and avoid problems of clarity.   Because you are trying to present a new or improved definition, you must strive above all for clarity. Ask yourself, "Who is my intended audience? What terms or parts of my definition are strange to them?" You don't help your audience, for example, by defining one campus slang expression in terms of other bits of unfamiliar slang. If, in other words, you discuss "mouse potatoes" as "Google bombers," you may be confusing some readers more than you are informing them. If your assignment doesn't specify a particular audience, you may find it useful to imagine one. You might pretend, for instance, that you're defining current campus slang for your parents, clarifying a local expression for a foreign visitor, or explaining a computer innovation to a technophobic friend. Remember that your definition is effective only if your explanation is clear not just to you but to those unfamiliar with the term or concept under discussion.

Use as many strategies as necessary to clarify your definition.   Depending on your subject, you may use any number of the following methods in your essay to define your term:

1. Describe the parts or distinguishing characteristics*
2. Offer some examples
3. Compare to or contrast with similar terms
4. Explain an operation or a process
5. State some familiar synonyms
6. Define by negation (that is, tell what the term doesn't mean)

---

* With some topics, it may also be useful to describe the genus, class, or species to which the subject belongs.

7. Present the history or trace its development or changes from the original linguistical meaning

8. Discuss causes or effects

9. Identify times/places of use or appearance

10. Associate it with recognizable people, places, or ideas

To illustrate some of the methods suggested here, let's suppose you wanted to write an extended definition of "crossover" country music. You might choose one or more of these methods:

- Describe the parts: lyrics, musical sound, instruments, typical subject matter
- Compare to or contrast with other kinds of music, such as traditional country music, Western swing, or "pop"
- Give some examples of famous "crossover" country songs and artists
- Trace its historical development from traditional country music to its present state

In the paper on "crossover" country music or in any definition essay, you should, of course, use only those methods that will best define your term. Never include methods purely for the sake of exhibiting a variety of techniques. You, the writer, must decide which method or methods work best, which should receive the most emphasis, and in which order the chosen methods of definition should appear.

Problems to Avoid

Here is a list of "don'ts" for the writer of extended definition essays:

Don't present an incomplete definition. An inadequate definition is often the result of choosing a subject too broad or complex for your essay. You probably can't, for instance, do a good job of defining "twentieth-century modern art" in all its varieties in a short essay; you might, however, introduce your reader to some specific school of modern art, such as cubism or surrealism. Always narrow your subject to a manageable size and then define it as thoroughly as possible.

Don't begin every definition essay by quoting Webster. If you must include a standard definition of your term, try to find a unique way of blending it into your discussion, perhaps as a point of contrast to your explanation of the word's meaning. Dictionary definitions are generally so overused as opening sentences that they often drive composition teachers to seek more interesting jobs, such as measuring spaghetti in a pasta factory. Don't bore your audience to death; it's a terrible way to go.

Don't define vaguely or by using generalities. As always, use specific, vivid details to explain your subject. If, for example, you define a shamrock as "a green plant with three leaves," you have also described hundreds of other plants, including poison ivy.

Consequently, you must select details that will make your subject distinct from any other. Including concrete examples is frequently useful in any essay but especially so when you are defining an abstract term, such as "pride," "patriotism," or "prejudice." To make your definition both interesting and clear, always add as many precise details as possible. (For a review of using specific, colorful language, see pages 116–118, 128–130, and 149–152.)

Don't offer circular definitions. To define a poet as "one who writes poetry" or the American Dream as "the dream most Americans hold dear" is about as helpful as a doctor telling a patient, "Your illness is primarily a lack of good health." Explain your subject; don't just rename it.

■ ESSAY TOPICS

Here are several suggestions for terms whose meanings are often unclear. Narrow any topic that seems too broad for your assignment, and decide before writing whether your definition will be objective or subjective. (Student writers, by the way, often note that abstract concepts are harder to define than the more concrete subjects, so proceed at your own risk, and remember to use plenty of specific detail in your essay.) For additional ideas, turn to the "Suggestions for Writing" section following the professional essay (page 243).

1. A current slang, campus, local, or popular-culture expression
2. A term from your field of study
3. A slob (or some other undesirable kind of roommate or friend)
4. Success or failure
5. A good/bad teacher, clerk, coach, friend, parent, date, or spouse
6. Heroism or cowardice
7. A term from science or technology
8. A kind of music, painting, architecture, or dance
9. A social label ("Goth," "Prep," "Skater," etc.)
10. A current fad or style or one from the past
11. A rebel or conformist
12. A family or hometown expression
13. A good/bad restaurant, store, movie theater, nightspot, class
14. Self-respect
15. Prejudice or discrimination
16. An important historical movement or group
17. A controversial political idea or term
18. A term from a hobby or sport
19. A medical term or condition

20. Select a painting or photograph in which you think the artist offers a visual definition of the subject matter. Explain this definition by examining the artist's choice and arrangement of details in the picture. (For example, study George Tooker's painting *The Subway*. What definition of urban life is being presented here? What parts of the picture illustrate and clarify this point of view? Or consider two other pictures in this text, *Migrant Mother* [page 322] or *The Scream* [page 111]. Other famous paintings that might work well for this assignment include Salvador Dali's surrealistic *Persistence of Memory* or any one of the many psychologically revealing self-portraits by Frida Kahlo.)

The Subway, 1950, by George Tooker

© 2000, Whitney Museum of American Art. Collection of the Whitney Museum of American Art, New York. Photography by Geoffrey Clements, NY.

A Topic Proposal for Your Essay

Selecting the right subject matter is important to every writer. To help you clarify your ideas and strengthen your commitment to your topic, here is a proposal sheet that asks you to describe some of your ideas about your subject before you begin drafting. Although your ideas may change as you write (they will almost certainly become more refined), thinking through your topic now may help you avoid several false starts.

1. What subject will your essay define? Will you define this subject objectively or subjectively? Why?

2. Why are you interested in this topic? Do you have a personal or professional connection to the subject? State at least one reason for your choice of topic.

3. Is this a significant topic of interest to others? Why? Who specifically might find it interesting, informative, or entertaining?

4. Is your subject a controversial, ambiguous, or new term? What will readers gain by understanding this term as defined from your point of view?

5. Writers use a variety of techniques to define terms. At this point, list at least two techniques you think you might use to help readers understand your topic.

6. What difficulties, if any, can you foresee during the drafting of this essay? For example, do you need to do any additional reading or interviewing to collect information for your definition?

■ Sample Student Essay

A student with an interest in running wrote the following essay defining "runner's high." Note that he uses several methods to define his subject, one that is difficult to explain to those who have not experienced it firsthand.

BLIND PACES

Introduction: An example and a general definition of the term

1   After running the Mile-Hi ten-kilometer race in my hometown, I spoke with several of the leading runners about their experiences in the race. While most of them agreed that the course, which passed through a beautifully wooded yet overly hilly country area, was difficult, they also agreed that it was one of the best races of their running careers. They could not, however, explain why it was such a wonderful race but could rather only mumble something about the tall trees, cool air, and sandy path. When pressed, most of them didn't even remember specific details about the course, except the start and finish, and ended their descriptions with a blank—but content—stare. This self-satisfied, yet almost indescribable, feeling is often the result of an experienced runner running, a feeling often called, because of its similarities to other euphoric experiences, "runner's high."

2   Because this experience is seemingly impossible to define, perhaps a description of what runner's high is not might, by contrast, lead

to a better understanding of what it is. I clearly remember—about
five years ago—when I first took up running. My first day, I donned
my tennis shorts, ragged T-shirt, and white discount-store tennis
shoes somewhat ashamedly, knowing that they were symbolic of my
novice status. I plodded around my block—just over a half mile—in a
little more than four minutes, feeling and regretting every painful
step. My shins and thighs revolted at every jarring move, and my
lungs wheezed uncontrollably, gasping for air, yet denied that
basic necessity. Worst of all, I was conscious of every aspect of my
existence—from the swinging of my arms to the slap of my feet on
the road, and from the sweat dripping into my eyes and ears and
mouth, to the frantic inhaling and exhaling of my lungs. I kept my
eyes carefully peeled on the horizon or the next turn in the road,
judging how far away it was, how long it would take me to get
there, and how much torture was left before I reached home. These
first few runs were, of course, the worst—as far from any euphoria or
"high" as possible. They did, however, slowly become easier as my
body became accustomed to running.

Definition by negation, contrast

3   After a few months, in fact, I felt serious enough about this new
pursuit to invest in a pair of real running shoes and shorts.
Admittedly, these changes added to the comfort of my endeavor, but
it wasn't until two full years later that the biggest change occurred—
and I experienced my first real "high." It was a fall day. The air was a
cool sixty-five degrees, the sun was shining intently, the sky was a
clear, crisp blue, and a few dead leaves were scattered across the
browning lawn. I stepped out onto the road and headed north
towards a nearby park for my routine jog. The next thing I
remember, however, was not my run through the park, but rather my
return, some forty-two minutes and six miles later, to my house. I
woke, as if out of a dream, just as I slowed to a walk, cooling down

Personal example

from my run. The only memory I had of my run was a feeling of floating on air—as if my real self was somewhere above and detached from my body, looking down on my physical self as it went through its blind paces. At first, I felt scared—what if I had run out in front of a car? Would I have even known it? I felt as if I had been asleep or out of control, that my brain had, in some real sense, been turned off.

Effects of the "high"

4   Now, after five years of running and hundreds of such mystical experiences, I realize that I had never lost control while in this euphoric state—and that my brain hadn't been turned off, or, at least, not completely. But what does happen is hard to prove. George Sheehan, in a column for Runner's World, suggests that "altered states," such as runner's high, result from the loss of conscious control, from the temporary cessation of left-brain messages and the dominance of right-brain activity (the left hemisphere being the seat of reason and rationality; the right, of emotions and inherited archetypal feelings) (14). Another explanation comes from Dr. Jerry Lynch, who argues, in his book The Total Runner, that the "high" results from the secretion of natural opiates, called beta endorphins, in the brain (213). My own explanation draws on both these medical explanations and is perhaps slightly more mystical. It's just possible that indeed natural opiates do go to work and consequently our brains lose track of the ins and outs of everyday activities—of jobs and classes and responsibilities. And because of this relaxed, drugged state, we are able to reach down into something more fundamental, something that ties us not only to each other but to all creation, here and gone. We rejoin nature, rediscovering the thread that links us to the universe.

Possible causes of the feeling: Two authorities

The writer's explanation

5   My explanation is, of course, unscientific and therefore suspect. But I found myself, that day of the Mile-Hi Ten K run, eagerly trying to discuss my experience with the other runners: I wanted desperately to discover where I had been and what I had been doing during the race for which I received my first trophy. I didn't discover the answer from my fellow runners that day, but it didn't matter. I'm still running and still feeling the glow—whatever it is.

Conclusion: An incomplete understanding doesn't hamper enjoyment

WORKS CITED*

Lynch, Jerry. The Total Runner: A Complete Mind-Body Guide to

Optimal Performance. Englewood Cliffs, NJ: Prentice Hall, 1987.

Sheehan, George. "Altered States." Runner's World. Aug. 1988: 14.

Professional Essay†

■ The Munchausen Mystery

Don R. Lipsitt

As a clinical professor of psychiatry at Harvard Medical School, Don R. Lipsitt has written over one hundred articles on mental health and coedited four books, including the *Handbook of Studies on General Hospital Psychiatry* (1991). In 2001 he was awarded a Lifetime Achievement Award from the Association of Academic Psychiatry. He published this article in *Psychology Today* in 1983.

1   In Thomas Mann's *Confessions of Felix Krull, Confidence Man*, young Felix fabricates an illness and convinces both his mother and the family doctor that he is sick. Felix describes the intense pleasure that his performance brings him. "I was delirious with the alternate tension and relaxation necessary to give reality, in my own eyes and others, to a condition that did not exist."

2   I estimate that in any given year in the United States, every general hospital with 100 or more beds admits an average of two patients who deliberately mimic symptoms of disease so convincingly that they deceive reasonably competent physicians. The patients'

---

* Editor's note: In a formal research paper, the "Works Cited" list appears on a separate page.
† To help you read this essay analytically, review pages 166–168.

ages range from 11 to 60, but most are men in their 20s and 30s. Often these strange imposters wander from hospital to hospital, but even if we count only one patient per hospital, we are left with the staggering figure of approximately 4,000 people each year who devote their energies to fooling medical practitioners. If each incurs a cost of $1,000 to $10,000—bills that are not unusual, and that are rarely paid—the annual drain on health services alone is between $4 million and $40 million.

3   What do these people hope to gain? Nothing more, experience and research suggest, than the opportunity to assume the role of patient—in some cases, all the way to the operating table.

4   Unlike hypochondriacs, who really believe that they are ill, these people intentionally use varied and often sophisticated deceptions to duplicate medical problems. These deceptions include: blood "spit up" from a rubber pouch concealed in the mouth; genital bleeding deliberately caused by sharp objects; hypoglycemia (low blood sugar) induced by insulin injections; and skin infections or abscesses caused by injecting oneself with feces, sputum, or laboratory cultures of bacteria. A patient who called himself "the Duncan Hines of American hospitals" logged about 400 admissions in 25 years. Another patient, dubbed the "Indiana cyclone," was hospitalized in at least 12 states and two countries. The dramatic fabrication and extensive wandering often observed in such individuals prompted the late British physician Richard Asher in 1951 to label their "condition" the Munchausen Syndrome, after a flamboyant 18th-century teller of tall tales fictionalized in *The Adventures of Baron von Munchausen*, by Rudolph Erich Raspe. But as Asher himself came to realize, the name is somewhat misleading. While stories of the Baron's escapades are always palpably absurd, the accounts of patients whose condition bears his name are generally quite feasible. "Indeed," says Asher, "it is the credibility of their stories that makes these patients such a perpetual and tedious problem."

5   For obvious reasons, Munchausen patients have been difficult to study—they usually flee once their fictions are exposed. But research to this point provides a minimal portrait. In addition to being primarily men in their 20s and 30s, most have high IQs (as their imaginative inventions indicate), often abuse but are not necessarily addicted to drugs, come from a background in which a doctor was an important figure, are employed in health care, and are productive citizens between episodes.

6   What produces their medical madness? There are three main explanations:

7   The psychoanalytic interpretation draws attention to the unconscious. The Munchausen patient, by feigning illness, presents himself simultaneously as victim and victimizer, and compulsively re-enacts unresolved conflicts: The weak child/patient is challenging and even defying the strong father/surgeon. Paradoxically, the weak patient controls the surgeon/parent—and risks death!—by "making" the doctor perform needless surgery. The psychoanalytic view also sees in the syndrome an attempt to continue into adulthood the game of "doctor," which characterizes a phase of childhood development.

8   A second explanation locates the source of Munchausen behavior in a personality trait known as borderline character disorder. According to Otto Kernberg, a psychoanalyst at Cornell who has most fully researched this trait, the core problems are untamed (often unconscious) rage and chronic feelings of boredom, two emotions that work against each other. The Munchausen character, for example, presents himself as a "sick" patient, a condition that should appeal to a dedicated physician—yet no accepting relationship can grow between a deceptive patient and a suspecting physician who is alternately idealized and despised.

9   The third explanation looks to excessive stress as the trigger that starts Munchausen patients on their medical odyssey. Many of them began their "wandering" and symptom mimicry in response to cumulative major disappointments, losses, or damage to self-image. One patient first sought surgery for questionable persistent stomach pains after being jilted by a medical-student lover, beginning a long string of lies and hospitalizations.

10   We are beginning to identify the reasons for the behavior of Munchausen patients, but we are still far from knowing how to free them of their remarkably creative compulsion for self-destructive behavior.

Questions on Content, Structure, and Style

1. Why does Lipsitt begin his essay with reference to Thomas Mann's character in *Confessions of Felix Krull, Confidence Man*?
2. What effect does the essay's title have on readers? Why didn't Lipsitt simply call this essay "Munchausen Disease"?
3. Why does Lipsitt feel this syndrome is important to understand? How does this problem affect the health-care system?
4. Why explain the origin of the syndrome's name?
5. Why does Lipsitt use specific examples of "deceptions" to develop his extended definition?
6. Similarly, why does Lipsitt offer examples of actual patients? Would additional examples be helpful?
7. How does Lipsitt use contrast as a technique of definition in paragraph 4?
8. What other strategy of definition does Lipsitt employ in paragraphs 6–9? Why might readers interested in understanding this syndrome want such discussion?
9. Evaluate the essay's conclusion. Is it an effective choice for this essay?
10. After reading Lipsitt's descriptive details, examples, and analysis, do you feel you now have a general understanding of a new term? If the writer were to expand his definition, what might he add to make your understanding even more complete? More statistics? Case studies? Testimony from doctors or patients themselves?

Suggestions for Writing

Try using Don Lipsitt's "The Munchausen Mystery" as a stepping-stone to your essay. Select a puzzling or "mysterious" subject from a field of study (e.g., black holes in space) or from an interest you have explored (or would like to explore). Write an extended definition, as Lipsitt did, that explains this mystery for your readers. As appropriate, include information about its characteristics, parts, history, possible causes, effects, solutions, benefits, or dangers. Or explore a well-known mystery, such as Stonehenge, the Bermuda Triangle, the Loch Ness monster, the Marfa lights, King Tut's "curse," Big Foot, the Roswell "aliens," or perhaps even a local ghost. Remember that your essay should offer in-depth explanation, not just general description.

Vocabulary

fabricates (1)	sputum (4)	psychoanalytic (7)
mimic (2)	palpably (4)	paradoxically (7)
incurs (2)	feasible (4)	odyssey (9)
hypochondriacs (4)		

■ A REVISION WORKSHEET

As you write your rough drafts, consult Chapter 5 for guidance through the revision process. In addition, here are a few questions to ask yourself as you revise your extended definition essay:

1. Is the subject narrowed to manageable size, and is the purpose of the definition clear to the readers?

2. If the definition is objective, is the language as neutral as possible?

3. If the definition is subjective, is the point of view obvious to the readers?

4. Are all the words and parts of the definition itself clear to the essay's particular audience?

5. Are there enough explanatory methods (examples, descriptions, history, causes, effects, etc.) used to make the definition clear and informative?

6. Have the various methods been organized and ordered in an effective way?

7. Does the essay contain enough specific details to make the definition clear and distinct rather than vague or circular? Where could additional details be added?

After you've revised your essay extensively, you might exchange rough drafts with a classmate and answer these questions for each other, making specific suggestions for improvement wherever appropriate. (For advice on productive participation in classroom workshops, see pages 106–109.)

Reviewing Your Progress

After you have completed your essay developed by definition, take a moment to measure your progress as a writer by responding to the following questions. Such analysis will help you recognize growth in your writing skills and may enable you to identify areas that are still problematic.

1. What do you like best about your essay? Why?

2. After considering the various methods of definition you used in your essay, which one do you think offered the clearest or most persuasive explanation of your topic? Why was that particular technique effective in this essay?

3. What part of your essay gave you the most trouble? How did you overcome the problem?

4. If you had more time to work on this essay, what would receive additional attention? Why?

5. What did you learn about your topic from writing this essay? About yourself as a writer?

■ Strategy Five: Development by Division and Classification

To make large or complex subjects easier to comprehend, we frequently apply the principles of *division* or *classification.*

Division

Division is the act of separating something into its component parts so that it may be better understood or used by the reader. For example, consider a complex subject such as the national budget. Perhaps you have seen a picture on television or in the newspaper of the budget represented by a circle or a pie that has been divided into parts and labeled: a certain percentage or "slice" of the budget designated for military spending, a another slice for social services, another for education, and so on. By studying the budget after it has been divided into its parts, taxpayers may have a better sense of how their money is being spent.

As a student, you see division in action in many of your college courses. A literature teacher, for instance, might approach a particular drama by dividing its plot into stages such as exposition, rising action, climax, falling action, and dénouement. Or your chemistry lab instructor may ask you to break down a substance into its components to learn how the parts interact to form the chemical. Even this textbook is divided into chapters to make it easier for you to use. When you think of *division,* then, think of dividing, separating, or breaking apart one subject (often a large or complex or unfamiliar one) into its parts to help people understand it more easily.

Classification

While the principle of division calls for separating one thing into its parts, *classification* systematically groups a number of things into categories to make the information easier to grasp. Without some sort of imposed system of order, a body of information can be a jumble of facts and figures. For example, at some point you've probably turned to the classified ads in the newspaper; if the ads were not classified into categories such as "houses to rent," "cars for sale," and "help wanted," you would have to search through countless ads to find the service or item you needed.

Classification occurs everywhere around you. As a student, you may be classified as a freshman, sophomore, junior, or senior; you may also be classified by your major. If you vote, you may be categorized as a Democrat, Republican, Independent, Socialist, or something else; if you attend religious services, you may be classified as Baptist, Methodist, Catholic, Jewish, and so on. The books you buy may be grouped and shelved by the bookstore into "mysteries," "Westerns," "biographies," "adventure stories," and other categories; the movies you see have already been typed as "G," "PG," "PG-13," "R," or "NC-17." Professionals classify almost every kind of knowledge: ornithologists classify birds; etymologists classify words by origins; botanists classify plants; zoologists classify animals. Remember that *classification* differs from division in that it sorts and organizes *many* things into appropriate groups, types, kinds, or categories. *Division* begins with *one* thing and separates it into its parts.

Developing Your Essay

A classification or division paper is generally easy to develop. Each part or category is identified and described in a major part of the body of the essay. Frequently, one body paragraph will be devoted to each category. Here are three additional hints for writing your essay:

Select one principle of classification or division and stick to it. If you are classifying students by major, for instance, don't suddenly switch to classification by college: French, economics, psychology, *arts and sciences*, math, and chemistry. A similar error occurs in this classification of dogs by breeds because it includes a physical characteristic: spaniels, terriers, *long-haired*, hounds, and retrievers. Decide on what basis of division you will classify or divide your subject and then be consistent throughout your essay.

Make the purpose of your division or classification clear to your audience. Don't just announce that "There are four kinds of 'X'" or that "'Z' has three important parts." Why does your particular audience need this information? Consider these sample thesis statements:

> By recognizing the three kinds of poisonous snakes in this area, campers and backpackers may be able to take the proper medical steps if they are bitten.

> Knowing the four types of spinning reels will allow those new to ice fishing to purchase the equipment best suited to their needs.

> Although karate has become a popular form of exercise as well as of self-defense, few people know what the six levels of achievement—or "belts" as they are called—actually stand for.

Organize your material for a particular purpose and then explain to your readers what that purpose is.

Account for all the parts in your division or classification. Don't, for instance, claim to classify all the evergreen trees native to your hometown and then leave out one or more species. For a short essay, narrow your ruling principle rather than omit categories. You couldn't, for instance, classify all the architectural styles in America in a short paper, but you might discuss the major styles on your campus. In the same manner, the enormous task of classifying all types of mental illness could be narrowed to the most common forms of childhood schizophrenia. However you narrow your topic, remember that in a formal classification, all the parts must be accounted for.

Like most rules, the preceding one has an exception. If your instructor permits, you can also write a satirical or humorous classification. In this sort of essay, you make up your own categories as well as your thesis. One writer, for example, recently wrote about the kinds of moviegoers who spoil the show for everyone else, such as "the babbling idiot," "the laughing hyena," and "the wandering dawdler." Another female student described blind dates to avoid, including "Mr. Neanderthal," "Timothy Timid," "Red, the Raging Rebel," and "Frat-Rat Freddie," among others. Still another student classified the various kinds of people who frequent the school library at 2 A.M. In this kind of informal essay, the thesis rule still holds true: though you start by making a humorous or satirical point about your subject, your classification must be more than mere silliness. Effective humor should ultimately make good sense, not nonsense.

Problems to Avoid

Avoid underdeveloped categories. A classification or division essay is not a mechanical list; each category should contain enough specific details to make it clearly recognizable and interesting. To present each category or part, you may draw on the methods of development you already know, such as example, comparison and contrast, and definition. Try to use the same techniques in each category so that no one category or part of your essay seems underdeveloped or unclear.

Avoid indistinct categories. Each category should be a separate unit; there should be no overlap among categories. For example, in a classification of shirts by fabric, the inclusion of flannel with silk, nylon, and cotton is an overlap because flannel is a kind of cotton. Similarly, in a classification of soft drinks by flavor, to include sugar-free with cola, root beer, orange, grape, and so on, is misleading because sugar-free drinks come in many different flavors. In other words, make each category unique.

Avoid too few or too many categories. A classification essay should have at least three categories, avoiding the either-or dichotomy. On the other hand, too many categories give a short essay the appearance of a list rather than a discussion. Whatever the number, don't forget to use transitional devices for easy movement from category to category.

■ ESSAY TOPICS

Narrow and focus your subject by selecting an appropriate principle of division or classification. Some of the suggestions below may be appropriate for humorous essays ("The Three Best Breeds of Cats for Antisocial People"). For additional ideas, see the "Suggestions for Writing" section following the professional essays (pages 254 and 257).

1. Friends or relatives
2. First-year college students
3. Heroes in a particular field
4. Summer or part-time jobs
5. Attitudes toward a current controversy
6. Kinds of popular tattoos

7. Specializations in your field of study

8. Approaches to studying a subject

9. Classmates, roommates, or dates

10. Dogs, cats, birds, or other pets

11. Popular kinds of movies, music, or video games (or types within a larger category: kinds of horror movie monsters or varieties of "heavy-metal" music)

12. Chronic moochers or fibbers

13. Vacations or Spring Break trips

14. Methods of accomplishing a task (ways to conduct an experiment, ways to introduce a bill into Congress)

15. Bosses or co-workers to avoid

16. Kinds of tools or equipment for a particular task in your field of study

17. Theories explaining "X" (the disappearance of the dinosaurs, for example)

18. Diets, exercise, or stress-reduction programs (or their participants)

19. Reasons people participate in some activity (or excuses for not participating)

20. Amateur athletes, coaches, or sports fans (including those you hope aren't sitting next to you at an athletic event)

Wisconsin Cheese Heads cheer on the Green Bay Packers.

A Topic Proposal for Your Essay

Selecting the right subject matter is important to every writer. To help you clarify your ideas and strengthen your commitment to your topic, here is a proposal sheet that asks you to describe some of your preliminary ideas about your subject before you begin drafting. Although your ideas may change as you write (they will almost certainly become more refined), thinking through your choice of topic now may help you avoid several false starts.

1. What is the subject of your essay? Will you write an essay of classification or division?

2. What principle of classification or division will you use? Why is this a useful or informative principle for your particular topic and readers?

3. Why are you interested in this topic? Do you have a personal or professional connection to the subject? State at least one reason for your choice of topic.

4. Is this a significant topic of interest to others? Why? Who specifically might find it interesting, informative, or entertaining?

5. List at least three categories you are considering for development in your essay.

6. What difficulties, if any, might arise from this topic during the drafting of your essay? For example, do you know enough about your topic to offer details that will make each of your categories clear and distinct to your readers?

■ Sample Student Essay

In the following essay, the student writer divided the Mesa Verde Indian Era into three time periods that correspond to changes in the people's domestic skills, crafts, and housing. Note the writer's use of description and examples to help the reader distinguish one time period from another.

THE INDIAN ERA AT MESA VERDE

1   Visiting Mesa Verde National Park is a trip back in time to two and a half centuries before Columbus. The park, located in southwestern Colorado, is the setting of a silent stone city, ten ruins built into protective seven-hundred-foot cliffs that housed hundreds of people from the pre-Columbian era to the end of the thirteenth century. Visitors to the park often enjoy its architecture and history more if they know a little about the various people who lived there. The

Introduction: Establishing a reason for knowing the classification

Principle of
division of the
Indian Era

Indian Era may be divided into three time periods that show growing sophistication in such activities as crafts, hunting, trade, and housing: Basket Maker (A.D. 1–450), Modified Basket Maker (A.D. 450–750), and Pueblo (A.D. 750–1300).*

Time period
one: Early
cliff life

2   The earliest Mesa Verdeans, the Basket Makers, whose ancestors had been nomads, sought shelter from the dry plains in the cliff caves and became farmers. During growing seasons they climbed up toeholds cut in the cliffs and grew beans and squash on the green mesa above. Settling down also meant more time for crafts. They didn't make pottery yet but instead wove intricate baskets that held water. Instead of depending on raw meats and vegetables, they could now cook food in these baskets by dropping heated rocks into the water. Because the Basket Makers hadn't discovered the bow and arrow yet, they had to rely on the inaccurate spear, which meant little fresh meat and few animal skins. Consequently, they wore little clothing but liked bone, seed, and stone ornaments.

Time period
two: New
crafts, trade,
and housing

3   The second period, A.D. 450–750, saw the invention of pottery, the bow and arrow, and houses. Pottery was apparently learned from other tribes. From crude clay baked in the sun, the Mesa Verdeans advanced to clay mixed with straw and sand and baked in kilns. Paints were concocted from plants and minerals, and the tribe produced a variety of beautifully decorated mugs, bowls, jars, pitchers, and canteens. Such pots meant that water could be stored for longer periods, and perhaps a water supply encouraged more trade with neighboring tribes. These Mesa Verdeans also acquired the bow and arrow, a weapon that improved their hunting skills, and

* Last summer I worked at Mesa Verde as a student-guide for the Parks Service; the information in this paper is based on the tour I gave three times a week to hundreds of visitors to the park.

enlarged their wardrobes to include animal skins and feather blankets. Their individual living quarters, called pithouses, consisted of twenty-foot-wide holes in the ground with log, grasses, and earthen framework over them.

4   The third period lasted until A.D. 1300 and saw the innovation of pueblos, or groups of dwellings, instead of single-family units. Nearly eight hundred dwellings show the large number of people who inhabited the complex tunneled houses, shops, storage rooms, courtyards, and community centers whose masonry walls, often elaborately decorated, were three and four stories high. At the spacious Balcony House pueblo, for example, an adobe court lies beneath another vaulted roof; on three sides stand two-story houses with balconies that lead from one room to the next. In back of the court is a spring, and along the front side is a low wall that kept the children from falling down the seven-hundred-foot cliff to the canyon floor below. Balcony House pueblo also contains two kivas, circular subterranean ceremonial chambers that show the importance of fellowship and religion to the people of this era. During this period the Mesa Verdeans were still farmers and potters, but cotton cloth and other nonnative products found at the ruins suggest a healthy trade with the south. But despite the trade goods, sophisticated pottery, and such innovations in clothing as the "disposable" juniper-bark diapers of babies, life was still simple; the Mesa Verdeans had no system of writing, no wheel, and no metal.

Time period three: Expanded community living and trade

5   Near the end of the thirteenth century, the cliff dwellings became ghost towns. Archaeologists don't know for certain why the Mesa Verdeans left their elaborate homes, but they speculate that a drought that lasted some twenty years may have driven them south

Conclusion: The importance of understanding Mesa Verde's people

into New Mexico and Arizona, where strikingly similar crafts and tools have been found. Regardless of their reason for leaving, they left an amazing architectural and cultural legacy. Learning about the people who lived in Mesa Verde centuries ago provides an even deeper appreciation of the cliff palaces that awe thousands of national park visitors every year.

Professional Essay: Classification*

■ The Plot against People

Russell Baker

Russell Baker has been a journalist and social commentator for over forty years. His "Observer" columns, written for *The New York Times* and syndicated throughout the country, have won him both the George Polk Award for Distinguished Commentary and a Pulitzer Prize for journalism. He has published twelve books, including *Growing Up* (1982), an autobiography that won him a second Pulitzer Prize; *The Good Times* (1989); and *Looking Back* (2002). This essay originally appeared in *The New York Times* in 1968.

1   Inanimate objects are classified into three major categories—those that don't work, those that break down and those that get lost.

2   The goal of all inanimate objects is to resist man and ultimately to defeat him, and the three major classifications are based on the method each object uses to achieve its purpose. As a general rule, any object capable of breaking down at the moment when it is most needed will do so. The automobile is typical of the category.

3   With the cunning typical of its breed, the automobile never breaks down while entering a filling station with a large staff of idle mechanics. It waits until it reaches a downtown intersection in the middle of the rush hour, or until it is fully loaded with family and luggage on the Ohio Turnpike.

4   Thus it creates maximum misery, inconvenience, frustration and irritability among its human cargo, thereby reducing its owner's life span.

5   Washing machines, garbage disposals, lawn mowers, light bulbs, automatic laundry dryers, water pipes, furnaces, electrical fuses, television tubes, hose nozzles, tape

---

* To help you read this essay analytically, review pages 166–168.

recorders, slide projectors—all are in league with the automobile to take their turn at breaking down whenever life threatens to flow smoothly for their human enemies.

6   Many inanimate objects, of course, find it extremely difficult to break down. Pliers, for example, and gloves and keys are almost totally incapable of breaking down. Therefore, they have had to evolve a different technique for resisting man.

7   They get lost. Science has still not solved the mystery of how they do it, and no man has ever caught one of them in the act of getting lost. The most plausible theory is that they have developed a secret method of locomotion which they are able to conceal the instant a human eye falls upon them.

8   It is not uncommon for a pair of pliers to climb all the way from the cellar to the attic in its single-minded determination to raise its owner's blood pressure. Keys have been known to burrow three feet under mattresses. Women's purses, despite their great weight, frequently travel through six or seven rooms to find hiding space under a couch.

9   Scientists have been struck by the fact that things that break down virtually never get lost, while things that get lost hardly ever break down.

10   A furnace, for example, will invariably break down at the depth of the first winter cold wave, but it will never get lost. A woman's purse, which after all does have some inherent capacity for breaking down, hardly ever does; it almost invariably chooses to get lost.

11   Some persons believe this constitutes evidence that inanimate objects are not entirely hostile to man, and that a negotiated peace is possible. After all, they point out, a furnace could infuriate a man even more thoroughly by getting lost than by breaking down, just as a glove could upset him far more by breaking down than by getting lost.

12   Not everyone agrees, however, that this indicates a conciliatory attitude among inanimate objects. Many say it merely proves that furnaces, gloves and pliers are incredibly stupid.

13   The third class of objects—those that don't work—is the most curious of all. These include such objects as barometers, car clocks, cigarette lighters, flashlights and toy-train locomotives. It is inaccurate, of course, to say that they never work. They work once, usually for the first few hours after being brought home, and then quit. Thereafter, they never work again.

14   In fact, it is widely assumed that they are built for the purpose of not working. Some people have reached advanced ages without ever seeing some of these objects—barometers, for example—in working order.

15   Science is utterly baffled by the entire category. There are many theories about it. The most interesting holds that the things that don't work have attained the highest state possible for an inanimate object, the state to which things that break down and things that get lost can still only aspire.

16   They have truly defeated man by conditioning him never to expect anything of them, and in return they have given man the only peace he receives from inanimate society. He does not expect his barometer to work, his electric locomotive to run, his cigarette lighter to light or his flashlight to illuminate, and when they don't, it does not raise his blood pressure.

17   He cannot attain that peace with furnaces and keys and cars and women's purses as long as he demands that they work for their keep.

Questions on Content, Structure, and Style

1. What is Baker's purpose in writing this classification? What reaction do you think Baker wants to evoke from his reading audience?

2. Where is Baker's thesis statement? Would his essay be more effective if his thesis were preceded by a fully developed lead-in? Why or why not?

3. Identify Baker's categories and principle of classification. What do these categories have in common?

4. Why does Baker give examples of items that belong to each category? Does this strengthen his essay? Why or why not?

5. Of the categories of inanimate objects discussed in the essay, which one is most effectively developed? List some examples of details.

6. Consider Baker's use of personification as he talks about inanimate objects. Give some examples of descriptions that give human qualities to these items. What effect does this have on tone and style?

7. How does Baker's word choice affect his tone? Would it be possible to write an effective essay about this subject from a more serious, informative standpoint? Why or why not?

8. What does Baker's title contribute to his tone and his readers' understanding of his classifying principle?

9. Evaluate Baker's conclusion. Is it effective or too abrupt?

10. What other categories of inanimate objects might you add to this essay? What items could you include under these new classifications?

Suggestions for Writing

Try using Russell Baker's "The Plot Against People" as a stepping-stone to your writing. To parallel Baker's criticisms of objects that inflict misery, think about kinds of people or forces that you feel are secretly conspiring to destroy your peace of mind. Consider, for example, kinds of crazed drivers who are contributing to road rage today. Annoying telephone solicitors? Obnoxious waiters or clerks? Grocery shoppers in the checkout line in front of you? Or consider the kinds of rules that govern your life. Inane parking regulations that ensure you will never find a space anywhere near campus? Financial aid red tape only an accounting genius could cut through? Your essay might be humorous, like Baker's, or quite serious, as you expose still another "plot" against humankind.

Vocabulary

inanimate (1)	locomotion (7)	constitutes (11)
cunning (3)	virtually (9)	conciliatory (12)
evolve (6)	inherent (10)	barometer (13)

Professional Essay: Division*

▪ A Brush with Reality: Surprises in the Tube

David Bodanis

A former teacher of intellectual history at the University of Oxford, David Bodanis speaks, writes, and conducts workshops on global trends in science and technology. Four of his books offer revealing insights into our bodies and homes: *The Body Book: A Fantastic Voyage to the World Within* (1984); *The Secret Garden: Dawn to Dusk in the Astonishing Hidden World of the Garden* (1992); *The Secret Family: Twenty-four Hours Inside the Mysterious World of Our Minds and Bodies* (1997); and *The Secret House* (1986), from which this excerpt is taken. His most recent book is *E=mc²: A Biography of the World's Most Famous Equation* (2000).

1   Into the bathroom goes our male resident, and after the most pressing need is satisfied, it's time to brush the teeth. The tube of toothpaste is squeezed, its pinched metal seams are splayed, pressure waves are generated inside, and the paste begins to flow. But what's in this toothpaste, so carefully being extruded out?

2   Water mostly, 30 to 45 percent in most brands: ordinary, everyday simple tap water. It's there because people like to have a big glob of toothpaste to spread on the brush, and water is the cheapest stuff there is when it comes to making big globs. Dripping a bit from the tap onto your brush would cost virtually nothing; whipped in with the rest of the toothpaste the manufacturers can sell it at a neat and accountant-pleasing $2 per pound equivalent. Toothpaste manufacture is a very lucrative occupation.

3   Second to water in quantity is chalk: exactly the same material that schoolteachers use to write on blackboards. It is collected from the crushed remains of long-dead ocean creatures. In the Cretaceous seas chalk particles served as part of the wickedly sharp outer skeleton that these creatures had to wrap around themselves to keep from getting chomped by all the slightly larger other ocean creatures they met. Their massed graves are our present chalk deposits.

4   The individual chalk particles—the size of the smallest mud particles in your garden—have kept their toughness over the aeons, and now on the toothbrush they'll need it. The enamel outer coating of the tooth they'll have to face is the hardest substance in the body—tougher than skull, or bone, or nail. Only the chalk particles in toothpaste can successfully grind into the teeth during brushing, ripping off the surface layers like an abrading wheel grinding down a boulder in a quarry.

5   The craters, slashes, and channels that the chalk tears into the teeth will also remove a certain amount of built-up yellow in the carnage, and it is for that polishing function that it's there. A certain amount of unduly enlarged extra-abrasive chalk fragments tear such cavernous pits into the teeth that future decay bacteria will be able to bunker down there and thrive; the quality control people find it almost impossible to screen out these errant super-chalk pieces, and government regulations allow them to stay in.

* To help you read this essay analytically, review pages 166–168.

6   In case even the gouging doesn't get all the yellow off, another substance is worked into the toothpaste cream. This is titanium dioxide. It comes in tiny spheres, and it's the stuff bobbing around in white wall paint to make it come out white. Splashed around onto your teeth during the brushing it coats much of the yellow that remains. Being water soluble it leaks off in the next few hours and is swallowed, but at least for the quick glance up in the mirror after finishing it will make the user think his teeth are truly white. Some manufacturers add optical whitening dyes—the stuff more commonly found in washing machine bleach—to make extra sure that the glance in the mirror shows reassuring white.

7   These ingredients alone would not make a very attractive concoction. They would stick in the tube like a sloppy white plastic lump, hard to squeeze out as well as revolting to the touch. Few consumers would savor rubbing in a mixture of water, ground-up blackboard chalk, and the whitener from latex paint first thing in the morning. To get around that finicky distaste the manufacturers have mixed in a host of other goodies.

8   To keep the glop from drying out, a mixture including glycerine glycol—related to the most common car antifreeze ingredient—is whipped in with the chalk and water, and to give *that* concoction a bit of substance (all we really have so far is wet colored chalk) a large helping is added of gummy molecules from the seaweed *Chondrus Crispus*. This seaweed ooze spreads in among the chalk, paint, and antifreeze, then stretches itself in all directions to hold the whole mass together. A bit of paraffin oil (the fuel that flickers in camping lamps) is pumped in with it to help the moss ooze keep the whole substance smooth.

9   With the glycol, ooze, and paraffin we're almost there. Only two major chemicals are left to make the refreshing, cleansing substance we know as toothpaste. The ingredients so far are fine for cleaning, but they wouldn't make much of the satisfying foam we have come to expect in the morning brushing.

10   To remedy that, every toothpaste on the market has a big dollop of detergent added too. You've seen the suds detergent will make in a washing machine. The same substance added here will duplicate that inside the mouth. It's not particularly necessary, but it sells.

11   The only problem is that by itself this ingredient tastes, well, too like detergent. It's horribly bitter and harsh. The chalk put in the toothpaste is pretty foul-tasting too for that matter. It's to get around the gustatory discomfort that the manufacturers put in the ingredient they tout perhaps the most of all. This is the flavoring, and it has to be strong. Double-rectified peppermint oil is used—a flavorer so powerful that chemists know better than to sniff it in the raw state in the laboratory. Menthol crystals and saccharin or other sugar simulators are added to complete the camouflage operation.

12   Is that it? Chalk, water, paint, seaweed, antifreeze, paraffin oil, detergent, and peppermint? Not quite. A mix like that would be irresistible to the hundreds of thousands of individual bacteria lying on the surface of even an immaculately cleaned bathroom sink. They would get in, float in the water bubbles, ingest the ooze and paraffin, maybe even spray out enzymes to break down the chalk. The result would be an uninviting mess. The way manufacturers avoid the final obstacle is by putting something in to kill the bacteria. Something good and strong is needed, something that will zap any accidentally intrudant bacteria into oblivion. And that something is formaldehyde—the disinfectant used in anatomy labs.

13   So it's chalk, water, paint, seaweed, antifreeze, paraffin oil, detergent, peppermint, formaldehyde, and fluoride (which can go some way toward preserving children's

teeth)—that's the usual mixture raised to the mouth on the toothbrush for a fresh morning's clean. If it sounds too unfortunate, take heart. Studies show that thorough brushing with just plain water will often do as good a job.

Questions on Content, Structure, and Style

1. How does this essay illustrate division rather than classification?

2. In additional to providing factual information, what is Bodanis's purpose in writing this essay? What response to his subject matter is he trying to produce in his readers?

3. How does Bodanis organize the parts of his division?

4. For what audience is Bodanis writing? How did an awareness of his audience influence his explanations?

5. As a reader, are you confident that Bodanis has accounted for all the parts in the subject of his division? If so, what gives you this sense of confidence?

6. In his explanation of an ingredient, Bodanis sometimes mentions its use in other products. Why does he do so?

7. How does Bodanis employ comparison and cause-and-effect explanations to clarify his subject and inform his readers?

8. What does Bodanis's word choice reveal about his attitude toward toothpaste manufacturing? Cite some examples of Bodanis's vivid language that transform this essay into more than a dry list of chemical ingredients.

9. Why does Bodanis use repetition in paragraphs 9, 12, and 13?

10. Evaluate Bodanis's conclusion. Does it provide an ending that is consistent with Bodanis's tone and point of view throughout the essay? Why/why not?

Suggestions for Writing

Use David Bodanis's essay "A Brush with Reality: Surprises in the Tube" as a stepping-stone to your essay. As a consumer, what other personal products would you like to know more about? What's really in our deodorant, cosmetics, or hair products? Consider any one of the many household cleaners or detergents. Or, if you prefer, think about food as a subject for a division essay. What is in lunch meat? Soft drinks? "Processed cheese food"? Or write an essay that nutritionally analyzes your favorite fast-food dinner. How healthy is a Happy Meal for our nation's children? Make your attitude toward your subject matter unmistakable, as Bodanis did, through your vivid details and word choice.

Vocabulary

splayed (1)	abrading (4)	errant (5)
extruded (1)	carnage (5)	gustatory (11)
lucrative (2)	cavernous (5)	intrudant (12)
aeons (4)		

■ A REVISION WORKSHEET

As you write your rough drafts, consult Chapter 5 for guidance through the revision process. In addition, here are a few questions to ask yourself as you revise your classification essay:

1. Is the purpose of the essay clear to the reader?

2. Is the principle of classification or division maintained consistently throughout the essay?

3. If the essay presents a formal division or classification, has the subject been narrowed so that all the parts of the subject are accounted for?

4. If the essay presents an informal or humorous division or classification, does the paper nevertheless make a significant or entertaining point?

5. Is each category developed with enough specific detail? Where might more details be effectively added?

6. Is each class distinct, with no overlap among categories?

7. Is the essay organized logically and coherently with smooth transitions between the discussions of the categories?

After you've revised your essay extensively, you might exchange rough drafts with a classmate and answer these questions for each other, making specific suggestions for improvement wherever appropriate. (For advice on productive participation in classroom workshops, see pages 106–109.)

Reviewing Your Progress

After you have completed your essay developed by classification or division, take a moment to measure your progress as a writer by responding to the following questions. Such analysis will help you recognize growth in your writing skills and may enable you to identify areas that are still problematic.

1. What is the best feature of your essay? Why?

2. Which category do you think is the clearest or most persuasive in your essay? Why does that one stand above the others?

3. What part of your essay gave you the most trouble? How did you overcome the problem?

4. If you had more time to work on this essay, what would receive additional attention? Why?

5. What did you learn about your topic from writing this essay? About yourself as a writer?

■ Strategy Six: Development by Causal Analysis

Causal analysis explains the cause-and-effect relationship between two (or more) elements. When you discuss the condition producing something, you are analyzing *cause;* when you discuss the result produced by something, you are analyzing *effect.* To find examples of causal analysis, you need only look around you. If your car stops running on the way to class, for example, you may discover the cause was an empty gas tank. On campus, in your history class, you may study the causes of the Civil War; in your economics class, the effects of teenage spending on the cosmetics market; and in your biology class, both the causes and effects of heart disease. Over dinner you may discuss the effects of some crisis in the Middle East on American foreign policy, and, as you drift to sleep, you may ponder the effects of your studying—or *not* studying—for your math test tomorrow.

To express it most simply, *cause* asks:

why did "X" happen?

or why does "X" happen?

or why will "X" happen?

Effect, on the other hand, asks:

what did "Y" produce?

or what does "Y" produce?

or what will "Y" produce?

Some essays of causal analysis focus primarily on the cause(s) of something; others mainly analyze the effect(s); still others discuss both causes and effects. If, for example, you wanted to concentrate on the major causes of the Wall Street crash of 1929, you might begin by briefly describing the effects of the crash on the economy, then devote your thesis and the rest of your essay to analyzing the major causes, perhaps allotting one major section (or one paragraph, depending on the complexity of the reasons) to each cause. Conversely, an effect paper might briefly note the causes of the crash and then detail the most important effects. An essay covering both the causes and effects of something often demands a longer paper so that each part will be clear. (Your assignment will frequently indicate which kind of causal analysis to write. However, if the choice is yours, let your interest in the subject be your guide.)

Developing Your Essay

Whether you are writing an essay that primarily discusses either causes or effects, or one that focuses on both, you should follow these rules:

Present a reasonable thesis statement. If your thesis makes dogmatic, unsupportable claims ("Medicare will lead to a complete collapse of quality medical treatment") or overly broad assertions ("Peer pressure causes alcoholism among students"), you won't convince your reader. Limit or qualify your thesis whenever necessary by using such phrases as "may be," "a contributing factor," "one of the main reasons," "two important factors," and so on ("Peer pressure is *one of the major causes* of alcoholism among students").

Limit your essay to a discussion of recent, major causes or effects. In a short paper you generally don't have space to discuss minor or remote causes or effects. If, for example, you analyzed your car wreck, you might decide that the three major causes were defective brakes, a hidden yield sign, and bad weather. A minor, or remote, cause might include being slightly tired because of less-than-usual sleep, less sleep because of staying out late the night before, staying out late because of an out-of-town visitor, and so on—back to the womb. In some cases you may want to mention a few of the indirect causes or effects, but do be reasonable. Concentrate on the most immediate, most important factors. Often, a writer of a 500-to-800-word essay will discuss no more than two, three, or four major causes or effects of something; trying to cover more frequently results in an underdeveloped essay that is not convincing.

Organize your essay clearly. Organization of your causal analysis essay will vary, of course, depending on whether you are focusing on the causes of something or the effects, or both. To avoid becoming tangled in causes and effects, you might try sketching out a drawing of your thesis and essay map before you begin your first draft. Here, for instance, are a couple of sketches for essays you might write on your recent traffic accident:

Thesis Emphasizing the Causes:

Cause (defective brakes)
Cause (hidden yield sign)   produced   Effect (my car wreck)
Cause (bad weather)

Thesis Emphasizing the Effects:

                                    Effect (loss of car)
Cause (my car wreck)   produced   Effect (doctor bills)
                                    Effect (higher insurance rates)

Sometimes you may discover that you can't isolate "the three main causes/effects of 'X'"; some essays do in fact demand a narrative explaining a chain reaction of causes and effects. For example, a paper on the rebellion of the American colonies might show how one unjust British law or restriction after another led to the war for independence. In this kind of causal analysis essay, be careful to limit your subject so that you'll have the space necessary to show your readers how each step in the chain led to the next. Here's a sketch of a slightly different car-wreck paper presented in a narrative or chain-reaction format:

Cause ⟶ 1st Effect ^{causes}→ 2nd Effect ^{causes}→ 3rd Effect

(bad weather)   (wet brakes)   (car wreck)   (doctor bills)

Sometimes the plan for organizing your causal analysis paper will be suggested by your subject matter; often, however, you'll have to devote some of your prewriting time to deciding, first, whether you want to emphasize causes or effects and, then, in what arrangement you will present your analysis.

Convince your reader that a causal relationship exists by showing how the relationship works. Let's suppose you are writing an essay in which you want to discuss the three major changes you've undergone since coming to college. Don't just state the changes and describe them; your job is to show the reader how college has *brought about* these changes. If, for instance, your study habits have improved, you must show the reader how the academic demands of your college courses caused you to change your habits; a simple description of your new study techniques is not enough. Remember that a causal analysis essay should stress *how* (and sometimes *why*) "X" caused "Y," rather than merely describing "Y" as it now exists.

Problems to Avoid

Don't oversimplify by assigning one all-encompassing cause to some effect. Most complex subjects have more than one cause (or effect), so make your analysis as complete and objective as you can, especially when dealing with your own problems or beliefs. For example, was that car wreck really caused only by the bad weather—or also because of your carelessness? Did your friend do poorly in astronomy class only because the instructor didn't like her? Before judging a situation too quickly, investigate your own biases. Then provide a thoughtful, thorough analysis, effectively organized to convince your readers of the validity of your viewpoint.

Avoid the *post hoc* fallacy. This error in logic (from the Latin phrase *post hoc, ergo propter hoc,* meaning "after this, therefore because of this") results when we mistake a temporal connection for a causal relationship—or in other words, when we assume that because one event follows another in time, the first event caused the second. Most of our superstitions are *post hoc* fallacies; we now realize that bad luck after walking under a ladder is a matter of coincidence, not cause and effect. The *post hoc* fallacy provided the basis for a rather popular joke in the 1960s' debates over decriminalizing marijuana. Those against argued that marijuana led to heroin because most users of the hard drug had first smoked the weed. The proponents retorted that milk, then, was the real culprit, because both marijuana and heroin users had drunk milk as babies. The point is this: in any causal analysis, you must be able to offer proof or reasoned logic to show that one event *caused* another, not just that it preceded it in time.

Avoid circular logic. Often causal essays seem to chase their own tails when they include such circular statements as "There aren't enough parking spaces for students on campus because there are too many cars." Such a statement merely presents a second half that restates what is already implied in the first half. A revision might say, "There aren't enough parking spaces for students on campus because the parking permits are not distributed fairly." This kind of assertion can be argued specifically and effectively; the other is a dead end.

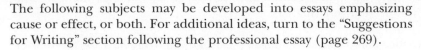

■ ESSAY TOPICS

The following subjects may be developed into essays emphasizing cause or effect, or both. For additional ideas, turn to the "Suggestions for Writing" section following the professional essay (page 269).

1. A pet peeve or bad habit

2. A change of mind about some important issue or belief

3. An accident, illness, or misadventure

4. A family tradition, ritual, or story

5. A trip or an experience in a different country or culture (for inspiration, read Julia Alvarez's "Snow" on page 440)

6. The best gift you ever received or ownership of a particular possession

7. A radical change in your appearance

8. A hobby, sport, or job

9. The best (or worst) advice you ever gave, followed, or rejected

10. An important decision or choice

11. An act of heroism or sacrifice

12. An important idea, event, or discovery in your field of study

13. A superstition or irrational fear

14. A place that is special to you

15. A disappointment or a success

16. Racism or sexism or some other kind of discrimination or prejudice

17. A friendship or influential person

18. A political action (campus, local, state, national), historical event, or social movement

19. A popular cultural trend (tattooing, piercing, clothing or hair styles)

20. A piece of visual art promoting a particular cause or point of view (Consider, for example, the famous image of Rosie the Riveter, who first appeared on a poster sponsored by the War Production Committee during World War II. Considering the gender roles of the time, why was such a poster needed? What effects was this image designed to have on both its male and female viewers? What specific elements in this picture produce these effects? What effect does this image have on viewers today? If you prefer, select another visual image reproduced in this text, such as *Migrant Mother* [page 322], or *The Subway* [page 237], or *Starry Night* [page 433], and analyze its major effects on the viewer.)

Rosie the Riveter, World War II poster

A Topic Proposal for Your Essay

Selecting the right subject matter is important to every writer. To help you clarify your ideas and strengthen your commitment to your topic, here is a proposal sheet that asks you to describe some of your preliminary ideas about your subject before you begin drafting. Although your ideas may change as you write (they will almost certainly become more refined), thinking through your choice of topic now may help you avoid several false starts.

1. What is the subject and purpose of your causal analysis essay? Is this subject appropriately narrowed and focused for a discussion of major causes or effects?

2. Will you develop your essay to emphasize primarily the effects or the causes of your topic? Or is a causal chain the most appropriate method of development?

3. Why are you interested in this topic? Do you have a personal or professional connection to the subject? State at least one reason for your choice of topic.

4. Is this a significant topic of interest to others? Why? Who specifically might find it interesting, informative, or entertaining?

5. List at least two major causes or effects that you might develop in the discussion of your topic.

6. What difficulties, if any, might arise during your drafting on this topic? For example, how might you convince a skeptical reader that your causal relationship is not merely a temporal one?

■ Sample Student Essay

In the following essay, a student explains why working in a local motel damaged her self-esteem, despite her attempts to do a good job. Note that the writer uses many vivid examples and specific details to show the reader how she was treated and, consequently, how such treatment made her feel.

IT'S SIMPLY NOT WORTH IT

Introduction: Her job as a motel maid

1   It's hard to find a job these days, and with our county's unemployment rate reaching as high as 5 percent, most people feel obligated to "take what they can get." But after working as a maid at a local motel for almost a year and a half, I decided no job is worth keeping if it causes a person to doubt his or her worth. My

Thesis: No appreciation, low pay, disgusting tasks (causes) produce damaged self-esteem and action (effects)

hard work rarely received recognition or appreciation, I was underpaid, and I was required to perform some of the most disgusting cleaning tasks imaginable. These factors caused me to devalue myself as a person and ultimately motivated me to return to school in hope of regaining my self-respect.

Cause one: Lack of appreciation

2   It may be obvious to say, but I believe that when a maid's hours of meticulous cleaning are met only with harsh words and complaints, she begins to lose her sense of self-esteem. I recall the care I took in making the motel's beds, imagining them as globs of

clay and molding them into impeccable pieces of art. I would teeter from one side of a bed to the other, over and over again, until I smoothed out every intruding wrinkle or tuck. And the mirrors—I would vigorously massage the glass, erasing any toothpaste splotches or oil smudges that might draw my customer's disapproval. I would scrutinize the mirror first from the left side, then I'd move to the right side, once more to the left until every possible angle ensured an unclouded reflection. And so my efforts went, room after room. But, without fail, each day more than one customer would approach me, not with praise for my tidy beds or spotless mirrors, but with nitpicking complaints that undermined my efforts: "Young lady, I just checked into room 143 and it only has one ashtray. Surely for $69.95 a night you people can afford more ashtrays in the rooms."

3   If it wasn't a guest complaining about ashtrays, it was an impatient customer demanding extra towels or a fussy stay-over insisting his room be cleaned by the time he returned from breakfast at 8:00 A.M. "Can't you come to work early to do it?" he would urge thoughtlessly. Day after day, my spotless rooms went unnoticed, with no spoken rewards for my efforts from either guests or management. Eventually, the ruthless complaints and thankless work began wearing me down. In my mind, I became a servant undeserving of gratitude.

4   The lack of spoken rewards was compounded by the lack of financial rewards. The $5.50/hour appraisal of my worth was simply not enough to support my financial needs or my self-esteem. The measly $2.75 I earned for cleaning one room took a lot of rooms to add up, and by the end of the month I was barely able to pay my bills and buy some food. (My mainstay became sixty-two cent, generic macaroni and cheese dinners.) Because the flow of travelers kept the motel full for only a few months of the year, during some weeks I

Cause two: Low pay

could only work half time, making a mere $440.00 a month. As a result, one month I was forced to request an extension on my rent payment. Unsympathetically, my landlord threatened to evict me if I didn't pay. Embarrassed, yet desperate, I went to a friend and borrowed money. I felt uneasy and awkward and regretted having to beg a friend for money. I felt like a mooch and a bum; I felt degraded. And the constant reminder from management that there were hundreds of people standing in lines who would be more than willing to work for $5.50 an hour only aided in demeaning me further.

Cause three: Repulsive duties

5   In addition to the thankless work and the inadequate salary, I was required to clean some of the most sickening messes. Frequently, conventions for high school clubs booked the motel. Once I opened the door of a conventioneer's room one morning and almost gagged at the odor. I immediately beheld a trail of vomit that began at the bedside and ended just short of the bathroom door. At that moment I cursed the inventor of shag carpet, for I knew it would take hours to comb this mess out of the fibers. On another day I spent thirty minutes dislodging the bed linen from the toilet where it had been stuffed. And I spent what seemed like hours removing from one of my spotless mirrors the lipstick-drawn message that read, "Yorktown Tigers are number one." But these inconsiderate acts were relaying another message, a message I took personally: "Lady, you're not worth the consideration—you're a maid and you're not worth respecting."

Conclusion: Review of the problem and a brief explanation of the solution she chose

6   I've never been afraid to work hard or do jobs that weren't particularly "fun." But the line must be drawn when a person's view of herself becomes clouded with feelings of worthlessness. The thankless efforts, the inadequate wage, and the disgusting work were just parts of a total message that degraded my character and caused me to question my worth. Therefore, I felt compelled to leave

this demeaning job in search of a way to rebuild my self-confidence. Returning to school has done just that for me. As my teachers and fellow students take time to listen to my ideas and compliment my responses, I feel once again like a vital, valued, and worthwhile person. I feel human once more.

Professional Essay*

■ How Mr. Dewey Decimal Saved My Life

Barbara Kingsolver

Barbara Kingsolver is a prize-winning novelist and essayist who was born in rural Kentucky. She holds a Master's Degree in biology and ecology and was for many years a journalist and science writer. Turning to fiction in the late eighties, she has published a number of highly praised novels, including *The Bean Trees* (1988), *Animal Dreams* (1990), *Pigs in Heaven* (1993), *The Poisonwood Bible* (1998), and *Prodigal Summer* (2000); her collections of essays include *High Tide in Tucson* (1995), from which this excerpt is taken, and *Small Wonder* (2002).

1   A librarian named Miss Truman Richey snatched me from the jaws of ruin, and it's too late now to thank her. I'm not the first person to notice that we rarely get around to thanking those who've helped us most. Salvation is such a heady thing the temptation is to dance gasping on the shore, shouting that we are alive, till our forgotten savior has long since gone under. Or else sit quietly, sideswiped and embarrassed, mumbling that we really did know pretty much how to swim. But now that I see the wreck that could have been, without Miss Richey, I'm of a fearsome mind to throw my arms around every living librarian who crosses my path, on behalf of the souls they never knew they saved.

2   I reached high school at the close of the sixties, in the Commonwealth of Kentucky, whose ranking on educational spending was I think around fifty-first, after Mississippi and whatever was below Mississippi. Recently Kentucky has drastically changed the way money is spent on its schools, but back then, the wealth of the county decreed the wealth of the school, and few coins fell far from the money trees that grew in Lexington. Our county, out where the bluegrass begins to turn brown, was just scraping by. Many a dedicated teacher served out earnest missions in our halls, but it was hard to spin silk purses out of a sow's ear budget. We didn't get anything fancy like Latin or Calculus. Apart from English, the only two courses of study that ran for four consecutive years, each one building upon the last, were segregated: Home Ec for girls and Shop for boys. And so I stand today, a woman who knows how to upholster, color-coordinate a table setting, and plan a traditional wedding—valuable skills I'm still waiting to put to good use in my life.

* To help you read this essay analytically, review pages 166–168.

3   As far as I could see from the lofty vantage point of age sixteen, there was nothing required of me at Nicholas County High that was going to keep me off the streets; unfortunately we had no streets, either. We had lanes, roads, and rural free delivery routes, six in number, I think. We had two stoplights, which were set to burn green in all directions after 6 P.M., so as not, should the event of traffic arise, to slow anybody up. . . .

4   I found myself beginning a third year of high school in a state of unrest, certain I already knew what there was to know, academically speaking—all wised up and no place to go. Some of my peers used the strategy of rationing out the Science and Math classes between periods of suspension or childbirth, stretching their schooling over the allotted four years, and I envied their broader vision. I had gone right ahead and used the classes up, like a reckless hiker gobbling up all the rations on day one of a long march. Now I faced years of Study Hall, with brief interludes of Home Ec III and IV as the bright spots. I was developing a lean and hungry outlook.

5   We did have a school library, and a librarian who was surely paid inadequately to do the work she did. Yet there she was, every afternoon, presiding over the study hall, and she noticed me. For reasons I can't fathom, she discerned potential. I expect she saw my future, or at least the one I craved so hard it must have materialized in the air above me, connected to my head by little cartoon bubbles. If that's the future she saw, it was riding down the road on the back of a motorcycle, wearing a black leather jacket with "Violators" (that was the name of our county's motorcycle gang, and I'm not kidding) stitched in a solemn arc across the back.

6   There is no way on earth I would have ended up a Violator Girlfriend—I could only dream of such a thrilling fate. But I was set hard upon wrecking my reputation in the limited ways available to skinny, unsought-after girls. They consisted mainly of cutting up in class, pretending to be surly, and making up shocking, entirely untrue stories about my home life. I wonder now that my parents continued to feed me. I clawed like a cat in a gunnysack against the doom I feared: staying home to reupholster my mother's couch one hundred thousand weekends in a row, until some tolerant myopic farm boy came along to rescue me from sewing-machine slavery.

7   Miss Richey had something else in mind. She took me by the arm in study hall one day and said, "Barbara, I'm going to teach you Dewey Decimal."

8   One more valuable skill in my life.

9   She launched me on the project of cataloging and shelving every one of the, probably, thousand books in the Nicholas County High School library. And since it beat Home Ec III by a mile, I spent my study-hall hours this way without audible complaint, so long as I could look plenty surly while I did it. Though it was hard to see the real point of organizing books nobody ever looked at. And since it was my God-given duty in those days to be frank as a plank, I said as much to Miss Richey.

10   She just smiled. She with her hidden agenda. And gradually, in the process of handling every book in the room, I made some discoveries. I found *Gone With the Wind*, which I suspected my mother felt was kind of trashy, and I found Edgar Allan Poe, who scared me witless. I found that the call number for books about snakes is 666. I found William Saroyan's *Human Comedy*, down there on the shelf between Human Anatomy and Human Physiology, where probably no one had touched it since 1943. But I read it, and it spoke to me. In spite of myself I imagined the life of an immigrant son who believed human kindness was a tangible and glorious thing. I began to think about words like *tangible* and *glorious*. I read on. After I'd read all the good ones, I went back and read Human Anatomy and Human Physiology and found that I liked those pretty well too.

11   It came to pass in two short years that the walls of my high school dropped down, and I caught the scent of a world. I started to dream up intoxicating lives for myself that I could not have conceived without the books. So I didn't end up on a motorcycle. I ended up roaring hell-for-leather down the backroads of transcedent, reeling sentences. A writer. Imagine that.

Questions on Content, Structure, and Style

1. What series of events caused an enormous change in the direction of Kingsolver's life?

2. What details does Kingsolver offer to describe her town, her educational opportunities, and her classmates? Why is it necessary for her to explain her background to the reader?

3. What sort of teenager was Kingsolver at sixteen? How was she similar to but also different from her classmates?

4. What future does Kingsolver think Miss Richey saw for her? What do you think Miss Richey really saw?

5. What is the Dewey Decimal system? What was Miss Richey's "hidden agenda"?

6. How did Kingsolver change? How does she use multiple examples to help explain this change?

7. Describe the tone of this essay. How does Kingsolver's use of dry humor, exaggeration, and "down-home" language affect the reader's attitude toward her?

8. Point out some examples of Kingsolver's figurative language (the similes and colorful images in paragraphs 4, 5, and 6, for instance) and explain what they add to the reader's understanding of this essay.

9. In the last paragraph Kingsolver puts a twist on what previous image? Is this an effective ending? Why/why not?

10. After studying Kingsolver's essay, reconsider her title and introductory paragraph. Did Mr. Dewey Decimal really save her life? Why does she begin her essay with an extended metaphor about drowning swimmers struggling to shore?

Suggestions for Writing

Use Barbara Kingsolver's essay "How Mr. Dewey Decimal Saved My Life" as a stepping-stone to your essay. Think of one or more books that greatly influenced you at some point in your life. Perhaps there was a book (or a series of books) in your childhood that first ignited your imagination or made you aware of a world outside of your own. Perhaps a book you read as a teenager encouraged personal dreams, adventures, or accomplishments. A story's character or plot might have allowed you to see entirely new possibilities in life or introduced you to future professional interests, just as Kingsolver's reading ultimately led her to become a writer. Write an essay explaining why and how a book changed or expanded your vision. (Or if you prefer to write about an influential person in your life, your own version of Miss Richey, you might find it helpful to turn to the "Suggestions for Writing" section that follows Maya Angelou's essay "Sister Flowers," on page 338.)

Vocabulary

rationing (4)	fathom (5)	myopic (6)
rations (4)	discerned (5)	tangible (10)
interludes (4)	surly (6)	transcendent (11)

■ A REVISION WORKSHEET

As you write your rough drafts, consult Chapter 5 for guidance through the revision process. In addition, here are a few questions to ask yourself as you revise your causal analysis essay:

1. Is the thesis limited to a reasonable claim that can be supported in the essay?

2. Is the organization clear and consistent so that the reader can understand the purpose of the analysis?

3. Does the essay focus on the most important causes or effects, or both?

4. If the essay has a narrative form, is each step in the chain reaction clearly connected to the next?

5. Does the essay convincingly show the reader *how* or *why* relationships between the causes and effects exist, instead of merely naming and describing them?

6. Does the essay provide enough evidence to show the connections between causes and effects? Where could additional details be added to make the relationships clearer?

7. Has the essay avoided the problems of oversimplification, circular logic, and the *post hoc* fallacy?

After you've revised your essay extensively, you might exchange rough drafts with a classmate and answer these questions for each other, making specific suggestions for improvement wherever appropriate. (For advice on productive participation in classroom workshops, see pages 106–109.)

Reviewing Your Progress

After you have completed your essay developed by causal analysis, take a moment to measure your progress as a writer by responding to the following questions. Such analysis will help you recognize growth in your writing skills and may enable you to identify areas that are still problematic.

1. What do you like best about your essay? Why?

2. After considering your essay's presentation of the major causes or effects, which part of your analysis do you think readers will find the most convincing? Why?

3. What part of your essay gave you the most trouble? How did you overcome the problem?
4. If you had more time to work on this essay, what would receive additional attention? Why?
5. What did you learn about your topic from writing this essay? About yourself as a writer?

Chapter 10

Argumentation

Almost without exception, each of us, every day, argues for or against something with somebody. The discussions may be short and friendly ("Let's go to this restaurant rather than that one") or long and complex ("Mandatory motorcycle helmets are an intrusion on civil rights"). Because we do argue our viewpoints so often, most of us realized long ago that shifting into high whine did not always get us what we wanted. On the contrary, we've learned that we usually have a much better chance at winning a dispute or having our plan adopted or changing someone's mind if we present our side of an issue in a calm, logical fashion, giving sound reasons for our position. This approach is just what a good argumentative essay does: it presents logical reasoning and solid evidence that will persuade your readers to accept your point of view.

Some argumentative essays declare the best solution to a problem ("Raising the drinking age will decrease traffic accidents"); others argue a certain way of looking at an issue ("Beauty pageants degrade women"); still others may urge adoption of a specific plan of action ("Voters should pass ordinance 10 to fund the new ice rink"). Whatever your exact purpose, your argumentative essay should be composed of a clear thesis and body paragraphs that offer enough sensible reasons and persuasive evidence to convince your readers to agree with you.

Developing Your Essay

Here are some suggestions for developing and organizing an effective argumentative essay:

Choose an appropriate topic. Selecting a good topic for any essay is important. Choosing a focused, appropriate topic for your argument essay will save you enormous time and energy even before you begin prewriting. Some subjects are simply too large and complex to be adequately treated in a three-to-five-page argumentative essay; selecting such a subject might produce a rough draft of generalities that will not be persuasive. If you have an interest in a subject that is too general or complex for the length of your assignment, try to find a more focused, specific issue within it to argue. For example, the large, controversial (and rather overdone) subject "capital punishment" might be narrowed and focused to a paper advocating time limits for the death-row appeal process or required use of DNA testing. A general opinion on "unfair college grading" might become a more interesting persuasive essay in which the writer takes a stand on the use of pluses and minuses (A–, B+, B–, etc.) on transcript grades. Your general annoyance with smokers might move from "All smoking should be outlawed forever" to an essay focused on the controversial smoking bans in open-air sports stadiums. In other words, while we certainly do debate large issues in our lives, in a short piece of writing it may be more effective, and often more interesting, to choose a focused topic that will allow for more depth in the arguments. You must ultimately decide whether your choice of subject is appropriate for your assignment, but taking a close, second look at your choice now may save you frustration later.

Explore the possibilities . . . and your opinions. Perhaps you have an interesting subject in mind for your argumentative essay, but you don't, as yet, have a definite opinion on the controversy. Use this opportunity to explore the subject! Do some research, talk to appropriate people, investigate the issues. By discovering your own position, you can address others who may be similarly uncertain about the subject.

Many times, however, you may want to argue for a belief or position you already hold. But before you proceed, take some time to consider the basis of your strong feelings. Not surprisingly, we humans have been known, on various occasions, to spout out opinions we can't always effectively support when challenged to do so. Sometimes we hold an opinion simply because on the surface it seems to make good sense to us or because it fits comfortably with our other social, ethical, or political beliefs. Or we may have inherited some of our beliefs from our families or friends, or perhaps we borrowed ideas from well-known people we admire. In some cases, we may have held an opinion for so long that we can't remember why we adopted it in the first place. We may also have a purely sentimental or emotional attachment to some idea or position. Whatever the original causes of our beliefs, we need to examine the real reasons for thinking what we do before we can effectively convince others.

If you have a strong opinion you want to write about, try jotting down a list of the reasons or points that support your position. Then study the list—are your points logical and persuasive? Which aren't, and why not? After this bit of prewriting, you may discover that although you believe something strongly, you really don't have the kinds of factual evidence or reasoned arguments you need to support your opinion. In some cases, depending on your topic, you may wish to talk to others who share your position or to research your subject (for help with research or interviewing, see Chapter 14); in other cases, you may just need to think longer and harder about your topic and your reasons for maintaining your attitude toward it. Keep an open mind; your exploration may lead you to a surprising new position. But with or without formal research, the better you know your subject, the more confident you will be about writing your argumentative essay.

Anticipate opposing views. An argument assumes that there is more than one side to an issue. To be convincing, you must be aware of your opposition's views on the subject and then organize your essay to answer or counter those views. If you don't have a good sense of the opposition's arguments, you can't effectively persuade your readers to dismiss their objections and see matters your way. Therefore, before you begin your first rough draft, write down all the opposing views you can think of and an answer to each of them so that you will know your subject thoroughly. If you are unfamiliar with the major objections to your position, now is the time to investigate your subject further. (For the sake of clarity throughout this chapter, your act of responding to those arguments against your position will be called *refuting the opposition;* "to refute" means "to prove false or wrong," and that's what you will try to do to some of the arguments of those who disagree with you.)

Know and remember your audience. Although it's important to think about your readers' needs and expectations whenever you write, it is essential to consider carefully the audience of your argumentative essay both before and as you write your rough drafts. Because you are trying to persuade people to adopt some new point of view or perhaps to take some action, you need to decide what kinds of supporting evidence will be most convincing to your particular readers. Try to analyze your audience by asking yourself a series of questions. What do they already know about your topic? What information or terms do they need to know to understand your point of view? What biases might they already have for or against your position? What special concerns might your readers have that influence their receptiveness? To be convincing, you should consider these questions and others by carefully reviewing the discussion of audience on pages 19–22 *before* you begin your drafts.

Decide which points of argument to include. Once you have a good sense of your audience, your own position, and your opposition's strongest arguments, try making a Pro-and-Con Sheet to help you sort out which points you will discuss in your essay.

Let's suppose you want to write an editorial on the sale-of-class-notes controversy at your school. Should professional note-takers be allowed to sit in on a course and then sell their notes to class members? After reviewing the evidence on both sides, you have decided to argue that your school should prohibit professional note-taking services from attending large lecture classes and selling notes. To help yourself begin planning your essay, you list all the pro-and-con arguments you can think of concerning the controversy:

My Side: Against the Sale of Class Notes	My Opposition's Side: For the Sale of Class Notes
1. Unfair advantage for some students in some classes	1. Helps students to get better test, course grades
2. Note-taking is a skill students need to develop	2. Helps students to learn, organize material
3. Rich students can afford and poor can't	3. Helps if you're sick and can't attend class
4. Prevents students from learning to organize for themselves	4. Shows students good models for taking notes and outlining them

My Side: Against the Sale of Class Notes	My Opposition's Side: For the Sale of Class Notes
5. Encourages class cutting	5. Other study guides are on the market, why not these?
6. Missing class means no chance to ask questions, participate in discussions	6. Gives starving graduate students jobs
7. Notes taken by others are often inaccurate	7. No laws against sale of notes, free country
8. Some professors don't like strangers in classroom	
9. Students need to think for themselves	

After making your Pro-and-Con Sheet, look over the list and decide which of your strongest points you want to argue in your paper and also which of your opposition's claims you want to refute. At this point you may also see some arguments on your list that might be combined and some that might be deleted because they're irrelevant or unconvincing. (Be careful not to select more arguments or counterarguments to discuss than the length of your writing assignment will allow. It's far better to present a persuasive analysis of a few points than it is to give an underdeveloped, shallow treatment of a host of reasons.)

Let's say you want to cover the following points in your essay:

- Professional note-taking services keep students from developing own thinking and organizational skills (combination of 4 and 9)
- Professional note-taking services discourage class attendance and participation (5 and 6)
- Unfair advantages to some students (1 and 3).

Your assignment calls for an essay of 750 to 1,000 words, so you figure you'll only have space to refute your opposition's strongest claim. You decide to refute this claim:

- Helps students to learn and organize material (2).

The next step is to formulate a working thesis. At this stage, you may find it helpful to put your working thesis in an "although-because" statement so you can clearly see both your opposition's arguments and your own. An "although-because" thesis for the note-taking essay might look something like this:

Although some students maintain that using professional note-taking services helps them learn more, such services should be banned from our campus *because* they prevent students from developing their own thinking and organizational skills, they discourage class attendance, and they give unfair advantages to some students.

Frequently your "although-because" thesis will be too long and awkward to use in the later drafts of your essay. But for now, it can serve as a guide, allowing you to see your overall position before the writing of the first draft begins. (To practice compiling a Pro-Con List and writing an "although-because" thesis, turn to the exercise on pages 285–286.)

Organize your essay clearly. Although there is no set model of organization for argumentative essays, here are some common patterns that you might use or that you might combine in some effective way.

Important note: For the sake of simplicity, the first two outlines present two of the writer's points and two opposing ideas. Naturally, your essay may contain any number of points and refuted points, depending on the complexity of your subject and the assigned length of your essay.

In Pattern A, you devote the first few body paragraphs to arguing points on your side and then turn to refuting or answering the opposition's claims.

Pattern A: Thesis

Body paragraph 1: you present your first point and its supporting evidence

Body paragraph 2: you present your second point and its supporting evidence

Body paragraph 3: you refute your opposition's first point

Body paragraph 4: you refute your opposition's second point

Conclusion

Sometimes you may wish to clear away the opposition's claims before you present the arguments for your side. To do so, you might select Pattern B:

Pattern B: Thesis

Body paragraph 1: you refute your opposition's first point

Body paragraph 2: you refute your opposition's second point

Body paragraph 3: you present your first point and its supporting evidence

Body paragraph 4: you present your second point and its supporting evidence

Conclusion

In some cases, you may find that the main arguments you want to present are the very same ones that will refute or answer your opposition's primary claims. If so, try Pattern C, which allows each of your argumentative points to refute one of your opposition's claims in the same paragraph:

Pattern C: Thesis

Body paragraph 1: you present your first point and its supporting evidence, which also refutes one of your opposition's claims

Body paragraph 2: you present a second point and its supporting evidence, which also refutes a second opposition claim

Body paragraph 3: you present a third point and its supporting evidence, which also refutes a third opposition claim

Conclusion

Now you might be thinking, "What if my position on a topic as yet has no opposition?" Remember that almost all issues have more than one side, so try to anticipate objections and then answer them. For example, you might first present a thesis that calls for a new traffic signal at a dangerous intersection in your town and then address hypothetical counter-arguments, such as "The City Council may say that a stop light at Lemay and

Columbia will cost too much, but the cost in lives will be much greater" or "Commuters may complain that a traffic light there will slow the continuous flow of north-south traffic, but it is precisely the uninterrupted nature of this road that encourages motorists to speed." By answering hypothetical objections, you impress your readers by showing them you've thought through your position thoroughly before you asked them to consider your point of view.

You might also be thinking, "What if my opposition actually has a valid objection, a legitimate point of criticism? Should I ignore it?" Hoping that an obviously strong opposing point will just go away is like hoping the IRS will cancel income taxes this year—a nice thought but hardly likely. Don't ignore your opposition's good point; instead, acknowledge it, but then go on quickly to show your readers why that reason, though valid, isn't compelling enough by itself to motivate people to adopt your opposition's entire position. Or you might concede that one point while simultaneously showing why your position isn't really in conflict with that criticism, but rather with other, more important, parts of your opponent's viewpoint. By admitting that you see some validity in your opposition's argument, you can again show your readers that you are both fair-minded and informed about all aspects of the controversy.

If you are feeling confident about your ability to organize an argumentative essay, you might try some combination of patterns, if your material allows such a treatment. For example, you might have a strong point to argue, another point that simultaneously answers one of your opposition's strongest claims, and another opposition point you want to refute. Your essay organization might look like this:

Combination: Thesis

Body paragraph 1: A point for your side

Body paragraph 2: One of your points, which also refutes an opposition claim

Body paragraph 3: Your refutation of another opposition claim

Conclusion

In other words, you can organize your essay in a variety of ways as long as your paper is logical and clear. Study your Pro-and-Con Sheet and then decide which organization best presents the arguments and counter-arguments you want to include. Try sketching out your essay following each of the patterns; look carefully to see which pattern (or variation of one of the patterns) seems to put forward your particular material most persuasively, with the least repetition or confusion. Sometimes your essay's material will clearly fall into a particular pattern of organization, so your choice will be easy. More often, however, you will have to arrange and rearrange your ideas and counterarguments until you see the best approach. Don't be discouraged if you decide to change patterns after you've begun a rough draft; what matters is finding the most effective way to persuade the reader to your side.

If no organizational pattern seems to fit at first, ask yourself which of your points or counter-arguments is the strongest or most important. Try putting that point in one of the two most emphatic places: either first or last. Sometimes your most important discussion will lead the way to your other points and, consequently, should be introduced first; perhaps more often, effective writers and speakers build up to their strongest point, presenting it last as the climax of their argument. Again, the choice depends on your material itself, though it's rare that you would want to bury your strongest point in the middle of your essay.

Now let's return to the essay on note-taking first discussed on page 275. After selecting the most important arguments and counter-arguments (pages 275–276), let's say that you decide that your main point concerns the development of students' learning skills. Since your opposition claims the contrary, that their service does promote learning, you see that you can make your main point as you refute theirs. But you also wish to include a couple of other points for your side. After trying several patterns, you decide to put the "thinking skills" rebuttal last for emphasis and present your other points first. Consequently, Pattern A best fits your plan. A sketchy outline might look like this:

- *Revised working thesis and essay map:* Professional note-taking services should be banned from our campus. Not only do they give some students unfair advantages and discourage class attendance, they prevent students from developing and practicing good learning skills.

- *Body paragraph 1 (a first point for the writer's side):* Services penalize some students—those who haven't enough money or take other sections or enroll in classes without lectures.

- *Body paragraph 2 (another point for the writer's side):* Services encourage cutting class and so students miss opportunities to ask questions, participate in discussion, talk to instructor, see visual aids, etc.

- *Body paragraph 3 (rebuttal of the opposition's strongest claim):* Services claim they help students learn more, but they don't because they're doing the work students ought to be doing themselves. Students must learn to think and organize for themselves.

Once you have a general notion of where your essay is going, plan to spend some more time thinking about ways to make each of your points clear, logical, and persuasive to your particular audience. (If you wish to see how one student actually developed an essay based on the preceding outline, turn to the sample student paper on pages 289–291.)

Argue your ideas logically. To convince your readers, you must provide sufficient reasons for your position. You must give more than mere opinion—you must offer logical arguments to back up your assertions. Some of the possible ways of supporting your ideas should already be familiar to you from writing expository essays; listed here are several methods and illustrations:

1. Give examples (real or hypothetical): "Cutting class because you have access to professional notes can be harmful; for instance, you might miss seeing some slides or graphics essential to your understanding of the lecture."

2. Present a comparison or contrast: "In contrast to reading 'canned' notes, outlining your own notes helps you remember the material."

3. Show a cause-and-effect relationship: "Dependence on professional notes may mean that some students will never learn to organize their own responses to classroom discussions."

4. Argue by definition: "Passively reading through professional notes isn't a learning experience in which one's mind is engaged."

The well-thought-out arguments you choose to support your case may be called *logical appeals* because they appeal to, and depend on, your readers' ability to reason and to recognize good sense when they see it. But there is another kind of appeal often used today: the *emotional appeal*.

Emotional appeals are designed to persuade people by playing on their feelings rather than appealing to their intellect. Rather than using thoughtful, logical reasoning to support their claims, writers and speakers using *only* emotional appeals often try to accomplish their goals by distracting or misleading their audiences. Frequently, emotional appeals are characterized by language that plays on people's fears, material desires, prejudices, or sympathies; such language often triggers highly favorable or unfavorable responses to a subject. For instance, emotional appeals are used constantly in advertising, where feel-good images, music, and slogans ("Come to Marlboro Country"; "The Heartbeat of America Is Today's Chevy Truck") are designed to sway potential customers to a product without them thinking about it too much. Some politicians also rely heavily on emotional appeals, often using scare tactics to disguise a situation or to lead people away from questioning the logic of a particular issue.

But in some cases, emotional appeals can be used for legitimate purposes. Good writers should always be aware of their audience's needs, values, and states of mind, and they may be more persuasive on occasion if they can frame their arguments in ways that appeal to both their readers' logic and their emotions. For example, when Martin Luther King, Jr., delivered his famous "I Have a Dream" speech to the crowds gathered in Washington in 1963 and described his vision of little children of different races walking hand-in-hand, being judged not "by the color of their skin but by the content of their character," he certainly spoke with passion that was aimed at the hearts of his listeners. But King was not using an emotional appeal to keep his audience from thinking about his message; on the contrary, he presented powerful emotional images that he hoped would inspire people to act on what they already thought and felt, their deepest convictions about equality and justice.

Appeals to emotions are tricky: you can use them effectively in conjunction with appeals to logic and with solid evidence, but only if you use them ethically. Too many appeals to the emotions are also overwhelming; readers tire quickly from excessive tugs on the heartstrings. To prevent your readers from suspecting deception, or feeling manipulated, support your assertions with as many logical arguments as you can muster, and use emotional appeals only when they legitimately advance your cause.

Offer evidence that effectively supports your claims. In addition to presenting thoughtful, logical reasoning, you may wish to incorporate a variety of convincing evidence to persuade your readers to your side. Your essay might profit from including, where appropriate, some of the following kinds of supporting evidence:

- Personal experiences
- The experiences or testimony of others whose opinions are pertinent to the topic
- Factual information you've gathered from research
- Statistics from current, reliable sources
- Hypothetical examples
- Testimony from authorities and experts
- Charts, graphs, or diagrams

You'll need to spend quite a bit of your prewriting time thinking about the best kinds of evidence to support your case. Remember that not all personal experiences or research materials are persuasive. For instance, the experiences we've had (or that our friends have had) may not be representative of a universal experience and consequently may lead to unconvincing generalizations. Even testimony from an authority may not be convincing if the person is not speaking on a topic from his or her field of expertise; famous football players, for instance, don't necessarily know any more about panty hose or soft drinks than anyone else. Always put yourself in the skeptical reader's place and ask, "Does this point convince me? If not, why not?" (For more information on incorporating research material into your essays, see Chapter 14. For more advice on the selection of evidence, see the section on critical thinking in Chapter 5.)

Find the appropriate tone. Sometimes when we argue, it's easy to get carried away. Remember that your goal is to persuade and perhaps change your readers, not alienate them. Instead of laying on insults or sarcasm, present your ideas in a moderate let-us-reason-together spirit. Such a tone will persuade your readers that you are sincere in your attempts to argue as truthfully and fairly as possible. If your readers do not respect you as a reasonable person, they certainly won't be swayed to your side of an issue. Don't preach or pontificate either; no one likes—or respects—a writer with a superior attitude. Write in your natural "voice"; don't adopt a pseudo-intellectual tone. In short, to argue effectively you should sound logical, sincere, and informed. (For additional comments on tone, review pages 144–146.)

Consider using Rogerian techniques, if they are appropriate. In some cases, especially those involving tense situations or highly sensitive issues, you may wish to incorporate some techniques of the noted psychologist Carl Rogers, who developed a procedure for presenting what he called the nonthreatening argument. Rogers believed that people involved in a debate should strive for clear, honest communication so that the problem under discussion could be resolved. Instead of going on the defensive and trying to "win" the argument, each side should try to recognize common ground and then develop a solution that will address the needs of both parties.

A Rogerian argument uses these techniques:

1. A clear, objective statement of the problem or issue

2. A clear, objective summary of the opposition's position that shows you understand its point of view and goals

3. A clear, objective summary of your point of view, stated in nonthreatening language

4. A discussion that emphasizes the beliefs, values, and goals that you and your opposition have in common

5. A description of any of your points that you are willing to concede or compromise

6. An explanation of a plan or proposed solution that meets the needs of both sides

By showing your opposition that you thoroughly understand its position and that you are sincerely trying to effect a solution that is in everyone's—not just your—best interests, you may succeed in some situations that might otherwise be hopeless because of their highly emotional nature. Remember, too, that you can use some of these Rogerian techniques in any kind of argument paper you are writing, if you think they would be effective.

Problems to Avoid

Writers of argumentative essays must appear logical or their readers will reject their point of view. Here is a short list of some of the most common *logical fallacies*—that is, errors in reasoning. Check your rough drafts carefully to avoid these problems.

Students sometimes ask, "If a logical fallacy works, why not use it? Isn't all fair in love, war, and argumentative essays?" The honest answer is maybe. It's quite true that speakers and writers do use faulty logic and irrational emotional appeals to persuade people every day (one needs only to look at television or a newspaper to see example after example). But the cost of the risk is high: if you do try to slide one by your readers and they see through your trick, you will lose your credibility instantly. On the whole, it's far more effective to use logical reasoning and strong evidence to convince your readers to accept your point of view.

■ Common Logical Fallacies

Hasty generalization: The writer bases the argument on insufficient or unrepresentative evidence. Suppose, for example, you have owned two poodles and they have both attacked you. If you declare that all poodles are vicious dogs, you are making a hasty generalization. There are, of course, thousands of poodles who have not attacked anyone. Similarly, you're in error if you interview only campus athletes and then declare, "University students favor a new stadium." What about the opinions of the students who aren't athletes? In other words, when the generalization is drawn from a sample that is too small or select, your conclusion isn't valid.

***Non sequitur* ("it doesn't follow"): The writer's conclusion is not necessarily a logical result of the facts.** An example of a *non sequitur* occurs when you conclude, "Professor Smith is a famous chemist, so he will be a brilliant chemistry teacher." As you may have realized by now, the fact that someone knows a subject well does not automatically mean that he or she can communicate the information clearly in a classroom; hence, the conclusion is not necessarily valid.

Begging the question: The writer presents as truth what is not yet proven by the argument. For example, in the statement "All useless laws such as Reform Bill 13 should be repealed," the writer has already pronounced the bill useless without assuming responsibility for proving that accusation. Similarly, the statement "Professors on our campus who are using their classroom solely for preaching their political ideas should be banned" begs the question (that is, tries like a beggar to get something for nothing from the reader) because the writer gives no evidence for what must first be argued, not merely asserted—that there are in fact professors on that particular campus using class time solely for spreading their political beliefs.

Red herring: The writer introduces an irrelevant point to divert the readers' attention from the main issue. This term originates from the old tactic used by escaped prisoners, of dragging a smoked herring, a strong-smelling fish, across their trail to confuse tracking dogs by making them follow the wrong scent. For example, roommate A might be criticizing roommate B for his repeated failure to do the dishes when it was his turn. To escape facing the charges, roommate B brings up times in the past when the other roommate failed to repay some money he borrowed. Although roommate A may indeed have a problem with remembering his debts, that discussion isn't relevant to the original argument about sharing the responsibility for the dishes. (By the way, you might have run across a well-known newspaper photograph of a California environmentalist group demonstrating for more protection of dolphins, whales, and other marine life; look closely to see, over in the left corner, almost hidden by the host of placards and banners, a fellow slyly holding up a sign that reads "Save the Red Herring!" Now, who says rhetoricians don't have a good sense of humor?)

Post hoc, ergo propter hoc. See page 261.

Argument *ad hominem* ("to the man"): The writer attacks the opponent's character rather than the opponent's argument. The statement "Dr. Bloom can't be a competent marriage counselor because she's been divorced" may not be valid. Bloom's advice to her clients may be excellent regardless of her own marital status.

Faulty use of authority: The writer relies on "authorities" who are not convincing sources. Although someone may be well known in a particular field, he or she may not be qualified to testify in a different area. A baseball player in an ad for laser surgery may stress his need for correct vision, but he may be no more knowledgeable about eye care than anyone else on the street. In other words, name recognition is not enough. For their testimony to count with readers, authorities must have expertise, credentials, or relevant experience in the area under discussion. (See also pages 281, 368–370, and "transfer of virtue" in the discussion of "bandwagon appeal" on page 284.)

Argument *ad populum* ("to the people"): The writer evades the issues by appealing to readers' emotional reactions to certain subjects. For example, instead of arguing the facts of an issue, a writer might play on the readers' negative response to such words as "communism," "fascism," or "radical," and their positive response to words like "God," "country," "liberty," or "patriotic." In the statement "If you are a true American, you will vote against the referendum on flag burning," the writer avoids any discussion of the merits or weaknesses of the bill and merely substitutes an emotional appeal. Other popular "virtue words" include "duty," "common sense," "courage," and "healthy." (Advertisers, of course, also play on consumers' emotions by filling their ads with pictures of babies, animals, status objects, and sexually attractive men and women.)

Circular thinking. See page 261.

Either/or: The writer tries to convince the readers that there are only two sides to an issue—one right, one wrong. The statement "If you don't go to war against Iceland, you don't love your country" is irrational because it doesn't consider the other possibilities, such as patriotic people's right to oppose war as an expression of love for their country. A classic example of this sort of oversimplification was illustrated in the 1960s' bumper sticker that was popular during the debate over the Vietnam War: "America: Love It or Leave It." Obviously, there are other choices ("Change It or Lose It," for instance, to quote another either/or bumper sticker of that era).

Hypostatization: The writer uses an abstract concept as if it were a concrete reality. Always be suspicious of a writer who frequently relies on statements beginning "History has always taught us . . ." or "Science has proven . . ." or "Research shows. . . ." The implication in each case is that history or science (or any other discipline) has only one voice, one opinion. On the contrary, "history" is written by a multitude of historians who hold a variety of opinions; doctors and scientists also frequently disagree. Instead of generalizing about a particular field, quote a respected authority or simply qualify your statement by referring to "many" or "some" scientists, historians, or other professionals.

Bandwagon appeal: The writer tries to validate a point by intimating that "everyone else believes in this." Such a tactic evades discussion of the issue itself. Advertising often uses this technique: "Everyone who demands real taste smokes Phooey cigarettes"; "Discriminating women use Smacky-Mouth lipstick." (The ultimate in "bandwagon" humor may have appeared on a recent Colorado bumper sticker: "Eat lamb—could 1000s of coyotes be wrong?") A variation of the "bandwagon" fallacy is sometimes referred to as "transfer of virtue," the sharing of light from someone else's sparkle. Advertisers often use this technique by paying attractive models or media stars to endorse their product. The underlying premise is this:

> Popular/beautiful/"cool"/rich people use/buy/wear "X"; if you use "X," you too will be popular/beautiful/etc.

Intelligent readers and consumers know, of course, to suspect such doubtful causal relationships.

Straw man: The writer selects the opposition's weakest or most insignificant point to argue against, to divert the readers' attention from the real issues. Instead of addressing the opposition's best arguments and defeating them, the writer "sets up a straw man"—that is, the writer picks out a trivial (or irrelevant) argument against his or her own position and easily knocks it down, just as one might easily push over a figure made of straw. Perhaps the most famous example of the "straw man" occurred in 1952 when, during his vice-presidential campaign, Richard Nixon was accused of misappropriating campaign funds for his personal use. Addressing the nation on television, Nixon described how his six-year-old daughter, Tricia, had received a little cocker spaniel named Checkers from a Texas supporter. Nixon went on about how much his children loved the dog and how, regardless of what anyone thought, by gosh, he was going to keep that cute dog for little Tricia. Of course, no one was asking Nixon to return the dog; they were asking about the $18,000 in missing campaign funds. But Nixon's canine gift was much easier for him to defend, and the "Checkers" speech is now famous as one of the most notorious "straw man" diversions.

Faulty analogy: The writer uses an extended comparison as proof of a point. Look closely at all extended comparisons and metaphors to see if the two things being compared are really similar. For example, in a recent editorial a woman protested the new laws requiring parents to use car seats for small children, arguing that if the state could require the seats, they could just as easily require mothers to breastfeed instead of using formula. Are the two situations alike? Car accidents are the leading cause of death of children under four; is formula deadly? Or perhaps you've read that putting teenagers in sex education classes is like taking an alcoholic to a bar. Is it? If readers don't see the similarity, the analogy may not be persuasive. Moreover, remember that even though a compelling analogy might suggest similarities, it alone cannot *prove* anything. (For more discussion of analogy, see pages 229–232.)

Quick fix: The writer leans too heavily on catchy phrases or empty slogans. A clever turn-of-phrase may grab one's attention, but it may lose its persuasiveness when scrutinized closely. For instance, a banner at a recent rally to protest a piece of antigun legislation read, "When guns are outlawed, only outlaws will have guns." Although the sentence had nice balance, it oversimplified the issue. The legislation in question was not trying to outlaw all guns, just the sale of the infamous Saturday Night Specials, most often used in crimes and domestic violence; the sale of guns for sport, such as hunting rifles, would remain legal. Other slogans sound good but are simply irrelevant: a particular soft drink, for example, may be "the real thing," but what drink isn't? Look closely at clever lines substituted for reasoned argument; always demand clear terms and logical explanations.*

■ **PRACTICING WHAT YOU'VE LEARNED**

A. Imagine that you are writing an argumentative essay addressing the controversial question "Should home-schooled students be allowed to play on public school athletic teams?" You have investigated the topic and have noted the variety of opinions listed here. Arrange the statements into two lists: A "Pro" list (those statements that argue for allowing home schoolers to play) and a "Con" list (those statements that are against allowing home schoolers to play). Cross off any inappropriate or illogical statements you find; combine any opinions that overlap.

   1. Parents of home schoolers pay same taxes as public school parents

   2. Public school kids must meet grade requirements to be eligible

   3. School rules prohibit nonenrolled youth on campus

---

* Sometimes advertisers get more for their slogans than they bargained for. According to one news source, a popular soft-drink company had to spend millions to revise its slogan after introducing its product into parts of China. Apparently the slogan "Come alive! Join the Blah-Blah-Cola Generation!" translated into some dialects as "Blah-Blah Cola Brings Your Ancestors Back from the Dead"!

4. Home schoolers shouldn't get benefits of a school they've rejected
5. Public school kids are bad influences on home schoolers
6. Home schoolers need the social interaction
7. Public school teams can always use more good athletes
8. More students will overburden athletic facilities
9. Home schoolers miss their public school friends, and vice versa
10. Ten states allow home schoolers to play on teams
11. Home schoolers will displace public school students on teams
12. Public school students have to meet attendance rules to be eligible
13. Athletic competition is good for everybody
14. Home schoolers often have controversial political beliefs that will cause fights
15. Team members need to share the same community on a daily basis
16. Home schoolers aren't as invested in school pride

Once you have your two lists, decide your own position on this topic. Then select two points you might use to argue your position and one opposing criticism you might refute. Put your working thesis into an "although-because" format, as explained on page 276. Compare your choices to those of your classmates.

B. Errors in reasoning can cause your reader to doubt your credibility. In the following mock essay, for example, the writer includes a variety of fallacies that undermine his argument; see if you can identify all his errors.

Ban Those Books!

1   A serious problem faces America today, a problem of such grave importance that our very existence as a nation is threatened. We must either cleanse our schools of evil-minded books, or we must reconcile ourselves to seeing our children become welfare moochers and homeless bums.

2   History has shown time and time again that placement of immoral books in our schools is part of an insidious plot designed to weaken the moral fiber of our youth from coast to coast. In Wettuckett, Ohio, for example, the year after books by Mark Twain, such as *Tom Sawyer* and *Huckleberry Finn,* were introduced into the school library by liberal free-thinkers and radicals, the number of students cutting classes rose by 6 percent. And in that same year, the number of high school seniors going on to college dropped from thirty to twenty-two.

3   The reason for this could either be a natural decline in intelligence and morals or the influence of those dirty books that teach our beloved children disrespect and irresponsibility. Since there is no evidence to suggest a natural decline, the conclusion is inescapable: once our children read about Twain's characters skipping school and running away from home, they had to do likewise. If they hadn't read about such undesirable characters as Huckleberry Finn, our innocent children would never have behaved in those ways.

4   Now, I am a simple man, a plain old farm boy—the pseudo-intellectuals call me redneck just like they call you folks. But I can assure you that, redneck or not, I've got the guts to fight moral decay everywhere I find it, and I urge you to do the same. For this reason I want all you good folks to come to the ban-the-books rally this Friday so we can talk it over. I promise you all your right-thinking neighbors will be there.

■ ASSIGNMENT

Search for the following:

1. An example of an advertisement that illustrates one or more of the fallacies or appeals discussed on pages 282–285;

2. An example of illogical or fallacious reasoning in a piece of writing (you might try looking at the editorial page or letters-to-the-editor section of your local or campus newspaper);

3. An example of a logical, persuasive point in a piece of writing.

Be prepared to explain your analyses of your samples, but do not write any sort of identifying label or evaluation on the samples themselves. Bring your ads and pieces of writing to class and exchange them with those of a classmate. After ten minutes, compare notes. Do you and your classmate agree on the evaluation of each sample? Why or why not?

■ ESSAY TOPICS

Write a convincing argument attacking or defending one of the following statements, or use them to help you think of your own topic. Remember to narrow and focus the topic as necessary. (Note that essays on some of the topics presented here might profit from research material; see Chapter 14 for help.) For additional ideas, see the "Suggestions for Writing" section following the professional essays (page 294).

1. Students should/should not work throughout high school.

2. To prepare students for a highly technical world, high schools should/should not extend their academic year.

3. Sixteen-year-olds should/should not be issued limited-privilege or "graduated" driver's licenses.

4. The movie rating system should/should not be revised.

5. All adoption records should/should not be open to adopted people over 18.

6. A school voucher system should/should not be used in this state.

7. Students who do poorly in their academic courses should/should not be allowed to participate in athletic programs.

8. All schools should/should not adopt a "repeat/delete" policy, allowing students to retake a course and substitute a higher grade on their record.

9. Televised instant replays should/should not be used to call plays in football and other sports.

10. National exams, such as the SAT, should/should not be required for college applicants.

11. The math requirement (or some other requirement, rule, or policy) at this school should/should not be changed.

12. Off-road recreational vehicles should/should not be banned from our national parks.

13. Telephone solicitation bans do/do not infringe on freedom of speech.

14. Public school students should/should not be required to wear uniforms.

15. The electoral system should/should not be used to select the U.S. president.

16. Controversial names or symbols of athletic teams ("Redskins," the Confederate flag, the tomahawk chop) should/should not be changed.

17. State-supported colleges should/should not be allowed to enroll exclusively male or female students.

18. Persons over 14 charged with crimes should/should not be tried as adults.

19. Men and women in the military should/should not serve in separate units.

20. Advertising for "Product X" rarely/often relies on use of emotional appeals and faulty logic. (Focus on one kind of product—cars, cosmetics, computers, soft drinks, cell phones, etc.—or on one especially popular brand, and collect a number of its ads to analyze. What does your analysis tell you about the major ways in which your particular product is advertised to its target audience? Do the ads appeal to consumers' reason or do they employ logical fallacies? Some combination? Which ads are more effective, and why? If it's helpful, start by considering the major appeals of the watch ad on page 304 or turn to the "Got Milk?" ad on page 186, part of a widely distributed series from the National Dairy Association.)

A Topic Proposal for Your Essay

Selecting the right subject matter is important to every writer. To help you clarify your ideas and strengthen your commitment to your topic, here is a proposal sheet that asks you to describe some of your preliminary ideas about your subject before you begin drafting. Although your ideas may change as you write (they will almost certainly become more refined), thinking through your choice of topic now may help you avoid several false starts.

1. What is the subject of your argumentative essay? Write a rough statement of your opinion on this subject.

2. Why are you interested in this topic? Is it important to your personal, civic, or professional life? State at least one reason for your choice of topic.

3. Is this a significant topic of interest to others? Why? Is there a particular audience you would like to address?

4. At this point, can you list at least two reasons that support your opinion of your topic?

5. Who opposes your opinion? Can you state clearly at least one of your opposition's major criticisms of your position?

6. What difficulties, if any, might arise during drafting? For example, might you need to collect any additional evidence through reading, research, or interviewing to support your points or to refute your opposition?

■ Sample Student Essay

The student who wrote this essay followed the steps for writing an argumentative paper discussed in this chapter. His intended audience was the readers of his school newspaper, primarily students but instructors as well. To argue his case, he chose Pattern A, presenting two of his own points and then concluding with a rebuttal of an important opposing view. Notice that this writer uses a variety of methods to convince his readers, including hypothetical examples, causal analysis, analogy, and testimony. Does the writer persuade you to his point of view? Which are his strongest and weakest arguments? What might you change to make his essay even more persuasive?

STUDENTS, TAKE NOTE!

1   A walk across campus this week will reveal students, professors, and administrators arguing about class notes like never before. But they're not engaged in intellectual debates over chemical formulas or literary images. They're fighting over the taking of the notes themselves, as professional note-taking services in town are applying for permission to sit in on large lecture courses and then sell their notes to the students in those classes. Although the prospect of having "canned" notes looks inviting to many students, our administration should nevertheless ban these services from campus. Not only do such businesses give certain students unfair advantages and discourage class attendance, but they also prohibit the development of students' important learning skills, despite the services' claims to the contrary.

Introduction: Presenting the controversy

Thesis

Essay map

A point for the writer's position: Note-taking services are unfair to some students

2   What is bothered for many of us about the professional-notes option is our sense of fair play. Let's face it: like it or not, school is, among other things, a place of competition, as students vie for the best academic records to send to prospective employers, graduate and professional schools, and in some cases, paying parents. In today's classes, all students have an equal opportunity to come to class, take notes, study, and pass or fail on their own merits. But the expensive professional notes, already organized and outlined, may give those with plenty of money some advantages that poorer students—those on scholarships or with families, for example—just can't afford. In addition, the notes may be available only to those students who take certain sections of a course and not others, thus giving some students an extra advantage. The same is true for students who satisfy a requirement by taking one course that has notes available rather than another that has not. Knowing that you're doing your own work may make you feel morally superior to a classmate who isn't, but frankly, on some other level, it just plain feels irritating and unfair, sort of like watching your roommate getting away with plagiarizing his paper for a class after you spent weeks researching yours.

Another point for the writer's position: Professional notes discourage students from attending and participating in class

3   In addition to being a potential source of conflict among students, the professional-note services aren't winning many friends among the faculty, either. Several instructors have complained that the availability of notes will encourage many students, especially the weaker ones, to cut classes, assuming that they have all the material necessary for understanding the lecture, discussion, or lab. But anyone who has ever had to use borrowed notes knows something vital is not there. Someone else's interpretation of the information is often hard or impossible to follow, especially if you must understand complex relationships and problems. Moreover, skipping class may mean missed opportunities for students to ask questions or to participate in experiments or in group discussions, all of which often help clarify concepts under study. Not seeing visual aids or diagrams in person

can also result in problems understanding the material. And, last, missing class can mean failure to become comfortably acquainted with the teacher, which, in turn, may discourage a student from asking for individual help when it's needed. All these possibilities are real; even Jeff Allridge, owner of the Quotable Notes service, has admitted to a campus reporter, "There *is* an incentive to skip class."

4   Despite the admission that professional note-taking encourages class-cutting, the services still promote themselves by claiming that students using their notes learn more. They support this claim by arguing that their notes offer students clearly organized information and, according to one advertising brochure, "good models" for students to follow in other classes. But such arguments miss the larger point: students should be learning how to develop their own note-taking, organizing, and thinking skills rather than swallowing the material whole as neatly packaged and delivered. Memorizing class material as outlined can be important, but it's not really as valuable in the long run as learning how to think about the material and use it to solve problems or come up with new ideas later. Taking your own notes teaches you how to listen and how to spot the important concepts; organizing your own notes teaches you how to pull ideas together in a logical way, all skills students will need in other classes, on jobs, and in life in general. Having memorized the outlines but not really mastered the thinking skills won't help the medical student whose patient's symptoms vary from the textbook description or the engineer whose airplane wings suddenly fail the stress test for no apparent reason.

Presentation and rebuttal of the opposition's claim that students learn more using professional notes

5   By appealing to students who believe professional notes will help them accomplish their educational goals easier and quicker, a variety of note-taking services now have franchises across the country. But our campus shouldn't allow them to move in. Students need to recognize that the difference between the services' definition of "learning" and the real learning experiences college can provide is of notable importance.

Conclusion: Restatement of thesis, ending on pun to emphasize the main idea

Professional Essays*

The following essays on the use of controversial free speech zones were first published together in *USA Today* in a "Today's Debate" column (May 27, 2003). The first essay represents the views of the newspaper's editorial board; the second essay was written by Robert J. Scott, a constitutional law attorney and legal commentator.

Although you may already hold an opinion on this controversy, try to remain objective as you analyze the strengths and weaknesses of both essays. Which points are most and least persuasive, and why?

■ *USA Today*'s View: Restrictions Overreach

1   Christopher Stevens wanted to hold a "pro-America rally" at his Glendora, Calif., college this month, but was blocked by campus rules curbing demonstrations. So he is suing the college, joining students nationwide forced to teach authoritarian educators a lesson in free speech. Andrew Wimmer was arrested in January for carrying an anti-war sign near a St. Louis warehouse where President Bush was speaking, instead of going to a designated protest zone blocks away. Other bystanders carrying pro-Bush signs were left alone.

2   The charges against Wimmer eventually were dropped, but the strategy employed by St. Louis police isn't likely to die. Local authorities increasingly are trying to herd citizens who seek to exercise their First Amendment rights into out-of-the-way sites where they're less likely to be seen or heard. Typically, officials point to a post-9/11 need for crowd control and security. And, certainly, the legal right to put reasonable limits on the time, place and manner of protests is well established. But when overzealous restrictions preclude robust and open debate, democracy isn't protected; it's hindered.

3   College officials are blunt about why they limit the areas where some forms of free speech can be practiced. "It makes it easier," a University of Mississippi dean explained. Police and municipal leaders are more subtle. They point to demonstrations that turned violent in recent years. But what's argued as reasonable restrictions can undercut the right to protest.

- In April, Martha Burk's protest of the men-only policies of the club hosting the prestigious Masters golf tournament was shunted off to a field a half-mile away, below street level and out of sight.
- In February, organizations hoping to protest the war in Iraq outside the United Nations building were penned instead in a nearby plaza.
- A growing number of campuses allow protests only in severely limited areas.

4   When challenged, several major universities have backed down. Yet local courts regularly allow limits on how close protestors can be to political rallies.

5   The Founders weren't trying to make life easier for college presidents and politicians when they enshrined freedom of speech and peaceable assembly in the

---

* For help reading these essays analytically, review pages 166–168.

Constitution. The were reacting to the excesses of British rulers, who jailed colonists for daring to speak out on issues of the day. A 1997 appeals court decision explained the basis for that freedom in a case involving anti-abortion activists barred from protesting at a presidential inaugural parade: "If . . . free speech . . . does not protect the right of citizens to 'inject' their own convictions and beliefs into a public event on a public forum, then it is difficult to understand why the Framers bothered including it at all."

6   Those seeking to set up areas where free speech can occur need to be reminded that the Constitution envisions one free-speech zone. It extends from Maine to Hawaii.

■ Robert J. Scott's Opposing View: Reasonable Limits Are Good

1 The use of "free speech zones" or "protest zones" is not new and does not present a significant threat to free-speech rights.

2   Protest zones have been used at political conventions and other major events, such as last year's Winter Olympics. By creating a protest zone, governments can ensure that those who wish to express their views have a place to do so while minimizing the disruptions protests may bring.

3   Given the violence and vandalism accompanying recent protests, there is a real, immediate threat of disorder justifying a reasonable governmental response. Most of downtown San Francisco was shut down for two days in March by demonstrators who blocked traffic, damaged businesses and held an organized "vomit-in" around the federal building. Across the bay in Oakland, protesters attempted to disrupt access to ships transporting munitions.

4   Such incidents remind us that the First Amendment is not a license to do and say anything, anywhere, at any time. The Constitution does not protect protesters who break windows, obstruct traffic, disrupt military supply lines or threaten the safety of other citizens.

5   It has long been recognized that governments can impose reasonable time, place and manner restrictions on speech. Obviously, the Secret Service should not be forced to allow protesters unlimited access to the president. College administrators should be able to make certain that protesters do not prevent other students from pursuing their studies.

6   Protest zones can be reasonable restrictions that allow free-speech rights to be expressed while decreasing safety concerns and preventing undue disruption. Our democracy is based first and foremost on the rule of law. Reasonable protest zones are actually consistent with the basic idea that civil liberties may only be guaranteed and protected by an organized society maintaining public order.

7   In the words of Theodore Roosevelt, "Order without liberty and liberty without order are equally destructive." The lawlessness, violence and vandalism seen at recent protests are the hallmarks of anarchy, not liberty. Requiring those expressing dissent to obey the law while doing so does not constitute repression.

Questions on Content, Structure, and Style

1. What specific issue do these two essays debate and what are their respective positions on this subject? What is the First Amendment right that stands at the center of this discussion?

2. Why does the *USA Today* editorial board oppose designated protest zones? What evidence does this editorial offer to support its growing concern regarding "overzealous restrictions"?

3. Why does the editorial present the exact words of the University of Mississippi dean? How might the editorial board have strengthened its claim regarding other college campuses that "allow protests only in severely limited areas"?

4. Why does the editorial board allude to the nation's Founders and the Constitution? Why do they quote the 1997 appeals court decision?

5. What are Robert Scott's main arguments for the use of "protest zones"?

6. In what ways do Scott's descriptions of protests differ from those offered by the editorial board? Why does he use the San Francisco and Oakland protests to argue his point of view? Are they representative examples of most protests in this country?

7. When Scott focuses on protests with "lawlessness, violence, and vandalism," could he be accused of diverting the argument from the issue of free speech zones for all protests? Explain your answer. Is Scott's analogy, comparing use of protest zones and the Secret Service's protection of the president, persuasive? Why/why not?

8. Does either essay acknowledge agreement with the opposing point of view? If so, where and why?

9. Why does Scott quote Theodore Roosevelt in his conclusion? Which of the two conclusions do you find more effective, and why?

10. Overall, what are the major strengths and weaknesses of these two essays? What advice might you offer to improve their arguments?

Suggestions for Writing

Use the *USA Today* editorial and Scott's response as a stepping-stone to your essay. Do you agree or disagree with one of the views on free speech zones? If you're not sure, try some role-playing. Imagine yourself as an administrator at your school. A highly controversial speaker will be on campus, and you must set the rules regarding protests that will ensure everyone's safety but also uphold the rights of free speech. Write an editorial for the school paper that announces and defends your policy. Or, if you prefer, turn the tables: a member of a hate-group such as the Aryan Nation wishes to recruit new followers on your campus. You and other students want to organize a peaceful protest, but the free speech zone on your campus is in an isolated area many blocks away. Write an essay directed to your school's administration, arguing for a change in policy.

If you don't know your college's policy on protest zones, controversial speakers, recruiters, or other free speech issues, take this opportunity to find out. Do you agree or disagree with the rules as they are now? Write an editorial arguing your position. (Public high schools are often in the news regarding free speech issues: what may a high school newspaper publish? Which groups may meet on campus and which may not? Has free speech been violated if t-shirts with certain printed messages or symbols are prohibited?) You might select any one of today's hotly debated free speech issues as the basis for your argumentative essay.

Vocabulary

USA Today's essay:

authoritarian (1)   robust (2)
overzealous (2)   shunted off (3)
preclude (2)   enshrined (5)

Robert J. Scott's essay:

munitions (3)   dissent (7)
anarchy (7)

■ Analyzing Advertisements

Because they are designed to be persuasive, advertisements use a variety of logical and emotional appeals. Ads might be considered arguments in brief form, as they frequently try to convince the public to buy a product, take an action, vote for or against something, join a group, or change an attitude or a behavior. By analyzing the ads that follow, you can practice identifying a variety of persuasive appeals and evaluating their effectiveness. After discussing these ads, apply what you've learned about logical appeals, target audiences, and choice of language to your argumentative essay.

Conflicting Positions: Gun Control

The three advertisements that follow address the controversial subject of gun control. The first ad is one of a series published by the National Rifle Association (NRA) to tell the public about its organization and its interpretation of the Second Amendment; other ads in this series have featured actor Charlton Heston and author Tom Clancy. The second ad ("Well-Regulated Militia") counters the NRA position. This ad features Sarah Brady, who, following the shooting of her husband, White House Press Secretary James Brady, during an assassination attempt on President Ronald Reagan, became chair of the Center to Prevent Handgun Violence. The third ad adopts an expository strategy and uses statistics to make its point about handgun regulation in America. Analyze the appeals used in each advertisement. Which methods of persuasion do you think are the most effective, and why? Do you find any of the logical fallacies previously described in this chapter?

REP. ALBERTO GUTMAN: Florida Legislator, Businessman, Husband, Member of the National Rifle Association.

"Being from a country that was once a democracy and turned communist, I really feel I know what the right to bear arms is all about. In Cuba, where I was born, the first thing the communist government did was take away everybody's firearms, leaving them defenseless and intimidated with fear. That's why our constitutional right to bear arms is so important to our country's survival.

"As a legislator I have to deal with reality. And the reality is that gun control does not work. It actually eliminates the rights of the law-abiding citizen, not the criminal. Criminals will always have guns, and they won't follow gun control laws anyway. I would like to see tougher laws on criminals as opposed to tougher laws on legitimate gun owners. We need to attack the problem of crime at its roots, instead of blaming crime on gun ownership and citizens who use them lawfully.

"It's a big responsibility that we face retaining the right to bear arms. That's why I joined the NRA. The NRA is instrumental in protecting these freedoms. It helps train and educate people, supporting legislation that benefits not only those who bear arms but all citizens of the United States. The NRA helps keep America free." **I'm the NRA.**

The NRA's lobbying organization, the Institute for Legislative Action, is the nation's largest and most influential protector of the constitutional right to keep and bear arms. At every level of government and through local grassroots efforts, the Institute guards against infringement upon the freedoms of law-abiding gun owners. If you would like to join the NRA or want more information about our programs and benefits, write J. Warren Cassidy, Executive Vice President, P.O. Box 37484, Dept. AG-15, Washington, D.C. 20013.

Paid for by the members of the National Rifle Association of America. Copyright 1986.

Reprinted with permission of the National Rifle Association.

IS THIS THE "WELL REGULATED MILITIA" PROTECTED BY THE SECOND AMENDMENT?

"A well regulated Militia, being necessary to the security of a free State, the right of the people to keep and bear Arms, shall not be infringed."

—Second Amendment to the U.S. Constitution

For years, the National Rifle Association has spread the myth that gun control laws violate the Second Amendment. Now self-styled "citizen militias" invoke the Second Amendment as they stockpile weapons and train for warfare against what they perceive as a "tyrannical" federal government. The NRA declares that the paramilitary activity of these groups is an exercise of their "right to keep and bear arms." Echoing the extremist rhetoric of the "militias," an NRA official has called the Second Amendment "a loaded gun...held to the head of government." This is a perversion of our Constitution.

When our Founding Fathers wrote the Second Amendment more than 200 years ago, the "well regulated militia" was not a privately organized army formed to resist the government of the United States. It was the military arm of state government, formed to maintain public order.

The Supreme Court has ruled that the "obvious purpose" of the Second Amendment was to protect the "militia which the States were expected to maintain and train," and that "the National Guard is the modern militia."

Because laws regulating firearms do not interfere with the modern militia, no gun control law has ever been overturned by the federal courts on Second Amendment grounds. That's why former Supreme Court Chief Justice Warren Burger has called the NRA's Second Amendment propaganda a "fraud on the American public."

The Second Amendment is not a barrier to reasonable gun control laws. Nor is it a license for those who disagree with government policies to resist them by force of arms. It's time for the NRA to stop its Second Amendment fraud.

The Second Amendment protects the National Guard, not private armies preparing to take the law into their own hands.

Sarah Brady, Chair of the Center to Prevent Handgun Violence

Dear Sarah, I want to support your national education campaign to fight the NRA's Second Amendment fraud. Enclosed is my contribution for:

☐ $15   ☐ $25   ☐ $50   ☐ Other _____

NAME _____

ADDRESS _____

CITY, STATE, ZIP _____

E-MAIL _____

Return to: Center to Prevent Handgun Violence, 1225 Eye Street, NW, Room 1100, Washington, DC 20005

Contributions to the Center to Prevent Handgun Violence are tax-deductible.

☐ **I'd like more information on the Second Amendment and the Center to Prevent Handgun Violence.**

NAME _____

ADDRESS _____

_____

CITY, STATE, ZIP _____

Return to: Center to Prevent Handgun Violence
1225 Eye Street, NW, Room 1100
Washington, DC 20005

Brought to you by the Center to Prevent Handgun Violence, Sarah Brady, Chair

Competing Products: Sources of Energy

The advertisement by the Metropolitan Energy Council presented on the following page argues for the use of oil to provide heating. The advertisement for nuclear energy on page 301 is part of a series sponsored by the U.S. Council for Energy Awareness to promote the building of more nuclear energy plants. What emotional appeals do you see in these ads? Are these appeals directed at the same readers? Overall, which ad do you find more persuasive, and why?

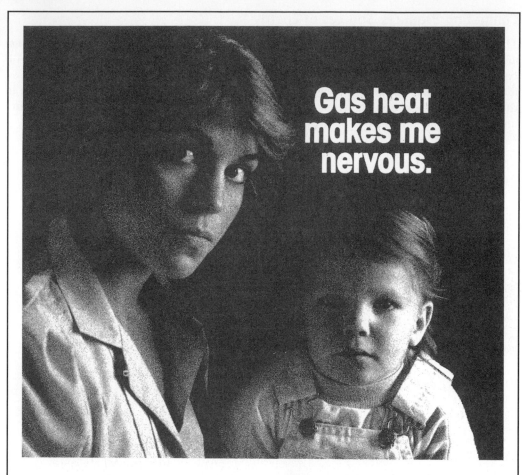

Gas heat makes me nervous.

Gas comes from the big utility.
They don't know my name.
They don't know my family.

If you need prompt service from them,
you have to say, "I smell gas."

That's what scares me most. I think gas heat
is dangerous . . . too dangerous
for my home, my kids.

I heat with oil.

 Oil heat...The Intelligent Choice
Metropolitan Energy Council, Inc.

SOME ARGUMENTS FOR NUCLEAR ENERGY ARE SMALLER THAN OTHERS.

Around the nuclear electric plant on Florida's Hutchinson Island, endangered wildlife have a safe haven. The baby sea turtles hatching on nearby beaches are more evidence of the truth about nuclear energy: it peacefully coexists with the environment.

America's 110 operating nuclear plants don't pollute the air, because they don't burn anything to generate electricity. Nor do they eat up valuable natural resources such as oil and natural gas.

Still, more plants are needed—to help satisfy the nation's growing need for electricity without sacrificing the quality of our environment. For a free booklet on nuclear energy, write to the U.S. Council for Energy Awareness, P.O. Box 66080, Dept. TR01, Washington, D.C. 20035.

NUCLEAR ENERGY MEANS CLEANER AIR.

© 1992 USCEA

As seen in April 1992 issues of The Washington Post, FORTUNE, and National Journal; May 1992 issues of TIME, Newsweek, Washington Post National Weekly and Congressional Quarterly; June 1992 issues of National Geographic, Smithsonian, New Choices and Christian Science Monitor; July 1992 issue of Forbes; August 1992 issue of World Monitor; September 1992 issue of Ladies' Home Journal and Natural History; October 1992 issues of Good Housekeeping, Atlantic and American Heritage; and November 1992 issue of Reader's Digest.

This advertisement is provided courtesy of the United States Council for Energy Awareness, Washington, D.C.

Popular Appeals: Spending Our Money

Although the products and target audiences are not at all similar, how might both of the advertisements that follow be said to employ variations of the "bandwagon" appeal? In the American Century ad, what sort of company identity is created with the story of the boss's lunch? Why might an investment service want this image? To what kind of person does this ad appeal?

The Omega watch ad appeals to a different audience in its use of movie star Pierce Brosnan, known for his portrayal of adventurous characters such as 007 spy James Bond. What effect is "Brosnan's choice" intended to have on the reader? What does the name of the watch style ("Seamaster Aqua Terra") contribute to the appeal of this ad?

AMERICAN VALUES

Every day, our founder has the same lunch. It isn't lobster tail. ⸻

It's a true story. At noon, he sits down in the cafeteria and eats a peanut butter sandwich. When he's done, he folds up his paper sack so it can be used again tomorrow.

It's a tradition around here. One of the many we've created in our 44 years of managing investments. Over time we've grown, but two things have remained constant. His lunch. And our values. Your success is still our first priority. The proof is in the peanut butter.

AMERICAN CENTURY.

Investment Managers

American Century Investment Services, Inc. © 2002 American Century Services Corporation

PIERCE BROSNAN'S CHOICE

www.omegawatches.com

SEAMASTER AQUA TERRA
Co-Axial Escapement
3 year extended warranty

The name Omega has always been closely associated with quality and reliability. The Seamaster Aqua Terra upholds this pioneering spirit. Its classic design houses the latest in watchmaking technology: the unique Co-Axial Escapement movement, which offers unrivalled long-term accuracy.

■ A REVISION WORKSHEET

As you write your rough drafts, consult Chapter 5 for guidance through the revision process. In addition, here are a few questions to ask yourself as you revise your argumentative essay:

1. Does this essay present a clear thesis limited to fit the assigned length of this paper?

2. Does this essay contain a number of strong, persuasive points in support of its thesis?

3. Is the essay organized in an easy-to-follow pattern that avoids repetition or confusion?

4. Does the essay present enough supporting evidence to make each of its points convincing? Where could additional examples, factual information, testimony, or other kinds of supporting material be added to make the arguments even more effective?

5. Will all the supporting evidence be clear to the essay's particular audience? Do any terms or examples need additional explanation or special definition?

6. Has at least one major opposing argument been addressed?

7. Does the essay avoid any logical fallacies or problems in tone?

After you've revised your essay extensively, you might exchange rough drafts with a classmate and answer these questions for each other, making specific suggestions for improvement wherever appropriate. (For advice on productive participation in classroom workshops, see pages 106–109.)

Reviewing Your Progress

After you have completed your argument essay, take a moment to measure your progress as a writer by responding to the following questions. Such analysis will help you recognize growth in your writing skills and may enable you to identify areas that are still problematic.

1. Which part of your essay do you like best? Why?

2. After analyzing your essay's reasoning and evidence, which particular argument or point do you consider the strongest? What makes it so convincing?

3. What part of your essay gave you the most trouble? How did you overcome the problem?

4. If you had more time to work on this essay, what would receive additional attention? Why?

5. What did you learn about your topic from writing this essay? About yourself as a writer?

Chapter 11

Description

The writer of description creates a word-picture of persons, places, objects, and emotions, using a careful selection of details to make an impression on the reader. If you have already written expository or argumentative essays in your composition course, you almost certainly have written some descriptive prose. Nearly every essay, after all, calls for some kind of description; for example, in the student comparison/contrast essay (pages 217–220), the writer describes two kinds of stores; in the professional process essay (pages 203–206), the writer describes the embalming procedure in great detail. To help you write better description in your other essays, however, you may want to practice writing descriptive paragraphs or a short descriptive essay.

■ How to Write Effective Description

When descriptive prose is called for in your writing, consider these four basic suggestions:

Recognize your purpose. Description is not free-floating; it appears in your writing for a particular reason—to help you inform, clarify, persuade, or create a mood. In some essays you will want your description as *objective*—without personal impressions—as you can make it; for example, you might describe a scientific experiment or a business transaction in straight factual detail. Other times, however, you will want to convey a particular attitude toward your subject; this approach to description is called *subjective* or *impressionistic*. Note the differences between the following two descriptions of a tall, thin boy: the objective writer sticks to the facts by saying, "The eighteen-year-old boy was 6'1" and weighed 155 pounds," whereas the subjective writer gives an impressionistic description: "The young boy was as tall and scrawny as a birch tree in winter." Before you begin describing anything, you must first decide your purpose and whether it calls for objective or subjective reporting.

Describe clearly, using specific details. To make any description clear to your reader, you must include a sufficient number of details that are specific rather than fuzzy or vague. If, for example, your family dog were missing, you wouldn't call the animal shelter to ask if they'd seen a "big brown dog with a short tail"—naturally, you'd mention every distinguishing detail about your pet you could think of: size, color, breed, cut of ears, and special markings. Similarly, if your car were stolen, you'd give the police as clear and as complete a description of your vehicle as possible. Look at the following sentence. Does it clearly identify a vaulting horse?

> A vaulting horse is a thing usually found in gyms that has four legs and a beam and is used by gymnasts making jumps.

If you didn't already know what a vaulting horse was, you might have trouble picking it out in a gymnasium crowded with equipment. A description with additional details would help you locate it:

> A vaulting horse is a piece of equipment used by gymnasts during competition to help propel them into the air when they perform any of a variety of leaps known as vaults. The gymnasts usually approach the vaulting horse from a running start and then place their hands on the horse for support or for a push off as they perform their vaults. The horse itself resembles a carpenter's sawhorse, but the main beam is made of padded leather rather than wood. The rectangular beam is approximately 5 feet, 3 inches long and 13½ inches wide. Supported by four legs usually made of steel, the padded leather beam is approximately 4 feet, ½ inch above the floor in men's competitions and 3 feet, 7 inches in women's competitions. The padded leather beam has two white lines marking off three sections on top: the croup, the saddle, and the neck. The two end sections—the croup and the neck—are each 15½ inches long. Gymnasts place their hands on the neck or croup, depending on the type of vault they are attempting.

Moreover, the reader cannot imagine your subject clearly if your description is couched in vague generalities. The following sentence, for example, presents only a hazy picture:

> Larry is a sloppy dresser.

Revised, the picture is now sharply in focus:

> Larry wears dirty, baggy pants, shirts too small to stay tucked in, socks that fail to match his pants or each other, and a stained coat the Salvation Army rejected as a donation.

Specific details can turn cloudy prose into crisp, clear images that can be reproduced in the mind like photographs.

Select only appropriate details. In any description the choice of details depends largely on the writer's purpose and audience. However, many descriptions—especially the more subjective ones—will present a *dominant impression;* that is, the writer selects primarily those details that communicate a particular mood or feeling to the reader. The dominant impression is the controlling focus of a description; for example, if you wrote a description of your grandmother to show her thoughtfulness, you would select only those details that convey an impression of a sweet, kindly old lady. Here are two brief descriptions illustrating the concept of dominant impression. The first writer tries to create a mood of mystery:

> Down a black winding road stands the abandoned old mansion, silhouetted against the cloud-shrouded moon, creaking and moaning in the wet, chill wind.

The second writer tries to present a feeling of joy and innocence.

> A dozen kites filled the spring air, and around the bright picnic tables spread with hot dogs, hamburgers, and slices of watermelon, Tom and Annie played away the warm April day.

In the description of the deserted mansion, the writer would have violated the impression of mystery had the sentence read,

> Down the black winding road stands the abandoned old mansion, surrounded by bright, multicolored tulips in early bloom.

Including the cheerful flowers as a detail in the description destroys the dominant mood of bleakness and mystery. Similarly, the second example would be spoiled had the writer ended it this way:

> Tom and Annie played away the warm April day until Tom got so sunburned he became ill and had to go home.

Therefore, remember to select only those details that advance your descriptive purpose. Omit any details you consider unimportant or distracting.

See if you can determine the dominant impression of each of the following descriptions:

> The wind had curled up to sleep in the distant mountains. Leaves hung limp and motionless from the silent trees, while birds perched on the branches like little statues. As I sat on the edge of the clearing, holding my breath, I could hear a squirrel scampering through the underbrush. Somewhere far away a dog barked twice, and then the woods were hushed once more.

> This poor thing has seen better days, but one should expect the sofa in a fraternity house den to be well worn. The large, plump, brown corduroy pillows strewn lazily on the floor and propped comfortably against the threadbare arms bear the pencil-point scars of frustrated students and foam-bleeding cuts of multiple pillow wars. No less than four pairs of rotting Nikes stand twenty-four-hour guard at the corners of its carefully mended frame. Obviously the relaxed, inviting appearance masks the permanent odors of cheap cigars from Thursday night poker parties; at least two or three guests each weekend sift through the popcorn kernels and Doritos crumbs, sprawl face down, and pass out for a nap. However, frequent inhabitants have learned to avoid the dark stains courtesy of the house pup and the red-punch designs of the chapter klutz. Habitually, they strategically lunge over the back of the sofa to an unsoiled area easily identifiable in flight by the large depression left by

previous regulars. The quiet *hmmph* of the cushions and harmonious squeal of the exhausted springs signal a perfect landing and utter a warm greeting from an old and faithful friend.

Make your descriptions vivid. By using clear, precise words, you can improve any kind of writing. Chapters 7 (on words) and 6 (on sentences) offer a variety of tips on clarifying your prose style. In addition to the advice given there, here are two other ways to enliven your descriptions, particularly those that call for a subjective approach:

Use sensory details. If it's appropriate, try using images that appeal to your readers' five senses. If, for example, you are describing your broken leg and the ensuing stay in a hospital, tell your readers how the place smelled, how it looked, what your cast felt like, how your pills tasted, and what noises you heard. Here are some specific examples using sensory details:

Sight	The clean white corridors of the hospital resembled the set of a sci-fi movie, with everyone scurrying around in identical starched uniforms.
Hearing	At night, the only sounds I heard were the quiet squeakings of sensible white shoes as the nurses made their rounds.
Smell	The green beans on the hospital cafeteria tray smelled stale and waxy, like crayons.
Touch	The hospital bed sheet felt as rough and heavy as a feed sack.
Taste	Every four hours they gave me an enormous gray pill whose aftertaste reminded me of the stale licorice my great-aunt kept in candy dishes around her house.

By appealing to the readers' senses, you better enable them to imagine the subject you are describing. Joseph Conrad, the famous nineteenth-century novelist, agreed, believing that all art "appeals primarily to the senses, and the artistic aim when expressing itself in written words must also make its appeal through the senses, if its highest desire is to reach the secret spring of responsive emotions." In other words, to make your readers feel, first make them "see."

Use figurative language when appropriate. As you may recall from Chapter 7, figurative language produces images or pictures in the readers' minds, helping them to understand unfamiliar or abstract subjects. Here are some devices you might use to clarify or spice up your prose:

1. Simile: a comparison between two things using the words "like" or "as" (see also pages 157–158)

   Example   Seeing exactly the video game he wanted, he moved as quickly as a starving teenager spotting pie in a refrigerator full of leftover vegetables.

2. Metaphor: a direct comparison between two things that does not use "like" or "as" (see also pages 157–158)

   Example   I was a puppet with my father controlling all the financial strings.

3. Personification: the attribution of human characteristics and emotions to inanimate objects, animals, or abstract ideas

   Example   The old teddy bear sat in a corner, dozing serenely before the fireplace.

4. Hyperbole: intentional exaggeration or overstatement for emphasis or humor

Example   The cockroaches in my kitchen had now grown to the size of carry-on luggage.

5. Understatement: intentional representation of a subject as less important than the facts would warrant (see also irony, pages 144–145)

Example   "The reports of my death are greatly exaggerated."—Mark Twain

6. Synecdoche: a part of something used to represent the whole

Example   A hundred tired feet hit the dance floor for one last jitterbug. [Here "feet" stand for the dancing couples themselves.]

Using figures of speech in appropriate places can make your descriptions clear, lively, and memorable. (For additional examples, see pages 157–158.)

Problems to Avoid

Keep in mind these three pieces of advice to solve problems that frequently arise in description:

Remember your audience. Sometimes the object of our description is so clear in our minds we forget that our readers haven't seen it, too. Consequently, the description we write turns out to be vague, bland, or skimpy ("The big tree was beautiful"). Ask yourself about your audience: what do they need to know to see this sight as clearly as I do? Then fill in your description with ample, precise details that reveal the best picture possible. Don't forget to define or explain any terms you use that may be puzzling to your audience. (For more advice on clear, vivid language, see Chapter 7.)

Avoid an erratic organization of details. Too often descriptions are a hodgepodge of details, jotted down randomly. When you write a lengthy description, you should select a plan that will arrange your details in an orderly fashion. Depending on your subject matter and your purpose, you might adopt a plan calling for a description of something from top to bottom, left to right, front to back, and so on. For example, a description of a woman might begin at the head and move to the feet; furniture in a room might be described as your eyes move from one side of the room to another. A second plan for arranging details presents the subject's outstanding characteristics first and then fills in the lesser information; a child's red hair, for example, might be his most striking feature and therefore would be described first. A third plan presents details in the order you see them approaching: dust, then a car, then details about the car, its occupants, and so on. Or you might describe a subject as it unfolds chronologically, as in some kind of process or operation. Regardless of which plan of organization you choose, the reader should feel a sense of order in your description.

Avoid any sudden change in perspective. If, for example, you are describing the White House from the outside, don't suddenly include details that could be seen only from the inside. Similarly, if you are describing a car from a distance, you might be able to tell the car's model, year, and color, but you could hardly describe the upholstery or reveal the mileage. It is, of course, possible for you—or your observer—to approach or move around the subject of your description, but the reader must be aware of this movement. Any shift in point of view must be presented clearly and logically, with no sudden, confusing leaps from a front to a back view, from outside to inside, and so on.

■ PRACTICING WHAT YOU'VE LEARNED

The following sketch, published in *The New York Times* in 2003, was written by Verlyn Klinkenborg, author of *Rural Life* (2003) and many other books, essays, newspaper and magazine articles. Analyze the effectiveness of this description: does the writer succeed in briefly re-creating this scene? What sort of world exists inside the noisy commuter car? Identify several uses of sensory details and figurative language and explain how they help readers "see" Klinkenborg's commuter colleagues.

■ Aboard the Sleeper

1   Nearly everyone on the commuter railroad platform looks immured in a sense of the coming day or, if it's an evening train, the day just past. Everyone projects a certain composure, an awareness of the unwritten rules of commuting, the cautious self-containment in the hopes that others will remain self-contained. The train pulls in. People board and quickly find their seats, and the wheels begin to rumble and clack. And one by one the commuters drop into sleep. Before long, the entire car is asleep, except for some wide-eyed first-time rider whose alertness looks like a kind of perversity. All that workday armor has been shuffled off, and though all the passengers are still wearing suits and ties and business ensembles, you can see the pajamas in their faces.

2   As long as I've been riding trains into New York—some 25 years now—I'm still struck by the collective intimacy of a passenger car full of sleeping strangers. It becomes clear at such moments—when the whole car is silent except for a dry gasp somewhere—that the human neck is a useless piece of anatomy, a stem unable to support the ripe fruit of the head. Some people lean against the window, and some just lean back, mouths agape, giving it the full Vesuvius.

3   A load of sleeping commuters is one of those scenes that make you stop short and marvel at the strangeness of humans. How is it that we plunge headlong into unconsciousness even with the lights staring down at us, the air-conditioning rushing, the wheels clattering, the conductor calling out the stations? Sleep is not only a blessing. It's also a wonderful joke, a truly sportive adaptation. I look around, watching bold chins receding, the appearance of every intention giving way to the haplessness, the aimlessness of sleep. Composure becomes discomposure. The avowed sincerity of wakefulness becomes the far greater sincerity of slumber. And then I, too, drift away, caught in the undertow, forgetful of the rain-streaked windows and the dark world outside.

■ ASSIGNMENT

Use this well-known painting, *Nighthawks* (1942), by American artist Edward Hopper, to practice your descriptive writing skills. What is the dominant impression or "mood" of this painting? What details in the picture support your interpretation? Consider, for example, the painting's setting (place, year, time); choice of colors and use of light and shadow; the people and their positions in the scene. In a short descriptive essay, re-create this painting as you see it for someone who is unfamiliar with the work.

Copyright © The Art Institute of Chicago. All rights Reserved.

Nighthawks, 1942, by Edward Hopper

■ ESSAY TOPICS

Here are some suggestions for a descriptive paragraph or essay; focus your topic to fit your assignment. Don't forget that every description, whether objective or subjective, has a purpose and that your details should support that purpose. For additional ideas, see "Suggestions for Writing" on page 321.

1. A favorite photograph or work of art (or choose a picture from this textbook)
2. Your best/worst job
3. A piece of equipment important to your major, a hobby, or favorite sport
4. A campus or local character
5. One dish or foodstuff that should be forever banned
6. Yourself (how you looked at a certain age or on a memorable occasion)

7. Your most precious material possession

8. The ugliest/most beautiful place on your campus or in town

9. A holiday dinner or ritual in your family

10. Your first or worst car or apartment

11. A piece of clothing that reveals the real "you"

12. A product that needs to be invented

13. An act of heroism or personal success

14. Your favorite recreation area (beach, hiking trail, park, etc.)

15. An unforgettable moment

16. An event, element, or critter in nature

17. A shopping mall, student cafeteria, or other crowded public place

18. The inside of your refrigerator, closet, or some other equally loathsome place in your home

19. A special collection or hobby display

20. Your Special Place (Perhaps your place offers you solitude, beauty, or renewed energy. The scene below was painted ten times by nineteenth-century artist Claude Monet, who loved this tranquil lily pond near his farmhouse in France. Re-create your special place for your readers by choosing the right descriptive words, just as Monet did with each brush stroke of color.)

The Water-Lily Pond, 1899, by Claude Monet

A Topic Proposal for Your Essay

Selecting the right subject matter is important to every writer. To help you clarify your ideas and strengthen your commitment to your topic, here is a proposal sheet that asks you to describe some of your preliminary ideas about your subject before you begin drafting. Although your ideas may change as you write (they will almost certainly become more refined), thinking through your choice of topic now may help you avoid several false starts.

1. What subject will your essay describe? Will you describe this subject objectively or subjectively? Why?

2. Why are you interested in this topic? Do you have a personal or professional connection to the subject? State at least one reason for your choice of topic.

3. Is this a significant topic of interest to others? Why? Who specifically might find it interesting, informative, or entertaining?

4. What is the main purpose of your description? In one or two sentences describe the major effect you'd like your descriptive essay to have on your readers. What would you like for them to understand or "see" about your subject?

5. List at least three details that you think will help clarify your subject for your readers.

6. What difficulties, if any, might arise during drafting? For example, what organizational strategy might you think about now that would allow you to guide your readers through your description in a coherent way?

■ Sample Student Essay

In her descriptive essay, this student writer recalls her childhood days at the home of her grandparents to make a point about growing up. Notice that the writer uses both figurative language and contrasting images to help her readers understand her point of view.

TREECLIMBING

1   It was Mike's eighteenth birthday and he was having a little bit of a breakdown. "When was the last time you made cloud pictures?" he asked me absently as he stared up at the ceiling before class started. Before I could answer, he continued, "Did you know that by the time you're an adult, you've lost 85 percent of your imagination?" He paused. "I don't want to grow up." Although I doubted the authenticity of his facts, I

Introduction: The conversation that triggers her memory

---

understood that Mike—the hopeless romantic with his long ponytail, sullen black clothes, and glinting dark eyes—was caught in a Peter Pan complex. He drew those eyes from the ceiling and focused on me: "There are two types of children. Tree children and dirt children. Kids playing will either climb trees or play in the dirt. Tree children are the dreamers—the hopeful, creative dreamers. Dirt children, they just stay on the ground. Stick to the rules." He trailed off, and then picked up again: "I'm a tree child. I want to make cloud pictures and climb trees. And I don't ever want to come down." Mike's story reminded me of my own days as a tree child, and of the inevitable fall from the tree to the ground.

2   My childhood was a playground for imagination. Summers were spent surrounded by family at my grandparents' house in Milwaukee, Wisconsin. The rambling Lannonstone bungalow was located on North 46th Street at Burleigh, a block away from center-city Milwaukee, two blocks from Schuster's department store and the Pfister hotel. In the winter, all the houses looked alike, rigid and militant, like white-bearded old generals with icicles hanging from their moustaches. One European-styled house after the other lined the streets in strict parallel formation, block after block.

The grandparents' neighborhood remembered in military images and sensory details

3   But in the summer it was different . . . softer. No subzero winds blew lonely down the back alley. Instead, kids played stickball in it. I had elegant, grass-stained tea parties with a neighborhood girl named Shelly, while my grandfather worked in his thriving vegetable garden among the honeybees, and watched sprouts grow. An ever-present warming smell of yeast filtered down every street as the nearby breweries pumped a constant flow of fresh beer. Above, the summer sky looked like an Easter egg God had dipped in blue dye.

4   Those summer trips to Milwaukee were greatly anticipated events back then. My brother and I itched with repressed energy throughout the long plane ride from the West Coast. We couldn't wait to see Grandma

and Papa. We couldn't wait to see what presents Papa had for us. We couldn't wait to slide down the steep, blue-carpeted staircase on our bottoms, and then on our stomachs. Most of all, we couldn't wait to go down to the basement.

5   The basement was better than a toy store. Yes, the old-fashioned milk cabinet in the kitchen wall was enchanting, and the laundry chute was fun because it was big enough to throw down Ernie, my stuffed dog companion, so my brother could catch him below in the laundry room, as our voices echoed up and down the chute. But the basement was better than all of these, better even than sliding down those stairs on rug-burned bottoms.

6   It was always deliciously cool down in the basement. Since the house was built in the 1930s, there was no air conditioning. Upstairs, we slept in hot, heavy rooms. My nightgown stuck to the sheets, and I would lie awake, listening to crickets, inhaling the beer-sweet smell of the summer night, hoping for a cool breeze. Nights were forgotten, however, as my brother and I spent hours every day in the basement. There were seven rooms in the basement; some darker rooms I had waited years to explore. There was always a jumbled heap of toys in the middle room, most of which were leftovers from my father's own basement days. It was a child's safe haven; it was a sacred place.

7   The hours spent in the basement were times of a gloriously secure childhood. Empires were created in a day with faded colored building blocks. New territories were annexed when either my brother or I got the courage to venture into one of those Other Rooms—the dark, musty ones without windows—and then scamper back to report of any sightings of monsters or other horrific childhood creatures. In those basement days everything seemed safe and wholesome and secure, with my family surrounding me, protecting me. Like childhood itself, entering the basement was like entering another dimension.

Marginal notes:

Use of parallel sentences to emphasize anticipation

The basement in contrast to other parts of the house

Adventures in the basement

The house
and
neighborhood
years later

8 Last summer I returned to Milwaukee to help my grandparents pack to move into an apartment. I went back at 17 to find the house—my kingdom—up for sale. I found another cycle coming to a close, and I found myself separated from what I had once known. I looked at the house. It was old; it was crumbling; it needed paint. I looked down the back alley and saw nothing but trash and weeds. I walked to the corner and saw smoke-choked, dirty streets and thick bars in shop windows, nothing more than another worn-out midwestern factory city. I went back to the house and down to the basement, alone.

The
basement
years later

9 It was gray and dark. Dust filtered through a single feeble sunbeam from a cracked window pane. It was empty, except for the overwhelming musty smell. The toys were gone, either packed or thrown away. As I walked in and out of rooms, the quietness filled my ears, but in the back of my head the sounds of childhood laughter and chatter played like an old recording.

10 The dark rooms were filled not with monsters but with remnants of my grandfather's business. A neon sign was propped against the wall in a corner: Ben Strauss Plumbing. Piles of heavy pipes and metal machine parts lay scattered about on shelves. A dusty purple ribbon was thumbtacked to a door. It said SHOOT THE WORKS in white letters. I gently took it down. The ribbon hangs on my door at home now, and out of context it somehow is not quite so awe-inspiring and mystifying as it once was. However, it does serve its purpose, permanently connecting me to my memories.

11 All children are tree children, I believe. The basement used to be my tree, the place I could dream in. That last summer I found myself, much to Mike's disappointment, quite mature, quite adult. Maybe Mike fell from his tree and was bruised. Climbing down from that tree doesn't have to be something to be afraid of. One needn't hide in the tree for fear of touching the ground and forgetting how to climb back up when necessary. I think there is a way to balance the two extremes. Climb down gracefully as you grow up, and if you fall, don't land in quicksand. I like to think I'm more of a shrubbery child: not so low as to get stuck in the mud and just high enough to look at the sky and make cloud pictures.

Conclusion: A return to the introduction's images and some advice

Professional Essay*

■ Still Learning from My Mother

Cliff Schneider

Cliff Schneider is a graduate of Cornell and a retired freshwater fisheries biologist, who worked for the Department of Environmental Conservation in New York. Much of his research and writing has focused on his work studying Lake Ontario. This essay, a personal tribute to his seventy-nine-year-old mother, was first published in the "My Turn" column of *Newsweek* magazine, in March 2000.

1   When I was a young boy growing up on New York's Long Island in the 1950s, it was common to see boys and their fathers gathering in the roads in front of their homes on warm summer evenings to "have a catch." That was the term we had for tossing a baseball while we talked about school, jobs and life in general. Although my dad and I had many catches together, my most memorable ones were with my mother. She would happily grab a glove, run out to the road and then fire fast balls at me that cracked my glove and left my hand stinging. She never showed any motherly concern, though, just a broad grin with the tip of her tongue exposed in the corner of her mouth. This was her game face. I can still recall how delighted I was tossing the ball with Mom and hearing the comments from my friends and neighbors: "Where did your mother learn to throw a ball like that?"

2   My mother, you see, was a jock long before Title IX unleashed the explosion of modern women's athletics. She lettered in field hockey and basketball while attending Hofstra University in the late 1930s. This was a time when it wasn't very fashionable

---

* To help you read this essay analytically, review pages 166–168. For two other professional essays in Part Two that make extensive use of description, see "To Bid the World Farewell" (pages 203–206) and "Two Ways of Viewing the River" (pages 227–228).

for women to go running after a ball and work up a sweat. Luckily for me, Mom never worried about what was fashionable. She loved sports, loved being active and, most of all, loved the competition. Mom was kind to her kids until we played ball. Then we'd notice this gleam in her eye, the broad grin and the familiar tongue that told us she was ready for action and ready to have some fun. No matter what game she played, Mom had class. She played hard, she laughed a lot and, win or lose, she was always gracious.

3   The years have diminished Mom's physical abilities, as they would have for anyone who is about to become an octogenarian. Her back is a little bent, and she complains occasionally about her hip. Her biggest concession to the aging process, however, is that she has had to lighten up on her bowling ball. As a young mother in suburban bowling leagues she toted a 15-pound ball, carried a 160 average and had a high game of 212. As she's grown older, her scores have declined. In recent years she's had to start using an eight-pound ball, which she protests is too light and "doesn't give enough pin action."

4   For years I have had to listen to my mother's perennial battle cry as she begins each new bowling season—"This is the year I'm going to bowl a 200 game!" I've always smiled and nodded in agreement, which was my way of acknowledging her determination. During our regular Thursday-evening phone conversations (she bowls on Thursdays), she gives me a frame-by-frame description of her games, and gripes that she can't bowl the way she used to. She almost always slips in the comment "I'm going to make 200 if it kills me." I try to explain that she should be satisfied that she is at least able to play the game. "Try to make some concession to your age, Mom," I say. Of course, she will have none of this talk and this year bought a 10-pound ball in pursuit of her dream. Vince Lombardi would be proud.

5   A week after she started bowling with her new ball, I called to check on her progress. She no sooner said "Hi" than I could tell something big had happened in her life. I could feel the smile all the way from Hendersonville, N.C., to upstate New York. I shouted, "You bowled a 200 game!" knowing it could be the only reason for such a happy voice. She corrected me: "Not a 200 game; I got a 220." It was her highest score ever! She gave me a strike-by-strike description of her game, and we both celebrated over the phone. As she signed off and said her goodbyes, I could still sense the smile on her face. Her grin will probably fade in another month or two.

6   After some reflection, I am amazed by my mother's accomplishment. Whether it is baseball, tennis, golf or even bowling, I have never heard of anyone's peaking at 79. Yes, there is some degree of luck in every game, but in Mom's case she had the best game of her life because she persevered. Mom's achievement has lifted her spirits and made her feel young again. For someone who is too frequently reminded that she can't do what she used to, this experience could not have come at a better time in her life. I guess I'm not surprised that I can still learn from Mom—that you are never too old to dream and never too old to realize those dreams. I am not surprised, either, that in our most recent calls she talks about bowling a 250 game.

Questions on Content, Structure, and Style

1. Is Schneider's description of his mother primarily objective or subjective? Cite an example of his language to support your answer.

2. Why was his mother's behavior unusual in the 1950s? What does "before Title IX" (paragraph 2) mean?

3. What "dominant impression" of his mother does Schneider present in this essay? What are some of the details Schneider provides to help us understand this woman's character?

4. How does Schneider physically describe his mother so that readers can easily imagine those early games of catch? Why does she have "class"?

5. Examine some of Schneider's word choices. What, for example, is the effect of writing that his mother would "fire fast balls at me that cracked my glove and left my hand stinging" (paragraph 1) instead of "mom could throw very hard"?

6. What does his mother's "perennial battle cry" at age 79 reveal about her? Why does Schneider think Vince Lombardi—the football coach who holds the record for the most NFL wins—would be proud of her?

7. What does Schneider's occasional use of dialogue add to this essay? Why, for example, does he quote his neighbors in paragraph 1 and his mother in paragraphs 3 and 4?

8. Why does Schneider organize his essay by starting with a description of his mother's younger days and concluding with a reference to "a 250 game"? How does this organization contribute to our understanding of his mother?

9. What has Schneider learned from his mother? In what way is this lesson an important part of this essay's purpose?

10. Did Schneider successfully create a picture of his mother? Could you suggest some ways he might improve his description? What language might have been more specific or vivid?

Suggestions for Writing

Try using Cliff Schneider's "Still Learning from My Mother" as a stepping-stone to your essay. Describe an unusual-but-wonderful relative or friend you admire for a particular trait. Consider including ample physical details, dialogue, and actions illustrating personality, as Schneider did, to make your description of this person vivid for your reader. Or write a description of an ancestor whose photograph has always intrigued you. What is the dominant impression of this picture? What does this person's face (or posture or choice of clothing) say to you about his or her character or style?

Perhaps you might choose to describe another mother figure, whose face is forever identified with the Great Depression. In 1936 photographer Dorothea Lange stopped on a dirt road in California to take a half-dozen pictures of a thirty-two-year-old woman and her children as they huddled in the rain under a lean-to tent. The woman told Lange they had been living off birds the children had killed and that she had just sold the tires off their car to buy food. Why do you think *Migrant Mother*, shown on page 322, is considered one of the most affecting photographs of all time?

Vocabulary

Title IX (2)   octogenarian (3)   toted (3)
diminished (3)   concession (3)   perennial (4)

Migrant Mother, 1936, Dorothea Lange

▪ A REVISION WORKSHEET

As you write your rough drafts, consult Chapter 5 for guidance through
the revision process. In addition, here are a few questions to ask yourself as you revise your description:

1. Is the descriptive essay's purpose clear to the reader?

2. Are there enough specific details in the description to make the subject matter distinct to readers who are unfamiliar with the scene, person, or object? Where might more detail be added?

3. Are the details arranged in an order that's easy to follow?

4. If the assignment called for an objective description, are the details as "neutral" as possible?

5. If the assignment called for a subjective description, does the writer's particular attitude come through clearly with a consistent use of well-chosen details or imagery?

6. Could any sensory details or figurative language be added to help the reader "see" the subject matter?

7. Does this essay end with an appropriate conclusion or does description merely stop?

After you've revised your essay extensively, you might exchange rough drafts with a classmate and answer these questions for each other, making specific suggestions for improvement wherever appropriate. (For advice on productive participation in classroom workshops, see pages 106–109.)

Reviewing Your Progress

After you have completed your descriptive essay, take a moment to measure your progress as a writer by responding to the following questions. Such analysis will help you recognize growth in your writing skills and may enable you to identify areas that are still problematic.

1. What is the best part of your essay? Why?

2. Which one descriptive detail or image do you think is the clearest or most vivid in your essay? Why does that one stand above the others?

3. What part of your essay gave you the most trouble? How did you overcome the problem?

4. If you had more time to work on this essay, what would receive additional attention? Why?

5. What did you learn about your topic from writing this essay? About yourself as a writer?

Chapter 12

Narration

When many people hear the word "narrative," they think of a made-up story. But not all stories are fiction. In this chapter we are not concerned with writing literary short stories—that's a skill to develop in a creative writing class—but rather with nonfiction *expository narratives,* stories that are used to explain or prove a point. We most often use two kinds of these stories:

1. the *extended narrative*—a long episode that by itself illustrates or supports an essay's thesis
2. the *brief narrative*—a shorter incident that is often used in a body paragraph to support or illustrate a particular point in an essay.

Let's suppose, for example, you wanted to write an essay showing how confusing the registration system is at your school. To illustrate the problems vividly, you might devote your entire essay to the retelling of a friend's seven-hour experience signing up for classes last fall, thus making use of extended narration. Or take another example: in an argumentative essay advocating mandatory use of side-door air bags in automobiles, you might include a brief narrative about a car wreck to support a paragraph's point about air bags' ability to save lives. Regardless of which type of narrative best fits your purpose, the telling of a story or an incident can be an interesting, persuasive means of informing your readers.

■ Writing the Effective Narrative Essay

Know your purpose. What are you trying to accomplish by writing this narrative essay? Are you, for example, offering an *objective* retelling of a historical event (the dropping of the atomic bomb) to inform your readers who may not be acquainted with the facts? Or are you presenting a *subjective* narrative, which persuasively tells a story (Susan B. Anthony's arrest for voting) from a clearly defined point of view? Perhaps your narrative is a personal story, whose lesson you wish readers to share. Whatever your choice—an objective, factual retelling or a subjective interpretation—your narrative's purpose should be clear to your readers, who should never reach the end of the story wondering "What was that all about?" Knowing your purpose will help you select the information and language best suited to meet your audience's needs.

Present your main point clearly. To ensure that readers understand their purpose, many writers first state a thesis claim followed by a narrative that supports it. Sometimes writers begin with their narrative and use their concluding paragraph to state or sum up the point or "lesson" of their story. Still others choose to imply a main point or attitude through the unfolding action and choice of descriptive details. An implied thesis is always riskier than a stated one, so unless you are absolutely convinced that your readers could not possibly fail to see your point, work on finding a smooth way to incorporate a statement of your main idea into your essay.

Follow a logical time sequence. Many narrative essays—and virtually all brief stories used in other kinds of essays—follow a chronological order, presenting actions as they naturally occur in the story. Occasionally, however, a writer will use the flashback technique, which takes the readers back in time to reveal an event that occurred before the present scene of the essay. If you decide to use shifts in time, use transitional phrases or other signals to ensure that your readers don't become confused or lost.

Use sensory details to hold your readers' interest. For example, if the setting plays an important role in your story, describe it in vivid terms so that your readers can imagine the scene easily. Suppose you are pointing out the necessity of life preservers on sailboats by telling the story of how you spent a stormy night in the lake, clinging to a capsized boat. To convince your readers, let them "feel" the stinging rain and the icy current trying to drag you under; let them "see" the black waves and the dark menacing sky; let them "hear" the howling wind and the gradual splitting apart of the boat. Effective narration often depends on effective description, and effective description depends on vivid, specific detail. (For more help on writing description, see Chapter 11; review Chapter 7 for advice on word choice.)

Create authentic characters. Again, the use of detail is crucial. Your readers should be able to visualize the people (or animals) in your narrative clearly; if your important characters are drawn too thinly or if they seem phony or stereotyped, your readers will not fully grasp the meaning of your story. Show your readers the major characters as you see them by commenting unobtrusively on their appearances, speech, and actions. In addition, a successful narrative may depend on the reader's understanding of people's motives—why they act the way they do in certain situations. A narrative about your hometown's grouchiest miser who suddenly donated a large sum of money to a poor family isn't very believable unless we know the motive behind the action. In other words, let your readers know what is happening to whom by explaining or showing why.

Use dialogue realistically. Writers often use dialogue, their characters' spoken words, to reveal action or personality traits of the speakers. By presenting conversations, writers show rather than tell, often creating emphasis or a more dramatic effect. Dialogue may also help readers identify with or feel closer to the characters or action by creating a sense of "you-are-there." If your narrative would profit from dialogue, be certain the word choice and the manner of speaking are in keeping with each character's education, background, age, location, and so forth. Don't, for example, put a sophisticated philosophical treatise into the mouth of a ten-year-old boy or the latest campus slang into the speech of a fifty-year-old auto mechanic from Two Egg, Florida. Also, make sure that your dialogue doesn't sound "wooden" or phony. The right dialogue can help make your story more realistic and interesting, provided that the conversations are essential to the narrative and are not merely padding the plot. (To see dialogue in narratives, read Maya Angelou's "Sister Flowers," pages 333–337, or Julia Alvarez's "Snow" on page 440. For help in punctuating dialogue, see pages 510–511 in Part Four.)

Problems to Avoid

Weak, boring narratives are often the result of problems with subject matter or poor pacing; therefore, you should keep in mind the following advice:

Choose your subject carefully. Most of the best narrative essays come from personal experience or study, and the reason is fairly obvious: it's difficult to write convincingly about something you've never seen or done or read about. You probably couldn't, for instance, write a realistic account of a bullfight unless you'd seen one or at least had studied the subject in great detail. The simplest, easiest, most interesting nonfiction narrative you can write is likely to be about an event with which you are personally familiar. This doesn't mean that you can't improvise many details or create a hypothetical story to illustrate a point. Even so, you will probably still have more success basing your narrative—real or hypothetical—on something or someone you know well.

Limit your scope. When you wish to use an extended narrative to illustrate a thesis, don't select an event or series of actions whose retelling will be too long or complex for your assignment. In general, it's better to select one episode and flesh it out with many specific details so that your readers may clearly see your point. For instance, you may have had many rewarding experiences during the summer you worked as a lifeguard, but you can't tell them all. Instead, you might focus on one experience that captures the essence of your attitude toward your job—say, the time you saved a child from drowning—and present the story so vividly that the readers can easily understand your point of view.

Don't let your story lag or wander. At some time you've probably listened to a story-teller who became stuck on some insignificant detail ("Was it Friday or Saturday the letter came? Let's see now . . ."; "Then Joe said to me—no, it was Sally—no, wait, it was . . ."). And you've probably also heard bores who insist on making a short story long by including too many unimportant details or digressions. These mistakes ruin the *pacing* of their stories; in other words, the story's tempo or movement becomes bogged down until the readers are bored witless. To avoid creating a sleeping tonic in word form, dismiss all unessential information and focus your attention—and use of detail—on the important events, people, and places. Skip uneventful periods of time by using such phrases as "A week went by before Mr. Smith called . . ." or "Later that evening, around nine o'clock. . . . " In short, keep the story moving quickly enough to hold the readers' interest. Moreover, use a variety of transitional devices to move the readers from one action to another; don't rely continuously on the "and then . . . and then . . ." method.

■ PRACTICING WHAT YOU'VE LEARNED

To practice collecting details that will strengthen your narrative, try this activity. First, study the painting below, *Tornado Over Kansas* by John Steuart Curry, and then list as many specific, descriptive details about the scene as you can see or imagine. For example, what do details about the setting and the

Tornado Over Kansas, 1929, by John Steuart Curry

Hackney Picture Fund Purchase, Muskegon Museum of Art, Muskegon, Michigan family's appearance reveal about these people and where they live? What unusual noises, colors, and smells might be present and how might they be vividly described? What does each person's facial expression and body language tell you about his or her thoughts at this very moment? What words might be spoken by each person and in what tone of voice? What role do the animals play in this scene?

Now think of a time in which you experienced a narrow escape or conquered a fearful moment, some event in your life that might be retold in an exciting narrative essay. Using the impressions recorded from the painting as a guide to prompt your memory, compile a similar list of vivid, sensory details describing the people, setting, dialogue, and action at the most dramatic point of your story.

■ ESSAY TOPICS

Use one of the following topics to suggest an essay that is developed by narration. Remember that each essay must have a clear purpose. For additional ideas, see the "Suggestions for Writing" section following the professional essay (page 338).

1. An act of courage or devotion
2. An event of historical, medical, or scientific importance
3. An interaction that changed your thinking on a particular subject
4. Your best holiday; special occasion; first or last day (school, job, camp, etc.)
5. A family story passed down through the generations
6. Your worst accident or brush with danger
7. An unforgettable childhood experience
8. A memorable event governed by nature
9. A time you gained self-confidence or changed your self-image
10. A meaningful event experienced in another culture or country
11. The day everything went wrong (or right)
12. An event that led to an important decision
13. Your experience with prejudice or with an act of charity or friendship
14. Giving in to or resisting peer pressure
15. A gain or loss of something or someone important
16. A risk that paid off (or a triumph against the odds)
17. A nonacademic lesson learned at school or on a job
18. An episode marking your passage from one stage of your life to another
19. A bad habit that got you into (or out of) trouble

20. Your day on September 11, 2001, showing how some specific aspect of the events informed or changed your thinking

The destruction of the World Trade Center Towers, September 11, 2001

A Topic Proposal for Your Essay

Selecting the right subject matter is important to every writer. To help you clarify your ideas and strengthen your commitment to your topic, here is a proposal sheet that asks you to describe some of your preliminary ideas about your subject before you begin drafting. Although your ideas may change as you write (they will almost certainly become more refined), thinking through your choice of topic now may help you avoid several false starts.

1. In a sentence or two, briefly state the subject of your narrative. Did you or someone you know participate in this story?

2. Why did you select this narrative? Does it have importance for you personally, academically, or professionally? In some other way? Explain your reason, or purpose, for telling this story.

3. Will others be informed or entertained by this story? Who might be especially interested in hearing your narrative? Why?

4. What is the primary effect you would like your narrative to have on your readers? What would you like them to feel or think about after they read your story? Why?

5. What is the critical moment in your story? At what point, in other words, does the action reach its peak? Summarize this moment in a few descriptive words.

6. What difficulties, if any, might this narrative present as you are drafting? For example, if the story you want to tell is long or complex, how might you focus on the main action and pace it appropriately?

■ Sample Student Essay

In this narrative a student uses a story about a sick but fierce dog to show how she learned a valuable lesson in her job as a veterinarian's assistant. Notice the student's good use of vivid details that make this well-paced story both clear and interesting.

NEVER UNDERESTIMATE THE LITTLE THINGS

1   When I went to work as a veterinarian's assistant for Dr. Sam Holt and Dr. Jack Gunn last summer, I was under the false impression that the hardest part of veterinary surgery would be the actual performance of an operation. The small chores demanded before this feat didn't occur to me as being of any importance. As it happened, I had been in the veterinary clinic only a total of four hours before I met a little animal who convinced me that the operation itself was probably the easiest part of treatment. This animal, to whom I owe thanks for so enlightening me, was a chocolate-colored chihuahua of tiny size and immense perversity named Smokey.

Introduction: A misconception

Thesis: Small preliminary details can be as important as the major action

2   Smokey could have very easily passed for some creature from another planet. It wasn't so much his gaunt little frame and overly large head, or his bony paws with nearly saberlike claws, as it was his grossly infected eyes. Those once-shining eyes were now distorted and swollen into grotesque balls of septic, sightless flesh. The only vague similarity they had to what we'd normally think of as the organs of vision was a slightly upraised dot, all that was left of the pupil, in the center of a pink and purply marble. As if that were not enough, Smokey had a temper to match his ugly sight. He also had surprisingly good aim, considering his largely diminished vision, toward any moving object that happened to place itself unwisely before his ever-inquisitive nose; with sudden and wholly vicious intent, he would snap and snarl at whatever blocked the little light that could filter through his swollen and ruptured blood vessels. Truly, in many respects, Smokey was a fearful dog to behold.

Description of the main character: His appearance

His personality

3   Such an appearance and personality did nothing to encourage my already flagging confidence in my capabilities as a vet's assistant. How was I supposed to get that little demon out of his cage? Jack had casually requested that I bring Smokey to the surgery room, but did he really expect me to put my hands into the cage of that devil dog? I suppose it must have been my anxious expression that saved me, for as I turned uncertainly toward the kennel, Jack chuckled nonchalantly and accompanied me to demonstrate how professionals in his line of work dealt with professionals in Smokey's. He took a small rope about four feet long with a no-choke noose at one end and unlatched Smokey's cage. Then cautiously he reached in and dangled the noose before the dog's snarling jaws. Since Smokey could only barely see what he was biting at, his attacks were directed haphazardly in a semicircle around his body. The tiny area of his cage led to his capture, for during one of Smokey's forward lunges, Jack dropped the noose over his head and moved the struggling creature out onto the floor. The fight had only just begun for Smokey, however, and he braced his feet against the slippery linoleum tiling and forced us to drag him, like a little pull toy on a string, to the surgery.

The difficulty of moving the dog to the surgery room

4   Once Smokey was in the surgery, however, the question that hung before our eyes like a veritable presence was how to get the dog from the floor to the table. Simply picking him up and plopping him down was out of the question. One glance at the quivering little figure emitting ominous and throaty warnings was enough to assure us of that. Realizing that the game was over, Jack grimly handed me the rope and reached for a muzzle. It was a doomed attempt from the start: the closer Jack dangled the tiny leather cup to the dog's nose, the more violent did Smokey's contortions and rage-filled cries become and the more frantic our efforts became to try to keep our feet and fingers clear of the angry jaws. Deciding that a firmer method had to be used, Jack instructed me to raise the rope up high enough so that Smokey would have to stand on his hind legs. This

The difficulty of moving the dog to the table

greatly reduced his maneuverability but served to increase his tenacity, for at this the little dog nearly went into paroxysms of frustration and rage. In his struggles, however, Smokey caught his forepaw on his swollen eye, and the blood that had been building up pressure behind the fragile cornea burst out and dripped to the floor. In the midst of our surprise and the twinge of panic startling the three of us, Jack saw his chance and swiftly muzzled the animal and lifted him to the operating table.

5   Even at that point it wasn't easy to put the now terrified dog to sleep. He fought the local anesthesia and caused Jack to curse as he was forced to give Smokey more of the drug than should have been necessary for such a small beast. After what seemed an eternity, Smokey lay prone on the table, breathing deeply and emitting soft snores and gentle whines. We also breathed deeply in relief, and I relaxed to watch fascinated, while Jack performed a very delicate operation quite smoothly and without mishap.

The difficulty of putting the dog to sleep before the surgery

6   Such was my harrowing induction into the life of a veterinary surgeon. But Smokey did teach me a valuable lesson that has proven its importance to me many times since: wherever animals are concerned, even the smallest detail is important and should never be taken for granted.

Conclusion: The lesson she learned

Professional Essay*

■ Sister Flowers

Maya Angelou

Maya Angelou is an American author, actress, civil-rights activist, poet, and professor. Recipient of many honorary degrees and awards, she was given the Presidential Medal of Arts in 2000. Angelou has written multiple volumes of poetry and a series of popular autobiographical works. This essay is a chapter from her first memoir, *I Know Why the Caged Bird Sings* (1969). Recent works include *A Song Flung Up to Heaven* (2002) and a children's book, *My Painted House, My Friendly Chicken, and Me* (2003).

---

* To help you read this essay analytically, review pages 166–168.

1 For nearly a year, I sopped around the house, the Store, the school and the church, like an old biscuit, dirty and inedible. Then I met, or rather got to know, the lady who threw me my first life line.

2 Mrs. Bertha Flowers was the aristocrat of Black Stamps. She had the grace of control to appear warm in the coldest weather, and on the Arkansas summer days it seemed she had a private breeze which swirled around, cooling her. She was thin without the taut look of wiry people, and her printed voile dresses and flowered hats were as right for her as denim overalls for a farmer. She was our side's answer to the richest white woman in town.

3 Her skin was a rich black that would have peeled like a plum if snagged, but then no one would have thought of getting close enough to Mrs. Flowers to ruffle her dress, let alone snag her skin. She didn't encourage familiarity. She wore gloves too.

4 I don't think I ever saw Mrs. Flowers laugh, but she smiled often. A slow widening of her thin black lips to show even, small white teeth, then the slow effortless closing. When she chose to smile on me, I always wanted to thank her. The action was so graceful and inclusively benign.

5 She was one of the few gentlewomen I have ever known, and has remained throughout my life the measure of what a human being can be.

6 Momma* had a strange relationship with her. Most often when she passed on the road in front of the Store, she spoke to Momma in that soft yet carrying voice, "Good day, Mrs. Henderson." Momma responded with "How you, Sister Flowers?"

7 Mrs. Flowers didn't belong to our church, nor was she Momma's familiar. Why on earth did she insist on calling her Sister Flowers? Shame made me want to hide my face. Mrs. Flowers deserved better than to be called Sister. Then, Momma left out the verb. Why not ask, "How *are* you, *Mrs.* Flowers?" With the unbalanced passion of the young, I hated her for showing her ignorance to Mrs. Flowers. It didn't occur to me for many years that they were as alike as sisters, separated only by formal education.

8 Although I was upset, neither of the women was in the least shaken by what I thought an unceremonious greeting. Mrs. Flowers would continue her easy gait up the hill to her little bungalow, and Momma kept on shelling peas or doing whatever had brought her to the front porch.

9 Occasionally, though, Mrs. Flowers would drift off the road and down to the Store and Momma would say to me, "Sister, you go on and play." As she left I would hear the beginning of an intimate conversation. Momma persistently using the wrong verb, or none at all.

10 "Brother and Sister Wilcox is sho'ly the meanest—" "Is," Momma? "Is"? Oh, please, not "is," Momma, for two or more. But they talked, and from the side of the building where I waited for the ground to open up and swallow me, I heard the soft-voiced Mrs. Flowers and the textured voice of my grandmother merging and melting. They were interrupted from time to time by giggles that must have come from Mrs. Flowers (Momma never giggled in her life). Then she was gone.

11 She appealed to me because she was like people I had never met personally. Like women in English novels who walked the moors (whatever they were) with their loyal dogs racing at a respectful distance. Like the women who sat in front of roaring fireplaces, drinking tea incessantly from silver trays full of scones and crumpets. Women

---

* "Momma" was the grandmother who raised Angelou and her brother in Stamps, Arkansas; she was the respected owner of a general store.

who walked over the "heath" and read morocco-bound books and had two last names divided by a hyphen. It would be safe to say that she made me proud to be Negro, just by being herself.

12   She acted just as refined as whitefolks in the movies and books and she was more beautiful, for none of them could have come near that warm color without looking gray by comparison.

13   I was fortunate that I never saw her in the company of po-whitefolks. For since they tend to think of their whiteness as an evenizer, I'm certain that I would have had to hear her spoken to commonly as Bertha, and my image of her would have been shattered like the unmendable Humpty-Dumpty.

14   One summer afternoon, sweet-milk fresh in my memory, she stopped at the Store to buy provisions. Another Negro woman of her health and age would have been expected to carry the paper sacks home in one hand, but Momma said, "Sister Flowers, I'll send Bailey* up to your house with these things."

15   She smiled that slow dragging smile, "Thank you, Mrs. Henderson. I'd prefer Marguerite, though." My name was beautiful when she said it. "I've been meaning to talk to her, anyway." They gave each other age-group looks.

16   Momma said, "Well, that's all right then. Sister, go and change your dress. You going to Sister Flowers'."

17   The chifforobe was a maze. What on earth did one put on to go to Mrs. Flowers' house? I knew I shouldn't put on a Sunday dress. It might be sacrilegious. Certainly not a house dress, since I was already wearing a fresh one. I chose a school dress, naturally. It was formal without suggesting that going to Mrs. Flowers' house was equivalent to attending church.

18   I trusted myself back into the Store.

19   "Now, don't you look nice." I had chosen the right thing, for once. . . .

20   There was a little path beside the rocky road, and Mrs. Flowers walked in front swinging her arms and picking her way over the stones.

21   She said, without turning her head, to me, "I hear you're doing very good school work, Marguerite, but that it's all written. The teachers report that they have trouble getting you to talk in class." We passed the triangular farm on our left and the path widened to allow us to walk together. I hung back in the separate unasked and unanswerable questions.

22   "Come and walk along with me, Marguerite." I couldn't have refused even if I wanted to. She pronounced my name so nicely. Or more correctly, she spoke each word with such clarity that I was certain a foreigner who didn't understand English could have understood her.

23   "Now no one is going to make you talk—possibly no one can. But bear in mind, language is man's way of communicating with his fellow man and it is language alone which separates him from the lower animals." That was a totally new idea to me, and I would need time to think about it.

24   "Your grandmother says you read a lot. Every chance you get. That's good, but not good enough. Words mean more than what is set down on paper. It takes the human voice to infuse them with the shades of deeper meaning."

25   I memorized the part about the human voice infusing words. It seemed so valid and poetic.

* Angelou's brother

26   She said she was going to give me some books and that I not only must read them, I must read them aloud. She suggested that I try to make a sentence sound in as many different ways as possible.

27   "I'll accept no excuse if you return a book to me that has been badly handled." My imagination boggled at the punishment I would deserve if in fact I did abuse a book of Mrs. Flowers'. Death would be too kind and brief.

28   The odors in the house surprised me. Somehow I had never connected Mrs. Flowers with food or eating or any other common experience of common people. There must have been an outhouse, too, but my mind never recorded it.

29   The sweet scent of vanilla had met us as she opened the door.

30   "I made tea cookies this morning. You see, I had planned to invite you for cookies and lemonade so we could have this little chat. The lemonade is in the icebox."

31   It followed that Mrs. Flowers would have ice on an ordinary day, when most families in our town bought ice late on Saturdays only a few times during the summer to be used in the wooden ice-cream freezers.

32   She took the bags from me and disappeared through the kitchen door. I looked around the room that I had never in my wildest fantasies imagined I would see. Browned photographs leered or threatened from the walls and the white, freshly done curtains pushed against themselves and against the wind. I wanted to gobble up the room entire and take it to Bailey, who would help me analyze and enjoy it.

33   "Have a seat, Marguerite. Over there by the table." She carried a platter covered with a tea towel. Although she warned that she hadn't tried her hand at baking sweets for some time, I was certain that like everything else about her the cookies would be perfect.

34   They were flat round wafers, slightly browned on the edges and butter-yellow in the center. With the cold lemonade they were sufficient for childhood's lifelong diet. Remembering my manners, I took nice little lady-like bites off the edges. She said she had made them expressly for me and that she had a few in the kitchen that I could take home to my brother. So I jammed one whole cake in my mouth and the rough crumbs scratched the insides of my jaws, and if I hadn't had to swallow, it would have been a dream come true.

35   As I ate she began the first of what we later called "my lessons in living." She said that I must always be intolerant of ignorance but understanding of illiteracy. That some people, unable to go to school, were more educated and even more intelligent than college professors. She encouraged me to listen carefully to what country people called mother wit. That in those homely sayings was couched the collective wisdom of generations.

36   When I finished the cookies she brushed off the table and brought a thick, small book from the bookcase. I had read *A Tale of Two Cities* and found it up to my standards as a romantic novel. She opened the first page and I heard poetry for the first time in my life.

37   "It was the best of times and the worst of times. . . ." Her voice slid in and curved down through and over the words. She was nearly singing. I wanted to look at the pages. Were they the same that I had read? Or were there notes, music, lined on the pages, as in a hymn book? Her sounds began cascading gently. I knew from listening to a thousand preachers that she was nearing the end of her reading, and I hadn't really heard, heard to understand, a single word.

38   "How do you like that?"

39   It occurred to me that she expected a response. The sweet vanilla flavor was still on my tongue and her reading was a wonder in my ears. I had to speak.

40   I said, "Yes, ma'am." It was the least I could do, but it was the most also.

41   "There's one more thing. Take this book of poems and memorize one for me. Next time you pay me a visit, I want you to recite."

42   I have tried often to search behind the sophistication of years for the enchantment I so easily found in those gifts. The essence escapes but its aura remains. To be allowed, no, invited, into the private lives of strangers, and to share their joys and fears, was a chance to exchange the Southern bitter wormwood for a cup of mead with Beowulf or a hot cup of tea and milk with Oliver Twist. When I said aloud, "It is a far, far better thing that I do, than I have ever done . . ." tears of love filled my eyes at my selflessness.

43   On that first day, I ran down the hill and into the road (few cars ever came along it) and had the good sense to stop running before I reached the Store.

44   I was liked, and what a difference it made. I was respected not as Mrs. Henderson's grandchild or Bailey's sister but for just being Marguerite Johnson.

45   Childhood's logic never asks to be proved (all conclusions are absolute). I didn't question why Mrs. Flowers had singled me out for attention, nor did it occur to me that Momma might have asked her to give me a little talking to. All I cared about was that she had made tea cookies for *me* and read to *me* from her favorite book. It was enough to prove that she liked me.

Questions on Content, Structure, and Style

1. What is Angelou's main purpose in this narrative? What does she want to show about Sister Flowers' effect on her?

2. How does Angelou use sensory details and imagery in paragraphs 2–4 to introduce Mrs. Flowers' character?

3. Why does Angelou emphasize the embarrassment she felt when Momma talked to Mrs. Flowers? What do these conversations reveal about Angelou's attitude toward her grandmother at this time?

4. As an adult, what does Angelou suspect about her grandmother's relationship to Mrs. Flowers that she didn't see as a child?

5. Why was Angelou impressed by Mrs. Flowers? To what kinds of women is she compared? Why is Angelou glad she had never seen Mrs. Flowers spoken to by white people?

6. What sort of young girl was Angelou before she became friends with Mrs. Flowers? Cite some evidence from the essay that supports your view of her character.

7. How does the description of Mrs. Flowers' house and possessions help communicate Angelou's childhood reverence for this woman? Why were the cookies and lemonade so important?

8. Why does Angelou choose to use dialogue in paragraphs 37–41 instead of just describing the scene?

9. Does Angelou use enough vivid details to make her narrative seem believable and her characters realistic? Cite two or three examples of descriptive language that you think are particularly effective.

10. Why does Angelou include paragraphs 42, 44, and 45 at the end of her essay? Would the extent of Mrs. Flowers' impact on the author be as clearly understood without them?

Suggestions for Writing

Try using Maya Angelou's "Sister Flowers" as a stepping-stone to your writing. Think of an adult who helped, guided, or "rescued" you when you were a child or young teen. How did this person make a difference in your life? This person might be a relative, a teacher, a neighbor, a coach, a friend's parent. Tell a story that captures an important moment in your relationship with this person: your first meeting, a crucial event, or an incident that crystallized your awareness of this person's influence on you. Or perhaps you have played an important role in the life of a child or older person. In either case, what insight about the value of intergenerational relationships might your narrative offer?

Vocabulary

voile (2)	chifforobe (17)	homely (35)
benign (4)	infuse (24)	aura (42)
gait (8)	boggled (27)	wormwood (42)
morocco-bound (11)	leered (32)	mead (42)

■ A REVISION WORKSHEET

As you write your rough drafts, consult Chapter 5 for guidance through the revision process. In addition, here are a few questions to ask yourself as you revise your narrative:

1. Is the narrative essay's purpose clear to the reader?

2. Is the thesis plainly stated or at least clearly implied?

3. Does the narrative convincingly support or illustrate its intended point? If not, how might the story be changed?

4. Does the story maintain a logical point of view and an understandable order of action? Are there enough transitional devices used to give the story a smooth flow?

5. Are the characters, actions, and settings presented in enough vivid detail to make them clear and believable? Where could more detail be effectively added? Would use of dialogue be appropriate?

6. Is the story coherent and well paced or does it wander or bog down in places because of irrelevant or repetitious details? What might be condensed or cut? Could bland or wordy description be replaced?

7. Does the essay end in a satisfying way or does the action stop too abruptly?

After you've revised your essay extensively, you might exchange rough drafts with a classmate and answer these questions for each other, making specific suggestions for improvement wherever appropriate. (For advice on productive participation in classroom workshops, see pages 106–109.)

Reviewing Your Progress

After you have completed your narrative essay, take a moment to measure your progress as a writer by responding to the following questions. Such analysis will help you recognize growth in your writing skills and may enable you to identify areas that are still problematic.

1. What do you like best about your narrative essay? Why?

2. After reading through your essay, select the description, detail, or piece of dialogue that you think best characterizes a major figure or most effectively advances the action in your story. Explain the reason for your choice in one or two sentences.

3. What part of your essay gave you the most trouble? How did you overcome the problem?

4. If you had more time to work on this essay, what would receive additional attention? Why?

5. What did you learn about your topic from writing this essay? About yourself as a writer?

Chapter 13

Writing Essays Using Multiple Strategies

In Part Two of this text, you have been studying essays developed primarily by a single mode or expository strategy. You may have, for example, written essays primarily developed by multiple examples, process analysis, or comparison/contrast. Concentrating on a single strategy in your essays has allowed you to practice, in a focused way, each of the patterns of development most often used in writing tasks. Although practicing each strategy in isolation this way is somewhat artificial, it is the easiest, simplest way to master the common organizational patterns. Consider the parallels to learning almost any skill: before you attempt a complex dive with spins and flips, you first practice each maneuver separately. Having understood and mastered the individual strategies of development, you should feel confident about facing any writing situation, including those that would most profit from incorporating multiple strategies to accomplish their goal.

Most essays *do* call upon multiple strategies of development to achieve their purpose, a reality you have probably discovered for yourself as you wrote and studied various essays in this text. In fact, you may have found it difficult—or impossible—to avoid combining modes and strategies in your own essays. As noted in the introduction to Part Two, writers virtually always blend strategies, using examples in their comparisons, description in their definitions, causal analysis in their arguments, and so on. Therein is the heart of the matter: the single patterns of development you have been practicing are *thinking* strategies—ways of considering a subject and generating ideas—as well as organizing tools. In most writing situations, writers study their tasks and choose the strategies that will *most effectively* accomplish their purpose.

In addition, some writing tasks, often the longer ones, will clearly profit from combining multiple strategies in distinct ways to thoroughly address the essay's subject, purpose, and audience. Suppose, for example, you are given a problem-solving assignment in a business class: selling the City Council on a plan to build a low-income housing project in a particular neighborhood. You might call upon your writing resources and use multiple strategies to

- Describe the project
- Explain the causes (the need for such a project)
- Argue its strengths; deflect opposing arguments
- Contrast it to other housing options
- Cite similar successful examples in other towns
- Explain its long-term beneficial effects on tenants, neighbors, businesses, etc.

Or perhaps you are investigating recent disciplinary action taken against Colorado high school seniors for decorating their graduation gowns. Your essay might combine strategies by first presenting examples of the controversy, explaining its causes and effects, and then contrasting the opinions of administrators, students, and parents. You might even conclude with a suggested process for avoiding future problems. In other words, many essay assignments—including the widely assigned summary-response paper*—might call for a multistrategy response.

As a writer who now knows how to use a variety of thinking and organizational methods, you can assess any writing situation and select the strategy—or strategies—that will work best for your topic, purpose, and audience.

Choosing the Best Strategies

To help you choose the best means of development for your essay, here is a brief review of the modes and strategies accompanied by some pertinent questions:

1. Example: Would real or hypothetical illustrations make my subject more easily understood?
2. Process: Would a step-by-step procedural analysis clarify my subject?
3. Comparison/Contrast: Would aligning or juxtaposing my subject to something else be helpful?
4. Definition: Would my subject profit from an extended explanation of its meaning?
5. Division/Classification: Would separating my subject into its component parts or grouping its parts into categories be useful?
6. Causal Analysis: Would explaining causes or effects add important information?
7. Argument: Would my position be advanced by offering logical reasons and/or addressing objections?

---

* For an in-depth look at this popular assignment, see pages 436–441.

8. Description: Would vivid details, sensory images, or figurative language help readers visualize my subject?

9. Narrative: Would a story best illustrate some idea or aspect of my subject?

Try using these questions as prompts to help you generate ideas and select those strategies that best accomplish your purpose.

Problems to Avoid

Avoid overkill. Being prepared to use any of the writing strategies is akin to carrying many tools in your carpenter's bag. But just because you own many tools doesn't mean you must use all of them in one project—rather, you select only the ones you need for the specific job at hand. If you do decide to use multiple strategies in a particular essay, avoid a hodgepodge of information that runs in too many directions. Sometimes your essay's prescribed length means you cannot present all you know; again, let your main purpose guide you to including the best or most important ideas.

Organize logically. If you decide that multiple strategies will work best, you must find an appropriate order and coherent flow for your essay. In the hypothetical problem-solving essay on the housing project mentioned earlier, for instance, the writer must decide whether the long-term effects of the project should be discussed earlier or later in the paper. In the student essay that follows, the writer struggled with the question of putting kinds of vegetarians before or after discussion of reasons for adopting vegetarianism. There are no easy answers to such questions—each writer must experiment with outlines and rough drafts to find the most successful arrangement, one that will offer the most effective response to the particular material, the essay's purpose, and the audience's needs. Be patient as you try various ways of combining strategies into a coherent rather than choppy paper.

■ Sample Student Essay

In the essay that follows, the student writer responds to an assignment that asked her to write about an important belief or distinguishing aspect of her life. The purpose, audience, and development of her essay were left to her; the length was designated at 750 to 1,000 words. As a confirmed vegetarian for well over a decade, she often found herself questioned about her beliefs. After deciding to clarify (and encourage) vegetarianism for an audience of interested but often puzzled fellow students, she developed her essay by drawing on many strategies, including causal analysis, example, classification, contrast, argument, and process analysis. Because she found her early draft too long, the writer edited out an extended narrative telling the story of her own "conversion" to vegetarianism, viewing that section as less central to her essay's main purpose than the other parts.

PASS THE BROCCOLI—PLEASE!

Introduction:
Famous examples

1   What do Benjamin Franklin, Charles Darwin, Leonardo da Vinci, Percy Bysshe Shelley, Mohandas Gandhi, Albert Einstein, and I have in common? In addition to being great thinkers, of course, we are all vegetarians, people who have rejected the practice of eating animals. Vegetarianism is growing rapidly in America today,

Thesis, purpose,
audience

but some people continue to see it as a strange choice. If you are thinking of making this decision yourself or are merely curious, taking time to learn about vegetarianism is worthwhile.

Contrast to
other parts
of the world

2   In a land where hamburgers, pepperoni pizza, and fried chicken are among our favorite foods, just why do Americans become vegetarians anyway? Worldwide, vegetarianism is often part of religious faith, especially to Buddhists, Hindus, and others whose spiritual beliefs emphasize nonviolence, karma, and reincarnation. But in this country the reasons for becoming

Causal analysis:
3 reasons

vegetarian are more diverse. Some people cite ecological reasons, arguing that vegetarianism is best for our planet because it takes less land and food to raise vegetables and grain than livestock. Others choose vegetarianism because of health reasons. Repeated studies by groups such as the American Heart Association and the American Medical Association show that diets lower in animal fats and higher in fiber decrease the risk of heart disease, cancer, diabetes, hypertension, and osteoporosis.

3   Still other people's ethical beliefs bring them to vegetarianism. These people object to the ways that some animals, such as cows and chickens, are confined and are often fed various chemicals, such as growth hormones, antibiotics, and tranquilizers. They object to the procedures of slaughterhouses. They object to killing animals for consumption or for their decorative body parts (hides, fur, skins, tusks, feathers, etc.) and to their use in science or

cosmetic experiments. These vegetarians believe that animals feel fear and pain and that it is morally wrong for one species to inflict unnecessary suffering on another. I count myself among this group; consequently, my vegetarian choices extend to wearing no leather or fur and I do not use household or cosmetic products tested on animals.

Personal example

4   Regardless of reasons for our choice, all vegetarians reject eating meat. However, there are actually several kinds of vegetarians, with the majority falling into three categories:

1. Ovo-lacto vegetarians eat milk, cheese, eggs, and honey;
2. Lacto vegetarians do not eat eggs but may keep other dairy products in their diet;
3. Vegans do not eat dairy products or any animal by-products whatsoever.

Classification: Three types

Many people, including myself, begin as ovo-lacto vegetarians but eventually become vegans, considered the most complete or pure type.

5   Perhaps the most common objection to any type of vegetarianism comes from a misconception about deficiencies in the diet, particularly protein. But it is a mistake to think only meat offers us protein. Vegetarians who eat dairy products, grains, vegetables, beans, and nuts receive more than enough nutrients, including protein. In fact, according to the cookbook The Higher Taste, cheese, peanuts, and lentils contain more protein per ounce than hamburger, pork, or a porterhouse steak. Many medical experts think that Americans actually eat too much protein, as seen in the revised food pyramid that now calls for an increase in vegetables, fruits, and grains over meat and dairy products. A vegetarian diet will not make someone a limp weakling. Kevin Eubanks, Tonight Show band leader, is, for

Argument: Refutation, evidence, examples

example, not only a busy musician but also a weightlifter. Some members of the Denver Broncos football team, according to their manager, no longer eat red meat at their training table.

6   For those who would like to give vegetarianism a try, here are a few suggestions for getting started:

Process:
4 steps to begin

1. Explore your motives. If you are only becoming a vegetarian to please a friend, for example, you won't stick with it. Be honest with yourself: the reasons behind your choice have a lot to do with your commitment.

2. Read more. The library can provide you with answers to your questions and concerns. There are hundreds of books full of ecological, medical, and ethical arguments for vegetarianism.

(More argument
and examples)

3. Eat! Another popular misconception is that vegetarianism means a life of eating tasteless grass; nothing could be less true. Visit a vegetarian restaurant several times to see how many delicious dishes are available. Even grocery stores now carry a variety of vegetarian entrees. Or try one of the many vegetarian cookbooks on the market today. You may be surprised to discover that tofu enchiladas, soy burgers, and stuffed eggplant taste better than you could ever imagine.

4. Start slowly. You don't have to become a vegan overnight if it doesn't feel right. Some people begin by excluding just red meat from their diets. Feeling good as time goes by can direct your choices. Books, such as <u>The Beginning Vegetarian</u>, and magazines, such as <u>Vegetarian Times</u>, can offer encouragement.

7   It's never too late to change your lifestyle. Nobel Prize–winning author Isaac Bashevis Singer became a vegetarian at age 58.

Making this choice now may allow you to live longer and feel better. In fifty years you may be like playwright George Bernard Shaw, who at 25 was warned against a vegetarian diet. As a vigorous old man, Shaw wanted to tell all those people they were wrong, but noted he couldn't: "They all passed away years ago"!

Conclusion: Additional famous examples, witty quotation

Professional Essay*

■ Don't Let Stereotypes Warp Your Judgments

Robert L. Heilbroner

Robert L. Heilbroner is a Professor of Economics, Emeritus, at the New School for Social Research in New York City. He is well known for his essays in *The New Yorker* and for over twenty books, including *The Worldly Philosophers* (1953), whose revised editions are still widely used in economics classes. Other books include *The Crisis of Vision in Modern Economic Thought* (1996) and *Economics Explained* (1998). This essay, published in *Reader's Digest*, uses multiple strategies to expose a social problem, explain its causes and effects, and offer some practical suggestions for change.

1   Is a girl called Gloria apt to be better-looking than one called Bertha? Are criminals more likely to be dark than blond? Can you tell a good deal about someone's personality from hearing his voice briefly over the phone? Can a person's nationality be pretty accurately guessed from his photograph? Does the fact that someone wears glasses imply that he is intelligent?

Can you find Cuthbert?

* For help reading this essay analytically, review pages 166–168.

2   The answer to all these questions is obviously, "No."

3   Yet, from all the evidence at hand, most of us believe these things. Ask any college boy if he'd rather take his chances with a Gloria or a Bertha, or ask a college girl if she'd rather blind-date a Richard or a Cuthbert. In fact, you don't have to ask: college students in questionnaires have revealed that names conjure up the same images in their minds as they do in yours—and for as little reason.

4   Look into the favorite suspects of persons who report "suspicious characters" and you will find a large percentage of them to be "swarthy" or "dark and foreign-looking"—despite the testimony of criminologists that criminals do *not* tend to be dark, foreign or "wild-eyed." Delve into the main asset of a telephone stock swindler and you will find it to be a marvelously confidence-inspiring telephone "personality." And whereas we all think we know what an Italian or a Swede looks like, it is the sad fact that when a group of Nebraska students sought to match faces and nationalities of 15 European countries, they were scored wrong in 93 percent of their identifications. Finally, for all the fact that horn-rimmed glasses have now become the standard television sign of an "intellectual," optometrists know that the main thing that distinguishes people with glasses is just bad eyes.

5   Stereotypes are a kind of gossip about the world, a gossip that makes us prejudge people before we ever lay eyes on them. Hence it is not surprising that stereotypes have something to do with the dark world of prejudice. Explore most prejudices (note that the word means prejudgment) and you will find a cruel stereotype at the core of each one.

6   For it is the extraordinary fact that once we have typecast the world, we tend to see people in terms of our standardized pictures. In another demonstration of the power of stereotypes to affect our vision, a number of Columbia and Barnard students were shown 30 photographs of pretty but unidentified girls, and asked to rate each in terms of "general liking," "intelligence," "beauty" and so on. Two months later, the same group were shown the same photographs, this time with fictitious Irish, Italian, Jewish and "American" names attached to the pictures. Right away the ratings changed. Faces which were now seen as representing a national group went down in looks and still farther down in likability, while the "American" girls suddenly looked decidedly prettier and nicer.

7   Why is it that we stereotype the world in such irrational and harmful fashion? In part, we begin to type-cast people in our childhood years. Early in life, as every parent whose child has watched a TV Western knows, we learn to spot the Good Guys from the Bad Guys. Some years ago, a social psychologist showed very clearly how powerful these stereotypes of childhood vision are. He secretly asked the most popular youngsters in an elementary school to make errors in their morning gym exercises. Afterwards, he asked the class if anyone had noticed any mistakes during gym period. Oh, yes, said the children. But it was the *unpopular* members of the class—the "bad guys"—they remembered as being out of step.

8   We not only grow up with standardized pictures forming inside of us, but as grown-ups we are constantly having them thrust upon us. Some of them, like the half-joking, half-serious stereotypes of mothers-in-law, or country yokels, or psychiatrists, are dinned into us by the stock jokes we hear and repeat. In fact, without such stereotypes, there would be a lot fewer jokes. Still other stereotypes are perpetuated by the advertisements we read, the movies we see, the books we read.

9   And finally, we tend to stereotype because it helps us make sense out of a highly confusing world, a world which William James* once described as "one great, blooming, buzzing confusion." It is a curious fact that if we don't *know* what we're looking at, we are often quite literally unable to *see* what we're looking at. People who recover their sight after a lifetime of blindness actually cannot at first tell a triangle from a square. A visitor to a factory sees only noisy chaos where the superintendent sees a perfectly synchronized flow of work. As Walter Lippmann† has said, "For the most part we do not first see, and then define; we define first, and then we see."

10   Stereotypes are one way in which we "define" the world in order to see it. They classify the infinite variety of human beings into a convenient handful of "types" towards whom we learn to act in stereotyped fashion. Life would be a wearing process if we had to start from scratch with each and every human contact. Stereotypes economize on our mental effort by covering up the blooming, buzzing confusion with big recognizable cutouts. They save us the "trouble" of finding out what the world is like—they give it its accustomed look.

11   Thus the trouble is that stereotypes make us mentally lazy. As S. I. Hayakawa, the authority on semantics, has written: "The danger of stereotypes lies not in their existence, but in the fact that they become for all people some of the time, and for some people all the time, *substitutes for observation.*" Worse yet, stereotypes get in the way of our judgment, even when we do observe the world. Someone who has formed rigid preconceptions of all Latins as "excitable," or all teenagers as "wild," doesn't alter his point of view when he meets a calm and deliberate Genoese,** or a serious-minded high school student. He brushes them aside as "exceptions that prove the rule." And, of course, if he meets someone true to type, he stands triumphantly vindicated. "They're all like that," he proclaims, having encountered an excited Latin, an ill-behaved adolescent.

12   Hence, quite aside from the injustice which stereotypes do to others, they impoverish ourselves. A person who lumps the world into simple categories, who type-casts all labor leaders as "racketeers," all businessmen as "reactionaries," all Harvard men as "snobs," and all Frenchmen as "sexy," is in danger of becoming a stereotype himself. He loses his capacity to be himself—which is to say, to see the world in his own absolutely unique, inimitable and independent fashion.

13   Instead, he votes for the man who fits his standardized picture of what a candidate "should" look like or sound like, buys the goods that someone in his "situation" in life "should" own, lives the life that others define for him. The mark of the stereotype person is that he never surprises us, that we do indeed have him "typed." And no one fits this strait-jacket so perfectly as someone whose opinions about *other people* are fixed and inflexible.

14   Impoverishing as they are, stereotypes are not easy to get rid of. The world we type-cast may be no better than a Grade B movie, but at least we know what to expect of our stock characters. When we let them act for themselves in the strangely unpredictable way that people do act, who knows but that many of our fondest convictions will be proved wrong?

---

* William James (1842–1910) was an American philosopher and psychologist.
† Walter Lippmann was a twentieth-century American journalist.
** Genoese refers to a citizen of Genoa, Italy.

15   Nor do we suddenly drop our standardized pictures for a blinding vision of the Truth. Sharp swings of ideas about people often just substitute one stereotype for another. The true process of change is a slow one that adds bits and pieces of reality to the pictures in our heads, until gradually they take on some of the blurriness of life itself. Little by little, we learn not that Jews and Negroes and Catholics and Puerto Ricans are "just like everybody else"—for that, too, is a stereotype—but that each and every one of them is unique, special, different and individual. Often we do not even know that we have let a stereotype lapse until we hear someone saying, "all so-and-so's are like such-and-such," and we hear ourselves saying, "Well—maybe."

16   Can we speed the process along? Of course we can.

17   First, we can become *aware* of the standardized pictures in our heads, in other peoples' heads, in the world around us.

18   Second, we can become suspicious of all judgments that we allow exceptions to "prove." There is no more chastening thought than that in the vast intellectual adventure of science, it takes but one tiny exception to topple a whole edifice of ideas.

19   Third, we can learn to be chary of generalizations about people. As F. Scott Fitzgerald* once wrote: "Begin with an individual, and before you know it you have created a type; begin with a type, and you find you have created—nothing."

20   Most of the time, when we type-cast the world, we are not in fact generalizing about people at all. We are only revealing the embarrassing facts about the pictures that hang in the gallery of stereotypes in our own heads.

Questions on Content, Structure, and Style

1. Why does Heilbroner begin his essay with a series of questions, references to criminal reports, and the Nebraska study? How does this introduction set up Heilbroner's thesis?

2. How does Heilbroner define stereotypes in paragraph 5? What do the studies at Barnard and Columbia University and at the elementary school (paragraph 7) illustrate about prejudice?

3. Why does Heilbroner use "we" and "us" so often in this essay instead of referring to "people who stereotype"? Is his choice a good one?

4. What explanation of causes does Heilbroner offer? How do stereotypes contribute to the ways we try to "define" the world?

5. In addition to the injustice inflicted on others, what negative effects does stereotyping have on those who employ it?

6. Throughout his essay, Heilbroner uses vivid, specific examples, both real and hypothetical. Cite and explain some of his most effective uses of this strategy.

7. Why does Heilbroner include a three-step process near the end of his essay?

8. Why does Heilbroner quote such well-known figures as William James, S. I. Hayakawa, Walter Lippmann, and F. Scott Fitzgerald in various places in his essay? What purposes do their words serve?

---

* F. Scott Fitzgerald (1896–1940) was an American writer, best known for his novel *The Great Gatsby*.

9. Evaluate this essay's conclusion. How does Heilbroner use figurative language to make a memorable last impression on his readers?

10. List the main strategies Heilbroner uses to develop his essay. Which do you find the most effective? If Heilbroner were to extend his essay, what other strategies might he incorporate in his exploration of stereotyping?

Suggestions for Writing

Try using Robert Heilbroner's "Don't Let Stereotypes Warp Your Judgments" as a stepping-stone to an essay of your own. Have you ever been the victim of someone's irrational or harmful standardized picture? Has anyone ever devalued your job or belittled your choice of activities? Or have you yourself been guilty of misjudging someone else? Remember that not all stereotypes are racial or ethnic; typecasting surrounds economic status (the "welfare moocher"), gender (the "dumb blonde"), locations (the redneck Texan), professions (the mousey accountant), and extracurricular activities (the "jock"), to name only a few areas. Write an essay that explores the topic of stereotyping or prejudice; use any of the modes or strategies you find helpful. You might, for example, describe an incident, explain causes or effects, argue for ways to solve the problem, or outline steps you once took to escape "the gallery of stereotypes" in your head.

Vocabulary

swarthy (4)	semantics (11)	chastening (18)
dinned (8)	vindicated (11)	edifice (18)
perpetuated (8)	impoverish (12)	chary (19)
synchronized (9)		

■ A REVISION WORKSHEET

As you write your rough drafts, consult Chapter 5 for guidance through the revision process. In addition, here are a few questions to ask yourself before and during the early stages of your writing:

1. What is my main purpose in writing this particular essay? Who is my audience?

2. Does my assignment or the subject itself suggest a primary method of development or would combining several strategies be more effective?

3. Have I considered my subject from multiple directions, as suggested by the questions on pages 342–343?

4. Have I selected the best strategies to meet the needs of my particular audience?

5. Would blending strategies help my readers understand my topic and my essay's purpose? Or am I trying to include too many approaches, move in too many directions, resulting in an essay that seems too scattered?

6. Have I considered an effective order for the strategies I've chosen? Do the parts of my essay flow together smoothly?

7. Have I avoided common weaknesses such as vague examples, fuzzy directions, circular definitions, overlapping categories, or logical fallacies, as discussed in the "Problems to Avoid" sections of Chapters 9–12?

After you've revised your essay extensively, you might exchange rough drafts with a classmate and answer these questions for each other, making specific suggestions for improvement wherever appropriate. (For advice on productive participation in classroom workshops, see pages 106–109.)

Reviewing Your Progress

After you have completed your essay, take a moment to measure your progress as a writer by responding to the following questions. Such analysis will help you recognize growth in your writing skills and may enable you to identify areas that are still problematic.

1. What do you like best about your essay? Why?

2. After considering the multiple strategies of development used in your essay, which one do you find most effective and why?

3. What part of your essay gave you the most trouble? How did you overcome the problem?

4. If you had more time to work on this essay, what would receive additional attention? Why?

5. What did you learn about your topic from writing this essay? About yourself as a writer?

Part 3

Special Assignments

The third section of this text addresses several kinds of assignments frequently included in many—but not all—composition classes. Chapter 14 will first explain ways to conduct formal research on a topic and then show you how to best incorporate your research into your essay. "Writing in Class: Exams and 'Response' Essays" confronts the anxiety that writing under pressure may bring by helping you respond quickly but effectively to a variety of timed essays and exams. This chapter also addresses one of the most widely used in-class assignments, the summary-response (or reaction) essay. Chapter 16, "Writing about Literature," illustrates several uses of poetry and short stories in the composition classroom and provides some guidelines for both close reading and analytical thinking. Similarly, Chapter 17, "Writing about Film," offers suggestions for essays based upon thoughtful analysis of movies. The last chapter in Part Three, "Writing in the World of Work," presents advice for effective business letters, memos, electronic-mail messages, and résumés.

If you have worked through Parts One and Two of this book, you have already practiced many of the skills demanded by these special assignments. Information in the next five chapters will build on what you already know about good writing. ■

Chapter 14

Writing a Paper Using Research

Although the words *research paper* have been known to produce anxiety worse than that caused by the sound of a dentist's drill, you should try to relax. A research paper is similar to the kinds of expository and argumentative essays described in the earlier parts of this book, the difference being the use of documented source material to support, illustrate, or explain your ideas. Research papers still call for thesis statements, logical sequences of paragraphs, well-developed evidence, smooth conclusions—or in other words, all the skills you've been practicing throughout this book. By citing sources in your essays or reports, you merely show your readers that you have investigated your ideas and found support for them. In addition, using sources affords your readers the opportunity to look into your subject further if they so desire, consulting your references for additional information.

The process described in the next few pages should help you write a paper using research that is carefully and effectively documented. This chapter also contains sample documentation forms for a variety of research sources and a sample student essay using MLA style.

■ Focusing Your Topic

In some cases, you will be assigned your topic, and you will be able to begin your research right away. In other cases, however, you may be encouraged to select your own subject, or you may be given a general subject ("health-care reform," "recycling," "U.S. immigration policies") that you must narrow and then focus into a specific, manageable topic. If the topic is your choice, you need to do some preliminary thinking about what interests you; as in any assignment, you should make the essay a learning experience from which both you and your readers will profit. Therefore, you may want to brainstorm for a while on your general subject before you go to the library, asking yourself questions about what you already know and don't know. Some of the most interesting papers are argumentative essays in which writers set about to find an answer to a controversy or to find support for a solution they suspected might work. Other papers, sometimes called "research reports," expose, explain, or summarize a situation or a problem for their audience.

Throughout this chapter, we will track the research and writing process of Amy Lawrence, a composition student whose writing assignment called for an essay presenting her view of a controversy in her major field of study. As a history major, Amy is particularly interested in the Russian Revolution of 1918, when the Romanov family, the last ruling family of Russia, was assassinated by the Bolsheviks, the Communist revolutionaries led by Lenin. The long-standing controversy surrounding the assassination of Czar Nicholas II and his family focused on the question of whether the two youngest Romanov children, the beautiful Anastasia and the sickly Alexei, escaped execution. A series of forensic and historical discoveries concerning the controversy had made news in the 1990s, so Amy decided to investigate the Romanov assassination for her topic. Because she already had some general knowledge of the controversy, Amy was able to think about her topic in terms of some specific *research questions:* What would research tell her about the possibility of the Romanov children's escape? Would the new forensic evidence support the theory of an escape—or would it put such a claim to rest forever? (Amy's completed essay appears on pages 397–406.)

■ Beginning Your Library Research

Once you have a general topic (and perhaps have some research questions in mind), your next step is familiarizing yourself with the school or public library where you may do all or part of your research. Most college libraries today have both print and electronic resources to offer researchers, as well as access to the Internet. Your library most likely has an online central information system, which may include a catalog of its holdings, a number of selected databases, gateways to other libraries, and other kinds of resources. With appropriate computer connections, this system may be accessed from other places on or off campus, which is handy for those times when you cannot be in the library.

Most libraries also have information (printed or online) that will indicate the location of important areas, and almost all have reference librarians who can explain the various kinds of programs and resources available to you. The smartest step you may take is asking a librarian for help before you begin searching. Library staff members may be able to save you enormous amounts of research time by pointing you in just the right direction. Do not be shy about asking the library staff for help at any point during your research!

Once you are familiar with your library, you may find it useful to consult one or more of the following research tools.

General Reference Works

If you need a general overview of your subject, or perhaps some background or historical information, you might begin your library research by consulting an encyclopedia, a collection of biographical entries, or even a statistical or demographic yearbook. You might use a comprehensive or specialized dictionary if your search turns up terms that are unfamiliar to you. These and many other library reference guides (in print and online) might also help you find a specific focus for your essay if you feel your topic is still too large or undefined at this point.

Online Catalogs

Today the online catalog has replaced the print catalog system as the primary guide to a library's holdings. You can access a library's catalog through on-site computer terminals or, in many cases, connect from off-site locations through the Internet to the library's Web page.

Most computer catalogs allow you to look for information by subject, author, and title as well as by keyword(s), by the ISBN (publisher's book number), by the call number, or by a series title (Time-Life books, for example). On-screen prompts will guide you through the process of searching. Because no two library catalog systems are exactly alike, never hesitate to ask a librarian for help if you need it.

Unless you are already familiar with authorities or their works on your topic, you might begin your search by typing in keywords or your general subject. For example, Amy Lawrence began her research on the Romanov assassination by looking under the subject heading for Nicholas II, the Russian czar. After typing in her subject, she discovered that the library had several books on the czar; one book looked especially promising, so she pulled up the following screen to see more information.

Record 3 of 5

Author	Radzinsky, Edvard.
Title	**The last Czar: the life and death of Nicholas II**
Publisher	New York: Anchor Books: Doubleday, 1992

LOCATION	CALL#	LAST CHECKED IN	STATUS
HRMY Nonfiction	947.083 Radzinsky, E. 1992	02-28-04	Checked In

Edition	1st Anchor Books ed.
Descript	vi, 475 p., [24] p. of plates : ill., maps : 24 cm.
Subject	Nicholas II, Emperor of Russia, 1868-1918 – Assassination
	Nicholas II, Emperor of Russia, 1868-1918 – Family
Note	Originally published: New York : Doubleday, 1992.
Bibliog.	Includes bibliographical references (p. [453]-457) and index.
ISBN	0385469624 : $14.95 ($18.95 Can.)

If you cannot find your topic in the subject catalog, you may have to look under several headings to find the specific one your library uses. (For example, Amy's library might have used "Romanov" instead of "Nicholas II" in its subject catalog.) If you can't find your subject under the headings that first come to mind, consult the *Library of Congress Subject Headings*, a common reference book that will suggest other names for your topic. Once you have a call number, a library map will help you find the book's location on the shelves.

Indexes

Indexes list magazines, journals, newspapers, audio and video sources, books, and collections that contain material you may wish to consult. Most of these indexes are now available as online databases; you will probably find the most current information there because databases are frequently updated. Some printed indexes, in contrast, may be revised and published only once a year.

Using the most appropriate index may save you valuable time as you research your subject. For example, if you think your topic has been the subject of general-interest magazines, you might consult the *Reader's Guide to Periodical Literature*; for newspaper articles, you might check *The New York Times Index* or the *National Newspaper Index*. Most specialized disciplines have their own indexes: the *Humanities Index*, the *Art Index*, the *Music Index*, the *Social Science Index*, the *Business Periodicals Index*, the *Applied Science and Technology Index*, and so on.

Databases

Most libraries across the country subscribe to different information services that will lead researchers to appropriate databases for their subjects. A *database* allows users to scan electronic indexes that list thousands of bibliographic sources, abstracts, summaries, and texts.

After you access your library's database information screen, you will find some general interest indexes and others that are more specialized. Page 359 shows a database screen from a shared city and community college library in Colorado.

Perhaps most helpful will be *full-text databases* that offer access to numerous academic and professional journals as well as magazines and newspapers. For example, under "Arts and Humanities," you might find this useful database:

Proquest—Magazine and newspaper articles from over 1,500 indexed publications, many of which are available in full text and full image format.

InfoTrac is another highly useful database that offers full-text articles from nearly 5,000 newspapers, general-interest magazines, trade publications, and scholarly journals. You can now conveniently access *InfoTrac College Edition* from your own Web browser by registering with the passcode packaged with all new copies of this textbook; this free four-month subscription is offered by Thomson Learning (for more information, visit www.infotrac-college.com).

Online databases are updated frequently and may therefore provide you with the most current sources for your research. Do note, however, that because libraries contract and

| databases | featured lists | interlibrary loan | my library account | catalog home |

city > library > catalog > selected databases

If you are looking for a particular magazine or journal title such as Consumer Reports, try:

If you are looking for a particular database such as Ancestry.com:

| Select Database from alphabetical list ... ▼ |

Databases by Category

Arts and Humanities	Health, Sciences and Technology (including car repair and career testing)	
Books and Literature		**Home Access**
Business and Investments	Homework	
Education	Magazines, Journals, Newspapers, Reports	
Genealogy and Local History	People	**In-Library Access**

pay a fee for database services, they must restrict some database access to on-site use or use by particular patrons (for example, enrolled students only at a campus library). Know, too, that each database may have its own search method. Always ask a librarian to help if you are struggling with a database search.

As you search your electronic sources, remember that you may have to try a variety of keywords (and their synonyms) to find what you need. Sometimes your keyword search may turn up too few leads—and sometimes you may be overwhelmed with too many matches! (For example, when Amy Lawrence typed in the keyword "Anastasia," she discovered too many irrelevant entries focusing on Hollywood movies about the princess.) To save time and effort, you may be able to broaden or narrow your search by typing in words called *Boolean operators**, as illustrated below:

AND (Nicholas II AND Anastasia)—narrows your search to those references containing both terms

OR (Nicholas II OR Anastasia)—broadens search to find items containing either term

NOT (Anastasia NOT movie)—excludes items irrelevant to your search

NEAR (Nicholas II NEAR assassination)—finds references in which the terms occur within a set number of words (This option is not always available.)

---

* Named for the nineteenth-century British mathematician and logician George Boole

Not all databases respond to Boolean operators, however, so it's always best to consult the searching advice offered by your particular information system.

Here is the InfoTrac "keyword" search screen Amy used to look for more information on the important Romanov DNA tests:

Keyword search

Click in the entry box and enter search term(s)

| Romanov AND DNA | Search | Clear Form |

Search for words ⊙ in title, citation, abstract ○ in entire article content
Type words to search for. You can use AND, OR, NOT. Results are sorted by date.

The InfoTrac search for "Romanov and DNA" produced these two titles, whose full-text articles Amy found useful.

Keyword search (in title, citation, abstract): Romanov AND DNA

—————— **Citations 1 to 2** ——————

☐ Mark all items on this page

☐ **DNA test confirms dead czar's identity.** (former Russian Czar Nicholas Romanov II)
Mark (Biology)(Brief Article)
Science News April 20, 1996 v149 n16 p255(1) (385 words)

☐ **Royal D-loops.** (remains of Russian Czar Nicholas II and family proved authentic with
Mark DNA) (1993 - The Year in Science) Josie Glausiusz.
Discover Jan 1994 v15 n1 p90(1) (474 words)

Once you have found useful information, remember that libraries have printers available to print out the on-screen data you wish to keep; you may have to pay a small fee for this printing, so it's a good idea to take some cash along, preferably in correct change. (Sometimes library users with personal computers at home can avoid this expense by e-mailing data to themselves.)

And once again, the very best advice bears repeating: never hesitate to ask your library staff for help.

The Internet

You may have access to the Internet through your library, through your school network, or through a personal account with a service provider of your choice. The Internet can offer great research opportunities, but in many cases, it may only supplement—not replace—the information you will need to collect through library sources.

The most effective approach to discovering useful material on the Internet may be through the use of "search engines" that produce a list of potential electronic documents or Web sites in response to your search. Some search engines (such as Yahoo!) offer a "subject directory," which organizes an enormous amount of information into broad categories, such as arts, education, health, humanities, or science. To research a topic, you move through general categories to more specific subcategories until you find the information you need (arts → literature → classics → Greek classics → *The Iliad*). You might wish to consult a subject directory early in your search when you are looking for general information on your topic.

Perhaps more useful in an advanced search are those search engines that operate in a more focused way: you type in your keyword(s); the search engine explores its database for word or phrase matches; it then presents you with a list of potential sources, which include the Internet addresses (called URLs—"uniform resource locators"). You may access the sources that seem most promising (often those that appear first on the list), and you may also connect to other material by clicking on any highlighted words (hypertext links) appearing within the text of a particular document. At this time, the most popular search engine is Google, but there are many, many more worldwide, including AltaVista, Yahoo!, AlltheWeb, Wisenut, and Teoma; some systems, such as Metacrawler and Kartoo, search multiple engines at once. Because each search engine pulls its results from a different (but often overlapping) pool of Web pages, and because each one offers distinct "extra features," it pays to try more than one. (If you aren't satisfied with your results, try another set of keywords before moving on.)

Most search engines have their own searching tips; to improve your chances for success, it's well worth the time to read the advice on advanced searches. For example, many search engines allow use of some or all of the Boolean operators (see page 359) to narrow or broaden your search. Some allow the use of plus and minus signs to show connected terms or unwanted matches:

Anastasia + Nicholas II (find sources containing both terms)

Anastasia – movie (find sources about Anastasia but exclude those that include the word "movie")

Some programs request quotation marks around a key term of multiple words ("Anne Frank"); some are case sensitive (capitalize proper nouns or not?); some use truncation to find various forms of a word (myth* will return *mythology* and *mythical*). Other search engines, such as Ask Jeeves, allow users to ask questions in natural language ("Who was Marie Romanov?"). As technology continues to improve, searching will no doubt become easier, so always take a moment to look at each search engine's current directions.

Here is one more hint for searching the Web: sometimes you can guess the URL you need. Simply fill in the name of a specific company, college, agency, or organization. Do not skip spaces between words (usnews.com).

Businesses: www.name of company.com

Universities: www.name of college.edu

Government agencies: www.name of agency.gov

Organizations: www.name of organization.org

You may also consult specialized directories to discover the addresses you need.

Once you find a useful document, you may print it, add the reference to your "bookmark" or "favorites" list, or copy it to a file, if you are using your own computer. Whether at the library or at home, always keep a list of your important sites, their addresses, and the date you accessed them. You may need this information for an easy return to a particular document and also for your working bibliography.

There are many other ways to use the Internet for research and for trading ideas with others. To explore the possibilities in more detail than may be presented here, invest in a current book on the Internet or go to one of the many sites offering research advice.

Words of Caution for Internet Users: Be Afraid, Be Very Afraid. . . .

The Internet offers researchers a wealth of information incredibly fast. However, the Internet poses problems, too. It may offer a great deal of information on your essay topic—but it may not offer the *best* information, which might be found in a classic text on your library shelf. Background information or historical perspective may not be available; Web site information may be out of date. Moreover, simply finding the specific information you need can be frustrating and time-consuming, especially if your keywords and links don't lead in useful directions. The information superhighway is congested with scores of irrelevant distractions, so beware the wild Web chase.

There is, however, another much more serious problem: not all material found on the Internet is accurate or reliable. When an article is printed in a respected journal, for example, readers have assurances that editors have reviewed the information, writers have checked their facts, and authorities have been quoted correctly. However, Web sites may be created by anyone on any subject, from gene splicing to Elvis sightings, without any sort of editorial review. Opinions—wise or crackpot—may be presented as facts; rumors may be presented as reality. Because there is no "quality control" of Web sites, writers of research papers must evaluate their sources extremely carefully to avoid gathering unreliable information. Always ask these questions of each source:

- What is the purpose of this Web site? (To inform, persuade, market a product or service, share an interest, entertain?) To whom is this site primarily directed, and why?

- Who is the sponsor, author, or creator of the site? (A business, an educational institution, a nonprofit organization, a government agency, a news bureau, an individual?) Is the sponsor or author known and respected in the particular content area?

- Does the sponsor or author reveal a clear bias or strong opinion? Does such a slant undercut the usefulness of the information?

- When was this site produced? When was it last updated or revised? If links exist, are they still viable? Up to date?

- Is the information accurate? How might the material be cross-checked and verified?

If you have doubts about the accuracy of any material you discover on the Internet, find another authoritative source to validate the information or omit it from your essay. Following the guidelines on pages 368–370 will help you evaluate *all* your potential research sources.

Special Collections

Your library may contain special collections that will help you research your subject. Some libraries, for example, have extensive collections of government documents or educational materials or newspapers from foreign cities. Other libraries may have invested in manuscripts from famous authors or in a series of works on a particular subject, such as your state's history. Remember, too, that some libraries contain collections of early films, rare recordings, or unique photographs. Consult your librarian or the information sources describing your library's special holdings.

■ Conducting the Personal Interview

Depending on your choice of topic, you may find all the information you need for your essay by exploring sources through library and online research. However, sometimes you may discover that an authority on your subject lives in your town or works on your campus. In this case, you may wish to conduct a *personal interview* to gather valuable information for your essay.

Preparation is the key word governing a good interview. Here are some suggestions that may help you collect useful data in the most effective way possible.

Before You Interview:

1. *Know your purpose.* If you have only a vague notion of why you are talking to the interviewee, you will waste everyone's time as the conversation roams like a lost hiker wandering from one clearing to the next. A close look at your essay's outline or your early drafts should tell you why and how this person might contribute to your research. Be certain that the person you have selected for an interview is, in fact, the best source for the kind of information you are seeking.

2. *Make an appointment.* Calling for an interview may make you a bit nervous, but remember that most people like to be asked for their opinions and are usually willing to help students with their research, if their schedules permit. Be sure the interviewee understands who you are, why you are asking for an interview, and approximately how much time you are requesting. Whenever possible, allow the interviewee to select the hour and place most convenient for him or her. Do adjust your schedule to give yourself time after the meeting in case the interview runs long and to allow yourself a few minutes to review and fill in your notes.

3. *Educate yourself.* Before the interview, read about your topic and your interviewee. You want to appear knowledgeable about your subject; you can also save time by skipping questions that have already been answered in print. Busy experts appreciate not having to explain basic information that you could have—and should have—already looked up.

4. *Plan some questions.* Unless you have an excellent memory, it is best to jot down some specific questions to which you can refer during the interview. Some interviewers write each question at the top of an index card, and then use the rest of the card for their notes on the answer. Others use a notebook in which they write a question (or key words) at the top of each page. Try to create questions that are specific, clear, and logically ordered. Avoid "yes/no" questions that don't lead to discussion. If you have a complicated or convoluted issue you want to discuss, try breaking it into a series of simpler questions that can be tackled by the interviewee one at a time.

During the Interview:

5. *Make a good first impression.* Always arrive on time, prepared with pens, paper, or other documents you need. Some interviewers like to use a small tape recorder, but you first must secure your interviewee's permission to use this equipment. (A recorder makes some people uncomfortably self-conscious and hesitant to speak freely, so consider whether the accuracy it may provide is more important than the spontaneity it may kill.) Always begin by thanking your interviewee for his or her time and briefly say again why you think he or she can provide helpful information to you.

6. *Ask, listen, ask.* Begin asking your prepared questions, but don't rush through them. Listen attentively to your interviewee's answers, and although it takes practice, try to maintain eye contact as you jot down abbreviated notes on the answers. Allow the interviewee to do almost all the talking; after all, you are there to collect information, not participate in a debate. Do politely ask for clarification (unfamiliar terms, spelling of names, unclear references, and so on) when you need it.

7. *Be flexible.* Sometimes your interviewee will talk about something fascinating that never occurred to you when you prepared your original list of questions. Be ready to adapt your plan and ask new questions that follow up on unexpected commentary.

8. *Silence is Golden but.* . . . If an interviewee is quiet or hesitates to give the kind of detailed responses you are seeking, you may need to use phrases of this kind to draw out longer answers:

Can you elaborate on that?

Tell me more about X.

Why did you think that?

How did you react to that?

When did you realize. . . ?

Why do you believe that?

What's your reading of that situation?

Would you explain that for me?

As you ask for more details, try to use a friendly, conversational tone that will put your interviewee at ease.

On the other hand, sometimes interviewees talk too much! They become stuck on one aspect of a topic, going into unnecessary depth, or perhaps they begin to drift off the subject completely. Be courteous but firm in your resolve to redirect the flow of conversation. To get back to your topic, you may need to re-ask the original question, using slightly different words.

9. *Conclude thoughtfully.* At the end of the interview, ask for any additional comments the interviewee would like to offer and for any information (or other sources) he or she thinks you might find useful. Ask the interviewee if you may contact him or her again if you should have another brief question; if such permission is granted, ask for the best means of contact (a telephone number or e-mail address). Give the interviewee your most sincere thanks for his or her time and assistance.

After the Interview:

10. *Review your notes immediately.* Fill in gaps in your notes while your memory is fresh, and write out acronyms or abbreviations whose meanings you might forget in a few days. Make some notes to yourself about using the information in your essay.

Later, if the interview figures prominently in your essay, consider sending your interviewee a copy of your work. Within days of the interview, however, it is ALWAYS polite to send your interviewee a short thank-you note, acknowledging his or her help with your research project.

■ Preparing a Working Bibliography

As you search for information about your essay topic, keep a list of sources that you may want to use in your essay. This list, called a *working bibliography*, will grow as you discover potential sources, and it may shrink if you delete references that aren't useful. Ultimately, this working bibliography will become the list of references presented at the end of your essay.

There are several ways to record your sources. Some students prefer to make an index card for each title; others compile a list in a research notebook; still others prefer to create a computer file or a folder of printouts. As you add sources to your working bibliography, note the following information as appropriate.

Book

1. Author's or editor's full name (and name of translator if given)
2. Complete title, including subtitle if one exists
3. Edition number
4. Volume number and the total number of volumes if the book is part of a series
5. Publisher
6. City of publication
7. Date of publication
8. Library call number or location of source
9. Chapter title or page numbers of the information you need

Article in a Journal, Magazine, or Newspaper

1. Author's full name (if given)
2. Title of the article
3. Title of the journal, magazine, or newspaper
4. Volume and issue number of the journal or magazine
5. Date of publication
6. Page numbers of the article (section and page numbers for newspaper)

Electronic Sources

1. Author's full name or name of sponsoring organization
2. Title of document
3. Information about print publication (book: place, publisher, date; periodical: title, volume and issue if given, date, pages)
4. Information about electronic publication (source, such as database, Web site, CD-ROM, etc.; name of service; date of publication or most recent update)
5. Access information (date of access and URL)

Interview

1. Interviewee's name and title
2. Interviewee's organization or company, job description, or other information regarding his or her expertise, including pertinent publications, studies, presentations, etc.
3. Subject of interview
4. Date, place, and method of interview (e.g., in person, by telephone, by e-mail)

Here are four sample index cards that might appear in Amy Lawrence's working bibliography:

Book

> Radzinsky, Edvard
> The Last Czar: The Life and Death of Nicholas II
> Doubleday Publishers, 1992
> New York, New York
> pp. 8–10, 315–434   Translated by
> call number: AN947.083   Marian Schwartz
> (CSU Library, East Wing)

Article in Magazine

> Elliott, Dorinda
> "The Legacy of the Last Czar"
> Newsweek, pp. 60–61
> Sept. 21, 1992

Electronic Source

> Varoli, John
> "Nemtsov: Bury Czar in St. Petersburg July 17"
> St. Petersburg Times
> St. Petersburg, Russia
> Feb. 9–15, 1998
> <http://www.spb.ru/times/336–337/nemtsov.html>
> Internet   (date of access: 2/26/04)

Interview

> *Wheeler, Anne (Dr.)*
>
> *Professor of History*
> *Department of History*
> *Colorado State University*
>
> *Teaches H456, Russian History and Culture*
>
> *Interview subject: Romanov assassination*
> *In-person interview: Feb. 15, 2004*
> *Office of Dr. Wheeler, Clark 305, campus, Ft. Collins, CO*

■ Choosing and Evaluating Your Sources

After you have found a number of promising sources, take a closer look at them. The strength and credibility of your research paper will depend directly on the strength and credibility of your sources. In short, a research paper built on shaky, unreliable sources will not convince a thoughtful reader. Even one suspect piece of evidence may lead your reader to wonder about the validity of other parts of your essay.

To help you choose your print and online sources, ask yourself the following questions as you try to decide which facts, figures, and testimonies will best support or illustrate your ideas.

What do I know about the author? Does this person have any expertise or particular knowledge about the subject matter? If the author of an article about nuclear fusion is a physics professor at a respected university, her views may be more informed than those of a writer of popular science. Although books and scholarly journals generally cite their author's qualifications, the credentials of journalists and magazine writers may be harder to evaluate. Internet sources, as mentioned earlier, may be highly suspect. In cases in which the background of a writer is unknown, you might examine the writer's use of his or her own sources. Can sources for specific data or opinions be checked or verified? In addition, the objectivity of the author must be considered: some authors are clearly biased and may even stand to gain economically or politically from taking a particular point of view. The president of a tobacco company, for instance, might insist that secondary smoke from the cigarettes of others will not harm nonsmokers, but does he or she have an objective opinion? Try to present evidence only from those authors whose views will sway your intelligent readers.

What do I know about the publisher? Who published your sources? Major, well-known publishing houses can be one indication of a book's credibility. (If you are unfamiliar with a particular publisher, consult a librarian or professor in that field.) Be aware that there are many publishers who only publish books supporting a specific viewpoint; similarly, many organizations support Web sites to further their causes. The bias in such sources may limit their usefulness to your research.

For periodicals, consider the nature of the journal, magazine, or newspaper. Who is its intended audience? A highly technical paper on sickle cell anemia, for example, might be weakened by citing a very general discussion of the disease from *Health Digest*; an article from the *Journal of the American Medical Association*, however, might be valuable. Is it a publication known to be fairly objective (*The New York Times*) or does it have a particular cause to support (*The National Sierra Club Bulletin*)? Looking at the masthead of a journal or other publication will often tell you whether articles are subjected to stringent review before acceptance for publication. In general, articles published in "open" or non-selective publications should be examined closely for credibility. For example, the newsletter for MENSA—a well-known international society for individuals who have documented IQs in the top 2 percent of the population—once created a furor when an article appeared recommending the euthanasia of the mentally and physically disabled, the homeless, and other so-called "nonproductive" members of society. The newsletter editor's explanation was that all articles submitted for publication were generally accepted.

Is my research reasonably balanced? Your treatment of your subject—especially if it is a controversial one—should show your readers that you investigated all sides of the issue before reaching a conclusion. If your sources are drawn only from authorities well known for voicing one position, your readers may be skeptical about the quality of your research. For instance, if in a paper arguing against a new gun-control measure, you cite only the opinions voiced by the officers of the National Rifle Association, you may antagonize the reader who wants a thorough analysis of all sides of the question. Do use sources that support your position, but don't overload your argument with obviously biased sources.

Are my sources reporting valid research? Is your source the original researcher or is he or she reporting someone else's study?* If the information is being reported second-hand, has your source been accurate and clear? Is the original source named or referenced in some way so that the information could be checked?

A thorough researcher might note the names of authorities frequently cited by other writers or researchers and try to obtain the original works by those authorities. This tip was useful for Amy Lawrence as she found the researcher Robert K. Massie mentioned in a number of magazine articles. Once she obtained a copy of his often-quoted book, she had additional information to consider for her paper.

Look too at the way information in your source was obtained in the first place. Did the

---

* Interviews, surveys, studies, and experiments conducted firsthand are referred to as *primary sources*; reports and studies written by someone other than the original researcher are called *secondary sources*.

original researchers themselves draw logical conclusions from their evidence? Did they run their study or project in a fair, impartial way? For example, a survey of people whose names were obtained from the rolls of the Democratic party will hardly constitute a representative sampling of voters' opinions on an upcoming election.

Moreover, be especially careful with statistics because they can be manipulated quite easily to give a distorted picture. A recent survey, for instance, asked a large sample of people to rate a number of American cities based on questions dealing with quality of life. Pittsburgh—a lovely city to be sure—came out the winner, but only if one agrees that all the questions should be weighted equally; that is, the figures gave Pittsburgh the highest score only if one rates "weather" as equally important as "educational opportunities," "number of crimes," "cultural opportunities," and other factors. In short, always evaluate the quality of your sources' research and the validity of their conclusions before you decide to incorporate their findings into your own paper. (And don't forget Mark Twain's reference to "lies, damned lies, and statistics.")

Are my sources still current? Although some famous experiments or studies have withstood the years, many topics demand research as current as possible. What was written two years or or even two weeks ago may have been disproved or surpassed since, especially in our rapidly changing political world and ever-expanding fields of technology. A paper on the status of the U.S. space program, for example, demands recent sources, and research on personal computer use in the United States would be severely weakened by the use of a text published as recently as 2001 for "current" statistics.

If they're appropriate, journals and other periodicals may contain more up-to-date reports than books printed several years ago; library database searches can often provide the most current information. On the other hand, you certainly shouldn't ignore a "classic" study on your subject, especially if it is the one against which all the other studies are measured. A student researching the life of Abraham Lincoln, for instance, might find Carl Sandburg's multivolume biography of over 60 years ago as valuable as more recent works. (Remember, too, that even though Web sites can be continually revised, they are sometimes neglected; always check to see if a "last updated" date has been posted or if the material contains current dates or references.)

✓ **REMEMBER:** For more advice to help you think critically about your sources, see Chapter 5.

■ Preparing an Annotated Bibliography

While you are gathering and assessing your sources, you may be asked to compile an annotated bibliography—a description of each important source that includes the basic bibliographic facts as well as a brief summary of each entry's content. After reading multiple articles or books on your subject over a period of days or even weeks, you may discover that the information you've found has begun to blur together in your head. Annotating each of your sources will help you remember the specific data in each one so that you can locate the material later in the planning and drafting stages of your writing process.

Here is a sample taken from Amy Lawrence's annotated bibliography:

Elliott, Dorinda. "The Legacy of the Last Czar." <u>Newsweek</u> 21 Sept. 1992: 60–61.

> Elliot offers the results of early forensic analysis of the Romanov grave site and a brief description of the events surrounding the executions. The article quotes forensic experts and historians and includes the views of Russian citizens on the significance of finding and identifying the remains of the Romanov family.

Compiling an annotated bibliography will also give you a clear sense of how complete and balanced your sources are in support of your ideas, perhaps revealing gaps in your evidence that need to be filled with additional research data. Later, when your essay is finished, your annotated bibliography might provide a useful reference for any of your readers who are interested in exploring your subject in more depth.

■ Taking Notes

As you evaluate and select those sources that are both reliable and useful, you will begin taking notes on their information. Most researchers use one or more of the following three methods of note-taking.

1. Some students prefer to make their notes on index cards rather than on notebook paper because a stack of cards may be added to, subtracted from, or shuffled around more easily when it's time to plan the essay. You may find it useful to label each card with a short topic heading that corresponds to a major idea in your essay. Then, as you read, put pertinent information on its appropriate card. Be sure to identify the source of all your notes. (Hint 1: If you have used bibliography cards, take your notes on cards of different sizes or colors to avoid any confusion; write on only one side of each card so that all your information will be in sight when you draft your essay.)

2. Other students rely on photocopies or printouts of sources, highlighting or underlining important details. (Hint 2: Copy a source's title page and other front matter so that you can clip complete bibliographic information to your pages.)

3. Students with personal computers may prefer to store their notes as computer files because of the easy transfer of quoted material from file to essay draft. (Hint 3: Always make a hard copy of your notes and back up your files frequently in case of a crash!) You will probably find yourself taking notes by hand on those occasions when you are without your computer (library, classroom, interview, public speech, etc.), so carry index cards with you and transcribe your notes into your files later.

Whichever note-taking method you choose, always remember to record bibliographic information and the specific page numbers (in printed sources) or paragraph numbers (in some electronic sources) from which your material is taken. Your notes may be one of the following kinds:

1. *Direct quotations.* When you use material word for word, you must always enclose it in quotation marks and note the precise page number of the quotation, if given.* If the quoted material runs from one printed page onto another, use some sort of signal to yourself, such as a slash bar (child/abuse) or arrow (→ p. 162) at the break so if you use only part of the quoted material in your paper, you will know on which page it appeared. If the quoted material contains odd, archaic, or incorrect spelling, punctuation marks, or grammar, insert the word *sic* in brackets next to the item in question; [*sic*] means "this is the way I found it in the original text," and such a symbol will remind you later that you did not miscopy the quotation. Otherwise, always double-check to make sure you did copy the material accurately and completely to avoid having to come back to the source as you prepare your essay. If the material you want to quote is lengthy or complex, you will find it easier—though not cheaper—to photocopy (or print out) the text rather than transcribe it.

2. *Paraphrase.* You paraphrase when you put into your own words what someone else has written or said. Please note: *paraphrased ideas are borrowed ideas, not your original thoughts, and, consequently, they must be attributed to their owner just as direct quotations are.*

To remind yourself that certain information in your notes is paraphrased, always introduce it with some sort of notation, such as a handwritten Ⓟ or a typed P//. Quotation marks will always tell you what you borrowed directly, but sometimes when writers take notes one week and write their first draft a week or two later, they cannot remember if a note was paraphrased or if it was an original thought. Writers occasionally plagiarize unintentionally because they believe only direct quotations and statistics must be attributed to their proper sources, so make your notes as clear as possible. (For more information on avoiding plagiarism, see pages 376–378.)

3. *Summary.* You may wish to condense a piece of writing so you can offer it as support for your own ideas. Using your own words, you should present in shorter form the writer's thesis and supporting ideas. You may find it helpful to include a few direct quotations in your summary to retain the flavor of the original work. Of course, you will tell your readers what you are summarizing and by whom it was written. Remember to make a note (sum:) to yourself to indicate summarized, rather than original, material. (For more information on writing a summary, see also pages 171–172.)

4. *Your own ideas.* Your notes may also contain your personal comments (judgments, flashes of brilliance, questions, notions of how to use something you've just read, notes to yourself about connections between sources, and so forth) that will aid you in the writing of your paper. In handwritten notes, you might jot these down in a different-colored pen or put them in brackets that you've initialed, so that you will recognize them later as your own responses.

---

* All tables, graphs, and charts that you copy must also be directly attributed to their sources, though you do not enclose graphics in quotation marks.

Distinguishing Paraphrase from Summary

Because novice writers sometimes have a hard time understanding the difference between paraphrase and summary, here is an explanation and a sample of each. The original paragraph that appears here was taken from a magazine article describing an important 1984 study still frequently cited:

> Another successful approach to the prevention of criminality has been to target very young children in a school setting before problems arise. The Perry Preschool Program, started 22 years ago in a low socioeconomic area of Ypsilanti, Michigan, has offered some of the most solid evidence to date that early intervention through a high-quality preschool program can significantly alter a child's life. A study released this fall tells what happened to 123 disadvantaged children from preschool age to present. The detention and arrest rates for the 58 children who had attended the preschool program was 31 percent, compared to 51 percent for the 65 who did not. Similarly, those in the preschool program were more likely to have graduated from high school, have enrolled in postsecondary education programs and be employed, and less likely to have become pregnant as teenagers.
>
> —from "Arresting Delinquency,"
> Dan Hurley, <u>Psychology Today</u>,
> March 1985, page 66

Paraphrase

A *paraphrase* puts the information in the researcher's own words, but it does follow the order of the original text, and it does include the important details:

> Quality preschooling for high-risk children may help stop crime before it starts. A 1984 study from the Perry Preschool Program located in a poor area of Ypsilanti, Michigan, showed that of 123 socially and economically disadvantaged children, the 58 who attended preschool had an arrest rate of 31 percent compared to 51 percent for those 65 who did not attend. The adults with preschool experience had also graduated from high school in larger numbers; in addition, more of them had attended postsecondary education programs, were employed, and had avoided teenage pregnancy (Hurley 66).

Summary

A *summary* is generally much shorter than the original; the researcher picks out the key ideas but often omits many of the supporting details:

> A 1984 study from the Perry Preschool Program in Michigan suggests that disadvantaged children who attend preschool are less likely to be arrested as adults. They choose more education, have better employment records, and avoid teenage pregnancy more often than those without preschool (Hurley 66).

☑ **REMEMBER:** Both paraphrased and summarized ideas must be attributed to their sources, even if you do not reproduce exact words or figures.

■ Incorporating Your Source Material

Be aware that a research paper is not a massive collection of quotations and paraphrased or summarized ideas glued together with a few transitional phrases. It is, instead, an essay in which you offer *your* thesis and ideas based on and supported by your research. Consequently, you will need to incorporate and blend in your reference material in a variety of smooth, persuasive ways. Here are some suggestions:

Use your sources in a clear, logical way. Make certain that you understand your source material well enough to use it in support of your own thoughts. Once you have selected the best references to use, be as convincing as possible. Ask yourself if you're using enough evidence and if the information you're offering really does clearly support your point. As in any essay, you need to avoid oversimplification, hasty generalizations, *non sequiturs*, and other problems in logic (for a review of common logical fallacies, see pages 282–285). Resist the temptation to add quotations, facts, or statistics that are interesting but not really relevant to your paper.

Don't overuse direct quotations. It's best to use a direct quotation *only* when it expresses a point in a far more impressive, emphatic, or concise way than you could say it yourself. Suppose, for instance, you were analyzing the films of a particular director and wanted to include a sample of critical reviews:

> As one movie critic wrote, "This film is really terrible, and people should ignore it" (Dennison 14).

The direct quotation above isn't remarkable and could be easily paraphrased. However, you might be tempted to quote the following line to show your readers an emphatically negative review of this movie:

> As one movie critic wrote, "This film's plot is so idiotic it's clearly intended for people who move their lips not only when they read but also when they watch TV" (Dennison 14).

When you do decide to use direct quotations, don't merely drop them in your prose as if they had fallen from a tall building onto your page. Instead, lead into them smoothly so that they obviously support or clarify what you are saying.

Dropped in	Scientists have been studying the ill effects of nitrites on test animals since 1961. "Nitrites produced malignant tumors in 62 percent of the test animals within six months" (Smith 109).
Better	Scientists have been studying the ill effects of nitrites on test animals since 1961. According to Dr. William Smith, head of the Farrell Institute of Research, who conducted the largest experiment thus far, "Nitrites produced malignant tumors in 62 percent of the test animals within six months" (109).

Vary your sentence pattern when you present your quotations. Here are some sample phrases for quotations:

In her introduction to <u>The Great Gatsby</u>, Professor Wilma Smith points out that Fitzgerald "wrote about himself and produced a narcissistic masterpiece" (5).

Wilma Smith, author of <u>Impact</u>, summarized the situation this way: "Eighty-eight percent of the sales force threaten a walkout" (21).

"Only the President controls the black box," according to the White House Press Secretary Wilma Smith.

As drama critic Wilma Smith observed last year in <u>The Saturday Review</u>, the play was "a rousing failure" (212).

Perhaps the well-known poet Wilma Smith expressed the idea best when she wrote, "Love is a spider waiting to entangle its victims" (14).

"Employment figures are down 3 percent from last year," claimed Senator Wilma Smith, who leads opposition to the tax cut (32).

In other words, don't simply repeat "Wilma Smith said," "John Jones said," "Mary Brown said."

Punctuate your quotations correctly. The proper punctuation will help your reader understand who said what. For information on the appropriate uses of quotation marks surrounding direct quotations, see pages 510–512 in Part Four. If you are incorporating a long quoted passage into your essay, one that appears as more than four typed lines in your manuscript, you should present it in block form without quotation marks, as described on page 381. To omit words in a quoted passage, use ellipsis points, explained on pages 517–518.

Make certain your support is in the paper, not still in your head or back in the original source. Sometimes when you've read a number of persuasive facts in an article or a book, it's easy to forget that your reader doesn't know them as you do now. For instance, the writer of the following paragraph isn't as persuasive as she might be because she hides the support for her controversial point in the reference to the article, forgetting that the reader needs to know what the article actually said:

> An organ transplant from one human to another is becoming an everyday occurrence, an operation that is generally applauded by everyone as a life-saving effort. But people are overlooking many of the serious problems that come with the increase in transplant surgery. A study shows that in Asia there may be a risk of traffic in organs on the Black Market. Figures recorded recently are very disturbing (Wood 35).

For the reader to be persuaded, he or she needs to know what the writer learned from the article: What study? What figures and what exactly do they show? Who has recorded these? Is the source reliable? Instead of offering the necessary support in the essay, the writer merely points to the article as proof. Few readers will take the time to look up the article to find the information they need to understand or believe your point. Therefore, when you use source material, always be sure that you have remembered to put your support on the page, *in the essay itself,* for the reader to see. Don't let the essence of your point remain hidden, especially when the claim is controversial.

Don't let reference material dominate your essay. Remember that your reader is interested in *your* thesis and *your* conclusions, not just in a string of references. Use your researched material wisely whenever your statements need clarification, support, or amplification. But don't use quotations, paraphrases, or summarized material at every turn, just to show that you've done your homework.

■ Avoiding Plagiarism

Unfortunately, most discussions of research must include a brief word about plagiarism. Novice writers often unintentionally plagiarize, as noted before, because they fail to recognize the necessity of attributing paraphrased, summarized, and borrowed ideas to their original owners. And indeed it is sometimes difficult after days of research to know exactly what one has read repeatedly and what one originally thought. Also, there's frequently a thin line between general or common knowledge ("Henry Ford was the father of the automobile industry in America") that does not have to be documented and those ideas and statements that do ("USX reported an operating loss of four million in its last quarter"). As a rule of thumb, ask yourself whether the majority of your readers would recognize the fact or opinion you're expressing or if it's repeatedly found in commonly used sources; if so, you may not need to document it. For example, most people would acknowledge that the Wall Street crash of 1929 ushered in the Great Depression of the 1930s, but the exact number of bank foreclosures in 1933 is not common knowledge and, therefore, needs documenting. Similarly, a well-known quotation from the Bible or Mother Goose or even the Declaration of Independence might pass without documentation, but a line from the vice-president's latest speech needs a reference to its source. Remember, too, that much of the material on the Internet is copyrighted. When in doubt, the best choice is to document anything that you feel may be in question.

To help you understand the difference between plagiarism and proper documentation, here is an original passage and both incorrect and correct ways to use it in a paper of your own:

Original
> It is a familiar nightmare: a person suffers a heart attack, and as the ambulance fights heavy traffic, the patient dies. In fact, 350,000 American heart-attack victims each year die without ever reaching a hospital. The killer in many cases is ventricular fibrillation, uncoordinated contraction of the heart muscle. Last week a team of Dutch physicians reported in <u>The New England Journal of Medicine</u> that these early deaths can often be prevented by administration of a common heart drug called lidocaine, injected into the patient's shoulder muscle by ambulance paramedics as soon as they arrive on the scene.
>
> —from "First Aid for Heart Attacks,"
> <u>Newsweek</u>, November 11, 1985,
> page 88

Plagiarized
> It is a common nightmare: as the ambulance sits in heavy traffic, a person with a heart attack dies, often a victim of ventricular

> fibrillation, uncoordinated contraction of the heart muscle. Today, however, these early deaths can often be prevented by an injection into the patient's shoulder of a common heart drug called lidocaine, which may be administered by paramedics on the scene.

This writer has changed some of the words and sentences, but the passage has obviously been borrowed and must be attributed to its source.

Also plagiarized   According to <u>Newsweek</u>, 350,000 American heart attack victims die before reaching help in hospitals ("First Aid for Heart Attacks" 88). However, a common heart drug called lidocaine, which may be injected into the patient by paramedics on the scene of the attack, may save many victims who die en route to doctors and sophisticated life-saving equipment.

This writer did attribute the statistic to its source, but the remainder of the preceding paragraph is still borrowed and must be documented.

Properly documented   Ambulance paramedics can, and often do, play a vital life-saving role today. They are frequently the first medical assistance available, especially to those patients or accident victims far away from hospitals. Moreover, according to a <u>Newsweek</u> report, paramedics are now being trained to administer powerful drugs to help the sick survive until they reach doctors and medical equipment. For instance, paramedics can inject the common heart drug lidocaine into heart attack victims on the scene, an act that may save many of the 350,000 Americans who die of heart attacks before ever reaching a hospital ("First Aid for Heart Attacks" 88).

This writer used the properly documented information to support her own point about paramedics and has not tried to pass off any of the article as her own.

Although plagiarism is often unintentional, it's your job to be as honest and careful as possible. If you're in doubt about your use of a particular idea, consult your instructor for a second opinion.

Here's a suggestion that might help you avoid plagiarizing by accident. When you are drafting your essay and come to a spot in which you want to incorporate the ideas of someone else, think of the borrowed material as if it were in a window.* Always frame the window at the top with some sort of introduction that identifies the author (or source) and frame the window on the bottom with a reference to the location of the material, as illustrated on the following page.

---

* I am indebted to Professor John Clark Pratt of Colorado State University for this useful suggestion. Professor Pratt is the author of *Writing from Scratch: The Essay* (1987) published by Hamilton Press, and the editor of the *Writing from Scratch* series.

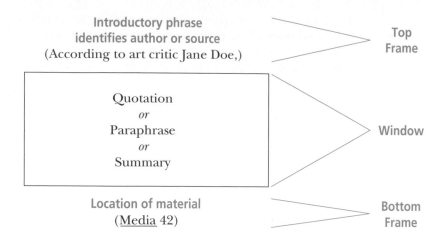

A sample might look like this:

Introductory phrase identifies author

As humorist Mike McGrady once said about housekeeping, "Any job that requires six hours to do and can be undone in six minutes by one small child carrying a plate of crackers and a Monopoly set—this is not a job that will long capture my interest" (13).

Window

Location

In a later draft, you'll probably want to vary your style so that all your borrowed material doesn't appear in exactly the same "window" format (see page 375 for suggestions). But until you acquire the habit of *always* documenting your sources, you might try using the "window" technique in your early drafts.

▪ PRACTICING WHAT YOU'VE LEARNED

As Amy Lawrence researched the Romanov execution, she found the following information about one of the earlier Romanov czars. To practice some of the skills you've learned so far, read the following passage on Alexander II of Russia (1855–1881) and do the tasks that are listed after it.

Alexander's greatest single achievement was his emancipation of some forty million Russian serfs, a deed which won him the title of "Tsar Liberator." To visit a rural Russian community in the earlier nineteenth century was like stepping back into the Middle Ages. Nine-tenths of the land was held by something less than one hundred thousand noble families. The serfs, attached to the soil, could be sold with the estates to new landlords, conscripted into the nobleman's household to work as domestic servants, or even sent to the factories in the towns for their master's profit. Though some nobles exercised their authority in a kindly and paternal fashion, others overworked their serfs, flogged them cruelly for slight faults, and interfered insolently in their private affairs and family relations. A serf could not marry without his master's consent, could not leave the estate without permission, and might be pursued, brought back, and punished if he sought to escape. He lived at the mercy of his master's caprice.

1. The book from which the preceding passage was taken contains the following information. Select the appropriate information and prepare a working bibliography card.

   <u>A Survey of European Civilization Part Two, Since 1660</u>
   Third Edition
   Houghton Mifflin Company, Publishers
   Boston
   First edition, 1936
   853.21
   1,012 pages
   Authors:
     Wallace K. Ferguson, The University of Western Ontario
     Geoffrey Brun, Formerly Visiting Professor of History, Cornell University
   Indexes: general, list of maps
   Picture Acknowledgments, xxvii
   copyright 1962
   page 716
   44 chapters

2. Paraphrase the first four sentences of the passage.

3. Summarize the passage, but do not quote from it.

4. Select an important idea from the passage to quote directly and lead into the quotation with a smooth acknowledgment of its source.

5. Select an idea or a quotation from the passage and use it as support for a point of your own, being careful not to plagiarize the borrowed material.

■ ASSIGNMENT

1. In your library, look up a newspaper* from any city or state and find the issue published on the day of your birth or on some other significant date. Prepare a bibliography card and then summarize an important article from the front page. (Don't forget to acknowledge the source of your summary.)

2. To practice searching for and choosing source material, find three recent works on your essay topic available in your library. If you don't have an essay

---

* If the newspaper is not accessible, you might substitute a weekly news magazine, such as *Time* or *Newsweek*.

topic yet, pick a subject that interests you, one that is likely to appear in both print and electronic sources (Baseball Hall of Fame, stamp collecting, the Titanic disaster, king cobras, etc.). If possible, try to find three different kinds of sources, such as a book, a journal or magazine article, and a Web site. After you have recorded bibliographic information for each source, locate and evaluate the works. Do each of these sources provide relevant, reliable information? In a few sentences explain why you believe each one would or would not be an appropriate source for your research essay.

■ Choosing the Documentation Style for Your Essay

Once you begin to write your paper incorporating your source material, you need to know how to show your readers where your material came from. You may have already learned a documentation system in a previous writing class, but because today's researchers and scholars use a number of different documentation styles, it's important that you know which style is appropriate for your current essay. In some cases, your instructors (or the audience for whom you are writing) will designate a particular style; at other times, the choice will be yours.

In this chapter, we will look at two widely used systems—MLA style and APA style—and also briefly review the use of the traditional footnote/bibliography format.

MLA Style

Most instructors in the humanities assign the documentation form prescribed by the Modern Language Association of America (MLA). Since 1984, the MLA has recommended a form of documentation that no longer uses traditional footnotes or endnotes to show references.* The current form calls for *parenthetical documentation,* most often consisting of the author's last name and the appropriate page number(s) in parentheses immediately following the source material in your paper. At the end of your discussion, readers may find complete bibliographic information for each source on a "Works Cited" page, a list of all the sources in your essay.

MLA Citations in Your Essay

Here are some guidelines for using the MLA parenthetical reference form within your paper.

1. If you use a source by one author, place the author's name and page number after the quoted, paraphrased, or summarized material. Note that the parentheses go *before* the end punctuation, and there is no punctuation between

---

* If you wish a more detailed description of the current MLA form, ask your local bookstore or library for the *MLA Handbook for Writers of Research Papers*, 6th ed. (New York: MLA, 2003) and also the *MLA Style Manual and Guide to Scholarly Publishing*, 2nd ed. (New York: MLA, 1998). The most up-to-date documentation information may be found on the MLA Web site <http://www.MLA.org>.

the author's name and the page number. (Use the author's name and omit the page reference when citing a complete work or a one-page work.)

Example   Although pop art often resembles the comic strip, it owes a debt to such painters as Magritte, Matisse, and de Kooning (Rose 184).

2. If you use a source by one author and give credit to that author by name in your paper, you need only give the page number in the parentheses.

Example   According to art critic Barbara Rose, pop art owes a large debt to such painters as Magritte, Matisse, and de Kooning (184).

3. If you are directly quoting material of more than four typed lines, indent the material one inch (or ten spaces) from the left margin, double-space, and do not use quotation marks. Do not change the right margin. Note that in this case, the parentheses appear *after* the punctuation that ends the quoted material.

Example   In addition to causing tragedy for others, Crane's characters who are motivated by a desire to appear heroic to their peers may also cause themselves serious trouble. For example, Collins, another Civil War private, almost causes his own death because of his vain desire to act bravely in front of his fellow soldiers. (Hall 16)

4. If you are citing more than one work by the same author, include a short title in the parentheses.

Example   Within 50 years, the Inca and Aztec civilizations were defeated and overthrown by outside invaders (Thomas, <u>Lost Cultures</u> 198).

5. If you are citing a work by two or three authors, use all last names and the page number.

Examples   Prisons today are overcrowded to the point of emergency; conditions could not be worse, and the state budget for prison reforms is at an all-time low (Smith and Jones 72).

Human infants grow quickly, with most babies doubling their birth weight in the first six months of life and tripling their weight by their first birthday (Pantell, Fries, and Vickery 52).

6. For more than three authors, use all the last names or use the last name of the first author plus *et al.* (Latin for "and others") and the page number. There is no comma after the author's name.

> **Example**   Casualties of World War II during 1940-45 amounted to more than twenty-five million soldiers and civilians (Blum et al. 779).

7. If you cite a work that has no named author, use the work's title and the page number.

> **Example**   Each year 350,000 Americans will die of a heart attack before reaching a hospital ("First Aid for Heart Attacks" 88).

8. If the work you are citing appears in a series, include the volume and page number with the author's name.

> **Example**   On August 28, 1963, King delivered his "I Have A Dream" address to more than 200,000 civil rights supporters in Washington, DC, a speech that added momentum to the passage of the 1964 Civil Rights Act (Lopez 1:270).

9. If your source is an electronic document, treat it as you would a print source. If you are citing an entire work from an electronic source that has no page, paragraph, or screen numbers, it is preferable to use the name of the author or editor in the text, rather than in a parenthetical reference. If the author's or editor's name is unavailable, use a short reference to the works's title.

> **Example**   Cannon College Economics Professor John Thompson argues a different view of the Chinese role in Indonesia's economy.

Some electronic documents include paragraph or screen numbers. When citing these documents, include the appropriate number, preceded by *par.* or *pars.* for paragraph(s), or *screen.*

> **Example**   The Chinese in Indonesia account for only 4% of the population but control 70% of the economy (Thompson, par. 6).

10. If the material you are citing contains a passage quoted from another source, indicate the use of the quotation in the parentheses.

> **Example**   According to George Orwell, "Good writing is like a window-pane" (qtd. in Murray 142).

11. If the work you are citing is a nonprint source with no reference markers, such as an interview, lecture, television show, film, or performance, include in the text the name of the person or the title (i.e., <u>60 Minutes</u>) that begins the corresponding entry in the Works Cited list.

> **Example**   In a March 5, 2003, telephone interview, ZipDrive president Charles Byrd denied persistent rumors of an impending merger.

Compiling a Works Cited List: MLA Style

If you are using the MLA format, at the end of your essay you should include a *Works Cited* page—a formal listing of the sources you used in your essay. (If you wish to show all the sources you consulted, but did not cite, add a *Works Consulted* page.) Arrange the entries alphabetically by the authors' last name; if no name is given, arrange your sources by the first important word of the title. Double-space each entry, and double-space after each one. If an entry takes more than one line, indent the subsequent lines one-half inch (or five spaces). Current MLA guidelines indicate one space following punctuation marks. (Some instructors still prefer two spaces, however, so you might check with your teacher on this issue.) See the sample entries that follow.

Sample Entries: MLA Style

Here are some sample entries to help you prepare a Works Cited page according to the MLA guidelines. Please note that MLA style recommends shortened forms of publishers' names: Holt for Holt, Rinehart & Winston; Harcourt for Harcourt Brace College Publishers; UP for University Press; and so forth. Also, omit business descriptions, such as Inc., Co., Press, or House.

Remember, too, when you type your paper, the titles of books and journals should be underlined even though you may see them printed in books or magazines in italics. The titles of articles, essays, and chapters should be enclosed in quotation marks. All important words in titles are capitalized.

Books

- Book with one author

  Keillor, Garrison. <u>WLT: A Radio Romance</u>. New York: Viking, 1991.

- Two books by the same author

  List books alphabetically by title. After the first entry, use three hyphens in place of the author's name.

  Keillor, Garrison. <u>Leaving Home</u>. New York: Viking, 1987.

  ---. <u>WLT: A Radio Romance</u>. New York: Viking, 1991.

- Book with two or three authors

  Pizzo, Stephen, and Paul Muolo. <u>Profiting from the Bank and Savings and Loan Crisis</u>. New York: Harper, 1993.

- Book with more than three authors

  You may use *et al.* for the other names or you may give all names in full in the order they appear on the book's title page.

  Guerin, Wilfred L., et al. <u>A Handbook of Critical Approaches to Literature</u>. New York: Harper, 1979.

- Book with author and editor

   Chaucer, Geoffrey. <u>The Tales of Canterbury</u>. Ed. Robert Pratt. Boston: Houghton, 1974.

- Book with corporate authorship

   National Fire Safety Council. <u>Stopping Arson before It Starts</u>. Washington: Edmondson, 1992.

- Book with an editor

   Knappman, Edward W., ed. <u>Great American Trials: From Salem Witchcraft to Rodney King</u>. Detroit: Visible Ink, 1994.

- Selection or chapter from an anthology or a collection with an editor

   Chopin, Kate. "La Belle Zoraide." <u>Classic American Women Writers</u>. Ed. Cynthia Griffin Wolff. New York: Harper, 1980. 250-73.

- One volume of a multivolume work

   Delaney, John J., ed. <u>Encyclopedia of Saints</u>. Vol. 4. New York: Doubleday, 1998.

- Work in more than one volume

   If the volumes were published over a period of years, give the inclusive dates at the end of the citation.

   Piepkorn, Arthur C. <u>Profiles in Belief: The Religious Bodies of the United States and Canada</u>. 2 vols. New York: Harper, 1976-78.

- Work in a series

   Berg, Barbara L. <u>The Remembered Gate: Origins of American Feminism</u>. Urban Life in Amer. Ser. 3. New York: Oxford UP, 1978.

- Translation

   Radzinsky, Edvard. <u>The Last Czar: The Life and Death of Nicholas II</u>. Trans. Marian Schwartz. New York: Doubleday, 1992.

- Reprint

   Note that this citation presents two dates: the date of original publication (1873) and the date of the reprinted work (1978).

   Thaxter, Celia. <u>Among the Isles of Shoals</u>. 1873. Ed. Leslie Dunn. Hampton, NH: Heritage, 1978.

- An introduction, preface, foreword, or afterword

Begin the citation with the name of the writer of the section you are citing; then identify the section but do not underline or use quotation marks around the word. Next, give the name of the book and the name of its author, preceded by the word "By" as shown below.

Soloman, Barbara H. Introduction. <u>Herland</u>. By Charlotte Perkins Gilman. New
    York: Penguin, 1992. xi–xxxi.

Periodicals (Magazines, Journals, Newspapers)

If an article is not printed on consecutive pages, use the first page number and a plus sign.

- Signed article in a monthly magazine

  Kaminer, Wendy. "Feminism's Identity Crisis." <u>Atlantic</u> Oct. 1993: 51-68.

- Unsigned article in a weekly magazine

  "The Wedding." <u>New Yorker</u> 11 Sept. 1989: 34-35.

- Signed article in a journal

  Lockwood, Thomas. "Divided Attention in <u>Persuasion</u>." <u>Nineteenth-Century
      Fiction</u> 33 (1978): 309-23.

- A review

  Spudis, Paul. Rev. of <u>To a Rocky Moon: A Geologist's History of Lunar Exploration</u>,
      by Don E. Wilhelms. <u>Natural History</u> Jan. 1994: 66-69.

- Signed article in newspaper

  Friedman, Thomas. "World Answer to Jobs: Schooling." <u>Denver Post</u>
      16 Mar. 1994: B9+.

- Unsigned article in newspaper

  "Blackhawks Shut Down Gretsky, Kings, 4–0." <u>Washington Post</u> 11 Mar. 1994: C4.

- Unsigned editorial in newspaper

  If the newspaper's city of publication is not clear from the title, put the location in brackets following the paper's name, as shown in the entry below.

  "Give Life after Death." Editorial. <u>Coloradoan</u> [Ft. Collins, CO] 23 Dec. 1995: A4.

- A letter to the newspaper

  Byrd, Charles. Letter. <u>Denver Post</u> 10 May 2004: A10.

Encyclopedias, Pamphlets, Dissertations

Use full publication information for reference works, such as encyclopedias and dictionaries, unless they are familiar and often revised. Delete volume and page numbers if the information is in alphabetical order.

- Signed article in an encyclopedia (full reference)

  Collins, Dean R. "Light Amplifier." McGraw-Hill Encyclopedia of Science and

  Technology. Ed. Justin Thyme. 3 vols. Boston: McGraw, 1997.

- Unsigned article in a well-known encyclopedia

  "Sailfish." Encyclopedia Britannica. 18th ed. 1998.

- A pamphlet

  Young, Leslie. Baby Care Essentials for the New Mother. Austin: Hall, 2004.

- A government document

  United States. National Institute on Drug Abuse. Drug Abuse Prevention.

  Washington: GPO, 1980.

- Unpublished dissertations and theses

  Harmon, Gail A. "Poor Writing Skills at the College Level: A Program for

  Correction." Diss. U of Colorado, 2004.

Films, Television, Radio, Performances, Recordings

- A film

  Begin with the title (underlined) followed by the director, the distributor, and the year of release. You may also include other data, such as the star performers, writer, or producer.

  Schindler's List. Dir. Steven Spielberg. Perf. Liam Neeson and Ben Kingsley.

  Universal, 1993.

  If you are referring to the contribution of a particular individual, such as the director, writer, actor, or composer, begin with that person's name. Cite a videocassette, DVD, or laser disc as a film but also include the medium, its distributor, and its distribution date.

  Spielberg, Steven, dir. Schindler's List. Perf. Liam Neeson and Ben Kingsley.

  Universal, 1993. DVD. Universal. 2004.

- A television or radio show

  Innovation. WNET, Newark. 12 Oct. 1985.

  If your reference is to a particular episode or person associated with the show, cite that name first, before the show's name.

"General Stonewall Jackson." <u>Civil War Journal</u>. Arts and Entertainment Network.
10 June 1992.

Moyers, Bill, writ. and narr. <u>Bill Moyers' Journal</u>. PBS. WABC, Denver. 30 Sept. 1980.

- Performances (plays, concerts, ballets, operas)

<u>Julius Caesar</u>. By William Shakespeare. Dir. Andrew St. John. Perf. Patrick Stewart.
Booth Theater, New York. 13 Oct. 1982.

If you are referring to the contribution of a particular person associated with the performance, put that person's name first.

Shao, En, cond. <u>Wiegenlied</u>. By Franz Schubert. Perf. Clare Stollak. Colorado
Symphony Orch. Boettcher Concert Hall, Denver. 18 Mar. 1994.

- A recording

If your source is not a compact disc, include the type of medium.

Marsalis, Wynton. "Oh, But on the Third Day." Rec. 27–28 Oct. 1988. <u>The Majesty
of the Blues</u>. Audiocassette. Columbia, 1989.

Letters, Lectures, and Speeches

- An unpublished letter, archived

Steinbeck, John. Letter to Elizabeth R. Otis. 11 Nov. 1944. Steinbeck Collection.
Stanford U Lib., Stanford, CA.

- A letter received by the author

Hall, Katherine. Letter to the author. 10 May 2004.

- A lecture or speech

Give the speaker's name and the title of the talk first, before the sponsoring organization (or occasion) and location. If there is no title, substitute the appropriate label, such as "lecture" or "speech."

Dippity, Sarah N. "The Importance of Prewriting." CLAS Convention. President
Hotel, Colorado Springs. 15 Feb. 2004.

Interviews

- A published interview

(Cite the person interviewed first and the title of the interview, if any. Use the word "Interview" if the interview has no title. The interviewer's name may be added if known and relevant. Conclude with publication information.)

Mailer, Norman. "Dialogue with Mailer." With Andrew Gordon. <u>Berkeley Times</u>
15 Jan. 1969: A12.

- A personal interview

  Give the name of the person interviewed, the kind of interview, and the date.

  Adkins, Camille. Personal interview. 11 Jan. 2004.

  Payne, Linda. Telephone interview. 13 Apr. 2004.

Electronic Sources: MLA Style

The purpose of a citation for an electronic source is the same as that for printed matter: identification of the source and the best way to locate it. All citations basically name the author and the work and identify publication information. Citations for various types of electronic sources, however, must also include different kinds of additional information—such as network addresses—to help researchers locate the sources in the easiest way.

It's important to remember, too, that forms of electronic sources continue to change rapidly. As technology expands, new ways of documenting electronic sources must also be created. The problem is further complicated by the fact that some sources will not supply all the information you might like to include in your citation. In these cases, you simply have to do the best you can by citing what is available.

The guidelines and sample entries that follow are designed merely as an introduction to citing electronic sources according to MLA style. If you need additional help citing other kinds of electronic sources, consult the most up-to-the-minute documentation guide available, such as the current *MLA Handbook for Writers of Research Papers* or the MLA Web site.

Before looking at the sample citations given here, you should be familiar with the following information regarding dates, addresses, and reference markers in online sources.

Use of multiple dates. Because online sources may change or be revised, a citation may contain more than one date. Your citation may present, for example, the original date of a document if it appeared previously in print form, the date of its electronic publication, or the date of its "latest update." Your entry should also include a "date of access," indicating the day you found the particular source.

Use of network addresses. The *MLA Handbook* recommends inclusion of network addresses (URLs) in citations of online works. Enclose URLs in angle brackets, and, if you must divide an address at the end of a line, break it only after a slash mark. Do not use a hyphen at the break as this will distort the address. URLs are often long and easy to misread, so take extra time to ensure that you are copying them correctly.

Use of reference markers. Unfortunately, many online sources do not use markers such as page or paragraph numbers. If such information is available to you, include it in your citations by all means; if it does not exist, readers must fend for themselves when accessing your sources. (Some readers might locate particular information in a document by using the "Find" tool in their computer program, but this option is not always available or useful.)

Scholarly Projects or Information Databases

An entry for an entire online scholarly project or information database may include the following information, *if available*: title of the project or database, editor's name, electronic publication information (including version number, publication date or latest update, name and place of sponsoring organization), date of access, and network address.

American Memory Project. 15 Nov. 2000. Lib. of Congress, Washington. 10 Jan. 2004

  <http://rs6.loc.gov/amhome.html>.

Granger's World of Poetry. 1999. Columbia UP. 10 Dec. 2003 <http://www.grangers.org>.

Documents within a Library or Subscription Database

To cite a source that you have found through one of your library's databases, begin with the author's name, if given. Follow the author's name with the name of the document, its publication information, the name of the database (underlined), the name of the subscription service, the name of the library you used (with its city, state abbreviation, or both if useful), and the date of access. If possible, conclude with the URL of the document; however, if the URL is impractically long, you may use the URL of the site's search page, as shown below. If no service URL is available, you may simply end with the date of access.

Smith, Lucinda. "Was She Anastasia or a World-Class Imposter?" Denver Post 18 July

  1993: 5D. ProQuest News & Magazines. ProQuest. Fort Collins Public Lib., Fort

  Collins, CO. 28 Feb. 2004 <http://0-proquest.umi.com.dalva.fcgov.com/>.

If you are using a source from a personal subscription service (e.g., America Online) that allows you to search by keyword, end the citation by writing "Keyword:" followed by the word itself.

"Pneumonia." Compton's Encyclopedia Online. Vers. 3.0. 2003. America Online. 2

  May 2004. Keyword: Compton's.

Articles in Online Periodicals (Magazines, Journals, Newspapers)

In citing online periodicals, begin with the author's name; if no author is given, begin with the title of the article. Continue with the name of the periodical (underlined), volume and issue number (if given), date of publication, the number range or total number of pages or paragraphs (if available), date of access, and network address.

- Signed article in a magazine

Goodman, David. "Forced Labor." Mother Jones Interactive Jan.-Feb. 2001. 2 Jan.

  2004 <http://www.motherjones.com/mother_jones/JFOL/labor.html>.

- Unsigned article in a magazine

"School Violence." U.S. News Online 6 July 2000. 21 Nov. 2003 <http://

  www.usnews.com/usnews/news/ctshoot.htm>.

- Article in a journal

Cummings, Robert. "Liberty and History in Jonson's 'Invitation to Supper.'" Studies

  in English Literature 40.1 (2000). 29 Dec. 2003 <http://muse.jhu.edu/

  journals/studies_in_english_literature/vo40/40.1/cummings.html>.

- Article in a newspaper or on a newswire

Kitner, John. "Widespread Opposition to Mideast Plan on Both Sides." <u>New York Times on the Web</u> 31 Dec. 2000. 1 Jan. 2004 <http://www.nytimes.com/ 2000/12/31/world/31MIDE.html/>.

- An editorial

"Success at Last." Editorial. <u>Front Range Times: Electronic Edition</u> 18 Jan. 2001. 12 Feb. 2004 <http://www.frtimes.com/ed/2001/01/18/p04.html>.

- A review

Ebert, Roger. Rev. of <u>What Women Want</u>, dir. Nancy Meyers. <u>Chicago Sun-Times Online</u> 15 Dec. 2000. 31 Dec. 2003 <http://www.suntimes.com/output/ ebert1/want15f.html>.

Personal or Professional Web Sites

In citing Web sites, begin with the name of the person who created the site, if appropriate. If no name is given, begin with the title of the site (underlined) or a description, such as "home page" (but do not underline or enclose a description in quotation marks). Continue with date of publication, or latest update, if given; the name of any organization associated with the site; date of access; and the network address.

Czepiel, Brad. Home page. 11 Mar. 2003. 22 Apr. 2004 <http:// www.chass.ucolorado.co:7070/~BC/>.

<u>Department of English Home Page</u>. May 1999. Colorado State U. 9 Jan. 2004 <http://colostate.edu/depts/English/english_ie4.htm>.

Note that in the first example, the phrase "home page" is used as a description of a personal Web site and is therefore *not* underlined; in the second example, "Home Page" is part of the site's title and *is* underlined.

To cite a home page for an academic course, begin the entry with the instructor's name, followed by the name of the course (do not underline or place in quotation marks). Continue with a description such as "Course home page" (again, do not underline or place in quotation marks), the dates of the course, the names of the department and the institution, the date of access, and the network address.

Wheeler, Jane. Advanced Expository Writing. Course home page. Jan.–May 2004. Dept. of English, Colorado State U. 10 Apr. 2004 <http://writing.colostate.edu./ JWheeler/ENG301A/002/Index.htm>.

Online Books

The texts of some books are now available online. Begin the citation with the author's name, the book's name, and any publication information given in the source (city of publication, publisher, date). Then list the title of the site (underlined), the name of the editor (if given), and the electronic publication information. Conclude with the date of access and the network address of the book itself, if possible.

> Baum, Frank L. <u>Glinda of Oz</u>. 1920. <u>Project Gutenberg</u>. Ed. Frances Stewart. June
> 1997. 6 May 2004 <ftp://ftp.archive.org/pub/etex/etex97/14woz10h.htm>.

Nonperiodical Publications on CD-ROM, Diskette, or Magnetic Tape

Nonperiodical electronic citations are similar to those for a print book, but also include the medium of publication (CD-ROM, diskette, magnetic tape). If you are citing a specific entry, article, essay, poem, or short story, enclose the title in quotation marks.

> "Acupuncture." <u>The Oxford English Dictionary</u>. 2nd ed. CD-ROM. Oxford UP, 1992.

E-Mail Communications

Begin with the name of the writer of the message, followed by the title taken from the subject line (if given), type of communication and its recipient, and date of the message.

> Clinton, Hillary. "Election News." E-mail to Jean Wyrick. 31 Oct. 2003.

APA Style

The American Psychological Association (APA) recommends a documentation style for research papers in the social sciences.* Your instructors in psychology and sociology classes, for example, may prefer that you use the APA form when you write essays for them.

The APA style is similar to the MLA style in that it calls for parenthetical documentation within the essay itself, although the information cited in the parentheses differs slightly from that presented according to the MLA format. For example, you will note that in the APA style the date of publication follows the author's last name and precedes the page number in the parentheses. Instead of a Works Cited page, the APA style uses a References page at the end of the essay to list those sources cited in the text. A Bibliography page lists all works that were consulted. Another important difference concerns capitalization of book and article titles in the reference list: in the MLA style, all important words are capitalized, but in the APA style, only proper names, the first word of titles, and the first word appearing after a colon are capitalized.

APA Citations in Your Essay

Here are some guidelines for using the APA parenthetical form within your paper:

1. APA style typically calls for an "author-publication year" method of citation, with the name and date inserted in the text at an appropriate place in the reference.

   Examples   A recent study (Jones, 2004) found no discernible differences in the
   absentee rate of men and women students on the main campus.

---

* If you wish a more detailed description of the APA style, you might order a copy of the *Publication Manual of the American Psychological Association*, 5th ed. (Washington, DC: American Psychological Association, 2001). The most up-to-date documentation forms may be found on the APA Web site <http://www.apa.style.org>.

Jones (2004) contrasted the absentee rates of men and women students on the main campus but found no discernible differences.

2. When you are quoting directly, place the author's name, the publication year, and the page number in parentheses following the quoted material. Note that in APA style, you place commas between the items in the parentheses, and you do include the "p." abbreviation for "page" (these are omitted in MLA style).

Example   One crucial step in developing an anti-social personality may, in fact, be "the experience of being caught in some act and consequently being publicly labeled as a deviant" (Becker, 1983, p. 31).

3. If you use a print source by one author and give credit to that author by name within your paper, you need give only the date and the page number in parentheses. Note that the publication date follows directly after the name of the author.

Example   According to Green (1994), gang members from upper-class families are rarely convicted for their crimes and are "almost never labeled as delinquent" (p.101).

4. If you are citing a work with more than two authors, but fewer than six, list all names in the first reference; in subsequent references, use only the first author's last name and *et al.* (which means "and others"). For six or more authors, use only the last name of the first author followed by *et al.* for all citations, including the first. Note the use of "&" instead of "and" within parentheses.

Example   *First reference:* After divorce, men's standard of living generally rises some 75% whereas women's falls to approximately 35% of what it once was (Bird, Gordon, & Smith, 1992, p. 203).

Subsequent references: Almost half of all the poor households in America today are headed by single women, most of whom are supporting a number of children (Bird et al., 1992, p. 285).

5. If you cite a work that has a corporate author, cite the group responsible for producing the work.

Example   In contrast, the State Highway Research Commision (2004) argues, "The return to the sixty-five-mile-an-hour speed limit on some of our state's highways has resulted in an increase in traffic fatalities" (p. 3).

6. Private interviews, e-mail messages, and other personal communications should be referred to in your text but *not* in your reference list. Provide the initials and

last name of the communicator, the words "personal communication," and the date in your paper.

Example   A. E. Wheeler acknowledged that until the most recent DNA work, most historians rejected belief in the Romanov children's escape (personal communication, February 23, 2004).

Compiling a Reference List: APA Style

If you are using the APA style, at the end of your essay you should include a page labeled References—a formal listing of the sources you cited in your essay. Arrange the entries alphabetically by the authors' last names; use initials for the authors' first and middle names. If there are two or more works by one author, list them chronologically, beginning with the earliest publication date. If an author published two or more works in the same year, the first reference is designated *a*, the second *b*, and so on (Feinstein 1999a; Feinstein 1999b).

Remember that in APA style, you italicize books and journal titles, volume numbers, and their associated punctuation, but you do not put the names of articles in quotation marks. Although you do capitalize the major words in the titles of magazines, newspapers, and journals, you do not capitalize any words in the titles of books or articles except the first word in each title, the first word following a colon, and all proper names.

Sample Entries: APA Style

Books

- Book with one author

  Gould, S. J. (1985). *The flamingo's smile*. New York: W. W. Norton.

- Book with two or more authors

  Forst, M. L., & Blomquist, M. (1991). *Missing children: Rhetoric and reality*. New York: Lexington Books.

- Books by one author published in the same year

  Hall, S. L. (1980a). *Attention deficit disorder*. Denver: Bald Mountain Press.

  Hall, S. L. (1980b). *Taming your adolescent*. Detroit: Morrison Books.

- Book with an editor

  Banks, A. S. (Ed.). (1988). *Political handbook of the world*. Binghamton, NY: CSA Publications.

- Selection or chapter from collection with an editor

    Newcomb, T. M. (1958). Attitude development as a function of reference groups: The Bennington study. In E. Maccoby, T. M. Newcomb, & E. L. Hartley (Eds.), *Readings in social psychology* (pp. 10–12). New York: Holt, Rinehart and Winston.

- A book with a corporate author

    Mentoring Group. (1997). *The new mentors and protégés: How to succeed with the new mentoring partnerships*. Grass Valley, CA: Author.

Articles (In Print)

Note that when a volume number appears, it is italicized, as is all associated punctuation. Use *p.* or *pp.* with page numbers in newspapers but not in magazines or journals.

- An article in a magazine

    Langer, E. T. (1989, May). The mindset of health. *Psychology Today, 48*, 1138-1241.

- An article in a journal

    Nyden, P. W. (1985). Democratizing organizations: A case study of a union reform movement. *American Journal of Sociology, 90*, 1119-1203.

- An article in a newspaper

    Noble, K. B. (1986, September 1). For ex-Hormel workers, no forgive and forget. *The New York Times*, p. A5.

Electronic Sources: APA Style

The most current guidelines for electronic citations appear on the APA Web site at <http://www.apastyle.org/elecsource.html>. Note that unlike MLA style, APA does not put a period at the end of the URLs nor enclose them in angle brackets. Only break a URL at a slash mark or at a period.

Internet Article Based on a Print Source

Most articles currently retrieved from online publications in psychology and the behavioral sciences are duplicates of those in print. However, if you have viewed the article only in its electronic form, add "Electronic version" in brackets after the article's title.

    Merrill, A. (2004). Use of group activities in first-year seminars [Electronic version]. *Journal of Nursing Instruction, 2*, 31-33.

If you are citing an online article that does differ from the print version (e.g., different format, additional information), add the date you retrieved the document from the URL.

Merrill, A. (2004). Use of group activities in first-year seminars. *Journal of Nursing Instruction, 2,* 31-33. Retrieved April 10, 2004, from http://jni.org/articles.html

Article in an Internet-Only Journal

Keen, M. L. (2003, April 5). Yoga for migraine headache relief. *Prevention & Treatment, 2,* Article 0001a. Retrieved December 29, 2003, from http://journalsapa.org/prevention/volume2/pre00030001a.html

Article Retrieved from a Database

Hall, K. E., Lind, S., & Michael, A. (2004). Sibling rivalry in adolescents. *Journal of American Psychology, 22,* 121–124. Retrieved February 26, 2004, from PsycARTICLES database.

Footnote and Bibliography Form

Most research papers today use a parenthetical documentation style, as illustrated in the MLA and APA sections of this chapter. However, in the event you face a writing situation that calls for use of traditional footnotes and bibliography page, here is a brief description of that format. This section will also help you understand the citation system of older documents you may be reading, especially those using Latin abbreviations.

If you are writing a paper using this format, each idea you borrow and each quotation you include must be attributed to its author(s) in a footnote that appears at the bottom of the appropriate page.* Number your footnotes consecutively throughout the essay (do not start over with "1" on each new page), and place the number in the text to the right of and slightly above the end of the passage, whether it is a direct quotation, a paraphrase, or a summary. Place the corresponding number, indented (one-half inch or five spaces) and slightly raised, before the footnote at the bottom of the page. Single-space each entry, and double-space after each footnote if more than one appears on the same page. Once you have provided a first full reference, subsequent footnotes for that source may include only the author's last name and page number. (See examples on the next page.)

You may notice the use of Latin abbreviations in the notes of some documents, such as *ibid.* ("in the same place") and *op. cit.* ("in the work cited"). In such documents, *ibid.* follows a footnote as a substitute for the author's name, title, and publication information; there will be a new page number only if the reference differs from the one in the previous footnote. Writers use *op. cit.* with the author's name to substitute for the title in later references.

---

* Some documents use endnotes that appear in a list on a page immediately following the end of the essay, before the bibliography page.

Sources are listed by author in alphabetical order (or by title if no author exists) in the Bibliography at the end of the document.

First footnote reference	[5]Garrison Keillor, <u>Leaving Home</u> (New York: Viking, 1987) 23.
Next footnote	[6]Keillor 79.
Later reference	[12]Keillor 135.
Bibliographic entry	Keillor, Garrison. <u>Leaving Home</u>. New York: Viking, 1987.

■ Using Supplementary Notes

Sometimes when writers of research papers wish to give their readers additional information about their topic or about a particular piece of source material, they include *supplementary notes*. If you are using the MLA or APA format, these notes should be indicated by using a raised number in your text (The study seemed incomplete at the time of its publication.[2]); the explanations appear on a page called "Notes" (MLA) or "Footnotes" (APA) that immediately follows the end of your essay. If you are using traditional footnote form, simply include the supplementary notes in your list of footnotes at the bottom of the page or in the list of endnotes following your essay's conclusion.

Supplementary notes can offer a wide variety of additional information.

Examples

[1]For a different interpretation of this imagery, see Spiller 1021-1023.

[2]Simon and Brown have also contributed to this area of investigation. For a description of their results, see <u>Report on the Star Wars Project</u> 98-102.

[3]It is important to note here that Brown's study followed Smith's by at least six months.

[4]Later in his report Carducci himself contradicts his earlier evaluation by saying, "Our experiment was contaminated from the beginning" (319).

Use supplementary notes only when you think the additional information would be truly valuable to your readers. Obviously, information critical to your essay's points should go in the appropriate body paragraphs. (See page 404 for additional examples.)

■ Sample Student Paper Using MLA Style

Here is the result of Amy Lawrence's research into the latest forensic and historical discoveries concerning the 1918 Romanov assassination. As you read her essay, ask yourself how effectively she uses research material to explain and support her view of the controversy surrounding the assassination and possible escape. Do you find her essay informative? Interesting? Convincing? Point out major strengths and weaknesses that you see. Does her method of structuring her essay—the step-by-step revelation of the new "clues"—add to her argument?

Remember that the paragraphs in Amy's essay have been numbered for easy reference during class discussion. Do *not* number the paragraphs in your own essay.

The Romanovs: Olga, Marie, Czar Nicholas II, Czarina Alexandra, Anastasia, Alexei, and Tatiana

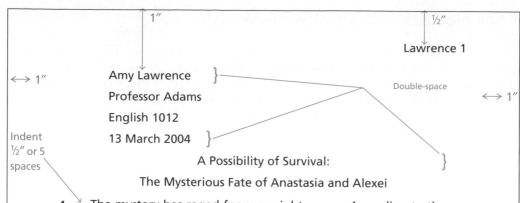

1"

½"

Lawrence 1

← 1" →

Amy Lawrence   }

Professor Adams

English 1012

Indent
½" or 5
spaces

13 March 2004   }

Double-space

← 1" →

A Possibility of Survival:

}

The Mysterious Fate of Anastasia and Alexei

1   The mystery has raged for over eighty years. According to the

history books, in 1918 Bolshevik revolutionaries brutally executed all

Introduction:
History of the
controversy
and the
research
questions

seven members of the Russian royal family, the Romanovs.

Immediately following the murders, however, rumors appeared

claiming that one, or perhaps two, of the Romanov children had

escaped the assassination. Is there any evidence to support even the

possibility that seventeen-year-old Anastasia and/or thirteen-year-old

Alexei were somehow secreted away from the murder scene? Or is

this merely a romantic story that has been repeated generation after

generation?

2   Over the years, many people have come forth to claim their

identities as either Anastasia or Alexei. Movies, plays, and even a ballet

have repeatedly captured the public's fascination with this story that

just won't die.[1] Until recently, many dismissed the story entirely as

pure fiction. However, political changes in the Soviet Union during the

1990s produced a government that is more open to research into the

haunting Romanov mystery. Today, historical information and

improved forensic research have provided exciting evidence that points

to a new conclusion based on facts, not rumors. It is indeed possible

Thesis

that Anastasia and Alexei survived the execution designed to end the

Romanov dynasty forever.

3   The first break in solving the mystery came in 1989 when the

↑ 1"

Lawrence 2

Russian government released important information about the
Romanovs' mass grave. Although the rumors had always insisted that
discovery of the secret grave would confirm that two Romanovs had
escaped, the location of the grave had never been revealed. In 1976 a
Soviet writer claimed that he had uncovered the common grave in
woods near the murder site, but its location was kept secret by the
Communist government (Kurth 100). The 1989 revelation of this
grave site was important to Romanov scholars because it did support
the often-retold escape stories: although <u>eleven</u> people were reported
executed (seven Romanov family members and four attendants), only
<u>nine</u> bodies were found in the grave (Massie 43). But was this really
the Romanov grave?

Release of evidence: The grave site

4   The next important historical information came in 1992 from
Edvard Radzinsky, a Russian playwright whose research on the
Romanovs could now be published. Radzinsky had spent two decades
studying the Central State Archives in Moscow, discovering the
unread diaries of the murdered Czar Nicholas II and Czarina
Alexandra and, even more important, the previously secret
"Yurovsky note." Yakov Yurovsky was the leader of the execution
squad, and his statement contained not only his description of the
horrible night but also testimony from other guards at the scene
(Radzinsky 373). The "Yurovsky note" clearly emphasized the chaos of
the execution and contributed to the possible explanation
surrounding the persistent rumors of two survivors.

More historical information uncovered: The "Yurovsky note"

5   According to Yurovsky, in the early hours of July 17, 1918, the
Romanov family--the Czar, the Czarina, four daughters, and son--were
taken with their personal physician and three servants into the
cellar in the house where they had been held prisoners by the

revolutionaries.² During the executions, the room filled with smoke and noise, and the bullets seemed to be oddly ricocheting, "jumping around the room like hail" (qtd. in Radzinsky 389). Although many bullets were fired at close range, Yurovsky mentions that the deaths of all five children were strangely hard to accomplish. Finally, as the guards hurriedly prepared to load the bodies onto a waiting truck, one of the guards heard a daughter cry out and then it was discovered that, amazingly, all the daughters were still alive (391). The daughters were then supposedly murdered by a drunken guard with a bayonet, who again experienced difficulty: "the point would not go through [the] corset" (qtd. in Radzinsky 391).

6   What the guards did NOT know until much later (at the grave site) was that at least three of the daughters, and possibly all the children, were wearing "corsets made of a solid mass of diamonds" (Radzinsky 373). The hidden Romanov jewels had acted like bullet-proof vests and were the reason the bullets and bayonet were deflected (373). Radzinsky argues that the chaos of the dark night, the drunken state of nervous, hurried guards, and the protective corsets cast serious doubt on the success of all the murder attempts (392).

7   The trip to the grave site was not smooth either. The truck broke down twice, and it was hard to move the bodies from the truck through the woods to the actual grave site. Yurovsky wrote that to lighten the load two bodies were cremated, supposedly the Czarina and her son, but he also claims that by mistake the family maid was confused with Czarina Alexandra (Radzinsky 410). Although the cremation story would account for the two bodies missing in the common grave, no remains or signs of a cremation site have ever been found. Consequently, many

Lawrence 4

Romanov researchers have another explanation. They argue that the
two youngest Romanovs, wounded but still alive thanks to their
protective corsets of jewels, were secretly removed from the truck
during a breakdown by guards who regretted their part in the killing
of the Romanov children (Smith). After all, why stop to burn only two
bodies? Why just two and not all? Wouldn't such a cremation have
taken valuable time and attracted attention? Why choose the boy and
not Nicholas, the hated Czar? Could Yurovsky have been covering up
the fact that by the time they reached the grave site two bodies were
missing--the boy and a female (Radzinsky 416)?

8   Although the newly recovered historical evidence added important   New forensic
pieces, it did not solve the puzzle. However, forensic research, using   research:
techniques not available until 1993, began to shed light on the   1. DNA
                                                                                 analysis
decades-old controversy. An international team of geneticists
conducted DNA analysis on the nine recovered skeletons. Through
mitochondrial-DNA sequencing, a process that analyzes DNA strains,
and comparison to DNA samples donated by living relatives of the
Romanovs, the team concluded in July 1993 that the skeletons were
indeed the remains of five members of the Romanov family and
four members of their household staff (Dricks). Yurovsky's story about
the cremation of the maid was therefore not true--two <u>Romanovs</u>
were missing!

9   Taking the next step, scientists used computer modeling to   2. Computer
superimpose facial photographs onto the skulls to determine structural   modeling
matches that would tell which family members the skeletons actually
were. The computer technology and dental work positively identified
the Czar and Czarina as two of the bodies. Then more news: all of the

remaining Romanov skeletons were of young females (Elliott 61).
Alexei, the heir to the throne, was one of the missing--just as the
rumors have always claimed.

3. Skeletal
measurements

10   To discover if the missing daughter was in fact Anastasia, the
scientists compared the size and age of the girls to the skeletons.
More controversy erupted. Although some Russian scientists argued
that the missing skeleton was that of daughter Marie, Dr. William
Maples, head of the American forensics team, strongly disagreed.
According to Dr. Maples, all the skeletons were too tall and too
developed to be Anastasia: "The bones we have show completed
growth, which indicates more mature individuals" (qtd. in Toufexis
65). Dr. Peter Gill, head of the British Forensic Science Service that
also studied the bones, agreed (O'Sullivan 6). According to these
respected scientists, Anastasia was definitely not in the grave.

More tests lead
to official
announcement

11   Six more years of sophisticated scientific experiments followed
these initial studies; DNA tests were replicated and results confirmed
(Glausiusz). Finally, in February 1998, a special federal commission
chaired by First Deputy Prime Minister Boris Nemtsov officially
announced its findings to Russian President Boris Yeltsin and the
world: the bones were, beyond a shadow of scientific doubt, those of
the Romanovs--but the bodies of Alexei and one sister (Anastasia?)
remained unaccounted for (Varoli).[3]

12   Throughout the years, stories speculating on the Romanov
assassination have always focused on the survival of the beautiful
Anastasia and her sickly brother, Alexei, often describing a devoted
guard smuggling them out through dark woods or secret passages.
Doubters have always said that the stories were folktales not worth
serious investigation. American and British forensic research, however,

Lawrence 6

argues this much: the real fate of Anastasia and Alexei is still unknown.
Therefore, their survival of the execution is still a possibility. Finally,
after the decades of rumors, there is a scientific basis for continuing the
search for the missing Romanovs. Someday, the mystery of their fate
will be solved and the controversy will rest in peace.

Conclusion:
The search
should
continue

Notes

[1] The most well-known story was told by Anna Anderson, a woman found in Berlin in 1920, who convinced many people throughout the world that she was indeed Anastasia. In 1956 her story was made into a popular movie starring Ingrid Bergman (Smith). The most recent treatment is the 1997 animated Fox film <u>Anastasia,</u> in which the young girl is saved by a servant boy, loses her memory, but is ultimately restored to her true identity (Rhodes).

[2] The Russian revolutionaries wanted to be rid of Czar Nicholas II and the entire Romanov family, which had ruled Russia since 1613. The Bolsheviks had held the family captive, charging Nicholas II with responsibility for Russia's poverty and social problems during World War I ("Romanov").

[3] The bones were officially buried on July 17, 1998, in the Peter and Paul Cathedral in St. Petersburg, resting place of all the Romanov czars since Peter the Great. The date marked the eightieth anniversary of the Romanov execution (Caryl).

Double-space

Lawrence 8

1″   ½″

Works Cited

Indent
½″ or 5
spaces →

Caryl, Christian. "Russia Buries the Czar but Not Its Squabbles." U.S.
      News Online 27 June 1998. 3 Mar. 2004 <http://
      www.usnews.com/usnews/issue/980727/27czar.htm>.

Dricks, Victor. "Part of Royal Murder Mystery May Be Solved—in
      Scottsdale." Phoenix Gazette 1 Oct. 1993: A1. ProQuest News &
      Magazines. ProQuest. Morgan Lib., Fort Collins, CO. 28 Feb. 2004
      <http://www.umi.com/proquest/>.

Elliott, Dorinda. "The Legacy of the Last Czar." Newsweek 21 Sept.
      1992: 60-1.

Glausiusz, Josie. "Royal D-loops." Discover 15.1 (1994): 90. InfoTrac
      College Edition. InfoTrac. 15 Feb. 2004 <http://
      infotrac-college.com>.

Kurth, Peter. "The Mystery of the Romanov Bones." Vanity Fair Jan.
      1993: 96+. Academic Search Premier. EBSCO. Morgan Lib., Fort
      Collins, CO. 28 Feb. 2004 <http://www.epnet.com>.

Massie, Robert K. The Romanovs: The Final Chapter. New York:
      Random, 1995.

O'Sullivan, Dermot. "The Romanov Riddle: DNA Tests Identify Bones
      of Czar and Family." Chemical and Engineering News 71 (1993):
      6-7.

Radzinsky, Edvard. The Last Czar: The Life and Death of Nicholas II.
      Trans. Marian Schwartz. New York: Doubleday, 1992.

Rhodes, Steve. Rev. of Anastasia, dir. Don Bluth. All-Reviews.Com 1997.
      28 Feb. 2004 <http://www.allreviews.com/videos/anastasia.htm>.

"Romanov." Encarta Online Encyclopedia. 2004. Microsoft. 16 Feb.
      2004 <http://encarta.msn.com/encyclopedia/Romanov.html>.

← 1″   ← 1″

↑ 1″

Smith, Lucinda. "Was She Anastasia or a World-Class Imposter?"
Denver Post 18 July 1993: 5D. ProQuest News & Magazines.
ProQuest. Fort Collins Public Lib., Fort Collins, CO. 28 Feb. 2004
<http://0-proquest.umi.com.dalva.fcgov.com/>.

Toufexis, Anastasia. "It's the Czar All Right, but Where's Anastasia?"
Time 14 Sept. 1992: 65.

Varoli, John. "Bury Tsar in St. Petersburg July 17." St. Petersburg
Times 9-16 Feb. 1998. 26 Feb. 2004 <http://www.spb.ru/
times/336-337/nemtsov.html>.

Chapter 15

Writing in Class: Exams and "Response" Essays

In-class writing assignments call for good writing skills, analytical reading skills, and confidence. When you write essays out of class, you have the luxury of time: you can mull over your ideas, talk about them with friends or classmates, prewrite, plan, revise, or even start over if you wish. Because essay assignments written in class must be planned and composed on the spot under the pressure of a time limit, they may induce anxiety in some students. (One composition-class student characterized his feelings of terror this way: "I felt like a slug caught in a sudden salt storm!")

Never fear! Hope reigns! By remembering what you already know about writing the short essay and by learning to analyze quickly the demands of the task you face, you can substantially reduce your anxiety level. With practice, you may discover that in-class writing assignments are not nearly as threatening as you once thought.

■ Steps to Writing Well under Pressure

   1. After you are assigned in-class writing, your first step is to **clarify for yourself the kind of task you face.** Sometimes your instructor will tell you about the assignment's format or general design in advance. Other times, however, figuring out the demands of the assignment on the spot and following the instructions carefully will be part of the task itself. Understanding the kind of exam or essay question you face

will help you prepare your response and boost your confidence. Here are some common formats for in-class assignments that call for your writing skills:

- **Short-answer exam questions**

    Your instructor might give an exam that asks you to write a well-developed paragraph or two to identify, define, or explain a term or idea. For example, a political science instructor might ask for paragraphs explaining the importance of certain treaties or laws; a literature teacher might ask for paragraphs that explain the significance of certain lines, characters, or symbols in a particular work; a science instructor might ask for extended definitions of important biological terms, and so on. The paragraph skills you learned in Chapter 3—focus, development, unity, and coherence—are all relevant here.

- **Essay exam questions**

    Frequently, questions appear on exams that call for more detailed discussion of specific material studied in a course. An essay question on a history exam might ask you to "Explain the major causes of the Civil War." Or in biology you might be asked to "Trace a drop of blood on its circulatory journey from the human heart throughout the body." You would be expected to shape your answer into a multi-paragraphed essay developed clearly in an easy-to-follow organizational pattern.

- **"Prompted" essays**

    Perhaps the most common in-class assignment in composition classes asks students to respond thoughtfully to some *prompt*—that is, students are asked to give their own opinion about a specific topic presented in a written passage or question, such as "Do you think teenage consumers are too influenced by television?" Other times, students will be asked to read a quotation or proverb ("All that glitters is not gold") and then respond in a personal essay. Other prompts include a statement of a current controversy (students should/should not be assessed a special fee for athletics on this campus) or the description of a hypothetical problem (the developer of a discount superstore has applied for a building permit on the edge of a wildlife preserve). Each student is responsible for explaining and supporting his or her position on the topic presented by the prompt.

- **Summary-and-response essays**

    Some in-class essays ask students to do more than voice their opinions in response to a short prompt. One common assignment is known as the *summary-and-response* essay or the *summary-reaction* essay. Students first read an essay by a professional writer (the reading may be done either in or out of class, depending on the instructor's preference). Once in class, students write an essay that begins with a clear summary of the essay they have just read (an activity that demonstrates analytical reading abilities), and then they present a reasoned argument that agrees or disagrees with the professional essay's ideas. Summary-and-response essays are often used as entrance or exit exams for composition classes at many schools throughout the country because they allow students to display both reading and writing skills. Because the summary-and-response essay is so frequently assigned today, additional discussion, illustrated by a student paper, is provided on pages 414–419 of this chapter.

There are numerous kinds and combinations of essay exams and in-class writing assignments. You can best prepare yourself mentally if you know in advance the purpose and format of the writing task you will face. If possible, ask your instructor to clarify the nature of your assignment before you come to class to write. (Also, some teachers allow students to bring dictionaries, outlines, or notes to class, but others don't. Consult your instructor.)

2. Arrive prepared. Before class, determine what items you need to take to respond to your writing assignment. For example, do you need loose paper or an exam book or will paper be provided? (If you are writing on your own notebook paper, always bring a paper clip or, better, one of those mini-staplers to fasten your pages together.) Were you asked to bring a copy of a reading or essay questions that were handed out in advance? Are dictionaries permitted? Note cards? The two essential items for every in-class assignment, regardless of type, are a watch, to help you gauge your writing time, and extra pens, to rescue you when yours inevitably runs dry. Having adequate supplies on hand keeps you from rustling around to borrow from your neighbors, which not only costs you valuable minutes but also disturbs the other writers around you. In addition, speaking to your classmates, especially during an examination, may be erroneously perceived as scholastic dishonesty. To avoid all such problems, bring the right tools to class.

Perhaps this is also a good place to say a little more about classroom atmosphere. Students often complain about their classmates' annoying behaviors during in-class writing assignments or examinations. Repeated pen-clicking, gum snapping, or chair kicking can make life miserable for other writers in the room. Empty pop cans noisily clanking down aisles, musical cell phones, beeping watches, and even crinkling candy wrappers can distract and derail someone else's complex thought. Please be *courteous:* leave the snack bar at home, spit out that gum, and turn off electronic equipment.

One more piece of advice: many in-class writing situations are "closed door." That is, at the appointed time for the class or exam to begin, the door is closed and no one is permitted to enter late. Consequently, try to arrive at least five minutes early, in case your instructor's watch is faster than yours, but also to have the extra minutes to settle yourself mentally as well as physically. ("Closed door" may also mean that no one is permitted to leave and return to the room during the writing session, even for restroom trips, so think carefully about that extra cup of coffee or can of pop just before your class.)

3. Once you are in class ready to write, **read the entire assignment with great care.** First, underline *key words* that are important to the subject matter of your essay; then circle the *directional words* that give you clues to the method of development you might use to organize your response.

Example	Explain the effects of the Triangle Shirtwaist Factory fire on child-labor laws in America from 1912 to 1915.
Example	In *The Grapes of Wrath,* John Steinbeck criticizes the unfair treatment of farmworkers by California land owners. Illustrate this criticism with three examples from the novel.

To help you identify some of the frequently used directional words and understand the approaches they suggest, study the following chart.

Directional Word or Phrase	Suggested Method of Development
Illustrate . . . Provide examples of . . . Show a number of . . . Support with references to . . .	Example
Explain the steps . . . Explain the procedure . . . Outline the sequence of . . . Trace the events . . . Review the series of . . . Give the history of . . .	Process or Narration
Discuss the effects of . . . Show the consequences of . . . Give the reasons for . . . Explain why . . . Discuss the causes of . . . Show the influence of . . .	Causal Analysis
Compare the following . . .* Contrast the positions of . . .* Show the differences between . . . Discuss the advantages and disadvantages . . . Show the similarities among . . . Relate X to Y . . .	Comparison/Contrast
Describe the following . . . Re-create the scene . . . Discuss in detail . . . Explain the features of . . .	Description
Agree or disagree . . . Defend or attack . . . Offer proof . . . Present evidence . . . Criticize . . . Evaluate . . . State reasons for . . . Justify your answer . . . What if . . .	Argument
Discuss the types of . . . Show the kinds of . . . Analyze the parts of . . . Classify the following . . .	Classification/Division
Define . . . Explain the meaning of . . . Identify the following . . . Give the origins of the term . . .	Definition

* Remember that the directional word "compare" may indicate a discussion of both similarities and differences; the directional word "contrast" focuses only on the differences.

Note that essay questions may demand more than one pattern of development in your response:

(Explain the meaning) of the term "hospice" and (show the differences) between the Hospice Movement in Great Britain and that of the United States. [definition and contrast]

(Discuss) Weber's three (types) of authority, giving (examples) of societies that illustrate each type. [classification and example]

(Explain) President Truman's (reasons) for bombing Japan during World War II and then (defend or attack) Truman's decision. [causal analysis and argument]

Learning to quickly recognize key directional words will help you organize as you begin to focus your essay. Always read the assignment at least twice and ask your instructor for clarification if some part of the assignment seems confusing to you.

4. Once you have read and fully understood the purpose and direction of your assignment, **prepare to write.** The following advice may be helpful:

- Think positively: remind yourself that the task you face is not unknown to you. You are being asked to write—yes, quickly—the same kind of essay that you have been practicing in your composition class. You *CAN* do this!

- If you are writing an in-class essay, take the first few minutes to think and plan. Many times it's helpful to formulate a thesis in a direct rephrasing of the exam question or "prompt" you have been assigned. For example:

  Assignment: After reading "How to Make People Smaller Than They Are" by Norman Cousins, write an essay agreeing or disagreeing with Cousins's suggestions for improving higher education today.

  Thesis: In his essay "How to Make People Smaller Than They Are," author Norman Cousins convincingly argues for requiring additional liberal arts courses for all students in college today. His suggestions for improving higher education are uniformly excellent and should be implemented immediately.

  Assignment: Discuss Weber's three types of authority, giving examples to clarify your answer.

  Thesis: Weber's three types of authority are traditional authority, charismatic authority, and legal authority. The three types may be exemplified, respectively, by the 19th-century absolute monarchs of Europe, by a variety of religious groups, and by the constitutional government of the United States.

- After deciding on your thesis, jot down on scratch paper a brief plan or outline that sketches out the main points that will appear in the body of your essay. You might scribble a few key words to remind yourself of the supporting evidence or important details you will use. Don't get too bogged down in detailed outlining—just use enough words to help you stay on track.

- You might also budget your time now—thinking "by 2:30 I should be done with two points in my discussion." Although such figuring is approximate at best, having a general schedule in mind might keep you from drifting or spending too much time on the first parts of your essay. In most cases, you should assume you will not be able to write a rough draft of your essay and then have the time to massively reorganize as you recopy it.

5. As you **begin writing,** remember what you have learned about paragraphing, topic sentences, and supporting evidence. If you have been given multiple tasks, be sure that you are responding to all parts of the assignment. If the assignment asks you to present your own opinion, focus your answer accordingly. In timed-writing situations, you can't take on the world, but you can offer intelligent commentary on selected ideas. If you only have an hour or less to complete your essay, consider aiming for three well-developed points of discussion. You may be writing a rather conventional five-paragraph essay, but frequently such a clear pattern of organization works best when nervous writers are under pressure and time is short.

Two more suggestions:

- It may be a good idea to write on one side of your paper only, leaving wide margins on both sides; consider, too, leaving extra lines between paragraphs. If you discover that you have time after finishing your essay, you might wish to add additional information to your exam answer or perhaps another persuasive example to a body paragraph. Leaving plenty of blank spaces will allow you to insert information neatly, instead of jamming in handwriting too small for your instructor to decipher.

- If you are writing an essay (rather than a short answer), do try to conclude in a satisfactory way. Your conclusion may be brief, but even a few sentences are better than an abrupt midsentence halt when time runs out.

6. In the time remaining after writing the complete draft of your essay, **read what you have written.** Aim for sufficient, appropriate content and clear organization. Insert, delete, or make changes neatly. Once you are reasonably satisfied with the essay's content and flow, take a few minutes to proofread and edit. Although most instructors do not expect an in-class essay to be as polished as one written out of class, you are responsible for the best spelling, grammar, and punctuation you can muster under the circumstances. Take care to apply what you know to sentence problems, especially the run-ons, comma splices, and twisted predicates that tend to surface when writers are composing in a hurry. After all, information too deeply hidden in a contorted sentence is information that may not be counted in your favor.

7. Tips. Before you turn in your work, be sure your name is on every page of your essay or exam so your instructor will know whom to praise for a job well done. If appropriate, include other pertinent information, such as your class section number or your student number. Number and clip or staple the loose pages of your essay or exam (do *not* rely on folded corners to hold your pages together!).

Problems to Avoid

Misreading the assignment. Always read the directions and the assignment completely and carefully before you start prewriting. Mark key and directional words. Do you have multiple tasks? Consider numbering the tasks to avoid overlooking any parts. Important choices to make? Neatly put a line through the options you don't want. Grossly misreading your assignment may give you as much chance at success as a pig at a barbecue.

Incomplete essay. Don't begin writing an in-class essay without a plan, even if you are excited about the topic and want to dive right in. Having a plan and budgeting your time accordingly will avoid the common problem of not finishing, which, in the end, may cost you dearly. Don't allow yourself to ramble off on a tangent in one part of the assignment. Stay focused on your plan and complete the entire essay or exam. If you have left blank space as described previously, you can return to a part of the essay to add more information if time permits. Wear a watch and consult it regularly! Don't depend on a classmate or your instructor to advise you of the time remaining.

Composition amnesia. Writing essays under time pressure causes some students suddenly to forget everything they ever knew about essay organization. This memory loss often wreaks havoc on paragraphing skills, resulting in a half-dozen one- and two-sentence string-bean paragraphs without adequate development; at other times, it results in one long super-paragraph that stretches for pages before the eye like the Mohave Desert, no relief or rest stop in sight. Emphasize your good ideas by presenting them in a recognizable organizational structure, just as you would do in an out-of-class assignment.

Gorilla generalizations. Perhaps the biggest problem instructors find is the lack of adequate, specific evidence to explain or support shaggy, gorilla-sized generalities roaming aimlessly through students' essays. If, for example, you argue, "Team sports are good for kids because they build character," *why* do you believe this? What particular character traits do you mean? Can you offer a personal example or a hypothetical case to clarify and support your claim? Remember what you learned in Chapter 3 about using evidence—examples, personal experience, testimony—to illustrate or back up any general claims you are making. Your goal is to be as clear and persuasive as you can be—*show* what you know!

▪ PRACTICING WHAT YOU'VE LEARNED

Underline the key words and circle the directional words or phrases in the following assignments. What pattern(s) of development are suggested in each assignment?

1. Discuss three examples of flower imagery as they clarify the major themes of Toni Morrison's novel *The Bluest Eye*.

2. Trace the events that led to the Bay of Pigs invasion of Cuba.

3. Discuss Louis B. Mayer's major influences on the American film industry during the "Golden Age of Moviemaking."

4. Agree or disagree with the following statement: "The 1957 launching of the Russian satellite Sputnik caused important changes in the American educational system."

5. Consider the similarities and differences between the surrealistic techniques of the American painter Peter Blume and those of Spanish painter Salvador Dali. Illustrate your answer with references to important works of both artists.

■ ASSIGNMENT

Practice planning an in-class essay by selecting one of the quotations on pages 43–44 in Chapter 2 as a brief "prompt" for a personal opinion essay developed by any method(s) you find appropriate. Allow yourself only ten minutes to write a working thesis and a sketch outline for your essay. Would you then be ready to turn your plan into a clearly organized and well-developed in-class essay? Continue to practice responding to the prompts in Chapter 2 until you gain confidence in your ability to think, plan, and write under time pressure.

■ Writing the Summary-and-Response Essay

The "summary-and-response essay" is such a common assignment today that it merits additional discussion and illustration. As noted earlier in this chapter, this kind of assignment frequently asks students to read a professional article, summarize its thesis and main points, and write a response expressing agreement or disagreement with the article's ideas.

You may have had experience with some form of this assignment before now. Many college entrance examinations have adopted this kind of essay to evaluate both reading comprehension and writing skills. Many colleges also use this format as their composition placement exam, to direct students into the appropriate writing class. Still other schools employ this kind of essay as a final exam or exit test for their composition requirement. And although this format is often assigned as in-class writing, it certainly is not limited to this use. Many composition classes and other academic courses include this type of essay as an out-of-class paper.

Though the format of this assignment may vary slightly depending on its purpose and occasion, throughout your college and professional life you will almost certainly be asked on more than one occasion to read information, summarize it for others, and then present your reaction to its ideas. To help you prepare for this kind of thinking and writing activity, here are a few suggestions, divided into three sections for clarity:

Reading the Assignment and the Article

1. Read your assignment's directions carefully to discover exactly what you are being asked to do. For example, are you being asked to present a one-paragraph summary of a professional article* first and then write a personal response? Or are you being asked to respond to the professional article's major points one at a time? Perhaps you are being asked to critique the author's style as well as ideas. Because formats vary, be sure you understand your complete assignment—all its required parts—before you begin writing.

2. Before you can intelligently respond to any reading you need to thoroughly understand its ideas. To review suggestions for close reading, take the time now to review Chapter 8, "The Reading-Writing Connection," in this text. This chapter will help you identify and evaluate an article's thesis, main points, supporting evidence, and other rhetorical techniques.

3. If you are given an article to read out of class, study it carefully, annotating it as outlined in Chapter 8. If reading the article is part of the in-class activity, you may have only enough time to read it carefully once, underlining and annotating as you move through each paragraph. Minimally, you should mark the thesis and the main ideas of the body paragraphs. Underline or star important claims or supporting evidence. Are the claims logical and well supported, or does the author rely on generalizations or other faulty reasoning? Overall, do you agree or disagree with the article? Would you call it a weak or strong piece of writing? Why? (For help evaluating claims and supporting evidence, review the discussion of logical fallacies in Chapter 10, pages 282–285.)

Writing the Summary Section

If you are to begin with a brief summary of the article, follow the guidelines listed under "Writing a Summary" on pages 171–172 of Chapter 8. Remember that a good summary presents the author's name and full title of the article in the first sentence, which also frequently presents the article's thesis (In his article "Free Speech on Campus," author Clarence Page argues that . . .). The next sentences of your summary should present the article's main ideas, found in the article's body paragraphs. Unless you need to quote a word or phrase for clarity or emphasis, use your own words to present a concise version of the article. Normally, your summary will be an objective treatment of the article's ideas, so save your opinions for the "response" section.

Writing the Response Section

1. Before you begin writing the "response" part of your essay, look at the underlining and any marginal notes you made on the article. What was your general assessment of the article? Do you agree or disagree with the author? Perhaps you only agree with some points and disagree with others? Or perhaps you agree with the main ideas but think that this particular essay is a weak defense of those ideas? After looking over the article and your notes, decide on your overall reaction to this article. This assessment will become your thesis in the "response" portion of your essay.

2. Once you have a working thesis in mind, plan the rest of your essay. For example, if you disagree with the article, you might want to note two or three reasons you

---

* To avoid confusion in this discussion between the professional essay used as a "prompt" and the student's response essay, the word "article" will be used to refer to the professional reading.

reject the author's opinion; these reasons may become the basis for your own body paragraphs. Important: Be sure you have evidence of your own to support your positions. Responding with personal examples is perhaps the most common kind of support for essays written in class, but if you know facts, statistics, testimony, or other information that would support your position, you may certainly include them.

3. If you have begun your essay with a summary, start the next paragraph with a sentence that clearly indicates the "response" section is now beginning. Present a smooth transition to your thesis and consider using an "essay map" to indicate to your readers the points you will discuss.

Example   Although in his article "Test!" Paul Perez correctly identifies a growing drug problem in our public schools, his plan to drug-test all students involved in campus activities should be rejected. Such a test could not be implemented fairly and is an unreasonable invasion of students' privacy.

4. In each of your own body paragraphs make clear which of the author's claims or ideas you are refuting or supporting by using "tag lines" to remind the reader.

Example   Although Foxcroft argues that the proposed tuition increase will not discourage prospective students, she fails to understand the economic situation of most IBC applicants, who are sacrificing income to return to school. In a recent survey. . . .

5. Once you have signaled the point in question and stated your position, develop each body paragraph with enough specific supporting evidence to make your claim convincing. If you disagree with a point, you must show why and present your position logically (you may wish to review Chapter 10 on argument). If you agree with the article, beware a tendency to simply restate the positions with which you are in agreement ("I think Brower is right when she says housing is too expensive on campus. She is also right about the lack of housing choices . . ."). Find other examples, reasons, or information that lend support to the points that you and the author think are valid.

6. Many assignments call for a straightforward personal opinion or "agree-disagree" response. In other assignments, you may be given the option of criticizing or praising an author's logic, style, or even tone. You might, for example, show that a particular argument is ineffective because it is based on a mass of overstated generalities, or you might show why the author's sarcastic tone alienates the reader. On the other hand, an author might deserve credit for a particularly effective supporting example or a brilliantly clever turn of phrase that captures the essence of an idea. Always check your assignment to see if this sort of critique is welcome or even required in your response.

7. Don't forget to write a brief concluding paragraph. If appropriate, you might emphasize the value of the article in question, or call for action for or against its ideas, or project its effects into the future (other suggestions for conclusions appear in Chapter 4). However you end your essay, your conclusion should always be consistent with your overall assessment of the article and its ideas.

■ Sample Student Essay

The essay that follows was written by a student who was assigned the article "Our Youth Should Serve" by Steven Muller (pages 169–171 in Chapter 8) and then asked to write a one-paragraph summary and a response essay, expressing her opinion of the article's proposal. Although the student thought the article itself could have been stronger, she liked Muller's suggestion for a volunteer youth service. Her approval of his proposal became her essay's thesis, which she then developed through use of her own experience.

After you read Muller's article and the student's summary-and-response essay, what suggestions for revision might you offer her?

YOUTH SERVICE: AN IDEA WHOSE TIME HAS COME

1   In "Our Youth Should Serve," former university president Steven Muller proposes a national volunteer youth service. This program would perform some of our country's public service tasks and also help high school graduates who have to choose between low-paying jobs or starting college with no clear direction. Although the pay would be low, volunteers would benefit through job training and by earning federal grants for college. Muller also argues that youth service would motivate volunteers to become better students and perhaps help them find a career. The greatest benefit, according to Muller, would be the self-esteem volunteers would gain from earning these benefits themselves.   *Summary*

2   Although Muller's article might have been more persuasive with some specific examples supporting its claims, Muller's national volunteer youth service is still a good idea, especially for students who have no money for college and no work experience. I was one of those students, and because of the year I spent after high school graduation working in a boring, dead-end job, I believe the Youth Service should be started as soon as possible.   *Response begins*   *Thesis*

3   After I graduated from high school, I didn't go to college because I didn't have any money saved and I was tired of school. I decided to work for a while to save up, but I didn't have any training for

Response to
the benefit
of earning
grant money

anything so I took a minimum-wage sales job in a mall clothing store.
I had to look good for work, but since my wardrobe consisted of jeans
and T-shirts, I had to buy new clothes. With clothes and transportation
to work and other bills, I was barely breaking even. If I had been in
Muller's program, my pay would also have been low but at least I
would have been earning grant money for college at the same time.

Response
to the
benefits of
meaningful
work, skills

4   Muller also makes a good point about people needing to feel that
what they are doing is important or meaningful. My job at the store
wasn't meaningful or challenging; it was, in fact, repetitive and
boring. For example, a typical day during the summer months
consisted of cleaning out dressing rooms and hanging up two-piece
swim suits thrown all over the floor. It took forever to match up the
right size tops and bottoms and then hang them back up on these
crazy little double hangers so that everything was facing the right
way with all the straps untwisted. In the winter it was pants and
sweaters. Unlike Muller's volunteers who would be helping society
while getting some valuable training themselves, I wasn't contributing
to anything meaningful, and I sure wasn't learning any skills for a
better future.

5   It didn't take me long to figure out that I wanted more out of life
than a low-paying, boring, going-nowhere job. So I talked to a
counselor here at Logan [Community College] who helped me explore

Response
to career
benefits

some of my interests, and now I am enrolled in the pre-nursing
program. In Muller's program I might have discovered this career
earlier by volunteering at a hospital or nursing home, plus getting
some on-the-job experience. I would have tuition grant money
instead of going into major debt from student loans like I am now. I
might also have worked for someone who might even hire me later.

and increased
self-esteem

And I'm absolutely positive I would have felt more useful and had
better self-esteem than I did hanging up clothes for eight months!

> **6** Although this program wasn't there to help me, my sister is getting ready to graduate and she is in the same situation I was two years ago—no money, no skills, no solid future goals. If Muller's program existed today, I'd tell her to look into it. The benefits of college money, job training, and better self-esteem are just too good to pass up.

Conclusion emphasizes benefits to a future volunteer

■ PRACTICING WHAT YOU'VE LEARNED

1. After reading Steven Muller's article "Our Youth Should Serve" (pages 169–171), write your own summary-and-response essay, drawing on your own knowledge and experience to support or reject his proposed program. In your opinion, would this be a worthwhile, feasible program? Why or why not?

2. Write a response to "Our Youth Should Serve" that presents at least one paragraph critiquing Muller's reasoning, use of supporting evidence, or other methods of persuasion. How might Muller have improved the arguments for his proposed youth service? Did he overlook any major problems or disadvantages that you see? (In other words, if Muller asked you for help during a revision workshop, what major suggestion for change or addition would you offer to assist him in writing a stronger draft?)

■ ASSIGNMENT

Read and annotate the selection "So What's So Bad about Being So-So?" on pages 189–191 of this textbook and then write your own summary-and-response essay, agreeing or disagreeing (wholly or in part) with the writer's view of competition today. Remember to support your position with logical reasons, persuasive examples, or relevant facts. (If you prefer, you may select some other professional essay from this textbook or from another source, such as a newspaper or magazine, but be sure to obtain your instructor's approval of your selection in advance.)

Chapter 16

Writing about Literature

People read literature for many, many reasons, including amusement, comfort, escape, new ideas, exploration of values, intellectual challenge, and on and on. Similarly, people write about literature to accomplish a variety of purposes. Literary essays may inform readers about the ideas in a work, analyze its craft, or focus on the work's relationship to the time or culture in which it was written. Other essays might explore biographical, psychological, archetypal, or personal readings of a work.

Although approaches to literature are diverse and may be studied in depth in other English courses, writing essays about literature is worthwhile in the composition classroom as well. Writing about literature offers an opportunity to practice the important skills of close reading, critical thinking, and effective expression of ideas.

■ Using Literature in the Composition Classroom

Teachers of writing most often use literature in their courses in two ways: as "prompts" to inspire personal essay topics and as subjects of interpretative essays.

1. *Prompts:* You might be asked to read a poem or short story and then use some aspect of it—its ideas or characters, for example—as a springboard to discover an essay topic of your own. For instance, after reading John Updike's "A & P," a story about a rather naive young man who receives a real-world lesson, you might write about a coming-of-age experience you had. Or your teacher might assign Shirley Jackson's "The Lottery" and ask you to agree or disagree with the author's views on unexamined conformity to tradition.

2. *Literary Analysis:* Rather than responding to a piece of literature in a personal essay, you might be assigned a literary analysis, asking you to study a piece of literature and then offer your interpretation—that is, your insight into the work (or some important part of it). Your insight becomes your thesis; the body of your essay explains this reading, supported by textual evidence (material from the work) to help your reader understand your view and perhaps gain greater pleasure in, and appreciation of, the work itself.

Literary analysis assignments may be focused in different ways, as well. Some common examples include essays whose main purpose is to show:

- how the various parts or elements of a piece of literature work together to present the main ideas (for example, how the choices of narrator, stanza form, and figurative language in a poem effectively complement each other);

- how one element fits into the complex whole (for example, how setting contributes to a story);

- how two works or two elements may be profitably read together (two poems with similar ideas but different forms; two characters from one story);

- how one interpretation is more insightful than another reading;

- how a work's value has been overlooked or misunderstood.

There are as many possibilities for essay topics as there are readers!

Regardless of the exact assignment, you should feel confident about writing an essay of literary analysis. Working through Part Two of this text, you have already practiced many of the strategies required. For example, to present a particular reading of a poem, you may organize your discussion by *dividing* it into its major literary elements: point of view, setting, structure, language, and so on. Your essay may offer specific lines or images from the work as *examples* illustrating your reading. Working with more than one piece of literature or literary element calls for *comparison and contrast* techniques. And every paper—whether it is a personal response or literary analysis—uses the skills you learned in Part One of this text: a clear thesis, adequate development of ideas, coherent organization, and effective use of language.

■ Suggestions for Close Reading of Literature

Writing about literature begins with careful reading—and, yes, rereading. The steps suggested here are certainly not exhaustive; one can ask literally hundreds of questions about a complex piece of literature. Rather, these questions are intended to give you a start. Practicing close reading and annotation should help you generate ideas and lead you to additional questions of your own.

Our discussion in this chapter is limited to poems and short stories because composition courses frequently do not have the time to include novels and plays (or long narrative poems, for that matter). However, many of the suggestions for reading short stories and poems may be applied to the reading of longer fiction and drama.

Before you begin reading the suggestions that follow, let's dispel the myth about "hidden meanings." A work of literature is not a trick or puzzle box wherein the author has hidden a message for readers to discover if they can just uncover the right clues. Literary works are open to discussion and interpretation; that's part of their appeal. They contain ideas and images that the author thought important, and some ideas or elements the writer may not have consciously been aware of. You, as the reader, will have insights into a poem or story that your classmates don't. It's your job as the writer of your literary analysis to explain not only *WHAT* you see but also *WHY* and *HOW*, supporting your interpretation in ways that seem reasonable, persuasive, and satisfying to your readers.

■ Steps to Reading a Story

If possible, make your own copy of the story and read with pen in hand. Prepare to make notes, underline important lines, circle revealing words or images, and put stars, question marks, or your own symbols in the margins.

1. Before you begin the piece, read any *biographical information* that may accompany the story. Knowing information about the author and when the story was written or published may offer some insight. Also, note the *title*. Does it offer intriguing hints about the story's content?

2. Read through the story at least once to clearly acquaint yourself with its *plot*, the series of actions and events that make up the narrative. In other words, what happened and to whom? Is there a conflict of some sort? Is it resolved or is the story left open-ended?

3. Many times you'll see words in a story you don't know. Sometimes you can figure them out from their context, but if you find unknown words that might indeed have a critical bearing on your understanding of a character, for example, look these up now.

4. Jot a few notes describing your initial reactions to the story's main idea(s) or major *theme(s)*. (If it's helpful, think of the story in terms of its "about-ness." What do you as reader think this story is about? Loss of innocence? The bitterness of revenge? The power of sympathy? Tragic lack of communication? The wonder of first love?) In other words, what comments or observations does this story make about the human condition?

5. As you review the story, begin to think about its parts, always asking yourself "why?": Why did the author choose to do it this way? What is gained (or lost) by writing it this way? What does "X" contribute to my understanding of the story? You might begin noting *point of view*—that is, who is narrating this story? Is a character telling this story or is it told by an all-knowing (omniscient) narrator? A narrator who is partially omniscient, seeing into the thoughts of only some characters? What is gained through the story's choice of narration?

6. Is the story's *structure* in chronological order or does the writer shift time sequences through flashbacks or multiple points of view? Does the story contain foreshadowing, early indications in the plot that signal later developments? Again, think about the author's choices in terms of communicating the story's ideas.

7. Think about the *characters*, their personalities, beliefs, motivations. How do they interact? Do any of them change—refuse or fail to change? Look closely at their descriptions, thoughts, and dialogue. Sometimes names are revealing, too.

8. What is the relationship between the *setting* of the story and its action or characters? Remember that setting can include place, time of year, hour of day or night, weather or climate, terrain, culture, and so on. Settings can create mood and even function symbolically to reveal character or foreshadow a coming event.

9. Look closely at the *language* of the story, paying attention to revealing images, metaphors, and similes (for help identifying these, see pages 310–311). Note any use of *symbols*—persons, places, or things that bear a significant meaning beyond their usual meaning. (For example, in a particular story, a dreary rain might be associated with a loss of hope; a soaring bird might emphasize new possibilities.) Overall, would you characterize the story's *style* as realistic or something else? What is the *tone* of the story? Serious? Humorous? Does irony, the discrepancy between appearance and reality, play a part?

10. After you've looked at these and any other important elements of the reading, review your initial reactions. How would you now describe the main ideas or major themes of this story? How do the parts of the story work together to clarify those themes?

Remember to add your own questions to this list, ones that address your specific story in a meaningful way. (For help writing essays of literary analysis, turn to pages 437–439.)

■ Annotated Story

Using the preceding guidelines, a composition student annotated the story that follows. Some of the notes she made on imagery became the basis for her short essay, which appears on pages 428–430. Before you read the story, however, cover the marginal notes with a sheet of paper. Then read the story, making your own notes. Next, uncover the student's notes and reread the story. Compare your reactions to those of the student writer. What new or different insights did you have?

■ The Story of an Hour

Kate Chopin

Kate Chopin was a nineteenth-century American writer whose stories appeared in such magazines as *The Atlantic Monthly*, *Century*, and *The Saturday Evening Post*. She published two collections of short stories and two novels; one of her novels, *The Awakening* (1899), was considered so shocking in its story of a married woman who desired a life of her own that it was removed from some library shelves. "The Story of an Hour" was first published in 1894.

similar theme

1   Knowing that Mrs. Mallard was afflicted with a heart trouble, great care was taken to break to her as gently as possible the news of her husband's death.

foreshadowing

2   It was her sister Josephine who told her, in broken sentences, veiled hints that revealed in half concealing. Her husband's friend Richards was there, too, near her. It was he who had been in the newspaper office when intelligence of the railroad disaster was received, with Brently Mallard's name leading the list of "killed." He had only taken the time to assure himself of its truth by a second telegram, and had hastened to forestall any less careful, less tender friend in bearing the sad message.

3   She did not hear the story as many women have heard the same, with a paralyzed inability to accept its significance. She wept at once, with sudden, wild abandonment, in her sister's arms. When the storm of grief had spent itself she went away to her room alone. She would have no one follow her.

storm imagery

4   There stood, facing the open window, a comfortable, roomy armchair. Into this she sank, pressed down by a physical exhaustion that haunted her body and seemed to reach into her soul.

Setting: closed room but open window

5   She could see in the open square before her house the tops of trees that were all aquiver with the new spring life. The delicious breath of rain was in the air. In the street below a peddler was crying his wares. The notes of a distant song which some one was singing reached her faintly, and countless sparrows were twittering in the eaves.

—spring
—trees, air
—songs
—blue sky

6   There were patches of blue sky showing here and there through the clouds that had met and piled each above the other in the west facing her window.

7   She sat with her head thrown back upon the cushion of the chair quite motionless, except when a sob came up into her throat and shook her, as a child who has cried itself to sleep continues to sob in its dreams.

Mrs M.: repression and strength

8   She was young, with a fair, calm face, whose lines bespoke repression and even a certain strength. But now there was a dull stare in her eyes, whose gaze was fixed away off yonder on one of those patches of blue sky. It was not a glance of reflection, but rather indicated a suspension of intelligent thought.

3rd person narrator— readers know her feelings.

9   There was something coming to her and she was waiting for it, fearfully. What was it? She did not know; it was too subtle and elusive to name. But she felt it, creeping out of the sky, reaching toward her through the sounds, the scents, the color that filled the air.

new insight from spring sky

10   Now her bosom rose and fell tumultuously. She was beginning to recognize this thing that was approaching to possess her, and she was striving to beat it back with her will—as powerless as her two white slender hands would have been.

conflict within herself

11   When she abandoned herself a little whispered word escaped her slightly parted lips. She said it over and over under her breath: "Free, free, free!" The vacant stare and the look of terror that had followed it went from her eyes. They stayed keen and bright. Her pulses beat fast, and the coursing blood warmed and relaxed every inch of her body.

*Revelation: freedom

images of vitality

12   She did not stop to ask if it were not a monstrous joy that held her. A clear and exalted perception enabled her to dismiss the suggestion as trivial.

13   She knew that she would weep again when she saw the kind, tender hands folded in death; the face that had never looked save with love upon her, fixed and gray and dead. But she saw beyond that bitter moment a long procession of years to come that would belong to her absolutely. And she opened and spread her arms out to them in welcome.

more "open" imagery

14   There would be no one to live for during those coming years; she would live for herself. There would be no powerful will bending her in that blind persistence with which men and women believe they have a right to impose a private will upon a fellow creature. A kind intention or a cruel intention made the act seem no less a crime as she looked upon it in that brief moment of illumination.

**self-assertion, wants to control her own life

15   And yet she had loved him—sometimes. Often she had not. What did it matter! What could love, the unsolved mystery, count for in face of this possession of self-assertion which she suddenly recognized as the strongest impulse of her being.

16   "Free! Body and soul free!" she kept whispering.

17   Josephine was kneeling before the closed door with her lips to the keyhole, imploring for admission. "Louise, open the door! I beg; open the door—you will make yourself ill. What are you doing, Louise? For heaven's sake open the door."

closed door, illness imagery vs "elixir of life" (potion that cures all), open window

18   "Go away. I am not making myself ill." No; she was drinking in a very elixir of life through that open window.

19   Her fancy was running riot along those days ahead of her. Spring days, and summer days, and all sorts of days that would be her own. She breathed a quick prayer that life might be long. It was only yesterday she had thought with a shudder that life might be long.

future: seasons of life, growth

20   She arose at length and opened the door to her sister's importunities. There was a feverish triumph in her eyes, and she carried herself unwittingly like a goddess of Victory. She clasped her sister's waist, and together they descended the stairs. Richards stood waiting for them at the bottom.

victory imagery

21   Some one was opening the front door with a latchkey. It was Brently Mallard who entered, a little travel-stained, composedly carrying his gripsack and umbrella. He had been far from the scene of accident, and did not even know there had been one. He stood amazed at Josephine's piercing cry; at Richards' quick motion to screen him from the view of his wife.

Is he associated with rain?

22   But Richards was too late.

23   When the doctors came they said she had died of heart disease—of joy that kills.

Irony: She may die from a "broken" heart all right, but readers know it's not from joy.

Initial Reactions: Mrs. Mallard is sad about her husband's death, though I'm not sure she really loved him all that much. He wasn't a bad guy—she just wants to be a "free" woman, back when women had few rights, little control over their lives. She dies—of shock? disappointment?—when he turns up alive.

After Re-Reading: I think Chopin wanted readers to see how confined some 19th-century women felt in their traditional roles. I felt sorry for Mrs. Mallard, whose realization that life will not be hers after all is so traumatic that it kills her.

Open window—lets in spring scenes, color, sounds of new life—symbol of future possibilities. Also, lots of sick-versus-well and life-versus-death imagery.

Question: Why is she named "Mallard"—a duck?

Nonchaloir (Repose) by John Singer Sargent, 1911

Repose, 1911, by John Singer Sargent

■ Sample Student Essay

After studying Chopin's story, this student writer decided to focus her essay on an important element in the work, the life-death imagery, to show how contrasting images reveal the main character's changes in attitude. Numbers in parentheses following direct quotations refer to the paragraphs in the story.

A BREATH OF FRESH AIR

Introduction: title and author identified; brief summary of plot and theme

    In Kate Chopin's 1894 story "The Story of an Hour" a young wife grieves over news of her husband's accidental death but soon discovers herself elated at the prospect of a life under her own control. The story ends tragically when the husband's sudden reappearance causes her weak heart to fail—not from joy—but from the devastating realization that her newfound freedom is lost. To help readers understand Mrs. Mallard's all-too-brief transformation to a

Thesis

hopeful "free" woman, Chopin contrasts images of illness and lifelessness with positive images of vitality and victory.

2   In the first line of the story, Mrs. Mallard is associated with illness because of her "heart trouble" (1). Following a "storm of grief" (3) on hearing of her husband's death, she isolates herself in her room, lifeless and numb behind a closed door. Chopin describes Mrs. Mallard

Images of illness and lifelessness, illustrated by lines from the story

as feeling "pressed down" (4) and "haunted" (4), exhausted in body and soul; she sits "motionless" (7) with a "dull stare" (8), except for an occasional sob. The lines in her strong, fair face "bespoke repression" (8) and indeed Mrs. Mallard is a young woman who, only the day before, hopelessly shuddered to think "that life might be long" (19).

3   In direct contrast with these images of lifelessness and emotional repression, Chopin introduces images of rebirth and hope. Mrs. Mallard's room has an open window, which becomes the key symbol

in the description of Mrs. Mallard's transformation. Chopin uses the open window to provide Mrs. Mallard with both a view of new life and with fresh air, paralleling the new hopeful feelings that come to her. Through this "open window" (4) Mrs. Mallard sees beyond her house to an "open square" (5) with "trees that were all aquiver with the new spring life" (5). The repetition of the word "open," the budding trees, and the spring season all emphasize the contrast between the world of possibilities and new life and Mrs. Mallard's enclosed room and enclosed spirit. The air after a life-giving spring rain has a "delicious breath" (5), and both people and birds are now singing. "Patches of blue sky" (6) are symbolically breaking through the clouds, but, as yet, Mrs. Mallard can only stare vacantly at the blue sky rather than respond to it.

Contrasting images of rebirth, supported by examples

4   Soon, however, Mrs. Mallard realizes that something—she's not sure what—is "creeping out of the sky, reaching toward her through the sounds, the scents, the color that filled the air" (9). She resists at first but ultimately allows herself the glorious revelation that she is free to live a new life as she, not others, wants it to be. The imagery associated with this revelation shows Mrs. Mallard becoming energized and healthy, in direct contrast to the imagery of lifelessness that characterized her before. The "vacant stare" (11) is replaced by eyes that are "keen and bright" (11). No longer beaten down, "her pulses beat fast, and the coursing blood warmed and relaxed every inch of her body" (11). In contrast to her previous hopeless view of the future, Mrs. Mallard joyfully thinks of the years ahead and "opened and spread her arms out to them in welcome" (13). This open gesture aligns her with the open window and open square, with their images of rebirth and hope.

Contrasting images of vitality, supported by examples and comparison

5   Chopin emphasizes the transformation even further by contrasting Mrs. Mallard's description to her sister Josephine's image of her.

Symbolically placed on the opposite side of the closed door from the open window and spring sky, her sister tells Mrs. Mallard that "you will make yourself ill" (17). But the images associated with the transformed Mrs. Mallard are not of illness but of health and victory. Through the open window, she is drinking in a "very elixir of life" (18), a potion that restores the sick to health, as she thinks of spring and summer, seasons of fertility and growth. She finally emerges from her room with "triumph in her eyes" (20), carrying herself "like a goddess of Victory" (20).

Contrast of illness imagery to images of health, victory

6   Mrs. Mallard's victory is cut short, however, as the return of Mr. Mallard destroys her hopes for her future life. The image of illness once again prevails, as doctors wrongly attribute her death to "heart disease—of joy that kills" (23). With this ironic last line echoing the story's first line, Chopin's imagery describing her character comes full circle, from illness to life and back to death, to emphasize for readers the tragedy of Mrs. Mallard's momentary gain and then the crushing defeat of her spiritual triumph.

Conclusion: Restatement of thesis showing purpose of the imagery

■ Steps to Reading a Poem

Close reading of a poem is similar to reading a story in many ways. Again, try to read with pen in hand so you can take notes, circle important words, and make comments in the margins.

1. Pay attention to any biographical information on the author and the date of publication, which may give you insight into the poem. Also note the title, as it may introduce the poem's main idea or tone.

2. Read through the poem at least twice. Poetry does differ from prose in that poets often compress or turn sentence structure in unusual ways, to create new images and fit rhyme and rhythm patterns. You might find it helpful to try to paraphrase (put into your own words) the lines of shorter poems (or summarize distinct parts) so that you have a clear understanding of the basic content. If you're lost in several lines, try to locate the subject, the verb, and objects of the action or description. And, always, before you begin to analyze a poem, be sure

you know the meaning of *all* the words. Looking up unfamiliar words is critical here—short poems are compact so every word counts.

3. Some poems are *narratives* and contain a plot; others, often referred to as *lyrics*, capture a scene, a series of images, an emotion, or a thought that has universal appeal. At this point, what action, situation, or ideas do you see presented in this poem? Is there a dominant tone or point of view expressed? Make some notes about your initial reactions to the poem's issues, themes, or ideas. As in fiction, poets often offer comments on the human condition or social values.

4. Now begin to analyze the elements of the poem. Identifying the *speaker* (or narrator) of the poem is a good place to start. Is it someone with recognizable characteristics or personality traits? Someone involved in the action of the poem? Young or old? Male or female? Mother, father, lover, friend? Tone of voice (angry, pleading, sad, joyful, etc.)? Remember that a speaker using "I" is not necessarily the poet but rather a persona or role the poet has assumed. Or is the speaker unidentified as she or he unfolds the poem for the reader? And to whom is the poem addressed? A specific person, a group of people, any readers?

5. What is the *setting* or *occasion* of the poem? Is the place, time, season, climate, or historical context important to understanding the poem? Why or why not?

6. What *characters*, if any, appear in the poem? What is the relationship between the speaker and others in the poem? What values, opinions, and motivations do these characters present? What conflicts or changes occur?

7. Look carefully at the poem's *diction* (choice of words). Most poems contain description and figurative language to create imagery, the vivid pictures that create meaning in the reader's mind. Look for similes and metaphors, as defined on page 310, that make abstract or unfamiliar images clear through comparisons, as well as personification and synecdoche (pages 310–311). Poets often use patterns or groups of *images* to present a dominant impression and concrete objects as *symbols* to represent abstract ideas within the poem (cold rain as death, a spring flower as rebirth). They also use *allusions*, brief references to other well-known persons, places, things, and literary works that shed light on their subject by comparison (for example, a reference to Romeo and Juliet might suggest ill-fated lovers). Underline or circle those words and images that you find most effective in communicating ideas or emotions.

8. How is the poem *structured*? There are too many poetic forms to define each one here (ballads, sonnets, odes, villanelles, etc.) so you might consult a more detailed handbook to help you identify the characteristics of each one. However, to help you begin, here is a brief introduction. Some poems are written in patterns called "fixed" or "closed" form. They often appear in stanzas, recognizable units often containing the same number of lines and the same rhyme and rhythm pattern in those lines. They often present one main idea per unit and have a space between each one. Some poems are not divided into stanzas but nevertheless have well-known fixed forms, such as the Shakespearean sonnet, which traditionally challenges the poet to write within fourteen lines, in a predictable line rhythm and rhyme scheme. Other poems are written in free verse

(or "open" form), with no set line length or regular rhyme pattern; these poems may rely on imagery, line lengths, repetition, or sound devices to maintain unity and show progression of ideas.

Study your poem and try to identify its form. How does its structure help communicate its ideas? Why might have the poet chosen this particular structure?

9. *Sound devices* may help unify a poem, establish tone, emphasize a description, and communicate theme. There are many kinds of rhyme (end, internal, slant, etc.), which often help unify or link ideas and parts of poems. For example, stanzas often have set patterns of end rhyme that pull a unit together; a quatrain (four-line stanza), for example, might rhyme *abab*, as shown here:

... free,	a
... sky,	b
... sea,	a
... fly.	b

Four other common sound devices include:

- *Alliteration:* repetition of consonant sounds at the beginning of words ("The Soul selects her own Society"), often used to link and emphasize a relationship among words;

- *Assonance:* repetition of vowel sounds ("child bride of time") to link and underscore a relationship among the words;

- *Onomatopoeia:* a word whose sound echoes, and thus emphasizes, its meaning (buzz, rustle, hiss, boom, sigh);

- *Repetition:* repetition of the same words, phrases, or lines for unity, emphasis, or musical effect ("Sing on, spring! Sing on, lovers!").

Sound devices not only unify poems but also add to their communication of images and meaning. Harsh-sounding, monosyllabic words ("the cold stone tomb") may slow lines and create a tone vastly different from one produced by multisyllabic words with soft, flowing sounds. Poets pick their words carefully for their sounds as well as their connotations and denotations. Ask yourself: What sound devices appear in the poem I'm reading, and why?

10. *Rhythm,* the repetition of stresses and pauses, may also play an important part in the creation of tone and meaning. A poem about a square dance, for example, might echo the content by having a number of quick stresses to imitate the music and the caller's voice. You can discover patterns of rhythm in lines of poetry by marking the accented (ˊ) and unaccented (˘) syllables:

My mistress' eyes are nothing like the sun

Many poems demand a prescribed rhythm as part of their fixed form; lines from a Shakespearean sonnet, as illustrated above, contain an often-used pattern called *iambic pentameter:* five units (called *feet*) of an unaccented syllable followed by an accented syllable.

Another device that contributes to the rhythm of a line is the *caesura*, a heavy pause in a line of poetry. Caesuras (indicated by a ‖ mark) may be used to isolate and thus emphasize words or slow the pace. Sometimes they are used to show strong contrasts, as in the following line: "Before, a joy proposed; ‖ behind, a dream." Caesuras may follow punctuation marks such as commas, semicolons, or periods, marks that say "slow down" to the reader.

After you have looked at the various elements of a poem (and there are many others in addition to the ones mentioned here), reassess your initial reaction. Do you understand the poem in a different or better way? Remember that the elements of an effective poem work together, so be sensitive to the poet's choices of point of view, language, structure, and so on. All these choices help communicate the tone and underscore the ideas of the poem. Ask yourself: What is gained through the poet's choice? What might be different—or lost—if the poet had chosen something else?

■ Annotated Poem

Using the suggestions of this chapter, a student responded to the Walt Whitman poem "When I Heard the Learn'd Astronomer" on the next page. The student essay on pages 434–437 presents an analysis developed from some of the notes shown there.

Starry Night, 1889, by Vincent Van Gogh

Digital Image © The Museum of Modern Art/Licensed by Scala/Art Resource, NY

Educated   _someone who studies the stars, sky_

■ When I Heard the Learn'd Astronomer

Walt Whitman

used here too

Walt Whitman was a nineteenth-century American poet whose free-verse poems often broke with conventional style and subject matter. Some of his most famous poems, including "Song of Myself," "Crossing Brooklyn Ferry," and "Passage to India," extol the virtues of the common people and stress their unity with a universal spirit. This poem was published in 1865.

speaker: "I" in audience

settings: inside lecture hall

When I heard the learn'd astronomer;
When the proofs, the figures, were ranged in columns
    before me;
When I was shown the charts and diagrams, to
    add, divide, and measure them;
When I, sitting, heard the astronomer, where he
    lectured with much applause in the lecture-room.

scientific images, repetition, long lines, slow pace

outside at night

5 How soon, unaccountable, I became tired and sick;
Till rising and gliding out, I wander'd off by myself,
In the mystical moist night-air, and from time to time,
Look'd up in perfect silence at the stars.

Contrast to 4 lines above: quicker, smoother sounds; nature imagery; appeals to senses, not brain

assonance   _multiple uses of alliteration_

Initial Reaction: The speaker of the poem (a student?) is listening to an astronomer's lecture—lots of facts and figures. He gets tired (bored?) and goes outside and looks at the nice night himself.

After re-reading: I see two ways of looking at the sky here, two ways of understanding. You can learn academically and you can use your own senses. I think Whitman prefers the personal experience in this case because the language and images are much more positive in the last lines of the poem when the speaker is looking at nature for himself.

The poem shows the contrast between the two ways by using two stanzas with different styles and tones, Cold vs. warm. Passive vs. active. Facts vs. personal experience.

■ Sample Student Essay

After studying the Whitman poem, the student writer wrote this essay to show how many poetic elements work together to present the main idea. Do you agree with his analysis? Which of his claims seems the most or least persuasive, and why? What different interpretation(s) might you suggest?

TWO WAYS OF KNOWING

1   In the poem "When I Heard the Learn'd Astronomer," nineteenth-century American poet Walt Whitman contrasts two ways people may study the world around them. They can approach the world through lectures and facts, and they can experience nature firsthand through their own senses. Through the use of contrasting structures, imagery, diction, and sound devices in this poem, Whitman expresses a strong preference for personal experience.

2   The poem's structure clearly presents the contrast between the two ways of experiencing the world, or in this specific case, two ways of studying the heavens. The eight-line, free-verse poem breaks into two stanzas, with the first four lines describing an indoor academic setting, followed by a one-line transition to three concluding lines describing an outdoor night scene. The two parts are unified by a first-person narrator who describes and reacts to both scenes.

3   In the first four lines the narrator is described as sitting in "a lecture-room" (l. 4) as part of an audience listening to an astronomer's talk. The dominant imagery of lines 2–3 is scientific and mathematical: "proofs," "figures," "charts," and "diagrams" are presented so that the audience "may add, divide, and measure them" (l. 3). The words, mostly nouns, appear without any colorful modifiers; the facts and figures are carefully arranged "in columns" (l. 2) for objective analysis. This approach to learning is clearly logical and systematic.

4   The structure and word choice of the first four lines of the poem also subtly reveal the narrator's attitude toward the lecture, which he finds dry and boring. To emphasize the narrator's emotional uninvolvement with the material, Whitman presents him passively "sitting" (l. 4), subject of the passive verb "was shown" (l. 3). Lines 2,

---

Introduction: title, author, brief overview of content

Thesis

Two-part structure

Stanza 1: Inside lecture hall

3, and 4, which describe the lecture, are much longer than the lines in the second stanza, with many caesuras, commas, and semicolons that slow the rhythm and pace (for example, l. 3: "When I was shown the charts and diagrams, to add, divide, and measure them;"). The slow, heavy pace of the lines, coupled with the four repetitions of the introductory "when" phrases, emphasizes the narrator's view of the lecture as long, drawn out, and repetitious. Even though the rest of the audience seems to appreciate the astronomer, giving him "much applause" (l. 4), the narrator becomes restless, "tired and sick" (l. 5), and leaves the lecture hall.

Slow pace to emphasize attitude

In the last three lines of the poem, the language and sound devices change dramatically, creating positive images of serenity, wonder, and beauty. The narrator leaves the hall by "rising and gliding out" (l. 6), a light, floating, almost spirit-like image that connects him with the "mystical" (l. 7) nature of the heavens. Whitman also uses assonance (repetition of the "i" sound) to strengthen the connection between the "r*i*sing and gl*i*ding" narrator and the "myst*i*cal . . . n*i*ght-air" (l. 7). In the lecture hall, the narrator was bored, passive, and removed from nature, but now he is spiritually part of the experience himself.

Stanza 2: Outside under stars

"mystical" imagery

6   Alone outside in the night, away from the noisy lecture hall, the narrator quietly contemplates the wonder of the sky, using his own senses of sight, touch, and hearing to observe the stars and feel the air. Positive words, such as "mystical" (l. 7) and "perfect" (l. 8), describe the scene, whose beauty is immediately accessible rather than filtered through the astronomer's cold "proofs" and "diagrams." Examples of alliteration tie together flowing images of natural beauty and serenity: "*m*ystical *m*oist night-air" (l. 7), "from *t*ime *t*o *t*ime" (l. 7), "*s*ilence at the *s*tars" (l. 8). Whitman's choice of the soft "m" and "s" sounds here

contrasting diction, flowing lines, smooth sounds

also adds to the pleasing fluid rhythm, which stands in direct, positive contrast to the harsher, choppier sounds ("charts," "add," "divide") and slow, heavy pauses found in the poem's first stanza.

7   Through careful selection and juxtaposition of language, sound, and structure in the two parts of this short poem, Whitman contrasts distinct ways of studying the natural world. One may learn as a student of facts and figures or choose instead to give oneself over to the wonders of the immediate experience itself. Within the context of this poem, it's no contest: firsthand natural experience wins easily over diagrams and lectures. Stars, 1; charts and graphs, 0.

Conclusion: Restatement of thesis and poem's main idea

■ Guidelines for Writing about Literature

Here are some suggestions that will improve any essay of literary analysis:

1. **Select a workable topic.** If the choice of subject matter is yours, you must decide if you will approach a work through discussion of several elements or if you will focus on some specific part of it as it relates to the whole work. You must also select a topic that is interesting and meaningful for your readers. If your topic is too obvious or insignificant, your readers will be bored. In other words, your essay should inform your readers and increase their appreciation of the work.

2. **Present a clear thesis.** Remember that your purpose is to provide new insight to your readers. Consequently, they need to know exactly what you see in the work. Don't just announce your topic ("This poem is about love"); rather, put forth your argumentative thesis clearly and specifically ("Through its repeated use of sewing imagery, the story emphasizes the tragedy of a tailor's wasted potential as an artist"). And don't waltz around vaguely talking about something readers may not have seen the first time through ("At first the warehouse scene doesn't look that important but after reading it a few times you see that it really does contain some of the meaningful ideas in the story"). Get on with it! cries your impatient reader. Tell me what you see!

3. **Follow literary conventions.** Essays of literary analysis have some customs you should follow, unless instructed otherwise. Always include the full name of the author and the work in your introductory paragraph; the author's last name is fine after that. Titles of short poems and stories are enclosed in quotation marks.

Most literary essays are written in present tense ("the poet presents an image of a withered tree"), from third-person point of view rather than the more informal first-person "I." So that your readers may easily follow your discussion, include a copy of the work or at least indicate publication information describing the location of the work (the name of volume, publisher, date, pages, and so forth).

Within your essay, it's also helpful to include a poem's line number following a direct quotation: "the silent schoolyard" (l. 10). Some instructors also request paragraph or page numbers in essays on fiction.

4. **Organize effectively.** Your method of organization may depend heavily on your subject matter. A poem, for example, might be best discussed by devoting a paragraph to each stanza; on the other hand, another work might profit from a paragraph on imagery, another on point of view, another on setting, and so on. You must decide what arrangement makes the best sense for your readers. Experiment by moving your ideas around in your prewriting outlines and drafts.

5. **Use ample evidence.** Remember that you are, in essence, arguing your interpretation—you are saying to your reader, "Understand this work the way I do." Therefore, it is absolutely essential that you offer your reader convincing evidence, based on reasonable readings of words in the work itself. The acceptance of your views depends on your making yourself clear and convincing. To do so, include plenty of references to the work through direct quotation and paraphrase. Don't assume that your reader sees what you see—or sees it in the way you do. You must *fight* for your interpretation by offering clearly explained readings substantiated with references to the work.

Unsupported claim: Robert feels sorry for himself throughout the story.

Claim supported with text: Robert's self-pity is evident throughout the story as he repeatedly thinks to himself, "No one on this earth cares about me" (4) and "There isn't a soul I can turn to" (5).

Ask yourself as you work through your drafts, am I offering enough clear, specific, convincing evidence here to persuade my reader to accept my reading?

6. **Find a pleasing conclusion.** At the end of your literary analysis, readers should feel they have gained new knowledge or understanding of a work or some important part of it. You might choose to wrap up your discussion with a creative restatement of your reading, its relation to the writer's craft, or even your assessment of the work's significance within the author's larger body of writing. However you conclude, the readers should feel intellectually and emotionally satisfied with your discussion.

Problems to Avoid

Don't assign meanings. By far the most common problem in essays of literary analysis involves interpretation without clear explanation of supporting evidence. Remember that your readers may not see what you see in a particular line or paragraph; in fact, they may see something quite different. The burden is on you to show cause—how you derived your reading and why it is a good one. Don't represent claims as truth even if they ever-so-conveniently fit your thesis: "It is clear that the moon is used here as a symbol of her family's loss." Clear to whom besides you? If it helps, each time you make an interpretative claim, imagine a classmate who immediately says, "Uh, sorry, but I don't get it. Show me how you see that?" Or imagine a hostile reader with a completely different reading who sneers, "Oh yeah, says who? Convince me."

Use quoted material effectively. Many times your supporting evidence will come from quotations from the text you're analyzing. But don't just drop a quoted line onto your page, as if it had just tumbled off a high cliff somewhere. You run the risk of your readers reading the quoted material and still not seeing in it what you do. Blend the quoted material smoothly into your prose, in a way that illustrates or supports your clearly stated point:

Dropped in: Miranda is twenty-four years old. "After working for three years on a morning newspaper she had an illusion of maturity and experience" (280). [What exact point do you want your reader to understand?]

Point clarified: Although Miranda is twenty-four and has worked on a newspaper for three years, she is not as worldly wise as she thinks she is, having acquired only the "illusion of maturity and experience" (280).

Review pages 374–375 for some ways to blend your quotations into your prose. Always double-check to ensure you are quoting accurately; refer to pages 381 and 510–512 for help with proper punctuation and block indention of longer quoted material.

Analysis is not plot summary. Sometimes you may want to offer your readers a brief overview of the work before you begin your in-depth analysis. And certainly there will be times in the body of your essay, especially if you are writing about fiction, that you will need to paraphrase actions or descriptions rather than quote long passages directly. Paraphrasing can indeed provide effective support, but do beware a tendency to fall into unproductive plot-telling. Remember that the purpose of your paper is to provide insight into the work's ideas and craft—not merely to present a rehash of the story line. Keep your eye on each of your claims and quote or paraphrase only those particular lines or important passages that illustrate and support your points. Use your editing pen as a sharp stick to beat back plot summary if it begins taking over your paragraphs.

■ PRACTICING WHAT YOU'VE LEARNED

A. Practice your skills of literary analysis on the short story that follows, taken from *How the Garcia Girls Lost Their Accents*, by Julia Alvarez. This novel tells of a family's adjustment after a move from the Dominican Republic to the United States; in this excerpt, called "Snow," daughter Yolanda has entered the fourth grade during the fall 1962 Cuban Missile Crisis, a tense time in American history. How does Alvarez communicate Yolanda's challenges in her new country? What does the snowflake simile in the last line contribute to our understanding of Alvarez's story?

■ Snow

Julia Alvarez

Julia Alvarez was born in New York City in 1950 but spent the first ten years of her life in the Dominican Republic. After her father was involved in an unsuccessful attempt to overthrow the dictatorship of Rafael Trujillo, her family fled back to the States. Since 1975 Alvarez has been a professor of creative writing and English at several schools, including the University of Vermont, the University of Illinois, and Middlebury College, and she continues to publish many works of poetry, essays, and fiction. Some of her novels are *How the Garcia Girls Lost Their Accents* (1991), *In the Time of Butterflies* (1994), *Yo!* (1997), and *Before We Were Free* (2002).

1   Our first year in New York we rented a small apartment with a Catholic school nearby, taught by the Sisters of Charity, hefty women in long black gowns and bonnets that made them look peculiar, like dolls in mourning. I liked them a lot, especially my grandmotherly fourth grade teacher, Sister Zoe. I had a lovely name, she said, and she had me teach the whole class how to pronounce it. *Yo-lan-da.* As the only immigrant in my class, I was put in a special seat in the first row by the window, apart from the other children so that Sister Zoe could tutor me without disturbing them. Slowly, she enunciated the new words I was to repeat: *laundromat, corn flakes, subway, snow.*

2   Soon I picked up enough English to understand holocaust was in the air. Sister Zoe explained to a wide-eyed classroom what was happening in Cuba. Russian missiles were being assembled, trained supposedly on New York City. President Kennedy, looking worried too, was on the television at home, explaining we might have to go to war against Communists. At school, we had air-raid drills: an ominous bell would go off and we'd file into the hall, fall to the floor, cover our heads with our coats, and imagine our hair falling out, the bones in our arms going soft. At home, Mami and my sisters and I said a rosary for world peace. I heard new vocabulary: *nuclear bomb, radioactive fallout, bomb shelter.* Sister Zoe explained how it would happen. She drew a picture of a mushroom on the blackboard and dotted a flurry of chalkmarks for the dusty fallout that would kill us all.

3   The months grew cold, November, December. It was dark when I got up in the morning, frosty when I followed my breath to school. One morning as I sat at my desk daydreaming out the window, I saw dots in the air like the ones Sister Zoe had drawn—random at first, then lots and lots. I shrieked, "Bomb! Bomb!" Sister Zoe jerked around, her full black skirt ballooning as she hurried to my side. A few girls began to cry.

4   But then Sister Zoe's shocked look faded. "Why, Yolanda dear, that's snow!" She laughed. "Snow."

5   "Snow," I repeated. I looked out the window warily. All my life I had heard about the white crystals that fell out of the American skies in the winter. From my desk I watched the fine powder dust the sidewalk and parked cars below. Each flake was different, Sister Zoe had said, like a person, irreplaceable and beautiful.

B. Read the poem that follows several times and then use the suggestions in this chapter to help you analyze the work. Who is speaking in this poem and what does he now understand?

■ Those Winter Sundays

Robert Hayden

Robert Hayden was a poet and professor at Fisk University and at the University of Michigan; he also served as Poetry Consultant to the Library of Congress. *A Ballad of Remembrance* (1962) first won him international honors at the World Festival of Negro Arts in Senegal; many other volumes of poetry followed, including *Words in Mourning Time* (1970), *American Journal* (1978), and *Complete Poems* (1985). This poem originally appeared in *Angle of Ascent, New and Selected Poems* (1975).

> Sundays too my father got up early
> and put his clothes on in the blueblack cold,
> then with cracked hands that ached
> from labor in the weekday weather made
> 5 banked fires blaze. No one ever thanked him.
>
> I'd wake and hear the cold splintering, breaking,
> When the rooms were warm, he'd call,
> and slowly I would rise and dress,
> fearing the chronic angers of that house,
>
> 10 Speaking indifferently to him,
> who had driven out the cold
> and polished my good shoes as well.
> What did I know, what did I know
> of love's austere and lonely offices?

Suggestions for Writing

The two stories and two poems reprinted in this chapter may be used as stepping-stones to your own essays. Some suggestions:

1. Write an essay that presents your interpretation of "Those Winter Sundays." Support your reading with specific references to the poem's images, structure, word choice, and other literary features.

2. Write an essay that discusses the major ways in which Julia Alvarez's "Snow" captures the difficulties of being an outsider in a particular cultural situation. How does she ultimately wish readers to feel about people who seem different from them? You might, for example, focus on characterization, setting, and Alvarez's use of figurative language, including the symbol of snow itself.

3. Use one of the works as a "prompt" for your own personal essay. For example, have you, like Mrs. Mallard in "The Story of an Hour," ever reacted to a situation in a way that was grossly misunderstood by those close to you? Or have you ever taken people for granted or devalued their help, as did the narrator in the Hayden poem? Perhaps the Whitman poem reminded you of a time when you learned something through hands-on experience rather than study? Or perhaps the opposite was true: you didn't fully appreciate an experience until you had studied it? As did Yolanda in "Snow," have you ever found yourself in a different culture or country? Or in some other "outsider" role? What did you learn from this experience? Did you have anyone like Sister Zoe to help guide you?

4. Write an essay analyzing some other important element(s) in "The Story of an Hour." For example, consider the other people in the story, including Mr. Mallard: how are they characterized, and why?

5. Find a poem or short story that you admire and, using this chapter as a guide, write your own essay of literary analysis. Be sure your readers have a copy of the work you choose.

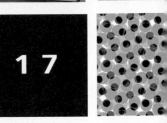

Chapter 17

Writing about Film

Millions of people see films of one kind or another every day. Because the movie screen has become such an important medium of communication, it is not surprising that so many college courses have added a variety of films—from educational documentaries to commercially produced "Hollywood" movies—to their syllabi.

As you know from visiting your local movie house, a powerful film can move its audience in many emotional and intellectual ways, leading its viewers to thoughtful consideration of its ideas, craft, and construction. Writing about film is simply the next step from something you have probably done for years. Moving from informally talking about a movie with your friends, you can now learn to use your analytical thinking skills to put your ideas into thoughtful essays so that others may respond to them.

■ Using Film in the Composition Classroom

Writing about film in academic classes may take many forms, depending upon its purpose and audience and the kind of course in which it is assigned. Here are some of the more common kinds of essay assignments using film found in composition and writing-across-the-disciplines courses:

1. *Prompted Response:* You might be shown a scene, a longer "clip" (that is, multiple shots or scenes), or a short film to help you find an interesting topic for your own writing. For example, a documentary on an inspirational figure might encourage you to write about a personal moment of courage, or you might write an essay about a memorable relative you recall after watching a fictionalized screen character or an interview with a famous author. Or perhaps you might

443

write about one of the important themes you saw expressed in a movie (for example, the importance of honesty or lessons learned from failure). Film, like literature, can be the springboard to all sorts of good essay topics.

2. *Review Essay:* Many composition courses offer students the chance to *evaluate* a commercial movie of their choice or one from an approved list. These review essays focus on why the writer does/does not think the movie is effective and whether it should be recommended to a particular audience. In these essays, writers usually select two or three important criteria by which a film may be judged (such as acting, plot, direction, special effects, etc.) and then offer evidence from the film to illustrate the reasons for their opinions. More than a simple yay/nay pronouncement, this kind of assignment is popular in writing classes because it allows writers to practice basic essay skills: a clear thesis, logical organization of persuasive claims, adequate development in support of those claims, and effective language.

3. *Strategy Practice:* You may also be offered the option of using film as subject matter in your essays as you practice mastering one or more of the organizational strategies discussed in Part Two of this text. For example, if you are practicing comparison/contrast, you might choose to write about a movie version of a literary work, an older movie and its current remake, a movie and its sequel, two movies with similar themes, or a Hollywood treatment of a historical event. Or you might practice causal analysis by explaining why a particular movie is your favorite or by showing how it influenced you at a crucial point in your life. Recalling a film you like (or hate!) can provide you with a wealth of examples and details while you practice developing essays in a number of ways.

4. *Formal Analysis:* Similar to essays of literary analysis discussed in Chapter 16, some assignments call for interpretation of one or more of the elements that make up a film, explaining how those elements help communicate a particular idea or mood. For example, you might analyze the setting in a particular scene and show what it adds to a movie's effectiveness (the house in *The Others*), or you might analyze a minor character to show his or her contribution to the viewer's understanding of the film's major themes (the little girl in the red coat in *Schindler's List*). Other kinds of analysis essay assignments might ask specific questions about a movie's political, cultural, or social ideas ("What criticisms of 1950s' American values does *Dr. Strangelove* offer its viewers?"; "Explain the concept of personal sacrifice as suggested in *It's a Wonderful Life*.").

There are, of course, many other kinds of essays written about film. In Film Studies classes, for example, you will often find students writing essays on film history (the influence of *Star Wars* on subsequent science fiction movies) or on the films of a particular actor or director (Spielberg's body of work), as well as many treatments of technical elements, such as editing, lighting, sound production, and special effects (computer-assisted fight scenes in *The Matrix*; use of innovative camera angles in *Citizen Kane*). These kinds of essay topics are fascinating, but they are often dependent upon expertise gained from research and in-depth study of film theory and production; consequently, they are not usually assigned in composition classes.

■ Guidelines for Writing about Film

Because the purposes of writing about film vary greatly, it is difficult to list suggestions that will apply to all assignments. However, if you are writing a movie review or an essay of film analysis, you may find some of these hints helpful.

1. **Pay close attention to your assignment.** Be sure you have a clear understanding of your purpose and audience. Are you, for example, writing a complete movie review or a more formal analysis of only certain elements? Does your assignment ask you to address any specific questions? Is your intended audience a group of general viewers, perhaps other students in your class, or are you writing for a particular audience, such as parents who might wish to know if this film is appropriate for their young children? Having a good understanding of the goals for this essay will help you focus your attention on the parts of the film relevant to your assignment.

2. **Prepare in advance of your first screening.** If you are writing a movie review or formal analysis, you may need to include certain kinds of production information about the film. To save time and stress (credits roll by quickly), obtain the information you need before you watch the film. It might be helpful, for example, to know the names of the director, the major actors, the screenwriter, the studio or film company, and the date of release. Does the movie fall into a particular genre, or category, such as horror, science fiction, mystery, adventure, musical, romantic comedy, or domestic drama? Some combination of genres (comedy-adventure) or a recognizable subcategory of a genre (buddy cops 'n robbers, teen-slasher horror flick, *film noir* mystery)? Some reviewers like to have a brief plot summary before they see the movie; other viewers want to experience the film free of preconceived ideas or expectations. (Hint: If the film is a classic, popular, or current movie, production information is often available online from the many studio, movie review, or film studies Web sites. Books on film in your library may also provide such information, although they will not contain facts about the most current movies.)

3. **Try to arrange multiple viewing opportunities.** It's difficult to write any kind of detailed treatment of a film you have seen only once, as most viewers need at least one screening just to take in plot and character development. If the choice of film is yours, you may find it much easier to write about one that is on videotape or DVD so that you can see it more than once as well as replay specific scenes for closer study. Multiple screenings may be necessary if you plan to quote dialogue, which must be presented accurately. (Remember that all kinds of films may be available, without charge, from your community's public library.)

4. **Take notes as you watch.** It's easier, of course, to take notes while watching a film at home than it is in a darkened movie theater or even in a classroom. But you can do it, even if you have to struggle to decipher some of your scrawl later. As you watch, take notes on the plot or story line, the sequence of events (told chronologically, in flashback, or in some other nontraditional way?), the time and places in which the narrative occurs, the character development and

interactions, and any cinematic elements (camera shots, lighting, sound, etc.) that seem especially striking. Jot down your reactions to key scenes, characters, or lines of dialogue in the film, and make notes on parts you may already know will be important to your particular assignment. As the film unfolds, do you see any commentary on particular values or cultural assumptions?

5. **Make more notes immediately after the screening**. While your memory is fresh, ask and try to answer questions for yourself. Did you like or dislike the film? Mixed reaction? Why? What were the best or worst parts? Try to record some specific reasons for your opinions. Begin to use your critical thinking skills here: what is the film "about"? That is, what larger themes, values, or point of view does this film communicate to its viewers? For example, does this film comment on the triumph of good over evil, the loss of innocence, the search for love in the modern world, materialism in our society? Even movies that one might view as "purely entertainment" have a point of view toward the actions and characters presented in their stories. What is your film saying about certain social, political, or personal values? Is the film positive, satiric, or cynical about these values? Do you agree or disagree with the stances taken in the film?

6. **Review your notes in light of your assignment's purpose**. At this point, do you have enough ideas to draft a tentative thesis (and perhaps an essay map) for your particular assignment? For example, if you are writing a review of a movie, do you have a clear idea of what the movie is about, your evaluation of it, and some reasons to offer for that opinion? You may need to reorganize your notes in order to focus your efforts at this stage. Remember, you can't talk about every aspect of a movie. Often movie review essays in composition classes will focus on two or three main points about the film. To help you select important discussion points, try rearranging your notes into useful groups (for example: notes on acting, notes on the screenplay, notes on the settings). Which ideas look most promising in order to illustrate and support your thesis? (One reviewer uses index cards to "bunch together" those notes that might make up a good discussion point; you could also type your notes on a computer and then move the similar notes together to see what you have.)

At this stage, many writers will have a working thesis in mind but now see the wisdom of screening the movie one or more times to clarify their supporting claims and to collect specific evidence to support those points.

7. **Watch the film again with a more analytical eye**. During this screening (and perhaps during repeated viewings of particular scenes), you can focus your attention on those specific aspects of the film you want to write about in your essay. If you already have a sense of the claims you want to make about the film, collect specific details you might use to illustrate and support your ideas.

If at this stage you are still searching for your thesis or main supporting points, try posing questions for yourself before you watch the film again. What parts of the film were confusing to you (e.g., a character's decision, an ambiguous ending) and why? Concentrate on the most powerful images that stuck with you from the first viewing. Or try to analyze the three most memorable scenes. What do these images or scenes contribute to your understanding of and response to the film? Why is the film titled as it is? Asking "why" as you watch a second time may uncover interesting questions about the film that your essay will answer, responses that will inform other viewers. (Incidentally, writing analytically about film has much in common with literary analysis, so you may find it helpful to review pages 421–424 in Chapter 16 for some general tips regarding common elements such as characterization, setting, point of view, and narrative structure.)

8. **As you begin to draft, be aware of certain conventions particular to writing about film**. For example, most movie review essays will include a brief summary of the movie's story. It may be clearer for folks who have not seen the movie to read the summary in a paragraph near the essay's beginning, though in some essays the plot may be effectively interwoven throughout the discussion. (*Special note*: if presenting a complete plot summary would give away a surprise ending, the name of the villain, or other information that would diminish the enjoyment of the potential moviegoer, you can acknowledge that you are holding back certain information. Or you can adopt the handy phrase "Spoiler Alert," which professional reviewers use to warn readers to skip the next sentence or two if they wish to remain in the dark about a particular detail.) In addition to a brief summary, reviews usually offer some production information, such as names of the leading actors and director and the year of the film; your essay may also present pertinent background or historical information about the film if it is relevant to the assignment.

    Another consideration for the writer is whether to use "I" in a movie review essay. Although some famous movie reviewers consistently use "I" and "my" in their reviews ("I am putting this movie on my 'All-Time Worst List'"), others do not, so ask your instructor which choice is preferable for your assignment.

9. **Use clear, precise language**. As you draft and revise, assume that your readers have not watched the film and consequently cannot visualize what you have seen unless you help them. Make your discussions as clear as possible, using details and vivid language to re-create the images you are recalling. For ease of discussion, writers on film sometimes make use of a few cinematic terms to help communicate what they saw ("Hollywood ending") or to describe how something was done on the screen ("voice-over"). A glossary at the end of this chapter provides vocabulary that might prove useful as you watch and write about film, though essays for a general audience should not become overly technical.

10. **In your final draft, it's wise to recheck the film to ensure your accuracy**. Be sure that you have the characters' names right and that any lines you quoted are correctly transcribed. (For help punctuating dialogue, see the guidelines for quoted material on pages 510–512 in Part Four.) Remember that the names of films are underlined or printed in italics, not placed within quotation marks.

Watching and thinking about films are enjoyable experiences for most people, and writing analytically about film can extend that pleasure as you offer your thoughtful opinions to others in an organized, persuasive way. Practice your good writing skills as you create an essay worthy of Four Stars!

Problems to Avoid

Don't be tempted to just "pun and run." Movie reviews are rather well known for offering critics the opportunity to throw out witty phrases or memorable one-liners to praise or slash actors, directors, or scripts. You may have read lines similar to "her acting ran the range of emotions from A to B" or "his performance was so wooden you could have boarded up the windows with it." Or perhaps you've just seen a "must flee" rather than a "must see" movie. Puns and vivid figurative language often do add humor and spice that increase our enjoyment of reading a review. However, witty one-liners, as on-target as they may be, are never a substitute for good analysis. Even if you think a movie is so frightfully bad that its screening could be used to threaten confessions out of hardened serial killers, you must offer some reasons for your evaluation. It isn't enough to say of a movie, "I just liked it" or "It was a tragic waste of two hours of my life"—explain your judgment and illustrate your claims with details from the film.

Keep your primary purpose in mind. Although you may need to include a plot summary in your essay, don't allow it to dominate your discussion. Remember that your larger purpose in a review or analytical essay is to offer an opinion—to give readers your recommendation and/or to interpret some important parts of the film. If your reaction to a film is mixed, you may certainly say so in a review essay as long as you avoid seeming wishy-washy. It's true that most bad films have at least one redeeming feature and many good films have flaws. But even if some aspect of the film bothered you to the point of wanting to pitch your popcorn (an annoying soundtrack, for example), ask yourself if that element alone merits a main point in your discussion. If, in fairness, you feel you must mention a strength in an overall negative review or point out a weakness in a generally positive review, then do so— but keep your main purpose and thesis in mind. Focus your discussion chiefly on those parts of your film that best support your overall evaluation or interpretation.

■ Sample Student Essay

In this essay a student recommends one of his favorite movies to his classmates. According to this writer, his hardest task was describing the mystery's twisting plot without spoiling the movie's surprises for the potential viewers. As you read this review, do you find that his comments encourage you to see this movie?

CATCH THE BLACK BIRD

1   Tired of watching movies with predictable plots, repetitive car chases, and excessive shoot-outs? Bored with lame performances and awful dialogue? As you stroll the aisles at your favorite movie rental store, leave

Introduction: Questions lead to thesis and map (plot, cast, dialogue)

those unoriginal stories and special effects behind. Reach for something new by reaching for something older. If you are looking for a crime caper with surprising plot twists, an unbeatable cast, and some of the best dialogue ever written, reach for <u>The Maltese Falcon</u> (1941).

2   Adapted from the detective novel by Dashiell Hammett, with direction and screenplay by John Huston, <u>The Maltese Falcon</u> is regarded as one of the first and best movies in the *film noir* genre, films popular from the early 1940s to the late 1950s (revisited by Hollywood more recently with <u>L.A. Confidential</u>, <u>Body Heat</u>, and <u>Chinatown</u>). These films typically tell dark stories of urban crime and are filled with seedy characters, often including a hard-boiled detective and a beautiful, treacherous woman. Frequently filmed in shadows and night scenes, these movies have a gritty visual style that emphasizes the bleak and corrupt atmosphere of their stories.

    Production and genre information

3   The plot of <u>The Maltese Falcon</u> is complex and unpredictable, mainly because throughout the film almost no character tells the truth the first time around . . . or even the second. The story begins in the office of tough-guy detective Sam Spade and his partner Miles Archer, hired by a beautiful Miss Wonderly to rescue her sister from a hoodlum named Thursby. Archer trails Thursby but is shot (at close range and with his coat buttoned over his gun). Spade is suspected of killing his partner because he has had an affair with Archer's wife, but then Thursby is killed too. The plot twists when Miss Wonderly admits (after trying out a few more phony stories) that she is really a thief named Brigid O'Shaughnessy, who claims she was double-crossed by Thursby, one of a handful of shady characters searching for a statue of a jewel-encrusted bird, now covered with a black veneer. Brigid convinces Spade to help her get the stolen bird, and an uneasy romantic relationship begins to grow. In pursuit of the mysterious falcon, Spade must outwit Brigid's dangerous enemies—the "Fatman," his murderous young henchman Wilmer, and Joel Cairo—not to mention a cop who hates Spade, Archer's angry widow, and Brigid herself. Characters make alliances one minute and then betray each other the next. By the movie's famous ending, Spade faces his toughest moral dilemma: whose side is he on?

    Supporting Point One: Surprising plot twists

    (Brief summary)

4   But it's not the plot twists that ultimately make this film so watchable—it's the fascinating cast of characters and the actors who play them perfectly. The best is Humphrey Bogart as the archetypal tough guy, whose un-pretty, no-nonsense face is an ideal match for the cold, cynical Spade. Bogart is totally believable as the unsentimental antihero: his reaction to his partner's brutal murder, for example, is a flat "yeah, tough break." Street smart and confident, he won't take guff from the cops, sees through Brigid's various poses, and knows how to manipulate the criminals in his own behalf. In one scene when the Fatman won't deal with him to his liking, he convincingly throws a violent fit of anger, smashes a glass, and stalks out—then grins all the way to the elevator, laughing over his successful act.

Supporting Point Two: Excellent cast

A. Bogart as antihero

5   The villains in the film are quirky and unforgettable too. Sidney Greenstreet is Kaspar Gutman, the huge "Fatman," whose chuckles and nice manners only partially hide his creepy obsession with the Black Bird. Peter Lorre plays bad guy Joel Cairo like a prissy little penguin with lethal craziness. And certainly Mary Astor as Brigid is much more than a Pretty Face. Like a quick-change artist, she's the Good/Bad Girl, who lies, tearfully admits her faults, and then lies again. When "helpless" Brigid begs Sam for protection, he replies, "You won't need much help . . . you're good. It's chiefly in your eyes, I think—and that throb you get in your voice. . . ." It takes a talented actress to play such a convincing liar, especially one who fools the audience every time she opens her mouth.

B. Memorable villains: Greenstreet, Lorre, Astor

6   The best part of the movie, however, may be the fast-paced, witty dialogue, full of wisecracks and sharp retorts. Sam gets most of the good lines, of course. Nobody's fool and slightly corrupt himself, he lets Brigid know he spotted her as a fake in his office from the beginning: "Oh, we didn't exactly believe your story . . . we believed your two hundred dollars." And he coolly answers an accusation of murder with the ironic question, "How'd I kill him, I forget." A lot of the humor is directed at Wilmer, the nasty young thug who is forever being needled by Spade. Relieving Wilmer of all his guns with a simple maneuver, Spade sneers, "Come on, this'll put you in solid with your boss" and then tells the Fatman how Wilmer lost his weapons: "a crippled newsy [newsboy] took 'em away

Supporting Point Three: Witty dialogue (examples)

from him but I made him give them back." To quote the famous lines of the last scene here would give away too much of the film's ending, but Sam's speech to the deceitful Brigid is so full of deliciously cold-blooded (but well-deserved) sarcasm that many film buffs know it by heart.

7   The movie's surprising conclusion wraps up a near-perfect film. Though it's not a warm, happy ending, it's a just one. Sam Spade may not always play fair or by the cops' rules, and he may be tempted by desire and money. Ultimately, however, he must follow a code of his own to maintain self-respect. He remains a hard-core detective to the end. Despite all the copycat detectives in films since 1941, there is truly only one Sam Spade. And as the Fatman explains as he agrees to sell out Wilmer to the cops, "There is only one Maltese falcon." So true, and its story is one of the best movies ever made.

Conclusion: An original hero in a compelling story make a great film

Humphrey Bogart, Peter Lorre, Mary Astor, and Sydney Greenstreet in *The Maltese Falcon* (1941)

■ **PRACTICING WHAT YOU'VE LEARNED**

Evaluate the effectiveness of the brief movie review that follows. Does the writer present a clear recommendation and overview of the film? Are all of the reasons for his opinion supported with enough details from the movie, or are you left unconvinced? Why? What changes or additions might make this a more informative, persuasive review?

■ *Cat in the Hat* Coughs Up Mayhem

By David Germain

David Germain writes movie reviews and entertainment features for The Associated Press news organization. This review first appeared in newspapers in November 2003.

1   The cat in the hat has come back, and he might put you and the kids in the mood for an evening alone with Dr. Seuss' original picture book to fumigate the stink of this feline's awful live-action adventure.

2   Shrill, boorish and witless, *Dr. Seuss' The Cat in the Hat* is as scenically crass and cluttered as its predecessor, *Dr. Seuss' How the Grinch Stole Christmas*, the first live adaptation of one of Theodor Geisel's children's tales. Yet *The Cat in the Hat* lacks the one saving grace of that earlier movie, Jim Carrey's whirlwind central character. As the Cat, Mike Myers is irritating and unamusing, caterwauling in a voice that channels Charles Nelson Reilly with traces of Bert Lahr's Cowardly Lion. And while the Grinch was meant to be a little menacing, the Cat ends up a scarier figure thanks to his rather creepy facial design and Myers' overly frisky demeanor, reminiscent of the goofy uncle who should never be left home alone with the kids.

3   First-time director Bo Welch, a production designer whose credits include *Edward Scissorhands* and the *Men in Black* flicks, crafts a visually overbearing movie. The performances he coaxes from Myers and the costars amount to distasteful tumult that's hard to endure. Screenwriters Alec Berg, David Mandel and Jeff Schaffer, who also adapted the *Grinch*, do a miserable job fleshing out the nuggets of Geisel's story to feature length. The characters they add are unpleasant, the expanded story details and sight gags vapid.

4   From a whimsical little rhyme about a feline in striped top hat who teaches two bored siblings a lesson on having fun, the filmmakers have strung together the insufferable story of a single mom (Kelly Preston), her control-freak daughter (Dakota Fanning) and reckless son (Spencer Breslin). The day mom's supposed to play host for her real-estate company's party, she's called in to work, leaving the kids with a narcoleptic baby-sitter and strict orders not to mess up the house. As the children cope with ennui, a sense of neglect and the machinations of mom's vile boyfriend (Alec Baldwin), the Cat pops in to spread mayhem and destruction. The frenzied pace fails to cover up the story's utter emptiness. The *Grinch* at least provided a protagonist with a character arc, who undergoes a real, though cartoonish, transformation. All *The Cat in the Hat* offers is the shallow message that to

have fun, you must know how. Fine for bedtime storybook reading, but piffling on the big screen.

5   The trappings Welch hangs on this thread of story are vulgar, a sensory overload of garish pastels and cloying characters. Sean Hayes is disagreeable on two fronts, as mom's germ-phobic boss and the voice of the family's whiny computer-animated goldfish. The Cat's helpers, Thing 1 and Thing 2, are in the running for most obnoxious looking and sounding creatures ever to appear in a family film.

6   The most alarming thing is that there's a ready-made sequel with Geisel's follow-up book, *The Cat in the Hat Comes Back.* Here's hoping this screen cat has just one life to live.

■ Suggestions for Writing

1. Select a film that's available on video or DVD and write a movie review that might appear in your local newspaper, addressed to a general audience. Explain your evaluation of the movie by providing at least two or three important reasons, each supported with details from the film. (Suggestion: As you decide on a movie to review, you might look at the American Film Institute Web site, containing their list of the top 100 American movies. Although you might not agree with the Institute, this ranking will suggest some films admired over the years by both critics and viewers. Now may be your chance to discover for yourself why a particular movie is considered a classic.)

2. Analyze one of your favorite movies. Write an essay explaining why you find it so satisfying. Or, if you prefer, tackle a movie that seems to be loved (or loathed) by everyone—but you. Write an essay that shows the world why your assessment is the better one.

3. Find a movie review (newspaper, magazine, online) with which you strongly disagree. Write an essay in which your analysis shows why the reviewer is off track in his or her evaluation of this movie.

4. Write an essay comparing/contrasting a literary work (novel, short story, or drama) you know well to its movie version (for example, one of the Harry Potter or *Lord of the Rings* movies, *The Grapes of Wrath, Gone with the Wind*), explaining how effectively you think the original story was captured on the Big Screen.

5. Think of a film story (fictional or factual) that deeply impressed you, one that you feel presents a thoughtful message, question, or challenge to its viewers. Explore this idea in a personal essay as it applies to values or choices in your own life. Or perhaps you have seen a film that changed your mind about an important topic. Explain how the film has affected your point of view.

■ Glossary of Film Terms

Camera angle The position of the camera in relation to the subject being filmed. Some common camera angles include the close-up (often of a face), the long shot, and the high angle.

Deus ex machina Refers to use of an improbable plot device to save the hero from a difficult situation (the cavalry or police arrive at just the right moment, for example). The phrase, meaning "god from the machine," came from ancient Greek drama when a crisis was solved by the appearance of a god, lowered onto the stage with ropes or other equipment. Today the term is most often used to criticize an unbelievable rescue in a weak script.

Dialogue The words spoken by the characters in a film.

Editing Technically, editing is the splicing together of different pieces of film. The order in which a filmmaker links shots in a single scene, and then links scenes together, to construct the entire film plays a crucial role in communicating the film's meaning.

Fade A transitional device in which the picture on the screen gradually darkens to black before another scene begins.

Flashback A scene or sequence of scenes that take the story into the past.

Genre Movies may be categorized into recognizable types that share similarities in themes, narrative structures, characters, style, mood, and other characteristics. Some common movie genres include horror, romantic comedy, Westerns, adventure, science fiction, crime, and mystery. Many movies are a blend of more than one genre.

"Guilty Pleasure" Refers to a movie that a reviewer enjoyed in spite of recognizing that the film has serious flaws (a comedy that is fun even though it is over-the-top silly or an action movie that is thrilling even though its special effects are ridiculously unbelievable).

Hero/Antihero The hero of a film is usually a major character who displays worthy values and admirable characteristics, often including courage and self-sacrifice for the good of others. An antihero rejects traditional values or societal norms, but may nevertheless appeal to audiences because of his/her individualism or adherence to a personal code of behavior.

"Hollywood Ending" Refers to a movie's happy ending that often seems contrived or tacked on merely to make audiences feel good as they leave the theater.

Location A film that is shot "on location" means that the movie was filmed in the geographical area that is present in the story, rather than being filmed in a studio.

Narrative structure Refers to the way a story's plot line is constructed, through arrangement of scenes and point of view.

Scene A period of screen activity in which the action is usually confined to one time and space.

Sets Constructed physical environments in scenes.

Setting Place and time (year, hour of day, month, season, etc.) of a particular scene or entire film. Lighting and sound effects may influence the mood of a particular setting.

Shot A single image on the screen; a variety of shots may be edited to form a sequence that makes up a scene.

Slow motion Film speed is slowed to produce a desired effect on the audience; frequently used in modern movies to underscore an emotional interaction between characters or to emphasize the horror of tragedy or violence. (In contrast, *fast motion* is often used for comedic effect or to show frenzied activity in a passage of time.)

Soft focus Refers to scenes in which the images on the screen appear slightly fuzzy or out of focus to the viewer; often used to create a romantic effect.

"Spoiler Alert" Phrase used by movie reviewers to warn those who have not seen the film that an important plot element (the identity of the murderer, for example) is about to be revealed.

Voice-over Refers to the commentary heard over the screen images, spoken by a narrator or character whose remarks directly address the audience.

Chapter 18

Writing in the World of Work

Imagine you are a manager of a business who receives the following memo from one of the sales representatives:

> Our biggest customer in Atlanta asked me to forward the shipment to the company warehouse and I said I could not realizing how serious a decision this was I changed my mind. This OK with you?

Did the salesperson mean to say that at first he thought he could send the shipment but then changed his mind? Or did he mean he thought he couldn't but then reconsidered? What would you do as the manager? Probably you would stop your current work and contact the salesperson to clarify the situation before you gave an OK. Because of the unclear communication, this extra effort will cost your business valuable time, energy, and perhaps even customer satisfaction.

The preceding scenario is not far-fetched; unclear writing hurts businesses and organizations in every country in the world. Consequently, here is a bold claim:

> Almost all workplaces today demand employees with good communication skills.

Although specific writing tasks vary from job to job, profession to profession, successful businesses rely on the effective passage of information among managers, coworkers, and customers. No employer ever wants to see confusing reports or puzzling memos that result in lost production time, squandered resources, or aggravated clients. To maximize their organization's efficiency, employers look for and reward employees who can demonstrate the very writing skills you have been practicing in this composition course. Without question, your ability to communicate clearly in precise, organized prose will give you a competitive edge in the world of work.

To help you address some of the most common on-the-job writing situations, this chapter offers general guidelines for business letters, office memos, and professional electronic-mail messages. A special section on the preparation of résumés at the end of the chapter will suggest ways to display your skills to any prospective employer.

■ Composing Business Letters

Letters in the workplace serve many purposes and audiences, so it isn't possible to illustrate each particular kind. However, it is important to note that all good business letters have some effective qualities in common. And although a business letter is clearly not a personal essay, they share many of the same features: consideration of audience, development of a main idea, organized paragraphs, appropriate tone and diction, and clear, concise expression of thoughts.

Before you begin any letter, prewrite by considering these important questions:

1. What is the main purpose of this letter? What do you want this letter to accomplish? Are you applying for a job, requesting material, offering thanks, lodging a complaint? Perhaps it is you who are answering a request for information about a product, procedure, service, or policy. The occasions for written correspondence are too many to list, but each letter should clearly state its purpose for the reader, just as a thesis in an essay presents your main idea.

2. Who is your "audience," the person to whom you are writing? As discussed in detail on pages 19–22 in Chapter 1, effective writers select the kinds of information, the level of complexity, and even the appropriate "voice" in response to their readers' needs, knowledge, and attitudes. Remember that no matter who your letter-reader happens to be, all readers want clarity, not confusion; order, not chaos; and useful information, not irrelevant chitchat. Put yourself in the reader's place: what should she or he know, understand, or decide to do after reading this letter?

3. What overall impression of yourself do you want your letter to present? All business correspondence should be courteous, with a tone that shows your appreciation for the reader's time and attention. Achieving this tone may be more difficult if you are writing a letter of complaint, but remember that to accomplish your purpose (a refund or an exchange of a purchase, for example), you

must persuade, not antagonize, your reader. If you're too angry or frustrated to maintain a reasonable tone, give yourself some time to cool off before writing. A respectful tone should not, on the other hand, sound phony or pretentious ("It is indeed regrettable but I must hereby inform you . . ."). Choose the same level of language you would use in one of your polished academic essays. In short, good business writing is clear, courteous, and direct.

Business Letter Format

Most traditional business letters are neatly typed on one side of 8½-by-11-inch white bond paper. Margins are usually set for a minimum of 1¼ inches at the top and at least one inch on the left and right sides and at the bottom. Almost all professional letters now use the "block form"—that is, lines of type are flush with the left margin and paragraphs are not indented. Envelopes should match the letter paper.

Business letters typically have six primary parts:

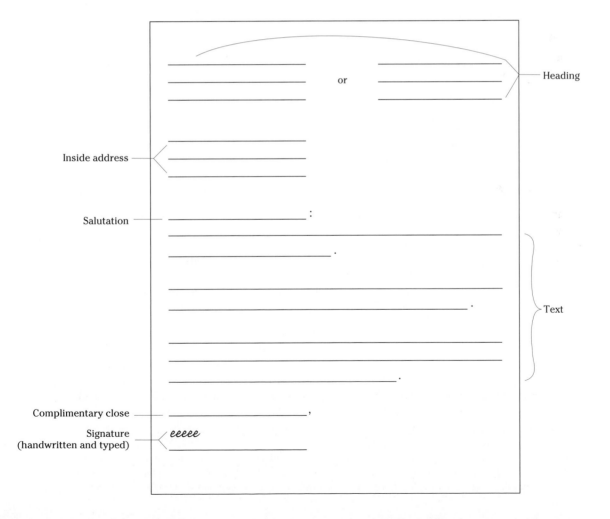

1. The **heading** of a letter is your address and the date, typed either above the inside address of the letter or in the upper right corner. If the heading is in the upper right position, the longest line should end at the one-inch margin on the right side of the page. All lines in your heading should begin evenly on the left. If you are using letterhead stationery (paper already imprinted with your business name, address, or logo), you need to add only the date.

2. The **inside address** contains the name of the person to whom you are writing, the person's title or position, the name of the company or organization, the full address (street or post office box, city, state, ZIP Code). The first line of the inside address should appear at least two spaces below the last line of the heading. (The inside address information should be repeated exactly on your letter's envelope.)

Correct use of titles and positions can be tricky. Sometimes a person has a title and an additional position; other times, the title is lengthy. In general, if a person's title has more than two words, put it on a separate line:

Professor Linda Payne
Dean, College of Liberal Arts
Colorado State University

Whenever possible, direct your letter to a specific person. If you do not know the name of the person and cannot discover it before your letter must be sent, you may address the correspondence to the position held by the appropriate person(s): General Manager, Graduate Advisor, Personnel Director, City Council, and so forth.

3. The **salutation** is your letter's greeting to your reader. Begin the salutation two spaces down from the inside address, and greet the person formally using the word "Dear" plus title and name (Dear Mr. Smith, Dear Ms. Jones,* Dear Dr. Black). The salutation is traditionally followed by a colon rather than the more informal comma:

Dear Dr. Montoya:
Dear Personnel Director:

A caution: be careful to avoid sexist assumptions in your salutations. If you do not know the gender of the person to whom you are writing (initials and many first names—Chris, Pat, Jordan—are used by both men and women), do some research, if possible. When in doubt, use the title or position and last name (Dear Professor Chieu). Use of the full name (Dear Xin Chieu) or organization name (Dear Safety Council) may be preferable to the impersonal "Dear Sir or Madam," a phrase that seems stilted today.

4. The **text** of your letter refers to the message that appears in the paragraphs. As in essays, think of your text as having a beginning, a middle, and an ending. Although

---

*If you know that the woman you are writing prefers to be addressed as Mrs. X, address her in this way. However, if you do not know her marital status or preferred title, Ms. may be the best choice. If possible, avoid the matter altogether by using her professional title: Dear Professor Smith, Dear Mayor Alvarez.

there is no rule about the number of paragraphs in any business letter, most letters contain:

- a first paragraph that clearly states the reason for writing (think about a thesis in an essay);
- one or more paragraphs that present the necessary details or explanation of the reason for writing (think body paragraphs in an essay);
- a last paragraph that sums up the message in a positive way, offers thanks if appropriate, and, on occasion, provides information to help reader and writer make contact (think conclusion in an essay).

Because professional people receive so much mail, business letters should be brief and to the point. *Above all, readers want clarity!* Scrutinize your prose for any words or phrases that might mislead or confuse your reader. Select precise words and create trim sentences that present your message in the clearest, most straightforward way possible. (For help writing clear, concise prose, review Chapters 6 and 7.)

If possible, without sacrificing clarity or necessary information, keep your letter to one page. Single-spaced paragraphs of eight lines or fewer are easiest to read. Skip a space between paragraphs. If you must go to a second page, type your name, the date, and the page number in an upper corner. If you discover that you have only one or two lines to carry over to the second page, try to condense your text or, if you must, squeeze or expand the margins just a bit. Try not to divide paragraphs between pages, and do not split a word between pages. Second and subsequent pages should be plain paper, without letterhead material.

5. The **complimentary closing** of a business letter is a conventional farewell to the reader, typed two spaces below the last line of the text. The two most common phrases for closing formal business correspondence are "Sincerely" and "Yours truly." Stick with these unless you have a more informal relationship with the person you are writing. In those cases, you might use such closings as "Cordially" or "Warm regards." The first letter of the first closing word is capitalized, and the closing is followed by a comma.

6. The **signature** part of a business letter contains both your handwritten name and, beneath that, your typed name (plus your title, if appropriate). Leave approximately four spaces for your handwritten name, which should be written in black ink:

Sincerely,

Jane Doe

Jane Doe
Professor of Philosophy

Do not forget to sign your letter! Such an oversight not only looks careless but may also suggest to the reader that this is merely a mass-produced form letter.

7. Some letters contain additional information below the signature. Typical notes include the word "enclosure" (or "encl.") to indicate inclusion of additional material (which may be named) or a distribution list to indicate other persons who are receiving a copy of this letter. Distribution is indicated by the word "copy" or by the letters *c*, *cc* (for "carbon copy"), or *xc* (for "Xeroxed copy"), followed by a colon and the name(s); if more than one person is listed, the names should appear in alphabetical order.

Copy: Mayor Sue Jones   Enclosure *or* Encl.
            or   *or*
cc: Mayor Sue Jones,   Enclosure: résumé
     Dr. Inga York

If someone else types your letter, put your initials in capital letters, a slash mark, and the typist's initials in lowercase:

JCW/ma

In formal business correspondence, avoid any sort of postscript (P.S.).

Some last advice: Most business letters today are written on a word processor, which can help writers find and fix typos without having to use correction fluid. But, as in any piece of writing, always proofread for errors carefully—and repeatedly! Never trust your spell-checker to catch all possible errors. Don't undercut the message you are sending by failing to revise misspelled words, inaccurate names, ungrammatical sentences, or sloppy punctuation. Also, be sure to select a clear, traditional type font (such as Times New Roman; no fancy script or gothic styles, please), set in a readable size (at least 12 point), and use only a printer that can produce dark, high-grade type.

■ PRACTICING WHAT YOU'VE LEARNED

Find a recent business letter you or someone you know has received. This letter might be a request for a charitable donation, an announcement of some school policy, a letter of recommendation, or even a parking-violation summons. Assess the effectiveness of the letter: Is it clear? Informative? To the point? Write a one-paragraph critique of the letter that identifies both its strengths and any weaknesses you see.

■ ASSIGNMENT

Writing business letters becomes easier with practice. Think of an upcoming occasion that will require you to write a professional letter. Perhaps you are asking for a job or accepting one? Applying for a scholarship, grant, or school loan? Requesting an interview or letter of recommendation? Complaining to your landlord? Ordering or returning a product? The choices are many but try to select a letter that you might indeed send sometime soon. Limit your letter to one page, and revise as many times as necessary to illustrate your good understanding of purpose, audience, format, and style. Don't forget to proofread carefully!

■ Sample Business Letter

Art Tech Studio
802 West Street
Fort Collins, CO 80525
May 10, 2004

Mr. Thomas Valdez
General Manager
Incredible Computers, Inc.
645 Monroe Avenue
Little Rock, AR 90056

Dear Mr. Valdez:

Thank you for your May 5 order for twenty of my hand-designed covers for computer monitors and for your advance payment check of $250. I am delighted that your company wishes to stock my painted canvas dust covers in both your Little Rock and Fayetteville stores.

The computer covers are being packed in individual boxes this week and should arrive by Air Flight Mail at your main office no later than May 25. If you wish for me to express-mail the covers to you for quicker arrival, please let me know.

Many thanks again for your interest in my work and for your recent order. I am planning to attend a marketing seminar in Little Rock, June 5–8; I will call you next week to see if we might arrange a brief meeting at your convenience on one of those days. Until then, should you need to contact me, please call my studio (970/555-6009).

Sincerely,

Rachel Zimmerman

Rachel Zimmerman

Enclosure: receipt

■ Creating Memos

A memo, short for "memorandum," is a common form of communication *within* a business or an organization. Memos are slightly more informal than business letters, and they may be addressed to more than one person (a committee, a sales staff, an advisory board, etc.). Memos may be sent up or down the chain of command at a particular workplace, or they may be distributed laterally, across a department or between offices. Although the format of the paper memo may vary slightly from organization to organization, it often appears arranged in this manner:

TO: name of recipient(s) and/or title(s)

FROM: name of sender and title; handwritten initials

DATE: day, month, year

SUBJECT: brief identification of the memo's subject matter

The message follows in one or more paragraphs.

Note that the name of the sender is usually accompanied by the sender's handwritten initials, rather than a full signature as in a business letter. Also, in some memos, the term "Re" ("in reference to") may be substituted for the word "Subject."

Many memos are brief, containing important bulletins, announcements, or reminders, as illustrated in this sample:

TO: Editorial Staff

FROM: Louise Presaria, Editor-in-Chief *LP*

DATE: April 22, 2004

RE: Silver Eagle Award Banquet

Because the current snowstorm is presenting problems with public transportation and also with heating outages in our building, the annual Silver Eagle Banquet originally scheduled for tomorrow night has been postponed for one week. It is now rescheduled for Thursday, April 29, beginning at 7:30 PM, in the Whitaker Conference room.

I look forward to seeing you all there. Each of you has done a marvelous job this year and greatly deserves to share the benefits that come with our industry's most prestigious award.

Other in-house memos—those explaining policies or procedures, for example—may be long and complex. Lengthy memos may begin with a summary or statement of general purpose and may use headings (such as "Background Information," "Previous Action," or "Recommendations") to identify various parts of the discussion.

All business memos, regardless of length, share a common goal: the clear, concise communication of useful information from writer to reader.

■ Sending Professional E-Mail

Although the world of work will never be totally "paperless," more businesses today are relying on computer-based communications to send or request information, both inside and outside their organizations.

Electronic mail, or e-mail, has a number of advantages over the business letter, memo, and telephone. It's faster and easier than postal service (humorously known to some as "snail mail"), as you can compose or forward a message to one person or many people, across the building or across the country, and receive a reply almost instantly. Messages may be sent anytime, day or night, and are held until the recipient is able to open them. Unlike the telephone, most e-mail has an "attachments" feature that may contain documents, forms, graphics, or pictures.

Because e-mail is so useful in so many ways to many different kinds of businesses and organizations, there is no one-size-fits-all format. Consequently, it's always a good idea to acquaint yourself with customary use of e-mail at your place of work. In addition, here are some suggestions for improving the quality of all electronic communications:

1. **Use a helpful subject line.** Successful business leaders today may receive scores of e-mail messages every day, so many that they are tempted to delete any unrecognizable mail that might be "spam" (an unsolicited message or sales offer) or a "virus" that might destroy their files. To ensure that your message will be opened and read, always use specific words in the subject line to clearly delineate the central focus or key words of your correspondence ("Project Thunderbolt contracts"). Using a specific subject line will also be helpful if your reader wants to reread your message later and needs to find it quickly in a long list of e-mails.

2. **Begin appropriately.** Unlike a business letter, e-mail needs no heading or inside address, but a new electronic communication should begin with an appropriate greeting, depending on the formality of the occasion. For example, if you are writing an officer of another company to ask for information, you might begin with a traditional salutation (Dear Mr. Hall:). An informal memo to a coworker might have a more casual greeting, depending on your relationship to that person (Hello, Bill; Good morning, Ms. Merrill). Some companies prefer the standard To-From-Date-Subject memo form discussed earlier in this chapter.

3. **Keep your message brief.** Long messages are difficult to read on screens; all that scrolling and flipping back and forth to check information can be tiresome. If possible, confine your message to one screen. Working people are busy, so try to follow the advice given previously in this chapter regarding business letters and memos: clearly state your purpose, explain in a concise manner, and conclude gracefully.

4. **Make it easy to read.** To avoid contributing to your reader's eyestrain, write messages that are visually pleasant. Keep your paragraphs short, and skip lines between

each paragraph. If your message is long, break it up with headings, numbered lists, or "bullets" (use lowercase "o"). Use a readable, plain font. Some e-mails will not allow a change in type, so to indicate boldface or italics you may use asterisks (*) around a word or phrase for emphasis—but do so sparingly.

5. Check your tone. Your e-mail messages should sound professional and cordial. Unlike personal e-mail that may contain slang, fragments, asides, or funny graphics, business e-mails should be written in good standard English and be straight to the point. If you're angry, resist the temptation to fly to the computer and "flame"; cool off and compose a thoughtful, persuasive response instead. Be especially careful about the use of irony or humor: without nonverbal clues, readers may misinterpret your words and react in a manner opposite the one you intended. In general, strive for a polite, friendly tone, using the clearest, most precise words you can muster.

6. Sign off. If your e-mail is performing a task similar to that of a business letter, you may wish to close in a traditional way:

Yours truly,

Scott Muranjan

You may also want to create a standard sign-off that not only includes your name but also your title, telephone and fax number, mailing and e-mail address. Such information is helpful for readers who wish to contact you later.

However, if your e-mail is more akin to an informal memo between coworkers, you may find it appropriate to end with a friendly thought or word of thanks and your first name:

I'm looking forward to working with you on the Blue file. See you at
Tuesday's meeting.
Scott

Allow your sense of occasion and audience to dictate the kind of closing each e-mail requires.

7. Revise, proofread, copy, send. The very ease of e-mail makes it tempting to send messages that may not be truly ready to go. All your professional correspondence should look just that: professional. Take some time to revise for clarity and tone; always proofread. Double-check figures and dates, and run the spell-checker if you have one. If time permits, print out a paper or "hard copy" of important messages to look over before you hit the Send button. If you need to keep track of your correspondence, make a computer file or a print copy for your office.

Problems to Avoid

Electronic mail has revolutionized the workplace, but it is not without its disadvantages. Computers crash, files vaporize, printers freeze, and so on. Work on developing patience and give yourself time to use other methods of communication if necessary. Meanwhile, here are two other tips:

Business E-mail Is Not Private. Perhaps because of individual passwords or because of experience with sealed postal mail, employees often believe that their e-mail is private correspondence. It is not! Employers have the legal right to read any e-mail sent from their organizations. Moreover, you never know when someone may be peering at a screen over the shoulder of the intended recipient. And there's always the danger of hitting the wrong button, sending your thoughts to an entire list of people when you meant to contact only one. To avoid embarrassing yourself—or even endangering your job—never send inappropriate comments, angry responses, petty remarks, or personal information through your business e-mail. Never send confidential or "top secret" business information through e-mail without proper authorization. Learn to use e-mail in a productive way that protects both you and your organization.

Mind Your Netiquette! Although no one requires that you don your white kid gloves to hit those computer keys, rules of etiquette for e-mail writers are taking form these days. Here are a few suggestions for well-behaved writers:

- Don't "shout" your messages in all capital letters. IT'S TOO HARD TO READ A SCREEN FULL OF SAME-SIZED LETTERS. Occasionally, you may type a word in capital letters for emphasis, but use this technique sparingly. (For more advice on proper tone, see previous page.)

- Be cautious about using Net shorthand or in-house abbreviations ("the TR6 project"), especially in messages to other organizations. If certain shorthand signs or phrases, such as BTW (by the way), FWIW (for what it's worth), or G2G (got to go), are routinely used in casual e-mail at your place of work, feel free to adopt them. However, most business correspondence is more formal and not all abbreviations may be universally recognized. When in doubt, spell it out. Business messages depend on clarity and a mutual understanding of all terms.

- Don't ever, ever use "emoticons" in business writing. Emoticons are typed "smiley" faces read sideways that many people find more annoying than ground glass in a sandwich. Instead of relying on these gaggingly cute symbols to communicate emotions of happiness, sadness, surprise, or irony, find the right words instead. Show off your writing skills, not your ability to group type!

- Never forward anyone else's e-mail message without permission, especially if that message contains controversial and/or hurtful statements or confidential material. (Because other people often break this rule, think twice before *you* write.)

■ Designing Résumés

A résumé is a document that presents a brief summary of your educational background, work experiences, professional skills, special qualifications, and honors; some résumés also contain a brief list of references. You may be asked to submit a résumé on a variety of occasions, most often to supplement your applications for jobs, interviews, promotions, scholarships, grants, fellowships, or other kinds of opportunities. Because prospective employers are the largest target audience for résumés, the following section offers advice to help job seekers design the most effective document possible.

Job seekers most frequently send their résumés with "cover letters" directed to particular employers. To prepare each cover letter, follow the basic steps for writing the traditional business letter, as outlined earlier in this chapter. In the first paragraph, clearly tell your reader why you are writing: the specific job you are applying for, and why. Devote one or more paragraphs in the "body" of your letter to noting your education or professional experience or both, explaining why you are a good match for the advertised position or how you might benefit the organization. Your concluding paragraph should express thanks for the employer's consideration and briefly reemphasize your interest in the job; in this paragraph you may also mention contact information or, in some situations, indicate your availability for an interview. If the employer is interested, he or she will scan your résumé for more details and possibly distribute copies to others involved in the hiring process.

Because employers today may receive hundreds of applications for a single job, it is important to present yourself as positively as possible in your letter and résumé. If your campus has a career center, seek it out as your first step. Career centers often have extraordinary resources: sample cover letters and résumés, hints for interviews, information on electronic job searching, and much more. Because there are multiple ways to arrange a résumé, you will find it useful to familiarize yourself with some representative samples before you begin working on your own.

Although there is no single blueprint for all résumés, there is one guiding principle: *select and arrange your information in the way that most effectively highlights your strengths to your prospective employer.* Think of your résumé as a one-page advertisement for yourself.

To find the best way to "sell" yourself to an employer, you might choose to adopt one of the two most popular arrangement styles:

- *Functional format:* This arrangement places the reader's focus more directly on the job seeker's education and skills than on limited work experience. It is better suited for job seekers who are new graduates or those just entering the workforce. Most résumés of this type are one page.

- *Experiential format:* This style emphasizes professional experience by placing work history in the most prominent position, listing the current or most important employment first. This format might be best for non-traditional students who have a work history before school or for those students who have worked throughout their college careers. If the list of relevant professional experience is lengthy, this kind of résumé may extend to a second page, if necessary.

Before you begin drafting your résumé, make a list of the information you want to include. Then think about the best ways to group your material, and select an appropriate title for each section. Some of the common content areas include the following:

1. **Heading.** Located at the top of your résumé, this section identifies you and presents your contact information: your full name, address, phone number, and e-mail address if you have one. You may wish to put your name in slightly bigger type or in bold letters.

2. **Employment objective.** Some job seekers choose to include a statement describing the kind of employment or specific position they are seeking. Others omit this section, making this information clear in their cover letters. If you do

include this section, always substitute a brief, specific objective for trite, over-blown language any job seeker in the world might write:

Trite: Seeking employment with a company offering intellectual challenges and opportunities for professional growth

Specific: A microbiology research position in a laboratory or center working on disease prevention and control

If you have the time and resources to customize a résumé for each job announcement you respond to, you can use this section to show that the position you most want matches the one advertised. However, if you plan to use one résumé for a variety of job applications, beware presenting an employment objective so narrowly focused that it excludes you from a particular application pool.

3. **Education.** If you have no extensive, relevant, or recent work experience, this section might best appear next on your résumé. Begin with the highest degree you have earned or, if you are about to graduate, you may present the anticipated graduation date. Include the name of the school and its location and, if relevant, your major, minor, or special concentration. Some graduates with a high grade point average also include that information. This section might also contain any professional certificates or licenses (teaching, real estate, counseling, etc.) you have earned or other educational information you deem relevant to a particular job search (internships, research projects, study-abroad programs, honors classes, or other special training).

4. **Professional experience.** If you wish to emphasize your work history, place this section after your heading or employment objective, rather than your educational background. In this section, list the position title, name of employer, city and state, and employment dates, with the most current job or relevant work experience first. Some résumés include brief statements describing the responsibilities or accomplishments of each position. If you choose to include such descriptions, try to be specific (Prepared monthly payroll for 35 employees) rather than general (Performed important financial tasks monthly); use action verbs (supervised, developed, organized, trained, created, etc.) that present your efforts in a strong way. Use past tense verbs for work completed and present tense for current responsibilities.

   Note that résumés traditionally do not use the word "I"; beginning brief descriptive phrases with a strong verb, rather than repeating "I had responsibility for . . . ," saves precious space on a résumé.

5. **Skills.** Because you want to stress your value to a prospective employer, you may wish to note relevant professional skills or special abilities you have to offer. This section may be especially important if you do not have a work history; many recent graduates place this section immediately following the education section to underscore the skills they could bring to the workplace. For example, you might list technical skills you possess or mention expertise in a foreign language if that might look useful to a company with overseas connections.

6. **Honors, awards, activities.** In this section, list those awards, scholarships, honors, and prizes that show others have selected you as an outstanding worker, student, writer, teacher, and so on. Here (or perhaps in a section for related skills

or experiences) you might also add leadership roles in organizations, and even certain kinds of volunteer work, if mentioning these would further your case. Although you don't want to trivialize your résumé by listing irrelevant activities, think hard about your life from a "skills" angle. Coordinating a campus charity project, for example, may indicate just the kinds of managerial skills an employer is looking for. Don't pad your résumé—but don't undersell yourself either.

7. **References.** Some employers ask immediately for references, persons they may contact for more information about you and your work or academic experiences; other employers ask for references later in the hiring process. If references are requested with the initial application letter, the information may be listed at the end of the résumé or on an attached page. Reference information includes the person's full name and title or position, the name and address of the person's business or organization, telephone number, and e-mail address, if available. Do not list friends or neighbors as references; résumé references should be academics or professionals who are familiar with your work.

Critique Your Page Appeal

Once you have decided on your résumé's content, you also need to consider its visual appeal. Because employers often scan résumés quickly, your page should be not only informative but also professional looking and easy to read. Unless you have a compelling reason for another choice, always laser print your résumé on high-quality white or off-white paper. You may highlight your section titles (education, work experiences, skills, etc.) by using boldface or large print, but don't overuse such print. Balance your text and white space in a pleasing arrangement.

If you have problems arranging your material (too much information jammed on the page or so little that your text looks lonely, for example), go back to the career center to look at ways others handled similar problems (some large copy shops also have sample books). A good page design, like a good haircut, can frame your best features in the most engaging way.

Most important: always proofread your résumé for errors in grammar, punctuation, spelling, spacing, or typing! Because you want your résumé to look as professional as possible, make a point of having several careful (human) readers proofread your final draft.

Problems to Avoid

Remain Ethical. Never lie on a résumé! Never, ever! Although you want to present yourself in the best possible ways, never fib about your experience, forge credentials you don't have, take credit for someone else's work, or overstate your participation in a project. No matter what you have heard about "puffery" in résumés ("everyone exaggerates so why shouldn't I?"), avoid embarrassment (or even legal action) by always telling the truth. Instead of misrepresenting yourself, find ways to identify and arrange your knowledge and skills in ways that best highlight your strengths.

Contact Your References in Advance. You *must* obtain permission from each person before you list him or her as a reference. Even if you know the person well, use your good manners here: in person or in a politely written note or letter, ask in advance of your job application if you may name him or her as a reference. Once permission is granted, it's smart to give your references your résumé and any other information that might help them help you if they are contacted by a prospective employer. (Although a former boss or teacher may remember you well, they may be hazy about your exact dates of employment or the semester of your course work. Give them a helpful list of places, dates, skills, and—though you may have to overcome your sense of modesty—tactfully remind them of any outstanding work you did.

It's also good manners (and smart) to send your references a thank-you note, expressing your appreciation for their part in your job search (such notes are absolutely *required* if people wrote letters of recommendation for you). Thank-you notes should be written on stationery and sent through the mail; e-mail notes are not appropriate.

Add Personal Information Thoughtfully. Federal law protects you: employers may not discriminate on the basis of ethnicity, race, religion, age, or gender. You should not include on your résumé any personal information (marital status, number of children, birth date, country of origin, etc.) that is not relevant to the job search. Although you may, if you wish, include information on your résumé about relevant personal interests (travel, theatrical experience, volunteer rescue work, etc.), you should be aware that employers may not consider such details useful. Don't squander your résumé space on unessential information! A better plan: if you've spent a great deal of your time in some after-work or extracurricular activity, identify the *skills* you have developed that will transfer to the workplace (customer relations, public speaking, editing, etc.). Instead of just describing yourself, show prospective employers what you can *do* for them.

Special Note: An increasing number of Web sites are helping employers and job-seekers find each other through the posting of jobs and résumés. If you do post your résumé on such a site, choose your words carefully. Many prospective employers now use applicant tracking software to look for keywords in résumés to match their needs. For example, a business seeking an accountant to assist its offices in Paris and Rome might flag only those résumés containing the words "CPA," "French," and "Italian." So, if you are interested in a particular job advertised on the Web, study the language of the job description and consider repeating, where appropriate, its key words in your résumé.

▪ Sample Résumés

The first résumé that follows was designed by a recent college graduate. Because he did not have an extensive work record, he chose a functional format to emphasize his education, business skills, and scholastic honors. The second résumé briefly notes specific skills from previous academic and work experiences that might interest a prospective employer.

■ Sample Résumé #1

Brent Monroe

417 Remington Street   (970) 555-4567
Fort Collins, CO 80525   BCMonroe@aol.com

Education

B.S. in Business Administration, Colorado State University, May 2004
A.S., Front Range Community College, May 2002

Professional Skills

Accounting
>   Spreadsheet programs
>   Amortization schedules
>   Payroll design and verification
>   Contracts and invoices

Computer
>   Word processing: Microsoft Word, WordPerfect
>   Spreadsheets: Excel, Select
>   Presentations: PowerPoint
>   Web site design

Awards and Activities

Outstanding Student Achievement Award, College of Business, Colorado State
    University, 2004
President's Scholarship, Colorado State University, 2003 and 2004
Treasurer, Business Students Association, Colorado State University, 2003

Employment

Assistant Manager, Poppa's Pizza; Ault, Colorado, 6/02-12/03

References

Professor Gwen Lesser	Professor Ralph Berber	Mr. Randy Attree
Department of Accounting	Department of Finance	Manager, Poppa's Pizza
Colorado State University	Colorado State University	630 E. Third Street
Fort Collins, CO 80523	Fort Collins, CO 80523	Ault, CO 80303
(970) 555-7890	(970) 555-2344	(970) 333-4839
Glesser@colostate.edu	Rberber@colostate.edu	

■ Sample Résumé #2

ROSEMARY SILVA

3000 Colorado Avenue
Boulder, Colorado 80303

(720) 555-6428
Rosesilva@netscape.net

Objective

To secure a full-time position as an admissions counselor at a mental health or addiction recovery facility

Education

B.A., University of Colorado at Boulder, May 2004. Major: Psychology. Minor: Spanish.

Internship and Research Experience

Intern Detoxification Counselor, Twin Lakes Recovery Center, Boulder, Colorado; January-May 2004.

Provided one-on-one counseling for in-patient residents; conducted admission interviews and prepared mental and physical evaluation reports; monitored physical vitals of patients; responded to crisis phone calls from out-patients; performed basic paramedical techniques; referred patients to other community agencies; supplied substance abuse information to patients and families.

Psychology Research Lab Assistant, University of Colorado at Boulder, under the direction of Professor Lois Diamond; September-December 2003.

Helped conduct experiments on CU student-volunteers to measure the relationship of memory and academic success: explained experiment procedures, set up computers, recorded student information, validated research credit slips.

Employment

Night Security Dispatcher, University of Colorado at Boulder, Campus Police Department; May 2002-April 2004.

Accurately received and responded to emergency and non-emergency calls and radio transmissions; communicated emergency information to appropriate agencies, such as Boulder Police and Rape Crisis Center; dispatched security units to handle crisis situations; wrote detailed records of incoming calls, security patrols, and responses.

References Available Upon Request

■ ASSIGNMENT

Prepare a one-page résumé for your professional use at this time or in the near future. While you are in school, you might use this résumé to apply for a scholarship, an internship, a summer job, or a part-time position. Arrange your information to emphasize your strengths, and don't forget to thoroughly proofread several times before you print your final draft. (If you keep a copy of this résumé handy and revise it regularly, you will be ready to respond quickly should a job or other opportunity unexpectedly present itself.)

■ Writing Post-Interview Letters

After you interview for a job you want, consider writing a follow-up note to the prospective employer. This letter should be more than a polite thank you for the interview, however. Use the opportunity to again emphasize your skills. Begin by thanking the person for his or her time, but move on to show that you think, now more than ever, that you are the right person for the position and for the organization. Illustrate this claim by showing that during the interview you really listened and observed: "After hearing about your goals for new product X, I know I could contribute because. . . ." Or remind your interviewer of reasons to hire you: "You stressed your company's need for someone with XYZ skills. My internship training in that area. . . ." In other words, use this follow-up letter not only to offer your thanks but also to gently advertise yourself (and your good writing skills) one more time.

Part 4

A Concise Handbook

In this section you will learn to recognize and correct the most common errors in grammar, punctuation, and mechanics. Each error will be explained as simply as possible, with a minimum of technical language. Beside each rule you will find the editing mark or abbreviation most often used to identify that error; each rule is also numbered for easy reference. Exercises throughout each chapter will help you practice your grammar and punctuation skills. ■

Chapter 19

Major Errors in Grammar

■ Errors with Verbs

19a Faulty Agreement   S-V Agr

Make your verb agree in number with its subject; a singular subject takes a singular verb, and a plural subject takes a plural verb.

Incorrect	*Lester Peabody*, principal of the Kung Fu School of Grammar, *don't* agree that gum chewing should be banned in the classroom.
Correct	*Lester Peabody*, principal of the Kung Fu School of Grammar, *doesn't* agree that gum chewing should be banned in the classroom.
Incorrect	The *actions* of the new senator *hasn't* been consistent with her campaign promises.
Correct	The *actions* of the new senator *haven't* been consistent with her campaign promises.

Compound subjects joined by "and" take a plural verb, unless the subject refers to a single person or a single unit.

Examples	*Bean sprouts* and *tofu are* dishes Jim Bob won't consider eating. ["Bean sprouts" and "tofu" are a compound subject joined by "and"; therefore, use a plural verb.]
	The *winner* and new *champion refuses* to give up the microphone at the news conference. ["Winner" and "champion" refer to a single person; therefore, use a singular verb.]

Listed here are some of the most confusing subject-verb agreement problems:

1. With a collective noun: a singular noun referring to a collection of elements as a unit generally takes a singular verb.

Incorrect	During boring parts of the Transcendental Vegetation lecture, the *class* often *chant* to the music of Norman Bates and the Shower Heads.
Correct	During boring parts of the Transcendental Vegetation lecture, the *class* often *chants* to the music of Norman Bates and the Shower Heads.
Incorrect	The *army* of the new nation *want* shoes, bullets, and weekend passes.
Correct	The *army* of the new nation *wants* shoes, bullets, and weekend passes.

2. With a relative pronoun ("that," "which," and "who") used as a subject: the verb agrees with its antecedent, the word being described.

Incorrect	The boss rejected a shipment of *shirts, which was* torn.
Correct	The boss rejected a shipment of *shirts, which were* torn.

3. With "each," "everybody," "everyone," and "neither" as the subject: use a singular verb even when followed by a plural construction.

Incorrect	*Each* of the children *think* Mom and Dad are automatic teller machines.
Correct	*Each* of the children *thinks* Mom and Dad are automatic teller machines.
Incorrect	Although only a few of the students saw the teacher pull out his hair, *everybody know* why he did it.
Correct	Although only a few of the students saw the teacher pull out his hair, *everybody knows* why he did it.
Incorrect	*Neither have* a dime left by the second of the month.
Correct	*Neither has* a dime left by the second of the month.

4. With "either . . . or" and "neither . . . nor": the verb agrees with the nearer item.

Incorrect	Neither rain nor dogs nor *gloom of night keep* the mail carrier from delivering bills.
Correct	Neither rain nor dogs nor *gloom of night keeps* the mail carrier from delivering bills.
Incorrect	Either Betty or her *neighbors is* hosting a come-as-you-are breakfast.
Correct	Either Betty or her *neighbors are* hosting a come-as-you-are breakfast.

5. With "here is (are)" and "there is (are)": the verb agrees with the number indicated by the subject following the verb.

Incorrect	*There is* only two good *reasons* for missing this law class: death and jury duty.
Correct	*There are* only two good *reasons* for missing this law class: death and jury duty.

Incorrect	To help you do your shopping quickly, Mr. Scrooge, *here are* a *list* of gifts under a dollar.
Correct	To help you do your shopping quickly, Mr. Scrooge, *here is* a *list* of gifts under a dollar.

6. With plural nouns intervening between subject and verb: the verb still agrees with the subject.

Incorrect	The *jungle*, with its poisonous plants, wild animals, and biting insects, *make* Herman long for the sidewalks of Topeka.
Correct	The *jungle*, with its poisonous plants, wild animals, and biting insects, *makes* Herman long for the sidewalks of Topeka.

7. With nouns plural in form but singular in meaning: a singular verb is usually correct.

Examples	*News travels* slowly if it comes through the post office.
	Charades is the exhibitionist's game of choice.
	Politics is often the rich person's hobby.

19b Subjunctive   V Sub

When you make a wish or a statement that is contrary to fact, use the subjunctive verb form "were."

Incorrect	I wish I *was* queen so I could levy a tax on men who spit.
Correct	I wish I *were* queen so I could levy a tax on men who spit. [This expresses a wish.]
Incorrect	If "Fightin' Henry" *was* a foot taller and thirty pounds heavier, we would all be in trouble.
Correct	If "Fightin' Henry" *were* a foot taller and thirty pounds heavier, we would all be in trouble. [This proposes a statement contrary to fact.]

19c Tense Shift   T

In most cases, the first verb in a sentence establishes the tense of any later verb. Keep your verbs within the same time frame.

Incorrect	Big Joe *saw* the police car coming up behind, so he *turns* into the next alley.
Correct	Big Joe *saw* the police car coming up behind, so he *turned* into the next alley.
Incorrect	Horace *uses* an artificial sweetener in his coffee all day, so he *felt* a pizza and a hot-fudge sundae *were* fine for dinner.
Correct	Horace *uses* an artificial sweetener in his coffee all day, so he *feels* a pizza and a hot-fudge sundae *are* fine for dinner.
Incorrect	Rex the Wonder Horse *was* obviously very smart because he *taps* out the telephone numbers of the stars with his hoof.
Correct	Rex the Wonder Horse *was* obviously very smart because he *tapped* out the telephone numbers of the stars with his hoof.

19d   Split Infinitive   Sp I

Many authorities insist that you never separate *to* from its verb; today, however, some grammarians allow the split infinitive except in the most formal kinds of writing. Nevertheless, because it offends some readers, it is probably best to avoid the construction unless clarity or emphasis is clearly served by its use.

Traditional	A swift kick is needed *to start* the machine properly.
Untraditional	A swift kick is needed *to* properly *start* the machine.
Traditional	The teacher wanted Lori *to communicate* her ideas clearly.
Untraditional	The teacher wanted Lori *to* clearly *communicate* her ideas.

19e   Double Negatives   D Neg

Don't use a negative verb and a negative qualifier together.

Incorrect	I *can't hardly* wait until Jim Bob gets his jaw out of traction, so I can challenge him to a bubble gum blowing contest.
Correct	I *can hardly* wait until Jim Bob gets his jaw out of traction, so I can challenge him to a bubble gum blowing contest.
Incorrect	Even when he flew his helicopter upside-down over her house, she *wouldn't scarcely* look at him.
Correct	Even when he flew his helicopter upside-down over her house, she *would scarcely* look at him.

19f   Passive Voice   Pass

"Active voice" refers to sentences in which the subject performs the action. "Passive voice" refers to sentences in which the subject is acted upon.

Active	The police *pulled* over the van full of stolen ski sweaters.
Passive	The van full of stolen ski sweaters *was pulled* over by the police.

Although conventions vary among disciplines, your prose style will improve if you choose strong, active-voice verbs over wordy or unclear passive constructions.

Wordy passive construction	For years Texas schoolchildren were taught by their teachers that the fifth food group was gravy.
Active	For years teachers taught Texas schoolchildren that gravy was the fifth food group.
Unclear passive construction	Much protest is being voiced over the new electric fireworks. [Who is protesting?]
Active verb	Members of the Fuse Lighters Association are protesting the new electric fireworks.

(For more examples of active- and passive-voice verbs, see page 125.)

■ PRACTICING WHAT YOU'VE LEARNED

Errors with Verbs

A. The following sentences contain subject–verb agreement errors. Correct the problems by changing the verbs. Some sentences contain more than one error.

1. A recent report on Cuban land crabs show they can run faster than horses.

2. The team from Snooker Hollow High School are considering switching from basketball to basket weaving because passing athletics are now required for graduation.

3. Neither of the students know that both mystery writer Agatha Christie and inventor Thomas Edison was dyslexic.

4. Each of the twins have read about Joseph Priestley's contribution to the understanding of oxygen, but neither were aware that he also invented the pencil eraser.

5. Clarity in speech and writing are absolutely essential in the business world today.

6. Some scholars believe that the world's first money, in the form of coins, were made in Lydia, a country that is now part of Turkey.

7. Bananas, rich in vitamins and low in fats, is rated the most popular fruit in America.

8. There is many children in this country who appreciate a big plate of hot grits, but none of the Hall kids like this Southern dish.

9. Either the cocker spaniel or the poodle hold the honor of being the most popular breed of dogs in the United States, say the American Kennel Club.

10. Many people considers Johnny Appleseed a mythical figure, but now two local historians, authors of a well-known book on the subject, argues he was a real person named John Chapman.

B. The following sentences contain incorrect verb forms, tense shifts, and double negatives. Correct any problems you see, and rewrite any sentences whose clarity or conciseness would be improved by using active rather than passive verbs.

1. He couldn't hardly wait to hear country star Sue Flay sing her version of "I've Been Flushed from the Bathroom of Your Heart."

2. "If you was in Wyoming and couldn't hear the wind blowing, what would people call you?" asked Jethro. "Dead," replies his buddy Herman.

3. It was believed by Aztec ruler Montezuma that chocolate had magical powers and can act as an aphrodisiac.

4. Tammy's favorite band is Opie Gone Bad so she always was buying their concert tickets, even though she can't hardly afford to.

5. Suspicions of arson are being raised by the Fire Department following the burning of the new Chip and Dale Furniture Factory.

■ Errors with Nouns   N

19g   Possessive with "-ing" Nouns

When the emphasis is on the action, use the possessive pronoun plus the "-ing" noun.

Example   He hated *my* singing around the house, so I made him live in the garage. [The emphasis is on *singing.*]

When the emphasis is not on the action, you may use a noun or pronoun plus the "-ing" noun.

Example   He hated *me* singing around the house, so I made him live in the garage. [The emphasis is on the person singing—me—not the action; he might have liked someone else singing.]

19h   Misuse of Nouns as Adjectives

Some nouns may be used as adjectives modifying other nouns: "horse show," "movie star," or "theater seats." But some nouns used as adjectives sound awkward or like jargon. To avoid such awkwardness, you may need to change the noun to an appropriate adjective or reword the sentence.

Awkward   The group decided to work on local *environment* problems.
Better   The group decided to work on local *environmental* problems.
Jargon   The executive began a *cost estimation comparison study* of the two products.
Better   The executive began a *comparison study* of the two products' costs.

(For more information on ridding your prose of multiple nouns, see page 131.)

■ Errors with Pronouns

19i   Faulty Agreement   Pro Agr

A pronoun should agree in number and gender with its antecedent (that is, the word the pronoun stands for).

Incorrect   To get a temperamental *actress* to sign a contract, the director would lock *them* in the dressing room.
Correct   To get a temperamental *actress* to sign a contract, the director would lock *her* in the dressing room.

Use the singular pronoun with "everyone," "anyone," and "each."

Incorrect	When the belly dancer asked for a volunteer partner, *everyone* in the men's gym class raised *their* hand.
Correct	When the belly dancer asked for a volunteer partner, *everyone* in the men's gym class raised *his* hand.
Incorrect	*Each* of the new wives decided to keep *their* own name.
Correct	*Each* of the new wives decided to keep *her* own name.

In the past, writers have traditionally used the masculine pronoun "he" when the gender of the antecedent is unknown, as in the following: "If a *spy* refuses to answer questions, *he* should be forced to watch James Bond movies until *he* cracks." Today, however, many authorities prefer the nonsexist "she/he," even though the construction can be awkward when maintained over a stretch of prose. Perhaps the best solution is to use the impersonal "one" when possible or simply rewrite the sentence in the plural: "If *spies* refuse to answer questions, *they* should be forced to watch James Bond movies until *they* crack." (For more examples, see pages 155–157.)

19j Vague Reference   Ref

Your pronoun references should be clear.

Vague	If the trained seal won't eat its dinner, throw *it* into the lion's cage. [What goes into the lion's cage?]
Clear	If the trained seal won't eat its dinner, throw *the food* into the lion's cage.
Vague	After the dog bit Harry, *he* raised such a fuss at the police station that the sergeant finally had *him* impounded. [Who raised the fuss? Who was impounded?]
Clear	After being bitten, *Harry* raised such a fuss at the police station that the sergeant finally had the *dog* impounded.

Sometimes you must add a word or rewrite the sentence to make the pronoun reference clear:

Vague	I'm a lab instructor in the biology department and am also taking a statistics course. *This* has always been difficult for me. [What is difficult?]
Clear	I'm a lab instructor in the biology department and am also taking statistics, a *course* that has always been difficult for me.
Clear	I'm a lab instructor in the biology department and am also taking a statistics course. Being a teacher and a student at the same time has always been difficult for me.

19k Shift in Pronouns   P Sh

Be consistent in your use of pronouns; don't shift from one person to another.

Incorrect	*One* shouldn't eat pudding with *your* fingers.
Correct	*One* shouldn't eat pudding with *one's* fingers.
Correct	*You* shouldn't eat pudding with *your* fingers.

| Incorrect | *We* left-handed people are at a disadvantage because most of the time *you* can't rent left-handed golf clubs or bowling balls. |
| Correct | *We* left-handed people are at a disadvantage because most of the time *we* can't rent left-handed golf clubs or bowling balls. |

(For additional examples, see pages 131–132.)

191   Incorrect Case   Ca

1. The case of a pronoun is determined by its function in the particular sentence. If the pronoun is a subject, use the nominative case: "I," "he," "she," "we," and "they"; if the pronoun is an object, use the objective case: "me," "him," "her," "us," and "them." To check your usage, all you need to do in many instances is isolate the pronoun in the manner shown here and see if it sounds correct alone.

Incorrect	Give the treasure map to Frankie and *I*.
Isolated	Give the treasure map to *I*. [awkward]
Correct	Give the treasure map to Frankie and *me*.
Incorrect	Bertram and *her* suspect that the moon is hollow.
Isolated	*Her* suspects that the moon is hollow. [awkward]
Correct	Bertram and *she* suspect that the moon is hollow.
Incorrect	The gift is from Annette and *I*.
Isolated	The gift is from *I*. [awkward]
Correct	The gift is from Annette and *me*.

Sometimes the "isolation test" doesn't work and you just have to remember the rules. A common pronoun problem involves use of the preposition "between" and the choice of "me" or "I." Perhaps you can remember this rule by recalling there is no "I" in "between," only "e's" as in "me."

| Incorrect | Just *between you and I*, the Russian housekeeper is a good cook but she won't iron curtains. |
| Correct | Just *between you and me*, the Russian housekeeper is a good cook but she won't iron curtains. |

In other cases, to determine the correct pronoun, you will need to add implied but unstated sentence elements:

Examples	Mother always liked Dickie more than *me*. [Mother liked Dickie more than *she liked* me.]
	She is younger than *I* by three days. [She is younger than I *am* by three days.]
	Telephone exchange: May I speak to Kate? This is *she*. [This is she *speaking*.]

2. To solve the confusing *who/whom* pronoun problem, first determine the case of the pronoun in its own clause in each sentence.

A. If the pronoun is the subject of a clause, use "who" or "whoever."

Examples   I don't know *who* spread the peanut butter on my English paper. ["Who" is the subject of the verb "spread" in the clause "who spread the peanut butter on my English paper."]
Rachel is a librarian *who* only likes books with pictures. ["Who" is the subject of the verb "likes" in the clause "who only likes books with pictures."]
He will sell secrets to *whoever* offers the largest sum of money. ["Whoever" is the subject of the verb "offers" in the clause "whoever offers the largest sum of money."]

B. If the pronoun is the object of a verb, use "whom" or "whomever."

Examples   *Whom* am I kicking? ["Whom" is the direct object of the verb "kicking."]
Sid is a man *whom* I distrust. ["Whom" is the direct object of the verb "distrust."]
Whomever he kicked will probably be angry. ["Whomever" is the direct object of the verb "kicked."]

C. If the pronoun occurs as the object of a preposition, use "whom," especially when the preposition immediately precedes the pronoun.

Examples   *With whom* am I speaking?
To whom is the letter addressed?
Do not ask *for whom* the bell tolls.

■ PRACTICING WHAT YOU'VE LEARNED

Errors with Nouns and Pronouns

A. In the sentences below select the proper pronouns.

1. Please buy a copy of the book *The Celery Stalks at Midnight* for my sister and (I, me).
2. Between you and (I, me), some people define Freudian slip as saying one thing but meaning your mother.
3. (Who, Whom) is the singer of the country song "You Can't Make a Heel Toe the Mark"?
4. Aunt Beulah makes better cookies than (I, me).
5. (Him and me, He and I) are going to the movies to see *Attack of the Killer Crabgrass.*
6. I'm giving my accordion to (whoever, whomever) is carrying a grudge against our neighbors.
7. The Botox surprise party was given by Paige Turner, Justin Case, and (I, me).

8. She is the kind of person for (who, whom) housework meant sweeping the room with a glance.

9. (Her and him, She and he) are twins.

10. The judge of the ugly feet contest found choosing between (him and her, she and he) too difficult.

B. The sentences below contain a variety of errors with nouns and pronouns. Some sentences contain more than one error; skip any correct sentences you may find.

1. The executive knew she was in trouble when her salary underwent a modification reduction adjustment of 50 percent.

2. Of whom did Oscar Wilde once say, "He hasn't a single redeeming vice"?

3. It was a surprise to both Mary and I to learn that Switzerland didn't give women the right to vote until 1971.

4. Each of the young women in the Family Life class decided not to marry after they read that couples today have 2.3 children.

5. Jim Bob explained to Frankie that the best way for him to avoid his recurring nosebleeds was to stay out of his cousin's marital arguments.

6. Those of us who'd had the flu agreed that one can always get a doctor to return your call quicker if you get in the shower, but let's keep this tip confidential between you and I.

7. The stranger gave the free movie tickets to Louise and I after he saw people standing in line to leave the theater.

8. The personnel director told each of the employees, most of who opposed him, to signify their "no" vote by saying, "I resign."

9. Clarence and me have an uncle who is so mean he writes the name of the murderer on the first page of mystery novels that are passed around the family.

10. One of the first movies to gross over one million dollars was *Tarzan of the Apes* (1932), starring Johnny Weismuller, a former Olympic star who became an actor. This didn't happen often in the movie industry at that time.

■ Errors with Adverbs and Adjectives

19m   Incorrect Usage   Adv   Adj

Incorrect use of adverbs and adjectives often occurs when you confuse the two modifiers. Adverbs qualify the meanings of verbs, adjectives, and other adverbs; they frequently end in "-ly," and they often answer the question "how?"

Incorrect	After Kay argued with the mechanic, her car began running *bad*.
Correct	After Kay argued with the mechanic, her car began running *badly*.

Adjectives, on the other hand, describe or qualify the meanings of nouns only.

Example	The *angry* mechanic neglected to put oil into Kay's car.

One of the most confusing pairs of modifiers is "well" and "good." We often use "good" as an adjective modifying a noun and "well" as an adverb modifying a verb.

Examples	*A Sap's Fables* is a *good* book for children, although it is not *well* organized.
	Bubba was such a *good* liar his wife had to call in the children at suppertime.
	After eating Rocky Mountain oysters, Susie yodels exceptionally *well*.
	Did you do *well* on your math test?

If you cannot determine whether a word is an adverb or an adjective, consult your dictionary.

19n Faulty Comparison   Comp

When you compare two elements to a higher or lower degree, you often add "-er" or "-r" to the adjective.

Incorrect	Of the two sisters, Sarah is the *loudest*.
Correct	Of the two sisters, Sarah is the *louder*.

When you compare more than two elements, you often add "-est" to the adjective.

Example	Sarah is the *loudest* of the four children in the family.

Other adjectives use the words "more," "most," "less," and "least" to indicate comparison.

Examples	Bela Lugosi is *more* handsome than Lon Chaney but *less* handsome than Vincent Price.
	Boris Karloff is the *most* handsome, and Christopher Lee is the *least* handsome, of all the horror film stars.

Beware using a double comparison when it is unnecessary:

Incorrect	It was the *most saddest* song I've ever heard.
Correct	It was the *saddest* song I've ever heard.

Note, too, that for most authorities, the word "unique" is a special adjective, one without a degree of comparison. Despite common usage to the contrary, an experience or thing may be unique—that is, one of a kind—but it may not be "very unique."

■ **PRACTICING WHAT YOU'VE LEARNED**

Errors with Adverbs and Adjectives

Choose the correct adverbs and adjectives in the sentences below.

1. After the optometrist pulled her eye tooth, Hortense didn't behave very (good, well) in the waiting room.

2. Which is the (worser, worse, worst) food, liver or buttermilk?

3. I didn't do (good, well) on my nature project because my bonsai sequoia tree grew (bad, badly) in its tiny container.

4. Don't forget to dress (warm, warmly) for the Arctic freestyle race.

5. Of the twins, Teensie is more (funner, fun) than Egore.

6. Watching Joe Bob eat candied fruit flies made Jolene feel (real, really) ill, and his table manners did not make her feel (more better, better).

7. The Roman toothpick holder was (very unique, the uniquest, unique).

8. That was the (funniest, most funniest) flea circus I have ever seen.

9. Does the instructional guide *Bobbing for Doughnuts* still sell (good, well)?

10. The Fighting Mosquitoes were trained (well, good), but they just didn't take practices (serious, seriously).

■ Errors in Modifying Phrases

19o Dangling Modifiers   DM

A modifying—or descriptive—phrase must have a logical relationship to some specific words in the sentence. When those words are omitted, the phrase "dangles" without anything to modify. Dangling modifiers frequently occur at the beginnings of sentences and often may be corrected by adding the proper subjects to the main clauses.

Dangling	Not knowing how to swim, buying scuba gear was foolish.
Correct	Not knowing how to swim, *we* decided that buying scuba gear was foolish.
Dangling	Feeling too sick to ski, her vacation to the mountains was postponed.
Correct	Feeling too sick to ski, *Laura* postponed her vacation to the mountains.

(For additional examples, see pages 120–121.)

19p   Misplaced Modifiers   MM

When modifying words, phrases, or clauses are not placed near the word they describe, confusion or unintentional humor often results.

Misplaced	Teddy swatted the fly still dressed in his pajamas.
Correct	Still dressed in his pajamas, Teddy swatted the fly.
Misplaced	There are many things people won't eat, especially children.
Correct	There are many things people, especially children, won't eat.

(For additional examples, see pages 119–120.)

■ PRACTICING WHAT YOU'VE LEARNED

Errors in Modifying Phrases

Correct the errors in dangling and misplaced modifiers by rearranging or rewriting the sentences below.

1. After boarding Hard Luck Airlines, the meals convinced us to return by ship.

2. Here is the new telephone number for notifying the fire department of any fires that may be attached to your telephone.

3. The prize-winning ice sculptor celebrated her new open-air studio in Aspen, where she lives with her infant daughter, purchased for $10,000.

4. The movie star showed off letters from admirers that were lying all over his desk.

5. Running too fast during a game of "Kick the Can," my face collided with the flagpole.

6. Eloise bought a computer from her neighbor with faulty memory.

7. Baggy, wrinkled, and hopelessly out of style, Jean tossed the skirt from her closet.

8. Forgetting to pack underwear, the suitcase had to be reopened.

9. Blanche plans to teach a course next spring incorporating her research into the mating habits of Big Foot on the campus of Slippery Rock College.

10. After spending all night in the library, Kate's friends knew she'd need a trip to Special Coffee.

11. Squeezing the can, the tomatoes didn't seem ripe to DeeDee.

12. From birth to twelve months, parents don't have to worry about solid food.

13. He didn't think the bicycles would make it over the mountains, being so old.

14. I've read that a number of modern sailors, like Thor Heyerdahl, have sailed primitive vessels across the ocean in books from the public library.

15. Proofreading carefully, dangling modifiers may be spotted and corrected easily.

■ Errors in Sentences

19q Fragments   Frag

A complete sentence must contain a subject and a verb. A fragment is an incomplete sentence; it is often a participial ("-ing") phrase or dependent clause that belongs to the preceding sentence. To check for fragments, try reading your prose, one sentence at a time, starting at the *end* of your essay. If you find a "sentence" that makes no sense alone, it's probably a fragment that should either be rewritten or connected to another sentence.

Incorrect	Bubba's parents refuse to send him to a psychiatrist. Although they both know he eats shoelaces and light bulbs.
Correct	Bubba's parents refuse to send him to a psychiatrist, although they both know he eats shoelaces and light bulbs.
Incorrect	This recording of the symphony's latest concert is so clear you can hear every sound. Including the coughs and whispers of the audience.
Correct	This recording of the symphony's latest concert is so clear you can hear every sound, including the coughs and whispers of the audience.
Incorrect	At Liz's most recent wedding, the photographer used an instant camera. Because her marriages break up so fast.
Correct	At Liz's most recent wedding, the photographer used an instant camera because her marriages break up so fast.

You can also try this test to see if a group of words is a fragment: say the phrase "It is true that" in front of the words in question. In most cases, a complete sentence will still make sense, but a fragment won't.

Example	At Liz's most recent wedding, the photographer used an instant camera. Because her marriages break up so fast.
	Which is a fragment?
	It is true that *at Liz's most recent wedding, the photographer used an instant camera.* [This sentence makes sense, so it's not a fragment.]
	It is true that *because her marriages break up so fast.* [Yes, this is a fragment.]

■ PRACTICING WHAT YOU'VE LEARNED

Fragment Sentence Errors

A. Using the "it is true that" test, identify the fragments and the complete sentences in the samples below.

1. The first drive-in theaters opened in New Jersey in 1933. Which was in the middle of the Great Depression when money was scarce.

2. By 1958 there were over 4,000 drive-ins in the United States. As recorded by the United Drive-in Theatre Owners Association.

3. The number of drive-ins has fallen drastically. Perhaps because escalating land prices make property too valuable for use in this way. Or the fact that they are only open during the summer months in some areas.

4. There are only 430 drive-ins left in the country. Including the American territories too.

5. Other outdoor summer activities are also endangered. For instance, the minature golf industry, down from 50,000 courses in the 1930s to fewer than 15,000 today.

B. Rewrite the following sentences so that there are no fragments.

1. The idea of a credit card first appeared in 1887. According to Lawrence M. Ausbel, author of "Credit Cards," in the *McGraw-Hill Encyclopedia of Economics.*

2. Originally an imaginary concept in a futurist novel by Edward Bellamy. The card allowed characters to charge against future earnings.

3. Around the turn of the twentieth century some American stores issued paper or metal "shoppers' plates." Although they were only used by retailers to identify their credit customers.

4. The first real credit card was issued in 1947 by a New York bank and was a success. Despite the fact that customers could only charge purchases in a two-block area in Brooklyn.

5. Travel and entertainment cards soon appeared that allowed customers to charge items and services across the country. For example, the American Express card in 1958 and Carte Blanche in 1959.

19r Run-On Sentence   R-O

Don't run two sentences together without any punctuation. Use a period, a semicolon, or a comma plus a coordinating conjunction (if appropriate), or subordinate one clause.

Incorrect	The indicted police chief submitted his resignation the mayor accepted it gratefully.
Correct	The indicted police chief submitted his resignation. The mayor accepted it gratefully.
Correct	The indicted police chief submitted his resignation; the mayor accepted it gratefully.
Correct	The indicted police chief submitted his resignation, and the mayor accepted it gratefully.
Correct	When the indicted police chief submitted his resignation, the mayor accepted it gratefully.

19s   Comma Splice   CS

A comma splice occurs when two sentences are linked with a comma. To correct this error, you can (1) separate the two sentences with a period, (2) separate the two sentences with a semicolon, (3) insert a coordinating conjunction ("for," "but," "and," "or," "nor," "so," "yet") after the comma, or (4) subordinate one clause.

Incorrect	Grover won a stuffed gila monster at the church raffle, his mother threw it away the next day while he was in school.
Correct	Grover won a stuffed gila monster at the church raffle. His mother threw it away the next day while he was in school.
Correct	Grover won a stuffed gila monster at the church raffle; his mother threw it away the next day while he was in school.
Correct	Grover won a stuffed gila monster at the church raffle, but his mother threw it away the next day while he was in school.
Correct	Although Grover won a stuffed gila monster at the church raffle, his mother threw it away the next day while he was in school.

(For more help on correcting comma splices, see pages 501–502; coordination and subordination are discussed in detail on pages 133–136.)

■ PRACTICING WHAT YOU'VE LEARNED

Run-On Sentence and Comma Splice Errors

A. Correct the run-on sentences below. Try to use several different methods of correcting the errors, as illustrated in section 19r.

1. Workers in the United States take an average of thirteen days of vacation a year in Italy they take forty-two.

2. In 1901 a school teacher named Annie Edson Taylor became the first person to go over Niagara Falls in a wooden barrel she is the only woman known to survive this risky adventure.

3. The minister preached his farewell sermon the choir sang "Break Forth into Joy."

4. The first microwave oven marketed in 1959 was a built-in unit it cost a whopping $2,595.

5. Coffee was considered a food in the Middle Ages travelers who found it growing in Ethiopia mixed it with animal fat.

B. Correct the comma splices that appear in the sentences below. Use more than one method of correcting the errors.

1. Most people know that the likeness of Susan B. Anthony appeared on an American dollar coin in the 1990s, fewer people know exactly who she was or why she is so important.

2. For most of her life Anthony fought for women to obtain the right to vote, she was an organizer of the world's first women's rights convention in 1848.

3. Anthony often risked her safety and her freedom for her beliefs, she was arrested in 1872 for the crime of voting in an election.

4. She also worked to secure laws to protect working women, at that time all of a woman's wages automatically belonged to her husband.

5. Unfortunately, Anthony did not live to see the 1920 passage of the Nineteenth Amendment giving women the right to vote, she died in 1906.

C. Correct any run-on sentences or comma splice errors you see. Skip any correct sentences you find.

1. My mother is very politically conservative, she's written in King George III for president in the last two elections.

2. Mary Lou decided not to eat the alphabet soup the letters spelled out "botulism."

3. A dried gourd containing seeds probably functioned as the first baby rattle, ancient Egyptian wall paintings show babies with such gourds clutched in their fingers.

4. Opportunists who came to the South after the Civil War were often called "carpetbaggers," they carried their belongings in cheaply produced travel bags made of Belgian carpet.

5. A friend of mine offers a good definition of nasty theater critics on opening night, according to him, they're the people who can't wait to stone the first cast.

6. When English scientist James Smithson died in 1829, he willed his entire fortune to the United States to establish a foundation for knowledge, that's how the Smithsonian Institution was started.

7. The word "jack-o'-lantern" may have come from the legend of Irish Jack, a mean old man in life, he was condemned after death to wander the earth carrying a hollow turnip with a lump of burning coal inside.

8. Americans forget how large the blue whale is it has a heart as large as a Volkswagen Beetle and can hold an elephant on its tongue.

9. According to a study by the Fish and Wildlife Service, Americans' favorite animals are dogs, horses, swans, robins, and butterflies; their least favorite are cockroaches, mosquitos, rats, wasps, and rattlesnakes.

10. The famous Eiffel Tower, built for the 1889 Paris Exposition, has inspired many crazy stunts, for example, in 1891 Silvain Dornon climbed the 363 steps on stilts.

19t   Faulty Parallelism   //

Parallel thoughts may be expressed in similar grammatical constructions. Repeated sentence elements, such as verbs, nouns, pronouns, and phrases, often appear in parallel form to emphasize meaning and to promote sentence fluency.

Examples

Parallel verbs: In his vaudeville act he *sang, danced,* and *juggled.*

Parallel prepositional phrases: She ran *through the door, across the yard,* and *into the limo.*

You may find it helpful to isolate the repeated elements in a sentence to see if they are parallel.

She ran

(1) through the door
(2) across the yard   } parallel
(3) into the limo

Faulty Parallelism	Boa constrictors like *to lie* in the sun, *to hang* from limbs, and *swallowing* small animals.
Isolated	(1) to lie (2) to hang (3) swallowing [not parallel to #1 and #2]
Revised	Boa constrictors like *to lie* in the sun, *to hang* from limbs, and *to swallow* small animals.
Faulty Parallelism	Whether *working* on his greasy car, *fistfighting* at the hamburger stand, or *in bed,* my brother always kept his hair combed.
Revised	Whether *working* on his greasy car, *fistfighting* at the hamburger stand, or *lounging* in bed, my brother always kept his hair combed.

■ PRACTICING WHAT YOU'VE LEARNED

Errors in Parallelism

Revise the sentences that follow so that the parallel ideas are expressed in similar grammatical constructions.

1. Is it true that Superman could leap tall buildings, run faster than a locomotive, and that bullets would bounce off his skin?

2. To celebrate the canned meat product called Spam, we attended the Texas Spamarama Festival to participate in the Spambalaya cook-off, the Spam-can toss, the Spam-jam session, and were dancing to such favorites as "Twist and Snout."

3. My Aunt Clara swears she has seen Elvis snacking at the deli, browsing at the supermarket, munching at the pizza parlor, and in the cookbook section of a local bookstore.

4. According to my husband, summer air in Louisiana is one part oxygen, nine parts water, and the rest is mosquitos, about 90 percent.

5. Many teachers believe that the most important keys to success for students in college include attending class, keep up with reading assignments, and being brave enough to ask questions.

6. Yoga encourages its participants to work on their flexibility, strength, and how they can reduce their stress levels.

7. Drivers should hang up their cell phones, refrain from eating, and drinking too, leaving the radio buttons alone.

8. Smart people learn from their own mistakes; learning from the mistakes of others is what even smarter people do.

9. Theater class helped me overcome my shyness, make new friends, and my confidence to do other activities was improved.

10. The writer Oscar Wilde, the dancer Isadora Duncan, the painter Max Ernst, and Jim Morrison, who was a rock star, are all buried in the same Paris cemetery.

19u False Predication   Pred

This error occurs when the predicate (that part of the sentence that says something about the subject) doesn't fit properly with the subject. Illogical constructions result.

Incorrect	The meaning of the sermon deals with love. [A "meaning" cannot deal with anything; the author, speaker, or work itself can, however.]
Correct	The sermon topic is love.
Incorrect	Energy is one of the world's biggest problems. ["Energy" itself is not a problem.]
Correct	The lack of fuel for energy is one of the world's biggest problems.
Incorrect	True failure is when you make an error and don't learn anything from it. [Avoid all "is when" and "is where" constructions. The subject does not denote a time, so the predicate is faulty.]
Correct	You have truly failed only when you make an error and don't learn anything from it.
Incorrect	My roommate is why I'm moving to a new apartment. [A roommate is not a reason.]
Correct	My roommate's habit of talking non-stop is driving me to find a new apartment.
Also Correct	Because of my annoying roommate, I'm moving to a new apartment.

| Incorrect | Her first comment after winning the lottery was exciting. [Her comment wasn't exciting; she was excited.] |
| Correct | Her first comment after winning the lottery expressed her excitement. |

(For other examples of faulty predication, see page 121.)

19v   Mixed Structure   Mix S

"Mixed structure" is a catchall term that applies to a variety of sentence construction errors. Usually, the term refers to a sentence in which the writer begins with one kind of structure and then shifts to another in midsentence. Such a shift often occurs when writers are in a hurry, and their minds have already jumped ahead to the next thought.

Confused	By the time one litter of cats is given away seems to bring a new one.
Clear	Giving away one litter of cats seems to tell the mother cat that it's time to produce a new batch.
Confused	The bank robber realized that in his crime spree how very little fun he was having.
Clear	The bank robber realized that he was having very little fun in his crime spree.
Confused	The novel is too confusing for what the author meant.
Clear	The novel is too confused for me to understand what the author meant.
Confused	Children with messages from their parents will be stapled to the bulletin board.
Clear	To find messages from their parents, children should look at the bulletin board.

(For other examples of mixed structure, see page 121.)

■ PRACTICING WHAT YOU'VE LEARNED

Errors of False Predication and Mixed Structure

Rewrite the following sentences so that each one is clear and coherent.

1. The team's quarterback A. M. Hall's broken finger, which sidelined him last week for the Raiders' game, is expected to play in tonight's game.

2. The groom is a graduate of Centerville High School where he lived all his life.

3. On my way to the doctor's office, my universal joint went out, causing even more body damage after hitting the tree.

4. An example of his intelligence is when he brought home a twenty-pound block of ice after ice fishing all day.

5. For those new residents who have children and don't know about it, the town offers low-cost daycare services.

6. According to the nineteenth-century cynic Ambrose Bierce, marriage is where there is "a master, a mistress, and two slaves, making in all, two."

7. A successful diet is when the mind triumphs over platter.

8. My drama teacher is the reason why I am a big star today.

9. Some folks argue that sound travels slower than light such as when advice parents give their teenagers doesn't reach them until they're forty.

10. Hearing his cries for help is how he came to be found in a ditch by some stray cows.

Chapter 20

A Concise Guide to Punctuation

Punctuation marks do not exist, as one student recently complained, to make your life complicated. They are used to clarify your written thoughts so that the reader understands your meaning. Just as traffic signs and signals tell a driver to slow down, stop, or go, so punctuation is intended to guide the reader through your prose. Look, for example, at the confusion in the following sentences when the necessary punctuation marks are omitted:

Confusing	Has the tiger been fed Bill? [Bill was the tiger's dinner?]
Clear	Has the tiger been fed, Bill?
Confusing	After we had finished raking the dog jumped into the pile of leaves. [Raking the dog?]
Clear	After we had finished raking, the dog jumped into the pile of leaves.
Confusing	The coach called the swimmers names. [Was the coach fired for verbally abusing the swimmers?]
Clear	The coach called the swimmers' names.

Because punctuation helps you communicate clearly with your reader, you should familiarize yourself with the following rules.

20a   The Period (.)   P

1. Use a period to end a sentence.

Examples   Employees at that company are not allowed to go on coffee breaks.
It takes too long to retrain them.

2. Use a period after initials and many abbreviations.

Examples   W. B. Yeats, 12 A.M., Dr., etc., M.A.

3. Only one period is necessary if the sentence ends with an abbreviation.

Examples   The elephant was delivered C.O.D.
To find a good job, you should obtain a B.S. or B.A.

20b   The Question Mark (?)   P

1. Use a question mark after every direct question.

Examples   May I borrow your boots?
Is the sandstorm over now?

2. No question mark is necessary after an indirect question.

Examples   Jean asked why no one makes a paper milk carton that opens without tearing.

Dave wondered how the television detective always found a parking place next to the scene of the crime.

20c   The Exclamation Point (!)   P

The exclamation point follows words, phrases, or sentences to show strong feelings.

Examples   Fire! Call the rescue squad!
The Broncos finally won the Super Bowl!

▪ PRACTICING WHAT YOU'VE LEARNED

Errors Using Periods, Question Marks, and Exclamation Points

Correct the following sentences by adding, deleting, or changing periods, question marks, or exclamation points, where appropriate.

1. The space program sent some cows into orbit last year I think they are now known as the herd shot around the world

2. Ms Anita Bath wants to know why erasers never outlast their pencils?

3. Her French class at St Claire's School on First Ave was taught by Madame Beau V Rhee, Ph.D..

4. Where do all the birds go when it's raining

5. I have wonderful news I won the lottery

20d   The Comma (,)   P

1. Use a comma to separate two independent clauses* joined by a coordinating conjunction. To remember the coordinating conjunctions, think of the acronym FANBOYS: "for," "and," "nor," "but," "or," "yet," and "so." Always use one of the FANBOYS and a comma when you join two independent clauses.

Examples   You can bury your savings in the backyard, *but* don't expect Mother Nature to pay interest.

I'm going home tomorrow, *and* I'm never coming back.

After six weeks Louie's diet was making him feel lonely and depressed, *so* he had a bumper sticker printed that said, "Honk if you love groceries."

Do *not* join two sentences with a comma only; such an error is called a comma splice. Use a comma plus one of the coordinating conjunctions listed previously, a period, a semicolon, or subordination.

Comma splice   Beatrice washes and grooms the chickens, Samantha feeds the spiders.

Correct   Beatrice washes and grooms the chickens, and Samantha feeds the spiders.

Correct   Beatrice washes and grooms the chickens. Samantha feeds the spiders.

Correct   Beatrice washes and grooms the chickens; Samantha feeds the spiders.

Correct   When Beatrice washes and grooms the chickens, Samantha feeds the spiders.

Comma splice   Jack doesn't like singing groups, he won't go with us to hear Fed Up with People.

Correct   Jack doesn't like singing groups, so he won't go with us to hear Fed Up with People.

Correct   Jack doesn't like singing groups. He won't go with us to hear Fed Up with People.

Correct   Jack doesn't like singing groups; he won't go with us to hear Fed Up with People.

Correct   Because Jack doesn't like singing groups, he won't go with us to hear Fed Up with People.

(For additional help, see page 492.)

2. Conjunctive adverbs, such as "however," "moreover," "thus," "consequently," and "therefore," are used to show continuity and are frequently set off by commas when they appear in midsentence.

---

* An independent clause looks like a complete sentence; it contains a subject and a verb, and it makes sense by itself.

Examples   She soon discovered, *however,* that he had stolen her monogrammed towels in addition to her pet avocado plant.

She felt, *consequently,* that he was not trustworthy.

When a conjunctive adverb occurs at the beginning of a sentence, it may be followed by a comma, especially if a pause is intended. If no pause is intended, you may omit the comma, but inserting the comma is never wrong.

Examples   *Thus,* she resolved never to speak to him again.

Thus she resolved never to speak to him again.

Therefore, he resolved never to speak to her again.

Therefore he resolved never to speak to her again.

Please note that "however" can never be used as a coordinating conjunction joining two independent clauses. Incorrect use of "however" most often results in a comma splice.

Comma splice   The police arrested the thief, *however,* they had to release him because the plant wouldn't talk.

Correct   The police arrested the thief; *however,* they had to release him because the plant wouldn't talk.

Also correct   The police arrested the thief. *However,* they had to release him because the plant wouldn't talk.

3. Set off with a comma an introductory phrase or clause.

Examples   After we had finished our laundry, we discovered one sock was missing.

According to the owner of the laundromat, customers have conflicting theories about missing laundry.

For example, one man claims his socks make a break for freedom when no one is watching the dryers.

4. Set off nonessential phrases and clauses. If the information can be omitted without changing the meaning of the main clause, then the phrase or clause is nonessential. Do *not* set off clauses or phrases that are essential to the meaning of the main clause.

Essential   He looked worse than my friend *who gets his clothes from the "lost and found" at the bus station.* [The "who" clause is essential to explain which friend.]

The storm *that destroyed Mr. Peartree's outhouse* left him speechless with anger. [The "that" clause is essential to explain which storm angered Mr. Peartree.]

The movie *now showing at the Ritz* is very obscene and very popular. [The participial phrase is essential to identify the particular movie.]

Nonessential   Joe Medusa, *who won the jalapeno-eating contest last year,* is this year's champion cow-chip tosser. [The "who" clause is nonessential because it only supplies additional information to the main clause.]

Black widow spiders, *which eat their spouses after mating,* are easily identifiable by the orange hourglass design on their abdomens. [The "which" clause is nonessential because it only supplies additional information.]

The juke box, *now reappearing in local honky-tonks,* first gained popularity during the 1920s. [The participial phrase is nonessential because it only supplies additional information.]

5. Use commas to separate items in a series of words, phrases, or clauses.

Examples   Julio collects coins, stamps, bottle caps, erasers, and pocket lint.

Mrs. Jones chased the burglar out the window, around the ledge, down the fire escape, and into the busy street.

Although journalists and some grammarians permit the omission of the last comma before the "and," many authorities believe the comma is necessary for clarity. For example, how many pints of ice cream are listed in the sentence below?

Please buy the following pints of ice cream: strawberry, peach, coffee, vanilla and chocolate swirl.

Four or five pints? Without a comma before the "and," the reader doesn't know if vanilla and chocolate swirl are (is?) one item or two. By inserting the last comma, you clarify the sentence:

Please buy the following pints of ice cream: strawberry, peach, coffee, vanilla, and chocolate swirl.

6. Use commas to separate adjectives of equal emphasis that modify the same noun. To determine if a comma should be used, see if you can insert the word "and" between the adjectives; if the phrase still makes proper sense with the substituted "and," use a comma.

Examples   She finally moved out of her cold, dark apartment.
She finally moved out of her cold and dark apartment.

I have a sweet, handsome husband.
I have a sweet and handsome husband.

He called from a convenient telephone booth.
But not: He called from a convenient and telephone booth. ["Convenient" modifies the unit "telephone booth," so there is no comma.]

Hand me some of that homemade pecan pie.
But not: Hand me some of that homemade and pecan pie. ["Homemade" modifies the unit "pecan pie," so there is no comma.]

7. Set off a direct address with commas.

Examples   Gentlemen, keep your seats.

Car fifty-four, where are you?

Not now, Eleanor, I'm busy.

8. Use commas to set off items in addresses and dates.

Examples   The sheriff followed me from Austin, Texas, to question me about my uncle.

He found me on February 2, 1978, when I stopped in Fairbanks, Alaska, to buy sunscreen.

9. Use commas to set off a degree or title following a name.

Examples   John Dough, M.D., was audited when he reported only $5.68 in taxable income last year.

The Neanderthal Award went to Samuel Lyle, Ph.D.

10. Use commas to set off dialogue from the speaker.

Examples   Alexander announced, "I don't think I want a second helping of possum."

"Eat hearty," said Marie, "because this is the last of the food."

11. Use commas to set off "yes," "no," "well," and other weak exclamations.

Examples   Yes, I am in the cat condo business.

No, all the units with decks are sold.

Well, perhaps one with a pool will do.

12. Set off interrupters or parenthetical elements appearing in the middle of a sentence. A parenthetical element is additional information placed as explanation or comment within an already complete sentence. This element may be a word (such as "certainly" or "fortunately"), a phrase ("for example" or "in fact"), or a clause ("I believe" or "you know"). The word, phrase, or clause is parenthetical if the sentence parts before and after it fit together and make sense.

Examples   Jack is, *I think*, still a compulsive gambler.

Harvey, *my brother*, sometimes has breakfast with him.

Jack cannot, *for example*, resist shuffling the toast or dealing the pancakes.

■ PRACTICING WHAT YOU'VE LEARNED

Comma Errors

A. Study the comma rules numbered 1–4 on pages 501–503. Correct any comma errors you see in the following sentences.

1. In 1886 temperance leader Harvey Wilcox left Kansas, he purchased 120 acres near Los Angeles to develop a new town.

2. Although there were no holly trees growing in that part of California Mrs. Wilcox named the area Hollywood.

3. Mrs. Wilcox may have named the place after a home, owned by a friend living in Illinois.

4. During the early years settlers who shared the Wilcoxes' values moved to the area and banned the recreational drinking of alcoholic beverages, however, some alcohol consumption was allowed for medicinal purposes.

5. Nevertheless by 1910 the first film studio opened its doors inside a tavern on Sunset Boulevard, within seven short years the quiet community started by the Wilcoxes had vanished.

B. Study the comma rules 5–12 on pages 503–504. Correct any comma errors you see in the following sentences.

1. Yes Hortense in the 1920s young women did indeed cut their hair raise their hemlines dab perfume behind their knees and dance the Charleston.

2. In 1873 Cornell University cancelled the school's first intercollegiate football game with Michigan when the president announced "I will not permit 30 men to travel 400 miles merely to agitate a bag of wind."

3. Jane Marian Donna Ann and Cissy graduated from high school on June 5 1964 in Texarkana Texas in the old Walnut Street Auditorium.

4. "I may be a man of few opinions" said Henry "but I insist that I am neither for nor against apathy."

5. Did you know for instance that early American settlers once thought the tomato was so poisonous they only used the plant for decoration?

C. The following sentences contain many kinds of comma errors, including the comma splice. Correct any errors you see by adding, deleting, or changing the commas as needed.

1. The father decided to recapture his youth, he took his son's car keys away.

2. Although ice cream didn't appear in America until the 1700s our country now leads the world in ice-cream consumption, Australia is second I think.

3. Last summer the large friendly family that lives next door flew Discount Airlines and visited three cities on their vacation, however, their suitcases visited five.

4. Researchers in Balboa, Panama have discovered that the poisonous, yellow-belly, sea snake which descended from the cobra, is the most deadly serpent in the world.

5. Lulu Belle, my cousin, spent the week of Sept. 1–7, 1986 in the woods near Dimebox, Texas looking for additions to her extinct, butterfly collection, however she wasn't at all successful in her search.

For additional practice correcting comma splice errors, see pages 492–493 in Chapter 19.

20e   The Semicolon (;)   P

1. Use a semicolon to link two closely related independent clauses.

Examples   Pierre has been cooking Cajun-style for years without realizing it; his specialty is blackened eggs.

Kate's mother does not have to begin a jogging program; she gets all the exercise she needs by worrying in place.

Avoid a "semicolon fragment" error by making sure there is an independent clause—a complete sentence, not a fragment—on either side of the semicolon.*

Semicolon fragment	Cutting your lawn with a push mower burns 420 calories; according to *Vitality* magazine. ["According to *Vitality* magazine" is a fragment. In this case, a comma, not a semicolon, is needed here.]
Correct	Cutting your lawn with a push mower burns 420 calories, according to *Vitality* magazine.

If you are unsure about recognizing a fragment, try using the "it is true that" test as described on page 490.

2. Use a semicolon to avoid a comma splice when connecting two independent clauses with words like "however," "moreover," "thus," "therefore," and "consequently."

Examples	Vincent Van Gogh sold only one painting in his entire life; however, in 1987 his *Sunflowers* sold for almost $40 million.
	All Esmeralda's plants die shortly after she gets them home from the store; consequently, she has the best compost heap in town.
	This town is not big enough for both of us; therefore, I suggest we expand the city limits.

3. Use a semicolon in a series between items that already contain internal punctuation.

Examples	Last year the Wildcats suffered enough injuries to keep them from winning the pennant, as Jake Pritchett, third baseman, broke his arm in a fight; Hugh Rosenbloom, starting pitcher, sprained his back on a trampoline; and Boris Baker, star outfielder, ate rotten clams and nearly died.
	Her children were born a year apart: Moe, 1936; Curley, 1937; and Larry, 1938.

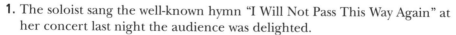

■ PRACTICING WHAT YOU'VE LEARNED

Semicolon Errors

Correct the sentences that follow by adding, deleting, or changing the semicolons.

1. The soloist sang the well-known hymn "I Will Not Pass This Way Again" at her concert last night the audience was delighted.

2. Apples have long been associated with romance for example, one legend says if you throw an apple peel over your shoulder, it will fall into the shape of your true love's initial.

---

* Some folks have noted that the semicolon might be better named the semi-period in that it functions like a weak period, joining two complete sentences together but with a weaker stop between thoughts than a period demands.

3. According to an 1863 book of etiquette, the perfect hostess will see to it that the works of male and female authors are properly separated on her bookshelves, however, if the authors happen to be married, their proximity may be tolerated.

4. Today, there are some 60,000 Americans older than 100 in 1960, there were only 3,222; according to *Health* magazine.

5. The sixth-grade drama club will present their interpretation of *Hamlet* tonight in the school cafeteria all parents are invited to see this tragedy.

6. Some inventors who named weapons after themselves include Samuel Colt, the Colt revolver, Henry Deringer, Jr., the derringer pistol, Dr. Richard J. Gatling, the crank machine gun, Col. John T. Thompson, the submachine or "tommy" gun, and Oliver F. Winchester, the repeating rifle.

7. My doctor failed in his career as a kidnapper, no one could read his ransom notes.

8. The highest point in the United States is Mt. McKinley at 20,320 feet, in contrast, the lowest point is Death Valley at 282 feet below sea level.

9. As we drove down the highway we saw a sign that said "See the World's Largest Prairie Dog Turn Right at This Exit," therefore we immediately stopped to look.

10. The next billboard read "See Live Jackalopes"; making us want to stop again.

20f The Colon (:) P

1. Use a colon to introduce a long or formal list, but do not use one after "to be" verbs.

Correct	Please pick up these items at the store: garlic, wolfbane, mirrors, a prayer book, a hammer, and a wooden stake.
Incorrect	Jean is such a bad cook that she thinks the four basic food groups are: canned, frozen, ready-to-mix, and take-out.
Correct	Jean is such a bad cook that she thinks the four basic food groups are canned, frozen, ready-to-mix, and take-out.

Avoid needless colons.

Incorrect	At the store I couldn't find: wolfbane or a wooden stake.
Correct	At the store I couldn't find wolfbane or a wooden stake.

2. A colon may be used to introduce a quotation or definition.

Examples	Ninteenth-century writer Ambrose Bierce offers this definition of a bore: "A person who talks when you wish him to listen." Critic Dorothy Parker was unambiguous in her review of the book: "This is not a novel to be tossed aside lightly; it should be thrown with great force."

In singer Jimmy Buffett's Margaritaville store in Key West, a sign warns: "Shoplifters will be forced to listen to Barry Manilow."

3. Use a colon to introduce a word, phrase, or sentence that emphatically explains, summarizes, or amplifies the preceding sentence.

Examples   Harriet knew the one ingredient that would improve any diet dinner: chocolate.

Zsa Zsa Gabor's advice for becoming a marvelous housekeeper is simple: every time you leave a relationship, keep the house.

Horace made a big mistake at the office party: he kissed his boss's wife hello and his job goodbye.

■ PRACTICING WHAT YOU'VE LEARNED

Errors with Colons

Correct the following errors by adding, deleting, or substituting colons for faulty punctuation. Skip any correct sentences.

1. Experts have discovered over 30 different kinds of clouds but have separated them into three main types cirrus, cumulus, and stratus.

2. To those folks who may talk too much, Abraham Lincoln gives the following advice: "It is better to remain silent and be thought a fool than to speak out and remove all doubt."

3. A recent Gallup poll found that Americans only consider one activity more stressful than visiting the dentist hosting a dinner party.

4. Because Hindu custom forbids the eating of beef, McDonald's restaurants in India often feature: veggie-burgers and mutton-burgers.

5. Please remember to buy the following at the pet store, one pound of cat food, two flea collars, kitty fang floss, a bag of cat nip, and thirty-six lint rollers.

6. A Director of Academic Services at Pennsylvania State University once nominated this sentence for Punctuation Error of the Year; "I had to leave my good friend's behind and find new ones."

7. Some of the cars manufactured between 1907 and 1912 that didn't achieve the popularity of the Model T were: the Black Crow, the Swallow, the Bugmobile, and the Carnation.

8. There's only one thing that can make our lawn look as good as our neighbor's; snow.

9. In a Thurmont, Maryland, cemetery can be found this epitaph "Here lies an Atheist, all dressed up, and no place to go."

10. George Bernard Shaw, the famous playwright, claimed he wanted the following epitaph on his tombstone: "I knew if I stayed around long enough, something like this would happen."

20g   The Apostrophe (')   AP

1. Use an apostrophe to indicate a contraction.

Examples   *It's* too bad your car burned.

Wouldn't the insurance company believe your story?

Many people today confuse "it's" (the contraction for "it is") and "its" (the possessive pronoun, which never takes an apostrophe).

Its = shows possession, functioning like "his" or "her"

It's = contraction for "it is"

Examples   The car is old, but *its* paint is new ["Its" shows the car's possession of paint.]

The car is old, but *it's* reliable. ["It's" is a contraction for "it is."]

If you are ever in doubt about your choice, read the sentence aloud, saying the words "it is" in place of the *its/it's* in question. If the sentence becomes nonsensical (The car is old but *it is* coat of paint is new), then the possessive form "its" is probably what you need.

Special note: Its' = no such word exists in the English language! Forget you even thought about it!

2. Add an apostrophe plus "s" to a noun to show possession.

Examples   *Jack's* dog ate the *cat's* dinner.

The *veterinarian's* assistant later doctored the *puppy's* wounds.

3. Add only an apostrophe to a plural noun ending in "s" to show possession.

Examples   Goldilocks invaded the *bears'* house.

She ignored her *parents'* warning about breaking and entering.

Be careful to avoid adding an apostrophe when the occasion simply calls for the plural use of a word.

Incorrect	*Apple's* are on sale now.
Correct	*Apples* are on sale now.
Incorrect	We ordered *chip's* and dip.
Correct	We ordered *chips* and dip.

4. In some cases you may add an apostrophe plus "s" to a singular word ending in "s," especially when the word is a proper name or for ease of pronunciation.

Examples   *Doris's* name was popular in the 1950s.

The silent screen *actress's* favorite flowers were mums.

5. To avoid confusion, you may use an apostrophe plus "s" to form the plurals of letters, figures, and words discussed as words; no apostrophe is also acceptable.

Examples   He made four *"C's"* last fall. [or *"Cs"*]

The right to resist the draft was a major issue in the *1960's.* [or *1960s*]

You use too many *"and's"* in your sentence. [or *"ands"*]

■ **PRACTICING WHAT YOU'VE LEARNED**

Errors with Apostrophes

A. Correct the apostrophe errors you see in the following phrases.

1. A horses' pajamas
2. The queens throne
3. A families' vacation
4. Ten students grades
5. The Depression of the 1930s' was over.
6. That dress of hers'
7. The childrens' toys
8. Worm's for sale
9. Bill Jones car
10. All essay's are due today.

B. Show that you understand the difference between "it's" and "its" by correcting any errors in the sentences that follow. Skip any correct use you see.

1. Its unfortunate that the game ended in a tie.
2. The tree lost its leaves.
3. Its beginning to feel like fall now.
4. The library was closing its' doors.
5. I realize its none of my business.

20h   Quotation Marks (" " and ' ')   P

1. Use quotation marks to enclose someone's spoken or written words.

Examples   The daughter wrote, "Remember, Daddy, when you pass on you can't take your money with you."

"But I've already bought a fireproof money belt," answered her father.

2. Use quotation marks around the titles of essays,* articles, chapter headings, short stories, short poems, and songs.

---

* Do *not*, however, put quotation marks around your own essay's title on either the title page or the first page of your paper.

Examples	"How to Paint Ceramic Ashtrays"
	"The Fall of the House of Usher"
	"Stopping by Woods on a Snowy Evening"
	"Yankee Doodle"

3. You may either underline or place quotation marks around a word, phrase, or letter used as the subject of discussion.

Examples	Never use "however" as a coordinating conjunction.
	The word "bigwig," meaning an important person, is derived from the large wigs worn by seventeenth-century British judges.
	Is your middle initial "X" or "Y"?
	Her use of such adjectives as "drab," "bleak," and "musty" gives the poem a somber tone.

4. Place quotation marks around uncommon nicknames and words used ironically. Do not, however, try to apologize for slang or clichés by enclosing them in quotation marks; instead, substitute specific words.

Examples	"Scat-cat" Malone takes candy from babies.
	Her "friend" was an old scarecrow in an abandoned barn.
Slang	After work Chuck liked to "simple out" in front of the television.
Specific	After work Chuck liked to relax by watching old movies on television.

5. The period and the comma go inside quotation marks; the semicolon and the colon go outside. If the quoted material is a question, the question mark goes inside; if the quoted material is a part of a whole sentence that is a question, the mark goes outside. The same is true for exclamation points.

Examples	According to cartoonist Matt Groening, "Love is a snowmobile racing across the tundra; suddenly it flips over, pins you underneath, and at night the ice weasels come."
	"Love is a snowmobile racing across the tundra; suddenly it flips over, pins you underneath, and at night the ice weasels come," says cartoonist Matt Groening.
	According to cartoonist Matt Groening, "Love is a snowmobile . . . suddenly it flips over, pins you underneath, and at night the ice weasels come"; Groening also advises that bored friends are one of the first signs that you're in love.
	Did he really say, "At night the ice weasels come"?
	Sally asked, "Do you think you're in love or just in a snowmobile?"

6. Use single quotation marks to enclose a quotation (or words requiring quotation marks) within a quotation.

Examples	Professor Hall asked his class, "Do you agree with Samuel Johnson, who once said that a second marriage represents 'the triumph of hope over experience'?"

"One of my favorite songs is 'In My Life' by the Beatles," said Jane.

"I'm so proud of the 'A' on my grammar test," Sue told her parents.

■ **PRACTICING WHAT YOU'VE LEARNED**

Errors with Apostrophes and Quotation Marks

Correct the following errors by adding, changing, or deleting apostrophes and quotation marks.

1. Its true that when famous wit Dorothy Parker was told that President Coolidge, also known as Silent Cal, was dead, she exclaimed, How can they tell?

2. When a woman seated next to Coolidge at a dinner party once told him she had made a bet with a friend that she could get more than two words out of him, he replied You lose.

3. Twenty-one of Elvis Presleys albums have sold over a million copies; twenty of the Beatles albums have also done so.

4. Cinderellas stepmother wasn't pleased that her daughter received an F in her creative writing class on her poem Seven Guys and a Gal, which she had plagiarized from her two friend's Snow White and Dopey.

5. Wasn't it Mae West who said, When choosing between two evils, I always like to try the one I've never tried before? asked Olivia.

6. Horace said Believe me, its to everybodies' advantage to sing the popular song You Stole My heart and Stomped That Sucker Flat, if thats what the holdup man wants.

7. A scholars research has revealed that the five most commonly used words in written English are the, of, and a, and to.

8. The triplets mother said that while its' hard for her to choose, O. Henrys famous short story The Ransom of Red Chief is probably her favorite.

9. Despite both her lawyers advice, she used the words terrifying, hideous, and unforgettable to describe her latest flight on Golden Fleece Airways, piloted by Jack One-Eye Marcus.

10. Its clear that Bubba didnt know if the Christmas' tree thrown in the neighbors yard was ours, theirs', or your's.

20i   Parentheses ( )   P

1. Use parentheses to set off words, dates, or statements that give additional information, explain, or qualify the main thought.

Examples   To encourage sales, some automobile manufacturers name their cars after fast or sleek animals (Impala, Mustang, and Thunderbird, for example).

Popular American author Mark Twain (Samuel Clemens) described many of his childhood experiences in *Tom Sawyer* (1876).

The Ford Motor Company once rejected the name Utopian Turtletop for one of its new cars, choosing instead to call it the Edsel (that name obviously didn't help sales either).

2. The period comes inside the close parenthesis if a complete sentence is enclosed; it occurs after the close parenthesis when the enclosed matter comes at the end of the main sentence and is only a part of the main sentence.

Examples   The Colorado winters of 1978 and 1979 broke records for low temperatures. (See pages 72–73 for temperature charts.)

Jean hates Colorado winters and would prefer a warmer environment (such as Alaska, the North Pole, or a meat locker in Philadelphia).

3. If you are confused trying to distinguish whether information should be set off by commas, parentheses, or dashes, here are three guidelines:

   a. Use commas to set off information closely related to the rest of the sentence.

Example   When Billy Clyde married Maybelle, his brother's young widow, the family was shocked. [The information identifies Maybelle and tells why the family was shocked.]

   b. Use parentheses to set off information loosely related to the rest of the sentence or material that would disturb the grammatical structure of the main sentence.

Examples   Billy Clyde married Maybelle (his fourth marriage, her second) in Las Vegas on Friday. [The information is merely additional comment not closely related to the meaning of the sentence.]

Billy Clyde married Maybelle (she was previously married to his brother) in Las Vegas on Friday. [The information is an additional comment that would also disturb the grammatical structure of the main sentence were it not enclosed in parentheses.]

   c. Use dashes to set off information dramatically or emphatically.

Example   Billy Clyde eloped with Maybelle—only three days after her husband's funeral—without saying a word to anyone in the family.

20j   Brackets [ ]   P

1. Use brackets to set off editorial explanations in the work of another writer.

Examples   According to the old letter, the treasure map could be found "in the library taped to the back of the portrait [of Gertrude the Great] that faces north."

The country singer ended the interview by saying, "My biggest hit so far is 'You're the Reason Our Kids Are Ugly' [original version by Sarah Bellham]."

2. Use brackets to set off editorial corrections in quoted material. By placing the bracketed word "sic" (meaning "thus") next to an error, you indicate that the mistake appeared in the original text and that *you* are not misquoting or misspelling.

Examples   The student wrote, "I think it's unfair for teachers to count off for speling [sic]." ["Sic" in brackets indicates that the student who is quoted misspelled the word "spelling."]

The highway advertisement read as follows: "For great stakes [sic], eat at Joe's, located right behind Daisy's Glue Factory." [Here, "sic" in brackets indicates an error in word choice; the restaurant owner incorrectly advertised "stakes" instead of "steaks."]

20k   The Dash (—)*   P

1. Use a dash to indicate a strong or sudden shift in thought.

Examples   Now, let's be reasonable—wait, put down that ice pick!

"It's not athlete's foot—it's deadly coreopsis!" cried Dr. Mitty.

2. Use dashes to set off parenthetical matter that deserves more emphasis than parentheses denote.

Examples   Wanda's newest guru—the one who practiced catatonic hedonism—taught her to rest and play at the same time.

He was amazed to learn his test score—a pitiful 43.

(To clear up any confusion over the uses of dashes, commas, and parentheses, see the guidelines on pages 512–513.)

3. Use a dash before a statement that summarizes or amplifies the preceding thought. (Dashes can also be used to introduce a humorous or ironic twist on the first idea in the sentence.)

Examples   Aged wine, delicious food, someone else picking up the check—the dinner was perfect.

Not everyone agrees with football coach Vince Lombardi, who said, "Winning isn't everything—it's the only thing."

According to Hollywood star Cher, "The trouble with some women is that they get all excited about nothing—and then marry him."

---

* Please note that in some typed work, a dash is indicated by *two* bar marks ("--"); one bar mark ("-") indicates a hyphen.

■ PRACTICING WHAT YOU'VE LEARNED

Errors with Parentheses, Brackets, and Dashes

Show that you understand the difference between parentheses, brackets, and dashes by using the best choice in the sentences that follow. Skip any correct sentences you see. (For additional practice, see also the exercise that appears on pages 518–519.)

1. George Eliot (the pen name of Mary Ann Evans) wrote the novel *Middlemarch.*

2. The Apostrophe Protection Society, founded in London in 2001, fights against the gross misuse of this mark of punctuation. Editor's note: For help with apostrophes, see pages 509–510 in this text.

3. A Russian woman holds the record for the highest number of children born to one mother: sixty-nine babies in a total of twenty-seven pregnancies sixteen pairs of twins, seven sets of triplets, and four sets of quadruplets.

4. More men holding first-class tickets on the *Titanic* were saved than childrens (sic) in the third-class section of the ship

5. Billy Clyde could stay married to Maybelle as long as he played his cards right [his Visa card, his Mastercard, his American Express card.]

20l   The Hyphen (-)   P

1. Use a hyphen to join words into a single adjective before a noun.

Examples   a wind-blown wig
the mud-caked sneakers
a made-for-television movie
a well-written essay
a five-year-old boy

Do *not* use a hyphen when the modifier ends in "ly."

Examples   a highly regarded worker
a beautifully landscaped yard

2. Writers who create original compound adjectives often join the words with hyphens.

Examples   Compulsive shoppers suffer from stuff-lust syndrome.
She prefers novels with they-lived-wretchedly-ever-after endings.

3. Some compound words are always spelled with a hyphen; check your dictionary when you're in doubt.

Examples   mother-in-law

president-elect

runner-up

good-for-nothing

twenty-one

Compound words made from combining verb forms are frequently hyphenated: The psychiatrist insisted his birthday presents be *shrink-wrapped.*

4. Some words with prefixes use a hyphen; again, check your dictionary if necessary. (Hint: If the second word begins with a capital letter, a hyphen is almost always used.)

Examples   ex-wife

self-esteem

all-American

non-English

5. Use a hyphen to mark the separation of syllables when you divide a word at the end of a line. Do not divide one-syllable words; do not leave one or two letters at the end of a line. (In most dictionaries, dots are used to indicate the division of syllables: va • ca • tion.)

Examples   In your essays you should avoid using fragment sentences.

Did your father try to help you with your homework?

■ PRACTICING WHAT YOU'VE LEARNED

Errors with Hyphens

Correct the errors in the phrases that follow by adding, deleting, or changing hyphens. Skip any correct uses you see. (For additional practice using hyphens, turn to the exercise on pages 518–519.)

1. A first class event
2. The well done steak
3. A self employed person
4. His completely fabricated story
5. Her one word answer
6. Pre-Columbian art
7. A once in a lifetime experience
8. A fifteen year-old girl
9. The overly-excited dog
10. His fifty sixth birthday

20m Underlining* (_____)   P

1. Underline, italicize, or place quotation marks around a word, phrase, or letter used as the subject of discussion. Whether you underline, italicize, or use quotation marks, always be consistent. (See also pages 510–511.)

Examples   No matter how I spell <u>offered</u>, it always looks wrong.

Is your middle initial <u>X</u> or <u>Y</u>?

Her use of such words as <u>drab</u>, <u>bleak</u>, and <u>musty</u> give the poem a somber tone.

2. Underline or italicize the title of books, magazines, newspapers, movies, works of art, television programs (but use quotation marks for individual episodes), airplanes, trains, and ships.

Examples   <u>Moby Dick</u>
<u>The Reader's Digest</u>
<u>Texarkana Gazette</u>
<u>Gone with the Wind</u>
<u>Mona Lisa</u>
<u>60 Minutes</u>
<u>Spirit of St. Louis</u>
<u>Titanic</u>

Exceptions: Do not underline the Bible or the titles of legal documents, including the United States Constitution, or the name of your own essay when it appears on your title page. Do not underline the city in a newspaper title unless the city's name is actually part of the newspaper's title.

3. Underline or italicize foreign words that are not commonly regarded as part of the English language.

Examples   He shrugged and said, "<u>C'est la vie</u>."
Under the "For Sale" sign on the old rusty truck, the farmer had written the words "<u>caveat emptor</u>," meaning "let the buyer beware."

4. Use underlining or italics sparingly to show emphasis.

Examples   Everyone was surprised to discover that the butler <u>didn't</u> do it.
"Do you realize that <u>your</u> son just ate a piece of my priceless sculpture?" the artist screamed at the museum director.

20n Ellipsis Points (. . . or . . . .)   P

1. To show an omission in quoted material within a sentence, use three periods, with spaces before and after each one.

---

* In some printed matter, including this textbook, words that might otherwise be underlined are presented in italics: She had just finished reading *The Great Gatsby*.

Original	Every time my father told the children about his having to trudge barefooted to school in the snow, the walk got longer and the snow got deeper.
Quoted with omission	In her autobiography, she wrote, "Every time my father told the children about his having to trudge barefooted to school . . . the snow got deeper."

2. Three points with spaces may be used to show an incomplete or interrupted thought.

Example   My wife is an intelligent, beautiful woman who wants me to live a long time. On the other hand, Harry's wife . . . oh, never mind.

3. If you omit any words at the end of a quotation and you are also ending your sentence, use three points plus a fourth to indicate the period. Do not add space before the first point.

Example   Lincoln wrote, "Four score and seven years ago our fathers brought forth upon this continent, a new nation. . . ."

4. If the omission of one or more sentences occurs at the end of a quoted sentence, use four points with no space before the first point.

Example   "The Lord is my shepherd; I shall not want. . . . he leadeth me in the paths of righteousness for his name's sake."

■ PRACTICING WHAT YOU'VE LEARNED

Errors with Parentheses, Brackets, Dashes, Hyphens, Underlining, and Ellipses

Correct the following errors by adding, changing, or deleting parentheses, brackets, dashes, hyphens, underlining, and ellipsis points.

1. Many moviegoers know that the ape in King Kong the original 1933 version, not the re-make was only an eighteen inch tall animated figure, but not everyone realizes that the Red Sea Moses parted in the 1923 movie of The Ten Commandments was a quivering slab of Jell O sliced down-the-middle.

2. We recall the last words of General John B. Sedwick at the Battle of Spotsylvania in 1864: "They couldn't hit an elephant at this dist   ."

3. In a person to person telephone call the twenty five year old starlet promised the hard working gossip columnist that she would "tell the truth . . . and nothing but the truth" about her highly-publicized feud with her exhusband, editor in chief of Meat Eaters Digest.

4. While sailing across the Atlantic on board the celebrity filled yacht Titanic II, Dottie Mae Haskell she's the author of the popular new self help book Finding Wolves to Raise Your Children confided that until recently she thought chutzpah was an Italian side dish.

5. During their twenty four hour sit in at the melt down site, the anti-nuclear protestors began to sing, "Oh, say can you see . . . "

6. Few people know that James Arness later Matt Dillon in the long running television series Gunsmoke got his start by playing the vegetable creature in the postwar monster movie The Thing 1951.

7. Similarly, the well known TV star Michael Landon he died of cancer in 1991 played the leading role in the 1957 classic I Was a Teenage Werewolf.

8. A French chemist named Georges Claude invented the first neon sign in 1910. For additional information on his unsuccessful attempts to use seawater to generate electricity, see pages 200–205.

9. When Lucille Ball, star of I Love Lucy, became pregnant with her first child, the network executives decided that the word expecting could be used on the air to refer to her condition, but not the word pregnant.

10. In mystery stories the detective often advises the police to cherchez la femme. Editor's note: Cherchez la femme means "look for the woman."

Chapter 21

A Concise Guide to Mechanics

21a Capitalization — Cap

1. Capitalize the first word of every sentence.

Example   The lazy horse leans against a tree all day.

2. Capitalize proper nouns—the specific names of people, places, and products—and also the adjectives formed from proper nouns.

Examples   John Doe
Austin, Texas
First National Bank
the Eiffel Tower
Chevrolets
Japanese cameras
Spanish class
an English major

3. Always capitalize the days of the week, the names of the months, and holidays.

Examples   Saturday, December 14
Tuesday's meeting
Halloween parties

Special events are often capitalized: Super Bowl, World Series, Festival of Lights.

   4. Capitalize titles when they are accompanied by proper names.

Examples   President Jones, Major Smith, Governor Brown, Judge Wheeler, Professor Plum, Queen Elizabeth

   5. Capitalize all the principal words in titles of books, articles, stories, plays, movies, and poems. Prepositions, articles, and conjunctions are not capitalized unless they begin or end the title.

Examples   "The Face on the Barroom Floor"
                    A Short History of the Civil War
                    For Whom the Bell Tolls

   6. Capitalize the first word of a direct quotation.

Examples   Shocked at actor John Barrymore's use of profanity, the woman said, "Sir, I'll have you know I'm a lady!"
                    Barrymore replied, "Your secret is safe with me."

   7. Capitalize "east," "west," "north," and "south" when they refer to particular sections of the country but not when they merely indicate direction.

Examples   The South has produced many excellent writers, including William Faulkner and Flannery O'Connor. ["South" here refers to a section of the country.]
                    If you travel south for ten miles, you'll see the papier-mâché replica of the world's largest hamburger. [In this case, "south" is a direction.]

   8. Capitalize a title when referring to a particular person;* do not capitalize a title if a pronoun precedes it.

Examples   The President announced a new national holiday honoring Frank H. Fleer, inventor of bubble gum.
                    The new car Dad bought is guaranteed for 10,000 miles or until something goes wrong.
                    My mother told us about a Hollywood party during which Zelda and F. Scott Fitzgerald collected and boiled all the women's purses.

■ PRACTICING WHAT YOU'VE LEARNED

Errors with Capitalization

A. Correct the errors in capitalization in the following phrases.

   1. delicious chinese food

   2. memorial day memories

   3. fiery southwestern salsa

---

* Some authorities disagree; others consider such capitalization optional.

4. his latest novel, *the story of a prince among thieves*

5. my son's Wedding at the baptist church

6. count Dracula's castle in transylvania

7. african-american heritage

8. a dodge van driven across the golden gate bridge

9. sunday morning newspapers

10. the british daughter-in-law of senator Snort

21b   Abbreviations   Ab

1. Abbreviate the titles "Mr.," "Mrs.," "Ms.," "St.," and "Dr." when they precede names

Examples   Dr. Scott, Ms. Steinham, Mrs. White, St. Jude

2. Abbreviate titles and degrees when they follow names.

Examples   Charles Byrd, Jr.; David Hall, Ph.D.; Dudley Carpenter, D.D.S.

3. You may abbreviate the following in even the most formal writing: A.M. (*ante meridiem*, before noon), P.M. (*post meridiem*, after noon), A.D. (*anno Domini*, in the year of our Lord), B.C. (before Christ), c.e. (common era), etc. (*et cetera*, and others), i.e. (*id est*, that is), and e.g. (*exempli gratia*, for example).

4. In formal writing, do *not* abbreviate the names of days, months, centuries, states, countries, or units of measure. Do *not* use an ampersand (&) unless it is an official part of a title.

Incorrect in formal writing	Tues., Sept., 18th century, Ark., Mex., lbs.
Correct	Tuesday, September, eighteenth century, Arkansas, Mexico, pounds
Incorrect	Tony & Gus went to the store to buy ginseng root.
Correct	Tony *and* Gus went to the A & P to buy ginseng root. [The "&" in "A & P" is correct because it is part of the store's official name.]

5. In formal writing, do *not* abbreviate the words for page, chapter, volume, and so forth, except in footnotes and bibliographies, which have prescribed rules of abbreviation.

(For additional information on proper abbreviation, consult your dictionary.)

21c   Numbers   Num

1. Use figures for dates, street or room numbers, page numbers, telephone numbers, percentages, and hours with A.M. and P.M.*

---

* 8:00 A.M. or 8 A.M., but eight o'clock in the morning

Examples   April 22, 1946
                      710 West 14th Street
                      page 242
                      room 17
                      476–1423
                      40 percent
                      10:00 A.M.

2. Some authorities say spell out numbers that can be expressed in one or two words; others say spell out numbers under one hundred.

Examples   ten thousand dollars or $10,000
                      twenty-four hours
                      thirty-nine years
                      five partridges
                      $12.99 per pair
                      1,294 essays

3. When several numbers are used in a short passage, use figures.

Examples   In the anchovy-eating contest, Jennifer ate 22, Juan ate 21, Pete ate 16, and I ate 6.

                      According to the U.S. Census Bureau, on an average day 11,000 babies are born, 6,000 people die, 7,000 couples marry, and 3,000 couples divorce.

4. Never begin a sentence with a figure.

Incorrect   50 spectators turned out to watch the surfing exhibition at Niagara Falls.
Correct   Fifty spectators turned out to watch the surfing exhibition at Niagara Falls.

5. When a date containing a day and a year appears within a sentence, always set off the year by placing commas on each side.

Examples   She married her first husband on February 2, 1978, in Texas.

                      The first birth on a commercial airliner occurred on October 28, 1929, as the plane cruised over Miami.

▪ PRACTICING WHAT YOU'VE LEARNED

Errors in Capitalization, Abbreviations, and Numbers

Correct the following errors by adding, deleting, or changing capitals, abbreviations, and numbers. Skip any correct words, letters, or numbers you may find.

1. Speaking to students at Gallaudet university, Marian Wright Edelman, Founder and president of the Children's Defense Fund, noted that an american child is born into poverty every thirty seconds, is born to a teen mother every 60 seconds, is abused or neglected every 26 seconds, is arrested for a violent crime every five minutes, and is killed by a gun every two hours.

2. My sister, who lives in the east, was amazed to read studies by Thomas Radecki, MD, showing that 12-year-olds commit 300 percent more murders than did the same age group 30 years ago.

3. In sixty-seven A.D. the roman emperor Nero entered the chariot race at the olympic games, and although he failed to finish the race, the judges unanimously declared him the Winner.

4. According to John Alcock, a Behavioral Ecologist at Arizona State University, in the U.S.A. the chance of being poisoned by a snake is 20 times less than that of being hit by lightning and 300 times less than the risk of being murdered by a fellow American.

5. The official chinese news agency, located in the city of xinhua, estimates that there are ten million guitar players in their country today, an amazing number considering that the instrument was banned during the cultural revolution, which lasted 10 years, from nineteen sixty-six to nineteen seventy-six.

6. 231 electoral votes were cast for James Monroe but only 1 for John Quincy Adams in the 1820 Presidential race.

7. The british soldier T. E. Lawrence, better known as "lawrence of arabia," stood less than 5 ft. 6 in. tall.

8. Drinking a glass of french wine makes me giddy before my 10 a.m. english class, held in wrigley field every other friday except on New Year's day.

9. When a political opponent once called him "two-faced," president Lincoln retorted, "if I had another face, do you think I would wear this one?"

10. Alexander Graham Bell, inventor of the telephone, died in nova scotia on aug. 2, 1922; 2 days later, on the day of his burial, for 1 minute no telephone in north america was allowed to ring.

21d Spelling   Sp

For some folks, learning to spell correctly is harder than trying to herd cats. Entire books have been written to teach people to become better spellers, and some of these are available at your local bookstore (and, no, not listed under witchcraft). Here, however, are a few suggestions that seem to work for many students:

1. Keep a list of the little beasties you misspell. After a few weeks, you may notice that you tend to misspell the same words again and again or that the words you misspell tend to fit a pattern—that is, you can't remember when the *i* goes

before the *e* or when to change the *y* to *i* before *ed*. Try to memorize the words you repeatedly misspell, or at least keep the list somewhere handy so you can refer to it when you're editing your last draft (listing the words on the inside cover of your dictionary also makes sense).

2. Become aware of a few rules that govern some of our spelling in English. For example, many people know the rule in the jingle "*I* before *E* except after *C* or when it sounds like *A* as in *neighbor* and *weigh*." Not everyone, however, knows the follow-up line, which contains most of the exceptions to that jingle: "Neither the weird financier nor the foreigner seizes leisure at its height."

3. Here are some other rules, without jingles, for adding suffixes (new endings to words), a common plague for poor spellers:

- Change final *y* to *i* if the *y* follows a consonant.

    bury → buried

    marry → marries

- But if the suffix is -*ing*, keep the *y*.

    marry + ing = marrying

    worry + ing = worrying

- If the word ends in a single consonant after a single vowel and the accent is on the last syllable, double the consonant before adding the suffix.

    occur → occurred

    cut → cutting

    swim → swimmer

- If a word ends in a silent *e*, drop the *e* before adding -*able* or -*ing*.

    love + able = lovable

    believe + able = believable

4. And here's an easy rule governing the doubling of letters with the addition of prefixes (new beginning syllables): most of the time, you simply add all the letters you've got when you mix the word and the prefix.

mis + spell = misspell

un + natural = unnatural

re + entry = reentry

5. Teach yourself to spell the words that you miss often by making up your own silly rules or jingles. For instance:

dessert (one *s* or two?): I always want two helpings so I double the *s*.

apparently (apparantly?): Ap*parent*ly, my *parent* knows the whole story.

separate (seperate?): I'd be *a rat* to sep*arat*e from you.

a lot (or alot?): A cot (not *acot*) provides *a lot* of comfort in a tent.

questionnaire (one *n* or two?): Questio*nn*aires have *n*umerous *n*umbered questions (two *n*'s).

And so on.

6. Don't forget to proofread your papers carefully. Anything that looks misspelled probably is, and deserves to be looked up in your dictionary. Reading your paper one sentence at a time from the end helps, too, because you tend to start thinking about your ideas when you read from the beginning of your paper. (And if you are writing on a word processor that has a spell program, don't forget to run it.)

Although these few suggestions won't completely cure your spelling problems, they may make a dramatic improvement in the quality of your papers and give you the confidence to continue learning and practicing other rules that govern the spelling of our language. Good luck!

Part 5

Additional Readings

Part Five offers thirty-six additional readings to help you improve your writing skills. In nine chapters, three selections illustrate each of the strategies previously explained in Part Two. In addition, Chapter 31 includes a speech and two essays illustrating multiple strategies for further analysis; Chapter 32 offers additional poetry and fiction to supplement literary assignments; Chapter 33 presents essays on writing and language. Overall, the readings in Part Five were selected not only to model methods of development but also to illustrate a variety of styles and tones, including humor and irony.

A close reading of these selections can help you become a better writer in several ways. Identifying the various methods by which these writers focused, organized, and developed their material may spark new ideas as you plan and shape your own essay. Familiarizing yourself with different styles and tones may encourage new uses of language. Analyzing the rhetorical choices of other writers will also help you revise your prose because it promotes the habit of asking questions from the reader's point of view. Moreover, reading the opinions or sharing the experience of these authors may suggest interesting topics for your own essays. In other words, to help yourself become a more effective writer, read as much and as often as you can. ■

Chapter 22

Exposition: Development by Example

■ Darkness at Noon

Harold Krents

Harold Krents was a Washington, D.C., attorney and activist for the rights of the disabled. Before his death in 1987, Krents served on the President's Committee on Employment of the Handicapped and was a member of the Vera Institute of Justice and Mainstream, Incorporated. His autobiography *To Race the Wind* was published in 1972; his life was the inspiration for the Broadway play and popular movie *Butterflies Are Free*. This essay originally appeared in *The New York Times* in 1976.

1   Blind from birth, I have never had the opportunity to see myself and have been completely dependent on the image I create in the eye of the observer. To date it has not been narcissistic.

2   There are those who assume that since I can't see, I obviously also cannot hear. Very often people will converse with me at the top of their lungs, enunciating each word very carefully. Conversely, people will also often whisper, assuming that since my eyes don't work, my ears don't either.

3   For example, when I go to the airport and ask the ticket agent for assistance to the plane, he or she will invariably pick up the phone, call a ground hostess and whisper: "Hi, Jane, we've got a 76 here." I have concluded that the word "blind" is not used for one of two reasons: Either they fear that if the dread word is spoken, the ticket agent's retina will immediately detach, or they are reluctant to inform me of my condition of which I may not have been previously aware.

531

4   On the other hand, others know that of course I can hear, but believe that I can't talk. Often, therefore, when my wife and I go out to dinner, a waiter or waitress will ask Kit if "*he* would like a drink" to which I respond that "indeed *he* would."

5   This point was graphically driven home to me while we were in England. I had been given a year's leave of absence from my Washington law firm to study for a diploma in law at Oxford University. During the year I became ill and was hospitalized. Immediately after admission, I was wheeled down to the X-ray room. Just at the door sat an elderly woman—elderly I would judge from the sound of her voice. "What is his name?" the woman asked the orderly who had been wheeling me.

6   "What's your name?" the orderly repeated to me.

7   "Harold Krents," I replied.

8   "Harold Krents," he repeated.

9   "When was he born?"

10   "When were you born?"

11   "November 5, 1944," I responded.

12   "November 5, 1944," the orderly intoned.

13   This procedure continued for approximately five minutes at which point even my saint-like disposition deserted me. "Look," I finally blurted out, "this is absolutely ridiculous. Okay, granted I can't see, but it's got to have become pretty clear to both of you that I don't need an interpreter."

14   "He says he doesn't need an interpreter," the orderly reported to the woman.

15   The toughest misconception of all is the view that because I can't see, I can't work. I was turned down by over forty law firms because of my blindness, even though my qualifications included a cum laude degree from Harvard College and a good ranking in my Harvard Law School class.

16   The attempt to find employment, the continuous frustration of being told that it was impossible for a blind person to practice law, the rejection letters, not based on my lack of ability but rather on my disability, will always remain one of the most disillusioning experiences of my life.

17   Fortunately, this view of limitation and exclusion is beginning to change. On April 16 [1976], the Department of Labor issued regulations that mandate equal-employment opportunities for the handicapped. By and large, the business community's response to offering employment to the disabled has been enthusiastic.

18   I therefore look forward to the day, with the expectation that it is certain to come, when employers will view their handicapped workers as a little child did me years ago when my family still lived in Scarsdale.

19   I was playing basketball with my father in our backyard according to procedures we had developed. My father would stand beneath the hoop, shout, and I would shoot over his head at the basket attached to our garage. Our next-door neighbor, aged five, wandered over into our yard with a playmate. "He's blind," our neighbor whispered to her friend in a voice that could be heard distinctly by Dad and me. Dad shot and missed; I did the same. Dad hit the rim: I missed entirely: Dad shot and missed the garage entirely. "Which one is blind?" whispered back the little friend.

20   I would hope that in the near future when a plant manager is touring the factory with the foreman and comes upon a handicapped and non-handicapped person working together, his comment after watching them work will be, "Which one is disabled?"

■ Black Men and Public Space

Brent Staples

Brent Staples is an editorial writer for *The New York Times* and has published essays in a number of other newspapers and magazines, including the *Chicago-Sun Times* and *The New York Review of Books*. He holds a Ph.D. in psychology from the University of Chicago, and his memoir *Parallel Time: Growing Up in Black and White* (1994) won the Anisfield Wolff Book Award. This essay first appeared in *Ms.* magazine in 1986.

1 My first victim was a woman—white, well dressed, probably in her late twenties. I came upon her late one evening on a deserted street in Hyde Park, a relatively affluent neighborhood in an otherwise mean, impoverished section of Chicago. As I swung onto the avenue behind her, there seemed to be a discreet, uninflammatory distance between us. Not so. She cast back a worried glance. To her, the youngish black man— a broad six feet two inches with a beard and billowing hair, both hands shoved into the pockets of a bulky military jacket—seemed menacingly close. After a few more quick glimpses, she picked up her pace and was soon running in earnest. Within seconds she disappeared into a cross street.

2 That was more than a decade ago, I was twenty-two years old, a graduate student newly arrived at the University of Chicago. It was in the echo of that terrified woman's footfalls that I first began to know the unwieldy inheritance I'd come into—the ability to alter public space in ugly ways. It was clear that she thought herself the quarry of a mugger, a rapist, or worse. Suffering a bout of insomnia, however, I was stalking sleep, not defenseless wayfarers. As a softy who is scarcely able to take a knife to a raw chicken—let alone hold one to a person's throat—I was surprised, embarrassed, and dismayed all at once. Her flight made me feel like an accomplice in tyranny. It also made it clear that I was indistinguishable from the muggers who occasionally seeped into the area from the surrounding ghetto. That first encounter, and those that followed, signified that a vast, unnerving gulf lay between nighttime pedestrians—particularly women—and me. And I soon gathered that being perceived as dangerous is a hazard in itself. I only needed to turn a corner into a dicey situation, or crowd some frightened, armed person in a foyer somewhere, or make an errant move after being pulled over by a policeman. Where fear and weapons meet—and they often do in urban America—there is always the possibility of death.

3 In that first year, my first away from my hometown, I was to become thoroughly familiar with the language of fear. At dark, shadowy intersections, I could cross in front of a car stopped at a traffic light and elicit the *thunk, thunk, thunk, thunk* of the driver— black, white, male, or female—hammering down the door locks. On less traveled streets after dark, I grew accustomed to but never comfortable with people crossing to the other side of the street rather than pass me. Then there were the standard unpleasantries with policemen, doormen, bouncers, cabdrivers, and others whose business it is to screen out troublesome individuals *before* there is any nastiness.

4 I moved to New York nearly two years ago and I have remained an avid night walker. In central Manhattan, the near-constant crowd cover minimizes tense one-on-one street encounters. Elsewhere—in SoHo, for example, where sidewalks are narrow and tightly spaced buildings shut out the sky—things can get very taut indeed.

5   After dark, on the warrenlike streets of Brooklyn where I live, I often see women who fear the worst from me. They seem to have set their faces on neutral, and with their purse straps strung across their chests bandolier-style, they forge ahead as though bracing themselves against being tackled. I understand, of course, that the danger they perceive is not a hallucination. Women are particularly vulnerable to street violence, and young black males are drastically overrepresented among the perpetrators of that violence. Yet these truths are no solace against the kind of alienation that comes of being ever the suspect, a fearsome entity with whom pedestrians avoid making eye contact.

6   It is not altogether clear to me how I reached the ripe old age of twenty-two without being conscious of the lethality nighttime pedestrians attributed to me. Perhaps it was because in Chester, Pennsylvania, the small, angry industrial town where I came of age in the 1960s, I was scarcely noticeable against a backdrop of gang warfare, street knifings, and murders. I grew up one of the good boys, had perhaps a half-dozen fistfights. In retrospect, my shyness of combat has clear sources.

7   As a boy, I saw countless tough guys locked away; I have since buried several, too. They were babies, really—a teenage cousin, a brother of twenty-two, a childhood friend in his mid-twenties—all gone down in episodes of bravado played out in the streets. I came to doubt the virtues of intimidation early on. I chose, perhaps unconsciously, to remain a shadow—timid, but a survivor.

8   The fearsomeness mistakenly attributed to me in public places often has a perilous flavor. The most frightening of these confusions occurred in the late 1970s and early 1980s, when I worked as a journalist in Chicago. One day, rushing into the office of a magazine I was writing for with a deadline story in hand, I was mistaken for a burglar. The office manager called security and, with an ad hoc posse, pursued me through the labyrinthine halls, nearly to my editor's door. I had no way of proving who I was. I could only move briskly toward the company of someone who knew me.

9   Another time I was on assignment for a local paper and killing time before an interview. I entered a jewelry store on the city's affluent Near North Side. The proprietor excused herself and returned with an enormous red Doberman pinscher straining at the end of a leash. She stood, the dog extended toward me, silent to my questions, her eyes bulging nearly out of her head. I took a cursory look around, nodded, and bade her good night.

10   Relatively speaking, however, I never fared as badly as another black male journalist. He went to nearby Waukegan, Illinois, a couple of summers ago to work on a story about a murderer who was born there. Mistaking the reporter for the killer, police officers hauled him from his car at gunpoint and but for his press credentials would probably have tried to book him. Such episodes are not uncommon. Black men trade tales like this all the time.

11   Over the years, I learned to smother the rage I felt at so often being taken for a criminal. Not to do so would surely have led to madness. I now take precautions to make myself less threatening. I move about with care, particularly late in the evening. I give a wide berth to nervous people on subway platforms during the wee hours, particularly when I have exchanged business clothes for jeans. If I happen to be entering a building behind some people who appear skittish, I may walk by, letting them clear the lobby before I return, so as not to seem to be following them. I have been calm and extremely congenial on those rare occasions when I've been pulled over by the police.

12   And on late-evening constitutionals I employ what has proved to be an excellent tension-reducing measure: I whistle melodies from Beethoven and Vivaldi and the more popular classical composers. Even steely New Yorkers hunching toward night-time destinations seem to relax, and occasionally they even join in the tune. Virtually everybody seems to sense that a mugger wouldn't be warbling bright, sunny selections from Vivaldi's *Four Seasons*. It is my equivalent of the cowbell that hikers wear when they know they are in bear country.

■ Relying on the Kindness of Strangers

Deborah Mathis

Deborah Mathis writes a nationally syndicated column covering politics, social issues, and family life. As an award-winning national correspondent for the Gannett News Service, she has appeared as a commentator on a host of broadcast news and public affairs programs, including *Frontline*, *Inside Washington*, and *America's Black Forum*. Her book, *Yet a Stranger*, on American race relations, was published in 2002. This essay appeared in newspapers across the country in 2000.

1   A scene from a pharmacy shortly before Christmas:

2   The shopping aisles are crowded. A nice-looking, middle-aged woman—auburn hair, brown coat, dark brown pumps—whispers an "Excuse me" as she wheels her cart past me. The woman stops farther down the aisle and, like me, begins scanning the shelves, obviously looking for something in particular. Having found my item, I push on up the aisle. As I'm about to pass the woman, I decide to say something—a little wisecrack about the store's piped-in music, which is festive but also obnoxiously loud. "You think I should ask the manager to turn that up a little?" I crack, facetiously. The auburn-haired, brown-coated woman turns with a smile. "Excuse me," she said through her teeth. "I'm minding my own business; would you mind doing the same?"

3   Now, I promise you, she looked normal as could be. No wild eyes, no frothing mouth, no dishevelment. Nothing about her forewarned that she would find a speck of innocent small talk—a two-second remark—to be intrusive on her "business." Unprepared for such a response, I reeled my smile back in and wheeled off from this odd woman, the type who puts the "strange" in "stranger."

4   For the next several days, I found myself hesitating to chat with strangers, as has been my habit, being Southern-born and the informal type anyway. I have often heard that "you act like you know everybody," a statement I have always taken as a clinical observation, if not a compliment, but which, as of the pharmacy encounter, began to reek a little of criticism. The woman's surprising reaction left me wondering whether I should be less comfortable with strangers, less familiar, less outgoing. Lord knows, I wouldn't want any of them to think I was prying into their "business," not when I have more than enough of my own, thank you very much. I resorted to smiling only.

5   Then I remembered a situation from a decade ago involving my supervisor's lenience with staff absentees. All we had to do was call in and explain that we couldn't make it to work that day and Jim let it go, no questions asked. He refused to be a stickler about counting sick days, deciding instead to go with the utterly humanitarian practice of giving us the benefit of the doubt.

6   One day, an absent employee, who was supposedly sick with flu, was spotted at the racetrack, having a high old time with the Daily Double. It was not the first time someone had taken advantage of Jim's easy policy, but the boss was determined it would be the last. "That's it," he angrily declared. "I'm not going to be nice to people about this anymore." To which I reminded Jim that, when one extends a kindness to another and the other abuses it, it is not the good-hearted one who has a problem that needs fixing, it's the other guy.

7   Somewhat reluctantly, Jim kept his no-questions-asked practice and, with rare exception, the staff took advantage of it sparingly.

8   So, while the pharmacy encounter, like the renegade employee story, are the kinds of things that give you pause, I suppose such disappointments should not shake our faith in human goodness nor strip us of what virtues we possess. Kindness is still a habit worth keeping.

9   A week after the mind-your-own-business event, I was in the produce aisle stocking up for New Year's dinner. Two onions I had selected fell out of the grocery basket and rolled across the floor, with me chasing them.

10   "Now why do you want to throw onions around the store?" came a voice. I turned to see an older woman's kindly face smiling. I thought about how the auburn-haired woman might have responded to that. "Trying to get in some last-minute exercise," I responded. We shared a chuckle and went our separate ways. And with that, my faith was restored as quickly as it had been dashed the week before.

11   Most strangers aren't jerks; most aren't too wrapped up in their own world to acknowledge a fleeting act of kindness; most don't mind being friends for a moment; and most aren't as strange as the name implies.

Chapter 23

Exposition: Process Analysis

■ The Jeaning of America

Carin C. Quinn

Carin C. Quinn is an essayist who received her Master of Arts degree in American Studies from California State University at Los Angeles in 1976. "The Jeaning of America—and the World," was first published in *American Heritage* magazine in 1978.

1   This is the story of a sturdy American symbol which has now spread throughout most of the world. The symbol is not the dollar. It is not even Coca-Cola. It is a simple pair of pants called blue jeans, and what the pants symbolize is what Alexis de Tocqueville called "a manly and legitimate passion for equality. . . ." Blue jeans are favored equally by bureaucrats and cowboys; bankers and deadbeats; fashion designers and beer drinkers. They draw no distinctions and recognize no classes; they are merely American. Yet they are sought after almost everywhere in the world—including Russia, where authorities recently broke up a teenaged gang that was selling them on the black market for two hundred dollars a pair. They have been around for a long time, and it seems likely that they will outlive even the necktie.

2   This ubiquitous American symbol was the invention of a Bavarian-born Jew. His name was Levi Strauss.

3   He was born in Bad Ocheim, Germany, in 1829, and during the European political turmoil of 1848 decided to take his chances in New York, to which his two brothers already had emigrated. Upon arrival, Levi soon found that his two brothers had exaggerated their tales of an easy life in the land of the main chance. They were

537

landowners, they had told him; instead, he found them pushing needles, thread, pots, pans, ribbons, yarn, scissors, and buttons to housewives. For two years he was a lowly peddler, hauling some 180 pounds of sundries door-to-door to eke out a marginal living. When a married sister in San Francisco offered to pay his way West in 1850, he jumped at the opportunity, taking with him bolts of canvas he hoped to sell for tenting.

4   It was the wrong kind of canvas for that purpose, but while talking with a miner down from the mother lode, he learned that pants—sturdy pants that would stand up to the rigors of the digging—were almost impossible to find. Opportunity beckoned. On the spot, Strauss measured the man's girth and inseam with a piece of string and, for six dollars in gold dust, had [the canvas] tailored into a pair of stiff but rugged pants. The miner was delighted with the result, word got around about "those pants of Levi's," and Strauss was in business. The company has been in business ever since.

5   When Strauss ran out of canvas, he wrote his two brothers to send more. He received instead a tough, brown cotton cloth made in Nîmes, France—called *serge de Nîmes* and swiftly shortened to "denim" (the word "jeans" derives from Gênes, the French word for Genoa, where a similar cloth was produced). Almost from the first, Strauss had his cloth dyed the distinctive indigo that gave blue jeans their name, but it was not until the 1870s that he added the copper rivets which have long since become a company trademark. The rivets were the idea of a Virginia City, Nevada, tailor, Jacob W. Davis, who added them to pacify a mean-tempered miner called Alkali Ike. Alkali, the story goes, complained that the pockets of his jeans always tore when he stuffed them with ore samples and demanded that Davis do something about it. As a kind of joke, Davis took the pants to a blacksmith and had the pockets riveted; once again, the idea worked so well that word got around; in 1873 Strauss appropriated and patented the gimmick—and hired Davis as a regional manager.

6   By this time, Strauss had taken both his brothers and two brothers-in-law into the company and was ready for his third San Francisco store. Over the ensuing years the company prospered locally, and by the time of his death in 1902, Strauss had become a man of prominence in California. For three decades thereafter the business remained profitable though small, with sales largely confined to the working people of the West—cowboys, lumberjacks, railroad workers, and the like. Levi's jeans were first introduced to the East, apparently, during the dude-ranch craze of the 1930s when vacationing Easterners returned and spread the word about the wonderful pants with rivets. Another boost came in World War II, when blue jeans were declared an essential commodity and were sold only to people engaged in defense work. From a company with fifteen salespeople, two plants, and almost no business east of the Mississippi in 1946, the organization grew in thirty years to include a sales force of more than twenty-two thousand, with fifty plants and offices in thirty-five countries. Each year, more than 250,000,000 items of Levi's clothing are sold—including more than 83,000,000 pairs of riveted blue jeans. They have become, through marketing, word of mouth, and demonstrable reliability, the common pants of America. They can be purchased pre-washed, pre-faded, and pre-shrunk for the suitably proletarian look. They adapt themselves to any sort of idiosyncratic use; women slit them at the inseams and convert them into long skirts, men chop them off above the knees and turn them into something to be worn while challenging the surf. Decorations and ornamentations abound.

7   The pants have become a tradition, and along the way have acquired a history of their own—so much so that the company has opened a museum in San Francisco. There was,

for example, the turn-of-the-century trainman who replaced a faulty coupling with a pair of jeans; the Wyoming man who used his jeans as a towrope to haul his car out of a ditch; the Californian who found several pairs in an abandoned mine, wore them, then discovered they were sixty-three years old and still as good as new and turned them over to the Smithsonian as a tribute to their toughness. And then there is the particularly terrifying story of the careless construction worker who dangled fifty-two stories above the street until rescued, his sole support the Levi's belt loop through which his rope was hooked.

■ Skiing Lessons: The Cold, Hard Facts

Dave Barry

Dave Barry is a contemporary humorist well known for his nationally syndicated newspaper column. He has published numerous collections of his columns, including *Dave Barry's Complete Guide to Guys* (1996), *Dave Barry Is from Mars and Venus* (1998), and *Dave Barry Is Not Taking This Sitting Down* (2000), and two novels, *Big Trouble* (1999) and *Tricky Business* (2002). This selection first appeared in newspapers throughout the country in 1989.

1   If you're looking for a vacation concept that combines the element of outdoor fun with the element of potentially knocking down a tree with your face, you can't do better than skiing. My family just got back from a ski trip to Vermont ("The Wind Chill Factor State"), and it was an adventure I'm sure we will remember fondly for many years while our various body parts heal.

2   The key to a successful ski trip, of course, is planning, by which I mean: money. For openers, you have to buy a special outfit that meets the strict requirements of the Ski Fashion Institute, namely: (1) it must cost as much as a medium wedding reception, (2) it must make you look like the Giant Radioactive Easter Bunny From Space and (3) it must be made of a mutant fiber with a name that sounds like the villain on a Saturday-morning cartoon show, such as "Gore-Tex," so as to provide the necessary resistance to moisture, which, trust me, will be gushing violently from all of your major armpits once you start lunging down the mountain. You also have to buy ski goggles costing upward of $50 per eyeball that are specially designed not to *not* fog up under any circumstances except when you put them on, at which time they become approximately as transparent as the Los Angeles telephone directory, which is why veteran skiers recommend that you do not pull them down over your eyes until just before you make contact with the tree. And you'll need ski boots, which are made from melted bowling balls and which protect your feet by preventing your blood, which could contain dangerous germs, from traveling below your shins.

3   As for the actual skis, you should rent them because of the feeling of confidence you get from reading the fine print on the lengthy legal document that the rental personnel make you sign, which states:

> The undersigned agrees that skiing is an *insanely dangerous activity,* and that the rental personnel were just sitting around minding their *own business* when the undersigned, who agrees that he or she is a *raving loon,* came *barging in uninvited,* waving a *loaded revolver* and demanding that he or she be given some rental skis for the express purpose of suffering *serious injury or death,* leaving the rental personnel with *no choice* but to . . . , etc.

4   OK! Now you're ready to "hit the slopes." Ski experts recommend you start by taking a group lesson because otherwise they would have to get real jobs. To start the lesson, your instructor, who is always a smiling 19-year-old named "Chip," will take you to the top of the mountain and explain basic ski safety procedures until he feels that the cold has killed enough of your brain cells that you will cheerfully follow whatever lunatic command he gives you. Then he'll ski a short distance down the mountain, just to the point where it gets very steep and swoosh to a graceful stop, making it look absurdly easy. It *is* absurdly easy for Chip, because underneath his outfit he's wearing an anti-gravity device. All the expert skiers wear them. You don't actually believe that "ski jumpers" can leap off those ridiculously high ramps and just float to the ground unassisted without breaking into walnut-sized pieces, do you? Like Tinkerbell or something? Don't be a cretin.

5   After Chip stops, he turns to the group, his skis hovering as much as three inches above the snow and orders the first student to copy what he did. This is the fun part. Woodland creatures often wake up from hibernation just to watch this part because even they understand that the laws of physics, which are strictly enforced on ski slopes, do not permit a person to simply stop on the side of a snow-covered mountain if his feet are encased in bowling balls attached to what are essentially large pieces of teflon. So they greatly enjoy watching as the first student cautiously pushes himself forward and almost instantly achieves Warp Speed, becoming an almost-invisible blur as he passes Chip and proceeds on into the woods, flailing his arms like a volunteer in a nerve-gas experiment. "That was good!" shouts Chip . . . then he turns to the rest of the group and says, "Next!" The group's only rational response, of course, would be to lie down in the snow and demand a rescue helicopter. But these are not rational beings; these are ski students. And so, one by one, they, too, ski into the woods, then stagger out sometimes with branches sticking out, antlerlike, from their foreheads, and do it again. "Bend your knees this time!" advises Chip, knowing that this will actually make them go faster. He loves his work.

6   Eventually, of course, you get better at it. If you stick with your lessons, you'll become an "intermediate" skier, meaning you'll learn to fall before you reach the woods. That's the level I'm on now, in stark contrast to my 8-year-old son, who has not yet studied gravity in school and therefore became an expert in a matter of hours. Watching him flash effortlessly down the slope, I found myself experiencing pride and hope; pride in his accomplishment, and hope that someday, somehow, he'll ski near enough to where I'm lying that I'll be able to trip him with my poles.

■ Autumn Leaves

Diane Ackerman

Diane Ackerman is the author of over twenty books of poetry and nonfiction, often blending her interests in nature, science, and natural history with her uses of figurative language. After publishing three books of poetry and earning her Ph.D. in English from Cornell University, Ackerman began to publish prose works, including *A Natural History of the Senses* (1990), from which this excerpt is taken; *A Slender Thread* (1997); *Deep Play* (1999); and *Cultivating Delight* (2001). Her most recent book of poetry is *Origami Bridges* (2002).

1   The stealth of autumn catches one unaware. Was that a goldfinch perching in the early September woods, or just the first turning leaf? A red-winged blackbird or a

sugar maple closing up shop for the winter? Keen-eyed as leopards, we stand still and squint hard, looking for signs of movement. Early-morning frost sits heavily on the grass, and turns barbed wire into a string of stars. On a distant hill, a small square of yellow appears to be a lighted stage. At last the truth dawns on us: Fall is staggering in, right on schedule, with its baggage of chilly nights, macabre holidays, and spectacular, heart-stoppingly beautiful leaves. Soon the leaves will start cringing on the trees, and roll up in clenched fists before they actually fall off. Dry seedpods will rattle like tiny gourds. But first there will be weeks of gushing color so bright, so pastel, so confettilike, that people will travel up and down the East Coast just to stare at it—a whole season of leaves.

2   Where do the colors come from? Sunlight rules most living things with its golden edicts. When the days begin to shorten, soon after the summer solstice on June 21, a tree reconsiders its leaves. All summer it feeds them so they can process sunlight, but in the dog days of summer the tree begins pulling nutrients back into its trunk and roots, pares down, and gradually chokes off its leaves. A corky layer of cells forms at the leaves' slender petioles, then scars over. Undernourished, the leaves stop producing the pigment chlorophyll, and photosynthesis ceases. Animals can migrate, hibernate, or store food to prepare for winter. But where can a tree go? It survives by dropping its leaves, and by the end of autumn only a few fragile threads of fluid-carrying xylem hold leaves to their stems.

3   A turning leaf stays partly green at first, then reveals splotches of yellow and red as the chlorophyll gradually breaks down. Dark green seems to stay longest in the veins, outlining and defining them. During the summer, chlorophyll dissolves in the heat and light, but it is also being steadily replaced. In the fall, on the other hand, no new pigment is produced, and so we notice the other colors that were always there, right in the leaf, although chlorophyll's shocking green hid them from view. With their camouflage gone, we see these colors for the first time all year, and marvel, but they were always there, hidden like a vivid secret beneath the hot glowing greens of summer.

4   The most spectacular range of fall foliage occurs in the northeastern United States and in eastern China, where the leaves are robustly colored, thanks in part to a rich climate. European maples don't achieve the same flaming reds as their American relatives, which thrive on cold nights and sunny days. In Europe, the warm, humid weather turns the leaves brown or mildly yellow. Anthocyanin, the pigment that gives apples their red and turns leaves red or red-violet, is produced by sugars that remain in the leaf after the supply of nutrients dwindles. Unlike the carotenoids, which color carrots, squash, and corn, and turn leaves orange and yellow, anthocyanin varies from year to year, depending on the temperature and amount of sunlight. The fiercest colors occur in years when the fall sunlight is strongest and the nights are cool and dry (a state of grace scientists find vexing to forecast). This is also why leaves appear dizzyingly bright and clear on a sunny fall day: The anthocyanin flashes like a marquee.

5   Not all leaves turn the same colors. Elms, weeping willows, and the ancient ginkgo all grow radiant yellow, along with hickories, aspens, bottlebrush buckeyes, cottonweeds, and tall, keening poplars. Basswood turns bronze, birches bright gold. Water-loving maples put on a symphonic display of scarlets. Sumacs turn red, too, as do flowering dogwoods, black gums, and sweet gums. Though some oaks yellow, most turn a pinkish brown. The farmlands also change color, as tepees of cornstalks and bales of shredded-wheat-textured hay stand drying in the fields. In some spots, one

slope of a hill may be green and the other already in bright color, because the hill-side facing south gets more sun and heat than the northern one.

6   An odd feature of the colors is that they don't seem to have any special purpose. We are predisposed to respond to their beauty, of course. They shimmer with the colors of sunset, spring flowers, the tawny buff of a colt's pretty rump, the shuttering pink of a blush. Animals and flowers color for a reason—adaptation to their environment—but there is no adaptive reason for leaves to color so beautifully in the fall any more than there is for the sky or ocean to be blue. It's just one of the haphazard marvels the planet bestows every year. We find the sizzling colors thrilling, and in a sense they dupe us. Colored like living things, they signal death and disintegration. In time, they will become fragile and, like the body, return to dust. They are as we hope our own fate will be when we die: Not to vanish, just to sublime from one beautiful state into another. Though leaves lose their green life, they bloom with urgent colors, as the woods grow mummified day by day, and Nature becomes more carnal, mute, and radiant. . . .

7   But how do the colored leaves fall? As a leaf ages, the growth hormone, auxin, fades, and cells at the base of the petiole divide. Two or three rows of small cells, lying at right angles to the axis of the petiole, react with water, then come apart, leaving the petioles hanging on by only a few threads of xylem. A light breeze, and the leaves are airborne. They glide and swoop, rocking in invisible cradles. They are all wing and may flutter from yard to yard on small whirlwinds or updrafts, swiveling as they go. Firmly tethered to earth, we love to see things rise up and fly—soap bubbles, balloons, birds, fall leaves. They remind us that the end of a season is capricious, as is the end of life. We especially like the way leaves rock, careen, and swoop as they fall. Everyone knows the motion. Pilots sometimes do a maneuver called a "falling leaf," in which the plane loses altitude quickly and on purpose, by slipping first to the right, then to the left. The machine weighs a ton or more, but in one pilot's mind it is a weightless thing, a falling leaf. She has seen the motion before, in the Vermont woods where she played as a child. Below her the trees radiate gold, copper, and red. Leaves are falling, although she can't see them fall, as she falls, swooping down for a closer view.

8   At last the leaves leave. But first they turn color and thrill us for weeks on end. Then they crunch and crackle underfoot. They *shush*, as children drag their small feet through leaves heaped along the curb. Dark, slimy mats of leaves cling to one's heels after a rain. A damp, stuccolike mortar of semidecayed leaves protects the tender shoots with a roof until spring, and makes a rich humus. An occasional bulge or ripple in the leafy mounds signals a shrew or a field mouse tunneling out of sight. Sometimes one finds in fossil stones the imprint of a leaf, long since disintegrated, whose outlines remind us how detailed, vibrant, and alive are the things of this earth that perish.

Chapter 24

Exposition:
Comparison / Contrast

■ My Real Car

Bailey White

Georgia-born Bailey White has published stories and essays in many magazines, but she is perhaps best known as a commentator on National Public Radio's award-winning news magazine, *All Things Considered*. Her essays and sketches have been collected in *Mama Makes Up Her Mind and Other Dangers of Southern Living* (1993) and *Sleeping at the Starlight Motel* (1995); her first novel is *Quite a Year for Plums* (1998). This selection was originally published in *Smithsonian* magazine in 1991.

1   It really makes you feel your age when you get a letter from your insurance agent telling you that the car you bought, only slightly used, the year you got out of college is now an antique. "Beginning with your next payment, your premiums will reflect this change in classification," the letter said.

2   I went out and looked at the car. I thought back over the years. I could almost hear my uncle's disapproving voice. "You should never buy a used car," he had told me the day I brought it home. Ten years later I drove that used car to his funeral. I drove my sister to the hospital in that car to have her first baby, and I drove to Atlanta in that car when the baby graduated from Georgia Tech with a degree in physics.

3   "When are you going to get a new car?" my friends asked me.

4   "I don't need a new car," I said. "This car runs fine."

5   I changed the oil often, and I kept good tires on it. It always got me where I wanted to go. But the stuffing came out of the backseat and the springs poked through, and

the dashboard disintegrated. At 300,000 miles the odometer quit turning, but I didn't really care to know how far I had driven. A hole wore in the floor where my heel rested in front of the accelerator, and the insulation all peeled off the fire wall. "Old piece of junk," my friends whispered. The seat-belt catch finally wore out, and I tied on a huge bronze hook with a fireman's knot.

6   Then one day on my way to work, the car coughed, sputtered and stopped. "This is it," I thought, and I gave it a pat. "It's been a good car."

7   The mechanic laughed at me. "You know what's wrong with that car?" he asked. "That car is out of gas." So I slopped some gas in the tank and drove ten more years.

8   The fuel gauge never worked again after that, but I got to where I could tell when the gas was low by the smell. I think it was the smell of the bottom of the tank. There was also a little smell of brake fluid, a little smell of exhaust, a little smell of oil and, after all the years, a little smell of me. Car smells.

9   And sounds. The wonderful sound when the engine finally catches on a cold day, and an ominous *tick tick* in July when the radiator is working too hard. The windshield wipers said, "Gracie Allen Gracie Allen Gracie Allen." I didn't like a lot of conversation in the car, because I had to keep listening for a little skip that meant I needed to jump out and adjust the carburetor. I kept a screwdriver close at hand, and a pint of brake fluid and a new rotor, just in case. "She's strange," my friends whispered. "And she drives so slow."

10   I don't know how fast I drove. The speedometer had quit working years ago. But when I would look down through the hole in the floor and see the pavement, a gray blur, whizzing by just inches away from my feet, and feel the tremendous heat from the internal-combustion engine pouring back through the fire wall into my lap, and hear each barely contained explosion, just as a heart attack victim is able to hear her own heartbeat, it didn't feel like slow to me. A whiff of brake fluid would remind me just what a tiny thing I was relying on to stop myself from hurtling along the surface of the Earth at an unnatural speed. When I arrived at my destination, I would slump back, unfasten the seat-belt hook with trembling hands and stagger out. I would gather up my things and give the car a last look. "Thank you, sir," I would say. "We got here one more time."

11   But after I received that letter I began thinking about buying a new car. I read the newspaper every night. Finally I found one that sounded good. It was the same make as my car, but almost new. "Call Steve," the ad said. I went to see the car. It was parked in Steve's driveway. It was a fashionable wheat color. There was carpet on the floor and the seats were covered with soft, velvety-feeling stuff. It smelled like acrylic, and vinyl, and Steve. I turned a knob. Mozart's Concerto for Flute and Harp poured out of four speakers. "But how can you listen to the engine with music playing?" I asked Steve.

12   I turned the key. The car started instantly. I fastened my seat belt. Nothing but a click. Steve got in the passenger seat, and we went for a test drive. We floated down the road. I couldn't hear a sound, but I decided it must be time to shift gears. I stomped around on the floor and grabbed Steve's knee before I remembered the car had automatic transmission.

13   "You mean you just put it in 'Drive' and drive?" I asked. Steve scrunched himself against his door and clamped his knees together. He tested his seat belt. "Have you ever driven before?" he asked.

14   I bought it. I rolled all the windows up by mashing a button beside my elbow, set the air-conditioning on "Recirc" and listened to Vivaldi all the way home.

15   So now I have two cars. I call them my new car and my real car. Most of the time I drive my new car. But on some days I go out to the barn and get in my real car. I shoo the rats out of the backseat and crank up the engine. Even without daily practice my hands and feet know just what to do. My ears perk up, and I sniff the air. I add a little brake fluid, a little water. I sniff again. It'll need gas next week, and an oil change. I back it out and we roll down the road. People stop and look. They smile. "Neat car!" they say.

■ Dearly Disconnected

Ian Frazier

Ian Frazier wrote for the *Harvard Lampoon* during his college days and then became a staff writer for *The New Yorker* magazine. Two collections of his humorous pieces from *The New Yorker* include *Coyote v. ACME* (1996) and *Dating Your Mom* (2003). He is also the author of *Great Plains* (1989), *On the Rez* (2000), and *The Fish's Eye* (2003) and the editor of *Best American Essays* (1996) and *Best American Travel Writing* (2003). This essay first appeared in *Mother Jones* magazine in 2000.

1   Before I got married I was living by myself in an A-frame cabin in northwestern Montana. The cabin's interior was a single high-ceilinged room, and at the center of the room, mounted on the rough-hewn log that held up the ceiling beam, was a telephone. I knew no one in the area or indeed the whole state, so my entire social life came to me through that phone. The woman I would marry was living in Sarasota, Florida, and the distance between us suggests how well we were getting along at the time. We had not been in touch for several months; she had no phone. One day she decided to call me from a pay phone. We talked for a while, and after her coins ran out I jotted the number on the wood beside my phone and called her back. A day or two later, thinking about the call, I wanted to talk to her again. The only number I had for her was the pay phone number I'd written down.

2   The pay phone was on the street some blocks from the apartment where she stayed. As it happened, though, she had just stepped out to do some errands a few minutes before I called, and she was passing by on the sidewalk when the phone rang. She had no reason to think that a public phone ringing on a busy street would be for her. She stopped, listened to it ring again, and picked up the receiver. Love is pure luck; somehow I had known she would answer, and she had known it would be me.

3   Long afterwards, on a trip to Disney World in Orlando with our two kids, then aged six and two, we made a special detour to Sarasota to show them the pay phone. It didn't impress them much. It's just a nondescript Bell Atlantic pay phone on the cement wall of a building, by the vestibule. But its ordinariness and even boringness only make me like it more; ordinary places where extraordinary events have occurred are my favorite kind. On my mental map of Florida that pay phone is a landmark looming above the city it occupies, and a notable, if private, historic site.

4   I'm interested in pay phones in general these days, especially when I get the feeling that they are about to go away. Technology, in the form of sleek little phones in our pockets, has swept on by them and made them begin to seem antique. My lifelong entanglement with pay phones dates me. When I was young they were just there, a given, often as stubborn and uncongenial as the curbstone underfoot. They were

instruments of torture sometimes. You had to feed them fistfuls of change in those pre-phone-card days, and the operator was a real person who stood maddeningly between you and whomever you were trying to call. And when the call went wrong, as communication often does, the pay phone gave you a focus for your rage. Pay phones were always getting smashed up, the receivers shattered to bits against the booth, the coin slots jammed with chewing gum, the cords yanked out and unraveled to the floor.

5   You used to hear people standing at pay phones and cursing them. I remember the sound of my own frustrated shouting confined by the glass walls of a phone booth—the kind you don't see much anymore, with a little ventilating fan in the ceiling that turned on when you shut the double-hinged glass door. The noise that fan made in the silence of a phone booth was for a while the essence of romantic, lonely-guy melancholy for me. Certain specific pay phones I still resent for the unhappiness they caused me, and others I will never forgive, though not for any fault of their own. In the C concourse of the Salt Lake City airport there's a row of pay phones set on the wall by the men's room just past the concourse entry. While on a business trip a few years ago, I called home from a phone in that row and learned that a friend had collapsed in her apartment and was in the hospital with brain cancer. I had liked those pay phones before, and had used them often; now I can't even look at them when I go by.

6   There was always a touch of seediness and sadness to pay phones, and a sense of transience. Drug dealers made calls from them, and shady types who did not want their whereabouts known, and otherwise respectable people planning assignations, and people too poor to have phones of their own. In the movies, any character who used a pay phone was either in trouble or contemplating a crime. Pay phones came with their own special atmospherics and even accessories sometimes—the predictable bad smells and graffiti, of course, as well as cigarette butts, soda cans, scattered pamphlets from the Jehovah's Witnesses, and single bottles of beer (empty) still in their individual, street-legal paper bags. Mostly, pay phones evoked the mundane: "Honey, I'm just leaving. I'll be there soon." But you could tell that a lot of undifferentiated humanity had flowed through these places, and that in the muteness of each pay phone's little space, wild emotion had howled.

7   Once, when I was living in Brooklyn, I read in the newspaper that a South American man suspected of dozens of drug-related contract murders had been arrested at a pay phone in Queens. Police said that the man had been on the phone setting up a murder at the time of his arrest. The newspaper story gave the address of the pay phone, and out of curiosity one afternoon I took a long walk to Queens to take a look at it. It was on an undistinguished street in a middle-class neighborhood, by a florist's shop. By the time I saw it, however, the pay phone had been blown up and/or firebombed. I had never before seen a pay phone so damaged; explosives had blasted pieces of the phone itself wide open in metal shreds like frozen banana peels, and flames had blackened everything and melted the plastic parts and burned the insulation off the wires. Soon after, I read that police could not find enough evidence against the suspected murderer and so had let him go.

8   The cold phone outside a shopping center in Bigfork, Montana, from which I called a friend in the West Indies one winter when her brother was sick; the phone on the wall of the concession stand at Redwood Pool, where I used to stand dripping and call my mom to come and pick me up; the sweaty phones used almost only by men in the hallway outside the maternity ward at Lenox Hill Hospital in New York; the phone

by the driveway of the Red Cloud Indian School in South Dakota where I used to talk with my wife while priests in black slacks and white socks chatted on a bench nearby; the phone in the old wood-paneled phone booth with leaded glass windows in the drugstore in my Ohio hometown—each one is as specific as a birthmark, a point on earth unlike any other. Recently I went back to New York City after a long absence and tried to find a working pay phone. I picked up one receiver after the next without success. Meanwhile, as I scanned down the long block, I counted half a dozen or more pedestrians talking on their cell phones.

9   It's the cell phone, of course, that's putting the pay phone out of business. The pay phone is to the cell phone as the troubled and difficult older sibling is to the cherished newborn. People even treat their cell phones like babies, cradling them in their palms and beaming down upon them lovingly as they dial. You sometimes hear people yelling on their cell phones, but almost never yelling at them. Cell phones are toylike, nearly magic, and we get a huge kick out of them, as often happens with technological advances until the new wears off. Somehow I don't believe people had a similar honeymoon period with pay phones back in their early days, and they certainly have no such enthusiasm for them now. When I see a cell-phone user gently push the little antenna and fit the phone back into its brushed-vinyl carrying case and tuck the case inside his jacket beside his heart, I feel sorry for the beat-up pay phone standing in the rain.

10   People almost always talk on cell phones while in motion—driving, walking down the street, riding on a commuter train. The cell phone took the transience the pay phone implied and turned it into VIP-style mobility and speed. Even sitting in a restaurant, the person on a cell phone seems importantly busy and on the move. Cell-phone conversations seem to be unlimited by ordinary constraints of place and time, as if they represent an almost-perfect form of communication whose perfect state would be telepathy.

11   And yet no matter how we factor the world away, it remains. I think this is what drives me so nuts when a person sitting next to me on a bus makes a call from her cell phone. Yes, this busy and important caller is at no fixed point in space, but nevertheless I happen to be beside her. The job of providing physical context falls on me; I become her call's surroundings, as if I'm the phone booth wall. For me to lean over and comment on her cell-phone conversation would be as unseemly and unexpected as if I were in fact a wall; and yet I have no choice, as a sentient person, but to hear what my chatty fellow traveler has to say.

12   Some middle-aged guys like me go around complaining about this kind of thing. The more sensible approach is just to accept it and forget about it, because there's not much we can do. I don't think that pay phones will completely disappear. Probably they will survive for a long while as clumsy old technology still of some use to those lagging behind, and as a backup if ever the superior systems should temporarily fail. Before pay phones became endangered I never thought of them as public spaces, which of course they are. They suggested a human average; they belonged to anybody who had a couple of coins. Now I see that, like public schools and public transportation, pay phones belong to a former commonality our culture is no longer quite so sure it needs.

13   I have a weakness for places—for old battlefields, car-crash sites, houses where famous authors lived. Bygone passions should always have an address, it seems to me. Ideally, the world would be covered with plaques and markers listing the notable events that occurred at each particular spot. A sign on every pay phone would describe how a woman broke up with her fiancé here, how a young ballplayer learned that he had

made the team. Unfortunately, the world itself is fluid, and changes out from under us; the rocky islands that the pilot Mark Twain was careful to avoid in the Mississippi are now stone outcroppings in a soybean field. Meanwhile, our passions proliferate into illegibility, and the places they occur can't hold them. Eventually pay phones will become relics of an almost-vanished landscape, and of a time when there were fewer of us and our stories were on an earlier page. Romantics like me will have to reimagine our passions as they are—unmoored to earth, like an infinitude of cell-phone messages flying through the atmosphere.

■ Once More to the Lake (August 1941)

E. B. White

Elwyn Brooks White was an editor and writer for *The New Yorker* and a columnist for *Harper's* magazine. He is well known for his essays, collected in volumes including *One Man's Meat* (1943), *The Second Tree from the Corner* (1954), and *The Points of My Compass* (1962), and for his children's books, *Charlotte's Web* (1952) and *Stuart Little* (1945). This essay, written in 1941, originally appeared in *Harper's*.

1   One summer, along about 1904, my father rented a camp on a lake in Maine and took us all there for the month of August. We all got ringworm from some kittens and had to rub Pond's Extract on our arms and legs night and morning, and my father rolled over in a canoe with all his clothes on; but outside of that the vacation was a success and from then on none of us ever thought there was any place in the world like that lake in Maine. We returned summer after summer—always on August 1st for one month. I have since become a salt-water man, but sometimes in summer there are days when the restlessness of the tides and the fearful cold of the sea water and the incessant wind which blows across the afternoon and into the evening make me wish for the placidity of a lake in the woods. A few weeks ago this feeling got so strong I bought myself a couple of bass hooks and a spinner and returned to the lake where we used to go, for a week's fishing and to revisit old haunts.

2   I took along my son, who had never had any fresh water up his nose and who had seen lily pads only from train windows. On the journey over to the lake I began to wonder what it would be like. I wondered how time would have marred this unique, this holy spot—the coves and streams, the hills that the sun set behind, the camps and the paths behind the camps. I was sure the tarred road would have found it out and I wondered in what other ways it would be desolated. It is strange how much you can remember about places like that once you allow your mind to return into the grooves which lead back. You remember one thing, and that suddenly reminds you of another thing. I guess I remembered clearest of all the early mornings, when the lake was cool and motionless, remembered how the bedroom smelled of the lumber it was made of and of the wet woods whose scent entered through the screen. The partitions in the camp were thin and did not extend clear to the top of the rooms, and as I was always the first up I would dress softly so as not to wake the others, and sneak out into the sweet outdoors and start out in the canoe, keeping close along the shore in the long shadows of the pines. I remembered being very careful never to rub my paddle against the gunwale for fear of disturbing the stillness of the cathedral.

3   The lake had never been what you would call a wild lake. There were cottages sprinkled around the shores, and it was in farming country although the shores of the lake were quite heavily wooded. Some of the cottages were owned by nearby farmers, and you would live at the shore and eat your meals at the farmhouse. That's what our family did. But although it wasn't wild, it was a fairly large and undisturbed lake and there were places in it which, to a child at least, seemed infinitely remote and primeval.

4   I was right about the tar: it led to within half a mile of the shore. But when I got back there, with my boy, and we settled into a camp near a farmhouse and into the kind of summertime I had known, I could tell that it was going to be pretty much the same as it had been before—I knew it, lying in bed the first morning, smelling the bedroom, and hearing the boy sneak quietly out and go off along the shore in a boat. I began to sustain the illusion that he was I, and therefore by simple transposition, that I was my father. This sensation persisted, kept cropping up all the time we were there. It was not an entirely new feeling, but in this setting it grew much stronger. I seemed to be living a dual existence. I would be in the middle of some simple act, I would be picking up a bait box or laying down a table fork, or I would be saying something, and suddenly it would be not I but my father who was saying the words or making the gesture. It gave me a creepy sensation.

5   We went fishing the first morning. I felt the same damp moss covering the worms in the bait can, and saw the dragonfly alight on the tip of my rod as it hovered a few inches from the surface of the water. It was the arrival of this fly that convinced me beyond any doubt that everything was as it always had been, that the years were a mirage and there had been no years. The small waves were the same, chucking the rowboat under the chin as we fished at anchor, and the boat was the same boat, the same color green and the ribs broken in the same places, and under the floor-boards the same fresh-water leavings and debris—the dead helgramite,* the wisps of moss, the rusty discarded fishhook, the dried blood from yesterday's catch. We stared silently at the tips of our rods, at the dragonflies that came and went. I lowered the tip of mine into the water, tentatively, pensively dislodging the fly, which darted two feet away, poised, darted two feet back, and came to rest again a little farther up the rod. There had been no years between the ducking of this dragonfly and the other one—the one that was part of memory. I looked at the boy, who was silently watching his fly, and it was my hands that held his rod, my eyes watching. I felt dizzy and didn't know which rod I was at the end of.

6   We caught two bass, hauling them in briskly as though they were mackerel, pulling them over the side of the boat in a businesslike manner without any landing net, and stunning them with a blow on the back of the head. When we got back for a swim before lunch, the lake was exactly where we had left it, the same number of inches from the dock, and there was only the merest suggestion of a breeze. This seemed an utterly enchanted sea, this lake you could leave to its own devices for a few hours and come back to, and find that it had not stirred, this constant and trustworthy body of water. In the shallows, the dark, water-soaked sticks and twigs, smooth and old, were undulating in clusters on the bottom against the clean ribbed sand, and the track of the mussel was plain. A school of minnows swam by, each minnow with its small individual shadow, doubling the attendance, so clear and sharp in the sunlight. Some of the other campers were in swimming, along the shore, one of them with a cake of soap,

*A helgramite is an insect sometimes used for bait.

and the water felt thin and clear and unsubstantial. Over the years there had been this person with the cake of soap, this cultist, and here he was. There had been no years.

7   Up to the farmhouse to dinner through the teeming, dusty field, the road under our sneakers was only a two-track road. The middle track was missing, the one with the marks of the hooves and the splotches of dried, flaky manure. There had always been three tracks to choose from in choosing which track to walk in; now the choice was narrowed down to two. For a moment I missed terribly the middle alternative. But the way led past the tennis court, and something about the way it lay there in the sun reassured me; the tape had loosened along the backline, the alleys were green with plantains and other weeds, and the net (installed in June and removed in September) sagged in the dry noon, and the whole place steamed with mid-day heat and hunger and emptiness. There was a choice of pie for dessert, and one was blueberry and one was apple, and the waitresses were the same country girls, there having been no passage of time, only the illusion of it as in a dropped curtain—the waitresses were still fifteen; their hair had been washed, that was the only difference—they had been to the movies and seen the pretty girls with the clean hair.

8   Summertime, oh summertime, pattern of life indelible, the fade-proof lake, the woods unshatterable, the pasture with the sweet-fern and the juniper forever and ever, summer without end; this was the background, and the life along the shore was the design, the cottages with their innocent and tranquil design, their tiny docks with the flagpole and the American flag floating against the white clouds in the blue sky, the little paths over the roots of the trees leading from camp to camp and the paths leading back to the outhouses and the can of lime for sprinkling, and at the souvenir counters at the store the miniature birch-bark canoes and the post cards that showed things looking a little better than they looked. This was the American family at play, escaping the city heat, wondering whether the newcomers in the camp at the head of the cove were "common" or "nice," wondering whether it was true that the people who drove up for Sunday dinner at the farmhouse were turned away because there wasn't enough chicken.

9   It seemed to me, as I kept remembering all this, that those times and those summers had been infinitely precious and worth saving. There had been jollity and peace and goodness. The arriving (at the beginning of August) had been so big a business in itself, at the railway station the farm wagon drawn up, the first smell of the pine-laden air, the first glimpse of the smiling farmer, and the great importance of the trunks and your father's enormous authority in such matters, and the feel of the wagon under you for a long ten-mile haul, and at the top of the last long hill catching the first view of the lake after eleven months of not seeing this cherished body of water. The shouts and cries of the other campers when they saw you, and the trunks to be unpacked, to give up their rich burden. (Arriving was less exciting nowadays, when you sneaked up in your car and parked it under a tree near the camp and took out the bags and in five minutes it was all over, no fuss, no loud wonderful fuss about trunks.)

10   Peace and goodness and jollity. The only thing that was wrong now, really, was the sound of the place, an unfamiliar nervous sound of the outboard motors. This was the note that jarred, the one thing that would sometimes break the illusion and set the years moving. In those other summertimes all motors were inboard; and when they were at a little distance, the noise they made was a sedative, an ingredient of summer sleep. They were one-cylinder and two-cylinder engines, and some were make-and-break and some

were jump-spark, but they all made a sleepy sound across the lake. The one-lungers throbbed and fluttered, and the twin-cylinder ones purred and purred, and that was a quiet sound too. But now the campers all had outboards. In the daytime, in the hot mornings, these motors made a petulant, irritable sound; at night, in the still evening when the afterglow lit the water, they whined about one's ears like mosquitoes. My boy loved our rented outboard, and his great desire was to achieve singlehanded mastery over it, and authority, and he soon learned the trick of choking it a little (but not too much), and the adjustment of the needle valve. Watching him I would remember the things you could do with the old one-cylinder engine with the heavy flywheel, how you could have it eating out of your hand if you got really close to it spiritually. Motor boats in those days didn't have clutches, and you would make a landing by shutting off the motor at the proper time and coasting in with a dead rudder. But there was a way of reversing them, if you learned the trick, by cutting the switch and putting it on again exactly on the final dying revolution of the flywheel, so that it would kick back against compression and begin reversing. Approaching a dock in a strong following breeze, it was difficult to slow up sufficiently by the ordinary coasting method, and if a boy felt he had complete mastery over his motor, he was tempted to keep it running beyond its time and then reverse it a few feet from the dock. It took a cool nerve, because if you threw the switch a twentieth of a second too soon you would catch the flywheel when it still had speed enough to go up past center, and the boat would leap ahead, charging bull-fashion at the dock.

11   We had a good week at the camp. The bass were biting well and the sun shone endlessly, day after day. We would be tired at night and lie down in the accumulated heat of the little bedrooms after the long hot day and the breeze would stir almost imperceptibly outside and the smell of the swamp drift in through the rusty screens. Sleep would come easily and in the morning the red squirrel would be on the roof, tapping out his gay routine. I kept remembering everything, lying in bed in the mornings—the small steamboat that had a long rounded stern like the lip of a Ubangi, and how quietly she ran on the moonlight sails, when the older boys played their mandolins and the girls sang and we ate doughnuts dipped in sugar, and how sweet the music was on the water in the shining night, and what it had felt like to think about girls then. After breakfast we would go up to the store and the things were in the same place—the minnows in a bottle, the plugs and spinners disarranged and pawed over by the youngsters from the boys' camp, the fig newtons and the Beeman's gum. Outside, the road was tarred and cars stood in front of the store. Inside, all was just as it had always been, except there was more Coca-Cola and not so much Moxie and root beer and birch beer and sarsaparilla. We would walk out with a bottle of pop apiece and sometimes the pop would backfire up our noses and hurt. We explored the streams, quietly, where the turtles slid off the sunny logs and dug their way into the soft bottom; and we lay on the town wharf and fed worms to the tame bass. Everywhere we went I had trouble making out which was I, the one walking at my side, the one walking in my pants.

12   One afternoon while we were there at that lake a thunderstorm came up. It was like the revival of an old melodrama that I had seen long ago with childish awe. The second-act climax of the drama of the electrical disturbance over a lake in America had not changed in any important respect. This was the big scene, still the big scene. The whole thing was so familiar, the first feeling of oppression and heat and a general air

around camp of not wanting to go very far away. In midafternoon (it was all the same) a curious darkening of the sky, and a lull in everything that had made life tick; and then the way the boats suddenly swung the other way at their moorings with the coming of a breeze out of the new quarter, and the premonitory rumble. Then the kettle drum, then the snare, then the bass drum and cymbals, then crackling light against the dark, and the gods grinning and licking their chops in the hills. Afterward the calm, the rain steadily rustling in the calm lake, the return of light and hope and spirits, and the campers running out in the joy and relief to go swimming in the rain, their bright cries perpetuating the deathless joke about how they were getting simply drenched, and the children screaming with delight at the new sensation of bathing in the rain, and the joke about getting drenched linking the generations in a strong indestructible chain. And the comedian who waded in carrying an umbrella.

13   When the others went swimming my son said he was going in too. He pulled his dripping trunks from the line where they had hung all through the shower, and wrung them out. Languidly, and with no thought of going in, I watched him, his hard little body, skinny and bare, saw him wince slightly as he pulled up around his vitals the small, soggy, icy garment. As he buckled the swollen belt suddenly my groin felt the chill of death.

Chapter 25

Exposition: Definition

■ The Heroes Among Us

Stephen M. Wolf

Stephen M. Wolf has been the chair and chief executive officer of United Airlines, Inc., and the chair of US Airways Group, Inc., and its airline, US Airways, Inc. In addition to his current work as a board member for the Altria Corporation, Wolf serves as a trustee for both Georgetown University and the World Wildlife Fund. This essay was first published in *Hemispheres* magazine in 1993.

1   Especially in today's world, our children need heroes. And we need to help them discover the kind of people who show us through their lives that the world is better than the headlines make us believe. Somewhere along the way, we seem to have confused celebrities with heroes. So we can hardly blame our children when the people they most admire do not live a life that is, as Webster defines it, "noted for courageous acts or nobility of purpose."

2   Historian Daniel Boorstin made the distinction between the hero and the celebrity clearly. "The hero was distinguished by his achievement; the celebrity by his image or trademark," he wrote. "The hero created himself; the celebrity is created by the media. The hero was a big man; the celebrity is a big name." Too often, the media manufactures celebrities and packages them as heroes. We learn little of their contributions to society and more than we need to about their fashions or love affairs. That is not to say some celebrities are not heroes. In fact, more than a few athletes, actors, and artists

have broken barriers and dedicated themselves to important humanitarian causes. Unfortunately, those actions command less attention than the latest scandal.

3   Television distorts reality and, in the process, obscures fundamental values. Children are often shown that wealth and beauty are the keys to happiness. They do not see people working hard for that wealth because that does not make for an exciting broadcast. And they rarely see programs featuring those whose beauty goes much deeper than the surface. Such programming offers children a world of shallow values, instant gratification, and quick fixes, with heroes who are always attractive and never work for what they have or want.

4   Instead of allowing children simply to focus on television or the movies in their search for heroes, we should encourage them to look closer to home. Extraordinary acts of courage and selflessness abound in communities everywhere. These stories deserve more than a few sentences buried in the back of Saturday's newspaper. Local heroes make up the fiber of a community's life; they provide its vitality, its strength. These people struggle to make their neighborhoods better places to live, to teach children after others have given up, to ensure the safety of those in violence-plagued communities.

5   I read an interesting article in *The Seattle Times,* about true heroes, individuals whom columnist Dale Turner described as people who "do not moan about how bad the world is, but they work for the good it was intended to be. They lift our society and do not lean upon it. Instead of cursing their genes, their parents, their circumstances or their luck, they buck the negatives and assume responsibility for their own lives and try to be helpful in the lives of others." Whether it is a teacher, a firefighter, a social worker, or an entrepreneur who fits that description, their courage and "nobility of purpose" is much more real—and important for children to see—than any celluloid cowboy or special effect could ever be.

6   We have the power and the means to expose more heroes and to address their human failures candidly, without dissecting every last flaw. No one is perfect, no matter how much we might wish them to be. Perhaps this is the most important lesson taught by the men and women who are true heroes. They show us how to be people of courage despite the odds, and to be people of grace, kindness, and nobility despite our humanity.

▪ Celebrating Nerdiness

Tom Rogers

Tom Rogers is a high school science teacher who has proudly raised a family of two "nerd" sons and a "nerd sympathizer" daughter in Greer, South Carolina. His essay, offering his own definition of the negative stereotype, was first published in the "My Turn" column of *Newsweek* magazine in December 2000.

1   I'm a nerd. While the Internet boom has lent some respectability to the term, narrow-minded and thoughtless stereotypes still linger. Nerds are supposedly friendless, book-smart sissies who suck up to authority figures. Some of our image problems stem from our obsession with mastering every inane detail of our interests. But to call us suck-ups is nonsense. We often horrify those in authority with our inability to understand, let alone follow, societal norms.

2   Like most nerds, I didn't know I was one until I started school. There I quickly found out that my enthusiasm for answering the teacher's questions made others feel I was deliberately trying to make them look bad. My classmates were not shy about expressing their feelings on the playground. Fortunately, I was tall and stood my ground, a bluff that helped repel bullies. But mostly I survived by learning to keep quiet in the classroom.

3   I became a high-school teacher because I realized there were lots of young nerds growing up who needed to know that being a nerd was not just OK but something wonderful. Unfortunately, they weren't likely to hear this even from teachers, although virtually every modern blessing from democracy to electric motors originated with a nerd. Some, like Thomas Paine, were idealistic; others, like Tesla, eccentric. Newton was arrogant and Einstein absent-minded. All of them are now considered geniuses. But make no mistake: 17-year-old versions of these men, placed in modern American high schools, would instantly be labeled as nerds.

4   I raised two nerd sons and a daughter, who describes herself as a nerd sympathizer, partly because I didn't have the cleverness to raise "cool" kids, but also because, selfishly, I wanted nerds to talk to. Every year I invite my Advanced Placement physics students to my house for study sessions before the AP test. Last year one student nerd's mother told me that her son had returned home and talked for hours about how awesome it was to have found a nerd family. Unfortunately, the world's response to our family has not always been so enthusiastic.

5   When my sons were still in school, they were often picked on by classmates. My older boy, a pale and unathletic kid, was an easy target. When his middle-school science teacher asked if anyone could name some elements, my son recited the periodic table from memory. Thanks to events like that, he endured nerd hell at the hands of bullies when waiting for the school bus every afternoon. We tried karate classes and pep talks to bolster his defenses, but he was never able to win his tormentors' respect. He was just too small.

6   My boys were often misunderstood by their teachers, too. My younger son's middle-school social-studies teacher rigidly insisted that he take notes. When he refused, she publicly told him he would never graduate from high school. My son was perfectly capable of taking notes, but in typical nerd fashion, he couldn't bring himself to comply because it was illogical. He could easily remember what the teacher had said. Writing it down cut into his thinking time.

7   Clearly, my son would have to give his teacher what she wanted, but it had to be done with style. We discussed options. These included taking notes in one of the foreign languages he studied as a hobby. I discouraged it because he had learned some colorful foreign terms and was capable of describing his teacher in ways that could make a sailor blush. Finally, we agreed he would write his notes backward.

8   For six months he transcribed his teacher's lectures backward. When I held my son's notes up to a mirror, they were perfectly readable. I shouldn't have been surprised. As a small child he'd entertained us by turning books upside down and reading them backward. I waited for a complaint from his teacher, but she never noticed.

9   Despite childhood trials, both of my sons remain devoted nerds. My older son became conversational in four foreign languages and has hitchhiked around Europe three times. And these days no one would mistake him for a sissy. On one occasion a

group of Russian policemen threw him a party after he accepted their invitation to take a mid-December dip in a spring filled with near-freezing water.

10   My younger son proved his teacher wrong and graduated from high school. He scored 1600 on the SAT and was asked to give a speech before 500 educators and politicians who had gathered to honor education. It was his one moment of visibility. As I waited for him to talk, my stomach flip-flopped. I had no idea what he was going to say. He rose from his seat and delivered 10 minutes of stand-up comedy on being a nerd. The audience laughed until they cried. I cried. Afterward a young nerd paid him his highest compliment: "Thank you for what you've done for our people." No, our kind doesn't fit the stereotypes, but yes, there is something wonderful about being a nerd.

■ What Is Poverty?

Jo Goodwin Parker

When George Henderson, a professor at the University of Oklahoma, was writing his 1971 book, *America's Other Children: Public Schools Outside Suburbia*, he received the following essay in the mail. It was signed "Jo Goodwin Parker" and had been mailed from West Virginia. No further information was ever discovered about the essay or its source. Whether the author of this essay was in reality a woman describing her own painful experiences or a sympathetic writer who had adopted her persona, Jo Goodwin Parker remains a mystery.

1   You ask me what is poverty? Listen to me. Here I am, dirty, smelly, and with no "proper" underwear on and with the stench of my rotting teeth near you. I will tell you. Listen to me. Listen without pity. I cannot use your pity. Listen with understanding. Put yourself in my dirty, worn out, ill-fitting shoes, and hear me.

2   Poverty is getting up every morning from a dirt- and illness-stained mattress. The sheets have long since been used for diapers. Poverty is living with a smell that never leaves. This is the smell of urine, sour milk, and spoiling food sometimes joined with the strong smell of long-cooked onions. Onions are cheap. If you have smelled this smell, you did not know how it came. It is the smell of the outdoor privy. It is the smell of young children who cannot walk the long dark way in the night. It is the smell of the mattresses where years of "accidents" have happened. It is the smell of the milk which has gone sour because the refrigerator long has not worked, and it costs money to get it fixed. It is the smell of rotting garbage. I could bury it, but where is the shovel? Shovels cost money.

3   Poverty is being tired. I have always been tired. They told me at the hospital when the last baby came that I had chronic anemia caused from poor diet, a bad case of worms, and that I needed a corrective operation. I listened politely—the poor are always polite. The poor always listen. They don't say that there is no money for iron pills, or better food, or worm medicine. The idea of an operation is frightening and costs so much that, if I had dared, I would have laughed. Who takes care of my children? Recovery from an operation takes a long time. I have three children. When I left them with "Granny" the last time I had a job, I came home to find the baby covered with fly specks, and a diaper that had not been changed since I left. When the dried diaper came off, bits of my baby's flesh came with it. My other child was playing with a sharp

bit of broken glass, and my oldest was playing alone at the edge of a lake. I made twenty-two dollars a week, and a good nursery school costs twenty dollars a week for three children. I quit my job.

4   Poverty is dirt. You say in your clean clothes coming from your clean house, "Anybody can be clean." Let me explain about housekeeping with no money. For breakfast I give my children grits with no oleo or cornbread without eggs and oleo. This does not use up many dishes. What dishes there are, I wash in cold water and with no soap. Even the cheapest soap has to be saved for the baby's diapers. Look at my hands, so cracked and red. Once I saved for two months to buy a jar of Vaseline for my hands and the baby's diaper rash. When I had saved enough, I went to buy it and the price had gone up two cents. The baby and I suffered on. I have to decide every day if I can bear to put my cracked, sore hands into the cold water and strong soap. But you ask, why not hot water? Fuel costs money. Hot water is a luxury. I do not have luxuries. I know you will be surprised when I tell you how young I am. I look so much older. My back has been bent over the wash tubs for so long, I cannot remember when I ever did anything else. Every night I wash every stitch my school age child has on and just hope her clothes will be dry by morning.

5   Poverty is staying up all night on cold nights to watch the fire, knowing one spark on the newspaper covering the walls means your sleeping children die in flames. In summer poverty is watching gnats and flies devour your baby's tears when he cries. The screens are torn and you pay so little rent you know they will never be fixed. Poverty means insects in your food, in your nose, in your eyes, and crawling over you when you sleep. Poverty is hoping it never rains because diapers won't dry when it rains and soon you are using newspapers. Poverty is seeing your children forever with runny noses. Paper handkerchiefs cost money and all your rags you need for other things. Even more costly are antihistamines. Poverty is cooking without food and cleaning without soap.

6   Poverty is asking for help. Have you ever had to ask for help, knowing your children will suffer unless you get it? Think about asking for a loan from a relative, if this is the only way you can imagine asking for help. I will tell you how it feels. You find out where the office is that you are supposed to visit. You circle that block four or five times. Thinking of your children, you go in. Everyone is very busy. Finally, someone comes out and you tell her that you need help. That never is the person you need to see. You go see another person, and after spilling the whole shame of your poverty all over the desk between you, you find that this isn't the right office after all—you must repeat the whole process, and it never is any easier at the next place.

7   You have asked for help, and after all it has a cost. You are again told to wait. You are told why, but you don't really hear because of the red cloud of shame and the rising black cloud of despair.

8   Poverty is remembering. It is remembering quitting school in junior high because "nice" children had been so cruel about my clothes and my smell. The attendance officer came. My mother told him I was pregnant. I wasn't but she thought that I could get a job and help out. I had jobs off and on, but never long enough to learn anything. Mostly I remember being married. I was so young then. I am still young. For a time, we had all the things you have. There was a little house in another town, with hot water and everything. Then my husband lost his job. There was unemployment insurance for a while and what few jobs I could get. Soon, all our nice things were repossessed and we

moved back here. I was pregnant then. This house didn't look so bad when we first moved in. Every week it gets worse. Nothing is ever fixed. We now had no money. There were a few odd jobs for my husband, but everything went for food then, as it does now. I don't know how we lived through three years and three babies, but we did. I'll tell you something, after the last baby I destroyed my marriage. It had been a good one, but could you keep on bringing children in this dirt? Did you ever think how much it costs for any kind of birth control? I knew my husband was leaving the day he left, but there were no good-byes between us. I hope he has been able to climb out of this mess somewhere. He never could hope with us to drag him down.

9   That's when I asked for help. When I got it, you know how much it was? It was, and is, seventy-eight dollars a month for the four of us; that is all I ever can get. Now you know why there is no soap, no needles and thread, no hot water, no aspirin, no worm medicine, no hand cream, no shampoo. None of these things forever and ever and ever. So that you can see clearly, I pay twenty dollars a month rent, and most of the rest goes for food. For grits and cornmeal, and rice and milk and beans. I try my best to use only the minimum electricity. If I use more, there is that much less for food.

10   Poverty is looking into a black future. Your children won't play with my boys. They will turn to other boys who steal to get what they want. I can already see them behind the bars of their prison instead of behind the bars of my poverty. Or they will turn to the freedom of alcohol or drugs, and find themselves enslaved. And my daughter? At best, there is for her a life like mine.

11   But you say to me, there are schools. Yes, there are schools. My children have no extra books, no magazines, no extra pencils, or crayons, or paper and the most important of all, they do not have health. They have worms, they have infections, they have pinkeye all summer. They do not sleep well on the floor, or with me in my one bed. They do not suffer from hunger, my seventy-eight dollars keeps us alive, but they do suffer from malnutrition. Oh yes, I do remember what I was taught about health in school. It doesn't do much good. In some places there is a surplus commodities program. Not here. The county said it cost too much. There is a school lunch program. But I have two children who will already be damaged by the time they get to school.

12   But, you say to me, there are health clinics. Yes, there are health clinics and they are in the towns. I live out here eight miles from town. I can walk that far (even if it is sixteen miles both ways), but can my little children? My neighbor will take me when he goes; but he expects to get paid, *one way or another.* I bet you know my neighbor. He is that large man who spends his time at the gas station, the barbershop, and the corner store complaining about the government spending money on the immoral mothers of illegitimate children.

13   Poverty is an acid that drips on pride until all pride is worn away. Poverty is a chisel that chips on honor until honor is worn away. Some of you say that you would do *something* in my situation, and maybe you would, for the first week or the first month, but for year after year after year?

14   Even the poor can dream. A dream of a time when there is money. Money for the right kinds of food, for worm medicine, for iron pills, for toothbrushes, for hand cream, for a hammer and nails and a bit of screening, for a shovel, for a bit of paint, for some sheeting, for needles and thread. Money to pay *in money* for a trip to town. And, oh, money for hot water and money for soap. A dream of when asking for help does not eat

away the last bit of pride. When the office you visit is as nice as the offices of other governmental agencies, when there are enough workers to help you quickly, when workers do not quit in defeat and despair. When you have to tell your story to only one person, and that person can send you for other help and you don't have to prove your poverty over and over and over again.

15   I have come out of my despair to tell you this. Remember I did not come from another place or another time. Others like me are all around you. Look at us with an angry heart, anger that will help you help me. Anger that will let you tell of me. The poor are always silent. Can you be silent too?

Chapter 26

Exposition: Division/Classification

■ Hoppers

Garrison Keillor

Garrison Keillor is a writer, storyteller, and humorist. He is best known as the host of National Public Radio's long-running *A Prairie Home Companion*, which presents the mythical town of Lake Wobegon, where "all the women are strong, all the men are good-looking, and all the children are above average." Keillor is the author of many essays, stories, and novels, including *Lake Wobegon Days* (1985), *WLT: A Radio Romance* (1991), *Wobegon Boy* (1997), and *Love Me* (2003). The following essay is from *We Are Still Married: Stories and Letters* (1989).

1   A hydrant was open on Seventh Avenue above 23rd Street last Friday morning, and I stopped on my way east and watched people hop over the water. It was a brilliant spring day. The water was a nice clear creek about three feet wide and ran along the gutter around the northwest corner of the intersection. A gaggle of pedestrians crossing 23rd went *hop hop hop hop hop* over the creek as a few soloists jaywalking Seventh performed at right angles to them, and I got engrossed in the dance. Three feet isn't a long leap for most people, and the ease of it permits a wide range of expression. Some hoppers went a good deal higher than necessary.

2   Long, lanky men don't hop, as a rule. The ones I saw hardly paused at the water's edge, just lengthened one stride and trucked on across—a rather flatfooted approach that showed no recognition of the space or occasion. Tall men typically suffer from an

excess of cool, but I kept hoping for one of them to get off the ground. Most of the tall men wore topcoats and carried briefcases, so perhaps their balance was thrown off. One tall man in a brown coat didn't notice the water and stepped off the curb into the fast-flowing Hydrant Creek and made a painful hop, like a wounded heron: a brown heron with a limp wing attached to a briefcase bulging full of dead fish. He crossed 23rd looking as though his day had been pretty much shot to pieces.

3   Short, fat men were superb: I could have watched them all morning. A typical fat man crossing the street would quicken his step when he saw the creek and, on his approach, do a little shuffle, arms out to the sides, and suddenly and with great concentration *spring*—a nimble step all the more graceful for the springer's bulk. Three fairly fat men jiggled and shambled across 23rd together, and then one poked another and they saw the water. They stepped forward, studying the angle, and just before the point man jumped for the curb his pals said something, undoubtedly discouraging, and he threw back his head and laughed over his shoulder and threw himself lightly, boyishly, across the water, followed—*boing boing*—by the others.

4   The women who hopped the water tended to stop and study the creek and find its narrows and measure the distance and then lurch across. They seemed dismayed that the creek was there at all, and one, in a beige suit, put her hands on her hips and glared upstream, as if to say, "Whose water *is* this? This is utterly unacceptable. I am *not* about to jump over this." But then she made a good jump after all. She put her left toe on the edge of the curb, leaned forward with right arm outstretched—for a second, she looked as if she might take off and zoom up toward the Flatiron Building—and pushed off, landing easily on her right toe, her right arm raised. The longest leap was made by a young woman in a blue raincoat carrying a plastic Macy's bag and crossing west on Seventh. She gathered herself up in three long, accelerating strides and sailed, her coat billowing out behind her, over the water and five feet beyond, almost creaming a guy coming out of Radio Shack. He shrank back as she loped past, her long black hair and snow-white hands and face right *there*, then gone, vanished in the crowd.

5   And then it was my turn. I waited for the green light, crossed 23rd, stopped by the creek flowing around the bend of curb and heard faint voices of old schoolmates ahead in the woods, and jumped heavily across and marched after them.

■ Party Manners

Richard Grossman

Richard Grossman is a psychotherapist, medical educator, and author. He has written a number of books, many on health-related issues, including *Choosing & Changing: A Guide to Self-Reliance* (1978) and *The Other Medicines* (1986). His most recent work is *A Year with Emerson* (2003), a daybook that introduces readers to the writings of philosopher-poet Ralph Waldo Emerson. This 1983 article first appeared in *Health* magazine as part of Grossman's column called "Richard's Almanac."

1   The Romans had their Colosseum, the Elizabethans their village promenades and their Globe Theater. For centuries the French and Germans had their spectacular court balls. Queens and Presidents have their state dinners, complete with chamber music. And we ordinary moderns? We have *parties*.

2   From college "mixers" to suburban cocktail "standarounds," from children's ice-cream splattered birthday celebrations to retirement dinners, from political fund-raisers to bridal showers, the party has become as ubiquitous an institution as the Internal Revenue Service. And familiar though it is, the party has a psychologically transforming effect on many of us. Somehow our attendance at a gathering called a "party" causes us to behave in ways we never do elsewhere, as though we were players in a drama meant to reveal some of the hidden parts of our personalities. The party setting seems to provide a license to unveil attitudes that we would never display at the office or the family dinner table. And though party behavior may not be a reliable guide to all our psychological tics, it is nevertheless a place to see how we "go public" with some of our unresolved problems. Consider this cast of characters, for example:

The Cartoonist

3   Here's the person who has no other arena in his life in which to be a vocal social critic, who sees every party as an opportunity to be the local Andy Rooney.* No dancing or merrymaking for this one, but rather a steady stream of mini-lectures on the foibles and deficiencies of all the other guests. The Cartoonist is someone who does not want to be part of the crowd, but needs to keep his distance and act the reporting observer, drawing verbal caricatures of "them" as though he were sending communiqués back to Mars on the tribal rituals of the "Earthlings." What's really going on, of course, is that the fear of spontaneity and the relaxation of conventions is just too threatening, so the only safe stance is to play the part of the uninvolved expert.

The Spotter

4   This character is the familiar shopper for greener pastures. She is talking to you, but is looking over your shoulder the whole time, ever alert to someone just a little more interesting or a little more important who may be on the other side of the room. This person is usually the inside-dopester, the one who craves the latest information, who drops the trendiest names, who goes to the hottest events. The Spotter has the attention span of an alcoholic mayfly and cannot wait to move on, fearful that she is missing out on something better. The usual result, of course, is that she has a terrible time at parties and can't understand why all those other folks are laughing.

The Performer

5   He's often known as "the life of the party" and is the one for whom every party is the high school play in which he didn't get a part. Parties for this type are only an opportunity to grab the spotlight that he wants desperately but is being denied elsewhere. There are variations, of course: The Practical Joker, The Bathroom Comedian, The Barroom Baritone, The Poor Man's Rich Little†—but all are revealing only one sad fact: They are yearning for notoriety and attention.

---

* Andy Rooney, a television commentator on *60 Minutes* for over twenty-five years, is known for his cranky observations on the annoyances of everyday life.

† Rich Little is a comedian known for his impersonations of famous celebrities.

The Wallflower

6   Here you have the reverse image of The Performer: The person who gains attention by a silent, martyred withdrawal from the center of the party. Sooner or later, someone will spot her standing in a corner with a rueful smile on her face, just waiting to be asked if something is wrong. If you should inquire, you'll hear that she "just isn't good in crowds," or "hates all that noise," or "never could learn to disco." Do not be deceived into thinking that you've discovered an authentically shy or lonely person. This routine is simply a device to get attention with a passive strategy. (The *really* shy one didn't come to the party.)

The Swashbuckler

7   Also known as "The Last of the Big Benders," this is a person who may be in real trouble. Something has gone drastically wrong somewhere in his life, and he is frightened or even desperate about the outcome. If he is not working on the problem in another corner of life or getting the help he really needs, then the only place for that terrified energy to go is into uncharacteristically heavy drinking and raucous, high-pitched haranguing. There are usually very real and troubling issues underlying this kind of behavior, and the party can, unfortunately, provide a convenient setting for acting out.

The Scarlet Pimpernel*

8   She's the person who sees every party invitation as an opportunity to project her romantic fantasy. Feeling frustrated by a humdrum, uneventful existence, such a person mentally writes out a script for Meryl Streep or Julie Christie† and goes off to the party prepared to try out the new role, altering the voice to sound sultry or provocative, speaking in cryptic or poetic language, gliding around the room like a visitor from the Court of St. James. Sometimes this is just playfulness or harmless flirtatiousness, but usually the pseudo-romantic is simply saying through her behavior that the rest of her life is dull and gray, and needs spicing up.

9   Now, a certain amount of nervousness and unease about going to a party is clearly normal, and it would be simple-minded to claim that even the types described above are necessarily displaying secret pathology. But if parties regularly call up odd or extraordinary behavior in you, or become a theater for exposing subterranean needs, it might be a good idea to look at the usual, non-partying areas of your life and see what's troubling you. Some parties are boring, to be sure, and a dose of silly, unplanned frolicking may liven them up. But we should remember that parties are usually designed as a means to gather in a friendly, open, genuine way; as a chance to enjoy the warmth and closeness of other human beings. If those are not reasons enough for going, if we need parties to ventilate other feelings, perhaps we should consider group therapy instead.

---

* This refers to a highly romantic 1905 novel by Baroness Emmuska Orczy, in which a British nobleman leads a double life as "the Scarlet Pimpernel," a sword-fighting rescuer of innocent people condemned to the guillotine during the French Revolution's Reign of Terror. Often credited as the first popular novel to establish the "dual identity" hero, the story paved the way for Superman, Batman, Zorro, and other modern superheroes in disguise.

† Meryl Streep is one of America's most highly regarded actresses, having won two Academy Awards; Julie Christie is a British actress, also an Academy Award winner, but possibly best known in this country for her role as Lara in the classic 1965 film *Dr. Zhivago*.

■ College Pressures

William Zinsser

As a faculty member at Yale, William Zinsser designed and taught the first course in nonfiction writing offered at that university. He is the author of sixteen books, including *On Writing Well: An Informal Guide to Writing Nonfiction* (1976) and *Writing to Learn: How to Write and Think Clearly About Any Subject at All* (1988). He is also the editor of a series of books that offer advice to writers of biography, children's literature, religion, memoir, and travel. His most recent work is *So Easy to Remember* (2001), a study of great American songwriters. This essay was originally published in *Country Journal* in 1979.

1   *Dear Carlos: I desperately need a dean's excuse for my chem midterm which will begin in about 1 hour. All I can say is that I totally blew it this week. I've fallen incredibly, inconceivably behind.*

2   *Carlos: Help! I'm anxious to hear from you. I'll be in my room and won't leave it until I hear from you. Tomorrow is the last day for . . .*

3   *Carlos: I left town because I started bugging out again. I stayed up all night to finish a take home make-up exam & am typing it to hand in on the 10th. It was due on the 5th. P.S. I'm going to the dentist. Pain is pretty bad.*

4   *Carlos: Probably by Friday I'll be able to get back to my studies. Right now I'm going to take a long walk. This whole thing has taken a lot out of me.*

5   *Carlos: I'm really up the proverbial creek. The problem is I really bombed the history final. Since I need that course for my major . . .*

6   *Carlos: Here follows a tale of woe. I went home this weekend, had to help my Mom, & caught a fever so didn't have much time to study. My professor . . .*

7   *Carlos: Aargh! Nothing original but everything's piling up at once. To be brief, my job interview . . .*

8   *Hey Carlos, good news! I've got mononucleosis.*

9   Who are these wretched supplicants, scribbling notes so laden with anxiety, seeking such miracles of postponement and balm? They are men and women who belong to Branford College, one of the twelve residential colleges at Yale University, and the messages are just a few of the hundreds that they left for their dean, Carlos Hortas—often slipped under his door at 4 A.M.—last year.

10   But students like the ones who wrote those notes can also be found on campuses from coast to coast—especially in New England and at many other private colleges across the country that have high academic standards and highly motivated students. Nobody could doubt that the notes are real. In their urgency and their gallows humor they are authentic voices of a generation that is panicky to succeed.

11   My own connection with the message writers is that I am master of Branford College. I live in its Gothic quadrangle and know the students well. (We have 485 of them.) I am privy to their hopes and fears—and also to their stereo music and their piercing cries in the dead of night ("Does anybody *ca-a-are?*"). If they went to Carlos to ask how to get through tomorrow, they come to me to ask how to get through the rest of their lives.

12   Mainly I try to remind them that the road ahead is a long one and that it will have more unexpected turns than they think. There will be plenty of time to change jobs, change careers, change whole attitudes and approaches. They don't want to hear such liberating news. They want a map—right now—that they can follow unswervingly to career security, financial security, Social Security and, presumably, a prepaid grave.

13   What I wish for all students is some release from the clammy grip of the future. I wish them a chance to savor each segment of their education as an experience in itself and

not as a grim preparation for the next step. I wish them the right to experiment, to trip and fall, to learn that defeat is as instructive as victory and is not the end of the world.

14   My wish, of course, is naive. One of the few rights that America does not proclaim is the right to fail. Achievement is the national god, venerated in our media—the million-dollar athlete, the wealthy executive—and glorified in our praise of possessions. In the presence of such a potent state religion, the young are growing up old.

15   I see four kinds of pressure working on college students today: economic pressure, parental pressure, peer pressure, and self-induced pressure. It is easy to look around for villains—to blame the colleges for charging too much money, the professors for assigning too much work, the parents for pushing their children too far, the students for driving themselves too hard. But there are no villains; only victims.

16   "In the late 1960s," one dean told me, "the typical question that I got from students was 'Why is there so much suffering in the world?' or 'How can I make a contribution?' Today it's 'Do you think it would look better for getting into law school if I did a double major in history and political science, or just majored in one of them?'" Many other deans confirmed this pattern. One said "They're trying to find an edge—the intangible something that will look better on paper if two students are about equal."

17   Note the emphasis on looking better. The transcript has become a sacred document, the passport to security. How one appears on paper is more important than how one appears in person. *A* is for Admirable and *B* is for Borderline, even though, in Yale's official system of grading, *A* means "excellent" and *B* means "very good." Today, looking very good is no longer good enough, especially for students who hope to go on to law school or medical school. They know that entrance into the better schools will be an entrance into the better law firms and better medical practices where they will make a lot of money. They also know that the odds are harsh. Yale Law School, for instance, matriculates 170 students from an applicant pool of 3,700; Harvard enrolls 550 from a pool of 7,000.

18   It's all very well for those of us who write letters of recommendation for our students to stress the qualities of humanity that will make them good lawyers or doctors. And it's nice to think that admission officers are really reading our letters and looking for the extra dimension of commitment or concern. Still, it would be hard for a student not to visualize these officers shuffling so many transcripts studded with *A*s that they regard a *B* as positively shameful.

19   The pressure is almost as heavy on students who just want to graduate and get a job. Long gone are the days of the "gentleman's C," when students journeyed through college with a certain relaxation, sampling a wide variety of courses—music, art, philosophy, classics, anthropology, poetry, religion—that would send them out as liberally educated men and women. If I were an employer I would rather employ graduates who have this range and curiosity than those who narrowly pursued safe subjects and high grades. I know countless students whose inquiring minds exhilarate me. I like to hear the play of their ideas. I don't know if they are getting *A*s or *C*s, and I don't care. I also like them as people. The country needs them, and they will find satisfying jobs. I tell them to relax. They can't.

20   Nor can I blame them. They live in a brutal economy. Tuition, room, and board at most private colleges now comes to at least $7,000, not counting books and fees. This might seem to suggest that the colleges are getting rich. But they are equally battered

by inflation. Tuition covers only 60 percent of what it costs to educate a student, and ordinarily the remainder comes from what colleges receive in endowments, grants, and gifts. Now the remainder keeps being swallowed by the cruel costs—higher every year— of just opening the doors. Heating oil is up. Insurance is up. Postage is up. Health-premium costs are up. Everything is up. Deficits are up. We are witnessing in America the creation of a brotherhood of paupers—colleges, parents, and students, joined by the common bond of debt.

21   Today it is not unusual for a student, even if he works part time at college and full time during the summer, to accrue $5,000 in loans after four years—loans that he must start to repay within one year after graduation. Exhorted at commencement to go forth into the world, he is already behind as he goes forth. How could he not feel under pressure throughout college to prepare for this day of reckoning? I have used "he" incidentally, only for brevity. Women at Yale are under no less pressure to justify their expensive education to themselves, their parents, and society. In fact, they are probably under more pressure. For although they leave college superbly equipped to bring fresh leadership to traditionally male jobs, society hasn't yet caught up with this fact.

22   Along with economic pressure goes parental pressure. Inevitably, the two are deeply intertwined.

23   I see many students taking pre-medical courses with joyless tenacity. They go off to their labs as if they were going to the dentist. It saddens me because I know them in other corners of their life as cheerful people.

24   "Do you want to go to medical school?" I ask them.

25   "I guess so," they say, without conviction, or "Not really."

26   "Then why are you going?"

27   "Well, my parents want me to be a doctor. They're paying all this money and . . ."

28   Poor students, poor parents. They are caught in one of the oldest webs of love and duty and guilt. The parents mean well: they are trying to steer their sons and daughters toward a secure future. But the sons and daughters want to major in history or classics or philosophy—subjects with no "practical" value. Where's the payoff on the humanities? It's not easy to persuade such loving parents that the humanities do indeed pay off. The intellectual faculties developed by studying subjects like history and classics—an ability to synthesize and relate, to weigh cause and effect, to see events in perspective— are just the faculties that make creative leaders in business or almost any general field. Still, many fathers would rather put their money on courses that point toward a specific profession—courses that are pre-law, pre-medical, pre-business, or, as I sometimes heard it put, "pre-rich."

29   But the pressure on students is severe. They are truly torn. One part of them feels obligated to fulfill their parents' expectations; after all, their parents are older and presumably wiser. Another part tells them that the expectations that are right for their parents are not right for them.

30   I know a student who wants to be an artist. She is very obviously an artist and will be a good one—she has already had several modest local exhibits. Meanwhile she is growing as a well-rounded person and taking humanistic subjects that will enrich the inner resources out of which her art will grow. But her father is strongly opposed. He thinks that an artist is a "dumb" thing to be. The student vacillates and tries to please everybody. She keeps up with her art somewhat furtively and takes some of the "dumb"

courses her father wants her to take—at least they are dumb courses for her. She is a free spirit on a campus of tense students—no small achievement in itself—and she deserves to follow her muse.

31   Peer pressure and self-induced pressure are also intertwined, and they begin almost at the beginning of freshman year.

32   "I had a freshman student I'll call Linda," one dean told me, "who came in and said she was under terrible pressure because her roommate, Barbara, was much brighter and studied all the time. I couldn't tell her that Barbara had come in two hours earlier to say the same thing about Linda."

33   The story is almost funny—except that it's not. It's symptomatic of all the pressures put together. When every student thinks every other student is working harder and doing better, the only solution is to study harder still. I see students going off to the library every night after dinner and coming back when it closes at midnight. I wish they could sometimes forget about their peers and go to a movie. I hear the clacking of type-writers in the hours before dawn. I see the tension in their eyes when exams are approaching and papers are due: *"Will I get everything done?"*

34   Probably they won't. They will get sick. They will get "blocked." They will sleep. They will oversleep. They will bug out. *Hey Carlos, help!*

35   Part of the problem is that they do more than they are expected to do. A professor will assign five-page papers. Several students will start writing ten-page papers to impress him. Then more students will write ten-page papers, and a few will raise the ante to fif-teen. Pity the poor student who is still just doing the assignment.

36   "Once you have twenty or thirty percent of the student population deliberately overexerting," one dean points out, "it is bad for everybody. When a teacher gets more and more effort from his class, the student who is doing normal work can be perceived as not doing well. The tactic works, psychologically."

37   Why can't the professor just cut back and not accept longer papers? He can, and he probably will. But by then the term will be half over and the damage done. Grade fever is highly contagious and not easily reversed. Besides, the professor's main concern is with his course. He knows his students only in relation to the course and doesn't know that they are also overexerting in their other courses. Nor is it really his business. He didn't sign up for dealing with the student as a whole person and with all the emotional baggage the student brought along from home. That's what deans, masters, chaplains, and psychiatrists are for.

38   To some extent this is nothing new: a certain number of professors have always been self-contained islands of scholarship and shyness, more comfortable with books than with people. But the new pauperism has widened the gap still further, for professors who actually like to spend time with students don't have as much time to spend. They also are overexerting. If they are young, they are busy trying to publish in order not to perish, hanging by their fingernails onto a shrinking profession. If they are old and tenured, they are buried under the duties of administering departments—as depart-mental chairmen or members of committees—that have been thinned out by the budg-etary axe.

39   Ultimately it will be the students' own business to break the circles in which they are trapped. They are too young to be prisoners of their parents' dreams and their class-mates' fears. They must be jolted into believing in themselves as unique men and women who have the power to shape their own future.

40   "Violence is being done to the undergraduate experience," says Carlos Hortas. "College should be open-ended: at the end it should open many, many roads. Instead, students are choosing their goal in advance, and their choices narrow as they go along. It's almost as if they think that the country has been codified in the type of jobs that exist—that they've got to fit into certain slots. Therefore, fit into the best-paying slot.

41   "They ought to take chances. Not taking chances will lead to a life of colorless mediocrity. They'll be comfortable. But something in the spirit will be missing."

42   I have painted too drab a portrait of today's students, making them seem a solemn lot. That is only half of their story; if they were so dreary I wouldn't so thoroughly enjoy their company. The other half is that they are easy to like. They are quick to laugh and to offer friendship. They are not introverts. They are usually kind and are more considerate of one another than any student generation I have known.

43   Nor are they so obsessed with their studies that they avoid sports and extracurricular activities. On the contrary, they juggle their crowded hours to play on a variety of teams, perform with musical and dramatic groups, and write for campus publications. But this in turn is one more cause of anxiety. There are too many choices. Academically, they have 1,300 courses to select from; outside class they have to decide how much spare time they can spare and how to spend it.

44   This means that they engage in fewer extracurricular pursuits than their predecessors did. If they want to row on the crew and play in the symphony they will eliminate one; in the '60s they would have done both. They also tend to choose activities that are self-limiting. Drama, for instance, is flourishing in all twelve of Yale's residential colleges as it never has before. Students hurl themselves into these productions—as actors, directors, carpenters, and technicians—with a dedication to create the best possible play, knowing that the day will come when the run will end and they can get back to their studies.

45   They also can't afford to be the willing slave of organizations like the *Yale Daily News*. Last spring at the one-hundredth anniversary banquet of that paper—whose past chairmen include such once and future kings as Potter Stewart, Kingman Brewster, and William F. Buckley, Jr.—much was made of the fact that the editorial staff used to be small and totally committed and that "newsies" routinely worked fifty hours a week. In effect they belonged to a club; newsies is how they defined themselves at Yale. Today's student will write one or two articles a week, when he can, and he defines himself as a student. I've never heard the word newsie except at the banquet.

46   If I have described the modern undergraduate primarily as a driven creature who is largely ignoring the blithe spirit inside who keeps trying to come out and play, it's because that's where the crunch is, not only at Yale but throughout American education. It's why I think we should all be worried about the values that are nurturing a generation so fearful of risk and so goal-obsessed at such an early age.

47   I tell students that there is no one "right" way to get ahead—that each of them is a different person, starting from a different point and bound for a different destination. I tell them that change is a tonic and that all the slots are not codified nor the frontiers closed. One of my ways of telling them is to invite men and women who have achieved success outside the academic world to come and talk informally with my students during the year. They are heads of companies or ad agencies, editors of magazines, politicians, public officials, television magnates, labor leaders, business executives, Broadway

producers, artists, writers, economists, photographers, scientists, historians—a mixed bag of achievers.

48   I ask them to say a few words about how they got started. The students assume that they started in their present profession and knew all along that it was what they wanted to do. Luckily for me, most of them got into their field by a circuitous route, to their surprise, after many detours. The students are startled. They can hardly conceive of a career that was not pre-planned. They can hardly imagine allowing the hand of God or chance to nudge them down some unforeseen trail.

C h a p t e r   27

Exposition: Causal Analysis

■ The Teacher Who Changed My Life

Nicholas Gage

Former investigative reporter for *The Wall Street Journal* and author of seven books, Nicholas Gage is best known for *Eleni* (1983), the story of his mother's life and execution in 1948 during the Greek civil war. The story of this murder and Gage's subsequent search for her killers was made into a well-received movie in 1985. The story of Gage's family, *A Place for Us: Eleni's Children in America* (1989), contains a version of the following essay, which also appeared in *Parade* magazine. Gage's recent books include *Greece: Land of Light* (1998) and *Greek Fire* (2000).

1   The person who set the course of my life in the new land I entered as a young war refugee—who, in fact, nearly dragged me onto the path that would bring all the blessings I've received in America—was a salty-tongued, no-nonsense schoolteacher named Marjorie Hurd. When I entered her classroom in 1953, I had been to six schools in five years, starting in the Greek village where I was born in 1939.

2   When I stepped off a ship in New York Harbor on a gray March day in 1949, I was an undersized nine-year-old in short pants who had lost his mother and was coming to live with the father he didn't know. My mother, Eleni Gatzoyiannis, had been imprisoned, tortured, and shot by Communist guerrillas for sending me and three of my four sisters to freedom. She died so that her children could go to their father in the United States.

3   The portly, bald, well-dressed man who met me and my sisters seemed a foreign, authoritarian figure. I secretly resented him for not getting the whole family out of

571

Greece early enough to save my mother. Ultimately, I would grow to love him and appreciate how he dealt with becoming a single parent at the age of fifty-six, but at first our relationship was prickly, full of hostility.

4   As Father drove us to our new home—a tenement in Worcester, Mass.—and pointed out the huge brick building that would be our first school in America, I clutched my Greek notebooks from the refugee camp, hoping that my few years of schooling would impress my teachers in this cold, crowded country. They didn't. When my father led me and my eleven-year-old sister to Greendale Elementary School, the grim-faced Yankee principal put the two of us in a class for the mentally retarded. There was no facility in those days for non-English-speaking children.

5   By the time I met Marjorie Hurd four years later, I had learned English, been placed in a normal, graded class and had even been chosen for the college preparatory track in the Worcester public school system. I was thirteen years old when our father moved us yet again, and I entered Chandler Junior High shortly after the beginning of seventh grade. I found myself surrounded by richer, smarter, and better-dressed classmates who looked askance at my strange clothes and heavy accent. Shortly after I arrived, we were told to select a hobby to pursue during "club hour" on Fridays. The idea of hobbies and clubs made no sense to my immigrant ears, but I decided to follow the prettiest girl in my class—the blue-eyed daughter of the local Lutheran minister. She led me through the door marked "Newspaper Club" and into the presence of Miss Hurd, the newspaper adviser and English teacher who would become my mentor and my muse.

6   A formidable, solidly built woman with salt-and-pepper hair, a steely eye, and a flat Boston accent, Miss Hurd had no patience with layabouts. "What are all you goof-offs doing here?" she bellowed at the would-be journalists. "This is the Newspaper Club! We're going to put out a *newspaper.* So if there's anybody in this room who doesn't like work, I suggest you go across to the Glee Club now, because you're going to work your tails off here!"

7   I was soon under Miss Hurd's spell. She did indeed teach us to put out a newspaper, skills I honed during my next twenty-five years as a journalist. Soon I asked the principal to transfer me to her English Class as well. There, she drilled us on grammar until I finally began to understand the logic and structure of the English language. She assigned stories for us to read and discuss; not tales of heroes, like the Greek myths I knew, but stories of underdogs—poor people, even immigrants, who seemed ordinary until a crisis drove them to do something extraordinary. She also introduced us to the literary wealth of Greece—giving me a new perspective on my war-ravaged, impoverished homeland. I began to be proud of my origins.

8   One day, after discussing how writers should write about what they know, she assigned us to compose an essay from our own experience. Fixing me with a stern look, she added, "Nick, I want you to write about what happened to your family in Greece." I had been trying to put those painful memories behind me and left the assignment until the last moment. Then, on a warm spring afternoon, I sat in my room with a yellow pad and pencil and stared out the window at the buds on the trees. I wrote that the coming of spring always reminded me of the last time I said goodbye to my mother on a green and gold day in 1948.

9   I kept writing, one line after another, telling how the Communist guerrillas occupied our village, took our home and food, how my mother started planning our escape when

she learned that children were to be sent to re-education camps behind the Iron Curtain, and how, at the last moment, she couldn't escape with us because the guerrillas sent her with a group of women to thresh wheat in a distant village. She promised she would try to get away on her own, she told me to be brave and hung a silver cross around my neck, and then she kissed me. I watched the line of women being led down into the ravine and up the other side, until they disappeared around the bend—my mother a tiny brown figure at the end who stopped for an instant to raise her hand in one last farewell.

10   I wrote about our nighttime escape down the mountain, across the minefields, and into the lines of the Nationalist soldiers, who sent us to a refugee camp. It was there that we learned of our mother's execution. I felt very lucky to have come to America, I concluded, but every year, the coming of spring made me feel sad because it reminded me of the last time I saw my mother.

11   I handed in the essay, hoping never to see it again, but Miss Hurd had it published in the school paper. This mortified me at first, until I saw that my classmates reacted with sympathy and tact to my family's story. Without telling me, Miss Hurd also submitted the essay to a contest sponsored by the Freedoms Foundation at Valley Forge, and it won a medal. The Worcester paper wrote about the award and quoted my essay at length. My father, by then a "five-and-dime-store chef," as the paper described him, was ecstatic with pride, and the Worcester Greek community celebrated the honor to one of its own.

12   For the first time, I began to understand the power of the written word. A secret ambition took root in me. One day, I vowed, I would go back to Greece, find out the details of my mother's death, and write about her life, so her grandchildren would know of her courage. Perhaps I would even track down the men who killed her and write of their crimes. Fulfilling that ambition would take me thirty years.

13   Meanwhile, I followed the literary path that Miss Hurd had so forcefully set me on. After junior high, I became the editor of my school paper at Classical High School and got a part-time job at the Worcester *Telegram and Gazette*. Although my father could only give me $50 and encouragement toward a college education, I managed to finance four years at Boston University with scholarships and part-time jobs in journalism. During my last year of college, an article I wrote about a friend who had died in the Philippines—the first person to lose his life working for the Peace Corps—led to my winning the Hearst Award for College Journalism. And the plaque was given to me in the White House by President John F. Kennedy.

14   For a refugee who had never seen a motorized vehicle or indoor plumbing until he was nine, this was an unimaginable honor. When the Worcester paper ran a picture of me standing next to President Kennedy, my father rushed out to buy a new suit in order to be properly dressed to receive the congratulations of the Worcester Greeks. He clipped out the photograph, had it laminated in plastic, and carried it in his breast pocket for the rest of his life to show everyone he met. I found the much-worn photo in his pocket on the day he died twenty years later.

15   In our isolated Greek village, my mother had bribed a cousin to teach her to read, for girls were not supposed to attend school beyond a certain age. She had always dreamed of her children receiving an education. She couldn't be there when I graduated from Boston University, but the person who came with my father and shared our

joy was my former teacher, Marjorie Hurd. We celebrated not only my bachelor's degree but also the scholarships that paid my way to Columbia's Graduate School of Journalism. There, I met the woman who would eventually become my wife. At our wedding and at the baptisms of our three children, Marjorie Hurd was always there, dancing alongside the Greeks.

16   By then, she was Mrs. Rabidou, for she had married a widower when she was in her early forties. That didn't distract her from her vocation of introducing young minds to English literature, however. She taught for a total of forty-one years and continually would make a "project" of some balky student in whom she spied a spark of potential. Often these were students from the most troubled homes, yet she would alternately bully and charm each one with her own special brand of tough love until the spark caught fire. She retired in 1981 at the age of sixty-two but still avidly follows the lives and careers of former students while overseeing her adult stepchildren and driving her husband on camping trips to New Hampshire.

17   Miss Hurd was one of the first to call me on December 10, 1987, when President Reagan, in his television address after the summit meeting with Gorbachev, told the nation that Elena Gatzoyiannis's dying cry, "My children!" had helped inspire him to seek an arms agreement "for all the children of the world."

18   "I can't imagine a better monument for your mother," Miss Hurd said with an uncharacteristic catch in her voice.

19   Although a bad hip makes it impossible for her to join in the Greek dancing, Marjorie Hurd Rabidou is still an honored and enthusiastic guest at all our family celebrations, including my fiftieth birthday picnic last summer, where the shish kebab was cooked on spits, clarinets and *bouzoukis* wailed, and costumed dancers led the guests in a serpentine line around our Colonial farmhouse, only twenty minutes from my first home in Worcester.

20   My sisters and I felt an aching void because my father was not there to lead the line, balancing a glass of wine on his head while he danced, the way he did at every celebration during his ninety-two years. But Miss Hurd was there, surveying the scene with quiet satisfaction. Although my parents are gone, her presence was a consolation, because I owe her so much.

21   This is truly the land of opportunity, and I would have enjoyed its bounty even if I hadn't walked into Miss Hurd's classroom in 1953. But she was the one who directed my grief and pain into writing, and if it weren't for her I wouldn't have become an investigative reporter and foreign correspondent, recorded the story of my mother's life and death in *Eleni* and now my father's story in *A Place for Us*, which is also a testament to the country that took us in. She was the catalyst that sent me into journalism and indirectly caused all the good things that came after. But Miss Hurd would probably deny this emphatically.

22   A few years ago, I answered the telephone and heard my former teacher's voice telling me, in that won't-take-no-for-an-answer tone of hers, that she had decided I was to write and deliver the eulogy at her funeral. I agreed (she didn't leave me any choice), but that's one assignment I never want to do. I hope, Miss Hurd, that you'll accept this remembrance instead.

■ They Have to Keep It: People Who Save Everything

Lynda W. Warren and Jonnae C. Ostrom

Lynda W. Warren holds a Ph.D. from the University of Minnesota and for many years was a professor of psychology at California State University, San Bernardino. She currently practices clinical psychology in California. Jonnae C. Ostrom is a social worker in Orange County, California, where she serves as Associate Director of Clinical Services for the Orange Resource Center and continues her research on human hoarding behavior. Warren and Ostrom originally published this article in *Psychology Today*, after which it was reprinted in the *San Francisco Chronicle* in 1988.

1   Most of us have more things than we need and use. At times they pile up in corners and closets or accumulate in the recesses of attics, basements or garages. But we sort through our clutter periodically and clean it up, saving only what we really need and giving away or throwing out the excess. This isn't the case, unfortunately, with people we call "pack rats"—those who collect, save or hoard insatiably, often with only the vague rationale that the items may someday be useful. And because they rarely winnow what they save, it grows and grows.

2   While some pack rats specialize in what they collect, others seem to save indiscriminately. And what they keep, such as junk mail, supermarket receipts, newspapers, business memos, empty cans, clothes or old Christmas and birthday cards, often seems to be worthless. Even when items have some value, such as lumber scraps, fabric remnants, auto parts, shoes and plastic meat trays, they tend to be kept in huge quantities that no one could use in a lifetime.

3   Although pack rats collect, they are different from collectors, who save in a systematic way. Collectors usually specialize in one of a few classes of objects, which they organize, display and even catalogue. But pack rats tend to stockpile their possessions haphazardly and seldom use them.

4   Our interest in pack rats was sparked by a combination of personal experience with some older relatives and recognition of similar saving patterns in some younger clients one of us saw in therapy sessions. Until then, we, like most people, assumed that pack rats were all older people who had lived through the Great Depression of the 1930s—eccentrics who were stockpiling stuff just in case another Depression came along. We were surprised to discover a younger generation of pack rats, born long after the 1930s.

5   None of these clients identified themselves during therapy as pack rats or indicated that their hoarding tendencies were causing problems in any way. Only after their partners told us how annoyed and angry they were about the pack rats' unwillingness to clean up the growing mess at home did they acknowledge their behavior. Even then, they defended it and had little interest in changing. The real problem, they implied, was the partner's intolerance rather than their own hoarding.

6   Like most people, we had viewed excessive saving as a rare and harmless eccentricity. But when we discussed our initial observations with others, we gradually came to realize that almost everyone we met either admitted to some strong pack-rat tendencies or seemed to know someone who had them. Perhaps the greatest surprise, however, was how eager people were to discuss their own pack-rat experiences. Although our observations are admittedly based on a small sample, we now believe that such behavior is

common and that, particularly when it is extreme, it may create problems for the pack rats or those close to them.

7   When we turned to the psychological literature, we found surprisingly little about human collecting or hoarding in general and almost nothing about pack-rat behavior. Psychoanalysts view hoarding as one characteristic of the "anal" character type, first described by Freud. Erich Fromm later identified the "hoarding orientation" as one of the four basic ways in which people may adjust unproductively to life.

8   While some pack rats do have typically anal-retentive* characteristics such as miserliness, orderliness and stubbornness, we suspect that they vary as much in personality characteristics as they do in education, socioeconomic status and occupation. But they do share certain ways of thinking and feeling about their possessions that shed some light on the possible causes and consequences of their behavior.

9   Why do some people continue to save when there is no more space for what they have and they own more of something than could ever be used? We have now asked that question of numerous students, friends and colleagues who have admitted their pack-rat inclinations. They readily answer the question with seemingly good reasons, such as possible future need ("I might need this sometime"), sentimental attachment ("Aunt Edith gave this to me"), potential value ("This might be worth something someday") and a lack of wear or damage ("This is too good to throw away"). Such reasons are difficult to challenge; they are grounded in some truth and logic and suggest that pack-rat saving reflects good sense, thrift and even foresight. Indeed, many pack rats proudly announce, "I've never thrown anything away!" or "You would not believe what I keep!"

10   But on further questioning, other, less logical reasons become apparent. Trying to get rid of things may upset pack rats emotionally and may even bring on physical distress. As one woman said, "I get a headache or sick to my stomach if I have to throw something away."

11   They find it hard to decide what to keep and what to throw away. Sometimes they fear they will get rid of something that they or someone else might value, now or later. Having made such a "mistake" in the past seems to increase such distress. "I've always regretted throwing away the letters Mother sent me in college. I will never make that mistake again," one client said. Saving the object eliminates the distress and is buttressed by the reassuring thought, "Better to save this than be sorry later."

12   Many pack rats resemble compulsive personalities in their tendency to avoid or postpone decisions, perhaps because of an inordinate fear of making a mistake. Indeed, in the latest edition of the psychiatric diagnostic bible (DSM-III-R), the kind of irrational hoarding seen in pack rats ("inability to discard worn-out or worthless objects even when they have no sentimental value") is described as a characteristic of people with obsessive-compulsive personality disorder.

13   Some pack rats seem to have a depressive side, too. Discarding things seems to reawaken old memories and feelings of loss or abandonment, akin to grief or the pain of rejection. "I feel incredibly sad—it's really very painful," one client said of the process. Another client, a mental-health counselor, said, "I don't understand why, but

---

* A psychoanalytic term describing a type of personality who shows traits such as meticulousness (being overly precise), greed, and stubbornness

when I have to throw something away, even something like dead flowers, I feel my old abandonment fears and I also feel lonely."

14   Some pack rats report that their parents discarded certain treasured possessions, apparently insensitive to their attachment to the objects. "My Dad went through my room one time and threw out my old shell collection that I had in a closet. It devastated me," said one woman we interviewed. Such early experiences continue to color their feelings as adults, particularly toward possessions they especially cherish.

15   It's not uncommon for pack rats to "personalize" their possessions or identify with them, seeing them as extensions of themselves. One pack rat defiantly said about her things, "This is me—this is my individuality and you are not going to throw it out!"

16   At times the possessions are viewed akin to beloved people. For example, one woman said, "I can't let my Christmas tree be destroyed! I love my Christmas ornaments—I adore them!" Another woman echoed her emotional involvement: "My jewelry is such a comfort to me. I just love my rings and chains." Discarding such personalized possessions could easily trigger fears, sadness or guilt because it would be psychologically equivalent to a part of oneself dying or abandoning a loved one.

17   In saving everything, the pack rat seems to have found the perfect way to avoid indecision and the discomfort of getting rid of things. It works—but only for a while. The stuff keeps mounting, and so do the problems it produces.

■ You Call This Progress?

Seth Shostak

Seth Shostak holds a degree in physics and a Ph.D. in astronomy. For much of his career, he has conducted radio astronomy research on galaxies, publishing forty professional papers as well as several hundred popular science articles on various topics in astronomy and technology. Currently the Public Programs Scientist at the SETI Institute, he is also the author of *Sharing the Universe* (1998) and *Cosmic Company* (2003). This 1999 essay appeared in the "My Turn" column of *Newsweek* magazine.

1   It's as ubiquitous as winter damp, a pernicious miasma that brings rot and ruin to society's delicate underpinnings. I speak of e-mail, the greatest threat to civilization since lead dinnerware addled the brains of the Roman aristocracy.

2   A technical byproduct of the Internet, e-mail lets 10 million Americans pound out correspondence faster than you can say QWERTY. One twitch of the finger is all it takes to dispatch missives to the next continent or the next cubicle at light speed. The result is a flood of what is loosely called communication, a tsunami of bytes that is threatening to drown white-collar workers everywhere. Masquerading as a better way to put everyone in touch, e-mail has become an incessant distraction, a nonstop obligation and a sure source of stress and anxiety. I expect that a public statement by the surgeon general is in the offing.

3   Mind you, e-mail started out cute and cuddly, an inoffensive spinoff from a government defense project. The technically inclined used it to send personal messages to colleagues without the need for a stamp or a wait. Only a small group of folks—mostly at universities—were plugged in to this select network. The amount of traffic was manageable. E-mail was something to be checked every week or so. But technology marches

on. Today access to the Internet is widespread, as common and accessible as a cheap motel. Everyone's wired, and everyone has something to say.

4   Unfortunately, this is not polite correspondence, the gentle art of letter writing in electronic form. E-mail is aggressive. It has a built-in, insistent arrogance. Because it arrives more or less instantaneously, the assumption is that you will deal with it quickly. "Quickly" might mean minutes, or possibly hours. Certainly not days. Failure to respond directly usually produces a second missive sporting the mildly critical plaint, "Didn't you get my last e-mail?" This imperative for the immediate makes me yearn for old-style written communication, in which a week might lapse between inquiry and response. Questions and discussion could be considered in depth. A reply could be considered (or mentally shelved, depending on circumstance). Today, however, all is knee-jerk reaction.

5   In addition, there is the dismaying fact that electronically generated mail, despite being easy to edit, is usually prose at its worst. Of every 10 e-mails I read, nine suffer from major spelling faults, convoluted grammar and a stunning lack of logical organization. ASCII graffiti. For years I assumed this was an inevitable byproduct of the low student test scores so regularly lamented in newspaper editorials. Johnny can't read, so it's not surprising that he can't write either. But now I believe that the reason for all this unimpressive prose is something else: e-mail has made correspondents of folks who would otherwise never compose a text. It encourages messaging because it is relatively anonymous. The shy, the introverted and the socially inept can all hunker down before a glowing computer and whisper to the world. This is not the telephone, with its brutally personal, audible contact. It's not the post, for which an actual sheet of paper, touched by the writer and displaying his imperfect calligraphic skills, will end up under the nose of the recipient. E-mails are surreptitiously thrown over an electronic transom in the dead of night, packaged in plain manila envelopes.

6   Still, it is not these esthetic debilities that make e-mail such a threat. Rather, it's the unstoppable proliferation. Like the brooms unleashed by the sorcerer's apprentice, e-mails are beginning to overwhelm those who use them. Electronic correspondence is not one to one. It is one to many, and that's bad news on the receiving end. The ease with which copies of any correspondence can be dispensed to the world ensures that I am "kept informed" of my co-workers' every move. Such bureaucratic banter was once held in check by the technical limitations of carbon paper. Now my colleagues just punch a plastic mouse to ensure my exposure to their thoughts, their plans and the endless missives that supposedly prove that they're doing their jobs.

7   Because of e-mail's many-tentacled reach, its practitioners hardly care whether I'm around or not. I'm just another address in a list. So the deluge of digital correspondence continues irrespective of whether I'm sitting in my cubicle doing the boss's business or lying on the Côte d'Azur squeezing sand through my toes. Either way the e-mail, like a horde of motivated Mongolians, just keeps a-comin'. Vacations have lost their allure, and I hesitate to leave town. Consider: if I disappear for two weeks of rest and recreation, I can be sure of confronting screenfuls of e-mail upon my return. It's enough to make a grown man groan. The alternative is to take a laptop computer along, in the desperate hope of keeping up with e-mail's steady drip, drip, drip. Needless to say, there's something unholy about answering e-mails from your holiday suite. A friend recently told me that he can't afford to die: the e-mail would pile up and nobody could handle it.

8   Today I will receive 50 electronic messages. Of that number, at least half require a reply. (Many of the others consist of jokes, irrelevant bulletins and important announcements about secret cookie recipes. I actually like getting such junk e-mails, as they allow the pleasure of a quick delete without guilt.) If I spend five minutes considering and composing a response to each correspondence, then two hours of my day are busied with e-mail, even if I don't initiate a single one. Since the number of Internet users is doubling about once a year, I expect that in the near future, I—and millions like me—will be doing nothing but writing e-mails. The collapse of commerce and polite society will quickly follow.

9   I'm as much in favor of technology as the next guy. Personally, I think the Luddites should have welcomed the steam looms. But if you insist on telling me that e-mail is an advance, do me a favor and use the phone.

Chapter 28

Argumentation

A Scientist: "I Am the Enemy"

Ron Kline

Ron Kline is a pediatric oncologist and former director of the bone marrow transplant program at the University of Louisville. Kline published the following essay in *Newsweek* magazine's "My Turn" column in 1989 when he was a biotechnology fellow in the Experimental Immunology Branch of the National Cancer Institute in Washington, D.C.

1   I am the enemy! One of those vilified, inhumane physician-scientists involved in animal research. How strange, for I have never thought of myself as an evil person. I became a pediatrician because of my love for children and my desire to keep them healthy. During medical school and residency, however, I saw many children die of leukemia, prematurity, and traumatic injury—circumstances against which medicine has made tremendous progress, but still has far to go. More important, I also saw children, alive and healthy, thanks to advances in medical science such as infant respirators, potent antibiotics, new surgical techniques and the entire field of organ transplantation. My desire to tip the scales in favor of the healthy, happy children drew me to medical research.

2   My accusers claim that I inflict torture on animals for the sole purpose of career advancement. My experiments supposedly have no relevance to medicine and are easily replaced by computer simulation. Meanwhile, an apathetic public barely watches, convinced that the issue has no significance, and publicity-conscious politicians increasingly give way to the demands of the activists.

3   We in medical research have also been unconscionably apathetic. We have allowed the most extreme animal-rights protesters to seize the initiative and frame the issue as one of "animal fraud." We have been complacent in our belief that a knowledgeable public would sense the importance of animal research to the public health. Perhaps we have been mistaken in not responding to the emotional tone of the argument created by those sad posters of animals by waving equally sad posters of children dying of leukemia or cystic fibrosis.

4   Much is made of the pain inflicted on these animals in the name of medical science. The animal-rights activists contend that this is evidence of our malevolent and sadistic nature. A more reasonable argument, however, can be advanced in our defense. Life is often cruel, both to animals and human beings. Teenagers get thrown from the back of a pickup truck and suffer severe head injuries. Toddlers, barely able to walk, find themselves at the bottom of a swimming pool while a parent checks the mail. Physicians hoping to alleviate the pain and suffering these tragedies cause have but three choices: create an animal model of the injury or disease and use that model to understand the process and test new therapies; experiment on human beings—some experiments will succeed, most will fail—or finally, leave medical knowledge static, hoping that accidental discoveries will lead us to the advances.

5   Some animal-rights activists would suggest a fourth choice, claiming that computer models can simulate animal experiments, thus making the actual experiments unnecessary. Computers can simulate, reasonably well, the effects of well-understood principles on complex systems, as in the application of the laws of physics to airplane and automobile design. However, when the principles themselves are in question, as is the case with the complex biological systems under study, computer modeling alone is of little value.

6   One of the terrifying effects of the effort to restrict the use of animals in medical research is that the impact will not be felt for years and decades: drugs that might have been discovered will not be; surgical techniques that might have been developed will not be, and fundamental biological processes that might have been understood will remain mysteries. There is the danger that politically expedient solutions will be found to placate a vocal minority, while the consequences of those decisions will not be apparent until long after the decisions are made and the decision makers forgotten.

7   Fortunately, most of us enjoy good health, and the trauma of watching one's child die has become a rare experience. Yet our good fortune should not make us unappreciative of the health we enjoy or the advances that make it possible. Vaccines, antibiotics, insulin, and drugs to treat heart disease, hypertension, and stroke are all based on animal research. Most complex surgical procedures, such as coronary-artery by-pass and organ transplantation, are initially developed in animals. Presently undergoing animal studies are techniques to insert genes in humans in order to replace the defective ones found to be the cause of so much disease. These studies will effectively end if animal research is severely restricted.

8   In America today, death has become an event isolated from our daily existence—out of the sight and thoughts of most of us. As a doctor who has watched many children die, and their parents grieve, I am particularly angered by people capable of so much compassion for a dog or a cat, but with seemingly so little for a dying human being. These people seem so insulated from the reality of human life and death and what it means.

9   Make no mistake, however: I am not advocating the needlessly cruel treatment of animals. To the extent that the animal-rights movement has made us more aware of the

needs of these animals, and made us search harder for suitable alternatives, they have made a significant contribution. But if the more radical members of this movement are successful in limiting further research, their efforts will bring about a tragedy that will cost many lives. The real question is whether an apathetic majority can be aroused to protect its future against a vocal, but misdirected, minority.

■ Sack Athletic Scholarships

Allen Barra

Allen Barra is a sports columnist for *The Wall Street Journal* and a contributor to newspapers and journals, such as *The New York Times*, the *Los Angeles Times*, and *American Heritage*. In addition to sports, Barra frequently writes about movies, books, history, and popular culture. His books include *Football by the Numbers* (1986), *That's Not the Way It Was* (1995), *Inventing Wyatt Earp* (1998), and *Clearing the Bases* (2002). This essay originally appeared in *The New York Times* in 1990.

1   "Of the making of reforms," Confucius is said to have said, "there is no end." With regard to college sports, he might have added: Especially when the reforms are half-hearted.

2   If the N.C.A.A. is serious about making reforms in college sports, there's one sweeping measure that is simple, fair and economically advantageous: Do away with athletic scholarships.

3   Scarcely a week goes by without news of some fresh scandal involving the football programs at our major schools. Steroids at Notre Dame. Chaos at Oklahoma. The off-campus activities of the Miami Hurricanes alone could have kept Don Johnson and the crew on "Miami Vice" busy for another season. And how serious is the N.C.A.A. about solving these problems?

4   The N.C.A.A.'s usual response, when it gets around to taking action, is to punish thousands of students and student athletes by barring their school's team from TV and post-season competition. Of course students and student athletes are easier to punish than coaches and administrators; they have no rights.

5   In a recent issue of *Sports Illustrated* the writer Douglas Looney suggested that a return to one-platoon football would cut the average school's athletic budget by nearly 25 percent, largely because the N.C.A.A.'s current limit of 95 scholarships per year could be reduced to 69.

6   Why not go a step further? Since most of the schools that compete in big-time football would lose money if not for TV, why not save everyone a lot more money by eliminating athletic scholarships entirely?

7   Today's college athletes are professionals in every significant way except one: they don't get paid. They are there not to learn but to make money for the colleges. The money is a fact of life and can't be done away with so long as millions of alumni and fans are willing to pay for tickets and turn on their TV's. What's to be done short of turning 18-year-olds into legitimate professionals?

8   For starters, colleges can get out of the business of being a cost-free minor league for the National Basketball Association and National Football League. The elimination of athletic scholarships would mean that football and basketball players would be ill-prepared for pro sports. But why should that concern colleges?

9   Colleges would be forced to try something new: to field teams comprising college students, not future pro draft picks. There would be no more preferential treatment for "scholar-athletes." Nevertheless, more athletes would graduate because they would be entering college as students, not athletes.

10   Without athletic scholarships, we'd really find out if students from Miami play football better than students from Notre Dame. More to the point, we'd find out if Miami and Notre Dame, once their recruiting machines are gone, are really better than, say, Northwestern and Georgia Tech.

11   The primary objections to this come, as you'd expect, from the coaches and N.C.A.A. administrators. It would cut down on revenues, they say. But why? Even if the networks paid less for a game played by nonscholarship athletes, the schools would still earn big bucks; certainly more than it would have cost them to field the teams . . . .

12   There may be nothing that can be done about the vast sums of money N.C.A.A. sports are bringing in, but something can be done about how it's spent. Most colleges put most of their basketball and football money back into their sports programs. Eliminate athletic scholarships and the money saved could go toward putting minority students in school. In this case, though, the minority students given aid would be ones with aptitudes for math instead of 20-foot jump shots.

13   Then, the millions brought in by college students would at least benefit college students. Instead of sending thousands of uneducated ex-jocks out to face a hostile society every year, colleges would have the chance to send thousands of professionals into a society that needs them badly.

■ Judging by the Cover

Bonny Gainley

Bonny Gainley is a marketing and management consultant, speaker, and author who writes on topics relating to the family and the workplace. In addition to articles based on her experiences in the high tech industry, she has published *Look Before You Step: Advice for Potential Stepparents and Their Partners* (2002). This essay originally appeared in 2003 as an opinion column in the Fort Collins, Colorado newspaper the *Coloradoan*.

1   Spring is in the air, and those about to graduate are looking for jobs just like many of the rest of us. Competition is tough, so jobs seekers must carefully consider their personal choices.

2   Every person has a need to be accepted, ideally just as he or she is. Our family and friends may do that, but the workplace does not. An editorial a while back in one of our high school newspapers claimed it is unfair for professions such as business, public relations, teaching and others to discourage visible tattoos. While not specifically mentioned, piercings and perhaps even certain hairstyles or garments would fall into the same category.

3   They say you can't judge a book by its cover, yet some people "cover" themselves in ways intended to convey certain messages. The message may be, "my uniform says I am a police officer" or "I like the latest fashions" or "I am a gang member."

4   We make assumptions about people based on their appearance every day, and often we assume exactly what they want us to assume. Just as people project messages about

themselves with their appearance, so do businesses. Dress codes and standards exist in the professional world for a number of reasons. Sometimes the issue is safety; sometimes it is a matter of what clients will accept. As long as parents don't want pre-school teachers waving visible skull or profanity tattoos in front of their small children, those tattoos will be deemed inappropriate for that profession.

5   Some say this is an issue of human rights and freedom, but it is really about free enterprise. The bottom line is that businesses exist to make money. Whether it seems fair or not, most employers do care about the personal appearances of the people they hire because those people represent the business to its customers.

6   Discrimination on the basis of factors an applicant can't control is wrong and illegal. Choosing the candidate who displays the attributes and skills that best match a job description is not. Just as runners would put themselves at a disadvantage by choosing to run the 100 meters in combat boots, people who choose to wear rings through their noses are putting themselves at a disadvantage in the professional job market. Each of us can choose whether to conform to the rules of any organization, but that organization is also free to choose whether they want us associated with it.

7   I don't personally have issues with visible tattoos or piercings, but as a hiring manager I was paid to choose the people who would make the best impression on our customers. It comes down to this—there are plenty of well-qualified applicants and most present themselves in a way my industry considers professional, so there was no compelling reason to choose someone who might offend my customers or poorly represent my company. Even though I may be open minded, I can't count on my customers to be.

8   If people continue to tattoo and pierce, attitudes about the appropriateness of those adornments in the professional workplace will change over time, in the same way that pants have become appropriate for women, for example. When tattoos and piercings are generally accepted in the business world, there will be new things that aren't—maybe nudity or some other trend we can't even imagine. Whether our personal choices will be accepted or not, we each have the right to make them, but must also be willing to accept the related consequences.

9   How we dress, tattoo or pierce is an expression of who we are and a message to the people we encounter. Freedom of choice is a dual-edged sword—individuals are free to present their desired image, and others are free to react to it.

10   There is nobody to blame but yourself if your set of choices does not match those desired by your preferred employers. No organization should have to change to accommodate a candidate simply because that person is unwilling to respect its standards, as long as its standards are legal.

Chapter 29

Description

■ A Day at the Theme Park

W. Bruce Cameron

W. Bruce Cameron began writing humorous features for the Denver newspaper *The Rocky Mountain News* in 1999; his column is now in syndication throughout the country. His book *The 8 Simple Rules for Dating My Teenage Daughter* (2001) was adapted into a television show of the same name, originally starring the late John Ritter. As the father of three teenagers, Cameron often writes about the challenges facing parents of adolescents, as illustrated in this column that first appeared in 1999.

1   One of the most endearing traits of children is their utter trust that their parents will provide them with all of life's necessities, meaning food, shelter, and a weekend at a theme park.

2   A theme park is a sort of artificial vacation, a place where you can enjoy all your favorite pastimes at once, such as motion sickness and heat exhaustion. Adult tolerance for theme parks peaks at about an hour, which is how long it takes to walk from the parking lot to the front gate. You fork over an obscene amount of money to gain entrance to a theme park, though it costs nothing to leave (which is odd, because you'd pay anything to escape). The two main activities in a theme park are (a) standing in line, and (b) sweating. The sun reflects off the concrete with a fiendish lack of mercy. You're about to learn the boiling point of tennis shoes. Your hair is sunburned, and when a small child in front of you gestures with her hand she smacks you in the face with her cotton candy; now it feels like your cheeks are covered with carnivorous sand.

3   The ride your children have selected for you is a corkscrewing, stomach-compressing roller coaster built by the same folks who manufactured the baggage delivery system at

DIA.* Apparently the theme of this particular park is "Nausea." You sit down and are strapped in so tightly you can feel your shoulders grinding against your pelvis. Once the ride begins you are thrown about with such violence it reminds you of your teenager's driving. When the ride is over your children want to get something to eat, but first the ride attendants have to pry your fingers off the safety bar. "Open your eyes, please, sir," they keep shouting. They finally persuade you to let go, though it seems a bit discourteous of them to have used pepper spray. Staggering, you follow your children to the Hot Dog Palace for some breakfast.

4   Food at a theme park is so expensive it would be cheaper to just eat your own money. You son's meal costs a day's pay and consists of items manufactured of corn syrup, which is sugar; sucrose, which is sugar; fructose, which is sugar; and sugar, which is sugar. He also consumes large quantities of what in dog food would be called "meat byproducts." When, after a couple of rides, he announces that he feels like he is going to throw up, you're very alarmed. Having seen his meal once, you're in no mood to see it again.

5   With the exception of that first pummeling, you manage to stay off the rides all day, explaining to your children that it isn't good for you when your internal organs are forcibly rearranged. Now, though, they coax you back in line, promising a ride that doesn't twist, doesn't hang you upside down like a bat, doesn't cause your brain to flop around inside your skull; it just goes up and then comes back down. That's it, Dad, no big deal. What they don't tell you is HOW it comes back down. You're strapped into a seat and pulled gently up into acrophobia, the city falling away from you. Okay, not so bad, and in the conversation you're having with God you explain that you're thankful for the wonderful view but you really would like to get down now.

6   And that's just how you descend: NOW. Without warning, you plummet to the ground in an uncontrolled free fall. You must be moving faster than the speed of sound because when you open your mouth, nothing comes out. Your life passes before your eyes, and your one regret is that you will not have an opportunity to punish your children for bringing you to this hellish place. Brakes cut in and you slam to a stop. You gingerly touch your face to confirm it has fallen off. "Wasn't that fun, Dad?" your kids ask. "Why are you kissing the ground?"

7   At the end of the day, you let your teenager drive home. (After the theme park, you are impervious to fear.)

■ Hush, Timmy—This Is Like a Church

Kurt Anderson

Kurt Anderson began a career in journalism at *Time*, ultimately becoming the magazine's architectural critic and an editor-at-large. Prior to his work as a cultural columnist for *The New Yorker* and editor-in-chief of *New York* magazine, he was cofounder and editor of *Spy* magazine. Anderson has also written television and stage productions and the novel *Turn of the Century* (1999). This article first appeared in *Time* in 1985.

---

* Denver International Airport

1   The veteran and his wife had already stared hard at four particular names. Now the couple walked slowly down the incline in front of the wall, looking at rows of hundreds, thousands more, amazed at the roster of the dead. "All the names," she said quietly, sniffling in the early-spring chill. "It's unreal, how many names." He said nothing. "You have to see it to believe it," she said.

2   Just so. In person, close up, the Vietnam Veterans Memorial—two skinny black granite triangles wedged onto a mound of Washington sod—is some kind of sanctum, beautiful and terrible. "We didn't plan that," says John Wheeler, chairman of the veterans' group that raised the money and built it. "I had a picture of seven-year-olds throwing a Frisbee around on the grass in front. But it's treated as a spiritual place." When Wheeler's colleague Jan Scruggs decided there ought to be a monument, he had only vague notions of what it might be like. "You don't set out and *build* a national shrine," Scruggs says. "It *becomes* one."

3   Washington is thick with monuments, several of them quite affecting. But as the Vietnam War was singular and strange, the dark, dreamy, redemptive memorial to its American veterans is like no other. "It's more solemn," says National Park Service Ranger Sarah Page, who has also worked at the memorials honoring Lincoln, Washington and Jefferson. "People give it more respect." Lately it has been the most visited monument in the capital: 2.3 million saw it in 1984, about 45,000 a week, but it is currently drawing 100,000 a week. Where does it get its power—to console, and also to make people sob?

4   The men who set up the Vietnam Veterans Memorial Fund wanted something that would include the name of every American killed in Vietnam, and would be contemplative and apolitical. They conducted an open design competition that drew 1,421 entries, all submitted anonymously. The winner, Maya Ying Lin, was a Chinese-American undergraduate at Yale: to memorialize men killed in a war in Asia, an Asian female studying at an old antiwar hotbed.

5   Opposition to Lin's design was intense. The opponents wanted something gleaming and grand. To them, the low-slung black wall would send the same old defeatist, elitist messages that had lost the war in the '60s and then stigmatized the veterans in the '70s. "Creating the memorial triggered a lot of old angers and rage among vets about the war," recalls Wheeler, a captain in Vietnam and now a Yale-trained government lawyer. "It got white hot."

6   In the end, Lin's sublime and stirring wall was built, 58,022 names inscribed. As a compromise with opponents, however, a more conventional figurative sculpture was added to the site last fall (at a cost of $400,000). It does not spoil the memorial, as the art mandarins had warned. The three U.S. soldiers, cast in bronze, stand a bit larger than life, carry automatic weapons and wear fatigues, but the pose is not John Wayne-heroic: these American boys are spectral and wary, even slightly bewildered as they gaze southeast toward the wall. While he was planning the figures, sculptor Frederick Hart spent time watching vets at the memorial. Hart now grants that "no modernist monument of its kind has been as successful as that wall. The sculpture and the wall interact beautifully. Everybody won." Nor does Lin, his erstwhile artistic antagonist, still feel that Hart's statue is so awfully trite. "It captures the mood," says Lin. "Their faces have a lost look." Out at the memorial last week, one veteran looked at the new addition and nodded: "That's us."

7   But it is the wall that vets approach as if it were a force field. It is at the wall that families of the dead cry and leave flowers and mementos and messages, much as Jews leave notes for God in the cracks of Jerusalem's Western Wall. Around the statue, people talk louder and breathe easier, snap vacation photos unselfconsciously, eat Eskimo Pies and Fritos. But near the wall, a young Boston father tells his rambunctious son, "Hush, Timmy—this is like a church." The visitors' processionals do seem to have a ritual, even liturgical quality. Going slowly down toward the vertex, looking at the names, they chat less and less, then fall silent where the names of the first men killed (July 1959) and the last (May 1975) appear. The talk begins again, softly, as they follow the path up out of the little valley of the shadow of death.

8   For veterans, the memorial was a touchstone from the beginning, and the 1982 dedication ceremony a delayed national embrace. "The actual act of being at the memorial is healing for the guy or woman who went to Vietnam," says Wheeler, who visits at least monthly. "It has to do with the felt presence of comrades." He pauses. "I always look at Tommy Hayes' name. Tommy's up on panel 50 east, line 29." Hayes, Wheeler's West Point pal, was killed 17 years ago this month. "I know guys," Wheeler says, "who are still waiting to go, whose wives have told me, 'He hasn't been able to do it yet.'" For those who go, catharsis is common. As Lin says of the names, chronologically ordered, "Veterans can look at the wall, find a name, and in a sense put themselves back in that time." The war has left some residual pathologies that the memorial cannot leach away. One veteran killed himself on the amphitheatrical green near the wall. A second, ex-Marine Randolph Taylor, tried and failed in January. "I regret what I did," he said. "I feel like I desecrated a holy place."

9   The memorial has become a totem, so much so that its tiniest imperfections make news. Last fall somebody noticed a few minute cracks at the seams between several of the granite panels. The cause of the hairlines is still unknown, and the builders are a little worried.

10   Probably no one is more determined than Wheeler to see the memorial's face made perfect, for he savors the startlingly faithful reflections the walls give off: he loves seeing the crowds of visitors looking simultaneously at the names and themselves. "Look!" he said the other day, gesturing at panel 4 east. "You see that plane taking off? You see the blue sky? No one expected that."

■ In the Land of "Coke-Cola"

William Least Heat-Moon

William Lewis Trogdon, who writes under the name of William Least Heat-Moon, was born in Kansas of English-Irish-Osage ancestry. After receiving his Ph.D. in literature and teaching for some years, Heat-Moon packed a van he called Ghost Dancing and traveled around the country on backroads marked in blue on his map; his experiences became the award-winning *Blue Highways: A Journey into America* (1982), from which this excerpt is taken. Later nonfiction includes *PrairyErth* (1999) and *River Horse* (2001).

1   In the land of "Coke-Cola" it was hot and dry. The artesian water was finished. Along route 72, an hour west of Ninety-Six, I tried not to look for a spring; I knew I wouldn't find one, but I kept looking. The Savannah River, dammed to an unnatural wideness, lay below, wet and cool. I'd come into Georgia. The sun seemed to press on the roadway,

and inside the truck, hot light bounced off chrome, flickering like a torch. Then I saw what I was trying not to look for: in a coppice, a long-handled pump.

2   I stopped and took my bottles to the well. A small sign: WATER UNSAFE FOR DRINKING. I drooped like warm tallow. What fungicide, herbicide, nematicide, fumigant, or growth regulant—potions that rebuilt Southern agriculture—had seeped into the ground water? In the old movie Westerns there is commonly a scene where a dehydrated man, crossing the barren waste, at last comes to a water hole; he lies flat to drink the tepid stuff. Just as lips touch water, he sees on the other side a steer skull. I drove off thirsty but feeling a part of mythic history.

3   The thirst subsided when hunger took over. I hadn't eaten since morning. Sunset arrived west of Oglesby, and the air cooled. Then a roadsign:

Swamp Guinea's Fish Lodge
All You Can Eat!

An arrow pointed down a country highway. I would gorge myself. A record would be set. They'd ask me to leave. An embarrassment to all.

4   The road through the orange earth of north Georgia passed an old, three-story house with a thin black child hanging out of every window like an illustration for "The Old Woman Who Lived in a Shoe"; on into hills and finally to Swamp Guinea's, a conglomerate of plywood and two-by-fours laid over with the smell of damp pine woods.

5   Inside, wherever an oddity or natural phenomenon could hang, one hung: stuffed rump of a deer, snowshoe, flintlock, hornet's nest. The place looked as if a Boy Scout troop had decorated it. Thirty or so people, black and white, sat around tables almost foundering under piled platters of food. I took a seat by the reproduction of a seventeenth-century woodcut depicting some Rabelaisian banquet at the groaning board.

6   The diners were mostly Oglethorpe County red-dirt farmers. In Georgia tones they talked about their husbandry in terms of rain and nitrogen and hope. An immense woman with a glossy picture of a hooked bass leaping on the front of her shirt said, "I'm gonna be sick from how much I've ate."

7   I was watching everyone else and didn't see the waitress standing quietly by. Her voice was deep and soft like water moving in a cavern. I ordered the $4.50 special. In a few minutes she wheeled up a cart and began offloading dinner: ham and eggs, fried catfish, fried perch fingerlings, fried shrimp, chunks of barbecued beef, fried chicken, French fries, hush puppies, a broad bowl of cole slaw, another of lemon, a quart of ice tea, a quart of ice, and an entire loaf of factory-wrapped white bread. The table was covered.

8   "Call me if y'all want any more." She wasn't joking. I quenched the thirst and then—slowly—went to the eating. I had to stand to reach plates across the table, but I intended to do the supper in. It was all Southern fried and good, except the Southern-style sweetened ice tea; still I took care of a quart of it. As I ate, making up for meals lost, the Old-Woman-in-the-Shoe house flashed before me, lightning in darkness. I had no moral right to eat so much. But I did. Headline: STOMACH PUMP FAILS TO REVIVE TRAVELER.

9   The loaf of bread lay unopened when I finally abandoned the meal. At the register, I paid a man who looked as if he'd been chipped out of Georgia chert. The Swamp Guinea. I asked about the name. He spoke of himself in the third person like the Wizard of Oz. "The Swamp Guinea only tells regulars."

10   "I'd be one, Mr. Guinea, if I didn't live in Missouri."

11   "Y'all from the North? Here, I got somethin' for you." He went to the office and returned with a 45 rpm record. "It's my daughter singin'. A little promotion we did. Take it along." Later, I heard a husky north Georgia voice let go a down-home lyric rendering of Swamp Guinea's menu:

> That's all you can eat
> For a dollar fifty,
> Hey! The barbecue's nifty!

And so on through the fried chicken and potatoes.

12   As I left, the Swamp Guinea, a former antique dealer whose name was Rudell Burroughs, said, "The nickname don't mean anything. Just made it up. Tried to figure a good one so we can franchise someday."

13   The frogs, high and low, shrilled and bellowed from the trees and ponds. It was cool going into Athens, a city suffering from a nasty case of the sprawls. On the University of Georgia campus, I tried to walk down Swamp Guinea's supper. Everywhere couples entwined like moon-flower vines, each waiting for the blossom that opens only once.

Chapter 30

Narration

■ 38 Who Saw Murder Didn't Call the Police

Martin Gansberg

Martin Gansberg was a reporter and editor for *The New York Times* for over 40 years, until his retirement in 1985. He also wrote for such magazines as *Diplomat*, *Catholic Digest*, and *Facts*. This often reprinted article was published in *The New York Times* in 1964, shortly after the murder of Kitty Genovese, a crime that has become synonomous with moral apathy.

1   For more than half an hour 38 respectable, law-abiding citizens in Queens watched a killer stalk and stab a woman in three separate attacks in Kew Gardens.

2   Twice the sound of their voices and the sudden glow of their bedroom lights interrupted him and frightened him off. Each time he returned, sought her out and stabbed her again. Not one person telephoned the police during the assault; one witness called after the woman was dead.

3   That was two weeks ago today. But Assistant Chief Inspector Frederick M. Lussen, in charge of the borough's detectives and a veteran of 25 years of homicide investigations, is still shocked.

4   He can give a matter-of-fact recitation of many murders. But the Kew Gardens slaying baffles him—not because it is a murder, but because the "good people" failed to call the police.

5   "As we have reconstructed the crime," he said, "the assailant had three chances to kill this woman during a 35-minute period. He returned twice to complete the job. If we had been called when he first attacked, the woman might not be dead now."

6   This is what the police say happened beginning at 3:20 A.M. in the staid, middle-class, tree-lined Austin Street area:

7   Twenty-eight-year-old Catherine Genovese, who was called Kitty by almost everyone in the neighborhood, was returning home from her job as manager of a bar in Hollis. She parked her red Fiat in a lot adjacent to the Kew Gardens Long Island Rail Road Station, facing Mowbray Place. Like many residents of the neighborhood, she had parked there day after day since her arrival from Connecticut a year ago, although the railroad frowns on the practice.

8   She turned off the lights of her car, locked the door and started to walk the 100 feet to the entrance of her apartment at 82–70 Austin Street, which is in a Tudor building, with stores on the first floor and apartments on the second.

9   The entrance to the apartment is in the rear of the building because the front is rented to retail stores. At night the quiet neighborhood is shrouded in the slumbering darkness that marks most residential areas.

10   Miss Genovese noticed a man at the far end of the lot, near a seven-story apartment house at 82–40 Austin Street. She halted. Then, nervously, she headed up Austin Street toward Lefferts Boulevard, where there is a call box to the 102nd Police Precinct in nearby Richmond Hill.

"He Stabbed Me"

11   She got as far as a street light in front of a bookstore before the man grabbed her. She screamed. Lights went on in the 10-story apartment house at 82–67 Austin Street, which faces the bookstore. Windows slid open and voices punctuated the early-morning stillness.

12   Miss Genovese screamed: "Oh, my God, he stabbed me! Please help me! Please help me!"

13   From one of the upper windows in the apartment house, a man called down: "Let that girl alone!"

14   The assailant looked up at him, shrugged and walked down Austin Street toward a white sedan parked a short distance away. Miss Genovese struggled to her feet.

15   Lights went out. The killer returned to Miss Genovese, now trying to make her way around the side of the building by the parking lot to get to her apartment. The assailant stabbed her again.

16   "I'm dying!" she shrieked. "I'm dying!"

A City Bus Passed

17   Windows were opened again, and lights went on in many apartments. The assailant got into his car and drove away. Miss Genovese staggered to her feet. A city bus, Q-10, the Lefferts Boulevard line to Kennedy International Airport, passed. It was 3:35 A.M.

18   The assailant returned. By then, Miss Genovese had crawled to the back of the building, where the freshly painted brown doors to the apartment house held out hope of safety. The killer tried the first door; she wasn't there. At the second door,

82–62 Austin Street, he saw her slumped on the floor at the foot of the stairs. He stabbed her a third time—fatally.

19 It was 3:50 by the time the police received their first call, from a man who was a neighbor of Miss Genovese. In two minutes they were at the scene. The neighbor, a 70-year-old woman and another woman were the only persons on the street. Nobody else came forward.

20 The man explained that he had called the police after much deliberation. He had phoned a friend in Nassau County for advice and then he had crossed the roof of the building to the apartment of the elderly woman to get her to make the call.

21 "I didn't want to get involved," he sheepishly told the police.

Suspect Is Arrested

22 Six days later, the police arrested Winston Moseley, a 29-year-old business-machine operator, and charged him with homicide. Moseley had no previous record. He is married, has two children and owns a home at 133-19 Sutter Avenue, South Ozone Park, Queens. On Wednesday, a court committed him to Kings County Hospital for psychiatric observation.

23 When questioned by the police, Moseley also said that he had slain Mrs. Annie May Johnson, 24, of 146–12 133d Avenue, Jamaica, on Feb. 29 and Barbara Kralik, 15, of 174–17 140th Avenue, Springfield Gardens, last July. In the Kralik case, the police are holding Alvin L. Mitchell, who is said to have confessed [to] that slaying.

24 The police stressed how simple it would have been to have gotten in touch with them. "A phone call," said one of the detectives, "would have done it." The police may be reached by dialing "O" for operator or SPring 7-3100. . . .

25 Today witnesses from the neighborhood, which is made up of one-family homes in the $35,000 to $60,000 range with the exception of the two apartment houses near the railroad station, find it difficult to explain why they didn't call the police. . . .

26 A housewife, knowingly if quite casually, said, "We thought it was a lover's quarrel." A husband and wife both said, "Frankly, we were afraid." They seemed aware of the fact that events might have been different. A distraught woman, wiping her hands in her apron, said, "I didn't want my husband to get involved."

27 One couple, now willing to talk about that night, said they heard the first screams. The husband looked thoughtfully at the bookstore where the killer first grabbed Miss Genovese.

28 "We went to the window to see what was happening," he said, "but the light from our bedroom made it difficult to see the street." The wife, still apprehensive, added: "I put out the light and we were able to see better."

29 Asked why they hadn't called the police, she shrugged and replied: "I don't know."

30 A man peeked out from a slight opening in the doorway to his apartment and rattled off an account of the killer's second attack. Why hadn't he called the police at the time? "I was tired," he said without emotion. "I went back to bed."

31 It was 4:25 A.M. when the ambulance arrived to take the body of Miss Genovese. It drove off. "Then," a solemn police detective said, "the people came out."

■ When Father Doesn't Know Best

Andrew Merton

Andrew Merton is a professor of English at the University of New Hampshire. In addition to work as a reporter and columnist for the *Boston Herald Traveler* and *The Boston Sunday Globe*, he has been a contributing editor of *Boston* magazine and poetry editor of *Conscience*. His essays have appeared in *The New York Times, Esquire, Ms.*, and other magazines, and his books include *Enemies of Choice* (1982) and *In Your Own Voice: A Writer's Reader* (1997).

1   On Nov. 25, 1983, the prizefighter Marvis Frazier, 23 and inexperienced, was knocked out by the heavyweight champion of the world, Larry Holmes, after 2 minutes and 57 seconds of the first round. Frazier was sucker-punched. Holmes faked a left jab and Frazier went for it, leaving himself open for the decisive punch, a right. Frazier managed to stay on his feet while Holmes pummeled him with 19 consecutive punches. Finally, with three seconds left in the round, the referee stopped the fight. At that moment, Marvis Frazier's father and manager, the former heavyweight champion Joe Frazier, embraced his son and repeated over and over: "It's all right. It's all right. I love you."

2   Later, responding to criticism that he had overestimated his son's abilities, Joe Frazier said, "I knew what I was doing." In the face of indisputable evidence to the contrary, Joe Frazier was unable to give up the notion that Marvis would succeed him as champion, that he would continue to reign through his son.

3   It is an insidious business, this drive for immortality, usually much more subtle than thrusting one's son naked into the ring. Often it is simply a matter of expecting the boy to repeat one's own boyhood, step for step.

4   In July 1983, my son Gabriel was 4 and extremely conscious of it. In fact, he defined and justified much of his behavior by his age: "Four-year-olds can buckle their own sandals." Or "I can run faster than Mike. That's because I'm 4 and he's only 3." A 4-year-old, I thought, was ready for a major-league baseball game. So on Saturday, July 16, I drove him to Boston to see the Red Sox play the Oakland A's.

5   It was a clear, hot day—very hot, in fact, setting a record for Boston on that date at 97 degrees—but, rare for Boston, it was dry. A good day for hitters. Jim Rice, Tony Armas, Carl Yastrzemski and Wade Boggs had been on a tear. I expected a slugfest. I had packed a bag with fruit and vegetables. Gabe slept through the entire 90-minute drive to Boston, a good sign; he'd be fresh for the game. Another good sign: I found a free, legal parking space. And as we entered the ball park, Gabe seemed excited. Gravely he heeded my advice to go to the bathroom now, so we would not have to move from our seat during the action.

6   As we walked through the catacombs beneath the stadium, I remembered my own first game, in Yankee Stadium in 1952. My only previous view of major-league baseball had come via the flickering images of black-and-white television. As my father and I emerged into the sun, I was overwhelmed by the vast, green expanse of the outfield. A stubble-faced pitcher named Vic Raschi fired strike after strike, a Yankee first baseman named Joe Collins hit a home run and the Yankees won, 3–2. The opponent had been the old Philadelphia Athletics, direct ancestors of the Oakland team. I felt joy

and anticipation as Gabe and I now emerged into the sun for his first look at the left-field wall at Fenway, the Green Monster. Gabe said nothing, but he must have felt the excitement.

7   We found our seats, on the right-field side of the park halfway between first base and the foul pole. Good seats, from which we could see every part of the playing field. We were about a half-hour early, and we settled down to watch the end of batting practice. Then, as the ground crew manicured the infield, Gabe said he was hungry. I gave him a carrot stick, which he munched happily. When he finished that, he asked what else I had in the bag. I gave him some grapes, then an apple. Within 15 minutes he had polished off most of the contents of the bag. And then he said: "I think I've had enough baseball. I want to go home now."

8   "But the game hasn't started yet," I said. "You haven't seen any baseball."

9   "Yes, I have. And I want to go home."

10   "That was only batting practice. Don't you want to see the real game?"

11   "No."

12   I considered staying anyway. It was *my* day with my son that was being ruined here, wasn't it?

13   But I knew better. I knew now that if I insisted on staying, it would be *his* day that would be ruined so Dad could watch a ball game. Submitting to the logic of this, I gritted my teeth. In a foul mood, I carried him out of the park on my shoulders just as the Red Sox took the field. I was muttering to myself, almost audibly, "It's *his* day, dammit."

14   "Daddy? Can I have an ice-cream cone?"

15   Without much grace, I bought him an ice-cream cone. Then we got in the car, and I drove away from my precious parking space, still fuming. He was well aware that I was upset; I could see the tentative look on his face, a combination of fear and pain. I hated that look. But I could not shake my mood. I was not looking forward to the drive back to New Hampshire.

16   Then on Storrow Drive, I spotted the Boston Museum of Science, just across the Charles River. Gabe had been there before, and he had loved it, although he still referred to it, quite seriously, as the "Museum of Silence." Still angry, I managed to say, "Gabe, would you like to go to the museum?"

17   "Yeah," he said.

18   We had the museum nearly to ourselves. As we walked through the wonderfully cool exhibition halls, I acknowledged to myself how much I wanted Gabe to be like me. He was supposed to like the baseball game, not for his sake, but for mine, and I had gotten angry at him when he didn't measure up to my expectations. It was those expectations, and not Gabe's actions, that were out of line. And it was those expectations that had to change.

19   I also thought about the competition between us: what had happened at the ball park was, after all, a battle of wills. He had won. He had prevailed because he was persistent and stubborn and stood up for what he thought was right.

20   We spent three quick hours at the museum, viewing the life-sized tyrannosaurus rex from different angles, trying out the space capsule, making waves and viewing exhibits on everything from centrifugal force to probability. Each time Gabe made a discovery, he called me over to share his excitement. And I *was* excited.

21   Son and father, together, had saved the day—he by holding out for something he enjoyed and I by having the sense, finally, to realize that he was right, and to let go of my dream of how things should be.

22   This time, anyway.

23   And then I remembered something else. When my own father took me to Yankee Stadium, I was 6 years old, not 4.

24   Maybe in a couple of years. . . .

■ The Talkies

James Lileks

James Lileks is a columnist for the *Minneapolis Star–Tribune* and a syndicated political humor columnist for Newhouse News Service. In addition to hosting a radio talk show, Lileks has published two novels, *Falling Up the Stairs* (1988) and *Mr. Obvious* (1995); two collections of essays, *Notes of a Nervous Man* (1991), from which this excerpt is taken, and *Fresh Lies* (1995); and a humorous look at cookbooks, *The Gallery of Regrettable Food* (2001).

1   I am a tolerant man. Especially at the movies. I do not complain when the seats are as plush as a Baptist pew, or the buttered popcorn tastes like packing material with a drizzle of melted crayon. I don't mind that I have to cash a bond to buy a box of Dots, and if I have to use solvents to free my feet from the floor at the end of the film, that's acceptable. I'm not happy when the man with the big yellow hat from the Curious George books sits directly in front of me and blocks my view, but accept it as the price you pay for a communal experience.

2   But people who talk in movies make me turn eight shades of mad. Plunk two talkers behind me and I start to pine for a decent billy club. Something well weighted with a comfortable grip. As I see it, there are two excuses for talking during movies: (*a*) you are on the screen; or (*b*) you have a rare neurological disease that causes you to blurt out statements like "I CAN'T BELIEVE SISKEL AND EBERT GAVE THIS TWO THUMBS UP!" at inappropriate times—and so you go to movie theaters where your affliction seems less bizarre.

3   Mind you, I am not discussing those who lean to their partner and whisper a few words or observations. Most of you whisper, or keep it to yourselves. The people to whom I refer are those who speak at a volume just a few decibels shy of the level you would use to warn someone in a crowd of a falling piano. The people who seem to expect their names to be listed in the credits under "Additional Dialogue."

4   Last week I went to see *Mississippi Burning*. I use the word "see" with precision, for I heard not a line of the dialogue. The entire row behind me talked all through the trailers.* That's fine. That's what trailers are for. Go on, get it out of your system. They also talked during the opening credits, but that was acceptable; they'd arrived late— I know this because one of them hit me in the head with her purse—and they were still flush with the excitement that comes with leaving the house three minutes before the film starts.

---

* A "trailer" is a preview of a forthcoming movie.

5   But as the film progressed, it became obvious that the row behind us was a group from the Institute for Pointing Out the Obvious, off on a field trip. The first image of the film, an early '60s-model car cresting a hill, prompted the gentleman behind me to note, "That's an old car." The appearance of several more cars of the same period gave the man an empirical Epiphany, and he could not help but burst out with his conclusion:

6   "This must be set in the past."

7   There was a period of silence, during which he may or may not have whispered, "Note how reflective and rectangular the screen is," to his partner. The slack was taken up by a group to his right, who were attempting to recall what this film was about, perhaps on the assumption that the plot, due to malicious filmmakers anxious for financial ruin, would remain inscrutable for the next two hours.

8   These folk soon shut up—after my buddy had turned around, locked eyes, and given his best I-taught-Manson-all-he-knows look. But the ones behind me were just beginning.

9   Nothing escaped comment. The streets in the rural Mississippi town were unpaved? Lo, hear them discuss the volume of dust raised by a passing car. The sheriff was fat? Lend an ear to "Looka that gut," and other biting witticisms (such as, "I mean it, how can he be that fat? I'll never get that fat."). Woe to any screen characters who fail to heed their judgments, and prolonged approval of those who do.

10   Often I was treated to a critical evaluation in process. At one point, Gene Hackman drives up to the house of a woman who knows something but isn't telling the Feds. This prompts the following speech:

11   "Oh, it's broad daylight, he'd better not go up to that house. People would talk and her husband would hear about it, don't you think?"

12   "I imagine so."

13   "Well, everyone knows that's his car."

14   "See, he's leaving."

15   "Yeah, he's turning around."

16   "Good. 'Cause he'd have gotten in trouble, and so would she."

17   Turning around and shouting "SHUT UP! SHUT UP AND REMAIN IN A STATE OF SHUTUPEDNESS!" would have done no good. I had spent the previous hour turning around and glaring, but they apparently took this to mean I was angry that they were speaking too softly, and hence depriving me of their views. For a while I was turning around, glaring and turning away with a heavy sigh, but given the classical decor of the theater, they probably interpreted this as a nostalgic sigh of regret for an idealized world long passed. Nothing worked. When the man issued a few racking coughs interspersed with words, I considered lighting up a cigarette and letting the smoke waft his way, but smoking, of course, is considered discourteous to others.

18   For a while I attempted to use telekinesis to loose a piece of plaster on the ceiling directly above them, but this did not work.

19   I finally turned around and said, "Quiet!" They nodded, as though I was describing an attribute to the theater. I might as well have said "Dark!" or "Chairs in rows!" They embarked anew on another discussion of whether or not that actor was in that Jack Nicholson film.

20   Actors, incidentally, were not allowed to have roles. When they discussed the motivations of Gene Hackman's character, they addressed him as Gene Hackman. "See, Gene Hackman wants to do it his way, that's the problem." This helped all of us within hearing range maintain our suspension of disbelief. Willem Dafoe, late of *Platoon*, was known only as "the guy in the glasses." They would occasionally bring out the depth in his character by asking, "Why is he always wearing a suit? It looks so warm, doesn't he sweat?"

21   If I seem to be exaggerating, I assure you I am not. These people babbled without cease, as though the fountain at the concession stand had added sodium pentothal to their beverages. I could not move, as there was not a decent seat to be had in the theater. I could barely concentrate on the film, as I was always steeled for another pronouncement. All I could do was entertain the idea of following them home, standing in the corner of their bedroom, and saying things like, "Oh, see, he has his arm around her shoulder, he likes her. Okay, well, she's getting ready for bed now, that's a nice set of sheets, I have ones like those at home. Say, that's quite a mole, I'd get that checked out if I had a mole like that," and so forth.

22   It would only be fair.

23   So, friends, if you're in a movie house, and you have something to say, ask yourself this: Do you, in the course of your day, constantly have to shout over the sound of a jackhammer, and should you now adjust your voice accordingly? Is what you have to say really necessary? Is the gentleman in front of you waving a flag on which is printed the nautical symbol for PUT A LID ON IT?

24   If you feel you still have to speak, ask yourself this: If this was World War II, and I was behind the German lines with Nazis everywhere, could the Nazis hear me if I spoke at this level, and subsequently submit me to horrible torture? If the answer is yes, tone it down. Or write it out and hand it to your partner, with the instructions to swallow it immediately.

25   Or, go on talking. Go ahead. You paid your money. Gab it up. And make sure you kick the seat in front of you when you cross your legs. You're only conforming to ancient tradition, after all. Movies are nothing more than modern versions of cavemen telling tales around the fire, and back then there were always a couple who talked all through the story.

26   We know this because of drawings on the walls of caves where they buried the talkers.

Chapter 31

Essays for Further Analysis: Multiple Strategies and Styles

■ I Have a Dream

Martin Luther King, Jr.

The Rev. Martin Luther King, Jr., president of the Southern Christian Leadership Conference, was the most well-known leader of the civil rights movement of the 1960s and the recipient of the 1964 Nobel Peace Prize. He was assassinated in 1968. King delivered this speech in 1963 at a celebration of the Emancipation Proclamation, before a crowd of 250,000 who had marched to the Lincoln Memorial in Washington, D.C.

1 Five score years ago, a great American, in whose symbolic shadow we stand, signed the Emancipation Proclamation. This momentous decree came as a great beacon light of hope to millions of Negro slaves who had been seared in the flames of withering injustice. It came as a joyous daybreak to end the long night of captivity.

2   But one hundred years later, we must face the tragic fact that the Negro is still not free. One hundred years later, the life of the Negro is still sadly crippled by the manacles of segregation and the chains of discrimination. One hundred years later, the Negro lives on a lonely island of poverty in the midst of a vast ocean of material prosperity. One hundred years later, the Negro is still languishing in the corners of American society and finds himself an exile in his own land. So we have come here today to dramatize an appalling condition.

3   In a sense we have come to our nation's capital to cash a check. When the architects of our republic wrote the magnificent words of the Constitution and the Declaration of Independence, they were signing a promissory note to which every American was to fall heir. This note was a promise that all men would be guaranteed the unalienable rights of life, liberty, and the pursuit of happiness.

4   It is obvious today that America has defaulted on this promissory note insofar as her citizens of color are concerned. Instead of honoring this sacred obligation, America has given the Negro people a bad check; a check which has come back marked "insufficient funds." But we refuse to believe that the bank of justice is bankrupt. We refuse to believe that there are insufficient funds in the great vaults of opportunity of this nation. So we have come to cash this check—a check that will give us upon demand the riches of freedom and the security of justice. We have also come to this hallowed spot to remind America of the fierce urgency of *now*. This is no time to engage in the luxury of cooling off or to take the tranquilizing drugs of gradualism. *Now* is the time to make real the promises of Democracy. *Now* is the time to rise from the dark and desolate valley of segregation to the sunlit path of racial justice. *Now* is the time to open the doors of opportunity to all of God's children. *Now* is the time to lift our nation from the quicksands of racial injustice to the solid rock of brotherhood.

5   It would be fatal for the nation to overlook the urgency of the moment and to underestimate the determination of the Negro. This sweltering summer of the Negro's legitimate discontent will not pass until there is an invigorating autumn of freedom and equality. Nineteen sixty-three is not an end, but a beginning. Those who hope that the Negro needed to blow off steam and will now be content will have a rude awakening if the nation returns to business as usual. There will be neither rest nor tranquillity in America until the Negro is granted his citizenship rights. The whirl-winds of revolt will continue to shake the foundations of our nation until the bright day of justice emerges.

6   But there is something that I must say to my people who stand on the warm threshold which leads into the palace of justice. In the process of gaining our rightful place we must not be guilty of wrongful deeds. Let us not seek to satisfy our thirst for freedom by drinking from the cup of bitterness and hatred. We must forever conduct our struggle on the high plane of dignity and discipline. We must not allow our creative protest to degenerate into physical violence. Again and again we must rise to the majestic heights of meeting physical force with soul force. The marvelous new militancy which has engulfed the Negro community must not lead us to distrust of all white people, for many of our white brothers, as evidenced by their presence here today, have come to realize that their destiny is tied up with our destiny and their freedom is inextricably bound to our freedom. We cannot walk alone.

7   And as we walk, we must make the pledge that we shall march ahead. We cannot turn back. There are those who are asking the devotees of civil rights, "When will you be satisfied?" We can never be satisfied as long as the Negro is the victim of the unspeakable horrors of police brutality. We can never be satisfied as long as our bodies, heavy with the fatigue of travel, cannot gain lodging in the motels of the highways and the hotels of the cities. We cannot be satisfied as long as the Negro's basic mobility is from a smaller ghetto to a larger one. We can never be satisfied as long as a Negro in Mississippi cannot vote and a Negro in New York believes he has nothing for

which to vote. No, no, we are not satisfied, and we will not be satisfied until justice rolls down like waters and righteousness like a mighty stream.

8   I am not unmindful that some of you have come here out of great trials and tribulations. Some of you have come fresh from narrow jail cells. Some of you have come from areas where your quest for freedom left you battered by the storms of persecution and staggered by the winds of police brutality. You have been the veterans of creative suffering. Continue to work with the faith that unearned suffering is redemptive.

9   Go back to Mississippi, go back to Alabama, go back to South Carolina, go back to Georgia, go back to Louisiana, go back to the slums and ghettos of our northern cities, knowing that somehow this situation can and will be changed. Let us not wallow in the valley of despair.

10   I say to you today, my friends, that in spite of the difficulties and frustrations of the moment I still have a dream. It is a dream deeply rooted in the American dream.

11   I have a dream that one day this nation will rise up and live out the true meaning of its creed: "We hold these truths to be self-evident; that all men are created equal."

12   I have a dream that one day on the red hills of Georgia the sons of former slaves and the sons of former slaveowners will be able to sit down together at the table of brotherhood.

13   I have a dream that one day even the state of Mississippi, a desert state sweltering with the heat of injustice and oppression, will be transformed into an oasis of freedom and justice.

14   I have a dream that my four little children will one day live in a nation where they will not be judged by the color of their skin but by the content of their character.

15   I have a dream today.

16   I have a dream that one day the state of Alabama, whose governor's lips are presently dripping with the words of interposition and nullification, will be transformed into a situation where little black boys and black girls will be able to join hands with little white boys and white girls and walk together as sisters and brothers.

17   I have a dream today.

18   I have a dream that one day every valley shall be exalted, every hill and mountain shall be made low, the rough places will be made plain, and the crooked places will be made straight, and the glory of the Lord shall be revealed, and all flesh shall see it together.

19   This is our hope. This is the faith with which I return to the South. With this faith we will be able to hew out of the mountain of despair a stone of hope. With this faith we will be able to transform the jangling discords of our nation into a beautiful symphony of brotherhood. With this faith we will be able to work together, to pray together, to struggle together, to go to jail together, to stand up for freedom together, knowing that we will be free one day.

20   This will be the day when all of God's children will be able to sing with new meaning

My country, 'tis of thee,
Sweet land of liberty,
   Of thee I sing:
Land where my fathers died,
Land of the pilgrims' pride,
From every mountain-side
   Let freedom ring.

21   And if America is to be a great nation this must become true. So let freedom ring from the prodigious hilltops of New Hampshire. Let freedom ring from the mighty mountains of New York. Let freedom ring from the heightening Alleghenies of Pennsylvania!

22   Let freedom ring from the snowcapped Rockies of Colorado!

23   Let freedom ring from the curvaceous peaks of California!

24   But not only that; let freedom ring from Stone Mountain of Georgia!

25   Let freedom ring from Lookout Mountain of Tennessee!

26   Let freedom ring from every hill and molehill of Mississippi. From every mountainside, let freedom ring.

27   When we let freedom ring, when we let it ring from every village and every hamlet, from every state and every city, we will be able to speed up that day when all of God's children, black men and white men, Jews and Gentiles, Protestants and Catholics, will be able to join hands and sing in the words of the old Negro spiritual, "Free at last! free at last! thank God almighty, we are free at last!"

■ Crossing the Great Divide

Peter Fish

Peter Fish is a senior editor and award-winning writer for *Sunset*, a magazine of Western living that began in 1898. During the last decade Fish has written over two hundred articles for the magazine on a wide range of subjects including travel, history, science, food, and nature, in addition to a number of interviews and book reviews. This essay appeared in Fish's column, called "Western Wanderings," in 1998.

1   I went to South Pass, Wyoming, to mark my son's 4-month birthday and my 43rd. People might think the middle of Wyoming a strange place to commemorate passing time, but I had my reasons. At 43, you look forward and backward, like a driver shifting his gaze from windshield to rearview mirror. At 4 months, you look straight ahead. From both my son's vantage point and mine, I thought South Pass would be enlightening.

2   We followed the Oregon Trail in from the east, past Independence Rock, where the wagon trains stopped to let emigrants carve their names in splintered granite. We crossed and recrossed the Sweetwater River. We rose with Wyoming toward the sky. At the end of a dirt road was a stone slab inscribed "Old Oregon Trail 1843–57." This was South Pass. Six generations ago my son's ancestors came here on their way to new lives in the West.

3   "South Pass is almost a religious experience," Terry Del Bene had told me a few days earlier. Before I dragged my wife and son into the sagebrush, I wanted to know where I was going. So I tagged along with Del Bene. He is an archaeologist for the Bureau of Land Management, the agency that manages South Pass National Historic Landmark, and he knows the place cold.

4   If South Pass did not exist, the history of the United States would be so different as to be unimaginable. The pass rests at 7,400 feet elevation and forms a broad gap in the otherwise unbroken mountain ranges we label the Rockies. It straddles the Continental Divide—"Splash your canteen and half the water would go the Atlantic and half to the Pacific," says Del Bene—but does so gently enough to allow wagon

travel. Without South Pass, there would have been no Oregon or Mormon or California Trail. The first emigrant wagon train came through in 1843. By the time the last recorded wagons rolled west (amazingly late, in 1912), 400,000 settlers had crossed South Pass.

5   Del Bene told me all this while steering his government truck down State Highway 28. He was dressed as a 19th-century sharpie in wool pants and a vest that resembled mattress ticking. Del Bene is not above spiking his history with theater, and perhaps South Pass needs that—though a national historic landmark, it is noticeably lacking in the visitor centers, interpretive trails, and gift shops with which Americans embalm their history.

6   But when Del Bene announced we had arrived at South Pass, I thought he was joking. This is not an uncommon response. "It ill comports with the ideas we have formed of a pass through the Rocky Mountains," wrote emigrant Cecelia Adams in 1852, "being merely a vast, level and sandy plain sloping a little on each side of the summit."

7   Del Bene must have noticed my expression. Enthusiasm is one of his skills, and he went to work. "Look there," he said. "That's the trail. At the peak of the westward movement, wagons rolled through four or five abreast. The wagons tend to push dirt to the side, so you get those marks. The reason you still see them is that we have such a short growing season up here. We have the best wagon ruts in the country."

8   I squinted at where Del Bene was pointing, but, as usual when somebody tries to show me something important, I couldn't see what he was talking about. Still, South Pass began to make itself felt. The very absence of modern man's tampering helped. At South Pass it's just you and the weight of hopes so numerous they dent the earth a century and a half later.

9   For every traveler who disparaged South Pass, there was one who knew the most important landmarks are those you don't recognize at first, who understood that he or she had reached the point of no return in a great journey. Some travelers fired rifles in the air and shouted, "Huzzah!" Others turned introspective. "We have forever taken leave of the waters running toward the home of our childhood and youth," one woman recorded in her diary. Another wrote, "Now we are on the other side of the world."

10   We got back in Del Bene's truck so he could show me a sadder sight. When Charlotte Dansie traveled the trail in 1862, she was 32 and pregnant with her eighth child. She went into labor about a mile east of the pass. The child lived only long enough to be christened. Charlotte died minutes later. Wyoming was hard on the immigrants, Del Bene said. "One out of 10 died. On average there should be a grave every tenth of a mile, but most of them are unmarked. Charlotte's is marked."

11   We were looking at the gravestone when we heard the crunch of tires on gravel. Three people got out of the car: a man in his 20s, his mother, her mother. Descendants of Charlotte Dansie, they had driven up from Salt Lake City to put flowers on the grave. They knew her story, of course, but Del Bene told them things they hadn't heard. One account had her pleading with her husband: "She could stand her suffering no longer and asked him to pray to God that she might be released and return to her maker." The grandmother said it was merciful that Charlotte had died so quickly.

12   That night I went back to a motel in Rock Springs. I knew I had a long drive the next morning to pick up my wife and son, and I wanted to fall asleep. Instead I lay on the ugly brocade bedspread pondering why Charlotte Dansie's descendants had driven

300 miles to honor sorrow so old, and why I felt it imperative that my son see South Pass before, say, Toys "R" Us. Venturing into the past is never about the past but about the present—we look for the courage and purity of intent that we cannot locate in the modern world.

13   It is bright and windy when I drive back to South Pass with my wife and son. Busty cumulus clouds tumble across a blue sky, and their shadows roll across the plain. Joseph is a good traveler: cheerful, unflappable. He squirms while his mother tells him ancestral stories—her ancestors, not mine, as she takes pains to point out. They were from Illinois, advised to go west by a family friend named Abraham Lincoln. It is good story, and possibly true.

14   We follow the dirt road and stop at the pass. I unbuckle Joseph from his car seat and lift him into the windy day. The world smells of sage and clean baby. His arrival was its own continental divide, and all the rivers of my life now run in a new direction. If there was water here, I would baptize us both, sprinkling droplets from the Atlantic slope and then from the Pacific. But all we have are sky and ground. I watch him take those in. "This is South Pass," I tell him. I want him to remember this place. I want it to be something he can carry with him on the rest of his trail.

■ Beauty: When the Other Dancer Is the Self

Alice Walker

A poet, essayist, novelist, editor, and teacher, Alice Walker is best known for her novel *The Color Purple*, which won both the Pulitzer Prize and the American Book Award in 1982. Some of her other works include *The Temple of My Familiar* (1989), *Possessing the Secret of Joy* (1992), *Anything We Love Can Be Saved* (1997), *Absolute Trust in the Goodness of the Earth: New Poems* (2003), and *Now Is the Time to Open Your Heart* (2004). The following selection comes from her 1983 collection of essays, *In Search of Our Mothers' Gardens*.

1   It is a bright summer day in 1947. My father, a fat, funny man with beautiful eyes and a subversive wit, is trying to decide which of his eight children he will take with him to the county fair. My mother, of course, will not go. She is knocked out from getting most of us ready: I hold my neck stiff against the pressure of her knuckles as she hastily completes the braiding and then beribboning of my hair.

2   My father is the driver for the rich old white lady up the road. Her name is Miss Mey. She owns all the land for miles around, as well as the house in which we live. All I remember about her is that she once offered to pay my mother thirty-five cents for cleaning her house, raking up piles of her magnolia leaves, and washing her family's clothes, and that my mother—she of no money, eight children, and a chronic earache—refused it. But I do not think of this in 1947. I am two and a half years old. I want to go everywhere my daddy goes. I am excited at the prospect of riding in a car. Someone has told me fairs are fun. That there is room in the car for only three of us doesn't faze me at all. Whirling happily in my starchy frock, showing off my biscuit-polished patent-leather shoes and lavender socks, tossing my head in a way that makes my ribbons bounce, I stand, hands on hips, before my father. "Take me, Daddy," I say with assurance: "I'm the prettiest!"

3   Later, it does not surprise me to find myself in Miss Mey's shiny black car, sharing the back seat with the other lucky ones. Does not surprise me that I thoroughly enjoy the fair. At home that night I tell the unlucky ones all I can remember about the merry-go-round, the man who eats live chickens, and the teddy bears, until they say: that's enough, baby Alice. Shut up now, and go to sleep.

4   It is Easter Sunday, 1950. I am dressed in a green, flocked, scalloped-hem dress (handmade by my adoring sister, Ruth) that has its own smooth satin petticoat and tiny hot-pink roses tucked into each scallop. My shoes, new T-strap patent leather, again highly biscuit-polished. I am six years old and have learned one of the longest Easter speeches to be heard that day, totally unlike the speech I said when I was two: "Easter lilies / pure and white / blossom in / the morning light." When I rise to give my speech I do so on a great wave of love and pride and expectation. People in the church stop rustling their new crinolines. They seem to hold their breath. I can tell they admire my dress, but it is my spirit, bordering on sassiness (womanishness), they secretly applaud.

5   "That girl's a little *mess*," they whisper to each other, pleased.

6   Naturally I say my speech without stammer or pause, unlike those who stutter, stammer, or, worst of all, forget. This is before the word "beautiful" exists in people's vocabulary, but "Oh, isn't she the *cutest* thing!" frequently floats my way. "And got so much sense!" they gratefully add . . . for which thoughtful addition I thank them to this day.

7   *It was great fun being cute. But then, one day, it ended.*

8   I am eight years old and a tomboy. I have a cowboy hat, cowboy boots, checkered shirt and pants, all red. My playmates are my brothers, two and four years older than I. Their colors are black and green, the only difference in the way we are dressed. On Saturday nights we all go to the picture show, even my mother; Westerns are her favorite kind of movie. Back home, "on the ranch," we pretend we are Tom Mix, Hopalong Cassidy, Lash LaRue (we've even named one of our dogs Lash LaRue); we chase each other for hours rustling cattle, being outlaws, delivering damsels from distress. Then my parents decide to buy my brothers guns. These are not "real" guns. They shoot "BBs," copper pellets my brothers say will kill birds. Because I am a girl, I do not get a gun. Instantly I am relegated to the position of Indian. Now there appears a great distance between us. They shoot and shoot at everything with their new guns. I try to keep up with my bow and arrows.

9   One day while I am standing on top of our makeshift "garage"—pieces of tin nailed across some poles—holding my bow and arrow and looking out toward the fields, I feel an incredible blow in my right eye. I look down just in time to see my brother lower his gun.

10   Both brothers rush to my side. My eye stings, and I cover it with my hand. "If you tell," they say, "we will get a whipping. You don't want that to happen, do you?" I do not. "Here's a piece of wire," says the older brother, picking it up from the roof; "say you stepped on one end of it and the other flew up and hit you." The pain is beginning to start. "Yes," I say. "Yes, I will say that is what happened." If I do not say this is what happened, I know my brothers will find ways to make me wish I had. But now I will say anything that gets me to my mother.

11   Confronted by our parents we stick to the lie agreed upon. They place me on a bench on the porch and I close my left eye while they examine the right. There is a tree growing from underneath the porch that climbs past the railing to the roof. It is the last thing my right eye sees. I watch as its trunk, its branches, and then its leaves are blotted out by the rising blood.

12   I am in shock. First there is intense fever, which my father tries to break using lily leaves bound around my head. Then there are chills: my mother tries to get me to eat soup. Eventually, I do not know how, my parents learn what has happened. A week after the "accident" they take me to see a doctor. "Why did you wait so long to come?" he asks, looking into my eye and shaking his head. "Eyes are sympathetic," he says. "If one is blind, the other will likely become blind too."

13   This comment of the doctor's terrifies me. But it is really how I look that bothers me most. Where the BB pellet struck there is a glob of whitish scar tissue, a hideous cataract, on my eye. Now when I stare at people—a favorite pastime, up to now—they will stare back. Not at the "cute" little girl, but at her scar. For six years I do not stare at anyone, because I do not raise my head.

14   Years later, in the throes of a mid-life crisis, I ask my mother and sister whether I changed after the "accident." "No," they say, puzzled. "What do you mean?"

15   *What do I mean?*

16   I am eight, and, for the first time, doing poorly in school, where I have been something of a whiz since I was four. We have just moved to the place where the "accident" occurred. We do not know any of the people around us because this is a different county. The only time I see the friends I knew is when we go back to our old church. The new school is the former state penitentiary. It is a large stone building, cold and drafty, crammed to overflowing with boisterous, ill-disciplined children. On the third floor there is a huge circular imprint of some partition that has been torn out.

17   "What used to be here?" I ask a sullen girl next to me on our way past it to lunch.

18   "The electric chair," says she.

19   At night I have nightmares about the electric chair, and about all the people reputedly "fried" in it. I am afraid of the school, where all the students seem to be budding criminals.

20   "What's the matter with your eye?" they ask, critically.

21   When I don't answer (I cannot decide whether it was an "accident" or not), they shove me, insist on a fight.

22   My brother, the one who created the story about the wire, comes to my rescue. But then brags so much about "protecting" me, I become sick.

23   After months of torture at the school, my parents decide to send me back to our old community, to my old school. I live with my grandparents and the teacher they board. But there is no room for Phoebe, my cat. By the time my grandparents decide there *is* room, and I ask for my cat, she cannot be found. Miss Yarborough, the boarding teacher, takes me under her wing, and begins to teach me to play the piano. But soon she marries an African—a "prince," she says—and is whisked away to his continent.

24   At my old school there is at least one teacher who loves me. She is the teacher who "knew me before I was born" and bought my first baby clothes. It is she who makes life bearable. It is her presence that finally helps me turn on the one child at the

school who continually calls me "one-eyed bitch." One day I simply grab him by his coat and beat him until I am satisfied. It is my teacher who tells me my mother is ill.

25   My mother is lying in bed in the middle of the day, something I have never seen. She is in too much pain to speak. She has an abscess in her ear. I stand looking down on her, knowing that if she dies, I cannot live. She is being treated with warm oils and hot bricks held against her cheek. Finally a doctor comes. But I must go back to my grandparents' house. The weeks pass but I am hardly aware of it. All I know is that my mother might die, my father is not so jolly, my brothers still have their guns, and I am the one sent away from home.

26   "You did not change," they say.

27   *Did I imagine the anguish of never looking up?*

28   I am twelve. When relatives come to visit I hide in my room. My cousin Brenda, just my age, whose father works in the post office and whose mother is a nurse, comes to find me. "Hello," she says. And then she asks, looking at my recent school picture, which I did not want taken, and on which the "glob," as I think of it, is clearly visible. "You still can't see out of that eye?"

29   "No," I say, and flop back on the bed over my book.

30   That night, as I do almost every night, I abuse my eye. I rant and rave at it, in front of the mirror. I plead with it to clear up before morning. I tell it I hate and despise it. I do not pray for sight. I pray for beauty.

31   "You did not change," they say.

32   I am fourteen and baby-sitting for my brother Bill, who lives in Boston. He is my favorite brother and there is a strong bond between us. Understanding my feelings of shame and ugliness he and his wife take me to a local hospital, where the "glob" is removed by a doctor named O. Henry. There is still a small bluish crater where the scar tissue was, but the ugly white stuff is gone. Almost immediately I become a different person from the girl who does not raise her head. Or so I think. Now that I've raised my head I win the boyfriend of my dreams. Now that I've raised my head I have plenty of friends. Now that I've raised my head classwork comes from my lips as faultlessly as Easter speeches did, and I leave high school as valedictorian, most popular student, and *queen*, hardly believing my luck. Ironically, the girl who was voted most beautiful in our class (and was) was later shot twice through the chest by a male companion, using a "real" gun, while she was pregnant. But that's another story in itself. Or is it?

33   "You did not change," they say.

34   It is now thirty years since the "accident." A beautiful journalist comes to visit and to interview me. She is going to write a cover story for her magazine that focuses on my latest book. "Decide how you want to look on the cover," she says. "Glamorous, or whatever."

35   Never mind "glamorous," it is the "whatever" that I hear. Suddenly all I can think of is whether I will get enough sleep the night before the photography session: if I don't, my eye will be tired and wander, as blind eyes will.

36   At night in bed with my lover I think up reasons why I should not appear on the cover of a magazine. "My meanest critics will say I've sold out," I say. "My family will now realize I write scandalous books."

37   "But what's the real reason you don't want to do this?" he asks.

38   "Because in all probability," I say in a rush, "my eye won't be straight."

39   "It will be straight enough," he says. Then, "Besides, I thought you'd made your peace with that."

40   And I suddenly remember that I have.

41   *I remember:*

42   I am talking to my brother Jimmy, asking if he remembers anything unusual about the day I was shot. He does not know I consider that day the last time my father, with his sweet home remedy of cool lily leaves, chose me, and that I suffered and raged inside because of this. "Well," he says, "all I remember is standing by the side of the highway with Daddy, trying to flag down a car. A white man stopped, but when Daddy said he needed somebody to take his little girl to the doctor, he drove off."

43   *I remember:*

44   I am in the desert for the first time. I fall totally in love with it. I am so overwhelmed by its beauty, I confront for the first time, consciously, the meaning of the doctor's words years ago: "Eyes are sympathetic. If one is blind, the other will likely become blind too." I realize I have dashed about the world madly, looking at that, storing up images against the fading of the light. *But I might have missed seeing the desert!* The shock of that possibility—and gratitude for over twenty-five years of sight—sends me literally to my knees. Poem after poem comes—which is perhaps how poets pray.

> ### On Sight
>
> I am so thankful I have seen
> The Desert
> And the creatures in the desert
> And the desert itself.
>
> The desert has its own moon
> Which I have seen
> With my own eye.
>
> There is no flag on it.
>
> Trees of the desert have arms
> All of which are always up
> That is because the moon is up
> The sun is up
> Also the sky
> The stars
> Clouds
> None with flags.
>
> If there *were* flags, I doubt
> the trees would point.
> Would you?

45   *But mostly, I remember this:*

46   I am twenty-seven, and my baby daughter is almost three. Since her birth, I have worried about her discovery that her mother's eyes are different from other people's. Will she be embarrassed? I think. What will she say? Every day she watches a television program called "Big Blue Marble." It begins with a picture of the earth as it appears

from the moon. It is bluish, a little battered-looking, but full of light, with whitish clouds swirling around it. Every time I see it I weep with love, as if it is a picture of Grandma's house. One day when I am putting Rebecca down for her nap, she suddenly focuses on my eye. Something inside me cringes, gets ready to protect myself. All children are cruel about physical differences, I know from experience, and that they don't always mean to be is another matter. I assume Rebecca will be the same.

47   But no-o-o-o. She studies my face intently as we stand, her inside and me outside her crib. She even holds my face maternally between her dimpled little hands. Then, looking every bit as serious and lawyerlike as her father, she says, as if it may just possibly have slipped my attention: "Mommy, there's a *world* in your eye." (As in, "Don't be alarmed, or do anything crazy.") And then, gently, but with great interest: "Mommy, where did you *get* that world in your eye?"

48   For the most part, the pain left then. (So what, if my brothers grew up to buy even more powerful pellet guns for their sons and to carry real guns themselves. So what, if a young "Morehouse man" once nearly fell off the steps of Trevos Arnett Library because he thought my eyes were blue.) Crying and laughing I ran to the bathroom, while Rebecca mumbled and sang herself off to sleep. Yes indeed, I realized, looking into the mirror. There *was* a world in my eye. And I saw that it was possible to love it: that in fact, for all it had taught me of shame and anger and inner vision, I *did* love it. Even to see it drifting out of orbit in boredom, or rolling up out of fatigue, not to mention floating back at attention in excitement (bearing witness, a friend has called it), deeply suitable to my personality, and even characteristic of me.

49   That night I dream I am dancing to Stevie Wonder's song "Always" (the name of the song is really "As," but I hear it as "Always"). As I dance, whirling and joyous, happier than I've ever been in my life, another bright-faced dancer joins me. We dance and kiss each other and hold each other through the night. The other dancer has obviously come through all right, as I have done. She is beautiful, whole and free. And she is also me.

Chapter 32

Literature

■ Child of the Americas

Aurora Levins Morales

Aurora Levins Morales is a contemporary poet and storyteller who was born in New York but raised in Puerto Rico. Of Jewish and Latina heritage, she often writes about cultural identity. In addition to teaching at the University of California, Berkeley, and the University of Minnesota, she has published *Getting Home Alive* (1986), *Medicine Stories* (1998), and *Remedios: Stories of Earth and Iron from the History of Puertorriquenas* (2001). This poem was written in 1986.

> I am a child of the Americas,
> a light-skinned mestiza of the Caribbean,
> a child of many diaspora, born into this
>   continent at a crossroads.
>
> 5   I am a U.S. Puerto Rican Jew,
> a product of the ghettos of New York I have
>   never known.
> An immigrant and the daughter
>   and granddaughter of immigrants.
> 10   I speak English with passion: it's the tongue
>   of my consciousness,
> a flashing knife blade of crystal, my tool,
>   my craft.

I am Caribeña, island grown. Spanish is in my flesh,
15   ripples from my tongue, lodges in my hips:
the language of garlic and mangoes,
the singing in my poetry, the flying gestures
   of my hands.
I am of Latinoamerica, rooted in the history
20   of my continent:
I speak from that body.

I am not african. Africa is in me, but I cannot return.
I am not taina. Taino* is in me, but there is no
   way back.
25   I am not european. Europe lives in me, but I
   have no home there.

I am new. History made me. My first language
   was spanglish.
I was born at the crossroads
30   and I am whole.

■ Ozymandias

Percy Bysshe Shelley

Percy Bysshe Shelley is considered one of the finest English poets and a major figure in the nineteenth-century Romantic movement. Born in 1792, Shelley was educated at Eton but was expelled from Oxford. He married Mary Wollstonecraft (later famous for her novel *Frankenstein*) and traveled in Europe, where he produced some of his best work, including "To a Skylark," "The Cloud," and "Ode to the West Wind." In 1822, at age 29, Shelley drowned in Italy. The sonnet presented here was written in 1818.

I met a traveler from an antique land
Who said: Two vast and trunkless legs of stone
Stand in the desert . . . Near them, on the sand,
Half sunk, a shattered visage lies, whose frown,
5   And wrinkled lip, and sneer of cold command,
Tell that its sculptor well those passions read
Which yet survive, stamped on these lifeless things,
The hand that mocked them, and the heart that fed:
And on the pedestal these words appear:
10   "My name is Ozymandias, king of kings:
Look on my works, ye Mighty, and despair!"
Nothing beside remains. Round the decay
Of that colossal wreck, boundless and bare
The lone and level sands stretch far away.

---

*Refers to a Native American people indigenous to Puerto Rico and other islands in the Caribbean; after 1492, the Taino nation saw its numbers greatly reduced in clashes with European explorers.

■ A Mystery of Heroism

Stephen Crane

Stephen Crane was a late-nineteenth-century American short story writer, novelist, poet, and journalist. His best-known novels are *Maggie, A Girl of the Streets* (1893), originally rejected by publishers because of Crane's sympathetic portrayal of the main character, and *The Red Badge of Courage* (1895), a Civil War story told so vividly that many veterans claimed participation in its fictional events. Some of Crane's stories include "The Open Boat," "The Blue Hotel," and "The Bride Comes to Yellow Sky." This story was first published in 1895.

1   The dark uniforms of the men were so coated with dust from the incessant wrestling of the two armies that the regiment almost seemed a part of the clay bank which shielded them from the shells. On the top of the hill a battery was arguing in tremendous roars with some other guns, and to the eye of the infantry the artillerymen, the guns, the caissons, the horses, were distinctly outlined upon the blue sky. When a piece was fired, a red streak as round as a log flashed low in the heavens, like a monstrous bolt of lightning. The men of the battery wore white duck trousers, which somehow emphasized their legs; and when they ran and crowded in little groups at the bidding of the shouting officers, it was more impressive than usual to the infantry.

2   Fred Collins, of A Company, was saying: "Thunder! I wisht I had a drink. Ain't there any water round here?" Then somebody yelled: "There goes th' bugler!"

3   As the eyes of half the regiment swept in one machinelike movement, there was an instant's picture of a horse in a great convulsive leap of a death wound and a rider leaning back with a crooked arm and spread fingers before his face. On the ground was the crimson terror of an exploding shell, with fibres of flame that seemed like lances. A glittering bugle swung clear of the rider's back as fell headlong the horse and the man. In the air was an odor as from a conflagration.

4   Sometimes they of the infantry looked down at a fair little meadow which spread at their feet. Its long green grass was rippling gently in a breeze. Beyond it was the grey form of a house half torn to pieces by shells and by the busy axes of soldiers who had pursued firewood. The line of an old fence was now dimly marked by long weeds and by an occasional post. A shell had blown the well-house to fragments. Little lines of grey smoke ribboning upward from some embers indicated the place where had stood the barn.

5   From beyond a curtain of green woods there came the sound of some stupendous scuffle, as if two animals of the size of islands were fighting. At a distance there were occasional appearances of swift-moving men, horses, batteries, flags, and with the crashing of infantry volleys were heard, often, wild and frenzied cheers. In the midst of it all Smith and Ferguson, two privates of A Company, were engaged in a heated discussion which involved the greatest questions of the national existence.

6   The battery on the hill presently engaged in a frightful duel. The white legs of the gunners scampered this way and that way, and the officers redoubled their shouts. The guns, with their demeanors of stolidity and courage, were typical of something infinitely self-possessed in this clamor of death that swirled around the hill.

7   One of a "swing" team was suddenly smitten quivering to the ground, and his maddened brethren dragged his torn body in their struggle to escape from this turmoil and danger. A young soldier astride one of the leaders swore and fumed in his saddle

and furiously jerked at the bridle. An officer screamed out an order so violently that his voice broke and ended the sentence in a falsetto shriek.

8   The leading company of the infantry regiment was somewhat exposed, and the colonel ordered it moved more fully under the shelter of the hill. There was the clank of steel against steel.

9   A lieutenant of the battery rode down and passed them, holding his right arm carefully in his left hand. And it was as if this arm was not at all a part of him, but belonged to another man. His sober and reflective charger went slowly. The officer's face was grimy and perspiring, and his uniform was tousled as if he had been in direct grapple with an enemy. He smiled grimly when the men stared at him. He turned his horse toward the meadow.

10   Collins, of A Company, said: "I wisht I had a drink. I bet there's water in that there ol' well yonder!"

11   "Yes; but how you goin' to git it?"

12   For the little meadow which intervened was now suffering a terrible onslaught of shells. Its green and beautiful calm had vanished utterly. Brown earth was being flung in monstrous handfuls. And there was a massacre of the young blades of grass. They were being torn, burned, obliterated. Some curious fortune of the battle had made this gentle little meadow the object of the red hate of the shells, and each one as it exploded seemed like an imprecation in the face of a maiden.

13   The wounded officer who was riding across this expanse said to himself: "Why, they couldn't shoot any harder if the whole army was massed here!"

14   A shell struck the gray ruins of the house, and as, after the roar, the shattered wall fell in fragments, there was a noise which resembled the flapping of shutters during a wild gale of winter. Indeed, the infantry paused in the shelter of the bank appeared as men standing upon a shore contemplating a madness of the sea. The angel of calamity had under its glance the battery upon the hill. Fewer white-legged men labored about the guns. A shell had smitten one of the pieces, and after the flare, the smoke, the dust, the wrath of this blow were gone, it was possible to see white legs stretched horizontally upon the ground. And at that interval to the rear where it is the business of battery horses to stand with their noses to the fight, awaiting the command to drag their guns out of the destruction, or into it, or wheresoever these incomprehensible humans demanded with whip and spur—in this line of passive and dumb spectators, whose fluttering hearts yet would not let them forget the iron laws of man's control of them—in this rank of brute-soldiers there had been relentless and hideous carnage. From the ruck of bleeding and prostrate horses, the men of the infantry could see one animal raising its stricken body with its forelegs and turning its nose with mystic and profound eloquence toward the sky.

15   Some comrades joked Collins about his thirst. "Well, if yeh want a drink so bad, why don't yeh go git it?"

16   "Well, I will in a minnet, if yeh don't shut up!"

17   A lieutenant of artillery floundered his horse straight down the hill with as little concern as if it were level ground. As he galloped past the colonel of the infantry, he threw up his hand in swift salute. "We've got to get out of that," he roared angrily. He was a black-bearded officer, and his eyes, which resembled beads, sparkled like those of an insane man. His jumping horse sped along the column of infantry.

18   The fat major, standing carelessly with his sword held horizontally behind him and with his legs far apart, looked after the receding horseman and laughed. "He wants to get back with orders pretty quick, or there'll be no batt'ry left," he observed.

19   The wise young captain of the second company hazarded to the lieutenant-colonel that the enemy's infantry would probably soon attack the hill, and the lieutenant-colonel snubbed him.

20   A private in one of the rear companies looked out over the meadow, and then turned to a companion and said, "Look there, Jim!" It was the wounded officer from the battery, who some time before had started to ride across the meadow, supporting his right arm carefully with this left hand. This man had encountered a shell, apparently, at a time when no one perceived him, and he could now be seen lying face downward with a stirruped foot stretched across the body of his dead horse. A leg of the charger extended slantingly upward, precisely as stiff as a stake. Around this motionless pair the shells still howled.

21   There was a quarrel in A Company. Collins was shaking his fist in the faces of some laughing comrades. "Dern yeh! I ain't afraid t' go. If yeh say much, I will go!"

22   "Of course, yeh will! You'll run through that there medder, won't yeh?"

23   Collins said, in a terrible voice: "You see now!" At this ominous threat his comrades broke into renewed jeers.

24   Collins gave them a dark scowl, and went to find his captain. The latter was conversing with the colonel of the regiment.

25   "Captain," said Collins, saluting and standing at attention—in those days all trousers bagged at the knees—"Captain, I want t' get permission to go git some water from that there well over yonder!"

26   The colonel and the captain swung about simultaneously and stared across the meadow. The captain laughed. "You must be pretty thirsty, Collins?"

27   "Yes, sir, I am."

28   "Well—ah," said the captain. After a moment, he asked, "Can't you wait?"

29   "No, sir."

30   The colonel was watching Collins' face. "Look here, my lad," he said, in a pious sort of voice—"Look here, my lad,"—Collins was not a lad—"don't you think that's taking pretty big risks for a little drink of water?"

31   "I dunno," said Collins uncomfortably. Some of the resentment toward his companions, which perhaps had forced him into this affair, was beginning to fade. "I dunno wether 'tis."

32   The colonel and the captain contemplated him for a time.

33   "Well," said the captain finally.

34   "Well," said the colonel, "if you want to go, why, go." Collins saluted. "Much obliged t' yeh."

35   As he moved away the colonel called after him. "Take some of the other boys' canteens with you, an' hurry back, now."

36   "Yes, sir, I will."

37   The colonel and the captain looked at each other then, for it had suddenly occurred that they could not for the life of them tell whether Collins wanted to go or whether he did not.

38   They turned to regard Collins, and as they perceived him surrounded by gesticulating comrades, the colonel said: "Well, by thunder! I guess he's going."

39   Collins appeared as a man dreaming. In the midst of the questions, the advice, the warnings, all the excited talk of his company mates, he maintained a curious silence.

40   They were very busy in preparing him for his ordeal. When they inspected him carefully, it was somewhat like the examination that grooms give a horse before a race; and they were amazed, staggered, by the whole affair. Their astonishment found vent in strange repetitions.

41   "Are yeh sure a-goin'?" they demanded again and again.

42   "Certainly I am," cried Collins at last, furiously.

43   He strode sullenly away from them. He was swinging five or six canteens by their cords. It seemed that his cap would not remain firmly on his head, and often he reached and pulled it down over his brow.

44   There was a general movement in the compact column. The long animal-like thing moved slightly. Its four hundred eyes were turned upon the figure of Collins.

45   "Well, sir, if that ain't th' derndest thing! I never thought Fred Collins had the blood in him for that kind of business."

46   "What's he goin' to do, anyhow?"

47   "He's goin' to that well there after water."

48   "We ain't dyin' of thirst, are we? That's foolishness."

49   "Well, somebody put him up to it, an' he's doin' it."

50   "Say, he must be a desperate cuss."

51   When Collins faced the meadow and walked away from the regiment, he was vaguely conscious that a chasm, the deep valley of all prides, was suddenly between him and his comrades. It was provisional, but the provision was that he return as a victor. He had blindly been led by quaint emotions, and laid himself under an obligation to walk squarely up to the face of death.

52   But he was not sure that he wished to make a retraction, even if he could do so without shame. As a matter of truth, he was sure of very little. He was mainly surprised.

53   It seemed to him supernaturally strange that he had allowed his mind to manoeuvre his body into such a situation. He understood that it might be called dramatically great.

54   However, he had no full appreciation of anything, excepting that he was actually conscious of being dazed. He could feel his dulled mind groping after the form and color of this incident. He wondered why he did not feel some keen agony of fear cutting his sense like a knife. He wondered at this, because human expression had said loudly for centuries that men should feel afraid of certain things, and that all men who did not feel this fear were phenomena—heroes.

55   He was, then, a hero. He suffered that disappointment which we would all have if we discovered that we were ourselves capable of those deeds which we most admire in history and legend. This, then, was a hero. After all, heroes were not much.

56   No, it could not be true. He was not a hero. Heroes had no shames in their lives, and, as for him, he remembered borrowing fifteen dollars from a friend and promising to pay it back the next day, and then avoiding that friend for ten months. When, at home, his mother had aroused him for the early labor of his life on the farm, it had often been his fashion to be irritable, childish, diabolical; and his mother had died since he had come to the war.

57   He saw that, in this matter of the well, the canteens, the shells, he was an intruder in the land of fine deeds.

58   He was now about thirty paces from his comrades. The regiment had just turned its many faces toward him.

59   From the forest of terrific noises there suddenly emerged a little uneven line of men. They fired fiercely and rapidly at distant foliage on which appeared little puffs of white smoke. The spatter of skirmish firing was added to the thunder of the guns on the hill. The little line of men ran forward. A color-sergeant fell flat with his flag as if he had slipped on ice. There was hoarse cheering from this distant field.

60   Collins suddenly felt that two demon fingers were pressed into his ears. He could see nothing but flying arrows, flaming red. He lurched from the shock of this explosion, but he made a mad rush for the house, which he viewed as a man submerged to the neck in a boiling surf might view the shore. In the air little pieces of shell howled, and the earthquake explosions drove him insane with the menace of their roar. As he ran the canteens knocked together with a rhythmical tinkling.

61   As he neared the house, each detail of the scene became vivid to him. He was aware of some bricks of the vanished chimney lying on the sod. There was a door which hung by one hinge.

62   Rifle bullets called forth by the insistent skirmishers came from the far-off bank of foliage. They mingled with the shells and the pieces of shells until the air was torn in all directions by hootings, yells, howls. The sky was full of fiends who directed all their wild rage at his head.

63   When he came to the well, he flung himself face downward and peered into its darkness. There were furtive silver glintings some feet from the surface. He grabbled one of the canteens and, unfastening its cap, swung it down by the cord. The water flowed slowly in with an indolent gurgle.

64   And now, as he lay with his face turned away, he was suddenly smitten with the terror. It came upon his heart like the grasp of claws. All the power faded from his muscles. For an instant he was no more than a dead man.

65   The canteen filled with a maddening slowness, in the manner of all bottles. Presently he recovered his strength and addressed a screaming oath to it. He leaned over until it seemed as if he intended to try to push water into it with his hands. His eyes as he gazed down into the well shone like two pieces of metal, and in their expression was a great appeal and a great curse. The stupid water derided him.

66   There was the blaring thunder of a shell. Crimson light shone through the swift-boiling smoke, and made a pink reflection on part of the wall of the well. Collins jerked out his arm and canteen with the same motion that a man would use in withdrawing his head from a furnace.

67   He scrambled erect and glared and hesitated. On the ground near him lay the old well bucket, with a length of rusty chain. He lowered it swiftly into the well. The bucket struck the water and then, turning lazily over, sank. When, with hand reaching tremblingly over hand, he hauled it out, it knocked often against the walls of the well and spilled some of its contents.

68   In running with a filled bucket, a man can adopt but one kind of gait. So, through this terrible field over which screamed practical angels of death, Collins ran in the manner of a farmer chased out of a dairy by a bull.

69   His face went staring white with anticipating—anticipation of a blow that would whirl him around and down. He would fall as he had seen other men fall, the life

knocked out of them so suddenly that their knees were no more quick to touch the ground than their heads. He saw the long blue line of the regiment, but his comrades were standing looking at him from the edge of an impossible star. He was aware of some deep wheelruts and hoofprints in the sod beneath his feet.

70   The artillery officer who had fallen in this meadow had been making groans in the teeth of the tempest of sound. These futile cries, wrenched from him by his agony, were heard only by shells, bullets. When wild-eyed Collins came running, this officer raised himself. His face contorted and blanched from pain, he was about to utter some great beseeching cry. But suddenly his face straightened, and he called: "Say, young man, give me a drink of water, will you?"

71   Collins had no room amid his emotions for surprise. He was mad from the threats of destruction.

72   "I can't!" he screamed, and in his reply was a full description of his quaking apprehension. His cap was gone and his hair was riotous. His clothes made it appear that he had been dragged over the ground by the heels. He ran on.

73   The officer's head sank down, and one elbow crooked. His foot in its brass-bound stirrup still stretched over the body of his horse, and the other leg was under the steed.

74   But Collins turned. He came dashing back. His face had now turned grey, and in his eyes was all terror. "Here it is! here it is!"

75   The officer was as a man gone in drink. His arm bent like a twig. His head drooped as if his neck were of willow. He was sinking to the ground, to lie face downward.

76   Collins grabbed him by the shoulder. "Here it is. Here's your drink. Turn over. Turn over, man, for God's sake!"

77   With Collins hauling at his shoulder, the officer twisted his body and fell with his face turned toward that region where lived the unspeakable noises of the swirling missiles. There was the faintest shadow of a smile on his lips as he looked at Collins. He gave a sigh, a little primitive breath like that from a child.

78   Collins tried to hold the bucket steadily, but his shaking hands caused the water to splash all over the face of the dying man. Then he jerked it away and ran on.

79   The regiment gave him a welcoming roar. The grimed faces were wrinkled in laughter.

80   His captain waved the bucket away. "Give it to the men!"

81   The two genial, skylarking young lieutenants were the first to gain possession of it. They played over it in their fashion.

82   When one tried to drink, the other teasingly knocked his elbow. "Don't Billie! You'll make me spill it," said the one. The other laughed.

83   Suddenly there was an oath, the thud of wood on the ground, and a swift murmur of astonishment among the ranks. The two lieutenants glared at each other. The bucket lay on the ground empty.

Chapter **33**

Writing and Language

■ Life at Close Range

Gretel Ehrlich

Gretel Ehrlich is the author of three volumes of poetry, two collections of essays, two collections of short stories, two memoirs, a novel, a novella for young adults, and many articles in publications such as *The Atlantic Monthly* and *Harper's*. Much of her writing has been influenced by her time as a Wyoming rancher and by her love of nature and travel. Some of her titles include *The Solace of Open Spaces* (1986), *Writing Down the River* (1998), and *This Cold Heaven* (2002). This essay was first published in 1990.

1   It's June and soon we'll be moving cattle to the high mountain pastures. Already the first slanting rains have come—black arrows that come back up as green grass. At this time of year it could still snow, but ducks and shorebirds stop over on our little lake to rest before going on to the Arctic or Canada. As soon as the mountain meltwater comes down, I go to work irrigating 125 acres of hay meadows and on the way, because I always carry binoculars, I keep track of what's on the pond: godwits, terns, mallards, teal, sora rails, snipes, and phalaropes. Coyotes come to drink early in the morning, vying with bald and golden eagles for a prairie dog on the way. It's not only what I do see as I set irrigation water, but what I don't see in the way of animals and birds that counts—those hidden ones like bears, mountain lions, badgers, ermine, and snakes who I know are here too, but I can't always see.

2   A writer's imagination must be like that: filled not just with literal truths, but with the unseen, the unknown whose shy presence is felt. What's underneath the lake water, the sod-bound fields, the lid of my skull, I wonder?

3   Yesterday lightning ignited a ridge above our ranch and, as quickly, a boisterous rain squall put it out. Then the hail came, dancing, blanching the land. The isolated ranch my husband and I inhabit often seems otherworldly: mist spills on us sweeping everything from sight, then on rising, the green-breasted earth steams. Last night the moon was so bright a moth inside the house beat against the window, trying to get out, and in the morning, at almost the same place, I found a blue luna moth, big as my hand, trying to get in. A writer's life must be like those moths, beating down obstructions to get at truths.

4   Sometimes when strangers ask what I do, I say I write, but around here, they think I said "ride." I do both of course, because most ranchwork is done on horseback. Writing is thought of as being cerebral work, while ranching, which takes up a good deal of my time, is mostly physical. But I couldn't write if I didn't ride and I'd find fourteen-hour days in the saddle quite tedious if I didn't have writing to come home to. In fact, I often write—notepad balanced on saddlehorn—gathering cattle, and when I'm in my writing room, a separate building on a hill with a view of the sorting corrals, I often get up mid-sentence to fix a panel of fence or change an irrigation dam, or put a stray horse away. This whole business of dividing body and mind is ludicrous. After all, the breath that starts the song of a poem, or the symphony of a novel—the same breath that lifts me into the saddle—starts in the body, and at the same time, enlivens the mind.

5   Our ranch is thirty miles from the nearest grocery store, eighty miles from a movie theater, a hundred and fifty miles from an airport, yet I feel as if I were at the center of things, "in media res." Our ranch, and the entire ecosystem in which it lies, is my laboratory. Wherever I am on it, whatever I'm doing, I'm always thinking, remembering, feeling, observing, absorbing, and listening—to wasps eating ants, to the eddies of wind above oceans of pines, to the pond ducks fighting at breeding time, to the whir of nighthawks driving down. But it's a curious laboratory, one in which I don't do experiments on nature, but nature experiments with me. I'm a land steward, but it's the land that tells me what's right and what's wrong, and I have to learn to listen.

6   If you live in a place—any place, city or country—long enough and deeply enough you can learn anything, the dynamics and interconnections that exist in every community, be it plant, human, or animal—you can learn what a writer needs to know. Here, as anywhere, the search for ways of knowing is a great discipline, an ultimate freedom in which you will find the entire world opens to you. When I began writing full time, I asked a well-known essayist his advice and he said, "Write from the heart," which was another way of saying, you must see through to the heart of things.

7   These days I do that by getting down on my hands and knees—literally and figuratively—and inspecting life at close range. From monitoring grass plants, soil quality, insects, and animals, as well as the health of entire watersheds, I've learned to scrutinize and savor the constructs of language, the points at which ideas, ethics, and sensations meet or collide, the way the tone of a piece of writing—like muscle tone, or the ecotone of a landscape—moves smoothly or drops out from under my pen. From diving into the midst of other lives, in nature and in the human realm, working as nurturer, student,

midwife, I've stumbled on the liberating sense of equality that exists everywhere and have been able to dismiss with great conviction the idiotic idea of human dominance over nature, and know it to be physically and intellectually absurd. With equality comes a sense of the holiness—sacred or secular—of every animate and inanimate thing.

8   Writing, like being a good hand with a horse, requires wakefulness and a willingness to surrender. I try to burn away preconception and let what is actually here come in. Any act of writing is a meditation on existence. It implies stopping, breathing in and out. "Do not write more clearly than you can think," the physicist Niels Bohr said. The truth is hard; no false décor allowed.

9   Riding out across a six-thousand-acre mountain pasture becomes an ambulation of mind. The body of the horse carries me into imagery, and memory, and, like the wind, I try to hone what has registered in me as a precision, making every word count, every word a tiny truth in itself. Roping a calf, I have to think ahead as the coil spins out, but at the same time, stay agile, flexible, alive in the present so that I can take my dallies with speed and care and not lose a thumb. Both jobs—writing and cowboying—take up the whole mind and heart. Weather pushes me the way I push at internal barriers and, after a decade or so, both jobs work together like mortar and pestle, the one pulverizing the other into clarity.

10   There is no knowing what makes a writer, what ingredients have contributed. Was it the stories my very urban (and urbane) grandfather told me over and over? Was it the frustration of being almost silent during my young life which fed the need to communicate, albeit on my own terms? Was it my inordinate love of animals and books—the one love growing alongside the other—that led me to this isolated, animal-rich place where the play of the mind and heart could take a far reach? It seems that any list of ingredients will do except deadness, frivolity, and refusal to enter silence and loneliness and listen to what is inside. A writer makes a pact with loneliness. It is her, or his, beach on which waves of desire, wild mind, speculation break. In my work, in my life, I am always moving toward and away from aloneness. To write is to refuse to cover up the rawness of being alive, of facing death.

11   Early in my life, maybe from reading D. H. Lawrence, I dedicated myself to "living fully," which included reading, keeping my standards high. To write and not read the best that has been written (and only the best; there's not time for anything less) is foolish. It's like a gardener putting in seeds where there is no ground. It is in the context of our ordinary, everyday lives that seeds germinate. In the larger sense, place ultimately becomes a mirror of mind.

12   In his notebooks, Henry James wrote: "The law of the artist is the terrible law of fructification, of fertilization, the law of acceptance of all experience, of all suffering, of all life, all suggestion and sensation and illumination." Looking out the windows of my writing room at this moment, I see an elk carrying mist on his shoulders, drifting out of a canyon; a duck diving for food; a meadowlark alighting on a fence post, tilting his head back and singing after a June rain.

13   A good hand on a ranch requires vigilance, acute powers of observation, readiness to anticipate what might go wrong or what's coming next, a taste for recklessness, intuitive skills, patience, and what cowboys look for when they buy a horse: a lot of heart. Aspiring to those qualities as a rancher, I can only hope my writing will benefit as well.

Notes on Punctuation

Lewis Thomas

A graduate of Harvard Medical School, Lewis Thomas practiced medicine and taught at several universities. His columns written for *The New England Journal of Medicine* were collected into *The Lives of a Cell* (1974), which won a National Book Award. This essay, part of his second collection, was published in *The Medusa and the Snail* (1979). His last works include *Late Night Thoughts on Listening to Mahler's Ninth Symphony* (1983) and *Et Cetera, Et Cetera: Notes of a Word-Watcher* (1990).

1   There are no precise rules about punctuation (Fowler* lays out some general advice (as best he can under the complex circumstances of English prose (he points out, for example, that we possess only four stops (the comma, the semicolon, the colon and the period (the question mark and exclamation point are not, strictly speaking, stops; they are indicators of tone (oddly enough, the Greeks employed the semicolon for their question mark (it produces a strange sensation to read a Greek sentence which is a straightforward question: Why weepest thou; (instead of Why weepest thou? (and, of course, there are parentheses (which are surely a kind of punctuation making this whole much more complicated by having to count up the left-handed parentheses in order to be sure of closing with the right number (but if the parentheses were left out, with nothing to work with but the stops, we would have considerably more flexibility in the deploying of layers of meaning than if we tried to separate all the clauses by physical barriers (and in the latter case, while we might have more precision and exactitude for our meaning, we would lose the essential flavor of language, which is its wonderful ambiguity)))))))))))).

2   The commas are the most useful and usable of all the stops. It is highly important to put them in place as you go along. If you try to come back after doing a paragraph and stick them in the various spots that tempt you you will discover that they tend to swarm like minnows into all sorts of crevices whose existence you hadn't realized and before you know it the whole long sentence becomes immobilized and lashed up squirming in commas. Better to use them sparingly, and with affection, precisely when the need for each one arises, nicely, by itself.

3   I have grown fond of semicolons in recent years. The semicolon tells you that there is still some question about the preceding full sentence; something needs to be added; it reminds you sometimes of the Greek usage. It is almost always a greater pleasure to come across a semicolon than a period. The period tells you that that is that; if you didn't get all the meaning you wanted or expected, anyway you got all the writer intended to parcel out and now you have to move along. But with a semicolon there you get a pleasant little feeling of expectancy; there is more to come; read on; it will get clearer.

4   Colons are a lot less attractive, for several reasons: firstly, they give you the feeling of being rather ordered around, or at least having your nose pointed in a direction you might not be inclined to take if left to yourself, and, secondly, you suspect you're in for one of those sentences that will be labeling the points to be made: firstly, secondly, and so forth, with the implication that you haven't sense enough to keep track of a sequence of notions without having them numbered. Also, many writers use this system loosely

---

* H. W. Fowler is the author of widely used reference books on language.

and incompletely, starting out with number one and number two as though counting off on their fingers but then going on and on without the succession of labels you've been led to expect, leaving you floundering about searching for the ninethly or seventeenthly that ought to be there but isn't.

5   Exclamation points are the most irritating of all. Look! they say, look at what I just said! How amazing is my thought! It is like being forced to watch someone else's small child jumping up and down crazily in the center of the living room shouting to attract attention. If a sentence really has something of importance to say, something quite remarkable, it doesn't need a mark to point it out. And if it is really, after all, a banal sentence needing more zing, the exclamation point simply emphasizes its banality!

6   Quotation marks should be used honestly and sparingly, when there is a genuine quotation at hand, and it is necessary to be very rigorous about the words enclosed by the marks. If something is to be quoted, the *exact* words must be used. If part of it must be left out because of space limitations, it is good manners to insert three dots to indicate the omission, but it is unethical to do this if it means connecting two thoughts which the original author did not intend to have tied together. Above all, quotation marks should not be used for ideas that you'd like to disown, things in the air so to speak. Nor should they be put in place around clichés; if you want to use a cliché you must take full responsibility for it yourself and not try to job it off on anon., or on society. The most objectionable misuse of quotation marks, but one which illustrates the dangers of misuse in ordinary prose, is seen in advertising, especially in advertisements for small restaurants, for example "just around the corner," or "a good place to eat." No single, identifiable, citable person ever really said for the record, "just around the corner," much less "a good place to eat," least likely of all for restaurants of the type that use this type of prose.

7   The dash is a handy device, informal and essentially playful, telling you that you're about to take off on a different tack but still in some way connected with the present course—only you have to remember that the dash is there, and either put a second dash at the end of the notion to let the reader know that he's back on course, or else end the sentence, as here, with a period.

8   The greatest danger in punctuation is for poetry. Here it is necessary to be as economical and parsimonious with commas and periods as with the words themselves, and any marks that seem to carry their own subtle meanings, like dashes and little rows of periods, even semicolons and question marks, should be left out altogether rather than inserted to clog up the thing with ambiguity. A single exclamation point in a poem, no matter what else the poem has to say, is enough to destroy the whole work.

9   The things I like best in T. S. Eliot's poetry, especially in the *Four Quartets,* are the semicolons. You cannot hear them, but they are there, laying out the connections between the images and the ideas. Sometimes you get a glimpse of a semicolon coming, a few lines farther on, and it is like climbing a steep path through woods and seeing a wooden bench just at a bend in the road ahead, a place where you can expect to sit for a moment, catching your breath.

10   Commas can't do this sort of thing; they can only tell you how the different parts of a complicated thought are to be fitted together, but you can't sit, not even take a breath, just because of a comma,

■ Mother Tongue

Amy Tan

Amy Tan is a native of California, born to parents who had emigrated from China only a few years before. After receiving an M.A. in linguistics, Tan worked as a business writer but ultimately turned to fiction; her first novel, *The Joy Luck Club* (1987), became both a best-seller and the winner of the National Book Award. Other popular works include *The Kitchen God's Wife* (1991), *The Hundred Secret Senses* (1995), *The Bonesetter's Daughter* (2000), and *The Opposite of Fate* (2003), a collection of speeches and reflections. "Mother Tongue" was a speech that was first printed in *The Threepenny Review* in 1990.

1   I am not a scholar of English or literature. I cannot give you much more than personal opinions of the English language and its variations in this country or others.

2   I am a writer. And by that definition, I am someone who has always loved language. I am fascinated by language in daily life. I spend a great deal of my time thinking about the power of language—the way it can evoke an emotion, a visual image, a complex idea, or a simple truth. Language is the tool of my trade. And I use them all—all the Englishes I grew up with.

3   Recently, I was made keenly aware of the different Englishes I do use. I was giving a talk to a large group of people, the same talk I had already given to half a dozen other groups. The nature of the talk was about my writing, my life, and my book, *The Joy Luck Club*. The talk was going along well enough, until I remembered one major difference that made the whole talk sound wrong. My mother was in the room. And it was perhaps the first time she had heard me give a lengthy speech, using the kind of English I have never used with her. I was saying things like, "The intersection of memory upon imagination" and "There is an aspect of my fiction that relates to thus-and-thus"—a speech filled with carefully wrought grammatical phrases, burdened, it suddenly seemed to me, with nominalized forms, past perfect tenses, conditional phrases, all the forms of standard English that I had learned in school and through books, the forms of English I did not use at home with my mother.

4   Just last week, I was walking down the street with my mother, and I again found myself conscious of the English I was using, and the English I do use with her. We were talking about the price of new and used furniture and I heard myself saying this: "Not waste money that way." My husband was with us as well, and he didn't notice any switch in my English. And then I realized why. It's because over the twenty years we've been together I've often used the same kind of English with him, and sometimes he even uses it with me. It has become our language of intimacy, a different sort of English that relates to family talk, the language I grew up with.

5   So you'll have some idea of what this family talk I heard sounds like, I'll quote what my mother said during a recent conversation which I videotaped and then transcribed. During this conversation, my mother was talking about a political gangster in Shanghai who had the same last name as her family's, Du, and how the gangster in his early years wanted to be adopted by her family, which was rich by comparison. Later, the gangster became more powerful, far richer than my mother's family, and one day showed up at my mother's wedding to pay his respects. Here's what she said in part:

6   "Du Yusong having business like fruit stand. Like off the street kind. He is Du like Du Zong—but not Tsung-ming Island people. The local people call putong, the river

east side, he belong to that side local people. The man want to ask Du Zong father take him in like become own family. Du Zong father wasn't look down on him, but didn't take seriously, until the man big like become a mafia. Now important person, very hard to inviting him. Chinese way, came only to show respect, don't stay for dinner. Respect for making big celebration, he shows up. Mean gives lots of respect. Chinese custom. Chinese social life that way. If too important won't have to stay too long. He come to my wedding. I didn't see, I heard it. I gone to boy's side, they have YMCA dinner. Chinese age I was nineteen."

7   You should know that my mother's expressive command of English belies how much she actually understands. She reads the Forbes report, listens to *Wall Street Week,* converses daily with her stockbroker, reads all of Shirley MacLaine's books with ease—all kinds of things I can't begin to understand. Yet some of my friends tell me they understand 50 percent of what my mother says. Some say they understand 80 to 90 percent. Some say they understand none of it, as if she were speaking pure Chinese. But to me, my mother's English is perfectly clear, perfectly natural. It's my mother tongue. Her language, as I hear it, vivid, direct, full of observation and imagery. That was the language that helped shape the way I saw things, expressed things, made sense of the world.

8   Lately, I've been giving more thought to the kind of English my mother speaks. Like others, I have described it to people as "broken" or "fractured" English. But I wince when I say that. It has always bothered me that I can think of no way to describe it other than "broken," as if it were damaged and needed to be fixed, as if it lacked a certain wholeness and soundness. I've heard other terms used, "limited English," for example. But they seem just as bad, as if everything is limited, including people's perceptions of the limited English speaker.

9   I know this for a fact, because when I was growing up, my mother's "limited" English limited *my* perception of her. I was ashamed of her English. I believed that her English reflected the quality of what she had to say. That is, because she expressed them imperfectly her thoughts were imperfect. And I had plenty of empirical evidence to support me: the fact that people in department stores, at banks, and at restaurants did not take her seriously, did not give her good service, pretended not to understand her, or even acted as if they did not hear her.

10   My mother has long realized the limitations of her English as well. When I was fifteen, she used to have me call people on the phone to pretend I was she. In this guise, I was forced to ask for information or even to complain and yell at people who had been rude to her. One time it was a call to her stockbroker in New York. She had cashed out her small portfolio and it just so happened we were going to go to New York the next week, our very first trip outside California. I had to get on the phone and say in an adolescent voice that was not very convincing, "This is Mrs. Tan."

11   And my mother was standing in back whispering loudly, "Why he don't send me check, already two weeks late. So mad he lie to me, losing me money."

12   And then I said in perfect English, "Yes, I'm getting rather concerned. You had agreed to send the check two weeks ago, but it hasn't arrived."

13   Then she began to talk more loudly. "What he want, I come to New York tell him front of his boss, you cheating me?" And I was trying to calm her down, make her be quiet, while telling the stockbroker, "I can't tolerate any more excuses. If I don't receive

the check immediately, I am going to have to speak to your manager when I'm in New York next week." And sure enough, the following week there we were in front of this astonished stockbroker, and I was sitting there red-faced and quiet, and my mother, the real Mrs. Tan, was shouting at his boss in her impeccable broken English.

14   We used a similar routine just five days ago, for a situation that was far less humorous. My mother had gone to the hospital for an appointment, to find out about a benign brain tumor a CAT scan had revealed a month ago. She said she had spoken very good English, her best English, no mistakes. Still, she said, the hospital did not apologize when they said they had lost the CAT scan and she had come for nothing. She said they did not seem to have any sympathy when she told them she was anxious to know the exact diagnosis, since her husband and son had both died of brain tumors. She said they would not give her any more information until the next time and she would have to make another appointment for that. So she said she would not leave until the doctor called her daughter. She wouldn't budge. And when the doctor finally called her daughter, me, who spoke in perfect English—lo and behold—we had assurances the CAT scan would be found, promises that a conference call on Monday would be held, and apologies for any suffering my mother had gone through for a most regrettable mistake.

15   I think my mother's English almost had an effect on limiting my possibilities in life as well. Sociologists and linguists probably will tell you that a person's developing language skills are more influenced by peers. But I do think that the language spoken in the family, especially in immigrant families which are more insular, plays a large role in shaping the language of the child. And I believe that it affected my results on achievement tests, IQ tests, and the SAT. While my English skills were never judged as poor, compared to math, English could not be considered my strong suit. In grade school I did moderately well, getting perhaps B's, sometimes B-pluses, in English and scoring perhaps in the sixtieth or seventieth percentile on achievement tests. But those scores were not good enough to override the opinion that my true abilities lay in math and science, because in those areas I achieved A's and scored in the ninetieth percentile or higher.

16   This was understandable. Math is precise; there is only one correct answer. Whereas, for me at least, the answers on English tests were always a judgment call, a matter of opinion and personal experience. Those tests were constructed around items like fill-in-the-blank sentence completion, such as, "Even though Tom was_____, Mary thought he was_____." And the correct answer always seemed to be the most bland combinations of thoughts, for example, "Even though Tom was shy, Mary thought he was charming," with the grammatical structure "even though" limiting the correct answer to some sort of semantic opposites, so you wouldn't get answers like, "Even though Tom was foolish, Mary thought he was ridiculous." Well, according to my mother, there were very few limitations as to what Tom could have been and what Mary might have thought of him. So I never did well on tests like that.

17   The same was true with word analogies, pairs of words in which you were supposed to find some sort of logical, semantic relationship—for example, "*Sunset* is to *nightfall* as _____is to_____." And here you would be presented with a list of four possible pairs, one of which showed the same kind of relationship: *red* is to *stoplight, bus* is to *arrival, chills* is to *fever, yawn* is to *boring*. Well, I could never think that way. I knew what the tests were asking, but I could not block out of my mind the images already created by the first pair, "*sunset*

is to *nightfall*"—and I would see a burst of colors against a darkening sky, the moon rising, the lowering of a curtain of stars. And all the other pairs of words—red, bus, stoplight, boring—just threw up a mess of confusing images, making it impossible for me to sort out something as logical as saying: "A sunset precedes nightfall" is the same as "a chill precedes a fever." The only way I would have gotten that answer right would have been to imagine an associative situation, for example, my being disobedient and staying out past sunset, catching a chill at night, which turns into feverish pneumonia as punishment, which indeed did happen to me.

18   I have been thinking about all this lately, about my mother's English, about achievement tests. Because lately I've been asked, as a writer, why there are not more Asian Americans represented in American literature. Why are there few Asian Americans enrolled in creative writing programs? Why do so many Chinese students go into engineering? Well, these are broad sociological questions I can't begin to answer. But I have noticed in surveys—in fact, just last week—that Asian students, as a whole, always do significantly better on math achievement tests than in English. And this makes me think that there are other Asian-American students whose English spoken in the home might also be described as "broken" or "limited." And perhaps they also have teachers who are steering them away from writing and into math and science, which is what happened to me.

19   Fortunately, I happen to be rebellious in nature and enjoy the challenge of disproving assumptions made about me. I became an English major my first year in college, after being enrolled as pre-med. I started writing nonfiction as a freelancer the week after I was told by my former boss that writing was my worst skill and I should hone my talents toward account management.

20   But it wasn't until 1985 that I finally began to write fiction. And at first I wrote using what I thought would be wittily crafted sentences, sentences that would finally prove I had mastery over the English language. Here's an example from the first draft of a story that later made its way into *The Joy Luck Club,* but without this line: "That was my mental quandary in the nascent state." A terrible line, which I can barely pronounce.

21   Fortunately, for reasons I won't get into today, I later decided I should envision a reader for the stories I would write. And the reader I decided upon was my mother, because these were stories about mothers. So with this reader in mind—and in fact she did read my early drafts—I began to write stories using all the Englishes I grew up with: the English I spoke to my mother, which for lack of a better term might be described as "simple"; the English she used with me, which for lack of a better term might be described as "broken"; my translation of her Chinese, which could certainly be described as "watered down"; and what I imagined to be her translation of her Chinese if she could speak in perfect English, her internal language, and for that I sought to preserve the essence, but neither an English nor a Chinese structure. I wanted to capture what language ability tests can never reveal: her intent, her passion, her imagery, the rhythms of her speech and the nature of her thoughts.

22   Apart from what any critic had to say about my writing, I knew I had succeeded where it counted when my mother finished reading my book and gave me her verdict: "So easy to read."

Credits

Readings

"Why the Leaves Turn Color in the Fall" from *A Natural History of the Senses* by Diane Ackerman, copyright © 1990 by Diane Ackerman. Used by permission of Random House, Inc.

"Hush Timmy—This Is Like a Church" by Kurt Anderson from *Time*, April 15, 1985. Copyright © 1985 Time Inc. Reprinted by permission.

"Snow" from *How the Garcia Girls Lost Their Accents*. Copyright © 1991 by Julia Alvarez. Published by Plume, an imprint of Penguin Group USA, and originally in hardcover by Algonquin Books of Chapel Hill. Reprinted by permission of Susan Bergholz Literary Services, New York. All rights reserved.

"Sister Flowers," copyright © 1969 and renewed 1997 by Maya Angelou, from *I Know Why the Caged Bird Sings* by Maya Angelou. Used by permission of Random House, Inc.

"The Plot Against the People" by Russell Baker from *The New York Times*, June 18, 1968. Copyright © 1968 The New York Times Co. Reprinted by permission.

"Sack Athletic Scholarships" by Allen Barra from *The New York Times*, Op-Ed, September 24, 1990. Copyright © 1990 The New York Times Co. Reprinted by permission.

"Skiing an Exercise...In Masochism" by Dave Barry as appeared in the *San Diego Union Tribune*, February 4, 1989. Copyright © 1989. Reprinted by permission of Tribune Media Services.

"A Brush with Reality" from *The Secret House* by David Bodanis. Copyright © by David Bodanis. Reprinted by permission of International Creative Management, Inc.

"Ditch Diving" from *Small Comforts* by Tom Bodett, pp. 22–24. Copyright © 1987 by Tom Bodett. Reprinted by permission of Perseus Books Publishers, a member of Perseus Books, L.L.C.

"A Day at the Theme Park" by Bruce Cameron, published in the *Rocky Mountain News*, August 22, 1999, p. 15F. Reprinted with permission of the Rocky Mountain News.

"Life at Close Range" by Gretel Ehrlich appeared in *The Writer On Her Work* edited by Janet Sternburg. Reprinted by permission of Darhansoff, Verrill, Feldman Literary Agents.

"Crossing the Great Divide" by Peter Fish from *Sunset* Magazine, May 1998, pp. 24, 28. Reprinted by permission of Sunset Publishing Corp.

"Dearly Disconnected" by Ian Frazier from *Mother Jones*, January/February 2000. Copyright © 2000, Foundation for National Progress. Reprinted by permission.

"The Teacher Who Changed My Life" by Nicholas Gage from *Parade*, December 17, 1989. Reprinted with permission from Parade, copyright © 1989, and permission from the author.

"38 Who Saw Murder and Didn't Call the Police" by Martin Gansberg from the *New York Times*, March 17, 1964. Copyright © 1964 The New York Times Co. Reprinted by permission.

"'Cat in the Hat' Coughs Up Mayhem" by David Germain as appeared in *The Coloradoan*, November 21, 2003. Reprinted with permission of The Associated Press.

"Party Manners" by Richard Grossman, originally appeared in *Health* Magazine, June 1983. Copyright © 1983 by Richard Grossman. Reprinted by permission of the author.

"Those Winter Sundays." Copyright © 1966 by Robert Hayden, from *Angle of Ascent: New and Selected Poems* by Robert Hayden. Used by permission of Liveright Publishing Corporation.

"Don't Let Stereotypes Warp Your Judgments" by Robert L. Heilbroner, originally appeared in *Reader's Digest*. Robert Heilbroner is the author of many books, including his best-known work, *The Worldly Philosophers*. Reprinted by permission of the author.

"Hoppers" from *We Are Still Married* by Garrison Keillor. Reprinted by permission.

"I Have a Dream" by Martin Luther King, Jr. Reprinted by arrangement with the Estate of Martin Luther King, Jr., c/o Writers House as agent for the proprietor New York, NY. Copyright © 1963 Dr. Martin Luther King, Jr., copyright renewed 1991 Coretta Scott King.

"How Mr. Dewey Decimal Saved My Life" from *High Tide in Tucson: Essays from Now or Never* by Barbara Kingsolver. Copyright © 1995 by Barbara Kingsolver. Reprinted by permission of HarperCollins Publishers Inc.

"A Scientist: I Am the Enemy" by Ronald M. Kline, MD. Originally published in *Newsweek*, December 18, 1989. Dr. Kline is the Director of Pediatric Bone Marrow Transplantation. Reprinted by permission of the author.

"The City Life: Aboard the Sleeper" by Verlyn Klinkenborg from *The New York Times*, September 4, 2003. Copyright © 2003 The New York Times Co. Reprinted by permission.

"Darkness at Noon" by Harold Krents from *The New York Times*, May 26, 1976. Copyright © 1976 The New York Times Co. Reprinted by permission.

"The Talkies" reprinted with permission of Atria Books, an imprint of Simon & Schuster Adult Publishing Group from *Notes of a Nervous Man* by James Lileks. Copyright © 1991 by James Lileks.

"The Munchansen Mystery" by Don R. Lipsitt from *Psychology Today*, February 1983. Reprinted with permission from Psychology Today Magazine. Copyright © 1983 Sussex Publishers, Inc.

"Relying on the Kindness of Strangers" by Deborah Mathis as appeared in *The Coloradoan*, January 6, 2000. Copyright © 2000. Reprinted by permission of Tribune Media Services.

"When Father Doesn't Know Best" by Andrew Merton as appeared in *The New York Times*, 1990. Reprinted by permission of Barbara Lowenstein Agency.

"To Bid the World Farewell" from *The American Way of Death* by Jessica Mitford. Reprinted by permission of The Estate of Jessica Mitford. Copyright © 1998 by the Estate of Jessica Mitford, all rights reserved.

"In the Land of Coke-Cola" from *Blue Highways* by William Least Heat Moon. Copyright © 1986, 1999 by William Least Heat-Moon. By permission of Little, Brown and Company, (Inc.).

"Child of the Americas" by Aurora Levins Morales from *Getting Home Alive*. Copyright © 1986 by Aurora Levins Morales and Rosario Morales. Reprinted by permission of Firebrand Books.

"Our Youth Should Serve" by Steven Muller as appeared in *Newsweek*, July 10, 1978. Reprinted by permission of the author.

"What Is Poverty?" by Jo Goodwin Parker in *America's Other Children: Public Schools outside Suburbia* by George Henderson. Reprinted by permission of University of Oklahoma Press.

"The Jeaning of America" by Carin Quinn from *American Heritage*, April 1978. Copyright © 1978. Reprinted by permission of American Heritage.

"Yobbish Prat Whinges On" by T. R. Reid in *The Washington Post*, May 10, 1998. Copyright © 1998, The Washington Post, reprinted with permission.

"Today's Debate: Free Speech 'Zones'" by Robert J. Scott as appeared in *USA Today*, May 27, 2003, p. 14A. Reprinted by permission of Robert J. Scott, Scott and Scott L.L.P.

"The Ultimate in Diet Cults: Don't Eat Anything at All" from the Bay Area Institute. Reprinted with permission.

"Let's Celebrate Nerdiness" by Tom Rogers from *Newsweek*, December 11, 2000. Copyright © 2000 Newsweek. All rights reserved. Reprinted by permission.

"I'm Still Learning from My Mother" by Cliff Schneider from *Newsweek*, March 20, 2000. Copyright © 2000 Newsweek. All rights reserved. Reprinted by permission.

"You Call This Progress?" by Seth Sostak from *Newsweek*, January 8, 1999. Copyright © 1999 Newsweek. All rights reserved. Reprinted by permission.

"Black Men in Public Space" first appeared in *Ms.* Magazine, 1986. Brent Staples writes editorials on politics and culture for *The New York Times* and is the author of the memoir *Parallel Time: Growing Up In Black And White*. Reprinted by permission of the author.

"So What's So Bad About Being So-So?" by Lisa Wilson Strick. First appeared in *Woman's Day* Magazine, April 14, 1984. Copyright © 1984 by Lisa Wilson Strick. Reprinted by permission of the author.

"Mother Tongue" by Amy Tan. Copyright © 1990 by Amy Tan. First appeared in *Threepenny Review*. Reprinted by permission of the author and the Sandra Dijkstra Literary Agency.

"Notes on Punctuation," copyright © 1979 by Lewis Thomas, from *The Medusa and the Snail* by Lewis Thomas. Used by permission of Viking Penguin, a division of Penguin Group (USA) Inc.

"Grant and Lee: A Study in Contrasts" by Bruce Catton. Copyright © U.S. Capitol Historical Society, all rights reserved. Rerpinted with permission.

"Beauty: When the Other Dancer Is the Self" from *In Search of Our Mothers' Gardens: Womanist Prose*, copyright © 1983 by Alice Walker, reprinted by permission of Harcourt, Inc.

"Rat Packs: World Class Savers" by Lynda Warren and Jonnae Ostrom from *Psychology Today*, February 1988. Reprinted with permission from Psychology Today Magazine. Copyright © 1988 Sussex Publishers, Inc.

"My Real Car" from *Mama Makes Up Her Mind and Other Dangers of Southern Living* by Bailey White, pp. 192-196. Copyright © 1993 by Bailey White. Reprinted by permission of Perseus Books Publishers, a member of Perseus Books, L.L.C.

"Once More to the Lake" from *One Man's Meat*, text copyright 1941 by E.B. White. Copyright renewed. Reprinted by permission of Tilbury House, Publishers, Gardiner, Maine.

"The Heroes Among Us" by Stephen M. Wolf from *Hemispheres* Magazine, June 1993. Reprinted courtesy of Hemispheres—the magazine of United Airlines.

"College Pressures" by William Zinsser from *Blair & Ketchum's Country Journal*, Vol. VI, No. 4, April 1979. Copyright © 1979 by William K. Zinsser. Reprinted by permission of the author.

Photos

4 © Roger Allyn Lee/SuperStock

25 © Giraudon/Art Resource, NY.

44 © Life Time Pictures/Getty Images

48 © Bettmann/CORBIS

74 © Lance Richbourg/SuperStock

84 © Bettmann/CORBIS

93 © Royalty-Free/CORBIS

111 Copyright © 1992 Munch Museum, Oslo/Eric Lessing/Art Resource, NY

116 © Robert Brenner/PhotoEdit

142 © Richard Orton/Index Stock Imagery

166 © Michael Newman/PhotoEdit

197 © Bettmann/CORBIS

216 © Life Time Pictures/Getty Images

237 Photography copyright © 2000, Whitney Museum of American Art. Collection of the Whitney Museum of American Art, New York. Photography by Geoffrey Clements, NY.

248 © Mark Richards/PhotoEdit

263 © CORBIS

313 © 2001 The Art Institute of Chicago. All rights reserved.

314 © SuperStock

322 Copyright © the Dorothea Lange Collection, Oakland Museum of California.

328 Hackney Picture Fund Purchase, Muskegon Museum of Art, Muskegon, Michigan.

330 © Reuters NewMedia, Inc./CORBIS

347 © Tom & Dee Ann McCarthy/CORBIS

396 © Bettmann/CORBIS

412 © Stockbyte/SuperStock

427 *Nonchaloir (Repose)* by John Singer Sargent, 1911. Oil on canvas. 63.8 × 76.2 cm (25 12/8" × 30"). National Gallery, Washington, DC. Gift of Curt H. Reisinger. 1948.16.1

433 Digital Image © The Museum of Modern Art/Licensed by Scala/Art Resource, NY

451 © Bettmann/CORBIS

458 © Yang Liu/CORBIS

Icons

Practicing What You've Learned © Canstock Images, Inc./Index Stock Imagery

Assignment © Photodisc/Ryan McVay/Getty Images

Applying What You've Learned to Your Writing © Keith Brofsky/Photodisc/Getty

Essay Topics © Hemera Photo Objects

A Revision Worksheet © Ryan McVay/Photodisc/Getty Images

Advertisements

Bears & Arms
From Violence Policy Center. Reprinted by permission.

Center to Prevent Handgun Violence
Brought to you by the Center to Prevent Handgun Violence, Sarah Brady, Chair.

Metropolitan Energy Council, Inc.
Courtesy of Metropolitan Energy Council, Inc.

NRA
Reprinted with permission of the National Rifle Association.

Nuclear Energy
This advertisement is provided courtesy of the United States Council for Energy Awareness, Washington, D.C.

Index

Abbreviations, 523–524
    in e-mail communications, 467
"Aboard the Sleeper" (Klinkenborg), 312
Accuracy, in word choice
    confused words, 141–142
    idiomatic phrases, 142–143
Ackerman, Diane, 540–542
Action, 16–17
Active verbs, 125
Active voice, 480
Actors, 16–17
Adjective clauses, 123
Adjectives, 486–488
    misuse of nouns as, 482
    modifying nouns, commas and, 503
    precise, 129
    strong, 150
Adverbs, 486–488
    conjunctive, 501–502
    precise, 129
Advertisements, analyzing
    competing products, 299–301
    conflicting positions, 296–298
    popular appeals, 302–304
Agreement
    pronouns, 482–483
    subject-verb, 477–479
Alliteration, 432
AlltheWeb, 361
Allusions, 431
AltaVista, 361
Although-because thesis, 276
Alvarez, Julia, 440–441
Analogy
    defined, 229
    faulty, 231, 285
    samples, 231–232
    usefulness of, 230–231
Analysis, 13, 14
    formal, 444
Analytical reading, 166–168, 175
Anderson, Kurt, 588–590
Angelou, Maya, 333–337

Annotated bibliography, 370–371
Annotated poem, 433–434
Annotated story, 424–427
Anxiety, 17
APA style of documentation, 391
    electronic sources, 394–395
    Reference works, 393
    sample entries, 393–394
Apostrophe ('), 103, 509–510
Application, use of some thing
    as essay topic, 13, 14
Applied Science and Technology Index, 358
Argument, 14
Argument ad hominem, 283
Argument ad populum, 283
Argumentation, 13, 342. See also
        Advertisements, analyzing
    advertisements, analysis of, 296–304
    although-because thesis, 276
    in analogy, 230
    defined, 177
    developing, 273–282
    emotional appeals, 280
    logical appeals, 279–280
    logical fallacies, 282–285
    organization of, 276–279
    Pro-and-Con Sheet, 275–276
    problems to avoid, 282
    professional samples, 292–294
    revision worksheet, 305
    Rogerian techniques, 281–282
    sample topics, 287–288
    student sample, 289–291
    supporting evidence, 280–281
    tone, 281
    topic proposal for, 288–289
Aristotle, 14
Art Index, 358
Ask Jeeves, 362
Assonance, 432
Audience, 275. See also Readers
    for business letters, 458
    clarity for, 234–235
    in descriptive essay, 311

discovering, 19
lead-in and, 82
revising for, 97
Augustine, St., 43
Authority, faulty use of, 283
"Autumn Leaves" (Ackerman), 540–542
Awkward diction, 142–143

Baker, Russell, 252–253
Bandwagon appeal, 284
Barra, Allen, 538–584
Barry, Dave, 539–540
"Beauty: When the Other Dancer Is the Self"
        (Walker), 606–611
Begging the question, 282–283
Between you and me, 484
Bias, 100
Bibliography
        annotated, 370–371
        documentation style, 395–396
        working, 365–368
Biographical data, 166
"Black Men and Public Space" (Staples),
        533–535
Bland verbs, 129
Block Pattern essay, 212–213, 220–223, 227–228
Bodanis, David, 255–257
Bodett, Tom, 208–209
Body, of the short essay. *See* Paragraphs
Body paragraphs, 47–78. *See also* Paragraphs
        coherence, 68–76
        composing, 50
        development, 59–62
        length, 62
        outline, 48–50
        planning, 47–50
        sequence, 76
        summary, 78
        supporting evidence, 59–62
        topic sentence, 50–58
        transitions between, 77
        unity, 64–66
Books
        APA citation style, 393–394
        MLA citation style, 383–385
        online, MLA citation style, 390–391
        working bibliography for, 366, 367
Boolean operators, 359–361
Boole, George, 359n

Boomerang, 10–11
Boredom
        of readers, 21
        of writers, 5
Bourke-White, Margaret, 216
Brackets [ ], 513–514
Brainstorming, 7, 11
*Breadline during the Louisville Flood, Kentucky
        1937* (photograph; Bourke-White), 216
Brief narrative, 325
Broun, Heywood Hale, 43
"Brush with Reality, A: Surprise in the Tube"
        (Bodanis), 255–257
Burke, Kenneth, 16
Business communication. *See* On-the-job
        writing assignments
Business jargon, 153
Business letters
        audience, 458
        block form, 459
        complimentary closing, 461
        enclosure/copy/postscript, 461–462
        format, 459–462
        heading, 460
        inside address, 460
        proofreading, 462
        purpose, 458
        salutation, 460
        sample, 463
        signature, 461
        text, 460–461
        tone, 458–459
Business Periodicals Index, 358

Caesura, 432
Calhoun, John C., 3
Cameron, W. Bruce, 587–588
Capitalization, 521–523
Capp, Al, 44
Case (pronouns), 484–485
"*Cat in the Hat* Coughs Up Mayhem"
        (Germain), 452–453
Catton, Bruce, 223–226
Causal analysis essay, 342
        defined, 259
        developing, 259–261
        problems to avoid, 261
        professional sample, 267–269
        revision worksheet, 270

sample topics, 262
    student sample, 264–267
    topic proposal for, 263–264
Cause-and-effect relationship. *See* Causal
        analysis essay
"Celebrating Nerdiness" (Rogers), 554–556
Center-of-gravity sentence, 9
Characters
    in narrative essays, 326–327
    in poems, 431
    in stories, 424
"Child of the Americas" (Morales), 613–614
Chopin, Kate, 424–427
Choppy Dick-and-Jane sentences, 122, 135, 215
Chronological order, 68–69, 194
Circular definitions, 236
Circular logic, 261
Clarity
    in analogy, 230
    in business letters, 461
    in causal analysis essay, 260–261
    in definition essays, 234–235
    editing for, 91
    in example essays, 180, 184
    in narrative essays, 326
    revising for, 101–102
    in sentences, 116–122
    of subjects, 214
Class discussions, of essays, 173–174
Classification essays. *See* Division/
        classification essays
Classroom critique, 106
Clemens, Samuel. *See* Twain, Mark
Cliches, 151, 158
Closed form (poetry), 431
Clustering, 11, 12
Coconuts, 119
Coherence, within paragraphs, 168
    in example essays, 184–185
    key words, repetition of, 71
    ordering of information, 68–70
    parallelism, 72
    pronouns substituted for key nouns, 71–72
    transition devices, variety of, 72–73
    transition words and phrases, 70–71
    See also individual topics
"College Pressures" (Zinsser), 565–570
Colloquial language, 143
Colon (:), 507–508

Comma (,)
    addresses and dates, 503
    adjectives modifying nouns, 503
    conjunctive adverbs and, 501–502
    coordinating conjunctions and, 501
    degree/title, 504
    dialogue, 504
    direct address, 503
    FANBOYS ("for," "and," "nor," "but," "or,"
        "yet," "so"), 501
    interrupters/parenthetical elements, 504
    introductory phrase/clause, 502
    nonessential phrase/clause, 502–503
    series, 503
    splice, 501, 502, 506
    weak exclamations, 504
Comma splice, 492, 501, 502, 506
Communication, with readers, 3–4
Compare, 410n
Comparison, 13, 70
    faulty, 487
Comparison/contrast essay, 342
    analogy, 229–232
    Block Pattern method, 212–213, 220–223,
        227–228
    developing, 211–213
    Point-by-Point method, 212, 213, 217–220,
        223–226
    problems to avoid, 214–215
    professional samples, 223–228
    revision worksheet, 229
    sample topics, 215–216
    student samples, 217–223
    topic proposal for, 217
Competing products, 299–301
Complimentary closing, 461
Composition amnesia, 413
Computer catalogs, 357–358
Computer classrooms, 95–96
Computer labs, 95–96
Computers (word processing), 93–95
Conciseness
    editing for, 91
    in sentences, 122–126
Concluding paragraph, 82, 196
    errors in, 84–85
    ideas for, 83–84
    in literary analysis, 438
Conflicting positions, 296–298

Confused words, 103, 141–142
Conjunctive adverbs, 501–502
Connotation, 146–147
Conrad, Joseph, 3, 310
Constructions (sentences)
    deadwood, 122–124
    mixed, 121–122
    overuse of one kind, 131
    straightforward, 119
Content, in sentences, 116–117
Contrast, 13, 70, 410n
Coordinating conjunctions (FANBOYS),
    133–134, 501
Coordination, 133–134
Copy notation, in letters, 461–462
Cover letters, 468
Crane, Stephen, 615–620
Credibility, 144
Critical thinking, in drafting and revision,
    98–100
Cross-examination, 14–16
"Crossing the Great Divide" (Fish), 604–606
Cubing, 11, 13–14
Curry, John Steuart, 328
Cuteness, 145

Dangling modifiers, 120–121, 488
"Darkness at Noon" (Krents), 531–532
Dash (—), 514
Databases (of research information), 358–361
    APA style of documentation, 395
    MLA style of documentation, 388–389
Davis, Bette, 84
"Day at the Theme Park, A" (Cameron),
    587–588
Deadwood constructions, 122–124
"Dearly Disconnected" (Frazier), 545–548
Deductive order, in paragraphs, 69
Definition essays, 232, 342
    developing, 233–235
    problems to avoid, 235–236
    professional sample, 241–243
    reasons for, 233
    revision worksheet, 244
    sample topics, 236–237
    student sample, 238–241
    topic proposal for, 237–238
Denotation, 146–147
Description, 13, 343
    appropriate, 308–310

defined, 177
dominant impression, 308–310
figurative language, 310–311
problems to avoid, 311–312
professional sample, 312, 319–320
purpose, 307–308
revision worksheet, 322–323
sample topics, 313–314
sensory details, 310
specific details, 308
student sample, 315–319
topic proposal for, 315
Details
    erratic organization of, 311
    in paragraph development, 59–62
    sensory, 310, 326
    specific, 308
Development, of paragraphs, 59–62. *See also*
    Exposition, development strategies for
Dialogue, 327
Dick-and-Jane sentences, 122, 135, 215
Diction, 142–143, 431
Dictionary, 103
Directional process essay
    defined, 193–194
    professional sample, 208–209
Directional words, in essay exam, 409–411
Direct quotations. *See* Quotations
Discovery draft, 31, 32–33, 39, 92
Dissertations, unpublished, citation for, 386
"Ditch Diving" (Bodett), 208–209
Division/classification essays, 342
    defined, 245–246
    developing, 246–247
    problems to avoid, 247
    professional samples, 252–257
    revision worksheet, 258
    sample topics, 247–248
    student sample, 249–252
    topic proposal for, 249
Documentation style
    APA, 391–395
    footnote/bibliography style, 395–396
    MLA, 380–391, 397–406
Dominant impression, 308–310
"Don't Let Stereotypes Warp Your Judgments"
    (Heilbroner), 347–350
Double negatives, 480
Drafting
    discovery draft, 31, 32–33, 39, 92

hints for, 92–93
revision process for, 96–98
summary, 176
word-processing programs and, 93–95
Writing Centers, computer labs, and
    computer classrooms, 95–96
Dramatizing the subject, 16–17
in analogy, 230

Editing
defined, 90–91
for errors, 102–103
in revision workshops, 106–109
Editing tools (word processors), 94–95
Either/or thinking, 284
Elbow, Peter, 8n
Electronic documents, citation of
APA style, 394–395
MLA style, 382, 388–391
Electronic sources. *See also* Electronic
    documents, citation of
databases, 358–361
Internet, 361–363
working bibliography for, 366, 367
Eliot, George (Mary Ann Evans), 43
Ellipsis points (. . . or . . . .), 517–518
E-mail communications, 465–467
APA style of documentation, 392–393
MLA style of documentation, 391
Emoticons, 467
Emotional appeal, 280
Emphasis, editing for, 91
Emphatic style, 133–136
Empty sentences, 117, 123, 135
Enclosures, in letters, 461–462
Encyclopedias, citation for, 386
Environment
for best writing, 4–5
as source of ideas, 5
Erlich, Gretel, 621–623
Essay exam questions, 408
Essay map, 41–42, 47, 49
Essays. *See also* Exposition, development
    strategies for; In-class writing
    assignments; Literary analysis; Modes
    and strategies; Research paper
annotated, sample, 168–171
body paragraphs, 47–78
checklist for, 104
conclusions, 82–85

critical thinking, 98–100
drafts, 92–98, 176
exams, 407–419
film reviews, 444
focus/purpose, 6–7
incomplete, 413
lead-ins, 79–82
multiple strategies for, 341–352
prewriting, 3–29
proofreading, 103
reading-writing connection, 165–176
revision, 89–91, 96–98, 100–103, 106–109
sentences, 115–139
summary of, 171–172
thesis statement, 31–46
titles, 85–86
weakness in, 59–60, 184–185
word logic, 141–164
See also individual topics and individual types
    of essays
Ethics, résumés and, 470
Euphemisms, 154–155
Evidence. *See also* Supporting information
in argumentative essays, 280–281
evaluating strength of, 99
in literary analysis, 438
in paragraph development, 59–62
revising and, 97–98
sources of, 60
specific, 99–100
to support opinions, 99
undermined by bias, 100
Example essay, 342
about, 180–183
developing, 183–184
problems to avoid, 184–185
professional sample, 189–192
revision worksheet, 192–193
sample topics, 185–186
student sample, 187–189
topic proposal for, 186–187
Exams. *See* In-class writing assignments
Exclamation point (!), 500
Exposition, development strategies for, 179
by causal analysis, 259–270
by comparison and contrast, 211–232
defined, 177
by definition, 232–245
by division or classification, 245–258
by example, 180–193

by process analysis, 193–211
professional samples, 202–210, 223–228, 241–243, 252–257, 267–269
student samples, 187–189, 198–202, 217–223, 238–241, 249–252, 264–267
See also individual topics
Expository narratives, 325
Extended definition, 233
Extended example, 181–182
Extended narrative, 325

Fact, opinion vs., 98–99
False predication, 495–496
FANBOYS ("for," "and," "nor," "but," "or," "yet," "so"), 133–134, 501
Faulty agreement
    pronouns, 482–483
    verbs, 477–479
Faulty analogy, 231, 285
Faulty comparison, 487
Faulty parallelism, 494
Faulty predication, 121–122
Faulty use of authority, 283
Feet (poetry), 432
Figurative language, 157–158
    types of, 310–311
Films, citation for, 382, 386
Film, writing about
    common assignments, 443–444
    conventions for, 447
    formal analysis, 444
    glossary of film terms, 454–455
    hints for, 445–447
    problems to avoid, 448
    prompted response, 443–444
    review essay, 444
    strategy practice, 444
    student sample, 448–451
Fish, Peter, 604–606
Fitzgerald, F. Scott, 350, 350n
Fixed form (poetry), 431
Flabby prose, 122
Flippancy, 145
Focus, 6–7
    of topic for research paper, 355–356
    of topic sentence, 53
"Foot in Mouth" prize, 161n

Footnote/bibliography form of documentation, 395–396
Formal language, 143–144
Formal outline, 48
Formal research paper, works cited, 241n
Fragments
    semicolon, 506
    sentence, 490–491
Frazier, Ian, 545–548
Free association, 7, 13
Free verse, 432
Freewriting, 7–9, 10–11, 16, 31
Full-text databases, 358

Gage, Nicholas, 571–574
Gainley, Bonny, 584–585
Gansberg, Martin, 593–595
Gender-specific references. *See* Sexist language
Generalities
    in definition essays, 235–236
    in example essays, 180
    hasty generalizations, 282
    in in-class writing assignments, 413
    in paragraphs, 60–62
    vague modifiers, 150
Generating ideas. *See* Prewriting
Germain, David, 452–453
Getting started. *See* Prewriting
Gibson, Althea, 44
Google, 361
Gorilla generalizations, 413
Government documents, citation for, 386
Graffiti, 232n
Grammar. *See also* Mechanics; Punctuation
    adjectives, 486–488
    adverbs, 486–488
    editing for errors, 90
    modifiers, 488–489
    nouns, 482
    pronouns, 482–486
    sentences, 490–497
    verbs, 477–481
    See also individual topics;
"Grant and Lee: A Study in Contrasts" (Catton), 223–226
Grossman, Richard, 562–564

Hasty generalizations, 282
Hayakawa, S.I., 349

Hayden, Robert, 441
Heading
    of business letter, 460
    of résumé, 468
Heilbroner, Robert L., 347–350
"Heroes Among Us, The" (Wolf), 553–554
Hidden meanings, 422–423
Hooks, 53, 55, 77
Hopper, Edward, 313
"Hoppers" (Keillor), 561–562
"How Mr. Dewey Decimal Saved My Life"
    (Kingsolver), 267–269
Humanities Index, 358
Humor, 145
"Hush, Timmy—This Is Like a Church"
    (Anderson), 588–590
Huxley, Aldous, 155
Hyperbole, 311
Hyphen (-), 515–516
Hypostatization, 284

Iambic pentameter, 432
Ibid, 395
Idea hooks, 53, 55, 77
Ideas
    main, 34
    repetitious, 60
    revising, 97–98
    self-evident or dead-ended, avoiding, 38
Ideas, sources of, 5, 7–17
    boomerang, 10–11
    clustering, 11, 12
    cross-examination, 14–16
    cubing, 11, 13–14
    dramatizing the subject, 16–17
    freewriting, 7–8
    interviewing, 14
    journal keeping, 25–28
    listing, 7
    looping, 8–10
    sketching, 16
Idiomatic phrases, 142–143
"I Have a Dream" (King), 601–604
Images, 431
Implied thesis, 37
Impressionistic description, 307
In-class writing assignments
    arrive prepared, 409
    common formats, 408–409
    directional words or phrases, 410

prepare to write, 411–412
problems to avoid, 413
read entire assignment, 409–411
read what you have written, 412
steps in process, 407–414
student sample, 417–419
summary-and-response essay, 408–409,
    414–416
tips, 412
Incomplete essay, 413
Indexes, 358
Inductive order, in paragraphs, 69–70
Infinitive phrases, *of* and, 124
Inflated language, 125–126
Informal language, 143
Informal outline, 48–50
Information, sources of. *See* Library research
Informative process essay
    defined, 194
    professional sample, 203–206
InfoTrac, 358
InfoTrac College Edition, 358, 360
Inside address, 460
"Insta-Prose," 151–152
Interest, 6
    in example essays, 180
    of writers, 5
Internet
    as research tool, 361–363
    as source of ideas, 5
Interrupters/parenthetical elements, 504
Interviews
    APA style of documentation, 392–393
    MLA style of documentation, 382,
        387–388
    as research tool, 363–365
    as source of ideas, 14
    working bibliography for, 366, 368
"In the Land of 'Coke-Cola'" (Least
    Heat-Moon), 590–592
Introductory phrase/clause, 502
Invective, 144
Inverted word order, 133
"I" pronoun, in essays, 131–132
Irony, 144–145
Irresponsible charges, avoiding, 38
ISBN, 357
"Isolation test" (pronouns), 484
It is, 123
It's/its, 103

James, William, 349, 349n
Jargon, 152–154
"Jeaning of America, The" (Quinn), 537–539
Jokes, 145
Journal articles, working bibliography for, 366
Journal keeping, 17, 25
    uses of, 26–28
Journals
        APA style of documentation, 394
        MLA style of documentation, 385, 389
"Judging by the Cover" (Gainley), 584–585

Kartoo, 361
Kerr, Jean, 3
Keillor, Garrison, 561–562
Keywords, 357, 361
King, Martin Luther, Jr., 44, 601–604
Kingsolver, Barbara, 267–269
Kline, Ron, 581–583
Klinkenborg, Verlyn, 312
Krents, Harold, 531–532

Laingen, Bruce, 44
Lange, Dorthea, 322
Language, levels of. *See also* Word choice; Words
        colloquial, 143
        formal, 143–144
        informal, 143
Leacock, Stephen, 44
Lead-in, 167. *See also* Thesis statement
        errors in, 81–82
        purpose of, 79–80
        suggestions for and examples of, 80–81
        thesis statement and, 81–82
Least Heat-Moon, William, 590–592
Lectures, citation for, 382, 387
Legal jargon, 153
Length, of paragraphs, 62
Letter, The (painting; Vermeer), 25
Letters. *See also* E-mail; Memos
        APA citation style, 392–393
        business, 458–463
        cover, 468
        MLA citation style, 387
        post-interview, 474
        thank-you, 471
Library of Congress Subject Headings, 358
Library research, 356
        computer catalogs, 357–358
        databases, 358–361

general reference works, 357
indexes, 358
Internet, 361–363
online catalogs, 357–358
special collections, 363
"Life at Close Range" (Ehrlich), 621–623
Lileks, James, 598–600
Lippmann, Walter, 349, 349n
Lipsitt, Don R., 241–243
Listening skills, 173
Listing, as source of ideas, 5, 7, 16
Literary analysis
        about, 422
        annotated poem and student essay, 433–437
        annotated story and student essay, 424–430
        careful reading tips, 422–423
        common assignments, 422
        conclusion, 438
        guidelines for, 437–438
        hidden meanings, 422–423
        literary conventions, 437–438
        literature in the composition classroom, 421–422
        organization, 438
        plot vs. summary, 439
        problems to avoid, 438–439
        prompts, 421
        quoted material, 439
        steps to reading a poem, 430–433
        steps to reading a story, 423–424
        supporting evidence, 438
        thesis, 437
        topic, 437
Literary conventions, 437–438
Lively style, 128–132
Logical appeal, 279–280
Logical fallacies, 100, 282–285
Logical time sequence, 326
Looping, 9–10
Lyrics, 431

Magazines
        APA style of documentation, 394
        MLA style of documentation, 385, 389
        working bibliography for, 366, 367
Maltese Falcon, The (photograph), 451
Mapping, essay map, 41–42, 47. *See also* Clustering

Mathis, Deborah, 535–536

McDonald, Wesley L., 161

Mechanics. *See also* Grammar; Punctuation
   abbreviations, 523–524
   capitalization, 521–523
   numbers, 524
   spelling, 525–527

Memos, 464–465

Mencken, H.L., 44

Mental blocks. *See* Writer's Block

Merton, Andrew, 596–598

Metacrawler, 361

Metaphor, 157–158, 310

Method, 16–17

Migrant Mother (photograph; Lange), 322

Misplaced modifiers, 119–121, 489

Mitford, Jessica, 203–206

Mixed constructions, 121–122

Mixed structure (sentences), 496

MLA Handbook for Writers of Research Papers, 380n

*MLA Style Manual and Guide to Scholarly
      Publishing*, 380n

MLA style of documentation
   electronic sources, 382, 388–391
   guidelines for, 380–382
   sample entries, 383–388
   student paper sample, 397–406
   Works Cited list, 383

Modern Language Association of America
      (MLA). *See* MLA style of documentation

Modes and strategies
   argumentation, 273–305
   description, 307–323
   exposition, 179–271
   multiple strategies, 341–352
   narration, 325–339
   See also individual topics

Modifiers
   dangling, 120–121, 488
   misplaced, 119–121, 489
   position of, 119
   precise, 129
   vague, 150

Molishever, Jay, 231

Monet, Claude, 314

Morales, Aurora Levin, 613–614

"Mother Tongue" (Tan), 626–629

Motive, 16–17

Muller, Steven, 169–171

Multiple strategies, 341
   choosing the best strategies, 342–343
   problems to avoid, 343
   professional sample, 347–350
   revision worksheet, 351–352
   student sample, 343–347

"Munchausen Mystery, The" (Lipsitt), 241–243

Munch, Eduard, 111

Mushy prose, 122

Music Index, 358

"My Real Car" (White), 543–545

"Mystery of Heroism, A" (Crane), 615–620

Name calling, avoiding, 38, 144

Narration, 343
   defined, 177
   hints/tips, 326–327
   kinds of stories, 325
   pacing, 328
   problems to avoid, 327–328
   professional sample, 333–337
   revision worksheet, 338–339
   sample topics, 329–330
   student sample, 331–333
   topic proposal for, 330

Narrative poems, 431

Narrowing a subject, 6, 35–36

National Newspaper Index, 358

Netiquette, 467

Newspapers
   APA style of documentation, 394
   MLA style of documentation, 385, 390
   working bibliography for, 366

New York Times Index, 358

Nighthawks (painting; Hopper), 313

Nixon, Richard, 284–285

Nominalizations, 153–154

Nonessential phrase/clause, 502–503

Nonperiodical publications on CD-ROM,
      diskette, or magazine tape, citation
      for, 391

Non sequitur, 282

"Notes on Punctuation" (Thomas), 624–625

Note-taking skills, 174, 371–373

Nouns
   adjectives as, 482
   misuse of, as adjectives, 482
   possessive with "-ing," 482
   pronouns substituted for, 71–72

specific, 150
vague, 149
Numbers, 524

Objective description, 307
Observation, 26
Occasion (of a poem), 431
Of and infinitive phrases, 124
"Once More to the Lake (August 1941)"
    (White), 548–552
Online catalogs, 357–358
Onomatopoeia, 432
On-the-job writing assignments, 457
    business letters, 458–463
    e-mail, 465–467
    memos, 464–465
    post-interview letters, 474
    résumés, 467–473
    See also individual topics
Op. cit., 395
Open form (poetry), 432
Opinion
    defined, 99
    fact vs., 98–99
    supporting, with evidence, 99
Ordering of information
    deductive order, 69
    inductive order, 69–70
    space, 69
    time, 68–69
Organization, 168
    of the argumentative essay, 276–279
    of details, erratic, 311
    in literary analysis, 438
    logical, 343
    revising for, 100–101
Orwell, George, 125
Ostrom, Jonnae C., 575–577
"Our Youth Should Serve" (Muller), 169–171
Outline
    of the argumentative essay, 277–279
    informal, 48–50
    value of, 49
Overkill, 343
Overpacked sentence, 118–119
Overuse of one kind of construction, 131
"Ozymandias" (Shelley), 614–615

Pacing, 328
Pamphlets, citation for, 386

Paragraphs. *See also* Body paragraphs;
        Concluding paragraph; Lead-in;
        Ordering of information
    in business letters, 460–461
    thesis statement and, 36–37
Parallelism, 72
Paraphrase, 372
    summary distinguished from, 373
Parentheses ( ), 512–513
Parenthetical documentation, 380
Parenthetical elements, 504
Parker, Dorothy, 80
Parker, Jo Goodwin, 556–559
Parks, Rosa, 197
"Party Manners" (Grossman), 562–564
Passive verbs, 125
Passive voice, 125, 480
Peer editing, 106
Performances, citation for, 382, 387
Period (.), 500
Periodicals, citation of
    APA style, 394
    MLA style, 385, 389–390
Personal interview (as resource tool), 363–365
Personification, 310
Perspective, change in, avoiding, 311–312
Persuasion
    in analogy, 230
    in example essays, 180, 184
Phrases
    idiomatic, 142–143
    overworked, 151
    there are and *it is*, 123
    to be, 124
    transition, 70–71
    unnecessary, 37–38
Pickering, Miles, 231
Placement, of topic sentence, 53–55
Plagiarism, 376–378
Plato, 44
Plot, 423
"Plot Against People, The" (Baker), 252–253
Poetry, 430–434
Point-by-Point essay, 212, 213, 217–220,
    223–226
Point of view, 423
    consistent, 131–132
Pomposity, 125, 146, 152
Popular appeals, 302–304
Post hoc, ergo propter hoc, 261

Post hoc fallacy, 261
Post-interview letters, 474
Postscript (P.S.) in letters, 462
Pratt, John Clark, 377n
Preachiness, 146
Preciseness, 22, 149–150
Predication, faulty, 121–122
Preparation, for in-class writing assignments, 409–412
Pretentiousness, 22, 125–126
Prewriting, 48
    boomerang, 10–11
    clustering, 11, 12
    cross-examination, 14–16
    cubing, 11, 13–14
    dramatizing the subject, 16–17
    focus/purpose, 6–7
    freewriting, 7–8
    getting ideas, 7–17
    getting started, 3–4
    interviewing, 14
    journal keeping, 25–28
    listing, 7
    looping, 8–10
    purpose, 6–7
    readers, analysis of, 19–22
    sketching, 16
    subject, selecting a, 4–6
    summary, 29
    thesis statement, 17–18
Primary sources, 369n
Pro-and-Con Sheet, 275–276
Process analysis essay, 342
    developing, 194–195
    directional, 193–194
    informative, 194
    problems to avoid, 196
    professional samples, 202–210
    revision worksheet, 210
    sample topics, 196–197
    student sample, 198–202
    topic proposal for, 198
Profanity, avoiding, 38, 144
Prompted essays, 408, 421
Prompted response, 443–444
Pronouns
    case, 484–485
    consistency, 483–484
    faulty agreement, 482–483
    shift in, 483–484

substituted for key nouns, 71–72
vague reference, 483
who/whom, 484–485
Proofreading, 103
    of business letters, 462
    defined, 91
    of e-mail communications, 466
    for spelling errors, 527
    word-choice decisions and, 95
Proquest, 358
Psychological jargon, 153
Publication information, 166
Publication Manual of the American Psychological Association, 391n
Pump-primer techniques, 7–17. *See also* Prewriting
Punctuation, 499. *See also* Grammar; Mechanics
    apostrophe, 509–510
    brackets, 513–514
    colon, 507–508
    comma, 501–505
    dash, 514
    editing for errors, 90
    ellipsis points, 517–518
    exclamation point, 500
    hyphen, 515–516
    parentheses, 512–513
    period, 500
    question mark, 500
    quotation marks, 510–512
    for quotations, 375
    semicolon, 505–506
    underlining, 517
Purpose
    of business letters, 458
    in definition essays, 233–234
    in descriptive essay, 307–308
    in division or classification essay, 246
    finding, 6–7
    in narrative essay, 326
    readers' role in, 19
    in reading-writing connection, 167
    revising for, 97

Question mark (?), 500
Questions, reporter's (interviewing), 14. *See also* In-class writing assignments
Quick fix, 285
Quinn, Carin C., 537–539

Quotation marks (" " and ' '), 510–512
Quotations
    direct, 372
    guidelines for, 374–376
    in literary analysis, 439

Radio show, citation for, 386–387
Read aloud, for editing, 102
Read backwards, for editing, 102
Reader review, 106
Readers
    analysis of, 19–21
    characteristics of, 21–22
    communication with, 3–4
    likes/dislikes, 21–22
Reader's Guide to Periodical Literature, 358
Reading
    analytical, 166–168, 175
    to become a better writer, 165–166
    of literature, 422–423
    of poems, steps in, 430–433
    of stories, steps in, 423–424
Reading-writing connection. *See* Reading
Reason, importance of, 38
Recordings, citation for, 387
Red herring, 283
Redundancies, 124–125
References, on résumé, 470–471
Reference works, 357
Refuting the opposition, 275
Re (in reference to), 464
Relevance, 183–184
"Relying on the Kindness of Strangers"
    (Mathis), 535–536
Repetition
    of key words, 71
    in poetry, 432
Repetitious ideas, 60
Reporter's questions, 14
Repose (painting; Sargent), 427
Research. *See* Library research; Research paper
Research paper. *See also* APA style of
    documentation; Library research; MLA
    style of documentation
    annotated bibliography, 370–371
    APA citation style, 391–395
    focusing the topic, 355–356
    footnote/bibliography style, 395–396
    library research, 356–363

MLA citation style, 380–391, 397–406
note-taking skills, 371–373
paraphrasing, 372, 373
personal interviews, 363–365
plagiarism, 376–378
quotations, 372, 374–376
source material, incorporating, 374–376
sources, choosing and evaluating, 368–370
student sample, 397–406
supplementary notes, 396
working bibliography, 365–368
works cited, 241n
Response (summary-and-response) essays,
    408–409, 414–416
Résumés, 467–473
Reviewers, in revision workshops, 108–109
Review essay, 444
Revision, 33. *See also* Drafting
    for clarity and style, 101–102
    computers and, 93–96
    critical thinking and, 98–100
    defined, 89–91
    editing for errors, 102–103
    in e-mail communications, 466
    for ideas and evidence, 97–98
    improving skills, 91
    of jargon, 153–154
    myths about, 90–91
    for organization, 100–101
    process for, 96–98
    proofreading, 103
    for purpose, thesis, and audience, 97
    summary, 113
    as thinking process, 89–90
    time-saving hints, 92–93
    when it occurs, 90
    in word choice, 159
    word processing programs and, 93–95
    workshops for, 106–109
Rhythm, 432–433
Richbourg, Lance, 74
Rogerian techniques, 281–282
Rogers, Carl, 281–282
Rogers, Tom, 554–556
Rogers, Will, 44
Romanov family (photograph), 397
Roosevelt, Eleanor, 44
Roosevelt, Franklin, 126
Rosie the Riveter (poster), 263

Rumsfeld, Donald, 161, 161n
Run-on sentences, 491

"Sack Athletic Scholarships" (Barra), 583–584
Salutation, 460
Sarcasm, 144
Sargent, John Singer, 427
Schneider, Cliff, 319–320
"Scientist, A: I Am the Enemy" (Kline), 581–583
Scope, 327
Scott, Robert J., 292–294
Scream, The (painting; Munch), 111
Screening (of films), 445–446
Search engines, 361
Search/find command, 95
Secondary sources, 369n
Semicolon (;), 505–506
Semicolon fragment, 506
Sensory details, 310, 326
Sentences, 115 *See also* Grammar; Mechanics;
       Punctuation; Thesis statement; Topic
       sentences
   center-of-gravity, 9
   choppy, 122, 133–134, 135
   clarity in, 116–122
   combining, 117, 135–136
   comma splice, 492
   conciseness, 122–126
   construction
          deadwood, 122–124
          mixed, 121–122
          overuse of one kind, 131
          straightforward, 119
          See also individual topics
   content, 116–117
   coordination, 133–134
   dangling modifiers, 120–121
   descriptive verbs, 129
   editing for sense, 90
   emphasize people, 130
   emphatic style, 133–136
   empty, 117, 123, 135
   false predication, 495–496
   faulty parallelism, 494
   faulty predication, 121–122
   fragments, 490–491
   fuzzy, 116
   inverted order, 133
   lively style in, 128–132
   misplaced modifiers, 119–120, 121

   mixed structure, 496
   modifiers, 119
   modifiers, precise, 129
   overpacked, 118–119
   passive verbs, 125
   point of view, 131–132
   pretentiousness, 22, 125–126
   redundancy, 124–125
   run-on, 491
   simple and direct, 118–119
   space wasters, 123
   specificity in, 117–118
   subordination, 134–136
   summary, 139
   vague vs. specific, 117–118
   vary style, 130–131
   wordiness, 123–124, 129
   word order, 119–121, 133
Sentimentality, 145
Sequence, 70
   logical, 326
   of paragraphs, 76
Setting, 16–17, 424, 431
Sexist language, 155–157
Shakespearean sonnet, 431, 432
Shaw, George Bernard, 43
S/he, 157n
Shelley, Percy Bysshe, 614–615
Short-answer exam questions, 408
Shorthand note-taking, 174
Shostak, Seth, 577–579
Signature, on business letter, 461
"Skiing Lessons: The Cold, Hard Facts"
       (Barry), 539–540
Simile, 157–158, 310
Simplicity, 118–119
"Sister Flowers" (Angelou), 333–337
Sketching, 16
Slang, 152
Sliding in Yankee Stadium (painting;
       Richbourg), 74
"Snow" (Alvarez), 440–441
Social Science Index, 358
Sociological jargon, 153
Sound devices, 432
Sources, of information. *See also* Library
       research
   choosing and evaluating, 368–370
   incorporating material, 374–376
   primary and secondary, 369n

"So What's So Bad about Being So-So?"
        (Strick), 189–192
So-what thesis problem, 214
Space, in ordering paragraphs, 69
Special collections, 363
Specificity. *See also* Example essay
        in descriptive essay, 308
        examples of, 180–181
        lack of, as weakness, 184
        in thesis statements, 36
        of topic sentence, 50
Speeches, citation for, 387
Spell-checker, 94, 103
Spelling, 525–527
        editing for errors, 90
Split infinitive, 480
Stanzas, 431
Staples, Brent, 533–535
Starry Night (painting; Van Gogh), 433
"Still Learning from My Mother" (Schneider),
        319–320
Stories, steps to reading, 423–424
"Story of an Hour, The" (Chopin), 424–427
Strategies. *See also* Exposition, development
        strategies for
        multiple, for essay writing, 341–352
        thinking, 341
Strategy practice, 444
Straw man, 284–285
Strick, Lisa Wilson, 189–192
Structure
        in poems, 431
        in stories, 423
Style, 168
        revising for, 101–102
Subject
        dramatizing, 16–17
        getting ideas, 7–17
        narrowing a, 6, 35–36
        purpose and focus, 6–7
        selecting a, 4–6
        thesis statement, 17–18
Subjective description, 307
Subject-verb agreement, 477–479
Subjunctive verbs, 479
Subordination, 134–136
Subway, The (painting; Tooker), 237
Summary, 372
        defined, 171
        guidelines for, 172

paraphrase distinguished from, 373
        sample, 172
Summary-and-response essays, 408–409, 414–416
Summary-reaction essay. *See* Summary-and-
        response essay
Summary-response papers, 342
Supplementary notes, 396
Supporting information, 59–62, 180. *See also*
        Evidence
Symbols, 424, 431
Synecdoche, 311

Tack-on words, 154
"Talkies, The" (Lileks), 598–600
Tan, Amy, 626–629
"Teacher Who Changed My Life, The" (Gage),
        571–574
Technical jargon, 152
Television shows, citation for, 382, 386–387
Tense shift, 479
Teoma, 361
Text, of business letter, 460–461
Theme, 423
There are and *It is* phrases, 123
There/they're, 103
Thesaurus, 94, 103
Theses, unpublished, citation for, 386
Thesis-map, 49–50
Thesis statement, 17–18, 31, 167, 196. *See also*
        Lead-in
        in causal analysis essay, 259–260
        changes of, 32–33
        clearly stated, 36
        defined, 32
        errors in, 37–39
        essay map and, 41–42
        fit to assignment, 35–36
        guidelines for, 33–37
        implied, 37
        in literary analysis, 437
        location of, 36–37
        narrowing of subject matter, 35–36
        one main idea, 34
        revising for, 97
        specific terms, 36
        summary, 45
        universalize, 35
        working vs. final, 32–33
        worthwhile idea, 34–35
        writer's opinion, 33

"They Have to Keep It: People Who Save Everything" (Warren and Ostrom), 575–577

"Thing," banishment of, 149n

Thinking strategies, 341

"38 Who Saw Murder Didn't Call the Police" (Gansberg), 593–595

Thomas, Lewis, 624–625

Thoreau, Henry, 43

"Those Winter Sundays" (Hayden), 441

Time
  logical sequence of, in narrative essay, 326
  in ordering paragraphs, 68–69

Titles, 85–86, 167, 423

To be phrases, 124

"To Bid the World Farewell" (Mitford), 203–206

Tolstoy, Leo, 43

Tone, 168
  in argumentative essays, 281
  of business letters, 458–459
  in e-mail communications, 466
  flippancy or cuteness, 145
  invective, 144
  irony, 144–145
  pomposity, 146
  preachiness, 146
  sarcasm, 144
  sentimentality, 145
  in stories, 424

Tooker, George, 237

Topic sentence, 167
  errors in, 55
  focus, 53
  functions, 50–53
  placement of, 53–55

Tornado Over Kansas (painting; Curry), 328

Transition devices, 55, 185. *See also* Coherence, within paragraphs
  common words/phrases, 70–71
  for comparison/contrast, 215
  between paragraphs, 77
  variety of, 72–73

Trendy expressions, 152

Trite expressions, 85, 151

Twain, Mark, 44, 227–228

"Two Ways of Viewing the River" (Twain), 227–228

"Ultimate in Diet Cults, The: Don't Eat Anything at All," 22–24

Underlining (_), 517

Understatement, 311

Unity, 168
  within paragraphs, 64–66

Universalize (in thesis statements), 35

Unnecessary phrases, 37–38

URLs (uniform resource locators), 361, 362, 388

Vague words, 149–150

Van Gogh, Vincent, 433

Vary sentence style, 130–131

Verbal litter, 153–154

Verbs
  active, 125
  active voice, 480
  bland, 129
  descriptive, 129
  double negatives, 480
  faulty agreement, 477–479
  passive, 125
  passive voice, 480
  split infinitive, 480
  subjunctive, 479
  tense shift, 479
  vague, 149
  vigorous, 150

Vermeer, Johannes, 25

Visualization, 16–17

Voice, 144
  active/passive, 480
  passive, 125

Walker, Alice, 606–611

Warren, Lynda W. 575–577

Water Lily Pond, The (painting; Monet), 314

Web sites
  citations for (APA and MLA), 390, 394–395
  résumé submission through, 471

"What Is Poverty?" (Parker), 556–559

"When Father Doesn't Know Best" (Merton), 596–598

"When I Heard the Learn'd Astronomer" (Whitman), 434

Which clauses, 123

White, Bailey, 543–545

White, E.B., 231–232, 548–552

Whitman, Walt, 434
Who and *which* clauses, 123
Who clauses, 123
Who's/whose, 103
Who/whom, 484–485
Wilde, Oscar, 44
Wisenut, 361
Wolf, Stephen M., 553–554
Word choice. *See also* Language, levels of; Tone
    accuracy, 141–143
    clichés, 151, 158
    confused words, 103, 141–142
    connotation, 146–147
    correct words, selecting, 141–147
    denotation, 146–147
    editing for errors, 90
    euphemisms, 154–155
    figurative language, 157–158
    fresh and original, 151–152
    idiomatic phrases, 142–143
    jargon, 153–154
    in poems, 431
    preciseness, 149–150
    in proofreading stage, 95
    revision and, 159
    sexist language, 155–157
    simple and direct, 152–154
    slang, 152
    trendy expressions, 152
    vague words, 149–150
    wordiness, 158–159
Wordiness, 129, 158–159
Word logic. *See* Word choice
Word order. *See also* Modifiers
    for clarity, 119–121
    in emphatic writing, 133
Word processors, 93–96

Words. *See also* Grammar; Phrases; Sentences; *specific usages of* Wordiness; Word order
    confused, 141–142
    direct, 37–38
    directional, 409–411
    jargon, 152–154
    nonexistent, 142
    repetition of, 71
    simple and direct, 22
    specificity of, 50
    tack-on, 154
    transition, 70–71
    trite expressions, 85
Working bibliography, 365–368
Working outline. *See* Informal outline
Working thesis statement. *See* Thesis statement
Workplace. *See* On-the-job writing assignments
Works cited, 241n
World Trade Center Towers, September 11, 2001 (photograph), 330
Writers, in revision workshops, 107–108
Writer's attitude, 3–4
Writer's Block, 17
    tips for working through, 110–113
Writing. *See also* Reading
    as an act of discovery, 32
    reasons for, 3–4
Writing about literature. *See* Literary analysis
Writing anxiety, 17
Writing Centers, 95–96

Yahoo!, 361
"You Call This Progress?" (Shostak), 577–579
Your/you're, 103

Zinsser, William, 565–570